McGRAW-HILL SERIES IN POLITICAL SCIENCE

Joseph P. Harris, CONSULTING EDITOR

THE LEGISLATIVE STRUGGLE

A Study in Social Combat

McGRAW-HILL SERIES IN POLITICAL SCIENCE

Joseph P. Harris, CONSULTING EDITOR

BONE: *American Politics and the Party System*
CHASE: *The United Nations in Action*
FERGUSON AND MCHENRY: *The American Federal Government*
FERGUSON AND MCHENRY: *The American System of Government*
FERGUSON AND MCHENRY: *Elements of American Government*
FIELD: *Governments in Modern Society*
FRANK: *Cases on the Constitution*
GROSS: *The Legislative Struggle*
HARTMANN: *Basic Documents of International Relations*
HARTMANN: *Readings in International Relations*
HOLLOWAY: *State and Local Government in the United States*
LEONARD: *International Organization*
NEUMANN: *European and Comparative Government*
REED: *Municipal Management*
RIEMER: *Problems of American Government*
STRAUSZ-HUPÉ AND POSSONY: *International Relations*
VANDENBOSCH AND HOGAN: *The United Nations—Background, Organization Functions, Activities*
WILSON: *The American Political Mind*
WILSON: *Police Administration*

THE LEGISLATIVE STRUGGLE

A Study in Social Combat

Bertram M. Gross

McGRAW-HILL BOOK COMPANY, INC.

New York Toronto London

1953

THE LEGISLATIVE STRUGGLE

Library of Congress Catalog Card Number: 52-11509

TO

Nora, David, Larry, Sammy, and Teddy

PREFACE

There are at least three motives behind the writing of "The Legislative Struggle."

First, while serving as a staff adviser to various Senate committees and later as an official in the Executive Office of the President, I long ago learned that many people felt the need for a book which could serve as a guide in the handling of concrete legislative problems.

True, many books were available on the organization, rules, and history of Congress, on the case histories of individual laws, on proposals for congressional reform, and on governmental operations as a whole. But none had ever attempted to deal in practical terms with the full gamut of problems that arise from questions of whether and when to seek legislative action to the final issues revolving around Presidential signature or veto.

Ignorance is not tolerated as an excuse for breaking the law. Yet ignorance accounts for the failure of many Americans to do their share in making the law. Baffled by the complexities of the lawmaking process, the average American finds it difficult to weigh the promises or appraise the accomplishments of the congressional candidates who seek his vote. He is easy prey for legislative double talk. When he is bestirred to petition the lawmakers directly, the result is often pathetic. The wastebaskets of Congressmen overflow with mail of the wrong kind to the wrong person on the wrong subject. The office buildings of Washington are filled with organizations that have never penetrated to the inner sanctum; their efforts for the most part end in futility. The lobbies of Capitol Hill teem with lawyers, public-relations men, and ex-government officials who accomplish little except to wrest large fees from gullible individuals, associations, and corporations.

Nor is the average public official given the clue to the mystery by virtue of his office. Many a well-meaning administrator, for want of knowledge concerning currents and soundings, has steered a government program on the legislative rocks. In fact, the expanding science of public administration is yielding large numbers of administrators, all well fitted for a world run entirely by administrators, but having little or no understanding of relations with legislators. Many a judge, too, in rendering a decision, will talk learnedly about "legislative intent," although his interpretation of the statute in question may be based upon an utterly naïve conception of how laws are born.

Some members of Congress never learn the secret of how to advance a legislative project. Many go through extended legislative battles without any clear idea of the forces that make for victory or defeat.

Second, through many years of behind-the-scenes work on legislation, I have often been urged to reveal what really happened on measures with which I have been connected.

The motive for doing this has always been compelling. For many years I had worked intensively on all sorts of legislative matters—developing ideas for legislation, drafting bills, arranging for committee hearings, interrogating witnesses, assisting in floor action, sitting in with legislative committees and conference committees in "marking up" bills and writing committee reports, preparing agency views on legislation, presenting agency budgets to the appropriations committees, participating in the process of Presidential clearance of legislative measures, and helping to prepare Presidential messages to Congress. I worked closely with Democrats and Republicans in both Houses of Congress, with government officials in the White House, the departments, the independent agencies, and state and local governments, and with representatives of corporations, labor unions, trade associations, and other private organizations. I became intimately involved with problems of legislative strategy and tactics. On a number of occasions, I experienced the unique thrill of seeing measures that I had initiated or collaborated on—such as the Employment Act of 1946, the Contract Settlement Act, the Surplus Property Act, the War Mobilization and Reconversion Act, the resolution setting up the Joint Committee on the Reorganization of Congress, the Defense Production Act and the National Capital Planning Act—approved by the Congress.

In all these situations I found that more things went on than were dreamed of by the most diligent observers, let alone by the general public. In his book "Congress Makes a Law," Stephen K. Bailey has described the legislative process as a drama played behind closed curtains. "It is much as though the citizenry were seated in a huge auditorium, allowed printed programs, but kept in total ignorance of what was happening on the stage. To the handful of citizens who have watched the show from the wings, this separation of players from audience is a dual tragedy: a tragedy for the players who might profit from audience reaction, a tragedy for the members of the audience who miss both entertainment and vitally needed education." In the drama of lawmaking there are as many competing directors and stage managers as there are would-be Hamlets. Nor are all the participants themselves privileged to see and hear the entire performance. Most of them give their orders or strut their bit and then take their places on the other side of the curtain to await the denouement. From his place in the wings Bailey proceeds to tell the story of the Employment Act of 1946, one of the dramas in which I played an active role. It seemed only natural that one of the characters should become an author.

But these two motives would scarcely have been sufficient by themselves. Far more important has been my growing belief in the need for a new and more realistic concept of the legislative process. I wrote the book mainly to develop such a concept—one that would emphasize people in action as the essence of legislative activity; that would analyze the role in the legislative process not only of members of Congress but also of Presidents and executive officials, judges, private organizations, and political parties; that would recognize the similarities between the legislative process and other governmental and social processes; and that would contribute to the development of better understanding of social behavior as a whole.

My basic aim has thus been to develop a theoretical structure, a systematic method of thinking about legislation. Yet I have always believed that if a theory does not work in a practical situation, it is a bad theory. I am, therefore, hopeful that the intellectual framework will stand up under the weight of practical application. If it does and if it therefore serves to promote more intelligent and more widespread participation in the writing of our laws, the effort will be amply rewarded.

In writing this book I have drawn extensively upon firsthand personal experience and upon secondhand experiences gleaned from discussions with other participants in the legislative process. I have also relied heavily upon the *Congressional Record,* congressional committee hearings and reports, and other publicly available records of legislative activity. My debt to other writers who have dealt with legislation is particularly great. The following have been the most helpful:

Arthur F. Bentley, "The Process of Government" (Bloomington, Indiana: Principia Press, 1949 reissue).

David B. Truman, "The Governmental Process" (New York: Knopf, 1951).

Woodrow Wilson, "Congressional Government" (Boston: Houghton Mifflin, 1885).

Stephen K. Bailey, "Congress Makes a Law" (New York: Columbia University Press, 1949).

Robert Luce's quartet: "Legislative Procedure," "Legislative Assemblies," "Legislative Principles," and "Legislative Problems" (Boston: Houghton Mifflin, 1922, 1930, 1930 and 1935, respectively).

Roland Young, "This Is Congress" (New York: Knopf, 1943).

George Galloway, "Congress at the Crossroads" (New York: Crowell, 1946).

James M. Burns, "Congress on Trial" (New York: Harper & Bros., 1949).

Joseph P. Chamberlain, "Legislative Processes: National and State" (New York: D. Appleton–Century, 1936).

Harvey Walker, "The Legislative Process" (New York: The Ronald Press, 1948).

Floyd M. Riddick, "The United States Congress: Organization and Procedure" (Washington, D.C.: National Capitol Publishers, 1949).

I must also express my indebtedness to those courageous friends who read carbon copies of the manuscript at various stages in its six years of growth and gave me the benefit of their advice and counsel. The hardiest of these souls are Ralph Goldman, of the American Political Science Association Cooperative Research Project on Convention Delegations, who assisted in reducing the first draft to a more suitable length; Stephen K. Bailey, of Wesleyan University; Arthur F. Bentley; Kurt Borchardt, of the House Committee on Interstate and Foreign Commerce; Kenneth Hechler, of Princeton University and the White House staff; Fritz Morstein Marx, of American University and the Bureau of the Budget; and Eve Zidel and Nora Gross, who wielded powerful vetoes by refusing to type anything that did not live up to their standards.

I am also grateful for the encouragement I have received from so many of my colleagues in the American Political Science Association. Participation in the Association's Committee on Political Parties and in the short-term special committees on Congressional Reapportionment and Soldier Voting has brought me into contact with some of the outstanding minds in American social science and has helped to deepen my understanding of governmental processes.

There may be those who believe that I have written too freely about confidential matters. My intention has been to write nothing that could be personally embarrassing to anyone. If there have been any deviations from this course, they have been accidental.

There are those whose writings on legislation and related matters have received too little attention in the text. For this I blame the rigorous limitations of space.

BERTRAM M. GROSS

ARLINGTON, VA.
JANUARY, 1953

CONTENTS

PART II. COMBAT ON THE LEGISLATIVE TERRAIN

THE LEGISLATIVE STRUGGLE

A Study in Social Combat

Chapter 1

THE TWOFOLD CHALLENGE: AN INTRODUCTION

EVERY YEAR the legislative process in Washington grinds out a bewildering variety of products. On the slight preeminence known as Capitol Hill, members of the Senate and the House of Representatives sponsor thousands of bills covering almost every conceivable subject. Many of these are unceremoniously ignored. Many become the focal point for energetic lobbying and propaganda, closed-door confabs, public hearings, and the making or unmaking of records, reputations, and election issues. Some win quiet acceptance in both houses. Others give rise to impassioned debate and voting, the forming and re-forming of political lines, or sharp disagreement between the two chambers.

Out of all the hubbub and confusion emerges a steady flow of bills to be signed by the Presiding Officer of the Senate and the Speaker of the House and carried by messenger up Pennsylvania Avenue to the White House. A few are stricken down by vetoes. Most are signed by the President and sent to the nearby Department of State where they are numbered, filed, and subsequently printed in the latest volume of an endless series entitled "United States Statutes at Large." These statutes embody decisions establishing a Federal budget which represents a huge share of the national income, regulating vast sectors of industry, agriculture, and labor, and extending the network of our economic, military, and political links with the rest of the world. They are the law of the land—to be administered for better or worse by the President and assorted bureaucrats; to be interpreted by the courts; to be praised, cursed, ignored, or supported by the American people; and sooner or later to be amended by other laws.

How do these laws really come into being? Why are these passed, and others not? Why was this clause voted down, and the proviso approved?

Does the national legislative process operate properly? How might it be improved?

These two sets of questions are not easy to answer. The legislative process is one of the methods of untying the Gordian knots created by the growing complexities of a highly organized capitalist society. Any attempt to describe it must recognize that it is closely interwoven with the full fabric of American life. Any effort to appraise and improve it must recognize that its weaknesses reflect underlying maladies, its strong points America's underlying strength. Yet for these very reasons the two sets of questions present a tempting challenge. Even partial success in discovering how the legislative process really operates would cast a penetrating light upon *homo americanus,* his folkways and mores, his place in today's sun. By grappling with proposals for improvement of the legislative process we can put ourselves in a better position to reflect upon his social ideals and ethics, to understand how his group life and conflicts determine the substance that fills the "interstices of democracy," and to help steer his path through the remaining decades of a troubled century.

The Problems of Description

Even in the physical sciences description is difficult. Every forward step in chemistry, physics, and biology has meant new challenges, new vistas for description and explanation. To meet these challenges and explore these vistas, physical scientists constantly must create new theoretical conceptions and new hypotheses that can be used to explain and organize the facts of physical life. They must develop new experiments and forms of observation to test their theories and hypotheses. They can rarely achieve complete certainty about anything fundamental. Progress is from one degree of possibility to a higher degree, with every basic theory being supplanted eventually by a new one that seems to provide a better explanation of reality.

In the social sciences observation is more difficult. Measurement is less frequently relevant. Controlled experiments are generally impossible, for the laboratory of the social scientist is society itself, and what happens in it is beyond his puny power to control. The intrusion of social and ethical values tends to blur the difference between "is" and "should be" and impedes the formulation of theories and hypotheses that can most fruitfully explain social processes. Hence the entire problem of social-science description and explanation is fraught with pitfalls.

The Inadequacy of a Formal Approach

One way to approach the problem of describing the legislative process is to look at the rules, procedures, and organizational structures. You will find some of them in the Constitution, many more in the Senate Manual, in the Rules of the House of Representatives, and in erudite tomes about Congress and the legislative process. If the rules really showed how the legislative process works, the inquiring analyst would have no choice but to grit his teeth and plow ahead through the heavy mass of detail. But the rules are merely fragmentary sources for finding out how some of the persons involved in the legislative process behave, claim to behave, or are expected to behave. One might just as well expect to learn about American and English literature by reading a dictionary. The only difference is that lawmakers break the rules of lawmaking far more frequently than writers depart from the spelling and definitions of the dictionary.

A slightly more sophisticated variant of this approach is to start with the assumption that the members of Congress make our laws. This assumption is buttressed by the first sentence in the first section of the American Constitution: "All legislative powers herein granted shall be vested in a Congress of the United States, which shall consist of a Senate and House of Representatives." It is reinforced by the fact that every bill introduced in Congress starts with the words: "Be it enacted by the Senate and House of Representatives of the United States of America in Congress assembled . . ." and, if passed, is then referred to as an "Act of Congress."[1] Yet the Constitution itself gives the President important legislative powers and functions: recommending, approving, disapproving. This practice, from the first weeks of the First Congress, has involved executive officials in the most intimate details of the legislative process. Judges also play an important role in the making of statutes; every interpretation of the Constitution or of an existing statute has a direct bearing upon the production of new statutes. All the agencies of government—Congress, the executive branch, the judiciary, and even the so-called "independent" boards and commissions, often referred to as the "fourth branch of government"—take part in the legislative process. You cannot learn much about it if you assume that the existence of separate agencies of the Federal government means that one of them has an exclusive franchise to operate the legislative process.

Nor is it very helpful to concede that all the branches of government help cook the legislative broth and therefore to assume that laws are made by government officials alone. Political parties are not a formal part of the government structure but they are a part of the legislative process. There is no place in the *Congressional Directory* or the Government Manual for interest groups and pressure groups, but there is a very real place for both in the process of lawmaking. Early in this century, one of the greatest of American political

[1] A law, of course, is not merely an act of Congress. No bill can become law without some act by the President also. When the first bill to be enacted under the Constitution was debated in Congress, the proposal was made that the President's name be included in the enacting clause. This proposal made no headway, probably because it called to mind the preamble used in England: "Be it enacted by the King's most Excellent Majesty, by and with the advice and consent of the Lords Spiritual and Temporal and Commons, in this present Parliament assembled. . . ." Senator Maclay wrote in his Journal: "This imitation of monarchy died a-borning." "Journal of William Maclay" (New York: Appleton-Century-Crofts, 1890), May 5, 1789, pp. 18–19.

writers, Arthur F. Bentley, pointed out the danger of trying to understand government by looking at government alone:

> A discussion of the work and defects of a state legislature carries one nowhere as long as the legislature is taken for what it purports to be—a body of men who deliberate upon and adopt laws. Not until the actual lawmaking is traced from its efficient demand to its actual application, can one tell just where the real law-creating work is done, and whether the legislature was Moses the law-giver or merely Moses the registration clerk.[2]

Bentley's comment applies just as well to the national legislative process.

A Realistic Approach

Another approach to the problem of description is to start with the recognition that the process of government is one of struggle as well as of cooperation. "There is no political process that is not a balancing of quantity against quantity. There is not a law that is passed that is not the expression of force and force in tension. There is not a court decision or an executive act that is not the result of the same process. Understanding any of these phenomena means measuring the elements that have gone into them." [3] From this viewpoint the production of statutes is far from a dull and static application of formal procedures to an issue of public policy. It is a dynamic process which, like any large-scale military operation, follows no rigid pattern. At every turn there are difficult choices to be made either on broad strategy or on daily tactics. The rules and procedures are the codes of battle. The agencies of government are instruments in the organization and disposition of contending forces. A statute is merely one of the things that can happen as a result of the struggle: a compromise, an armed truce, a prelude to the next conflict, or, more rarely, an all-out victory for one side.

It would be possible to describe this process with more euphemistic words, such as "adjustment" or "bargaining." Both could probably be interpreted in a manner that would give the full flavor of group conflict. Yet "adjustment" overemphasizes the end result of given conflicts and does too little justice to the motives and methods of the actors in the drama. "Bargaining," while bet-

[2] Arthur L. Bentley, "The Process of Government: A Study of Social Pressures" (Bloomington, Ind.: University of Chicago Press, 1908; reissued, Principia Press, 1935 and 1949), p. 163. Until recently, this book has been one of the neglected classics in the literature of social science. See this author's review of the 1949 reissue in *American Political Science Review,* Vol. 44, No. 3, September, 1950. "The Governmental Process," by David B. Truman (New York: Knopf, 1951), restates Bentley's approach in more up-to-date terms. An excellent application of this approach to the history of a single legislative contest is made by Earl Latham in "The Group Basis of Politics: A Study in Basing-point Legislation" (Ithaca, N.Y.: Cornell University Press, 1952).

[3] Bentley, *op. cit.,* p. 202.

ter oriented toward the activities of the participants, is too narrow a concept. Just as "competition" has long since proved itself as one of the most expressive terms in economics, "struggle" is the most useful term with which to describe the process of government. In this struggle men and women tend to align themselves in various groupings rather than operate as isolated individuals.

All phenomena of government are phenomena of groups pressing one another, forming one another, and pushing out new groups and group representatives (the organs or agencies of government) to mediate the adjustments. It is only as we isolate these group activities, determine their representative values, and get the whole process stated in terms of them, that we approach to a satisfactory knowledge of government.[4]

Individuals, it must be recognized, are of great importance—but their importance stems from their actual or potential relationship to groups. They are the bedrock materials from which groups are organized. They supply the ideas and leadership needed for successful group operations or, for that matter, even for rudimentary group organization. This does not mean that individual ability and personality are unimportant; they are often decisive factors. It means that individual leadership can be understood only in its relationship to group activities.

It is for this reason that Part I of this book is entitled "The Contestants." Without giving primary attention to people and to types of people, government becomes a lifeless landscape instead of the vital and human drama that it really is. The contestants in the legislative process are, in the first place, persons like the rest of us. They become *special* persons, with *special* criteria of choice, as a result of their membership in certain groups or kinds of groups; for example, the legislature itself, a political party, a privately organized association or "pressure group," one of the other branches of government, etc. They act as members of one or another of these groups, and frequently this action becomes a formalized part of the legislative process. More frequently their actions must be described as "informal" and "typical," at all times difficult to extricate from the maze of legislative pushing and pulling. A shift of the eye will move our attention from the individuals as group members to the groups themselves.

There are all sorts of groups engaged in this struggle: organized groups and potential groups, formal ones and informal ones, private organizations, political parties, government agencies, and blocs or factions within any of them. Some of these are transitory; others are hoary with age. Some are local in character; others are large and sprawling groups with supply and communication lines extending like a network across America and into many other countries.

Group conflict has often been described in terms of economic classes. James Madison took this approach in his famous Federalist Paper, No. 10:

[4] *Ibid.*, p. 300.

A landed interest, a manufacturing interest, a mercantile interest, a moneyed interest, with many lesser interests, grow up of necessity in civilized nations, and divide them into different classes, actuated by different sentiments and views. The regulation of these various and interfering interests forms the principal task of modern legislation, and involves the spirit of party and faction in the necessary and ordinary operations of the government.[5]

Oliver Wendell Holmes made a similar observation early in his juristic career:

The more powerful interests must be more or less reflected in legislation. The objection to class legislation is not that it favors a class, but either that it fails to benefit the legislators, or that it is dangerous to them because a competing class has gained in power, or that it transcends the limits of self-preference which are imposed by sympathy. . . . But it is no sufficient condemnation of legislation that it favors one class at the expense of another; for much or all legislation does that. . . .[6]

It would be a serious oversimplification, however, to assume that all the important groups are highly organized "classes" in the Marxist sense of the term. Only a few have class consciousness. Many of the most cohesive groups have very narrow purposes far removed from the idea of class domination of American society. Instead of standing alone in tight isolation, most of them develop close relations with other groups, forming an intricate pattern of clusters and coalitions. Some are interested mainly in the process of mediating between conflicting groups. Few make exclusive claims upon the loyalties of their members; overlapping membership is the rule rather than the exception. Nor can the purposes of many groups be fitted into a watertight set of compartments such as economic, political, sectional, religious, or nationalistic; most of them tend to represent a combination of two or more of these.

The most generalized method of describing the purpose of all these groups is to regard the struggle as one to win a larger share of power or maintain their present share. From this viewpoint the term power must be regarded in its broadest sense as including (1) political power of the formal type, (2) control of worldly goods of all types, machinery, know-how, and the monetary claims to any of these forms of wealth, and (3) the power to impress one's ideas upon a larger part of one's community, win security, and obtain deference. Political scientists tend to concentrate on the production and distribution of power; economists on the production and distribution of wealth; but neither special approach should obscure the fact that the basic struggles in society are power contests.

If the entire process of government can be described as one of group struggle for power, how does the legislative process differ from the administrative

[5] "The Federalist" (New York: Modern Library Series, Random House, 1937), p. 56.

[6] Oliver Wendell Holmes, "The Gas Stokers' Strike," *American Law Review,* Vol. 7, 1873, pp. 583–584.

process and the judicial process? When viewed at a high enough level of abstraction, there is little or no difference. Both the contestants in the struggle and their objectives are generally the same. At a more specific level of description, however, the difference is that the legislative struggle is fought on a different battlefield. This calls for a more specialized use of general weapons and a development of specialized strategy, tactics, rules, procedures, and organizational forms.

From this viewpoint, an analysis of the formalized aspects of the legislative process becomes tremendously significant. It is every bit as important as is the analysis of the terrain to a historian whose task it is to record a great military engagement. Many of the fundamental conflicts in the legislative struggle are fought over the procedures and forms of government. Formal changes can be of great influence upon the course of the victories won, the defeats suffered, the compromises fashioned, and the truces solemnized. It is for this very reason that the participants in the legislative struggle concern themselves with the most minute details of rules, procedures, and organization. This, too, explains why proposed changes in the rules, procedures, and organizational forms are bitterly contested and why many "improvements," which abstract logic would seem to require, simply never take place.

The Obstacles to a Realistic Approach

It is the realistic approach upon which the activities of the more effective leaders in legislative conflicts have always been based. With few exceptions, they approach the task of legislation as one of social engineering, of the organization of power for the purpose of attaining a specific objective. To operate on any other assumption would mean a waste of their time.

Yet the fact that someone operates on the assumption that the legislative process is one of group struggle does not mean that he is consciously aware of this assumption or capable of accurately describing it. This is a basic obstacle to a realistic look at government. There are undoubtedly many participants in this struggle who are sincerely carried away by the river of words written or uttered about the legislative process by themselves, their associates, or their opponents.

> We have in this world many lawyers who know nothing of law making. They play their part, and their learning is justified by their work. We have many lawmakers who know nothing of law. They too play their part and their wisdom—though they may not be able to give it verbal expression—is nonetheless real. But the practical lore of neither of these types of men is a scientific knowledge of society nor by putting the two layers together do we make an advance. It is they themselves we must study and know, for what they are, for what they represent.[7]

[7] Bentley, *op. cit.*, p. 164.

Furthermore, the more one is embroiled in the legislative struggle or any other form of social combat, the more he knows that everything he says is a weapon that can be used on his behalf or, if he is not on his guard, can be used against him. Hence the proclivity of every group spokesman to describe his activities as being above the realm of narrow partisan interests and wholly and unselfishly dedicated to the welfare of everybody. Hence the habitual insistence of persons in all branches of government that they are above the madding throng and wholly dedicated to advancing the national interest irrespective of the pressures exerted upon them.

Another obstacle is the blunt fact that the legislative struggle is unbelievably complex. Many of the most sophisticated and acute observers can participate in a legislative battle without ever succeeding in obtaining a clear idea of the forces that make for victory or defeat. Two of the persons who were in the center of the conflict involved in the Atomic Energy Act of 1946 put it this way:

> The historian who attempts to recreate this drama is appalled by the confused and chaotic nature of the action. The scene that confronts him resembles the description of the Battle of Borodino in Tolstoy's "War and Peace." The hosts gather, impelled by some impulse deeper than they comprehend, seeking a goal they do not altogether understand. The struggle that ensues takes on a life of its own, independent of any individual's will or direction. The conflict swirls and eddies and becomes not one but scores of battles, each appearing crucial to its participants. The field is a confused jumble of motion, the whole is obscured in smoke, and even the commanding generals have little understanding of developments, much less any effective control of them. The motives of the contestants are frequently obscure; the action is extended over weeks or months, rather than hours; there are sometimes not two but several armies engaged; alliances are shifted in the heat of battle; and in the end the issue is not decided on the field at all but in some clandestine meeting among rival leaders.[8]

This quotation illustrates the difficulty of following the course of only one of the battles that took place in 1946. During the same year, as in any year, there was not one but scores of Borodinos. To describe the legislative struggle as a whole in any year would be to give a complete cross section of American society.

A third obstacle in the description and explanation of governmental and legislative processes arises from the tendency to confuse realism with cynicism. Charges of "cynicism" and "immorality" have been levied against Machiavelli; yet few writers have contributed more to our understanding of political realities. In the present account of the legislative process there will be ample opportunity for similar charges. For example, the objectivity with which judges do and *do not* arrive at decisions is discussed. The "myth" of objectivity is distinguished from the realities in language that may be vigorous for the sake

[8] James R. Newman and Byron S. Miller, "The Control of Atomic Energy" (New York: McGraw-Hill, 1948), p. 9.

of emphasis. Similar editorialization and use of examples and language appear throughout this book. The object is *not* to be cynical and destructive but to state an observation with force and to give a slant upon the truth which stems from many years of personal participation in the processes being described. After all, most of our laws, rules, and "understandings" about the processes of government are really myths and fictions whose acceptance, tongue in cheek or otherwise, is necessary for making national and group life and disputes bearable for all.

The Problem of "Should Be"

One of the major differences between the physical and the social sciences is that in addition to dealing with "has been," "is," and "may be," the latter focuses directly on "should be" also. In the physical sciences social values may affect the selection of one's field of specialization. In the social sciences they are part of any field one selects. To neglect their consideration is to deal with the material in an incomplete fashion or else to have one's normative judgments traipse around in the guise of factual observations.

No Absolute Standards

One of the most persistent of all ideas about social change is the delusion that intelligence or education can provide objective solutions to problems of public policy. As standard-bearers of the one and purveyors of the other, social scientists should therefore, it is claimed, be able to advise on maladjustments in the social organisms as authoritatively as physicians handle diseases of the body. If capable social scientists disagree or even line up in dramatically opposite camps, the reason is given that someone's methodology is out of joint, a "mature discipline" has not yet been developed, or that the foundations have not furnished enough money to support essential research.

The effort to establish absolute standards, of course, is made every day. It is a habitual part of every propaganda campaign, one that is used in the legislative struggle itself every time the claim is made that this or that bill is the ultimate method of saving freedom and democracy or making the Government efficient. Yet if rules, procedures, and organizational structures are merely the more formalized methods through which the legislative struggle is conducted, they can be judged only in terms of their function as instruments in the struggle. A rule or procedure can be "good" only in the light of its utility in facilitating the efforts of given groups to achieve given objectives. It can be "bad" only because it frustrates, or inadequately facilitates, such objectives. To regard it as good or bad in itself would be a rejection of the realistic approach to the problem of description.

If the realistic approach to the legislative process is accepted, one can then obtain absolute standards of judgment only by regarding as absolute the aims and views of one social group, or cluster of groups, among the contestants in the legislative struggle. This is entirely justifiable and indeed praiseworthy—but one deludes himself when he thinks that his own social standards are capable someday of revealing themselves in a blaze of glory to everyone else and of commanding the same broad acceptance as the proposition that two plus two makes four. Conflicting standards of judgment are inherent in the structure of the democratic society; every reconciliation of conflicting standards is usually merely the prelude to a new clash in the future. The only final decisions are made on the basis of power in one form or another. Once they are made, it is then the province of historians to carry on endless debates on whether Might made Right.

There are those to whom one or another set of abstract forms of government is enshrined as a moral absolute and who, if these abstractions are seriously deprecated, find themselves tottering on the edge of moral cynicism and emptiness. The trouble here is a lack of self-recognition, for the deep attachment to abstract forms is itself a reflection of group values and affiliations.

There are also those who stick to abstractions in the effort to avoid substantive controversy and to be constructive without seeming to leave the confines of the ivory tower. Yet the abstractions themselves, if they are at all meaningful, are in some way tied in with the partisan controversies of one's era. From the time of Plato and Aristotle to the present, the greatest writers on government have been protagonists of one or another social viewpoint and have dealt with governmental forms as instruments for achieving their objectives.

The Author's Standards

It is entirely possible to regard "should be" judgments of the legislative process as themselves data to be scientifically described. One can analyze the motivations behind a proposal, its probable effect, and the reasons for resistance to it. In this manner one can best understand the significance of various proposals for change and relate normative judgments to the process of group conflict.

Yet it is impossible to decree a divorce of head from heart in order to describe these judgments and proposals in a purely objective manner. No matter how carefully one may seek to balance the scales, he can scarcely avoid weighing the scales on the side he favors. Even the selection of the proposals to be explained, the order in which they are discussed, and the amount of attention given to each tend to reflect personal biases. True objectivity consists not of trying to withhold judgment but of recognizing one's biases. Straightforward analysis requires an effort to state these biases as candidly as possible.

A full statement of the author's personal values would require another book. For the present purposes it is probably sufficient to list several of the author's "inarticulate major premises." One is deep-rooted support for those who speak and act to provide the underprivileged, the underorganized, and the underrepresented with a greater share of material goods and of power to affect the decisions that shape their lives. Another is an instinctive support for governmental operations designed to provide more adequate opportunities for individual growth and security and to help prevent the scourges of depression, inflation, and war. Still another is the placement of a high moral value upon the diversity and pluralism of American society, as distinguished from the deadliness of any society in which one group achieves complete domination. This is coupled with strong attachments to certain group values and allegiances and a strong propensity—nourished by an overfondness for the excitements of combat and by years of self-restraint in the civil service—to advance these views through all available channels of academic, nonpartisan, political, unofficial, and official activity. Finally, as a guide to such activity, is the conviction that power without idealism is barbarity and that idealism without power is futility.

The Method of Presentation

One method of attacking the twofold problem of description and prescription would be to jump directly into the middle of things and deal with such matters as the birth and drafting of legislative proposals.

Yet these activities can scarcely be seen in three-dimensional reality unless one focuses upon the people and groups who bring about the birth, do the drafting, and carry on the legislative process in all its many phases. It is, therefore, more meaningful to begin at the beginning and to introduce rather fully the actors in the drama.

This is done in Part I, "The Contestants: Reality and Reform." Two chapters deal with the private organizations (Chaps. 2 and 3), two with the political parties (Chaps. 4 and 5), and two with the government agencies (Chaps. 6 and 7). The first chapter in each pair presents a descriptive survey and a discussion of the role of each set of actors in the legislative drama. The second chapter in each pair presents a survey of reform proposals relevant to each type of contestant. As a result of this related handling of description and prescription, it is hoped that the subsequent account of the legislative struggle in process will take on sharper meaning.

At the end of Part I comes "The Contestants and Their Power" (Chap. 8).

Here the effort is made to indicate the sources of the power exercised by the various contestants in the legislative struggle and to indicate how this power may be extended through various sorts of combinations.

Part II, "Combat on the Legislative Terrain," attempts to capture the movement and vigor of the legislative struggle. It points up the basic decisions that need to be made by the various contestants in it and tells of the long and muddy marches which are the daily lot of those actively involved. Shall a bill be introduced into the congressional hopper, or shall some other arena of social combat be selected (Chap. 9)? Whence and when shall it originate (Chap. 10)? What words and ideas shall go into the design of a bill as a combat vehicle (Chap. 11)? How and by whom shall the legislative troops be organized and led (Chap. 12)? How shall the arsenal of propaganda and pressure best be employed (Chap. 13)? What are the strategies and the tactics of the infighting that occurs in congressional committees (Chaps. 14–16)? What happens as the battle front moves onto the floor of Congress (Chaps. 17–18)? After Congress registers its approval of a bill, how does the legislative struggle sweep on to the choice to be made by the President (Chap. 19)? And, finally, having gone over the battleground that is Congress, what comments may be made regarding the improvement of the rules of on-the-ground legislative warfare (Chap. 20)?

In each of these chapters generalizations and examples are liberally mixed together. To describe the legislative process through a series of case studies would not have permitted sufficient interpretation. An abstract presentation of different phases of the process would hardly present it in its full flavor and variety.

While Part II describes scores of problems that are faced by participants in the legislative process, it should not be thought for a moment that all or even most of them arise in connection with an individual bill. Also, there is a danger of reading into the picture a more conscious awareness of strategies and tactical considerations than really exists. Most contestants deal with the majority of problems on the basis of habit and rote and engage in active calculation on only a handful of problems.

Part III provides a brief conclusion devoted to a general appraisal of the potentialities for future change in the legislative process (Chap. 21).

Much of the material presented in these chapters is relevant to the legislative process in the states. Occasional references are made to state experiences. However, the analysis deals directly with the national process only.

In the preparation of these chapters, considerable use has been made not only of the publicly available records concerning legislative activity, but also of personal experiences that can scarcely be documented by references to other sources. Other writings dealing directly or indirectly with the legislative process have also been drawn upon extensively. The major references which the author would recommend as most pertinent to a general understanding of the legislative process are as follows:

1. Arthur F. Bentley, "The Process of Government" (Bloomington, Ind.: Principia Press, 1949 reissue).
2. David B. Truman, "The Governmental Process" (New York: Knopf, 1951).
3. Woodrow Wilson, "Congressional Government" (Boston: Houghton Mifflin, 1885).
4. Stephen K. Bailey, "Congress Makes a Law" (New York: Columbia University Press, 1949).
5. Robert Luce's quartet: "Legislative Procedure," "Legislative Assemblies," "Legislative Principles," and "Legislative Problems" (Boston: Houghton Mifflin, 1922, 1930, 1930, and 1935, respectively).
6. Roland A. Young, "This Is Congress" (New York: Knopf, 1943).
7. George Galloway, "Congress at the Crossroads" (New York: Crowell, 1946).
8. James M. Burns, "Congress on Trial" (New York: Harper, 1949).
9. Joseph P. Chamberlain, "Legislative Processes: National and State" (New York: Appleton-Century-Crofts, 1936).
10. Harvey Walker, "Legislative Process; Lawmaking in the United States" (New York: Ronald, 1948).
11. Floyd M. Riddick, "The United States Congress: Organization and Procedure" (Washington, D.C.: National Capitol Publishers, 1949).

PART I

THE CONTESTANTS: REALITY AND REFORM

Chapter 2

THE PRIVATE ORGANIZATIONS

THE SIMPLEST method of classifying the groups that take part in the legislative struggle is to divide them into private organizations, parties, and government agencies. The first term covers such private groups as the American Federation of Labor and the General Motors Corporation, the Baptist church and the American Wild Life Institute. The second refers to the Democratic and Republican parties, the various minor parties, and the wings and factions in all of them. The third covers the Congress, the executive branch, the judiciary, and local and foreign governments.

Yet the formal quality of this classification should not lead one to overlook certain fundamental similarities. The term "group"—whether it applies to a private organization, a party, or a government agency—merely provides a way of talking about people acting in concert. When we say that a corporation has started a propaganda campaign, a party has drawn up a platform, or a government agency has spent its funds wastefully, we are talking in each case about the actions of individual persons. There is no such thing as an organization, party, or agency consciousness or philosophy apart from the individuals who make up the group. "Collective consciousness and behavior," as Allport has pointed out, "are simply the aggregation of those states and reactions of individuals which, owing to similarities of constitution, training, and common stimulations, are possessed of a similar character." [1] Each group represents an organization of individual opinions. It is the welter of diversified sets of opinions which is the reality behind the much-abused term "public opinion." As John Dickinson observed many years ago: "The larger number of members of any political society have no opinion, and hence no will, on nearly all the matters on which government acts. The only opinion, the only will, which exists is the opinion, the will, of special groups." [2]

The person who has a degree of responsibility in one of these groups may seem to represent—and in a way does represent—much more than himself.

[1] Floyd Henry Allport, "Social Psychology" (Boston: Houghton Mifflin, 1924), p. 6.

[2] John Dickinson, "Democratic Realities and Democratic Dogmas," *American Political Science Review,* Vol. 24, February, 1930, p. 291.

Essentially he is a human being and, despite the halo of importance that may encircle his brow, he is subject to the same drives, impulses, and failings as are other human beings.[3] Each type of group provides both leaders and members with an opportunity to solve inner conflicts by losing themselves in a "cause" and building the sense of security that can be derived only from working in cooperation with others. Each can be subdivided into smaller groups that lead and larger ones that follow.[4] Each opens up avenues toward personal advancement—whether that advancement be measured in terms of profit, power, prestige, or any combination of these. All tend to serve as vehicles for pursuing the immediate interests of their leaders and members rather than what others may conceive of as their "ultimate" interest or the "national" interest.[5] This tendency cannot be disputed on the ground that "material" interests, measured in terms of money, are often far weaker than such "nonmaterial" interests as the drive to achieve greater power, status, admiration, or self-respect; these latter interests are often the most immediate and compelling of all.

There is a profound difference between interests as such and organized groups. An interest by itself has neither eyes, voice, nor motive power. If, at a given moment, it should be to the immediate interest of domestic sugar producers to prevent the importation of Cuban sugar, the mere existence of that interest does not mean that anything will be done. Rather, it indicates a potentiality for the organization or operation of some group based upon the desire to restrict the importation of Cuban sugar. It provides an opportunity for private organizations, politicians, and government officials to organize sugar growers and in one way or another to do something about their interest. For almost every underlying interest of any importance there are competing organizations seeking to build upon that interest, or competing organizers seeking to start a group of some sort. The more pronounced these interests and the more deeply they are felt, the greater is the probability that an organization may be built to represent a large portion of those who share the interest in common. Yet the complete organization of people with common

[3] The Great Man, of course, usually succeeds in concealing this fact from most people, particularly himself. The aura of semidivinity often becomes so impressive that not even his closest associates—with the possible exception of wife, mistress, or psychiatrist—realize how much he resembles other human beings.

[4] The classic description of the oligarchic tendencies within social groups is found in Robert Michels, "Political Parties" (Glencoe, Ill.: The Free Press, 1949 ed.).

[5] ". . . if the conduct of human beings was determined by no other interested considerations than those which constitute their 'real' interest, neither monarchy nor oligarchy would be such bad governments as they are. . . . It is not what their interest is, but what they suppose it to be, that is the important consideration with respect to their conduct. . . . As Coleridge observes, the man makes the motive, not the motive the man." John Stuart Mill, "Considerations on Representative Government" (New York: Macmillan, 1947 ed.), pp. 183–184.

interests rarely takes place. Organizers and leaders have their limitations. Many people with interests in common tend to be lethargic or concerned mainly with other problems. As a result, organized groups are usually but an imperfect organization of underlying interests.

"Pressure Groups" and the Legislative Process

In recent years it has become customary, both in colloquial language and in the learned writings of political science and economics, to refer to private organizations as "special-interest groups" or "pressure groups."

Yet both these terms have an invidious connotation that impairs their utility in objective analysis. The "special interests" or the "vested interests" are organizations one looks upon with disfavor as contrasted with organizations with which one sympathizes and therefore regards as laboring in the "public" or "national" interest. "Pressure groups," similarly, usually turn out to be those which exert pressure in the "wrong" direction. Those which exert the "right" kind of pressure are educational bodies working on behalf of the majority of the people.[6]

Neither term, moreover, is a precise label. Both refer to characteristics shared by parties and government agencies. The Republican party and the Department of Agriculture, for example, have as many special interests as the United States Chamber of Commerce and, in their own way, also make use of pressure techniques. Hence, the most serviceable label is simply "private organizations."

Who They Are

"Americans of all ages, all conditions, and all dispositions, constantly form associations. They have not only commercial and manufacturing companies, in which all take part, but associations of a thousand other kinds—religious, moral, serious, futile, extensive or restricted, enormous or diminutive."[7]

If private organizations of this type played a significant role in the young capitalist society observed by De Tocqueville, they became even more significant with the growth of American civilization during the subsequent century. Through them, people organize to make a living, achieve social status, provide for material aid and self-protection, and engage in cultural, religious, and self-expressive activities. They have become a dominant part of the

[6] A splendid attack on the invidious connotation of "special interests" is contained in Dickinson, *op. cit.*, p. 292.

[7] Alexis de Tocqueville, "Democracy in America" (New York: Oxford, 1947 ed.), p. 319. It is an interesting commentary on the ambiguity of the term "public" that De Tocqueville habitually refers to these associations as "public" associations. "Public" is used to distinguish both the general public from the government and government agencies from private agencies.

structure of American society, relegating the family group to a somewhat more subordinate position and providing an indispensable foundation for the organization of political parties and government agencies.

The most powerful and the most intimately developed organizations are those composed of businessmen. The basic business grouping is the corporation, "a means whereby"—to quote the classic study on the modern corporation—"the wealth of innumerable individuals has been concentrated into huge aggregates and whereby control over this wealth has been surrendered to a unified direction."[8] Many corporations are "holding companies" rather than organizations directly engaged in business operations; through the pyramiding of stock ownership they control the business activities of many lesser corporations. The largest corporations are vast economic empires with financial resources greater than those of most states. Also, in almost every phase of manufacturing, mining, transportation, construction, distribution, foreign commerce, and finance, there are firmly established trade associations; most of these are controlled by the management of the larger corporations among their membership. Finally there are the peak associations, such as the National Association of Manufacturers and the United States Chamber of Commerce, which purport to act on behalf of business as a whole. In these organizations, as well, the dominant influence is that exercised by certain corporate members.

Next in importance come the organizations in the farm and labor fields. There are special associations for individual agricultural-commodities groupings, such as milk, fruit and vegetable, cattle, wheat, cotton, wool, and sugar. Many of these are quite similar to the trade associations on the business front. This similarity derives not only from the fact that farmers are business entrepreneurs but also from the extensive agricultural holdings of insurance companies and other nonagricultural business organizations. Nationally, there are at least four major peak farm organizations: the American Farm Bureau Federation, the National Grange, the Farmers Educational and Cooperative Union (usually referred to as the National Farmers Union), and the National Council of Farmer Cooperatives.

Labor unions also are organized by individual lines of business activity. Some are associations of craftsmen, such as machinists, bricklayers, and electricians. Others—and the trend has been increasingly in this direction—are industrial unions covering such fields as coal mining, steel, shipbuilding, and textiles. Most of these are affiliated with one of the two major national groups: the American Federation of Labor or the Congress of Industrial Organizations. A number of unions, such as the Brotherhood of Railroad Trainmen, maintain an independent and unaffiliated status. Most of the craft unions in the railroad in-

[8] Adolf Berle and Gardner Means, "The Modern Corporation and Private Property" (New York: Macmillan, 1937), p. 2.

dustry, including both independents and A.F.L. affiliates, are represented in the Railway Labor Executives Association.

There are also hosts of other private organizations that may not measure up to the business, farm, and labor groups in general significance but are nevertheless an integral part of American life. In the religious field there is a vast array of organized churches, church societies interested in causes that go far beyond the purely religious, and church affiliates for both women and younger people. Veterans are organized into two huge groups: the American Legion and the Veterans of Foreign Wars, and into a number of smaller and competing bodies. There are also separate veterans' organizations for each war in which the United States has taken part, for various categories of veterans—overseas, wounded, and disabled—and for veterans of different religions. There are special organizations for Negroes, Italians, Irishmen, and other nationality or racial groups; for women, youth, the aged, and the physically handicapped. There are professional groups like the American Bar Association, the American Medical Association, the National Education Association, and the American Political Science Association. There are organizations which speak the views of the Left, such as Americans for Democratic Action, and others which advance the philosophy of the Right, such as the Committee for Constitutional Government. There are organizations established for the sole purpose of serving as fronts, allies, preceptors, scouts, and trial-balloon testers for other groups who stay behind the scenes and pull the strings.

Private organizations defy any ready-made classification. Many of those that might be regarded as primarily economic organizations engage in cultural activities. Nationality and minority groups usually have clear-cut economic objectives. A sense of fervor and consecration that merits description by the term "religious" can be found in many organizations completely outside the formal church groups. Almost all have political objectives of one sort or another. Even the categories "reactionary," "conservative," "liberal," and "radical" are hard to apply. American society is fluid rather than highly stratified. At any one time most of these organizations contain conflicting currents within them, and the strength of these currents varies with the shifting trends in the economic development of the country and in the business cycle, with the pendulum swing between war and peace, and with the unpredictable influence of leaders and organizers.

Upon first examination the difference in the way these groups organize—entirely apart from social objectives—appears bewildering. The variations in type of membership, in the election of officers, in the relationship between central offices and local units, and in the discharge of legislative, executive, and judicial functions are every bit as great (and as fascinating) as those between the governments of nations. Underlying these differences, however, are at least three striking similarities. First, each is subject to internal struggles over positions of leadership, particularly between the "ins" and the "outs," but also among the "ins" and among the "outs." Second, the loyalty of most leaders and members of each group is shared with other groups; overlapping group membership has the dual effect of promoting internal conflict and serving as a "balancing force in the politics of a multigroup society such as the United States." [9] Third, each represents a combination of formalized structure which tends to become crystallized in constitutions and bylaws and of informal arrangements that are never recorded in the rules and seldom meet the eye. Recognition of these traits is fundamental to an understanding of the role of private associations in the legislative struggle.

Their Role in the Legislative Struggle

In other countries private organizations have at times been formally given a central position in the structure of the state. The separate houses or "estates" of legislative bodies have themselves been the vehicles for group organization. Thus, to pick an extreme example, the early Swedish constitution provided for five separate houses, one for the great landlords, one for the bishops, one for the landed gentry, one for the representatives of the burghers of the town, and one for representatives of the farmers and peasants. In the development of fascism during the period between World Wars I and II a basic principle called for turning over governmental functions to organizations of private businessmen. In Italy these bodies were known as "corporations" and they were supposed to represent labor as well as business. In Germany the central role was given to the cartels and the peak associations.

In the United States the formal position given to private associations has been either temporary or incidental. For a brief period under the NRA codes, vast governmental authority was vested in trade associations. This period was brought to a halt by a unanimous Supreme Court decision in which the judges, while declaring that the code-making authority conferred on the President was "an unconstitutional delegation of legislative power," also took time out to criticize the role of private groups.[10] Both executive agencies and congressional committees have from time to time set up advisory committees composed mainly of the official representatives of business, agricultural, la-

[9] David B. Truman, "The Governmental Process" (New York: Knopf, 1951), p. 520. For an interesting discussion of overlapping membership and its implications, see all of Chaps. 6 and 16.

[10] ". . . would it be seriously contended that Congress should delegate its legislative authority to trade or industrial associations or groups so as to empower them to enact the laws they deem to be wise and beneficent for the rehabilitation and expansion of their trade or industries? . . . The answer is obvious. Such a delegation of legislative power is unknown to our law and is utterly inconsistent with the constitutional prerogatives and duties of Congress." *Schechter Poultry Corporation v. United States,* 1935.

bor, or professional organizations. In the case of certain executive agencies, some of these committees have at times been given a formal veto power over governmental decisions.[11]

The informal role of private organizations, however, has been so intensive that observers constantly—and ruefully—refer to "government by pressure groups." Private organizations make themselves felt in the political parties by influencing the selection of candidates and the drafting of campaign platforms, by campaign contributions, and by electioneering. At times, their leaders become personally active in political parties. They play an important role in influencing appointments to executive and judicial positions and to congressional committees. They organize "blocs" in Congress: farm blocs, mining blocs, labor blocs, and others. Occasionally their leaders themselves win posts in the Government, or, what amounts to almost the same thing, members of Congress or executive officials are given official positions of leadership in private organizations. On matters of public policy in which they are interested they collect facts and statistics, develop new ideas and angles, and draft proposed bills and regulations. The larger organizations hire experts, technicians, and contact men (these are the lobbyists) who sometimes come to know more about their subject than anyone else in the country, even including the specialists in the executive branch of the Government. Finally (and it is this point of their activity which is most conspicuous) they conduct campaigns to achieve their objectives at all stages of the legislative process—from the decision on whether or not to have a bill to the time of Presidential signature or veto.

Hardly a year goes by without a hue and cry being raised against the lobbyists who represent private organizations. In February, 1947, for example, Representative Adolph Sabath of Illinois made a nationwide broadcast in which he demanded a sweeping investigation of lobbies, lobbyists, and propagandists. "When I first came to Congress 40 years ago," he declared, "I found the ever-present railroad lobby, the banking lobby, the shipping lobby, and, most vicious of all, the power lobby, and others too numerous to mention. Not only are all those lobbies still operating, but scores more have joined the battle of pressures. . . ."[12] Later in the same year, in a message sent to Congress after he had reluctantly signed the Rent Decontrol and Housing Act, President Truman attacked the real-estate lobby as "subversive of representative government" and called for a congressional investigation.[13]

Behind both these attacks was a disagreement with the objectives of specific pressure groups. The fact that Representative Sabath was really opposed to

[11] Under the Hospital Survey and Construction Act of 1946, for example, the Surgeon General is required to prescribe certain regulations "with the approval of the Federal Hospital Council." Most of the members of the Federal Hospital Council, set up in the same Act, are representatives of hospital and health organizations.

[12] *Congressional Record* (daily edition), Feb. 26, 1947, pp. A753–A754.

[13] *The New York Times,* July 1, 1947.

only certain types of lobbies was revealed in a somewhat piquant statement later in the same broadcast. "The detrimental effect on the country of all these skilled and ruthless private-interest pressure groups has forced veterans, consumers, law, women, and even religious groups to counteract these other poisonous influences and work for the public interest."[14] President Truman's blast was more sophisticated, being aimed only at the lobbies opposing rent control and public housing. The fact that neither of the two requests for investigations was granted is testimony to the weakness of the pressure groups favored by Messrs. Sabath and Truman. Historically, lobby investigations themselves come into being largely as the result of lobbying. The 1913 investigation of the National Association of Manufacturers was the product of the American Federation of Labor's campaign for the Clayton Act. Senator Nye's investigation of munitions makers was a triumph for the women's peace societies. Senator Black's probe of the private-power lobby was strongly backed by the public-power lobby. Senator La Follette's civil-liberties investigation was strongly backed by the labor lobby.

The methods by which private groups influence legislation have also been under constant attack. In 1910, revelations of bribes accepted by Congressmen in exchange for votes resulted in the Corrupt Practices Act. Secrecy of operation, allegedly unethical operations within the law, exaggerated claims as to an organization's effectiveness or the number of people for whom it speaks—all these have been struck at through efforts to bring the facts before the public view. Investigations by congressional committees have been one method. Another has been the requirement of registration with a designated public officer. In 1940, as a defense measure, all representatives of foreign governments were compelled to register with the Department of State. The Legislative Reorganization Act of 1946, in a rather loosely worded passage, provided for the quarterly filing of financial statements with the Secretary of the Senate and the Clerk of the House by persons who receive or spend money for the principal purpose of influencing legislation. In an equally ambiguous section any person "who shall engage himself for pay or for any consideration" for the purpose of attempting to influence legislation is to register quarterly with the Secretary of the Senate and the Clerk of the House.

The private associations as such—as distinguished from their representatives and their methods of operating—have also been subjected to criticism. Stuart Chase has penned the following indictment: "Pressure groups have long been the despair of patriots. They have been responsible for some of the darkest days in Washington. . . . They continually pervert, twist and halt the path of progress in the Republic."[15]

[14] *Congressional Record* (daily edition), Feb. 26, 1947, p. A754.

[15] Stuart Chase, "Democracy under Pressure" (New York: Twentieth Century Fund, 1945), p. 9.

Yet no competent observers have ever gone so far as to suggest that direct action be taken to abolish the role of private associations in the legislative process. To do so would mean an attack on traditional American conceptions of the right of petition and free speech and of other civil liberties. Furthermore, the inevitable tendency is toward increased specialization and more marked concentration of economic power. One of the accompanying factors, both cause and result, is the growing strength of private associations, particularly business and labor organizations. One of the automatic by-products is the broadening of governmental activities and a steadily more active role by private organizations in the processes of government. Aside from registration requirements to provide more public information about them, the only feasible way to counteract objectional activities of private groups is to develop counterpressures on the part of other contestants in the legislative struggle. This means a strengthening of certain organizations at the expense of others. Or it means stronger political parties or government agencies. But parties and government agencies cannot become significantly stronger without the support of private organizations. Hence, these two latter alternatives imply no fundamental subordination of private associations but only another way of changing organizational alignments and modifying the channels through which they affect the governmental process.

Their Future Role in Society

The importance of private organizations in the legislative process derives from their general role in American society.

Deep fears have often been expressed concerning the continuation of conflict among private groups and the dire consequences that could result from its intensification. In the light of these fears, various ideas have been developed concerning the possibilities for a larger role for individuals, for a more cooperative relationship among groups, or for government planning as an escape from the tyranny of private pressures. While each of these ideas goes far beyond the legislative process, and even beyond the sphere of government as a whole, their consideration is nonetheless vital to an analysis of the legislative structure.

The Dangers in Group Conflict

There are three types of "dire consequences" that can be seen from a continuation—particularly if in sharpened form—of the conflict among private groups: deadlock, violence, and dictatorship. Moreover, there is genuine justification for believing that any or all of these three might come to pass, although it must be recognized that dark visions of each or all are an inevitable part of the sales kit of anyone with a panacea to peddle.

In a sense, the possibility of deadlock—or, to use a closely related term, stasis—is inherent in the democratic process of peaceful group conflict. When few victories are ever complete, when power is widely dispersed among many "veto groups," when every solution is a compromise that is objectionable to many, and when every settlement itself creates new problems, you have the makings of a stalemate. In the sphere of American economic organization, for example, as organized labor increases its strength and stands on a more equal plane with organized business groups, the opportunities for one-sided victories by the business community become slimmer and the potentialities for deadlock become greater. This is one of the great risks whenever the weak become stronger.

This kind of deadlock, of course, is not limited to the conflicts between organized business and organized labor. A prime example of deadlock can be found in the controversy over Federal aid to education that has been going on for many years. The proponents of Federal aid for public schools have been able to prevent legislation that would provide aid to parochial schools. Yet apart from certain emergency programs for schools in defense areas, their antagonists have been able to stymie legislation that would provide aid for any school. Similar examples could be given in the field of civil rights and natural resources. Perhaps the most dramatic example is found in the problem of dealing with inflationary trends. At any time when government expenditures are sharply rising, and particularly when an increasing volume of goods is being diverted away from civilian use into building up the armed forces, almost any major group in society is in a strategic position to stymie a stabilization effort. If businessmen insist on profiteering, there is little that can be done about wages or farm prices. If farm groups insist on getting as much as they can while the getting is good, the problem of holding the dike against inflation at other points becomes much more difficult. If labor tries to get as much as it can, it might wreck efforts to deal with businessmen and farmers. This kind of deadlock leads to protracted inflation. In the field of foreign affairs, similar deadlocks can lead to a fluctuating foreign policy that puts our representatives in a difficult position in dealing with other nations.

Widespread violence is less of a likelihood in America than deadlock, but it is always a possibility. Behind the peaceful struggle among the groups that compose society there always lies the possibility that any group or cluster of groups may resort at times to some form of force. Americans with a knowledge of the history of their country can never forget this fact. America's own Civil War came after many years of repeated efforts to adjust differences between the North and the South through the legislative process. One compromise after another failed and bloodshed ensued. We have also seen the use of violence as a method of preventing labor organization and as a weapon used on both sides during the course of strikes. "The essential and central problem of representative democracy," according to Laski, "is the question of what 'the better' classes can do when some claim is made which, in their judgment, they cannot 'safely' concede." [16] During the Roosevelt New Deal, thunderous talk of violent action could often be heard on the extreme right. Yet potentialities for violent action are usually present in some form on all sides, for there is almost always some limit beyond which no group can be forced without its contemplating the most drastic of countermeasures.

The third danger is closely related to the other two. After a period of protracted deadlock on issues of importance to many people, dictatorship becomes a method of getting things done. While it must use violence either as a method of achieving power or as a threat against dissidents, an effective dictatorship can provide an outward appearance of peacefulness.

It is difficult for Americans to take the danger of dictatorship very seriously. True, there are a few states in which dictatorial groups have taken control of state and local governments and suppressed opposition by the use of one or another form of violence. Yet these are rare exceptions, and short-lived at that. When we look at the world about us, the possibility seems more real. There are innumerable examples of domination of whole nations by small groups which have seized the reins of government and literally annihilated all sources of effective opposition. Also, the international military situation always threatens the continuation of normal relationships within American society. In time of war or near war, dictatorial or at least semidictatorial forms of government become more and more expedient as a means of organizing mobilization activities and protecting against internal divisions that might undermine national security.

As one reflects upon these three "dire consequences," one is tempted to join with Justice Holmes in proclaiming "I have no faith in panaceas and almost none in sudden ruin." And, indeed, a measure of skepticism is undoubtedly warranted. Yet ruin in any of these forms can come on slow and silent feet. Preventives ought to be discussed regardless of their avowed inadequacies. The discussion can serve to test and summarize the brief descriptive account of American private associations in the legislative process and sharpen our perceptions of trends into the future in this area of political behavior. Retaining Justice Holmes's skepticism about panaceas and sudden ruin, one may observe three recommended escapes from the dangers of group conflict: a return to individualism, the substitution of group cooperation instead of conflict, and governmental planning.

[16] Harold J. Laski, "Parliamentary Government in England" (New York: Viking, 1947), p. 7.

Back to the Individual

If there are dangers for society in organized groups, why cannot we hope for more from individuals as such rather than from organizations?

This question has a persistent appeal. It is answered in affirmative tones by those who plead for "return" to laissez-faire economics. Yet this is a call for a return to a nonexistent society. The so-called days of *laissez faire* were days when group organization and group conflict were also essential parts of the social structure. For Adam Smith, the mythical beauties of the free market constituted valuable propaganda in the campaign for private business organizations against state-fostered monopolies. The early days of so-called free and competitive private enterprise in America were days when organized groups used state subsidies of one form or another—particularly protective tariffs and land grants—to extend their power and strengthen their organization. The "break-them-down approach" of the Sherman Antitrust Act has itself been merely a part of the campaign against certain business organizations by other, and sometimes weaker, business groups, by farm organizations, and by labor organizations. The attack upon the extension of labor organizations is itself a part of the campaign of business organizations. The modern call for a rebirth of "rugged individualism" usually comes from propagandists or from powerful private organizations who use this symbol in campaigning activities against any threatening sources of opposition.[17]

The overwhelming probabilities for the future are all on the side of more organization of social relationships rather than less. In fact, it is only through an acceptance of group struggle and participation in the process that anyone with conviction concerning the path this struggle should take can make progress toward carrying his convictions into practice.

The yearning for individual action as opposed to group action is evidenced also in the recurrent idea that the way out for the dog-eat-dog battle of the major groups in society is for disinterested thinkers to work out a solution for our problems. Perhaps the most classic presentation for this viewpoint is found in a book by Stuart Chase.

> Sometimes I have a clear picture of the way the Agenda for 1950 could be presented to the people. I see, perhaps, a hundred leading Americans, men and women, meeting in some high, quiet place to prepare it. They are not the kind of people who are active in Me First groups. They are scientists, judges, teachers, university people, philosophers of business, lovers of the land, statesmen; and they think in terms of the whole community.[18]

[17] If a return to rugged individualism should ever really take place, the result would probably be a breakdown in moral values and an increase in all varieties of corruption.

[18] Chase, *op. cit.*, p. 133.

These thoughtful citizens, dreamed Chase, would get together amid the beauty and remoteness of Sun Valley and would draft a program for America. A delightful prospect! Particularly for the participants! But the keenest minds in America could get together and prepare a general program for America or even a little program dealing with a single problem and, unless the participants represented important groups in the social conflict, or had guidelines for conveying their ideas to these groups, their proposals would be neglected. In so far as the proposals really tied up with interests of organizations with power, they would themselves be another incident in the group struggle. Actually many conferences of this type have taken place and no more can be expected from them than the production of occasional reading matter, propaganda for one side or another, or a rather purified version of the round-table conference approach discussed in the next chapter.

Individuals have a major role in group conflict. There can be no doubt about this, but their role is in the process as leaders, subleaders, and followers —not outsiders. The only active role that individuals can play is in the guidance or direction of the efforts of this or that group or set of groups.

A still more rarefied emphasis on the individual is found in the hope that somehow or other the forces of Intelligence, of Reason, or of Science will bring order out of chaos. During the first years of disillusionment that followed in the wake of World War I, James Harvey Robinson urged "the liberation of Intelligence" as the first and most essential step in dealing with "the shocking derangement of human affairs which now prevails in most civilized countries. . . ."[19]

Walter Lippmann enlarged upon the idea by proposing a network of government "Intelligence Bureaus" manned by experts with lifetime tenure and insulated against the pressures of either congressional committees or department heads.[20] Since then, the dramatic achievements of physical scientists have suggested to many that these achievements might be transferred to the field of human relations and group conflict.

If intelligence and science are viewed as abstract forces apart from either individuals or groups, then they are the products of dreamy-eyed mysticism and deserve little further discussion. If they are viewed as characteristics or power of individuals in splendid isolation, they can have as little effect as the men on Stuart Chase's mountaintop. If they are viewed as qualities and characteristics of individuals who serve as leaders of groups, then they are meaningful—and of tremendous potency. But one simple fact cannot be forgotten: intelli-

[19] James Harvey Robinson, "The Mind in the Making, the Relation of Intelligence to Social Reform" (New York: Harper, 1921). See Chaps. 1 and 2, pp. 3–29.

[20] Walter Lippmann, "Public Opinion" (New York: Macmillan, 1922). See Part 8, "Organized Intelligence."

gence, science, and reason can be used by both or many sides. By themselves they do not necessarily weight the scales in favor of a milder form of conflict any more than more effective armaments or generalship can be regarded as weighting the scales in favor of less bloody warfare.

Groups without Conflict

Once the fact of large groups in society is taken for granted, then the thought occurs that some means might be developed for escaping the dangers of deadlock, violence, or dictatorship, by promoting more amicable relations among them.

At one extreme one finds one of the greatest pipe dreams of all time: Karl Marx's vision of a classless society in which, with the instruments of production taken over by the proletariat, there would no longer be any basis for economic class war. In the Marxian scheme of things, this has the double merit of picturing "pie in the sky" after the fighting on the barricades is over, and of serving as the basis for Marx's theory of the "withering away of the state," which has provided an intellectual appeal to the anarchists and other anti-state theorists whose support was sought by Marx and his followers. From the strict Marxian standpoint, as interpreted by Lenin and his followers, this state of grace is no alternative to, but rather a consequence of, violence and dictatorship.

Even from the point of view of evolutionary, as contrasted to revolutionary, socialism, the classless-society prospect makes little sense. The socialization of the means of production, even if carried to the full extreme, as in the Soviet Union, can merely change the economic conditions under which groups emerge and the struggle for power takes place. Max Nomad has stated this from the class-struggle point of view in terms more logically consistent than those used by Marx and Lenin:

> The permanent change of masters and the accompanying striving of the masses in the direction of an ever greater *approach* towards equality in the enjoyment of the good things of life forms the basic content of the historical process. That process knows of no millennium when full harmony has been achieved once for all eternity. There is no "happy ending" just as there is no "final revolution" that will eliminate all further class struggles.[21]

The major American variant is found in the vision of cooperation among the leaders of organized groups. This vision takes many forms. At times it appears in the administrative terms of a national economic council or some other piece of machinery which will bring group leaders together. But such

[21] Max Nomad, "Masters—Old and New," in V. F. Calverton (ed.), "The Making of Society" (New York: Modern Library, 1937), p. 893.

machinery, as indicated in the next chapter's discussion of proposals for formal group representation in the structure of government, can do no more than bring people together, as in a back alley or a boxing ring; it cannot determine how they behave when they get there.

An extremely interesting variant is found in the writings of Edwin G. Nourse, who has repeatedly pictured the tremendous potentialities that could come from the exercise of more economic wisdom by the leaders of business, labor, and agriculture. Nourse pictures a future in which each of them "will seek to make their best contribution to maximize total production and then will cooperate in those patterns of distribution that will do most to keep the productive process going with both vigor and efficiency." [22]

This is all very well and good as far as it goes. But it does not go very far. First of all, there are different views, even among the most expert of experts, of what the best contribution of various groups might be, either toward the maximization of total production or the development of sound distribution patterns. Economics cannot resolve these matters; it can only provide refined technical instruments for the development and presentation of one or another point of view. Any philosophy capable of translating itself into reality must be backed by power, and power can come only from direct participation in group conflict.

The vision of more cooperation and less bitterness in the struggle among the groups that make up society is a valuable one. It provides a goal which can probably be regarded as the only substitute for the three dangers of deadlock, violence, or dictatorship. But it is too valuable a goal to be dissipated by suggesting that it can be obtained by administrative gadgetry, sermonizing, or learning more about textbook economics. It can come only through development of the group struggle itself, for the vicissitudes of this struggle create the conditions that promote cooperation and make it possible. From the world viewpoint, the emergence of threats to national survival creates conditions under which—depending upon the degree of the threat—there is more inclination toward amicable and cooperative domestic group relationship. From the internal viewpoint, the expansion of real national income to a point where there will be much more for all groups can also create conditions under which the law of the jungle will recede into the background, and group collaboration can become more feasible. Yet this development itself is the cart and not the horse, for it can be obtained only through the organization of sufficient power to oppose those groups in the economy who prefer scarcity to abundance and to put into effect concrete programs that will achieve the desired goal of genuine economic growth.[23]

[22] Edwin G. Nourse, "The 1950's Come First" (New York: Holt, 1951), p. 179.

[23] For a fuller statement by this author on Nourse's viewpoint, see his "The 1950's Come First," a book review, *American Political Science Review,* Vol. 45, No. 3, September, 1950, pp. 867–874.

An interesting approach toward development of group cooperation has been presented by Stuart Chase on the basis of human-relations studies undertaken in many fields of social science. In a book written eight years after the presentation of his "mountaintop" proposal referred to a few pages back, he accepts the existence of group combat and group tensions as a major factor to be reckoned with and offers the following five principles upon which group agreement can be based:

1. The principle of participation
2. The principle of group energy
3. The principle of clearing communication lines
4. The principle of facts first
5. The principle that agreement is much easier when people feel secure [24]

As more knowledge on human relations is added to the storehouse, Chase maintains we can become "better prepared to meet the two chief tasks which have always faced mankind: coming to terms with nature, and coming to terms with our fellows."

Here again we find observations which are extremely useful but suffer serious limitations. The greatest limitation flows from Chase's failure to recognize that agreement among people also depends upon the development of objectives for group action and that such objectives usually conflict in some manner with objectives of others. Still more specifically, there is nothing like a common enemy and a "clear and present danger" to make people work together in genuine cooperation. When these facts are kept in mind, it then becomes apparent that the limited set of principles offered by Chase is of value not as a means of eliminating group combat and tensions, but as a means of organizing group action as a part of social combat.

Government Planning [25]

Government planning often comes to the fore as an antidote for the jungle conflict between competing groups of American society, and, more specifically, as a means of bringing order and purpose into the legislative process. Toward

[24] Chase, "Roads to Agreement" (New York: Harper, 1951), pp. 235–240.

[25] The following are leading books in the growing literature on government planning: Herman Finer, "Road to Reaction" (Boston: Little, Brown, 1945); Friedrick Hayek, "The Road to Serfdom" (Chicago: University of Chicago Press, 1944); John Jewkes, "Ordeal by Planning" (New York: Macmillan, 1948); Karl Mannheim, "Freedom, Power and Democratic Planning" (New York: Oxford, 1950); John P. Millet, "The Process and Organization of Government Planning" (New York: Columbia University Press, 1948); Theo Surányi-Unger, "Private Enterprise and Governmental Planning" (New York: McGraw-Hill, 1950); Barbara Wootton, "Freedom under Planning" (Chapel Hill, N.C.: University of North Carolina Press, 1945); and Ferdinand Zweig, "The Planning of Free Societies" (London: Secker and Werburg, 1943).

the end of the troubled 1930's, for example, Rexford G. Tugwell called for an integration of all forces of society, maintaining that "the articulation of the whole is the emergent need of society" and that the planning arts are "the only available resource in the crisis." [26] In Donald Blaisdell's pioneering study, "Economic Power and Political Pressures," the strengthening of planning is listed—along with lobby registration, the development of advisory councils, and the improvement of government administration—as a major method of coping with the economic and political power of private organizations.

For many years there has been an unending stream of suggestions for new departures in government planning. In scope, these range from proposals to deal with the totality of economic life to proposals dealing with such specific problems as defense mobilization, the prevention of depression, the control of inflation, the scheduling of public works, or the development of river-valley basins. Some center upon planning by officials of the executive branch, others upon planning in Congress, others upon the development of new planning agencies apart from both the executive branch and Congress, and still others favor more ambitious planning by local and state governments. Some propose the vast extension of governmental functions, while others are aimed at more adequate performance of present functions. Many such proposals are hidden under words that have proved less controversial than the word "planning"—words like "coordination," "integration," "general policy making," or "programming." The fact that the Government has long been involved in many planning activities in no way diminishes the interest which exists in new proposals.

Practically all conceptions of government planning are subject to two divergent interpretations. According to one interpretation, planning provides escape from the pressure and propaganda activities of private organizations. This view is buttressed by the techniques of planning themselves, which emphasize the compilation of fact and the application of professional skills. It is supported by the arguments of many technicians who, undoubtedly, like to view their skills as sufficient to produce inevitable conclusions and as enabling government to close its ranks against group pressures. Some plans are so breath-taking in their scope and imaginative quality that they stir up semi-religious emotions of order and balance and seem to place the planning process upon a pinnacle far removed from the sordid aspects of social combat. This is the idealistic interpretation of planning, one which, if not counterbalanced by powerful injections of realism, leads to useless plans and frustrated planners.

In the second interpretation, planning is a method of organizing power to achieve given objectives. Schattschneider illustrated this more realistic viewpoint very aptly in a discussion of planning for full employment:

[26] Rexford G. Tugwell, "The Fourth Power" *Planning and Civil Comment,* April–June, 1939, p. 2.

. . . what is required is that an organized and systematic attempt be made to use political methods to produce an amplitude of power to do all that needs to be done. Power is emphasized because all plans and policies for the maintenance of high-level employment imply power; without the power to do something about it, planning is a mere form of wishful thinking. All planning and all policies imply power. However, power in turn implies politics; for it is the business of politics to produce power.[27]

The production of power, in turn, involves the obtaining of support, either directly or indirectly, from various groups in society. Obviously support by governmental agencies is indispensable; a planning agency with no allies within the Government is indeed an orphan. As Schattschneider has pointed out at great length, the mobilization of power through political parties is also relevant. Private organizations, too, must be brought into the planning process in one manner or another. This is why the more successful type of planners talk about "participation" and "public relations." They realize the necessity not only of selling their plans to private groups, but of drawing them into the entire operation so that their responsible support can be assured. Some plans, of course, rely to an important degree upon the support of relatively unorganized groups or groups which come into being intermittently. But this merely means that the character of the relationship between planning and private organizations varies from time to time, not that the relationship is nonexistent.

One of the reasons why the idea of planning has been so controversial is the fact that it becomes so intensively involved in conflicts between private organizations. Planners inevitably take sides, and inevitably in a democratic society there are competing plans and competing planners. Planning often means concrete shifts in power—gains for some and losses for others. Those who are afraid of losing power wail about their loss of "freedom," which becomes a more euphemistic term for describing power they wish to preserve. The push and pull of private interests operates upon both plans and planners. Few successful plans are developed without a careful eye toward balancing the interests and groups that might be affected by the plan. In other words, the plan becomes a tentative or semifinal resolution of conflicts between various groups, including private organizations. If the process of group conflict is not sufficiently reflected in the development of the plan, it will make itself felt rather sharply when the time comes to take action upon the plan. At this stage the pressures will either tear the plan to pieces or modify it. Planners who seek to prevent this contingency can avoid complete failure only by dealing with basic group conflicts in the early stages of the planning process.

Planning can be an escape from the pressure and propaganda activities of private organizations only if it degenerates into the development of paper plans which are politically unrealistic or if it is backed up by that dictatorial

[27] E. E. Schattschneider, "Party Government and Employment Policy," *American Political Science Review,* Vol. 39, No. 6, December, 1945, p. 1149.

use of force which threatens or perpetrates acts of violence to suppress the activities of private groups. On the other hand, planning is an indispensable method for democratically organizing private groups—not to suppress their differences and create a barren uniformity, but to achieve certain objectives that are unattainable without a more rationally developed power structure. More extensive planning is needed for purposes of military defense, of providing more efficiently the governmental services which are needed, of providing more effective representation for the weaker and less organized groups in the country. But always the questions must be asked, planning for what, planning for whom, planning by whom, and even planning against whom?

It has often been suggested that the basic approach of government to problems created by the power of private organizations should be to support the weak against the strong so that they can contend on a more equal basis. Actually, the activities of government agencies of necessity must affect the distribution of power in one way or another. It is natural, therefore, for weaker groups to seek governmental support and for governmental agencies to strengthen themselves by relations of this type. This is illustrated by government action which has facilitated the organizational activities of union labor, supplemented the organizational activities of farmers through financial assistance, or provided financial support for banking institutions.

Government planning often becomes a means of doing all this on a broader scale. Some plans would turn increased power over to business organizations. Other plans would enhance the power of weakly organized groups or provide representation for the interests of those who come together to express themselves on only few occasions other than at the ballot box during national elections. "Government planning" along the latter lines has succeeded in making the term a *bête noire* to the minds of many conservative citizens.

Quis custodiet ipsos custodes? This is the recurring question that all proponents of planning must meet. Who will plan for the planners? If government planners are to obtain the power needed to carry out their plans, what protection is there against an overwhelming concentration of power in their hands?

The question is not one that can be answered in abstract terms. The problem has relevance only as it bears upon the kind of planning that is proposed and the present and potential distribution of power in existing societies. If one thinks in terms of all-powerful governmental planning, there can be no satisfactory answer. The "guardians" will do as they please until they fall out among themselves, are stricken from power by an internal revolt, or become weak as a result of clashes with other nations.

If one thinks of limited planning, the answer depends upon the nature of the limitations or—to put the matter in other words—the actual distribution of power between competing forces in society. "Guardianship will emerge," writes David B. Truman in the last sentence of his book, "out of the affiliations of the guardians." [28] Through this extremely suggestive phrase Truman points out that the overlapping groups to which the planners themselves may have loyalties are a protection against planning that might go too far in the interests of any one group or coalition. One might well carry the matter a little further and add that guardianship will also emerge "out of the group conflicts in society." The process of group combat itself—harsh and cruel though it may be—provides a check-and-balance system of protection far more powerful and meaningful than the constitutional arrangements envisaged by the Founding Fathers against the harshness and cruelties of unguarded guardians.

[28] Truman, *op. cit.*, p. 535.

Chapter 3

THE PRIVATE ORGANIZATIONS: REFORMING THEIR METHODS

IF THE process of group combat is so central to "guarding the guardians," clearly its procedures and practices are vital to the preservation of a democratic legislative system. The behavior of private groups and organizations, therefore, has been of particular interest to those who would either preserve or change these procedures and practices. Generally their interest has been grounded upon a fear of the growing power of Big Business, Big Labor, the Farm Lobby, and other groups. It has been nurtured by the realization that every group has specialized interests of its own and cannot be depended upon to use its power in behalf of other groups or, to use a term which usually serves as a method of referring to the interests of a particular congeries of groups, the "general welfare."

The specific proposals that have been advanced concerning private organizations may be divided into three groups. The first deals with certain aspects of their legislative campaigning activities. The second deals with the question of whether they should be given a more formal status within government itself. The third deals with the dangers inherent in group conflict and various admonitions to the effect that private organizations should either vanish from the scene or behave themselves.

THEIR CAMPAIGNING ACTIVITIES

The campaigning activities of private organizations are extremely extensive. They include the organization of group support, the application of pressure, the dissemination of propaganda, and all the arts of leadership that are needed to make these elements effective. The major proposals thus far presented deal with the existence of financial bonds between private organizations and government officials, contributions to the campaign funds of candidates for Congress and the Presidency, the activities of lobbyists, and the control of the major channels of communication.

Financial Bonds with Government Officials [1]

American history is full of recurring exposés of how private groups have purchased government favors—including favorable action on legislative proposals—by lining the pockets of government officials. The extent of such direct financial bonds between private groups and government officials has probably declined sharply over the decades, particularly as nonfinancial bonds have come into being to take the place of the direct financial nexus. V. O. Key has observed:

> It may be that bribery . . . occurs on a large scale only in a relatively chaotic society in which new interests are forging upward, rapid realignments of wealth are being formed, the introduction of new inventions, social and technological, is rapidly upsetting the old economic order, society is relatively unstratified, or old class alignments are being shifted and re-formed. . . . The rise of the propaganda and public-relations experts of the pressure groups in some ways contribute toward the reduction in the reliance on corrupt techniques. Results, formerly secured by bribery or kindred methods, may be secured by more or less legitimate methods.[2]

Yet it would be a mistake to assume that direct financial connections will decline steadily to the point of becoming inconsequential. The more intensive organization of society in fact multiplies the interest of many private groups in the buying of favors, and does nothing of itself to diminish the widespread tendency to use hook or crook to advance one's own personal interests if one can get away with it. Nor has wealth in the United States become, as many radical commentators have charged, so consolidated and so powerful that it can rely on the more accepted forms of influence alone. Furthermore, corruption itself is not merely tolerated but, as Robert C. Brooks pointed out several decades ago, it is justified by many on the grounds that it is good for business, that "it may be more than compensated for by the high efficiency otherwise of those who engage in it," [3] that it is a useful technique of getting things done.

Accordingly, proposals are continuously being made for dealing with the problem. The more important proposals deal with such matters as codes of ethics, disqualification requirements, the disclosure of outside sources of in-

[1] One of the most useful documents on this subject, as indicated by the frequent quotations and references on the following pages, is "Ethical Standards in Government," a report of the Douglas subcommittee of the Senate Committee on Labor and Public Welfare, 82d Cong., 1st Sess., 1951. See also, "Establishment of a Commission on Ethics in Government," Hearings before a subcommittee to study S. Con. Res. 21, 82d Cong., 1st Sess., 1951.

[2] V. O. Key, Jr., "Politics, Parties, and Pressure Groups" (New York: Crowell, 1942). The chapter on pecuniary sanctions, from which this quotation is taken, has been omitted from the 1947 edition of this book, probably because the rash of exposés in the aftermath of World War II suggested that this thesis on the decline of bribery might call for reexamination.

[3] Robert C. Brooks, "Corruption of American Politics and Life" (New York: Dodd, Mead, 1910). This is an excellent sociological and political analysis of this field.

come, bribery and corruption laws, and larger rewards through the government service itself.

Codes of Ethics. Early in 1951 dramatic exposés of highly questionable activities by executive officials led to the repeated suggestion that codes of ethics should be established for the public service, which would be comparable to those that have been commonly accepted in medicine, law, and other professions. In fact, a number of members of Congress began to prepare sample codes governing members of Congress themselves.

After long hearings on the subject of ethics in government, a Senate subcommittee headed by Senator Douglas recommended the creation of a Commission on Ethics in Government. Without the leadership and assistance of a high status commission, the subcommittee did not believe the work of formulating the needed ethical codes would go forward as it should. The subcommittee also listed the following arguments on behalf of ethical codes:

> (1) They would clarify new or complex situations where the application of basic moral principles is far from obvious; (2) they would anticipate issues so that difficulties could be foreseen and basic policy decided when rational consideration is possible (*i.e.*, the rules of the game must be approved before play begins); (3) the enhancement of the influence of the more progressive elements of the group who will tend to bring the whole group up to higher standards; (4) they would be a basis for discipline if the group had enough leadership and pride to act; (5) they would furnish a basis for instructing new members of the group as to their professional obligations (Hippocrates required all of his disciples to take the oath); and (6) they would instruct the public as to what it should expect of the principal elements in the realm of public affairs.[4]

An additional argument, not mentioned by the subcommittee, but one of great importance, is that ethical codes can include principles of conduct which are extremely difficult or even impossible to enforce, and which therefore cannot practicably be included in more formalized requirements.

It is obvious, of course, that codes of this type can provide no ironclad protection against undesirable financial bonds between private groups and government officials. They could be neither applicable to all situations that develop nor susceptible of rigorous enforcement. Furthermore, high standards of personal conduct are bound to come into conflict with contradictory standards which are widely held.

Disqualification. It has long been customary to disqualify executive officials from the handling of governmental affairs that directly affect their personal financial interests, and former government officials from conducting relations with government agencies on matters which they had previously handled when in the government service. The Douglas subcommittee proposed that, in the case of executive officials, disqualification provisions of this type be considera-

[4] "Ethical Standards in Government," p. 35.

bly extended. It urged that nonsalaried officials who are brought in from industry should not be assigned to positions that require them to deal with their former industries. It called for the permanent "disbarment" of former Federal officials from appearing before executive agencies in connection with any cases which they had previously handled during their period of government service. It recommended "disbarment" for a two-year period of all former officials who wish to appear before an agency with which they formerly worked on any cases whatsoever.

In the case of members of Congress, a disqualification provision has been in existence in the Rules of the House of Representatives since 1789. Rule VIII provides that every member of the House "shall vote on each question put, unless he has a personal or pecuniary interest in the event of such question." Yet only in the rarest of instances has a Speaker of the House ever decided that, because of personal interest, a member could not vote. Nor have members of the House asked that this rule be enforced or extended to cover committee as well as floor action.

Disclosure. Another method of dealing with financial relations between private groups and government officials is found in the highly controversial proposal that Congress should add "glass pockets to the appurtenances of office." In sponsoring a proposal for the registration of the amounts and sources of Congressmen's incomes, Senator Wayne Morse of Oregon put the case as follows:

> I believe a legislator's viewpoint may be influenced—no matter how honest he is—by his own personal interests. Therefore I believe the public has a right to know from whom and from where we get our money. My own actions show that I do not think it improper for a senator to receive money over and above his salary. I lecture and write for fees. Neither do I say or believe that sources from which my colleagues receive money are improper. That's not the point. The point is that the people have a right to know what influences the attitudes of their representatives. They need to know this in order to decide whether we truly represent them.[5]

Four years later, in a special message to Congress, President Truman presented the same proposal in broader terms, asking that disclosure requirements cover not only members of Congress, but also the Federal judiciary, top executive officials, and the top officials of the national political parties.

> If an official of an executive agency knew that he would have to disclose the fact that he accepted a gift or loan from a private company with which he has public business, or if a Member of Congress who is on a committee concerned with a certain industry knew that he would have to disclose the fact that he accepted a fee from a company in that industry, I believe the chances are that such gifts or fees would not be accepted.[6]

[5] Quoted in editorial by James C. Derieux, *Collier's,* Sept. 20, 1947.
[6] White House press release, Sept. 27, 1951.

A veil of secrecy, of course, will always cover the full facts on the financial relations between government officials and private organizations. Income flowing to a wife or brother or to a firm of which one has been a member will always be difficult to pin down. Understandings concerning future rewards in the form of personal employment are too tenuous to be uncovered ahead of time. Moreover, the recording of certain facts on outside sources of income—no matter how comprehensive they might turn out to be—would by no means destroy or even significantly curtail the relations between government officials and private groups. It would probably result in still more use of the less direct financial relationship. Nor would it by itself throw a "spotlight of publicity" on these officials. It would merely make certain facts available for interpretation and use by various contestants in the legislative struggle. These facts would probably be used in most cases by those groups in society with the weakest financial resources and might often be used with great effectiveness.

Penalties for Bribery and Corruption. In addition to the many other points covered in its report, the Douglas subcommittee recommended a thorough study of changes needed in the provisions of the Criminal Code dealing with bribery and corruption. To facilitate such a study the subcommittee included in its report a draft of a bill to amend the criminal laws.

One of the major changes in the proposed bill would strengthen the Criminal Code by broadening the definition of "bribe" to include "other considerations just as useful to bribers as hard cash," such as any "emoluments, fee, profit, advantage, benefit, position, future position, employment, future employment, opportunity, future opportunity, advancement, or future advancement." Another provision would cover public officials who "receive things of substantial value not for doing things which come within their official capacity, but for using their influence with other persons in the government." Also, bribers would be treated as harshly as the bribed. Just as the latter are subject to disqualification from henceforth holding an office, honor, or trust under the United States, the former would be henceforth prohibited from participating in any substantial business activity with the Federal government. Existing penalties would be sharply increased. In the case of employees of executive agencies, administrative sanctions were recommended by the subcommittee so that, entirely apart from any criminal action, employees who had used their official position for purposes of personal profit or who had accepted bribes of any sort could be promptly dismissed without extended hearings or appeals procedures.

Action along these lines would face innumerable obstacles. In so far as members of Congress are concerned, the enforcement of criminal provisions is particularly difficult. Administrative officials are naturally loath to risk tangling with members of Congress. This is particularly true inasmuch as "Congress adheres pretty faithfully to the theory that mistakes will happen, and when a member slips on the banana peel of mischance and lands all sprawled out before the gaze of his countrymen, the disposition is to form a circle about him and hide his confusion." [7] Bribery and corruption, moreover, are extremely hard to prove. The line between minor foibles and crimes is, in this area, extremely hard to draw. The difficulty is made worse by the existence of what Brooks has called "auto-corruption" and "smokeless sin," the one involving no direct associates in a legitimate transaction and the other being of a nature that attracts no attention and can rarely be found out. The difficulty is also compounded by the fact that the greater felonies are often legalized. As stated in the old English quatrain:

> The law locks up both man and woman
> Who steals the goose from off the common,
> But lets the greater felon loose
> Who steals the common from the goose.

Larger Rewards through Government Service Itself. Another approach toward weakening financial bonds between government officials and private organizations is found in action that would increase salaries and retirement benefits.

As far back as 1945, the Heller Report advocated $25,000 per year for members of Congress. A closely related proposal called for retirement benefits after age fifty-five of $1,000 for each full year of congressional service, up to a maximum of $10,000 a year. One of the reasons given—euphemistically phrased—was: "In providing such security, the country at least partially safeguards the legislative function from possible deficiencies resulting from efforts of members to protect themselves against the time when they are not reelected." [8] Many similar proposals have been made for increasing the financial rewards and economic security of employees in the executive branch.

From the viewpoint of wealthier groups, action along these lines is intended to make government posts more attractive to men who might otherwise gravitate toward well-paying private jobs, although, for men of real wealth, a few thousand dollars more or less in one's salary is a minor matter. In the case of persons from the lower-income groups, higher government salaries might serve as a counterbalance against the influence of wealthy interests. In either case, the extraordinary expenses involved in being a member of Congress, even with salary increases, will probably continue to make difficult a life of luxury from the rich man's viewpoint.

[7] H. H. Wilson, "Congress: Corruption and Compromise" (New York: Rinehart, 1951), p. 245.

[8] Robert Heller, "Strengthening the Congress" (Washington, D.C.: National Planning Association, January, 1945), p. 35. Since the issuance of this report, salaries of members of Congress have been raised and a retirement system has been established, but both salaries and benefits are considerably below the levels proposed in the report.

Yet substantial opposition to proposals of this type can always be expected. Higher salaries and retirement benefits, whether in the executive or congressional branches, are anathema to those who see in them one more step toward an all-powerful state and an overheavy Federal budget. Efforts to raise congressional remuneration must always reckon with the potential embarrassment faced by members of Congress who publicly vote for an increase in their own pay or retirement benefits in the face of the frequent denunciation of such proposals by a few members of Congress who proudly proclaim their desire to serve their country irrespective of remuneration.

Contributions to Political Campaigns [9]

A special type of financial bond between private groups and government officials is found in campaign contributions. Candidates for Congress and the Presidency need money in order to conduct their election campaigns. Many private groups are always eager to meet this need in the hope that their contributions may yield a substantial return in the form of support for the legislative objectives.

Accordingly, repeated efforts have been made to deal with this problem by various prohibitions, by requirements for the registration of facts concerning campaign contributions and expenditures, and by various forms of public financing of political campaigns.

Prohibitions. The prohibitions thus far brought into effect have dealt with three aspects of campaign financing: sources of contributions, amounts of contributions, and expenditures. Corporations and unions have been prohibited from contributing money to political campaigns. It has been made illegal to intimidate Federal employees into contributing to campaign funds. The amount any person can contribute to an individual candidate or campaign has been limited to $5,000. In so far as expenditures are concerned, candidates for the Senate operate under a $25,000 ceiling, candidates for the House of Representatives under a $10,000 ceiling, and national-party committees under a ceiling of $3,000,000 during any calendar year. Campaign expenditures by both corporations and unions have been prohibited. Naturally, the direct purchase of votes has long been illegal.

It is doubtful whether any provisions of law have ever been so systematically evaded as the above prohibitions. It is certain that no provisions of law have ever been so thoroughly evaded by political leaders and government officials. The prohibitions on sources of contributions are evaded by the device of having the money flow from individuals and groups associated with corporations

[9] Although the literature on this subject is vast, the following references will serve to provide background for proposals in this field: Key, *op. cit.*, 1947 ed., Chap. 15, "Party Finance"; Louise Overacker, "Presidential Campaign Funds" (Boston: Boston University Press, 1946); and James K. Pollock, "Party Campaign Funds" (New York: Knopf, 1926).

or unions, rather than from the corporations or unions themselves. The limitations on personal contributions are evaded by having the money given in smaller sums by various members of a family, rather than in one large sum. The limitations on expenditures are evaded by the development of a large number of campaign committees.

Many changes are obviously needed. Among those recommended are more rigorous enforcement of the present prohibitions; recognition that the existing ceilings on personal contributions and on expenditures are unrealistic, not only because the value of the dollar has declined, but also because new methods of mass communication and development of larger constituencies have made campaigning more expensive; and discontinuance of all prohibitions, with the exception of those on political assessment and vote buying.

Disclosure. Present prohibitions are accompanied by registration provisions designed to deal with contributions and expenditures through the disclosure method. Yet the wholesale evasion of the intent, if not the letter, of the requirements is so great as to suggest that more is concealed than disclosed.

Many proposals have been developed for strengthening registration provisions. The following list synthesizes the most constructive of these proposals:

1. Include campaigns for nominations as well as for elections
2. Include loans as well as gifts
3. Include contributions to, and expenditures by, all campaign organizations
4. Provide for more adequate reporting before primaries, conventions, and elections
5. Develop more uniform methods of reporting
6. Provide a central repository for the filing of statements
7. Provide for the prompt auditing, compilation, and analysis of this material and for its publication within each state as well as in Washington

In reflecting upon the significance of these proposals, it should be kept in mind that dollar contributions to political campaigns are by no means an accurate indication of the power exerted by contributors upon electoral or legislative decisions. Small contributions, strategically placed, may win more power than large contributions that flow haphazardly or are not actively followed up. The flow of campaign contributions may reveal nothing whatsoever of the campaigning done directly by business, labor, religious, and other organizations or of the many campaign resources stemming from the prerogatives of office and enjoyed exclusively by incumbents running for reelection. In many cases, the "spotlight of publicity" upon large campaign contributions might turn out to be merely a feeble glimmer competing with hundreds of other flashes, sparked by groups seeking advantage in the legislative process.

Public Support. Back in 1907, President Theodore Roosevelt sent a message to Congress in which he suggested that the Federal government subsidize most of the "proper and legitimate expenses of each of the great national parties." [10]

[10] *Congressional Record,* 60th Cong., 1st Sess., Dec. 3, 1907, p. 78.

The purpose of this proposal was clearly to free candidates from overdependence upon contributions from private organizations and to provide more equality in campaign resources. It has always enjoyed a widespread appeal. The Douglas subcommittee on Ethics in Government, for example, concluded that "some form of public support is justified" and that it "would be less expensive than the indirect costs of allowing candidates and parties to be solely dependent upon the support of well-heeled special interests."[11]

In a few states candidates are given free or low-cost space in publicity pamphlets which are printed and distributed to all voters by the state governments. Senator Benton of Connecticut and others have proposed that the franking privilege be made available to *all candidates* for Congress. A still more significant proposal would provide political candidates with a limited amount of free television and radio time.

It is suggested that the Federal government could appropriate the money and transfer specified sums to the television and radio stations. Or the Federal Communications Commission could require its licensees, as a condition for receiving access to the airways, to provide a certain amount of free political time—and this approach might be associated with indirect subsidy in the form of tax concessions.[12] An extremely indirect form of Federal assistance could be provided through action to reduce campaign costs, since newspapers often charge political candidates higher advertising rates than commercial advertisers, and television and radio stations habitually raise the rates for political candidates. Another minor form of public assistance could be provided through the indirect method of allowing candidates, in computing their Federal income taxes, to deduct up to a fixed amount of their personal campaign expenses as an expense of doing business. At present, because of a bare 5 to 4 decision of the Supreme Court, this is not allowed.[13] Attention should also be given to the possibility of allowing individuals to deduct from taxes up to a certain amount of money spent in campaign contributions. A final method of diminishing the dependence of political candidates upon funds supplied by private organizations would be to increase, by systems of regular dues payments, the amount of funds made available through party sources themselves.

Lobbying[14]

Legislative provisions dealing with lobbying differ from campaign laws in that they have been on the statute books for a shorter period of time and con-

[11] "Ethical Standards in Government," p. 63.

[12] "Establishment of a Commission on Ethics in Government," pp. 464–468.

[13] *McDonald v. Commission of Internal Revenue,* 63 Sup. Ct. 96 (1944).

[14] The following items are particularly relevant: Hearings of Select Committee on Lobbying Activities of the House of Representatives, 81st Cong., 2d Sess., 1950; this same committee's "General Interim Report," H. Rept. 3138; "Report and Recommendations on Fed-

tain neither prohibitions nor ceilings. Yet the experience with these requirements since their enactment in 1946 has been similarly disillusioning and has led to many proposals for more effective disclosure of facts concerning lobbying and for a number of prohibitions.

Disclosure. The information on organizations, individuals, contributions, and expenditures under it, printed four times a year in the *Congressional Record*, is a miscellaneous array of undigested facts, often extremely misleading. Only a meager reflection is given of activities of the richer, multipurpose organizations like the National Association of Manufacturers or the American Federation of Labor, whose influence on legislation is far greater than that of special groups set up to work on legislation alone.

If all the problems of coverage, accuracy, and compilation were solved, the question might well be asked: What would be the use of this highly complex mass of information?

The answer hardly lies, as some of the ardent advocates of disclosure have maintained, in the possibility that large numbers of people who might be described as "the public" will have time or interest to read, understand, react to, or act upon this information. Nor does it lie in the possibility that disclosure requirements will inhibit large-scale lobby operations; the probability is rather that the bulk of legislative campaigning by private organizations would go on as always, with somewhat more attention paid to techniques of channeling funds and activities in a manner that would evade disclosure.

The best answer to the question, as with the disclosure of facts concerning political contributions, probably lies in the potential use to which the disclosed information can be put by various participants in the legislative process, including not only members of Congress and executive officials, but also the leaders of private organizations and the lobbyists themselves. The information would be of greatest use to those participants in the legislative process whose sources of intelligence are meager and whose power might be buttressed by facts of this type concerning other participants. In short, the information could, to some extent, serve to deprive some participants, particularly the stronger ones, of the advantages achieved through more complete secrecy and add a minor increment to the power of the weaker participants.

The suggestion has often been made that the disclosure operation be extended to cover private attempts to influence executive action. It is argued not only that administrative decisions are important but also that legislative decisions are often influenced via executive officials. The Buchanan Committee dealt with this matter merely by proposing that Congress authorize investiga-

---

eral Lobbying Act," H. Rept. 3239; "Report and Recommendations on Federal Lobbying Act, Minority Views," H. Rept. 3239, pt. 2. Also, Belle Zeller, "The Federal Regulation of Lobbying Act," *American Political Science Review,* Vol. 42, No. 2, April, 1948, pp. 239–271.

tions of various private attempts to influence executive action.[15] The Douglas subcommittee, as part of its work on the problem of ethics, suggested that anyone spending more than $10,000 a year in connection with representation before the Government be required to file expenditure details with the agency involved.[16]

It has occasionally been suggested that the registration system be extended to cover the legislative activities of Federal executive officials themselves. In rejecting this proposal, the Buchanan Committee commented that "Congress, through the proper exercise of its powers to appropriate funds and to investigate conditions and practices of the executive branch, as well as through its financial watchdog, the General Accounting Office, can and should remain vigilant against any improper use of appropriated funds and any invasion of the legislative prerogatives and responsibilities of the Congress." [17]

Regulation. In so far as regulation is concerned, three proposals can be mentioned briefly—and quickly dismissed.

One is the idea that misrepresentation in legislative propaganda, like misrepresentation in drug advertisements, should be prohibited. Though superficially appealing, this proposal is rendered both unfeasible and undesirable by the fact that the distinction between "good" and "bad" and "true" and "false," in the realm of legislative propaganda, is almost entirely subjective.

The second is the proposal that contingent-fees contracts with respect to legislative activities be prohibited. The use of such arrangements is objected to by many members of Congress because of their dislike of any remuneration system which seems to brand their actions as the "effect" and the activities of specific individuals or groups as the "cause." Yet if working to influence legislation is a legitimate form of employment or business activity, as all observers seem to agree it is, it is difficult to find any sound basis for special public regulation of the methods or amounts of remuneration. If exorbitant contingent fees are charged, one can always go to a court of equity.[18]

The third is the proposal that former members of Congress be denied access to the floor of the Senate and the House if they appear there as lobbyists. Although access to the floor is a minor form of access to power and not one which necessarily confers a major advantage upon any ex-member of Congress, a change in the rules would seem unquestionably in order. Congressional reluctance to change the rules probably stems from the desire of incumbent mem-

15 "Report and Recommendations on Federal Lobbying Act," p. 35.

16 "Ethical Standards in Government," pp. 49–50.

17 "Report and Recommendations on Federal Lobbying Act," p. 36.

18 There are a number of cases on record in which courts have refused to enforce contingent-fees contracts calling for exorbitant fees. By sleight-of-hand reasoning these cases are sometimes used in backing up the argument that contingent-fees contracts in the field of legislative influence should be made illegal.

bers themselves, when no longer in office, to be able to visit the scenes of their former glory, whether to indulge in nostalgia or to carry on personal business.

Control of the Major Channels of Communication[19]

As major weapons in the arsenal of social combat, newspapers, television, radio, and cinema are mainstays of the argumentation and propaganda which are vital to the wars of words and influence in the legislative process, particularly in a democratic society. Throughout his career each legislator time and again must decide whether or not to try to break into the headlines, whether or not, when, and where he should be seen and heard inside the legislature and out, whether or not his appeals for personal or policy support should be made "on the stump," over television, in the magazines, or by book and pamphlet, and to which audiences. Usually these choices and the accessibility to him of the communications media are influenced by his relations with private and party organizations or by his status as a public official. Nor is the legislator the only one in the legislative process to make use of the major channels of communication. Leaders and members of the private organizations, the parties, and the other government organizations are equally significant as users.

Yet it is too readily forgotten that the owners and operators of the media are themselves a group as well as members of a variety of other groups and that they have their own interpretations of their private interests and those of the public. Each of these channels of communication rests upon business enterprises involving heavy investments and substantial financial backing. In each there has been a well-defined tendency toward concentration of power into major units and the development of close financial bonds with the more powerful business groupings in the country.

As a result, many individuals and groups have outlined standards which they would like communication enterprises to conform with and have proposed various forms of private or governmental action to compel adherence to these standards or change the pattern of control.

Standards. In its 1923 Code of Ethics, the American Society of Newspaper Editors listed "independence of private interests" as a major standard. Although the code in which it was embodied has probably been something of a dead letter, the concept itself has shown great staying power and widespread appeal.

[19] One of the most valuable of the many books written on this subject—one that will serve as an admirable starting point for anyone who is interested in penetrating further into this fascinating subject—is "A Free and Responsible Press: A General Report on Mass Communication" by the Commission on Freedom of the Press (Chicago: University of Chicago Press, 1947). The other volumes in this series provide rich source materials on newspapers; radio, motion-picture, magazine, and book industries; freedom of the press; and international communications.

A more broad-gauged approach is found in the following five standards developed by the Commission on Freedom of the Press:

"1. A truthful, comprehensive, and intelligent account of the day's events in a context which gives them meaning
"2. A forum for the exchange of comment and criticism
"3. The projection of a representative picture of the constituent groups in the society
"4. The presentation and clarification of the goals and values of the society
"5. Full access to the day's intelligence" [20]

The great advantage of this approach is that it fully recognizes the pluralistic character of American society. Instead of fastening its hopes upon the spurious standards of independence from private interests, it suggests that all interests in society should have access to the major channels of communication. It is based upon a conception of "freedom of the press" which insists that in the freedoms enjoyed by communication enterprises lie reciprocal responsibilities, and that those who have something worth saying should be free to have a public hearing.

A major response to the promulgation of these standards has been to point out that by and large the performance of the American communication industries in the United States is far superior to that of other countries. Another is to indicate that the public is being given what it wants, and that anyone is unrealistic who seeks to impose standards of performance which are far different from those of the average men and women of the country. The critics of the communication industries, however, have not been convinced. Many of them would agree with the Commission on Freedom of the Press when it stated that while the communication industry "has displayed remarkable ingenuity in gathering its raw material and in manufacturing and distributing its finished product" and that "extraordinarily high quality of performance has been achieved by the leaders in each field of mass communications," the industry as a whole "is not meeting the needs of our society." [21]

Codes of Conduct. Most of the communication industries have adopted minimum codes designed to protect against indecency and other flagrant violations of the mores of the community. Yet these codes rarely attempt to set forth goals of public responsibility or ideal performance. The Commission on Freedom of the Press, therefore, attempted to outline in ideal terms the responsibilities of the communication industries. Without asking them to do what can be done more properly by other private groups or more effectively by the Government, the Commission recommended that each of the communication

[20] Commission on Freedom of the Press, "A Free and Responsible Press," Chap. 2, "The Requirements," pp. 20–29.
[21] *Ibid.*, p. 68.

enterprises develop ideal codes of conduct similar to those of the established professions of law and medicine.

Among the other recommendations set down by the Commission were those advocating "That the agencies of mass communication assume the responsibility of financing new, experimental activities in their field . . . that the members of the press engage in vigorous mutual criticism . . . that the press use every means that can be devised to increase the competence, independence, and effectiveness of its staff . . . that the radio industry take control of its programs, and that it treat advertising as it is treated by the best newspapers." [22]

Organization of Weaker Interests. Under the heading of "What can be done by the public" the Commission on Freedom of the Press recommended three lines of action that would tend to provide somewhat greater access to the major channels of communication by the weaker interests in society. The Commission called for greater use of the major communication channels by schools and other nonprofit institutions, for the creation of "academic-professional centers of advanced study, research, and publication in the field of communications," and "the establishment of a new and independent agency to appraise and report annually upon the performance" of the communication industries.[23]

One of the most discerning critics of radio performance, Jerome Spingarn, has urged a localized form of the national agency advocated by the Commission on Freedom of the Press.[24] He emphasizes that the air waves belong to the public and that the public ultimately pays all of radio's bills. He therefore urges that community radio councils be established not only to protest unbalanced radio programs but also to advise community groups on how to use the radio in a competent, interesting fashion. Whatever potentialities there may be in this approach seem to lie in more attention to radio and other channels of communication by existing organizations formed for other purposes. This is borne out by the experience of various religious, racial, and national groups which have been formed for other purposes but which have been extremely effective at times in forcing communication enterprises to eliminate material which they regard as offensive.

Government Control. There are four major methods through which the Government, apart from any direct communication activities of its own, can control the major channels of communication: antitrust action, the enforcement of certain performance standards, censorship, and antilibel sanctions.

Among those who advocate central economic planning or who cater to the whims of large concerns, it is often fashionable to cast sly aspersions upon the value of antitrust action. These aspersions are usually based upon the

[22] *Ibid.*, pp. 90–96.

[23] *Ibid.*, pp. 96–102.

[24] Jerome Spingarn, "Radio Is Yours," Public Affairs Pamphlet, No. 121 (New York· Public Affairs Committee, 1946).

rather obvious fact that a broadside effort to break down bigness and to prevent newspapers from owning radio stations and other forms of joint ownership would clearly be a backward step. Nevertheless, antitrust action, used selectively, can be an invaluable tool. It can open up opportunities for new enterprises which otherwise would not be able to come into being or survive in the face of concentrated competition. It can be used to prevent overpowering concentrations of control in the hands of a few interests and to break down restrictions on the extension of new services or the use of new technological improvements.

Antitrust action can be particularly effective when backed up by economic assistance to smaller enterprises. Morris Ernst has proposed special tax exemptions for small communications enterprises to assist them in building up the capital needed for effective competition with larger groups. In connection with small newspapers and magazines, he has proposed sliding scales of postal rates which would favor smaller companies.[25]

The most ambitious attempt to establish standards of performance for any communication industry is found in the "blue book" of the Federal Communications Commission. The Commission indicated that in considering the renewal of licenses of broadcast stations, it would give particular consideration to various "service factors relevant to the public interest." One of these service factors was "the carrying of sustaining programs" (which in many cases consist of programs dealing with the pros and cons of public issues), while another was "the carrying of programs devoted to the discussion of public issues." [26] As a result of vigorous resistance from the radio industry, the Commission has walked gingerly, as though on eggshells, in carrying out these policies.

A specific method through which the Commission tried at one time to develop a policy of equal treatment was its "Mayflower decision" prohibiting editorializing by radio stations. This was defended on the ground that it prevented undue power over public-policy decisions on the part of those few individuals who are given a franchise to use the air waves and of the large advertisers who support them. If it did not prevent indirect propaganda, at least it prevented direct and open propagandizing. If it prevented the expression of views by a minority of liberal broadcasters, it also prevented a great social imbalance from developing through giving more freedom of action to the great majority of conservative broadcasters. Finally it was argued that the requirement that a station licensee must not be an advocate is inseparable from the policy that stations present all sides of controversial issues.

[25] Morris Ernst, "The First Freedom" (New York: Macmillan, 1946), pp. 254–255, 258–259.

[26] Federal Communications Commission, "Public Service Responsibility of Broadcast Licensees," pp. 12–36, 39–40.

The Commission formally dropped its anti-editorializing policy in 1949 after it was vigorously attacked on many scores. In its place it repeated its policy standard that a reasonable percentage of broadcasting time be devoted to the discussion of public issues, and set forth the requirement that "such programs be designed so that the public has a reasonable opportunity to hear different opposing positions on the public issues of interest and importance in the community." Commissioner Hennock dissented from this decision on the ground that "The standard of fairness . . . is virtually impossible of enforcement by the Commission." [27]

The difficulties in enforcing such standards upon the radio industry are illustrated by the rather remarkable fact that scarcely anyone has seriously proposed the extension of the same principles to the other communications industries. Probably the only such proposal has come from J. B. S. Hardman, an editor of a trade-union newspaper, who proposed that a Free Press Authority be set up to regulate the entire network of communication channels. One of the major functions of the Authority would be to ascertain the relative strength of majority and minority opinions and to compel where necessary adequate expression of minority views.[28] According to Chafee, this proposal "offers to a government the most magnificent opportunity to fetter the press which has ever existed in English-speaking countries." [29]

Censorship is one of the most powerful instruments of control that any government can use. In any full-blown dictatorship the power of censorship is an indispensable weapon, one that assures that views other than those of the group in power have no opportunity to be presented through the major channels of communication. In the past there has been little danger of censorship in America. Yet every war has produced censorship in one form or another. The possibility of partial military mobilization over long periods of time holds the threat of at least partial censorship in some areas. This is a problem that will require serious attention in future years.

Libel laws are a means of self-defense for individuals and groups who feel they have been seriously hurt by statements concerning them made through some channel of communication. The Commission on Freedom of the Press criticized present libel proceedings as "expensive, difficult, and encumbered with technicalities," and therefore proposed, as an alternative, "legislation by which the injured party might obtain a retraction or a restatement of the facts by the offender or an opportunity to reply." [30] The Commission also in-

[27] *Federal Communications Commission's revised ruling* (1 *June*, 1949) *in the matter of Editorializing by Broadcast Licensees* (FCC-49-769 36009).

[28] J. B. S. Hardman, in Harold L. Ickes (ed.), "Freedom of the Press Today" (New York: Vanguard, 1941), pp. 130–131.

[29] Commission on Freedom of the Press, "Government and Mass Communications," Vol. 2, p. 696.

[30] "A Free and Responsible Press," pp. 86–87.

dicated its opposition to proposals that have been made in various states for group libel laws, insisting that libel actions should be confined to civil suits brought by individuals who can prove that they were specifically damaged by false statements. Otherwise, according to the Commission, libel laws could be used to suppress legitimate public controversy among various social groupings.

Government Communication Activities. The most direct form of government participation in communication activities is the conversion of a communication industry into a government monopoly. In England, for example, the British Broadcasting Company, a government corporation, owns and operates the radio broadcasting facilities of the country.

In the United States nothing so far-reaching has been seriously proposed. Outside the radio industry, not even limited forms of Government operation have been suggested. In radio the only serious approach toward Government-owned radio stations for domestic broadcasting has been made by Jerome Spingarn who proposes that the Government establish three stations which would set yardsticks by which to judge private stations.[31]

Government informational activities represent the most effective and acceptable form of direct communication on the part of the government. For the most part, these activities use the established channels of communication; the only major production facility owned by the Government is the Government Printing Office, which produces a wealth of specialized literature that is generally noncompetitive with commercial newspapers and magazines. The Commission on Freedom of the Press favored activities of this sort as a method through which government could improve the level of communications.

> We recommend that the government, through the media of mass communication, inform the public of the facts with respect to its policies and that, to the extent that private agencies of mass communications are unable or unwilling to supply such media to the government, the government itself may employ media of its own.[32]

THEIR PARTICIPATION IN GOVERNMENT [33]

Since private organizations play an inescapable role in the processes of government, the question is sometimes raised as to whether or not they should be given a more directly recognized type of participation. The geographical basis of representation in Congress, it is pointed out, is not capable of reflect-

[31] Spingarn, "Is Your Radio On Now?" *Ladies' Home Journal,* May, 1948, p. 61.

[32] "A Free and Responsible Press," pp. 88–89.

[33] For general material on this subject, see the following: Avery Leiserson, "Administration Regulation" (Chicago: University of Chicago Press, 1942); Lewis Lorwin, "Advisory Economic Councils" (Washington, D.C.: Brookings Institution, 1931); and Fritz Nova, "Functional Representation" (Dubuque, Iowa: Wm. C. Brown, 1950).

ing the multiple interests of a highly differentiated society. It is therefore suggested that the extralegal structure of private organizations, particularly those representing national economic interests, should be incorporated in some manner into the structure and processes of government, either by placing private groups or their representatives in positions of formal power or casting them in advisory roles.

Positions of Formal Power

Here one finds an interesting combination of totally impractical ideas for the reconstruction of government as well as ideas firmly grounded in the practicalities of power politics.

On the impractical side are various proposals—more frequently offered in other countries, less frequently in America—for organizing Congress, or at least one house of Congress, along economic, rather than geographical, lines.[34] One such proposal suggests that for a state with 6,000,000 population and 20 seats in the House of Representatives, the members of the House might be selected from economic groups in the following manner: [35]

Category	*Population*	*No. of Members*
Agriculture	2,100,000	7
Mining	600,000	2
Manufacturing	1,500,000	5
Transportation	300,000	1
Retail distribution	600,000	2
Professional service	600,000	2
Public service and utilities	300,000	1
	6,000,000	20

Other proposals, more along the lines of the corporate state theories used by the theorists of Italian Fascism during the 1920's and 1930's, would supplement the present structure of Congress with a new body set up along functional lines. Inspired by the NRA experience, one writer envisions the creation of a "commonwealth of industry" based upon the trade associations as the unit of organization. The many units would then be organized into six supertrade associations. Each would send two representatives to a National Economic Council. With this structure we could then have self-government by industry, with far less intervention and control by the Government than under the NRA.[36] Another writer proposes a system of Federal charters for trade, pro-

[34] For a general discussion of proposals of this type see William A. Hobson, "Functional Representation," *Encyclopaedia of the Social Sciences,* Vol. 6, pp. 518–520.

[35] Harvey Walker, "Legislative Process; Lawmaking in the United States" (New York: Ronald, 1948), p. 134.

[36] Benjamin A. Javits, "The Commonwealth of Industry" (New York: Harper, 1936), *passim.*

fessional, labor, farm, and consumer organizations. "These autonomous legal entities will have elected in a democratic manner several hundred delegates to a Supreme Council that shall have been permanently established in Washington to cooperate with the President and Congress in making social and economic plans to govern our society. . . ." [37]

There have also been various proposals for bringing conflicting economic groups directly into individual agencies of government. "The principal groups in our free society should get together to solve their mutually dependent problems instead of either neglecting them or leaving them to a centrally constituted governmental bureaucracy to try and solve." [38] This philosophy, varied at times by leaders of some segments of organized labor, is developed in more specific terms in the industry council plan which Philip Murray submitted to President Roosevelt in behalf of the Congress of Industrial Organizations in December, 1940.[39] Under this plan defense mobilization would be put under the direction of a "National Defense Board" consisting of an equal number of representatives of industry and labor unions, over which the President or his designee would be the chairman. The major administrative agencies would be industry councils representing management and organized labor in each industry, with a government representative to serve as chairman.

In discussions of such proposals, the technical difficulties in setting up a system of this type are usually pointed out. "The principal difficulty would be the determination of the action to be taken in cases of divided economic interest. . . . Divided residence is rare. Divided economic loyalties would not be unusual." [40] On a more substantive level, Key refers to "the anarchy of groups that would arise with the delegation of public authority to private associations." [41]

Among the more workable proposals are those that arise when the functions of government are being extended into areas previously handled by private groups, particularly in time of national emergency. Such proposals often call for some method of fusion between these groups and the Government. This can be done through "delegating" powers to a private association, making the private group a quasi-government agency, or placing its representatives at key positions in the Government.

A special approach is the formal participation of opposing groups within the governing body of an agency. During both World War II and the mobilization program following the invasion of Korea in 1950, it was felt that much

[37] Michael O'Shaughnessey, "Economic Democracy and Private Enterprise" (New York: Harper, 1945), pp. 38–39.

[38] Clinton S. Golden and Harold J. Ruttenberg, "The Dynamics of Industrial Democracy" (New York: Harper, 1942), pp. 329–330.

[39] *Ibid.*, pp. 343–347.

[40] Walker, "The Legislative Process" (New York: Ronald, 1948), p. 135.

[41] Key, *op. cit.*, p. 149.

was to be gained by bringing the management-labor bargaining process directly into the structure of the Government. This was done by setting up tripartite boards to develop wage policies and handle labor disputes. These boards consisted of labor representatives, business representatives, and public members who served as mediators between the other members. This approach has the effect of maintaining or strengthening the power of the private groups involved, which is why it is so frequently advocated by business and professional organizations. It also supplies the Government with skilled and experienced manpower and an opportunity to avoid head-on conflicts with certain powerful groups. This is the reason why it is frequently welcomed by Government.

Advisory Positions

"Could representatives of the more important occupational and cultural groups," asks Galloway, "be brought together in some council or federation which would provide a forum for the reconciliation of inter-group controversies and advise Congress on their areas of agreement?" [42]

Proposals for advisory councils bringing together the representatives of divergent groups have enjoyed a remarkably wide vogue. In fact, proposals of this type have probably been as frequent in America as proposals for thoroughgoing functional representation systems have been in other countries. One of the earliest was offered by Senator Robert M. La Follette of Wisconsin who, in 1931, introduced legislation that would have set up a National Economic Council. The Council would have been composed of 15 persons appointed by the President from lists submitted by industrial, financial, agricultural, transportation, and labor organizations. A similar proposal was advanced by Senator Bulkley of Ohio in 1935. In subsequent years the idea received recurring support from national leaders who hoped that some such device would ameliorate the pushing and pulling among divergent groups. It was given a prominent place among the conclusions reached by the chairman of the Temporary National Economic Committee.[43]

In 1944 in the War Mobilization and Reconversion Act, a national group of this type was finally established. The War Mobilization and Reconversion Board was composed of three leaders of farm groups, three leaders of labor groups, three businessmen, and three representatives of the public at large. In actual practice, many of the high hopes held out for such an agency were frustrated. First of all, since its deliberations took place behind closed doors, as they necessarily had to be, the Board's activities did little or nothing to bring private pressures out into the open. Second, it was found while the members

[42] George Galloway, "Congress at the Crossroads" (New York: Crowell, 1946), p. 309.
[43] Final print of the TNEC, Mar. 31, 1941, p. 48.

might at times agree when recommending policies to adjust competing interests, they often failed to obtain the support of their organizations. Third, by the time the Board expired in 1947, many of its members had wearied of attending meetings. By and large, its experience showed that the best to be expected from such a group was an opportunity to exchange information on current problems and test reactions to possible solutions.

Another function for groups of this type is suggested by the following quotation from one of the most irreverent and penetrating analysts of governmental processes:

> Where a separate institution has arisen in order to represent an ideal by separating it from the practical situation, it is never able to reach any conclusion leading to practical action. Its failure to reach such a conclusion is part of its function because the debate convinces everyone that nothing could be done about the practical situation without further study and prayer.[44]

Proposals are always being made that private organizations take part in advisory operations in connection with *individual fields* of government activity. But in such cases there is rarely any thought that by so doing the role of private groups in the processes of government can somehow be improved. Rather, advisory committees of one sort or another are recognized as an invaluable method of organizing support for specific projects. From the point of view of the private groups that take part they are recognized as a potential device for enhancing a group's status and power and wielding more decisive influence upon governmental decisions. In fact, many a so-called "advisory committee" has been the real locus of power in governmental operations. Hence, proposals to place private groups in advisory positions are frequently adopted as a normal part of both the administrative and legislative processes of government rather than as techniques of reform and improvement.

Avery Leiserson has offered an interesting set of conditions to govern interest-group representation in executive agencies:

> Generally three preconditions may be stated as necessary adjuncts to any plan providing for representation of organized groups. There should be an independence of administrative initiative which serves as a compelling incentive for affected groups to co-operate. Second, either through the terms of the grant of authority or in specific declarations of policy, the statute should make it clear that administrative responsibility is wider in scope than any one group interest. Third, administrative officials should be able to calculate consequences of particular group proposals and to secure modifications of these proposals if necessary so that they will be acceptable to other groups. Obviously this concept of administrative ability includes the capacity of persuading particular interests to appreciate the necessity of accepting and conforming

[44] Thurman Arnold, "The Folklore of Capitalism" (New York: New York University Press, 1937), p. 363.

to a positive program of public welfare, which almost inevitably embodies something other than the groups' original demands.[45]

Whether in formal or in advisory capacities, the private organizations will continue to have a major influence upon governmental and legislative action. They will continue to campaign in behalf of their conceptions of their own and the public interest. As agreements and disagreements unfold among these private groups so will the proposals for reforming their behavior and limiting their choices. At times these proposals will be weapons in the armories of distinct groups; less often they will transcend all lesser group interests in order that the larger community may survive.

[45] Leiserson, *op. cit.*, pp. 284–285.

Chapter 4

THE POLITICAL PARTIES

POLITICAL parties in America[1] have never been entirely respectable. In his famous farewell address, George Washington warned against "the baneful effects" and "horrid enormities" of the party spirit. We still hear about the "mire of party politics." "Nonpartisan" is usually used as a term of approval, in contrast with the evils of partisanship. "Politician" is a term of disapproval, and a "statesman," in the words of Speaker "Uncle Joe" Cannon, is a politician who has been dead a long time. According to Schattschneider, so many writers have explained democracy, sovereignty, laws, constitutions, suffrage, representation, liberty, and so on, without reference to parties, that the parties at one time became "the orphans of political philosophy."[2]

Yet parties have always been with us. In the prerevolution days the colonial leaders divided into Whigs and Tories, much along the same lines as in England. Washington's condemnation of parties was sound Whig doctrine. The revolution against the British was organized by party formations. The Committees of Correspondence, organized under the lead of the Virginia House of Burgesses, were the predecessors of our state central committees.[3] At the Constitutional Convention and throughout the bitter struggle over ratification, rival party groups were already emerging. In subsequent years they

> substantially abolished the electoral college, created a plebiscitary presidency and contributed greatly to the extra-constitutional growth of that office. . . . As the political entrepreneurs who have mobilized and organized the dynamic forces of American

[1] For basic material on political parties see Wilfred E. Binkley, "American Political Parties" (New York: Knopf, 1947); Committee on Political Parties, American Political Science Association, "Toward a More Responsible Two-party System," *American Political Science Review,* Vol. 44, No. 3, Part II, Supplement, September, 1950; Pendleton Herring, "The Politics of Democracy" (New York: Rinehart, 1940); Arthur N. Holcombe, "Our More Perfect Union" (Cambridge, Mass.: Harvard University Press, 1950), Chaps. 4 and 5; V. O. Key, Jr., "Parties, Politics and Pressure Groups" (New York: Crowell, 1947); E. M. Sait, "American Parties and Elections" (New York: Appleton-Century-Crofts; rev. ed. by Penniman, 1948); E. E. Schattschneider, "Party Government" (New York: Rinehart, 1942).

[2] Schattschneider, *op. cit.*, p. 10.

[3] Henry Jones Ford, "The Rise and Growth of American Politics" (New York: Macmillan, 1898), p. 8.

public life, these parties have presided over the transformation of the government of the United States from a small experiment in republicanism to the most powerful regime on earth, vastly more liberal and democratic than it was in 1789. They have supervised or adapted themselves to the conquest of a continent, the transformation of the economic system, the absorption of the largest immigrant population in the history of the world, a series of economic crises, and the rise of the modern administrative state, to mention only a few of the developments in which the parties have participated.[4]

Organization and Activities

Who They Are

It is easy for anyone to make a list of the political parties in America. The two major parties, Democratic and Republican, and the more widely advertised minor parties, Communist and Socialist, come quickly to mind. By glancing at a local ballot or reading the papers at the time of a Presidential election, one can pick up the names of lesser-known minor parties. But knowing the names of the parties tells us very little about them. To find out who the parties really are, one must discover what groups of people comprise them, how these groups differ from other social groupings, and how they differ among themselves.

A popular conception of a political party is that it is made up of all voters who participate in a party primary or support a party candidate. The leaders who comprise the party organization—or "machine"—are merely the agents of the party voters. This concept is actively promoted by party leaders, much as the managers of a large corporation often promote the idea that their corporation is really the property of widows, orphans, and everyone else who owns a share of stock. Yet, as Schattschneider has pointed out, this is precisely what parties are not.

> Whatever else the parties may be, they are not associations of voters who support the party candidate. That is to say, the Democratic party is not an association of the twenty-seven million people who voted for Mr. Roosevelt in November, 1940. To describe the party as if it were this sort of association of voters is to produce confusion, and, moreover, to be victimized by a promotional device so old that it should deceive no one. The concept of the parties as a mass association of partisans has no historical basis and has little relation to the facts of party organization. . . . Would it not be to our advantage to abandon the whole concept of party membership, the mental image of the party as an association of all partisans, and to recognize frankly that the party is the property of the "organization"? [5]

The major party organizations are built along similar lines. Each is a cluster or confederation of separate organizations. The most numerous of these are

[4] Schattschneider, *op. cit.*

[5] *Ibid.*, pp. 53–54, 61.

local party groups organized on a geographical basis to conform to the pattern of local governmental units. State groups are made up of the leaders of the local machine. These groups are invariably made up of officeholders, would-be officeholders, and individuals hoping for other forms of personal benefit from their labors on behalf of the organization. The formal structure of local and state groups consists of an intricate network of geographical committees and of party clubs and societies. The actual control is more apt to be found in the hands of a small informal group. Invariably there is a leader—the "boss" —who may or may not have a formal position in the party and who may be a local or state official, a member of Congress, or a completely nonofficial power. The essence of control is the power to pick the party candidate for office. Since the growth of the primary system (which is essentially a method of resolving differences between opposing groups seeking control of the party organization), this has come to mean the power to mobilize sufficient votes in party primaries.

The local and state machines, which are the basic party units, come together in various national groups. First, there is a national committee which is a loose alliance of state and local leaders brought together to perform certain functions with respect to the Presidential elections. Second, there are party organizations in the Senate and House respectively: caucuses or conferences, steering committees and policy committees, party leaders and whips, and congressional campaign committees. These organizations, composed of members of Congress whose political roots are found in local and state organizations, assign party members to committees, consult on the legislative agenda and on legislative policy, and work on campaigns for reelection to Congress.

In the case of the Administration party, there is a third element in the cluster, namely, the President and his associates. The President, by virtue of the powers of office, is invariably the leader of his party. He can hand-pick the chairman of the national committee and run the national office as his personal organization. Depending upon circumstances, he can exercise varying degrees of influence on the local and state party organizations and on the party organizations in Congress. In the case of the anti-Administration party, the Presidential candidate defeated in the last election is called the "titular leader." But the title has little meaning, and leadership is apt to be divided among the local and state organizations and the Senate and House leaders. In both parties, all the various clusters are brought together every four years in a National Convention for the purpose of selecting candidates for President and Vice-President.

Organizationally, the minor parties differ from the major parties in that they usually have a single national body which exercises firm control over its entire operations. This is a corollary of the fact that their local organizations are extremely weak and are seldom able to elect local or state officials or members of Congress.

Many organizations that are called parties scarcely merit the name. Note V. O. Key's description of the Democratic party's organizations in the South:

> . . . the Democratic party in most states of the South is merely a holding-company for a congeries of transient squabbling factions, most of which fail by far to meet the standards of permanence, cohesiveness, and responsibility that characterize the political party. The restriction of all significant political choices in the South to the Democratic primaries enables the South to maintain its constancy to Democratic presidential candidates, but it has not enabled the South to maintain social groupings equivalent to political parties within the Democratic party. In the conduct of campaigns for the control of legislatures, for the control of governorships, and for representatives in the national Congress, the South must depend for political leadership, not on political parties, but on lone-wolf operators, on fortuitous groupings of individuals usually of a transient nature, on spectacular demagogues odd enough to command the attention of considerable numbers of voters, on men who have become persons of political consequence in their own little bailiwicks, and on other types of leaders whose methods to attract electoral attention serve as substitutes for leadership of a party organization.[6]

Parties, Private Organizations, and Government Agencies

How do parties differ from private associations and government agencies? This question cannot be answered without first understanding how much they resemble these other groups. Viewed from one perspective, the parties are themselves private associations closely allied with other associations whose interests they represent in one way or another and from whom they derive indispensable support. Viewed from the perspective of their role in manning the key positions in government, they can be regarded as part of the government structure itself. In fact, the people who man the parties are largely the leaders of other private organizations and of government agencies, plus a certain amount of specialized party personnel who make the machinery run. Nor is the existence of machines and bosses and the use of patronage and other favors anything peculiar to parties. No organization, including private associations and government agencies, can be effective without the development of machines and bosses of some sort or can be held together without the ability to provide specific benefits to its supporters.

The most distinguishing function of a party organization is that it serves as a vehicle for winning or maintaining control of the key positions in government through participation in the electoral process. Whether the purpose of winning control is to obtain personal advantage or to carry out certain policies is not particularly relevant; in fact, both motives are usually insepa-

[6] V. O. Key, Jr., "Southern Politics in State and Nation" (New York: Knopf, 1949), p. 16.

rably entwined. The important thing is that the group needs to select the persons who occupy the key positions. To achieve this objective, party organizations engage in two kinds of activity. First of all, they nominate candidates. Schattschneider regards the nominating process as the most important activity of the party. Although other groups influence the nominating process, it is the nomination of candidates that brings a party together more than anything else.

> The nomination may be made by a congressional caucus, a delegate convention, a mass meeting, a cabal, an individual, or a party election. The test is, does it bind? Not, how was it done? Unless the party makes authoritative and effective nominations, it cannot stay in business, for dual or multiple party candidacies mean certain defeat. As far as elections are concerned, the united front of the party, the party concentration of numbers, can be brought about only by a binding nomination. The nominating process thus has become the crucial process of the party.[7]

Second, parties play a specialized role in campaigning for candidates. They do not monopolize political campaigns, for the campaign activities of business, labor, and farm groups often dwarf the activities of party organizations. But they do supply the basic machinery through which other groups take part in election campaigns; they do provide an organization which is interested more in the electoral process than anything else; and they do provide a connective tissue that brings electoral considerations into the processes of government between elections.

Parties, of course, are not the only groups interested in winning or maintaining control of the key positions in government. The leaders of the most powerful and ambitious private organizations have similar objectives. But they seek to fulfill this by working in cooperation with party groups, particularly in matters relating to elections. The fact that they may control a party, or even two parties, does not mean that they themselves have become parties. They would become parties only if they converted their own organizations into vehicles for seeking power rather than using a specialized organization for this purpose. This is rarely done. In England, for example, where organized labor provides the basic support for the Labour party, there is a clear organizational distribution between the Trade Union Congress and the Labour party. In America the purpose of the various political organizations set up by the A.F.L. and the C.I.O. is to influence and support the activities of party organizations rather than to supplant them.

Despite their conflicts, the parties have numerous common characteristics. First, all parties that unite to work in terms of political power develop a community of interest among the members of the party organization. They become self-help societies oriented toward achieving major personal advantage for the leaders and minor personal advantage for the rank and file. It is this

[7] Schattschneider, *op. cit.*, p. 64.

factor which makes the party always something more than a mere representative of other groups and interests.

Second, any party that is interested in winning majority support throughout the country must appeal to a wide variety of competing groups and interests. In a sense, it must try to become all things to all men. The local groups must give representation to the interests that are strongest locally. Nationally, it must find means of accommodating local party groups with divergent interests and outside support from divergent interests.

Third, there is always a strong tendency for nonparty organizations to work through competing parties. By so doing they can achieve their objectives better, no matter which party wins out. Finally, there are many areas of the country where, by reason of historical traditions and economic and social structure, there is only one party which ever has much of a chance to win elections. In those areas, competing groups all tend to work through the dominant party, thus contributing to intraparty diversity and interparty similarity. All these forces militate against any black-and-white differences between the major parties and tend to make the major point of variance the fact that one is made up of "ins" and the others of "outs."

Yet the contrast between the two major parties in America has rarely been simply one of "ins" versus "outs." The two major parties have never been based upon an identical combination of groups and interests. At times the major differences have been merely reflections of divergent sectional and national interests among business groups or among agricultural groups. At other times, depending upon the changing character of American society and upon the political strategy adopted by group leaders, the differences have been more striking. When Jefferson's Republican party was waging its campaign against the Federalists, the conflict was mainly between agricultural and business interests. In recent years, with the growing strength of organized labor, the business interests are finding their best expression through the modern Republican party and the labor interests through the Democratic party. In both cases, however, it would be a great oversimplification to define the opposing parties in terms of single competing interests. There were certain agricultural groups supporting the Federalists and there are certain labor groups supporting the Republicans today. No party can be properly identified except in terms of a complete analysis of the various groups and subgroups from which it derives support. Moreover, such an analysis must be made not only in terms of business, agriculture, and labor but also in terms of all the other groups and interests into which the people of the country are divided.[8]

[8] As examples of detailed analyses of the group bases of political parties see Charles A. Beard, "The Economic Origins of Jeffersonian Democracy" (New York: Macmillan, 1916); Arthur N. Holcombe, "Political Parties of Today" (New York: Harper, 1924); and Key, "Politics, Parties and Pressure Groups," Chap. 9.

Their Legislative Activities

One of the minor myths about American government centers around the role of political parties in the legislative process. Each party, so the story goes, formulates the principles to which it is devoted and selects candidates to carry these principles to the people at election time. The people then decide by majority vote which party is to be entrusted with the reins of government. The victorious party, with a popular mandate behind it, is then responsible for putting its program into action. On the legislative front, the ties of party loyalty, supported by disciplinary measures, bridge the separation between the Presidency and the Congress and bring the two into cooperative action to carry out party policies. If these policies are not carried out, it is because the party leaders have blundered or because they were never really sincere in their campaign pledges. When the next elections roll around, the opposing parties once again present their case to the people and once again the people make their choice.

The presentation of party policy is just not this simple. Party candidates appeal to voters not only in terms of policy but also in terms of their personalities—their winsome smile, their family life, their sense of humor, and goodfellowship. When they deal with policies, neither candidate nor platforms can, in the very nature of things, cover the entire gamut of major legislative issues, deal with the detailed intricacies of any of them, anticipate the new issues that may arise between elections, or separate the national from the local or the international. They must necessarily deal mainly in abstract terms which, depending on one's point of view, may be regarded as "fundamental principles" or "glittering generalities." [9] Even apart from the problem of vagueness and ambiguity, there is the problem of conflicting commitments. Presidential candidates often take positions that differ from the national platform on which they run. The national platform is not regarded as binding upon candidates for Congress, who may refuse to support certain provisions or directly oppose them. At mid-term elections, the major parties have not been accustomed to the promulgation of national platforms, and each candidate for the House or Senate is even more on his own. Most candidates make private commitments that are never publicly broadcast and may, either directly or through unofficial spokesmen, make contradictory commitments to conflicting groups.

The electoral process is not this simple either. Millions of citizens of vot-

[9] A perfect example is the following plank in the Republican party platform of 1944: "We pledge the establishment by Federal legislation of a permanent Fair Employment Practices Commission." This sounded like a clear-cut, unqualified commitment. However, when legislation to establish a Fair Employment Practices Commission came up in Congress shortly after the 1944 election, it became evident that one of the major issues in this area was not whether such a commission should be established but rather whether such a commission should have regulatory powers or confine itself instead to educational activities.

ing age stay away from the polls. In 1940, 1944, and 1948, the percentage of potential voters, twenty-one years of age and over, who voted in the Presidential elections was, respectively, 62, 56, and 54. One reason for the stay-at-homes is apathy—as evidenced by the fact that the figures for the congressional elections of 1942, 1946, and 1950, when the excitement of a national campaign was lacking, were still lower: 34, 39, and 43. Another reason is found in the many barriers that still exist between the people and the polls. These range from poll taxes, discriminatory literacy tests, and threats of violence against Negroes to onerous residence and registration requirements, polling places that are open for an insufficient number of hours or are geographically inaccessible, and inadequate absentee provisions.

Furthermore, each vote actually cast is not given equal weight. This is not merely a matter of the use of fraudulent and corrupt practices, which seem to be a persistent, though immeasurable, part of the political scene. By constitutional requirement, two Senators are elected in each state regardless of population. The districts from which members of the House of Representatives are elected are of varying size and are frequently gerrymandered to distort the actual vote. Presidents are elected not by popular vote but by the antiquated electoral-college system which can at times give the Presidency to a candidate with less than the greatest number of popular votes and which on all occasions gives extra weight to every vote cast in the "doubtful states." Finally, there are many areas of the country in which one party is so strong that there are really no election contests worth the name. In some of these areas, one-party control of the elections is duplicated in the party primaries, where one party group dictates the party candidates, and opposition in the primaries by competing groups is usually futile.

Thirdly, the parties seldom have full hold upon the reins of the Government. One party may win the Presidency but lose out in the Senate or the House of Representatives. At mid-term elections the opposition party may win a majority in Congress, or in one house, without even getting a chance to capture the White House. If a party has nominal control of both the White House and the Congress, there is still the possibility that a majority of the members of the Supreme Court may declare its legislation unconstitutional. But these are merely the more obvious obstructions to party control. Of much greater significance is the fact that formal party control—even though it may cover all branches of the Federal government, including the Supreme Court—is often merely a façade behind which one finds bitterly antagonistic groups and interests. In recent years, for example, the Democratic party has had formal control of the Government, and again and again we have seen Democratic Presidents, both Roosevelt and Truman, go in one direction on major legislative issues, while Congress, controlled by a coalition of conservative Republicans and Democrats, has gone in another direction. Under such circumstances, within Congress itself, party leadership is also weak. "Steering committees seldom meet and never steer," generalized ex-Senator James Byrnes.[10] When policy committees meet, the Senate and House groups may move in opposite directions—as in 1946 when the Senate Policy Committee approved the Wagner-Ellender-Taft Housing Bill and the House Republicans fought it. The chairman and ranking members of legislative committees reach their positions of power through seniority and are neither responsible to, nor necessarily a part of, party leadership. Party caucuses or conferences invariably reveal deep splits on legislative issues among a party's members. Hence, they are only infrequently convened on matters of policy; when they are, decisions are seldom regarded as binding.[11]

In the great majority of legislative struggles the major parties are observers on the side lines. When attempts are made to enroll them as combatants, they prove adept at preserving their neutrality. If drawn in momentarily, the next moment they may be back on the side lines. When they really get into a legislative struggle, it is usually at an advanced stage in combat, rarely before the battle positions of conflicting contestants have been crystallized. Sometimes a tacit bipartisan understanding yields a party battle staged like a professional wrestling match. Spokesmen for opposing parties will grunt and groan through a series of phony routines, applying holds that are dramatic to the spectators in the gallery but harmful to nobody and ending up with a preordained finale. Most "bipartisan" policies, moreover, are nothing of the sort. Instead of being agreements reached on the basis of negotiations between authorized representatives of the two parties and ratified by appropriate party organs, they are usually policies on which at least one party has officially taken no position, and on which there has never been any official party negotiations. They are bipartisan only in the sense that they are supported by individuals in both parties.

[10] James L. Byrnes, "Streamlining Congress," *The American Magazine,* February, 1945.

[11] Statistical interpretations of party loyalty in terms of congressional votes can be very misleading. The line-up on floor votes often fails completely to indicate the actual influences brought to bear by members of Congress, particularly in committees. (See discussion in Chap. 18.) Nevertheless, statistical tabulations on "party loyalty" are constantly being attempted. For example, see the *Congressional Quarterly,* which publishes its own party-loyalty tabulation for important issues at every congressional session; Key, "Southern Politics in State and Nation," Chaps. 16 and 17, on Senate and House voting behavior of Southern Democrats, non-Southern Democrats, and Republicans; Robert A. Dahl, "Congress and Foreign Policy" (New York: Harcourt, Brace, 1950), pp. 45–50; Julius Turner, "Responsible Parties: A Dissent from the Floor," *American Political Science Review,* Vol. 45, No. 1, March, 1951; and—an incisive analysis by an extremely competent newspaperman—Richard Strout, "The Elephant, the Donkey and the Tariff," *Christian Science Monitor,* Sept. 17, 1949 (Magazine), p. 5. The earliest systematic study of this sort was prepared by A. L. Lowell, "The Influence of Party upon Legislation in England and America," *Annual Report of American Historical Association,* 1901, Vol. 1.

It would be a great mistake, however, to come to the conclusion that the political parties have no role in the legislative struggle. They always have a certain role, no matter how limited. The party organization always provides a certain degree of connective tissue among the party leaders and followers in Congress, the executive branch, and the Federal courts. Some legislative matters become genuine party issues. On many legislative matters the struggle between divergent party factions becomes a crucial part of the legislative process. In nominating candidates, the parties select a small group of men from whom key contestants in the legislative struggle will be drawn, thereby defining the choices that are submitted to the voters. If these men sometimes appeal for votes mainly on the basis of character, charm, and other personal traits, it is nevertheless true that there is no sharp line to be drawn between personality and policy. The nomination of a solid, stolid candidate with a safe-and-sane family and religious background is often merely another way of entering a campaign on the basis of safe-and-sane, standpat conservatism. The drafting of party platforms is part of the push-and-pull process that lines up the conflicting forces in the legislative process. The inclusion of a specific legislative objective in a major party platform can give crucial impetus to a legislative campaign. Inclusion in a minor party platform often serves as a trial balloon for ideas that are subsequently taken over by a major party.

Although elections are a far cry from legislative referenda, they unquestionably have legislative implications. While they never comprise all the elements that are weighed, they always tilt the legislative scales in one direction or another—if only in the direction of speed as opposed to sluggishness. The conduct of electoral campaigns is itself a method of organizing people into groups. From the viewpoint of group structure it is one of the lowest forms of organization, just a few notches above the organization of participants in a parade or of customers for a certain brand of cigarettes or breakfast cereal. From the viewpoint of the group struggle, however, it is a far more important operation, one which has come to be identified with democratic government itself. It not only brings divergent groups together for the purpose of pooling their resources for mutual advantage, but also opens up the processes of government to under-represented interests. Electoral campaigns are a method of organizing the unorganized. Just as the advertising firm that seeks a mass market for a cigarette or breakfast cereal cannot be content with merely keeping present customers, the political party conducting an election campaign must seek to organize the support of those who have been inactive, undecided, or even followers of a rival party.

It would also be a mistake to think that any one description can precisely describe the legislative role of the political parties. At any one time, there may be stronger party control in one house and weaker party control in the other, stronger party control within one party and weaker within the other. At one time, the role of the parties may be relatively unimportant; at another it may become exceedingly important. The factors that determine these variations are the economic, social, and cultural development of the country, the diverse changing interests of the American people, and the manner in which these interests are organized by the leaders not only of the political parties but also of the private associations and government agencies.

The Party "System"

A discussion of party "systems" can be extremely misleading if it gives the impression that we can legislate or otherwise decree a "one-party system" or a "two-party system" into being. The number of parties that operate in any area, their role in government, and the differences between them—these are the result of group conflicts, social traditions, and the strategy and tactics used by the various participants in the social struggle.

Ideas concerning the kind of party system that is desirable are understandably influenced by one's substantive goals in life and one's ideas concerning the best methods of attaining these goals. Those who are satisfied with governmental policies and their own position in the power structure will tend to be more or less satisfied with whatever party line-up exists. Those who want to "change the world" or "get ahead in the world" are apt to think differently. As Holcombe aptly observes: "There will always be ambitious politicians and discontented factions watchfully waiting for opportunities to break up the established factional combinations and bring about a new alignment of the major parties in which their own prospects of influence would be greater." [12]

start Fri

The Number of Parties

The simplest way to discuss the number of parties that may be regarded as desirable is to start with zero and move up the line to one-party domination, the two-party system, and a multiparty setup.

No Parties. The idea that we should have no parties at all was rather strongly presented early in American history by the Federalists. This, however, is merely another way of saying that the dominant political group at that time looked with disfavor upon the development of a strong opposition. Both among the Founding Fathers and their Whig counterparts in England, the most vocal opponents of parties as such were members of a dominant group which developed the habit of attacking opposing groups on the ground that they were fomenting partisanship.

In many local communities in America there has developed a "nonpartisan" approach to local politics. The nonpartisan theory is that local elections should

[12] Holcombe, *op. cit.*, p. 143.

be fought strictly on the basis of the ability of the rival candidates and not by parties as such. At times, however, this point of view becomes an attack on national parties, with some recognition of the partisan functions of local private organizations. Usually a nonpartisan movement is strong where the "nonpartisans" have developed an organization, loose though it may be, which is essentially a local party and which has probably developed an alliance with the weaker of the established parties as a means of beating the dominant or formerly dominant "machine."

In some communities, the nomination of local candidates by the local wings of the national parties is prohibited by law, an arrangement which is ardently sought by many nonpartisans. If such prohibitions effectively eliminated party candidates, they would in fact confer a political monopoly on the nonpartisan organizations and create a local one-party system. In practice, however, the regular parties take part in supposedly nonpartisan elections by informally sponsoring candidates and by entering into all sorts of alliances and understandings with other groups and factions.

The opponents of nonpartisanship at the local level charge that it introduces an anarchic note into local government and that it weakens the two-party system nationally. The proponents maintain that nonpartisan local officials can be just as responsible as party representatives and that the national two-party system is not affected, and may even be strengthened, by local nonpartisanship. The specific character of the influence upon national parties varies substantially from one community to another.

One-party. If the idea of no parties has been frequently talked about but never carried into practice, the idea of one-party domination has often been carried into practice but—in America at least—is rarely advocated. Even in the one-party states and congressional districts, those who benefit from and participate in the quasi monopoly enjoyed by the dominant party usually talk glibly about the virtues of a two-party system and justify such a position by pointing out that a second party, weak though it may be, exists. Or else they claim that internal conflicts over the nomination of candidates by the dominant party sometimes approach the dimensions of two-party conflict.

The most open defense of a one-party system comes from the Russians. One of the leading Soviet theorists, G. F. Aleksandrov, argues first that in capitalist countries such as the United States or in England the major parties "do not differ in principle on many quite important contemporary questions." Hence, there is really no genuine two-party system in these countries. Secondly, he argues that under a two-party system, each party really tries to obtain all the elected posts held by the opposition. The only reason two-party systems persist is that neither party has succeeded in carrying out its objectives. The Communist party of the Soviet Union has merely succeeded in doing what the bourgeois parties in England and the United States have tried to do but without success.[13]

The answer to this argument, of course, is that in neither England nor the United States has either party tried to suppress its rivals through the use of force and violence, as the Communist party has done in Russia. In both countries, moreover, there are matters on which the two major parties disagree as well as matters on which they agree.

One-party domination can mean one of three things. It can mean a social structure in which the dominant group has few rivals of any importance and power. It can reflect the suppression of political competition and rivalry through trickery, disenfranchisement, or open violence. It can serve as a façade for inner-party conflict which develops to the point where it may at times become almost as meaningful as direct competition between rival parties.[14]

Two-party. The two-party system is one of the most revered of all the sacred cows in American thought. The defense of the two-party system has become an emotional undertaking akin to the protection of the Constitution and the home. This emotion is based upon the solid interest of party leaders who oppose the formation of new parties which might split their own support rather than that of their rivals. It is also based upon conservative opposition to the radical ideas often associated with the minor parties. Some of the most vocal defenders of the two-party system are those who are active leaders of the dominant party in states where there is no meaningful opposition to one-party domination. Under these circumstances the second party often becomes a useful tool and ally of the top-dog party. From the liberal standpoint, too, there is good reason to support the idea of a two-party system so long as it provides an instrument for carrying liberal ideas into action through a political party capable of winning not only the Presidency but also a genuine liberal majority in Congress.

Perhaps the most forcibly presented argument in favor of the two-party system stems from the manageable number of leadership alternatives that it presents for selection by the electorates. The "yes-no" range of choice thus provided is generally about all that millions of voters can handle effectively by way of the ballot box. Two parties, rooted as they are in single-district systems of representation operating on the "winner-take-all" principle, are also

[13] G. F. Aleksandrov, "The Pattern of Soviet Democracy" (Washington, D.C.: Public Affairs Press, 1948), pp. 22*ff*.

[14] "One-party states, however, vary in the degree to which their factual systems approach the nature of a two-party system. North Carolina, for example, is in reality quite as much a two-party state as some non-southern states, while Arkansas and South Carolina present examples of one-party factionalism in almost pure form. . . ." Key, "Southern Politics in State and Nation," p. 299. The chapter from which this quotation is taken (pp. 298–311) provides a penetrating analysis of this entire subject.

supposed to absorb some of the more disruptive shocks of intergroup political strife as a result of their tendency to limit these choices and of their need to be broadly representative of the population as a whole.

Many Parties. Like one-party domination, the idea of a multiparty system in the United States is something that is rarely advocated. Even the proponents of minor parties and new parties (and the number of such proponents seems to be declining) base their political thinking upon the hope that someday they will become major parties. It is generally recognized that a multiplicity of parties leads to internal instability. The major recognition given to the multiparty setup in American political thought lies in the observation that minor parties represent a germinating center for ideas that are often picked up and used by the major parties.

Party Government

"Why not try party government?" writes E. E. Schattschneider. "The potentialities of the party are very great. Moreover, party government is good democratic doctrine because the parties are the special form of political organization adapted to the mobilization of majorities. How else can the majority get organized? If democracy means anything at all, it means that the majority has the right to organize for the purpose of taking over the government."[15]

The case for party government is also justified on a number of other grounds. The political party, it is argued, is the only instrument that can present alternatives to the voters and give them meaningful choices on Election Day. It is the only body capable of bridging the separation between the branches of government or even of bringing consistency to the policies of the executive branch. It is far better that party activities be brought out into the open through party government rather than have party bosses hold the strings from behind the scenes where they cannot be held accountable for their actions. Finally, it is felt that party government provides a means for realizing in America a political system akin to that of cabinet government in England, which has been fondly regarded by many political scientists as the best of all systems.

These arguments are somewhat unrealistic. First of all, no majority organizes expressly for the purpose of taking over the government. Parties are organized not by majorities but by small groups of leaders. While one group of leaders may win majority support in an election, this does not mean that the people who voted for these leaders can be described as a party organization. Further, there is a danger in placing too much reliance on the theory that a mandate at the polls can be specific enough to serve as a charter for the development of national policy. When elections deal with principles they can deal with them

[15] Schattschneider, *op. cit.*, p. 208.

only in general terms and cannot serve as a guide in the development of all important details. Many issues of national policy simply cannot be brought to focus in election contests.

Moreover, the sheer bulk of conflicts in American society is so great that the parties could be expected to carry the entire burden of government only by developing a concentration of political power which, in the views of most individuals and most groups, would be highly undesirable. If the parties should ever become the arena for the reconciliation of the major conflicts in American life, this would be a far cry from bringing governmental operations out into the open. While it would clearly identify the importance of the party leaders, such a change would transfer into the secret sessions of the parties and of the party bureaucracies many of the conflicts that now receive much more airing in the halls of Congress as well as in the activities of various executive agencies.

A final question might be raised as to the accuracy of the term "party government" as a description of the British system of *cabinet* government. True, the British Cabinet is usually composed of the leaders of the majority party in the House of Commons. Yet to conclude from this observation that the British have "party government" is to minimize the influence of the King, the House of Lords, the Civil-Service bureaucracy, and the private organizations which, in England as in America, wield a huge influence upon the operations of government.

Tweedledum and Tweedledee

There is another school of thought which, although more realistic than that of the party government advocates, is equally sterile as a guide to action. In 1944 Pendleton Herring wrote a brilliant description of the operations of American government. Looking at the party system, he expressed considerable satisfaction with the lack of clear-cut lines of demarcation between the Republican and Democratic parties: "If all those wanting change," he wrote, "were able to gang up and force through a sweeping party program, while all those of the party against change were expected to stand by until an election occurred two or three years hence, the pent-up feeling and the resulting clash would probably blow the dome off the Capitol." [16] A few years later, this theme was stated in even stronger terms by one of the early New Dealers, David Cushman Coyle, who abhorred "the ghastly choice of a communist-infiltrated 'liberal' party versus a fascist-infiltrated 'conservative' one." [17] Herbert Agar has written a vivid history of American government for the

[16] Herring, *op. cit.*, pp. 113–114.

[17] David Cushman Coyle, "Reorganizing Congress," *Virginia Quarterly Review*, Winter, 1947.

purpose of illustrating his thesis that parties without programmatic unity are the price we pay for union.[18]

The most complete statement of the tweedledum-tweedledee thesis comes from Arthur Holcombe.

> Perhaps the best party system would be one in which each of the major parties was as nearly as possible a fair sample of all the important factional interests in the country. Under such a party system the voters would possess the greatest freedom of choice between the candidates for important offices on grounds of merit and fitness. Under the existing system much freedom of choice is restricted by the necessity of choosing between the parties as well as between the candidates. Perhaps under a new party alignment each of the major parties might be a truer sample of the whole body of people than is either of the present major parties.[19]

There are obvious virtues in this approach. It emphasizes acceptance of "reality" rather than impractical departures. It is well suited to those who are essentially conservative or to those who, if liberal, prefer to take their liberalism in very small doses. It is well geared to the goals of those who prefer middle-class domination of the political scene and are wary about the implications of a growing labor movement and labor's emerging political power. Finally, it provides a formula which, if followed faithfully and never abandoned, would prevent America from coming under the sway of a dictatorial government of either the Right or the Left.

The approach also has many defects. It minimizes the significant differences that have often developed among the parties, particularly during the 1930's and the 1940's. The differences between the two major parties are rarely clean-cut, but nevertheless existent. Those who ask for a straight tweedledum-tweedledee line-up would probably be interested more in a return to some "good old days" than in a maintenance of the *status quo.*

Another defect in this approach is the automatic inference that party conflict must lead to intolerable stresses upon society. While Agar seems to claim that the Civil War resulted from the fact that the parties began to have meaning in the ten years before 1860, it is also possible to maintain that the weakness and decentralization of the parties contributed to the outbreak of hostilities between the states. Roy Franklin Nichols places a major share of the blame for the Civil War upon the disruption of the Democratic party.[20] Agar lends credence to this interpretation in a passage which, clashing with his own major thesis, bewails the fact that neither Pierce nor Buchanan were able to invoke the "mighty spell" of party loyalty.[21]

[18] Herbert Agar, "The Price of Union" (Boston: Houghton Mifflin, 1950), pp. 689–690.

[19] Holcombe, *op. cit.,* p. 145.

[20] Roy Franklin Nichols, "The Disruption of American Democracy" (New York: Macmillan, 1948).

[21] Agar, *op. cit.,* pp. 354–355.

Whether or not social conflict is fanned by the operations of a party with clear-cut positions on major issues depends, of course, on what these issues are. It also depends upon the dynamics of party relationships at a given time and the quality of leadership evidenced by party rivals. A case might well be made, for example, that a Democratic party with more internal unity on liberal programs would have the effect not of fanning sharper conflicts with the Republican party, but of bringing about a softening and liberalization of conservative forces in America. The growth of the Labour party in England has by no means meant that a communist-dominated party has faced a fascist-infiltrated party, nor has it tended to blow the dome off the House of Commons. Rather, it has placed the business interests and the Conservative party in a position where they long ago discovered the expediency of taking more progressive positions on many fronts. This is the basic explanation of the fact that the British Conservatives have often proved themselves far more liberal than the New Deal or Fair Deal wings of the Democratic party in the United States.

A case can also be made that a more unified Democratic party would operate to the right rather than to the left of the Democratic party's present liberal wing. The price of unity would unquestionably be paid in terms of a rapprochement with the Southern middle-of-the-roaders. This would mean that the Democratic party would have to forgo many of the more advanced positions taken by its Northern liberals but, in return, would be in a better position to obtain legislative action on moderately advanced policies. Stronger parties, therefore, might well lead to the development of two parties, one liberal and one conservative, but both with definite leanings toward the center. This has already been the path of development in both England and Sweden, where strong and rather well-disciplined parties have opposed one another for many years and where the political atmosphere has been characterized by relative stability and peacefulness.

More Party Responsibility

In its report of September, 1950, the Committee on Political Parties of the American Political Science Association steered away from the idea of "party government" which had been earlier advocated by the chairman of the committee, E. E. Schattschneider. It also disassociated itself from the tweedledum-tweedledee school. In contrast, it brought forth a middle-of-the-road concept that, without becoming monolithic in character, each of the two major parties ought to become more "responsible." Responsibility was spelled out in terms that emphasized the inevitability of gradualism, that is, of changes by small degrees. The report calls for a stronger party system in which the parties, first, "are able to bring forth programs to which they commit themselves," and, second, "possess sufficient internal cohesion to carry out these programs." It also called for an organized party opposition as well as for parties with greater resistance to pressures, more internal party loyalty, and more opportunities for discussion of party policy among the various leaders throughout the party. The report recognizes that there are and must be both nonpartisan and bipartisan issues and that the process of adjustment between conflicting groups cannot be entirely channeled through the parties.

The great value of this approach is that it projects a party system ideally suited to the needs of many groups. For the liberal Democrats it provides a rationale for liberalizing the South and developing a genuine two-party system in that region. For the conservative Republicans it provides a rationale for suppressing or combating the activities of the "me-too" liberals in Republican ranks. From the point of view of those who are interested in developing a more consistent approach in foreign affairs, it suggests a structure in which American policies on foreign affairs and national security could be more firmly grounded upon party decisions.

The limitations upon this approach are two in number. First, there is the question of feasibility. The desire of party leaders to appeal to the broadest possible section of the American electorate, the interests of private organizations in getting support within both parties, the strategic advantages that are often obtained by party disunity—these and other factors are considerable obstacles in the path of any who seek to make either one of the major parties a more responsible organization.

Second, any program implies concrete action to strengthen one or another party. It is not quite accurate to say that action to strengthen the responsibility of the Democratic party sets an example which forces the Republican party to be more responsible. The dominant consideration in political combat is to strengthen one's supporters and divide one's opponents. This inevitably leads to the use of coalition-party strategy. The legislative combat on domestic legislation has been characterized for many decades by crystallization, with varying degrees of clarity and precision, of a bipartisan conservative coalition and a bipartisan liberal coalition. Politics of this type are unquestionably here to stay and are by no means inconsistent with the development of more responsibility within any one major political party.

Chapter 5

THE PARTIES: PROPOSALS FOR CHANGE

WHILE MOST of its proposals follow the "more responsible parties" orientation, the report "Toward a More Responsible Two-party System" of the Committee on Political Parties of the American Political Science Association serves as an excellent jumping-off point for general consideration of normative and reform attitudes toward the role of political parties in the legislative process.

Proposals have been made for changes *outside* Congress as well as *inside.* These are pointed up here because it is believed that the relevance of party developments outside the arena called Congress is not so far removed as some would think. The operations of local primaries, national conventions, and other agencies of the national party have their effect upon the legislative struggle, later if not sooner.

PROPOSALS FOR CHANGES OUTSIDE CONGRESS

The Local Primaries

The local primaries operate at the roots of party life. Through them, candidates for Congress are nominated and the basic decisions are thus made on the variety of people and viewpoints that may be represented within the congressional ranks of each party.

Objections to Primaries as Such. A wide variety of arguments has been leveled against the primary system. While it was first advocated as a method of attacking or controlling local party machines, it has become evident that local party bosses can often succeed in dominating the local primaries. Moreover, the primary contests cost money and, combined with the campaigning necessities of the election itself, make candidates for Congress all the more dependent upon contributions from private organizations. Finally, the primary system represents a serious obstacle toward the development of unified national parties. Anybody who can succeed in winning a primary contest is automatically the candidate of the party no matter how much he may disagree with the party's national position.

There are many advocates of party responsibility who have, therefore, long yearned for the abandonment of the primary system and who would prefer to see the central party organizations picking party candidates for Congress as is done to a large extent by the English parties. They feel that as long as the present system is maintained, any Administration party which is sincerely interested in winning the support of dissident members of Congress is compelled by the force of circumstances to place major reliance upon patronage, the allocation of funds for local projects, and favorable handling of constituents' complaints. This undermines the Civil-Service system, prevents the independent exercise of Executive judgment in choosing administrators and employees, and introduces an arbitrary or capricious note into the determination of Executive policy.

Yet open opposition to the direct primaries is rare indeed. The number of reasons that can be added up against the primary system never seems to provide enough support for a frontal attack. One of the most vocal advocates of stronger national parties satisfies himself with a wistful eying of the English system where "nominations are made informally, privately, and simply" and "once a candidate has been adopted by the local party association in a constituency he is entitled, in practice, to be the party candidate permanently until he retires voluntarily, whether he is elected to Parliament or not." [1] In fact, the Committee on Political Parties concluded: "[The direct primary] is a useful weapon in the arsenal of intra-party democracy. No workable substitute has been found for it and it probably can be adapted to the needs of parties unified in terms of national policy." [2]

The only seriously entertained proposals concerning the primary system in America deal not with its possible abandonment but with possible adaptations. Among these, the major proposals relate to whether or not the primary should be "open" or "closed," whether or not they should be preceded by a preprimary designation of official candidates, and whether or not national party leaders should intervene in local primary contests.

Open versus Closed Primaries. The American Political Science Association report contains a useful summation of the debate concerning open versus closed primaries:

> In an open primary the voter is not required to register his party affiliation ahead of time or to disclose it when he applies for a primary ballot. He receives the ballots of all parties, and in the secrecy of the polling booth makes his decision. Party affiliation is thus a "some time" thing which may be changed from primary to primary. In more than three-fourths of the states some variation of the closed primary is used, voters

[1] E. E. Schattschneider, "Party Government" (New York: Rinehart, 1942), p. 99.

[2] Committee on Political Parties, American Political Science Association, "Toward a More Responsible Two-party System," *American Political Science Review,* Vol. 44, No. 3, Part II, Supplement, September, 1950, p. 71.

being required either to register their affiliations beforehand or to declare their affiliation, subject to challenge, when they apply for ballots at the primary.

Supporters of the open primary argue that it preserves the full secrecy of the ballot, prevents intimidation, and avoids disfranchising the independent voter, who is unwilling to declare himself a member of one or another. In support of the closed primary it is urged that party members should be willing to "stand up and be counted," that it prevents raids in terms of participation by members of other parties, and that it is impossible to develop party responsibility if nominations may be controlled by those with no continuing allegiance to the party.[3]

The report favors the closed primary,[4] but two qualifications seem essential. First, the closed primary can be used in many states as a method of buttressing the power of a state organization which is strongly at odds with the national organization of the same party. Secondly, given favorable circumstances, a well-organized and well-financed group of party leaders can and have been known to operate effectively in an open primary or even under systems where party labels themselves are completely abandoned.

Preprimary Designations. One of the earliest proposals for improving the party system came from Charles Evans Hughes in 1910. Hughes proposed that party committees be given the duty of recommending candidates for nomination.

> If such a party committee did its duty well there would be no necessity for a double campaign. Its choice would be ratified on primary day without contest. . . . If it ignored the sentiment of the party voters, if it appeared that some ulterior or sinister purpose had been served, if the candidates, or any of them, which it selected were unworthy, then there should be opportunity for the party members, immediately and without difficulty, to express themselves in opposition and on primary day to have a chance to show whether or not the designation of the organization party was approved.[5]

In similar vein, the report of the Committee on Political Parties states that "the formal or informal proposal of candidates by preprimary meetings of responsible party committees or party councils is a healthy development." The statement itself indicates that there has been considerable action along the lines of the Hughes proposals.

Joseph P. Harris has proposed a fundamental revision of the present direct primary system, one which rests largely upon preprimary designations. The political parties under the Harris plan would be authorized to hold conferences or conventions before the primaries and recommend candidates to be voted on at the primary election. The names of the candidates so designated,

[3] *Ibid.*, p. 71.

[4] *Ibid.*, pp. 71–72.

[5] Charles Evans Hughes, "The Fate of the Direct Primary," *National Municipal Review*, Vol. 10, 1921, pp. 23–31.

together with any other candidates for whom petitions might be filed, would then appear on a single ballot. The candidates who received a majority of all votes cast for the office in the primary would be declared elected. If no one received a majority, the two highest candidates would compete at the regular election.[6] In many cases, therefore, the preprimary designating process would in effect become the primary, and the primary would be converted into the final election.

National Intervention in Local Primaries. The Committee on Political Parties also strongly endorsed "the principle that it is proper for a nationally representative party organ to discuss possible nominees for office which are of national rather than local concern."[7] In contrast, the guiding principle of the major national parties seems to be never to intervene in local primary contests or, if on rare occasions such action seems imperative, to do so surreptitiously. The results of President Roosevelt's ill-fated attempt to purge anti-New Deal Democrats in the 1938 congressional primaries are recalled whenever the matter is raised. Yet with the growing emphasis on national issues and national campaigning via television and radio, the principle favored by the Committee on Political Parties will probably gain ground.

Another proposal would have all congressional primaries held after the party conventions. When a local primary is held before a party's Presidential candidate is selected and its campaign platform promulgated, there is somewhat less chance that the platform decisions of the convention may be regarded as binding. With the nomination already in his pocket, a party candidate is free either to disavow his party's pledges or pay them only lip service. If all primaries were held after the political conventions, then the platforms could be used as principles to which candidates for the congressional nomination would be required to pledge themselves as a condition of national support.

The National Conventions

The national conventions of the major parties operate at the highest level of party life. Through them, four men are nominated from whom the next President and Vice-President of the United States will be selected, and the one occasion is provided on which the heterogeneous groups that make up each party can meet each other face to face.

Objections to Conventions as Such. The national conventions of the major parties have been on the receiving end of far more open attack than have the local primaries. Its hurly-burly atmosphere, its unwieldy size, and its unrep-

[6] Joseph P. Harris, "A New Primary System," *State Government*, Vol. 21, No. 7, July, 1948.

[7] "Toward a More Responsible Two-party System," p. 73.

resentative composition have led many critics to agree with Ostrogorski, whose final word, after describing the operations of the national party convention, was: "God takes care of drunkards, of little children, and of the United States." [8]

After emerging victoriously from the ordeal of a major national convention and the subsequent campaign, Woodrow Wilson included in his first annual address to Congress a recommendation for dropping the convention as an instrument for nominating a Presidential candidate:

> . . . I urge the prompt enactment of legislation which will provide for primary elections throughout the country at which the voters of the several parties may choose their nominees for the presidency without the intervention of nominating conventions. I venture the suggestion that this legislation should provide for the retention of party conventions, but only for the purpose of declaring and accepting the verdict of the primaries in formulating the platforms of the parties. . . .[9]

This proposal has received little serious attention. The most that has happened as a result of the efforts of those who agreed with Wilson has been the development in a number of states of preferential primaries, through which convention delegates are given a mandate of sorts whom they should support when they arrive at the convention. The major use of these preferential primaries has been to serve as a battleground for preliminary skirmishes between contenders for the nomination at the convention itself.

Many observers have leaped to the defense of the national convention. Pendleton Herring maintains that the national convention "is admirably suited to testing the talents of our politicians. It demands organizational skill and manipulative genius—both of which qualities are exceedingly useful in democratic government." And again: "The party convention is one institutional expression of human beings competing by their wits and emotions for some of the prizes available under popular government." [10] Conventions are also a unifying force in national politics. They bring people together from all parts of the country and attract national attention to the problems and personalities in the coming Presidential election.

Here the reform situation is much like that of the local primaries. Despite all the criticism, both open and latent, no one seriously proposes any more to abolish the national convention. Those proposals that merit consideration are therefore aimed at the improvement of the institution.

More Frequent Meetings. The first proposal, made by the Committee on

[8] Moisei Yakovlevich Ostrogorski, "Democracy and the Organization of Political Parties" (New York: Macmillan, 1902), Vol. II, p. 279.

[9] First Annual Address to Congress, Dec. 2, 1913.

[10] Pendleton Herring, "The Politics of Democracy" (New York: Rinehart, 1940), pp. 238–239.

Political Parties, is that the national conventions "should meet at least biennially instead of only quadrennially as at present, with easy provisions for special meetings." [11]

There is considerable weight behind this recommendation. One of the most important factors making for futility in party platforms is the fact that it is impossible to project meaningful policies—even though they are, at best, compromises—over a period as long as four years. No matter how much effort and skill are channeled into the writing of a party platform, the march of events will inevitably render its major provisions irrelevant in one or two years. National conventions in the mid-term election years would not only serve to bring party platforms up to date but would also lend more national significance to the mid-term congressional elections. In 1950, a mid-term election year, both the Democratic and Republican national parties held various regional conferences which served as instruments for underscoring the views of both parties on current issues of national policy. To many observers, these conferences appeared to be important steppingstones toward a subsequent system of full-fledged biennial conventions.

In attacking the conventions as both unwieldy and unrepresentative, the committee also proposes an entirely new structure. "Much better results could be obtained," the report suggests, "with a convention of not more than 500–600 members, composed mostly of delegates elected directly by the party voters on a more representative basis (300–350 members), a substantial number of ex-officio members (the national committee, state and party chairmen, congressional leaders—probably about 150 altogether), and a selected number of prominent party leaders outside the party organizations (probably 25)." [12]

From the viewpoint of political dynamics the most important part of this package is the proposal that delegates be elected on a more representative basis. The other changes in composition represent no significant shift in political power. A representative apportionment of delegates among the states, however, based more upon the number of party voters in each state and less on the apportionment of Presidential electors, would have the effect of providing greater power at the Democratic Party Convention for the urban centers and lesser power at the Republican National Convention for delegates from the Southern states.

The National Agencies

The problem of developing a strong national organization to guide national election campaigns and to provide leadership between national conventions

[11] "Toward a More Responsible Two-party System," p. 38.
[12] *Ibid.*, p. 38.

has also received considerable attention. Four proposals along this line deserve discussion.

Party Councils. It has been proposed that each major party establish a Party Council to serve as the major organ of party leadership between national conventions. This proposal was first made many decades ago by Charles E. Merriam, who suggested a Party Council of about 600 members,[13] an agency which would be larger than the abbreviated national conventions that have been proposed by others. The Committee on Political Parties trimmed down Merriam's proposals and offered instead a Party Council of 50 members. This Party Council would be made up of representatives of five main groups: "the national committee (probably 5, chosen by the committee); the congressional party organizations (5 from each House, chosen by the respective organizations); the state committees (10, chosen on a regional basis by the regional groups, if any, otherwise by the national convention); the party's governors (5, chosen by them); and other recognized party groups, such as Young Republican and Young Democrats' groups as well as the party following at large (20, with the majority chosen by the national convention and the remainder by the particular groups)."[14] The President and some cabinet officers designated by him would serve as ex-officio members of the Party Council of the Administration party. In the case of the anti-Administration party the ex-officio positions would go to the Presidential candidate or, as the case may be, the defeated Presidential candidate and his running mate.

The merit of proposals of this type is that they underscore the desirability of developing working relationships between party leaders operating in separate and disconnected areas. The national committees of the major parties cannot by themselves perform this function, inasmuch as they are both organized strictly on the basis of representing state organizations. The weakness of these proposals is that they underestimate the possibility of accomplishing the same objective through making better use of the national committee and its national-headquarters organizations. From time to time various officers of both national committees have, in fact, attempted to develop closer working relations with House and Senate party members, the party's state organizations, and various national leaders of the party. A more effective effort along these lines could achieve the same objectives as are sought by the proposals for a formalized Party Council.

A major obstacle to effectiveness, however, is the understandable opposition that most Presidents have evidenced toward the clustering of other, and potentially rival, party leaders into a potent organization. There is little doubt that an organization of this type might trim a President's wings. Nor is this

[13] Charles E. Merriam with Harold F. Gosnell, "The American Party System" (New York: Macmillan, 1949), 4th ed., pp. 356–360.

[14] "Toward a More Responsible Two-party System," p. 43.

merely a personal question of the President versus Party. A stronger national-party organization might well become the vehicle of a somewhat different aggregation of group interests and purposes than of the President himself.

In the case of the anti-Administration party there is an obstacle of an entirely different sort. The "titular leader," as the defeated Presidential candidate is euphemistically called, is rarely recognized as a *de facto* leader. There are so many rivals for nomination at the next Presidential Convention that the centrifugal forces within the party are extremely strong. Under those circumstances the chances of pulling the party together into a tighter national party are exceedingly slim. It has occasionally been proposed that the national-leadership vacuum in the anti-Administration party be remedied by giving a place of high honor and dignity—say, a nonvoting seat in the United States Senate—to the defeated Presidential candidate. Yet it is hard to see how a device of this sort would go very far toward making up for the power and prestige lost by a candidate's defeat or toward dampening the aspirations of Senators, governors, and other ambitious party leaders.

The National Committees. It has also been proposed that "the members of the national committee reflect the actual strength of the party within the areas they represent." [15] This could be done by having each member of a national committee cast a vote equal to the total party vote in areas he or she represents. This would reduce the voting power of those members of the national committee from the states with smaller populations and with lesser support among the voters. This proposal, however, seems to be based upon the presumption that the national committees decide on important matters by casting ballots. This is done only in rare instances when representatives of dissident state organizations are refused seats on the national committee. For the most part the national committees do not deal with policy decisions. If the national committees should become more active, naturally the problem of representation and voting methods would become more acute. However, it is doubtful whether any formalized change in the basis of representation would ever be feasible. Probably the best method of activating the national committees and of introducing a more representative quality into their work would be to use them as instruments for bringing together party leaders from Congress, the executive branch, and other spots in the party structure.

The National Headquarters Staff. A third proposal is that each of the major parties maintain rounded staffs on a permanent basis. The Committee on Political Parties pointed out:

> Staff development at party headquarters provides the essential mechanism to enable each party to concern itself appropriately with its continuing responsibilities. The availability of professionally trained staffs in particular makes it more readily possible for the party leadership to grasp issues clearly, to see trends and problems in

[15] *Ibid.*, p. 39.

perspective, and to consider the far-flung interests of the party as a whole. . . . What is needed is a much stronger full-time research organization adequately financed and working on a year-in, year-out basis.[16]

Expenditures of National Committees. It has been proposed that the legal ceiling of 3 million dollars upon the annual expenditures of the national committees should be repealed. "Repeal of these restrictions," comments the committee, "would make it possible for a national body to assume more responsibility in the field of party finance." [17] If this proposal should eventually be adopted, it would be interesting to note the extent to which funds, as a result, flow in greater volume toward the national committees and in lesser volume to independent-party and nonparty committees. In either case there is little likelihood that the source of the funds and the interests of those who put up the money will in any way be modified.

Proposals for Changes inside Congress

In Congress the parties operate year in and year out within a major center of national attention. Here their weaknesses, particularly those relating to the legislative process, are most apparent. As a result, the bulk of attention on party reform has tended to center on such matters as the structure of congressional party leadership and the role of the parties in the struggle for committee power and congressional time.

Congressional Party Leadership

This rather complex subject can best be discussed if reference is first made to (1) the party leaders, (2) the party-leadership committees, and (3) caucuses and conferences.

The Party Leaders. In what was probably the only complacent portion of its entire report, the Committee on Political Parties gave its hearty endorsement to the informal meetings between the President and the Big Four, that is, the Speaker of the House, the Majority Leader of the House, the Vice-President, and the Majority Leader of the Senate. The committee argued that the Big-Four meetings "have provided an essential tie between Congress and the executive branch" and that "it would be an error to attempt to supplant the relationship between the Big Four and the President by some new body to carry on the same function." [18]

The committee also endorsed the occasional doubling of the Big Four into an eight-man group including the leadership of the anti-Administration party

[16] *Ibid.*, pp. 50, 81.
[17] *Ibid.*, p. 75.
[18] *Ibid.*, p. 58.

and recommended that this should be done more frequently on bipartisan issues.

Moreover, the committee took the position that both the Speaker of the House and the Majority and Minority Leaders should be regarded as spokesmen for one or the other party as a whole. It specifically endorsed Presidential interest in the selection of these leaders. This is in sharp contrast to the attitude of Vice-President Garner on Roosevelt's intervention in the effort to obtain the election of Senator Alben Barkley as Senate Democratic Leader in 1937: "It is an encroachment on the prerogatives of members of the legislative branch no President of the United States ought to engage in." [19]

The Party-leadership Committees. "Each house should establish a Majority Policy Committee," advised Heller, "composed of the chairman of each major standing committee and let the chairman be the majority leader, and a minority policy committee composed of ranking minority members." [20] The obvious theory here is that since committee chairmen and ranking minority members occupy positions of greater strategic strength, the best way to obtain strong party-policy committees is to establish them from among these gentlemen. One might just as validly maintain that the way to get weak party-policy committees is to place in them members of Congress who are in the best position to go their own way and fight established party policies. The Joint Committee on the Organization of Congress seemed to follow the second line of reasoning.[21]

The Committee on Political Parties dealt with this problem by recognizing the existing proliferation of party leadership in committees and then calling for the consolidation of existing party-leadership committees into four committees with specific powers both with respect to the committee structure and to legislative schedules. A related recommendation suggested that "the four party leadership committees meet jointly at the beginning of every session as a Joint Committee on the President's Program. Such a committee could consider the entire program embodied in the President's three principal annual messages and furnish guidance to the general line of action on the part of the various legislative committees." [22]

Caucuses and Conferences. "Whether they be called caucuses or conferences," suggested the Committee on Political Parties, "more frequent meetings of the party membership in each House should be held. Otherwise, there can be no real discussion of party positions and no real participation in or check upon the decisions of the party leadership. Without such discussion

[19] Bascom N. Timmons, "John N. Garner's Story," *Collier's,* Feb. 28, 1948.

[20] Robert Heller, "Strengthening the Congress" (Washington, D.C.: National Planning Association, January, 1945), pp. 13–14.

[21] Joint Committee on the Organization of Congress, H. Rept. 1011, 79th Cong., 2d Sess., Mar. 4, 1946.

[22] "Toward a More Responsible Two-party System," p. 60.

and participation, efforts to make party operations more responsible will be futile."[23] There is no doubt that strong party leadership needs caucuses or conferences as a means of mobilizing the support of their members. Where leadership is weak, however, or where there is a fundamental split among party membership, these meetings of party members may accomplish little except to fan the flames of dissension.

The question has often been debated furiously whether or not a decision arrived at at these meetings of party members should be regarded as binding upon the party membership when the matter later comes up on the floor of either house. On the one hand, it has been pointed out that through the instrumentality of a binding caucus decision a bare majority of a majority-party caucus may comprise only 51 per cent of a party having only 51 per cent in the entire house and yet may dictate the decision of that house.[24] It has also been charged that binding caucus decisions would transfer the deliberative processes of Congress from the more leisurely and less secret committee and floor sessions to the cloistered haste of the caucus room. On the other hand, it is claimed that unless party members subordinate their views to those of the majority of the party membership, effective party leadership in Congress will continue to be impossible.

The tendency of party leaders in both houses and in both parties is to dodge this issue, calling few caucuses and only occasionally attempting to develop binding decisions. They have resolved the problem at various times by regarding a caucus decision as binding only when there is a two-thirds vote in favor of a particular proposition. The Democratic House Caucus rules allow members to evade a decision when they regard it as unconstitutional or when it conflicts with clear instructions from their constituents or clear promises made by them during their election campaigns.

Parties and the Struggle for Committee Power

The formal structure of party-leadership committees is far less important than the extent to which the party leadership can affect the structure of committee power. Some of the most important proposals concerning party leadership in Congress, therefore, relate to the role of the parties in determining the party line-up on committees, assigning members to committees, and selecting committee chairmen.

Party Line-up on Committees. Woodrow Wilson believed that it was a mistake to have both parties represented on legislative committees. He felt that the majority party should take full responsibility for committee work and

[23] *Ibid.*, p. 60.

[24] See the attack on the closed caucus in Glenn Haines, "Your Congress" (Washington, D.C.: National Capitol Press, 1915), pp. 75–86.

that members of the minority party should be excluded. At the other extreme, it has occasionally been proposed that the two parties be given equal representation on the committees. In the case of an occasional subcommittee, joint committee, or congressional commission, this practice has been adopted.

As a practical matter, however, the problem boils down to a series of decisions by majority-party leaders regarding the additional margin of seats they will assign to their party members on this or that committee. Certain mathematical limits are set by the size of each committee and by the fact that, with the exception of only a few minor committees, each Senator may serve on only two committees and each Representative on only one. A party with a slender majority is thus unable to achieve a substantial committee majority in all committees and must therefore carefully select the points at which to concentrate its strength. In the interests of party responsibility, therefore, it would seem desirable to weaken the limitations on committee service as a means of strengthening party representation within the committees.

A large margin of majority members on a committee, however, does not necessarily provide a means of party control. In some cases party leaders can rely upon sympathetic viewpoints in the ranks of the other party and dominate a committee with a one-member margin only. In other cases, a large nominal margin will be completely negated by the existence of vigorous dissidents within the party ranks.

Assignments to Committees. Of all the proposals to give party leaders more definite responsibility with respect to committee assignments, the first to originate in Congress and win considerable congressional support was the proposal which George Norris and his insurgent colleagues fashioned back in 1910 when they were planning their revolt against Speaker Cannon. The Republican rebels attached to the resolution that stripped Speaker Cannon of many of his powers a provision converting the House Rules Committee into a joint-party-leadership body with the power and the duty of appointing the members of all the legislative committees of the House. The Democrats opposed this provision, however, and in order to obtain their support, which was essential to the success of the anti-Cannon campaign, Norris was forced to remove the constructive part of his resolution and limit it to a negative restraint on the powers of the Speaker.[25]

Norris's old idea is revived in the recommendations of the Committee on Political Parties. In keeping with its recommendation on the consolidation of the various party-leadership committees, it urged that the function of preparing slates of committee assignments be handled by the party-policy committees themselves rather than by any special committee or committees.[26]

[25] "Fighting Liberal, The Autobiography of George Norris" (New York: Macmillan, 1946), pp. 114–119.

[26] "Toward a More Responsible Two-party System," pp. 62–63.

Although the committee indicated that slates of committee assignments should be presented to party caucuses or conferences for approval or modification, it did not deal directly with the fact that the rules call for election of committee members by the entire membership of each house. Thus, a small minority within a party's ranks may hold on to positions of considerable committee power by the tacit threat of joining with the other party in taking control of the committee structure. A truly logical system of party responsibility would, therefore, dispense with the requirement that committee assignments be voted upon in each house and would leave the matter entirely up to each party caucus or conference.

Selection of Chairmen. The practice of selecting committee chairmen on the basis of seniority has been a consistent target for criticism. Yet it is generally conceded that it is easier to criticize the seniority system than to devise a workable substitute. The Joint Committee on the Organization of Congress came to the conclusion that on this question, as with the powers of the House Rules Committee, it would be impossible to iron out the conflicting views among the committee members.

Writing a year later, George Galloway dealt with the matter as follows:

> . . . the best method of selection in the final analysis would be the appointment of committee chairmen by the majority leaders in each house . . . They should also be empowered by the party caucus to remove chairmen who refuse to cooperate in the execution of the party's legislative program. In this way, the line of party responsibility and accountability for legislative action would be clearly drawn. . . .[27]

The Committee on Political Parties took a similar position. In so doing, it conceded that "advancement within a committee on the basis of seniority makes sense, other things being equal" and opposed the idea that seniority as such should be abolished.

It also recognized that as long as party dissidents succeed in getting regularly reelected to Congress, it will be extremely difficult to amass enough power to dislodge them from important committee posts.[28]

Parties and the Struggle for Congressional Time

Another index of the power of congressional party leaders is their ability to affect the scheduling of floor operations. For those who seek a strengthening of party leadership, therefore, proposals to give the party leaders a greater role in the struggle for congressional time are almost as important as proposals to give them greater power over the congressional committee structure.

The House Rules Committee. Along with the seniority system and the Sen-

27 George Galloway, "Congress at the Crossroads" (New York: Crowell, 1946), p. 194.
28 "Toward a More Responsible Two-party System," pp. 61–62.

ate filibuster, the House Rules Committee ranks as a major target for those who criticize congressional operations. Critics of the Rules Committee have often made the unwarranted assumption that traffic direction in Congress can somehow or other be separated from policy decisions. "It seems to me," testified Representative Herter of Massachusetts, "the Rules Committee job is more that of a traffic director than one to pass on the merits of the bills that have been heard very completely by the individual committees." [29]

Legislative traffic in Congress cannot be compared to that of automobiles on a highway, where the right of way is generally given without examination of a vehicle's destination or cargo. The applicable simile is that of a railroad system. An examination of the merits of bills reported from committees is as much a part of the decision to recommend consideration on the floor as such an examination is a part of decisions by legislative committees.

One proposal is to cut down the powers of the Rules Committee. This could be done by regarding as "privileged" any bill which has a unanimous committee endorsement, or by requiring that all committee-reported measures be given some sort of rule by the Rules Committee. This objective could also be attained by organized revolts against, and amendments of, the rules proposed by the Rules Committee.

A second approach, advocated by the Committee on Political Parties, is to substitute open party control for control by the Rules Committee or by individual chairmen. The committee pointed out that there are many ways to do this. At one extreme, the Rules Committee could be abolished and its functions be taken over by two party-leadership committees in the House of Representatives acting jointly. Or else the majority leaders might be allowed the choice of either using the Rules Committee as its instrument or bypassing it.

A short-lived change in rules during the life of the Eighty-first Congress allowed the committee chairmen to bypass the Rules Committee under certain circumstances. But this reform, in taking power away from the Rules Committee, transferred more power to committee chairmen rather than to the party leaders.

Legislative Scheduling. In the House, there are scheduling problems outside the sphere of the Rules Committee. In the Senate, as contrasted with the House, the problem is one of looseness in legislative scheduling. The Committee on Political Parties has dealt with this question by stressing the inseparability of policy and steering functions and advocating a comprehensive scheduling operation by the party-leadership committees: "Scheduling should include not only what measures are to be taken from the calendar for floor action but also the general scheduling of major hearings. Schedules should be openly explained on the floor in advance. They should apply to all issues, not just party

[29] Hearings before the Joint Committee on the Organization of Congress, 79th Cong., 1st Sess., p. 104.

issues." [30] A specific proposal along these lines was offered some years ago by former Senator Myers of Pennsylvania.[31]

Party leaders have usually been aloof to proposals of this type. The task of holding things together is already so difficult, particularly in the Senate, that the thought of a more ambitious effort is a little disconcerting. Some of them have probably felt that their ability to control the floor schedule depended upon surprise action and that a more openly handled scheduling operation would weaken them. There has probably also been a feeling that the end-of-the-season log jam which results from inadequate scheduling during the course of a session places them in an unusually strategic position to decide what shall and what shall not be considered.

Discharging Committees. The strongest invective of the incumbent leaders of a majority party is always reserved for proposals to liberalize the House discharge rule. The majority leaders of the House usually argue that a discharge rule allowing less than a majority to bring a bill out of a committee would break down party discipline.

One of the greatest defenders of the discharge rule has advocated that, instead of requiring an affirmative vote of the majority of the House membership, "no more than an ordinary majority of those voting should be required." While this proposal appears to be "antiparty," Hasbrouck justifies it on the very ground that it would tend to strengthen the two-party system. Hasbrouck also suggests that if existing parties cannot adapt themselves to new conditions, the new rule "would provide a parliamentary outlet for the forces of change." [32]

A liberalized discharge process could be used effectively as a means of getting action on a party measure that has been bottled up by a bipartisan coalition. It can also become a protection against an overconcentration of party power. "If we generally develop a more responsible party structure in the House of Representatives, then we would not only have conditions under which you could afford to have a better discharge system, but we would need a method of making the party leadership more accountable to the members." [33]

30 "Toward a More Responsible Two-party System," p. 64.

31 S. Con. Res. 62, 80th Cong., 2d Sess.

32 Paul Hasbrouck, "Party Government in the House of Representatives" (New York: Macmillan, 1927), pp. 212, 216–217.

33 Bertram M. Gross, "Organization and Operation of Congress," Hearings before the Senate Committee on Expenditures in the Executive Departments, 82d Cong., 1st Sess., p. 283.

Chapter 6

THE AGENCIES OF GOVERNMENT

ANOTHER of the many fictions concerning politics is the idea that government agencies are above the daily conflict among competing groups and interests. If private organizations and political parties, having special ends in view, stir up conflicts, government is said to appear on the scene to serve the national or public interest and to make peace. This idea has considerable psychological value in winning acceptance of government decisions and is of obvious utility to the officials of government agencies themselves. Yet to realize how fictitious this is, one should go back to James Madison's famous Federalist Paper, No. 10. "What are the different classes of legislators," he asked ruefully, fresh from his experience in the Virginia House of Delegates, "but advocates and parties to the causes which they determine?" [1] He might well have asked the same rhetorical question about the other officers of government. During his lifetime he saw the Federal courts packed with advocates of Federalist doctrines and as Chief Executive himself became an advocate of causes which he helped to determine.

In the present era of "Big Government," it has become increasingly evident that each part of the vast and complex structure of government has a dual role as a contestant in the struggle among competing groups. On the one hand, it reflects or represents various nongovernment groups and interests which provide its basic support. On the other, it develops specialized interests of its own, for government is the one group in the world furthest from being a single homogeneous mass; it is rather a conglomeration of assorted groups divided by an endless series of inner conflicts. If the function of many of these groups is to serve as mediator, there is almost always one or more rival groups eager and willing to impose a rival brand of mediation.

THE MEMBERS OF CONGRESS

The stock Congressman, for many cartoonists, wears a broad-brimmed hat, a potbelly in front, a shaggy mane of hair behind, and delights in demagoguery.

[1] "The Federalist" (New York: Modern Library Series, Random House, 1937), p. 56.

He is elected through the machinations of a corrupt political boss. He acts in accordance with instructions from people who pull the wires.

Although it would be a comforting thought to brand this character as pure myth, a few days in the congressional galleries and committee hearings will always uncover a number of Congressmen who seem to be modeled after the cartoon character. Yet these are far from being typical. In fact, there is no such animal as a typical or average member of the Congress. Congress is made up of people—96 Senators and 435 Representatives—people whose characteristics and practices are infinitely varied. This is one of the reasons why Congress—to drop the distinctive "the" which is invariably used by members of Congress—has always been and always will be a favorite target for jokes, jibes, and lampoons.

Background

Although these people are not a cross section of American life, they are closely associated with important social groupings. Most of the lawyers, businessmen, bankers, and farmers in Congress—and these are the great majority [2] —maintain their occupational pursuits. If some withdraw from an active role, others, particularly lawyers and insurance men, expand their activities as a result of the contacts made through their official positions. Many members of Congress serve as officials of trade associations, farm groups, and organizations set up to obtain some specific kind of legislative measure. Many more obtain substantial remuneration from speeches and lecture tours arranged by friendly outside groups. The basic bonds, of course, are the political relationships between the individual member and his constituency. This means close ties not only with a party machine but also with the more important private organizations in the state or district. Are members so close to local interests that they have little direct concern with the great national and international issues? "Sometimes we wish to vote for measures of national good," confessed Representative Charles L. Gifford of Massachusetts in a speech acquainting new members with the problems faced by the average Representative, "but somehow there are people back home pulling the strings, are there not? . . . Sometimes we have that appalling decision to make: shall I vote for my country as a whole

[2] A statistical justification of this observation is found in the table entitled "Occupational Distribution of the Membership of the 79th Congress, 1st Session," in George Galloway, "Congress at the Crossroads" (New York: Crowell, 1946), p. 349. In the 79th Congress, the table indicates, lawyers alone accounted for 55 per cent of the House and 65 per cent of the Senate. The affinity thus suggested between the legal profession and the function of legislation is based to a large degree upon the fact that lawyers often have (1) flexible working schedules into which political activity can be readily (and often profitably) inserted, (2) business connections which can be helpful in raising campaign funds and experience in representing the interests of others, (3) experience that is as serviceable to constituents as it is to clients.

or must I vote to protect my own particular district? Which should I represent? Your conscience must be your guide. But you can almost always subdue your conscience, you can always educate your conscience." [3]

It should be remembered, however, that most local organizations are interested in issues which have a broad geographical significance. Some of these are regional issues, as in the cases of textile manufacturers who want higher tariffs and the tobacco growers who seek more ample foreign markets. The bulk of the more powerful local groups is associated with national organizations whose viewpoint is anything but geographically restricted. Thus, a member of Congress cannot sink political roots in his locality without concerning himself with many national and international issues. A Southern Senator may obtain strong financial support from Northern industrial interests. A Northern Representative may have to win the support of national labor bodies before obtaining sufficient backing from organized labor at home.

Burdens

The tasks expected of Congressmen are exceptionally onerous. During the sessions of the Eighty-first Congress, for example, there were 921 public and 1,103 private bills that became law, 455 recorded votes on the floor of the Senate, and 275 recorded votes on the floor of the House. In addition, every member had hundreds of decisions to face in unrecorded votes, committee sessions, correspondence, and other individual legislative activities. In no other walk of life and in no other branch of government, with the single exception of the President's office, are men called upon to make so many decisions so quickly. And every decision, it must be remembered, is not merely an intellectual exercise; it is the Congressman's answer to the private, party, and governmental groups who are competing with one another to pressure and persuade him to act in accordance with their wishes. But legislative activities are not the only part of a Congressman's duties. The members of Congress not only make laws but also participate in the country's greatest public forum. They investigate public conduct and survey the administration of specific laws. Senators confirm hundreds of appointments in the executive and judicial branches. Members of both houses are vitally interested in the character and distribution of other Presidential appointments. In addition, constituents expect all sorts of help in obtaining jobs, settling cases before administrative agencies, and obtaining Federal funds for various local projects. In 1940, Representative Luther Patrick of Alabama made a speech on the floor of the House in which he described the burden of placating constituents:

> A congressman has become an expanded messenger boy, an employment agency, getter-out of the Navy, Army, Marines, ward heeler, wound healer, trouble shooter,

[3] *Congressional Record,* Jan. 27, 1947, p. 668.

law explainer, bill finder, issue translator, resolution interpreter, controversy oil pourer, gladhand extender, business promoter, convention goer, civic ills skirmisher, veterans' affairs adjuster, ex-serviceman's champion, watchdog for the underdog, sympathizer with the upper dog, namer and kisser of babies, recoverer of lost baggage, soberer of delegates, adjuster for traffic violators—voters straying into Washington and into toils of the law—binder up of broken hearts, financial wet nurse, good samaritan, contributor to good causes—there are so many good causes—cornerstone layer, public building and bridge dedicator, ship christener—to be sure he does get in a little flag waving—and a little constitutional hoisting and spread-eagle work, but it is getting harder every day to find time to properly study legislation—the very business we are primarily here to discharge, and that must be done above all things.[4]

Another task that absorbs the time of most members of Congress is running for office. The exceptions, of course, are those members from one-party districts who are so firmly entrenched that they have no real opposition in the primaries. By the time a member of the House takes his seat at the beginning of any Congress, the date of the primaries for the next election in his home district is only about fifteen months away. Members of the Senate have more breathing time, but any Senator who is lulled into a false sense of job security by reason of his six-year tenure is courting disaster. A Senator's political fences extend across a whole state and need constant tending.

Finally, much time is taken up by conflicts among congressional competitors for a place in the sun: between Senators who want to be nominated as Presidential candidates; between Representatives from the same state who want to be Senators; between Senators from the same state who want to achieve preeminence at home; and between members of both houses from all states who are competing to perform public service, to obtain power, prestige, and publicity, or to enhance their personal finances.

The burdensome character of the congressional job is made still more difficult by the survival of an old tradition that, except in time of war, Congress should meet for only a portion of the year and then adjourn. After four or five months of every session, there develops a deep-seated and persistent yearning for adjournment. Their motives are to secure relief from the strain; to get close to the grass roots; to carry on investigations or political campaigns; or to prepare for the legislative battles of the next session. Although a few energetic individuals in Congress always complain publicly that Congress shirks its duty by going home and leaving its business unfinished (which it always does), most members are impatient with any congressional action that might delay adjournment. In fact, once adjournment is in sight, the legislators start to fold their tents and quietly steal away. It is sometimes difficult to get a quorum for the act of adjournment.

[4] *Congressional Record,* 76th Cong., 3d Sess., p. 3028.

Behavior

Congressmen react to their burdens in different ways. Some take every decision seriously; the result is ceaseless overwork and nervous strain. Some react like the doctor so familiar with human anatomy that nothing upsets his equanimity. A blasé shell is their protection. They can take part in the most heated debates without real inward concern over the outcome. Many choose special fields and give only perfunctory interest to the rest. Some become creative participants through the introduction of innumerable bills, while others have no interest whatsoever in introducing measures or, if they do, in trying to get them enacted. Some glory in the excitement of floor debate and examination of witnesses at public hearings, while others labor only behind the scenes. A growing number resort to expert assistance for advice on technical matters, although the more old-fashioned members still shun staff assistance as a confession of ignorance. Some develop faculties of comprehension and analysis unequaled elsewhere in public life, while others operate on an intellectual level akin to that of the Crustacea. Some become inveterate straddlers; others specialize in meeting certain issues squarely.

Most, of necessity, acquire an intensive interest in learning the other man's viewpoint and develop thereby high proficiency in bargaining, yielding, and working out compromises. For self-protection practically every member learns how to evade decisions, to blur issues, and to crawl back after being pushed out on a limb. At times, all members act as the direct agents of powerful groups without bothering to exercise personal discretion, a line of action which has the merit—not to be scorned in a hectic world—of ease and simplicity. On other occasions, they rely on their own discretion.[5] At times they yield to pressure or propaganda and accept the views of others—a line of action which is facilitated by the sheer impossibility of having personal views on all the issues that arise in Congress. On other occasions they stand by personal convictions that have been firmly bred into them by their cultural background and lifetime associations. The extent to which personal discretion and conviction enter

[5] A long-standing controversy centers around the question of whether a legislator should be an instructed agent of his constituents, bound by an "imperative mandate," or a representative who, in the words Edmund Burke used in his famous speech to the Electors of Bristol, will sacrifice his "unbiased opinion, his mature judgment, his enlightened conscience" to no set of men living. The first alternative is often advocated by groups who feel their interests are being neglected, the latter by those who resent specific outside influences. In the early days of the French Estates and English Parliament, the monarchs often demanded that the members be uninstructed so that they might be free to vote for the king's policy, while the rising opposition groups usually favored binding mandates from their constituencies. Actually, the issue is not a real one, for every agent must use discretion and every representative must be flexible in opinions and judgments. The dispute over the abstract question of how a legislator should behave usually resolves itself into a contest between groups with opposing substantive interests.

into the life of the individual member varies with the character of the issue, the political and legislative situation at any given time, and the personality of the individual member.

There is a Senate at the northern end of the Capitol; a House at the southern end.

> As bodies they are strangers to each other. Save for conference committees, they might as well sit at the opposite extremes of the continent, or at different times of the year. The leaders confer once in a while, no doubt, but for the rank and file there is neither acquaintance nor interest. Rarely does a Senator deign to enter the House. Rarely does a Representative go to the other end of the Capitol from motives other than those of curiosity, unless he has occasion to consult a Senator from his own State in some personal or political matter.[6]

One of the few institutional forces that join the two houses together is congressional rivalry with the executive branch, especially the President. But this is counterbalanced by an undercurrent of institutional hostility between the House and the Senate. Members of the House are jealous of the powers exclusively reserved to the Senate: confirmation of Presidential nominations and the ratification of treaties. They are also jealous of Senators' greater influence over patronage, greater access to channels of publicity, and habitual domination of joint committees. Senators, in turn, frequently resent House prerogatives on the initiation of revenue and appropriations measures. Members of each house are often conspicuously patronizing toward the other house —an attitude which itself promotes conflict. "The Senate," Speaker Thomas B. Reed is alleged to have said, "is a nice, quiet sort of a place where good Representatives go when they die." Countless wisecrack variations on this theme are coined every year.

There are a number of interesting organizational differences between the two houses. In the House, with its larger membership, the very need to get action by a large group of men has called into being a tighter degree of control than in the Senate. Its rules and traditions tend to promote expeditious action at the expense of the personal prerogatives of individual members. In the Senate the emphasis is more toward a deliberative atmosphere and personal privilege. This attitude stems not only from the tradition that Senators are "ambassadors of the sovereign states" but from the fact that the Senators themselves, facing reelection only once every six years, have more time at their disposal.

When the Constitution was drawn up, it was thought that the House would be closer to the people and therefore the more liberal body, while the Senate would be the more conservative influence. The story is told that Washington described the difference between the two houses by saying, "We pour legislation into the senatorial saucer to cool it." Since the constitutional amend-

[6] Robert Luce, "Legislative Procedure" (Boston: Houghton Mifflin, 1922), p. 141.

ment providing for the choice of Senators by popular vote instead of by the state legislatures, this concept has completely broken down. There have been many periods in which the Senate has been the liberal body and the House the saucer to cool the senatorial tea.

Organized labor has had less influence, and conservative business and farm groups more influence, in the House. While every Senator represents a combination of both rural and urban areas, many Representatives represent only rural areas, areas in which there are no organized labor groups of any consequence and in which the dominant farm groups frequently work in close cooperation with business groups. The districting of seats has been controlled by the state legislatures, which usually allocate more congressional seats to rural areas than is warranted by the size of the rural population. In Ohio, for example, one rural congressional district contains only 166,932 people, while one district of the city of Cleveland contains 908,403 people. This discrepancy is not accidental; it results from the fact that the state legislatures themselves are organized on the basis of overrepresentation for rural areas and are used by conservative farm and business groups to achieve a similar structure in the House of Representatives.[7]

It is misleading to talk about Congress as a whole. It is just as misleading to think of either house as acting under the direction of its formal leadership. The highest official of the Senate—despite his two high-sounding titles of "Vice-President of the United States" and "President of the Senate"—is little more than a figurehead. The first Vice-President, John Adams, spoke for all Vice-Presidents when he lamented that "My country has in its wisdom contrived for me the most insignificant office that ever the invention of man contrived, or his imagination conceived." The President pro tem of the Senate, who serves when the Vice-President is absent or has moved into the White House, is somewhat more of a senatorial leader because he is chosen by members of the Senate themselves rather than superimposed upon them by a national election.

The real direction of the Senate, in so far as there is direction, is found in the positions of party leadership and in the chairmen and ranking members of committees. The ceaseless tug of war within each party, however, often makes it difficult, if not impossible, to determine exactly who is really the Majority Leader. Party leadership is divided between the Majority Leader, the chairman of the majority steering committee, the chairman of the majority policy committee, and the chairman of the majority caucus or conference. During the Eightieth Congress Senator Robert A. Taft, who served as chairman of both the policy and steering committees of the Republican party, was the acknowledged leader on domestic policy, while Senator Arthur Van-

[7] On this, see Arthur N. Holcombe, "The Middle Classes in American Politics" (Cambridge, Mass.: Harvard University Press, 1940), p. 100.

denberg, President pro tem of the Senate, was the acknowledged leader on foreign policy. Senator Wallace White, although elected as Majority Leader, had the name but not the power.

In the House of Representatives the top official is the Speaker, who is elected by the majority party at the beginning of each session. While the Speaker is always a far more significant figure in congressional life than the Vice-President, he is no longer the czar he was before 1911, the year in which a coalition of Democratic and Republican progressives forced a revision of the rules to clip the wings of Speaker "Uncle Joe" Cannon. The Speaker shares his leadership not only with the Majority Leader and Whip, the majority caucus and conference, and whatever steering or policy committees may be set up, but also with the powerful House Rules Committee and the members of the more important legislative committees.

The legislative committees of both houses, in turn, are founded upon a Balkanization of power that outshines any of the crazy-quilt patterns ever developed in the Balkans.[8] While each party contrives to get its due share of representation on every committee, there is no clear-cut centralization of the appointive power in the hands of the party leadership. Even when committee members hold their positions as a result of party decisions, there is no real sense of accountability. The Republican or Democratic members on a given committee are seldom regarded as responsible to the Republican and Democratic parties. This practice favors those members of Congress who manage to get reelected often and is thus of particular benefit to the dominant groups and interests in one-party areas of the country.

The real legislative leadership in Congress lies with those who have behind them the strongest array of organized backing by groups outside Congress, that is, private organizations, party groups, and executive agencies. If this backing is given to a majority party leader or a committee chairman, we then see examples of party or committee leadership. If it is achieved by a President—and on some issues Presidents are in a unique position to organize such backing—then the President becomes the leader of Congress. The secret of success is usually the organization of a coalition—in most cases a coalition between like-minded members of both the major parties, and, in all cases, a coalition of supporting private and governmental organizations. Sometimes such coalitions are of fleeting duration, coming into being for action on one or two bills. Sometimes they represent long-term understandings and arrangements and cover a broad variety of mutual interests. The shifting nature of these coalitions is further explained in part by the altering views taken by the leaders of organized groups and by the changing distribution of group strength among the senatorial and congressional districts.

The manner in which the individual members of Congress balance the in-

[8] The structure of committee power is discussed at length in Chap. 14.

terests of conflicting groups is of central importance. Only a small number of members have such strong backing from one set of interests that they can afford complete consistency. For most members the price of survival is for the member to try to do something for every organized interest in his constituency, even though his actions seem inconsistent when judged on the basis of abstract principles. Hence the wry witticism so often heard in the halls of Congress: "There comes a time in the life of every member when he must rise above conviction." Hence, too, the spectacle of outstanding liberals at times working hand in glove with the most conservative interests in the country and that of deep-dyed reactionaries occasionally behaving like liberals.

The Executive Officials

"The third house of Congress" is a metaphorical phrase variously applied to congressional conference committees, the Supreme Court, the Washington lobbyists, and the press. If its purpose is to indicate the extent of direct and continuous activity in the legislative struggle, it is particularly applicable to the executive branch of the Federal government. In the President and the people around him, in the high officials of the many agencies and bureaus, and in the vast staff of miscellaneous administrators and experts we find an aggregate of people who not only far outnumber the members of Congress and their employees but also spend an incalculably greater total of man-hours in the production of bills and statutes.

Presidents

A President, of course, is many men. "The 'President Roosevelt' of history, for example," as Bentley said with reference to Roosevelt I, "is a very large amount of official activity, involving many people. Any other 'President Roosevelt' of public life, physical, temperamental, moral, is but a limited characterization of that activity." [9] The same observation might be made concerning Roosevelt II or any of his successors, the only difference being that Presidents are now a still larger amount of activity involving a much larger number of people.

In pictorial and formal terms, these people can be described as a series of concentric circles. At the center are the members of the White House staff, which has grown considerably in recent years. Next come the top officials of the Bureau of the Budget, the Council of Economic Advisers, the National Security Resources Board, and the National Security Council.[10] Then come

[9] Arthur F. Bentley, "The Process of Government" (Bloomington, Ind.: Principia Press, 1949 reissue), p. 176.

[10] For an interesting discussion of the Executive Office of the President in which these agencies are located see F. Morstein Marx (ed.), "Federal Executive Reorganization Re-examined: A Symposium," *American Political Science Review*, Vol. 40, 1946, pp. 1124*ff*.

the heads of the Departments, who collectively comprise the Cabinet and meet with the President regularly, and the officials of the other agencies, boards, and commissions. On the outermost rim, in the informal sense, are the members of Congress, party officials, personal friends, and various leaders of industry, agriculture, labor, and other private organizations.

These circles, however, are constantly undulating and overlapping. "Our twentieth century President," writes a White House correspondent, "is like a fortress under constant siege."[11] Every now and then various besiegers succeed in penetrating into the inner circles. The President, for his part, usually sets up circles of his own, picking this selected group for one purpose and that group for another, playing one off against the other, never allowing anyone else to capture too much power. It is this shadowy set of groups that is often called the "Kitchen Cabinet," a colorful phrase indicating that the members of the formal Cabinet are frequently overshadowed in importance by people who are much closer to the President. The phrase should not lead one to regard the President's closest intimates as a compact and nonfluctuating body. Most of them serve only for fixed purposes, and all of them run the risk of being charged off as expendable at any moment and being summarily removed from the throne room and propelled into the outer darkness.

In function also the President is many men. He is the single living symbol of the national government; and everything connected with him, his family and the house he lives in and works in, rivals Hollywood as an object of public attention, discussion, and gossip. He is Commander in Chief of the Army and Navy. He conducts our foreign relations. He is the head of a major political party. He is supposed to administer laws and interpret them in the process. In addition to all this he is a legislative leader—in fact, the most important single legislative leader in the Government. Except in wartime, Presidents are now judged more by the quality of the legislation they propose or succeed in getting enacted than by their records as Executives.

In part, the President's legislative activities are based squarely on the provisions of the Constitution. Under the Constitution the President "shall give to the Congress Information of the State of the Union and recommend to their Consideration such Measures as he shall judge necessary and expedient." He may convene special sessions of either or both houses to consider his legislative proposals. He may wield a limited veto over measures adopted in Congress—a power which can be exercised not only in a negative and defensive fashion but also as an affirmative and aggressive weapon in the legislative struggle.

Upon this foundation has been erected an elaborate structure of Presidential recommendations for legislative action. The President now sends three general messages to Congress at the beginning of every year. They are (1) a

[11] Merriman Smith, "A President Is Many Men" (New York: Harper, 1948), p. 9.

State of the Union Message outlining the general nature of his program for Federal action, including legislation; (2) an Economic Report which includes legislative proposals supposedly geared to the maintenance of maximum employment, production, and purchasing power; and (3) a Budget Message which contains his proposals for appropriation acts, both in general terms and in specific legislative language. He sends to Congress every year scores of special messages dealing with individual legislative matters, many on his own initiative, others in conformance with the requirements of individual statutes. He makes many legislative proposals through both correspondence and conferences with official congressional leaders, chairmen of congressional committees, and many individual members. Veto messages themselves often become vehicles for alternative proposals.

In great part, also, a President's legislative activities are based on functions and powers unmentioned in the Constitution (although most became quite familiar to those Founding Fathers who later became Presidents). Among these is a President's ability to influence congressional action through the manipulation of patronage, the allocation of Federal funds and projects, and the handling of constituents' cases in which members of Congress are interested. Still more important is the power which he enjoys as leader of his party and chief election campaigner and by reason of occupying a strategic position for promoting broad coalitions of social groups and interests.

Every President is a complex combination of strength and weakness. Even those who seem to enjoy the greatest power and to be most suited temperamentally for its aggressive exercise have proved utterly unable to cope with many situations. For one thing, a President is like an Oriental potentate who has a harem of a thousand wives. While he is theoretically free to give attention to all of them, there are only so many hours a day and so many days a year. Although the President and the people around him usually do their best to cover the water front, the time always comes quickly when they must make the choice between exercising their powers of office on important matters or risking a nervous breakdown.[12] Then again there is an institutional rivalry between Presidents and members of Congress, many of whom can best develop public stature by demonstrating their ability to "clip the President's wings." "There can be no doubt," writes Harold Laski, "that in its own eyes, Congress establishes its prestige when it either refuses to let the President have his own way, or compels him to compromise with it." [13] This institutional analysis can

[12] "Men of ordinary physique and discretion cannot be Presidents and live if the strain be not somehow relieved. We shall be obliged always to be picking our chief magistrates from among wise and prudent athletes,—a small class." Woodrow Wilson, "Constitutional Government in the United States" (New York: Columbia University Press, 1911 ed.), pp. 79–80.

[13] Harold J. Laski, "The American Presidency: An Interpretation" (New York: Harper, 1940), p. 116.

easily be carried too far. In fact, it has been carried too far by many writers on American government, particularly Laski, who, despite his background as a Marxian, seems to regard the institutional factor as the whole story and to neglect the significance of social groups able to use the members of one government agency against the members of another.

The battle line-up and the disposition of contesting groups always have a material effect on a President's strength. Bentley writes:

> If group interests tend in a certain direction and are checked in their course through Congress, they will find their way through the presidency. If the group interests take permanently a form which makes Congress an inadequate agency for them, then the presidency will consolidate its power. If, on the other hand, the shifting of interests or the change in Congress makes the latter agency adequate, then the presidency's power will readjust itself accordingly. . . . If the executive yields to a group organization gathering force from without, before the legislature yields, it will gain in power as compared to the legislature, until the legislature yields in its turn.[14]

Binkley puts it this way: "It can be set down as a fundamental principle that whether Congress or the executive is dominant in the government depends upon which of the two, in a given period, is the more adequate medium of governmental control for the dominant interests of the nation."[15]

The manner in which various groups express themselves through the Presidency or the Congress is closely connected with the electoral system. The under-representation of the urban population in Congress tends to make Congress a more adequate medium for farm groups and for the business groups which have succeeded in obtaining the support of farm organizations against their fellow urbanites, the organized workers.

> The clash of President and Congress is intensified by the striking differences between the ways in which pressures play upon the Congress on the one hand and upon the President on the other. For example, important elements such as labor, racial and certain other groups are peculiarly weak in urging their desires upon Congress. Consequently they quite naturally and properly seek to exert a leverage on the government through their voting strength as balances of power in presidential elections. Indeed, here is a counterbalance against the immense advantage the interests of property and production hold in Congress due to the under-representation of urban voters in Congress and to the fact that the practice of seniority in determining control of the House of Representatives reduces considerably the power of the urban voters. Such is the predominance of rural constituencies that the majority of Congressmen can ignore the desires of the urban masses with impunity while the President does so only at his peril.[16]

[14] Bentley, *op. cit.*, pp. 351, 358–359.

[15] Wilfred E. Binkley, "The President and Congress," *Journal of Politics*, Vol. 11, February, 1949, p. 69.

[16] *Ibid.*, p. 76.

Other Executive Officials

Entirely apart from whatever services they may render as part of the Presidential team, the officials of the various executive agencies are inextricably involved in the legislative struggle. In the daily process of administering legislation, they run into countless problems that can be solved only through amendments or new legislation. They constitute a vast reservoir of information and know-how needed in the legislative process. Success in obtaining the funds upon which their agencies exist depends upon their ability to justify favorable appropriation legislation every year. And so the officials of the various agencies can be found spending large portions of their time in preparing recommendations for legislation, writing detailed reports in support of legislation, presenting testimony before congressional committees, and actively organizing support for their legislative efforts.

A bogeyman has been created of a vast Executive bureaucracy with such power and influence that the President can use it to dominate Congress and obtain whatever legislation he wants. One reason that this is not so is that no President has ever been able to avoid or overcome serious conflicts between the heads of the various agencies. From the days of the historic battles between Secretary of the Treasury Alexander Hamilton and Secretary of State Thomas Jefferson we have seen rival agency heads pitted against one another. Many of these have been able to go their own ways irrespective of Presidential direction, thumbing their noses at the President, yet surviving. The Army Corps of Engineers is the prize example of successful insubordination.

> Almost without exception, the Corps has disregarded the orders of its Presidents. It has set itself above its commander-in-chief. It calls itself "the consulting engineer to and contractor for" the Congress, and it considers itself an arm of the legislative branch. Franklin D. Roosevelt, generally regarded as a strong President, lost every round he fought with the Corps. Although the Champ swung angrily and often, he never laid a glove on the Army Engineers. . . . The Corps has the whole-hearted support of the so-called "Rivers and Harbors Bloc," led largely by men from the lower Mississippi area. . . . Staunchly behind the "Rivers and Harbors Bloc" is the National Rivers and Harbors Congress—an organization dedicated to the principle that no stream is too small for a Federal handout, no levee tall enough, no channel deep enough, no harbor improved enough. It is a comprehensive lobby group, an involuted sort of affair which includes among its membership representatives and senators—the lobbied—as well as the contractors, and state and local officials—the lobby.[17]

Many Cabinet members and heads of agencies regard themselves as more responsible to certain members of Congress than to the President. When Rep-

[17] Robert de Roos and Arthur A. Maass, "The Lobby That Can't Be Licked," *Harper's Magazine,* August, 1949.

resentative Carl Vinson was chairman of the House Naval Affairs Committee he spoke fondly—and not wholly inaccurately—of "my Navy" and referred to Cabinet members as "the best (or worst) Secretary of the Navy I ever had." [18] Within the Departments, also, one finds firmly established heads of bureaus and divisions who within their own walls are lords of the manor and have learned through many years of experience how to evade or act counter to instructions from their superiors. "Matters of routine organization are of primary importance and if you ever want to run the United States of America," writes a newspaperman who had a splendid opportunity to observe Washington agencies during World War II, "never mind about the top jobs, take over the spots at the operating level and you'll really have your hands on the controls. . . . In any government organization, the operating man is likely to find himself in possession of an effective veto power over the policy man." [19]

Each agency and each part of an agency tends to develop a special interest of its own, with its people ever alert to see how they can best strengthen their personal positions. This tendency is immeasurably strengthened by the fact that many agencies themselves are established only in response to the pressure of private organizations and their representatives in Congress and can continue in existence only by working with and serving such groups. Alliances of this type are fortified by requirements for senatorial confirmation of Presidential appointments, by limitations on the President's power to remove the members of so-called "independent" boards and commissions, and by statutory provisions placing the appointive power for various second-level positions with the President rather than with the agency heads. As a result of these diverse and often conflicting allegiances, there are more checks and balances within the executive branch itself than the Founding Fathers ever dreamed of when they wrote the Constitution.

The Judges

Although the legislative, judicial, and administrative processes of government are all interrelated parts of one complex struggle between competing groups and interests, there is a tendency among lawyers and law-school teachers to regard the courts as the end of the road and legislative activity as merely a preliminary action that provides materials used by the judges.

Yet from the viewpoint of the legislative process, judicial decisions are often merely incidents in the production of statutes. If it is true that one can never be positive concerning the meaning of a statute until a controversial question

[18] Jim G. Lucas, "Vinson the Invincible," *Washington Daily News*, Oct. 17, 1949.

[19] Bruce Catton, "The War Lords of Washington" (New York: Harcourt, Brace, 1948), pp. 232–233.

of interpretation has been settled by the courts, it is also true that those who disagree with a court interpretation can, and often do, immediately proceed to obtain a reversal of court action by an amendment of the original statute or by a new law. A judicial decision can serve the purpose of terminating efforts to obtain action through legislation and diverting efforts to other means. This occurs in matters of interpretation as well as when the Federal courts overthrow a law on the ground that it is unconstitutional. Decisions of executive officials in the administration of a law have a direct bearing upon the legislative process, but it is probably true that a larger proportion of judicial decisions have a more direct impact on the legislative process.

But does this mean that the judges are actually contestants in the legislative process? The theory that government officials can be neutral and objective mediators between contesting forces is nowhere more full-blown than with respect to the Federal judiciary. It is buttressed by three specialized fictions which often seem to have as much force in modern times as that once enjoyed by the concept of the divine right of kings. The first, which has been developed by the judges themselves with the valiant aid of the courtroom lawyers, is the idea that judges are able to grasp and interpret the intent of the legislators. The second fiction is that, with the Constitution as its finely drawn yardstick, the judges declare a law unconstitutional only when it goes beyond the legislative powers given to the Federal government under the Constitution. The third is that when a man is appointed to a life-term position, he is thereby immunized against the virus of personal ambition and insulated against the influence of group allegiances and pressures.

Yet in the misleading judicial jargon, "the intent of Congress" is little more than a method of rationalizing the views of the judges themselves. Every statute leaves broad room for interpretation. The issues litigated before the courts are usually ones which never arose during the course of the legislative process, were scarcely considered by the legislators, or upon which the Congress as a whole would certainly never have had an "intent." In fact, many issues which are determined "in accordance with the intent of Congress" were in the first instance deliberately left unsolved because any effort to resolve them in Congress would have made too many people unhappy.

The yardstick theory with respect to matters of constitutionality is still more hollow. Members of the Constitutional Convention had very little "intent" that was applicable to the problems of later decades. They were wise enough to write a document which could be flexibly interpreted. They even left it wide open as to whether or not the Supreme Court itself could declare a Federal statute unconstitutional. Although Alexander Hamilton's Federalist Paper, No. 78, explained the Constitution as giving the Supreme Court this power, the explanation itself was a matter of creative interpretation. Not a single word in the document deals directly with the matter. The Supreme

Court's power to overthrow a Federal statute is itself a prime example of extra-Constitutional action which is taken in the name of the Constitution.

As for lifetime tenure,[20] it is interesting to note that in most other contexts security against replacement is usually regarded as providing stronger entrenchment for a given social viewpoint. This is true with respect to those members of Congress who, coming from one-party areas, face no real opposition in the primaries. It is too seldom realized that similar realities lie behind the lifetime tenure of judges. A result of the constitutional provision that "Judges, both of the supreme and inferior Courts, shall hold their Offices during good Behavior" has undoubtedly been to maintain a group of people who could protect the interests of property against officers of the Government chosen through more popular methods and who are thereby more susceptible to the influence of the less propertied groups.

Many aspects of the judicial branch are inevitably partisan. It is impossible for a man to rise to the point of being considered for appointment to the bench without entering in a prominent fashion into partisan struggles, whether as a corporation lawyer, a member of Congress, an Attorney General, or a law-school professor. If appointed to a lower court, he may well play his cards so as to lead toward a subsequent seat on a higher court. If appointed to the Supreme Court, he can scarcely help realizing that the Supreme Court is often regarded as a reservoir of potential Presidential candidates. If he has no ambition for future political advancement, he cannot help but regard his position as an opportunity to translate into action the social convictions he has developed during the course of his lifetime. Few justices can avoid developing a vested interest in the judicial branch and becoming partisans in the competition of roles among judges, Congressmen, and executive officials.

There have always been and will always be sharp conflicts within the judicial branch: the circuit courts reversing the district courts, the supreme courts reversing the circuit courts, and the members of the Supreme Court perpetually squabbling among themselves. There have always been and will always be dramatic instances of a court taking one position at one time and then later on executing a dramatic about-face. This may be lamented by those who would like to find somewhere in our governmental system a firm and unchanging Rock of Gibraltar.[21] But it cannot be otherwise. What Robert Jack-

[20] The impeachment of judges is so rare that it is questionable whether reference to it in a broad discussion of the role of the judicial branch as a limitation on lifetime tenure merits more than a footnote.

[21] Jerome Frank suggests that one of the major reasons why people seek unrealizable certainty in the law is because "they have not yet relinquished the childish need for an authoritative father and unconsciously have tried to find in the law a substitute for those attributes of firmness, sureness, certainty and infallibility ascribed in childhood to the father." "Law and the Modern Mind" (New York: Tudor Publishing Co., 1935), p. 21.

son wrote about the Supreme Court before he became a member is applicable to the entire judicial branch:

> The ultimate function of the Supreme Court is nothing less than the arbitration between fundamental and ever-present rival forces or trends in our organized society. . . . Conflicts which have divided the Justices always mirror a conflict which pervades society. In fact, it may be said that the Supreme Court conference chamber is the forum where each fundamental cause has had its most determined and understanding championship. . . .[22]

The Local and Foreign Governments

When the Constitution was drafted it was contemplated that state governments would have indirect participation in the work of the Federal government through their role both in the ratification of constitutional amendments and in the designation of the members of the Senate. Participation of this type still continues. With the popular election of Senators, though, the influence of the state legislatures is concentrated in the House, the composition of which is materially affected by the manner in which the states set up their congressional districts.

Yet beyond these formal functions, the states have become exceedingly active in influencing the course of national legislative action. Within their given fields, organizations such as the American Association of State Highway Officials and the Conference of State and Territorial Health Officers have been able to determine the character of national legislation, even in the face of Presidential opposition. The Council of State Governments serves as an active vehicle for advancing the interests of the state governments as such.

The influence of state agencies, however, is complicated by the growth of urban governments and the steadily increasing power of organizations such as the United States Conference of Mayors. The state and local groups join arms in fighting to have Federal funds for local projects spent through local rather than Federal agencies, but they are in continuous conflict as to whether Federal aid for localities is to be channeled through state agencies or made available directly to the cities.

To an advancing degree, the actions of both "unfriendly" and "friendly" nations have a major impact upon American policy. When a major power takes an aggressive step that seems to threaten American interests, it obviously exercises a powerful influence on behalf of increased armament appropriations. In addition, the major powers, without exception, take direct steps of intervention in our legislative process. The Russians see to it that their supporters in America agitate vigorously against legislative action that opposes

[22] Robert Jackson, "The Struggle for Judicial Supremacy" (New York: Knopf, 1941), pp. 311–312.

Russian interests. The anti-Russian countries play an equally active role. The Washington embassies and legations of foreign governments are traditionally the organizing centers for these activities. Embassy and legation officials hire the services of American lawyers, research agencies, and lobbyists; organize support of nationality groups, American affiliates of international church bodies, American corporations with international business interests, and American affiliates of foreign corporations; and generally develop sources of legislative influence in the same manner as any domestic group or local government.

Midway between foreign governments and the American government stands a large array of international agencies, such as the International Bank for Reconstruction and Development, the Food and Agriculture Organization, the International Labor Organization, and the United Nations. Their functions depend to a high degree on legislative ratification of Executive agreements and Senate ratification of treaties. Often their major financial sustenance is derived from American appropriations, relying to a large extent upon the legislative activities of the various agencies of the Federal government and the business, farm, and labor groups with a direct interest in their world-wide activities.

Chapter 7

GOVERNMENT AGENCIES: RELATIONSHIPS AND REFORMS

As ONE LEAVES the area of private organizations and political parties and considers proposals for changes in government agencies, he finds those that deal with the election of Congressmen and Presidents, the relations among the various branches of the Federal government, and the relations between the administrative and legislative processes.

THE ELECTORAL SYSTEM

The electoral system has an obvious bearing not only upon the choice of members of Congress and of Presidents but also upon their behavior. It affects the scope of their interests, the sources of their political support, and their attitude toward specific issues and conflicts. Changes in the electoral system, therefore, are often regarded as an important method of strengthening or impairing the position of various contestants in the legislative struggle. In a democracy, of course, the system for elections provides the ultimate sounding board for the attitudes of the community regarding the character of its political leadership and many of the basic orientations of its public policy. Here, too, the meaning of elections for the legislative struggle is profound. The discussion that follows will serve merely to make the reader aware of the range of this impact and of the areas of controversy regarding changes.

The Election of Members of Congress

Apportionment and Districting. The basis of representation in the Senate constitutes the most obvious violation of the democratic ideal that voters should have equal representation in an elected legislature. The justification for the unequal basis of representation in the Senate is that at the Constitutional Convention it was conceded to the smaller states as a matter of expediency, that it placed the senatorial representation of the smaller states in a privileged position that they would not willingly abdicate, that the present setup could scarcely be circumvented short of a veritable national emergency, and that the unequal basis of representation in the Senate has never produced and is never likely to produce such an emergency.

When one looks at the House of Representatives, one finds another series of representation problems with which it is easier to grapple. Every ten years in the light of the population shifts that have taken place between the states, Congress faces the very practical question of how to decide upon the number of seats assigned to each state. If the population of each state were an exact multiple of the average-sized House district, there would be no problem on the apportionment of seats among the states. The average-sized district would be divided into the population of a state, and the resulting figure would be the number of seats to which the state would be entitled. Population changes, however, never conform to meet mathematical patterns. The ratio of population to representatives will never divide exactly into the population of each state. There is always a fraction left over. Many complex mathematical formulas have been developed to allocate these fractions one way or another. Schmeckebier lists 16 different formulas, and many more probably could be devised.[1] The major contenders among the competing mathematical formulas are the methods of major fractions and of equal proportions. The latter method was written into the apportionment legislation of 1941.

However, disputes concerning the apportionment of House seats among the states sometimes tend to distract attention from the much more important problem of districting within each state. The tendency, as indicated in Chap. 6, is for redistricting within states to lag seriously behind the population shifts which enlarge the population of urban districts and decrease the population of rural districts. The political effect is to maintain political influence in rural districts far beyond that warranted by their population.

In 1950, as an outgrowth of the recommendation of its Committee on Political Parties, the American Political Science Association set up a special committee to study the problem.

The committee's basic proposals were as follows:

1. "That the standard requiring districts to be 'compact and contiguous,' found in the 1911 apportionment statute and omitted in the 1929 statute, should be included in a new law.

2. "That the statute should include a standard limiting to a certain percentage the deviation of any district within the State, upward or downward, from the average of all districts for the State; and that an effort should be made to keep the deviation of any district from the average of all districts for the State within a limit of 10%; but in any event such deviation should not be permitted to exceed 15%. [The practical effect of this recommendation would be to allow districts to vary over a range of about 100,000—that is from about 300 to 400 thousand.]

[1] Laurence F. Schmeckebier, "Congressional Apportionment" (Washington, D.C.: Brookings Institution, 1941), Chaps. 3–5, pp. 12–85.

3. "That the evasion of the above standards by electing Congressmen-at-large be prohibited." [2]

The committee then appraised various sanctions that might be used to force the states to live up to these standards. It then proposed a procedure designed to help bring the matter to a head in Congress:

First, the States should be required to do their own redistricting soon after Congress passes the Apportionment Act; this would give Congress ample time to consider whether this action by the States complies with the statutory standards of approximate equality.

Second, the President should transmit the results of State redistricting to Congress and to all the States, with information showing how any particular State has violated the statutory standards of approximate equality. Since the President's statement will appear in the press, unequal districting will be subjected to the powerful sanction of publicity.

Third, Congress may then take such action as it deems proper. Congress may order the State to do the job over again. Or Congress may redistrict the State itself.

The committee recognized that these sanctions applied more to districts of unequal size than to gerrymandered districts. Because it felt that precise standards on what is and is not gerrymandering are impossible, the committee recommended no specific action on the subject. The essence of the committee's proposals was adopted by President Truman in his regular decennial message dealing with apportionment.[3] Their adoption would tend to lead to a House of Representatives with a greater number of Congressmen from urban constituencies, a lesser number from rural constituencies, and a new power balance among the groups covered within the rural-urban rubrics.

Smaller or Larger Districts. In 1951, one proposal was to increase the size of the House from 435 to 509. This would have preserved the existing number of seats for all states with declining populations and would have rewarded faster-growing states with an additional 74 new seats. The compromise proposal would have enlarged the House to 450 seats, thereby reducing in part the individual losses that otherwise loomed over states with declining populations. In defense of these proposals, the argument is always made that smaller districts will allow individual members to maintain closer personal relationships with their constituents. It is also stated at times that greater membership will help the House of Representatives to handle its steadily growing burden.

Basically, however, proposals of this type constitute methods of avoiding sound apportionment and redistricting. They are effectively answered in the report of the Committee on the Reapportionment of Congress.[4]

[2] Committee on Reapportionment of Congress, "The Reapportionment of Congress," *American Political Science Review,* Vol. 14, No. 1, March, 1951, pp. 153–157.

[3] Message of Jan. 9, 1951.

[4] "The Reapportionment of Congress," p. 153.

In the course of a polemical debate with Friedriek Hayek over economic planning, Herman Finer proposed that the membership of the House of Representatives be increased to about 750.[5] According to William Y. Elliott, the forty-eight states should be brought together into a much smaller number of regional "commonwealths," each of which would be represented in a national House of Representatives on the basis of population. The broadening of the area in which a candidate might stand for office "would tend to defeat the purely local character of representatives." Furthermore, the recognition of "sectional areas as the primary bases of a new Federal system . . . would revive our groping federalism and stay the present march of centralization in Washington." [6]

Multimembered Districts. In some other countries, particularly in France, there has been continuous controversy on the merits of the single-member district versus the multimember district. Single-member districts, it is pointed out, give an unfair advantage to the majority party and greatly handicap the development of any third parties. For this very reason they are defended by the proponents of the two-party system.[7]

The use of multimembered districts (districts from which two or more of the legislative body are to be chosen at the same election) always raises the question of whether elections should be held on the basis of a general ticket or of proportional representation. Under the first alternative, the party with the highest number of votes on its side will send its complete slate to the legislature. Under the second alternative, all parties will send representatives to the legislature in proportion to their voting strength.

During the first fifty years of the American Republic these were live issues. Close to the middle of the nineteenth century, however, this problem was solved by requiring each state to establish congressional districts. This system has served well and it should be continued. The only departures that are made from this system occur on certain occasions when state legislatures dodge redistricting by providing for Congressmen at Large. As suggested by the Committee on Reapportionment of Congress in the report referred to above, this practice should be prohibited.

Terms of Office. The most far-reaching proposal for changes in the terms of office would synchronize Presidential elections and congressional elections. One advocate of complete realignment writes:

> The four-year term of office for all Congressmen, Representatives and Senators alike, would afford, as a rule, an opportunity for the Administration to pursue its

[5] Herman Finer, "Road to Reaction" (Boston: Little, Brown, 1945), p. 213.

[6] William Y. Elliott, "The Need for Constitutional Reform" (New York: McGraw-Hill, 1935), pp. 182–208.

[7] See E. E. Schattschneider, "Party Government" (New York: Rinehart, 1942), pp. 69–84 for a useful analysis of the "single-member-district-system-plus-plurality-elections."

projects and plans untrammeled by partisan prejudice, pettiness, and opposition, thereby making possible a constructive, more nearly unified policy; and at the same time would place the responsibility for the management of affairs where it belongs—squarely on the shoulders of the leaders in power.[8]

In so far as the shortening of senatorial terms is concerned, this approach has received little favorable attention in Congress. The case for extending the terms of members of the House of Representatives, however, is more popular. Members from contested districts have scarcely any breathing space between elections. Four-year terms would unquestionably give them more time to devote to the legislative process. The proposal is particularly attractive to those who see in the mid-term elections a barrier to effective Presidential and party leadership, but under present political circumstances the desire of House members for longer terms of office is scarcely strong enough to override the strong opposition in the House to any increase in Presidential power. Furthermore, scores of members of Congress have been elected on the same day that Presidents were and have found it unnecessary to stand together with the President during the election campaign.

The Election of Presidents

How the Votes Are Counted. Many arguments have been made for abolishing the electoral-college system of electing our Presidents, on the ground that the electors selected in each state are not only useless but also dangerous. In some elections, as has happened occasionally, electors might switch their votes. They might withhold them. They might involuntarily create national problems by dying before the day arrived to cast their votes. They might become storm centers of litigation over electoral qualifications.

A more important target of criticism—one that would remain even if electors as such were eliminated—is the bloc-voting or "winner-take-all" system of electoral votes. Under this system the total amount of electoral votes of every state goes to the candidate who has received the largest number of votes, and the candidate with less than a plurality gets no electoral votes whatsoever. This enhances the political power of "swing" groups in the most populous states, since large masses of electoral votes can be moved *in toto* into one column or the other. It provides little incentive for voting or for Presidential campaigning in the so-called "safe states," for here the vote for a minority candidate can rise from 10 to 49 per cent of the total without making one bit of difference in the electoral vote by which the Presidential contest is decided. Moreover, through this disenfranchisement of minority voters within each state,

[8] Pearl Olive Ponsford, "Evil Results of Mid-term Congressional Elections and a Suggested Remedy" (Los Angeles: University of Southern California Press, 1937), p. 70.

it becomes possible, on occasion, for a candidate with the greatest number of popular votes to lose the election.

Theoretically, no constitutional amendment is necessary in order to break down this bloc-voting system. The Founding Fathers wrote nothing in the Constitution suggesting that the electoral vote in any state be given in entirety to the candidate obtaining the plurality. Under the Constitution, the states decide how their electoral votes are allocated. During the first years of the Republic the votes were divided among the congressional districts in each state. The bloc-voting system developed in 1800 when a number of Federalist states adopted it as a method of reducing the voting power of Jefferson's supporters. The Jeffersonians countered by trying to amend the Constitution to prevent Federalist use of this device. Failing to obtain a two-thirds majority in Congress, they then adopted the bloc-voting system themselves in the Jeffersonian states in order to reduce the voting power of the Federalists. During the subsequent years, the bloc-voting system became frozen into the electoral system through legislation in every state.

The effort to change the voting method used in Presidential contests by use of a constitutional amendment has been the greatest lost cause in the history of all efforts to amend the Constitution. From 1800 to 1950 almost 400 resolutions to change the system were introduced in the Congress. The proposals are of three basic types: The first is to have a direct popular vote, the most democratic method of electing a President. The adoption of this type is generally regarded as beyond the realm of probability. The fact that it would involve substantial shifts in political power alone would make it unfeasible. The second type is to return to the district system. This would go a few steps in the direction of distributing the electoral vote more in accordance with the popular vote. In one-party states, however, where the minority party often fails to capture even one congressional seat, it is unlikely that the district system would effect any significant change. It would also extend into Presidential elections the influence of gerrymandering. The third type is to allocate the electoral vote in each state in accordance with the number of voters. Thus, in a state with ten electoral votes, a candidate who obtains 40 per cent of the votes cast would be credited with four electoral votes. This proposal has sometimes been confused with proportional representation but it is entirely different. Proportional representation applies only to elections in which two or more persons are elected on the basis of the voting strength behind each candidate. In this case there is still only one person to be elected and no minority representation is possible. It has also been charged that this proposal would give great additional power to minority parties. Yet, in exchange for a paper showing on the final talley sheets, the minority parties would in fact be nudged out of the balance-of-power positions in what are now pivotal states.

An interesting suggestion on how to steer electoral-college reform through the shifting shoals of opposition has been designed by Samuel Huntington who has suggested that the Lodge-Gossett reform be combined with a constitutional amendment requiring congressional districts of approximately equal population.[9]

A subordinate, though fascinating, question of electoral-college reform is whether or not a full majority of the total vote, rather than a mere plurality, should be required as a condition of election. Recent proposals for a proportional system of allocating the electoral vote within each state, therefore, have provided that no candidate could become President without winning a given percentage of all electoral votes—usually 40 per cent. A closely related problem is the present provision for having the election determined in the House of Representatives if no candidate obtains the required number of electoral votes. It is often proposed, therefore, that any election in the House of Representatives be made by the vote of the entire membership only. A still more attractive proposal is that the selection be made by the membership of both houses of Congress voting together as a unit.

Number of Terms. In 1950, with the ratification of the Twenty-second (anti-third-term) Amendment to the Constitution, the venerable two-term tradition, so decisively broken by Franklin D. Roosevelt, came back into its own.

What effect the anti-third-term amendment may have remains to be seen. It will probably make it more difficult for a second-term President to obtain legislative support in Congress. On the other hand, it may turn out that a President, whose nomination at the next convention is thus forestalled, may yet exercise a strategic influence over the selection of his party's Presidential candidate and thereby maintain considerable power during his second term. There is also the possibility that in some cases the new prohibition will encourage the growth of contenders for party leadership. When a President can be reelected repeatedly, there is always the danger that the functions of the party leadership will devolve upon his shoulders alone.

A hoary proposal which still seems to have a long life ahead of it is that Presidents be limited to one term of six years each. One of its latest proponents is Harold Laski.[10] Others have been Representatives Hobbs and Gossett, whose minority views attached to the House Judiciary Committee report on the anti-third-term amendment argued that a single term of six years "would eliminate, as far as it is possible to do so, political considerations from the execution of office." [11] This is much like eliminating water as a consideration in the life of a fish.

[9] Samuel Huntington, "Electoral Reform: Congress and President" (unpublished paper, Harvard University, February, 1951).

[10] Harold J. Laski, "The American Democracy" (New York: Viking, 1948), pp. 122–124.

[11] "Proposed Amendment to the Constitution of the United States Relating to Terms of Office of the President," 80th Cong., 1st Sess., H. Rept. 17, Feb. 5, 1947.

Succession and the Vice-Presidency. Since death itself plays a role in the selection of Presidents, many minds have pondered over the question of how to get Vice-Presidents who are best equipped to take over when tapped by the finger of fate.

There is little reason to change the present constitutional provisions regarding the Vice-President. An elected Vice-President is certainly better than one who is appointed. A designated successor is certainly better than a period of interregnum and possible chaos during which a new election would be held.

It is often argued that the party conventions should nominate Vice-Presidential candidates who are highly qualified to serve as President and who have more to offer than an appeal to various groups whose support is needed for the Presidential campaign. Yet the necessities of politics will inevitably continue to produce "balanced tickets" made up of Presidential and Vice-Presidential candidates with differing points of view on national issues.

It is also suggested that the Vice-President become the key link between the President and the Congress. Some Vice-Presidents have already served in this capacity and others will undoubtedly play a similar role. Yet, in many cases, political differences between the President and the Vice-President make such a relationship impossible.

A more formidable suggestion calls for legislation to designate the Vice-President "as the President's chief assistant in the over-all direction of the administrative branch." The Vice-President might even be given the task of planning the annual budget and transmitting it to Congress. Finally, the President would be expected to invite the Vice-President to sit regularly with the Cabinet and to transfer various administrative duties to him by Executive order. With these additions to Vice-Presidential prestige and responsibility, the national conventions would probably be induced to nominate more first-rate men to serve as Vice-Presidential candidates.[12]

What about the line of succession in the event of the death of both the President and Vice-President? Here a convincing argument can be made for remedial action. Under legislation passed in 1947, the Speaker of the House and subsequently the President pro tempore of the Senate are next in the line of succession. This is a very unsatisfactory arrangement. The Speaker of the House might be a member of an opposing party, as was in fact the case when the law was passed. The present law should be amended to restore the previous arrangement whereby various high-ranking Cabinet officers are designated as the next in line.[13]

[12] Clinton Rossiter, "The Reform of the Vice-Presidency," *Political Science Quarterly,* Vol. 43, No. 3, September, 1948, pp. 383–403.

[13] Joseph E. Kallenbach, in "The New Presidential Succession Act," *American Political Science Review,* Vol. 41, No. 5, October, 1947, pp. 931–941, points out the need for clarifying the question of how Presidential disability should be established and of what procedure should be followed in the event that Presidential or Vice-Presidential candidates die be-

The Voters

Behind the members of Congress and the President stand the men and women whose votes placed them in office or almost elected their opponents. Since large numbers of eligible voters customarily stay away from the polls, the case is often urged that larger turnouts are needed.

The Case for More Voters. In abstract terms of general principles, the case for more voters is a very appealing one. President Truman in December, 1950, wrote to the president of the American Political Science Association:

> The strength of democracy stems from popular participation in the government and popular support of our free institutions. Unfortunately, in the past ten years we have seen a marked decline in the percentage of eligible voters who go to the polls. This is a serious matter which challenges the interest of all citizens, regardless of party affiliation.[14]

Still on the level of abstract principle, the case is occasionally made against a large turnout at the polls. Francis G. Wilson has suggested that a high percentage of participation in voting would be a symptom of dangerous social struggles.

> In a society in which only fifty percent of the electorate participates, it is clear that politics does satisfy in a way the desires of the mass of individuals in the state. As the percentage of participation rises above, let us say, ninety percent, it is apparent that the tensions of political struggle are stretching to the breaking point the will toward the Constitution.[15]

In support of this thesis, it can be pointed out that mass participation in European elections has resulted from struggles that threatened—sometimes successfully—the very structure of democracy.

Calculations as to the implications of increases in voting have entered into all the historic conflicts over extension of suffrage. The removal of property-owning and taxpaying qualifications was the outcome of a long struggle for more political power on the part of Western settlers and lower-income groups. The drive for woman suffrage, finally consummated in the Nineteenth Amendment to the Constitution, was opposed not only by men who wanted to preserve their masculine prerogatives but also by liquor interests sensitive to feminine hostility to their business and by corporations fearful that women with votes would add to the strength of labor organizations. The still-continuing

---

tween Election Day and the formal casting of electoral ballots. These and related questions should probably become a specific subject for study by an expert committee or a special congressional commission.

[14] *American Political Science Review,* Vol. 45, March, 1951, p. 165.

[15] Francis G. Wilson, "The Inactive Electorate and Social Revolution," *Southwestern Social Science Quarterly,* Vol. 16, No. 4, 1936, pp. 73–84.

struggle over Negro suffrage has been characterized by opposition, particularly from the black belt counties of the Deep South, to the idea of more political power in the hands of Negro leaders. It has also been accompanied by less outspoken opposition to the idea of greater political activity by the lower-income elements generally, whether white or Negro. Practically all proposals for the extension of suffrage have been opposed by leaders of entrenched political organizations with anxieties about how an increased electorate might affect their power.

The available evidence seems to indicate that the greatest number of stay-at-homes on Election Day are to be found among lower-income groups. "In breaking the native-white group down into its economic constituents," reported Edward Litchfield in his classic study of voting in Detroit between 1930 and 1938, "it was learned that its laxness during non-presidential years was confined entirely to the lower and middle-income groups." As for Presidential elections, "The participation data revealed the existence of a direct relationship between income and the amount of participation. The higher the income the higher the percentage of participation. . . ." [16] It is therefore evident that the largest increment of additional votes is to be found among the lower-income groups generally and particularly among lower-income women and Negroes. Any party which successfully appeals to these elements of the population will thereby win a major advantage in election contests. On the other hand, any party which depends for the bulk of its support upon the lower-income groups will usually be seriously hurt by a low turnout at the polls.

Above all, it should be kept in mind that the size of the vote is not a causative factor. It is rather a reflection—in statistical and therefore in limited terms—of the concrete achievements of competing organizations, each one of which is presumably concentrating on getting out the vote for its candidates. To analyze the meaning of the turnout at a given election, therefore, one must look at its composition.

The composition of the vote in any election, in turn, is a result of the political struggle that has taken place before the election. To some extent, the character of this struggle is determined by social conditions. It is also determined by the character of the campaigning. Not only do allegiances shift but many American voters have little or no allegiances. Attractive candidates, skillful campaigning, and organizational unity can do wonders in winning conservative support for Democrats or liberal supporters for Republicans.

Methods for Widening Participation. Whether or not it seems doctrinally

[16] Edward Litchfield, "Voting Behavior in a Metropolitan Area" (Ann Arbor, Mich.: University of Michigan Press, 1941), p. 66; see also G. M. Connelly and H. H. Field, "The Non-voter—Who He Is, What He Thinks," *Public Opinion Quarterly*, Vol. 8, 1944, pp. 175–187; and Julian L. Woodward and Elmo Roper, "Political Activity of American Citizens," *American Political Science Review*, Vol. 44, No. 4, December, 1950, pp. 872–885.

sound to have more people vote at a particular time or in a particular situation in a democracy such as ours, the compulsions to widen participation in the community's decisions are ever present and will remain so as long as opportunity remains for new leaders to arise through the social structure and for the poor and the disenfranchised to obtain more than a modicum of education. Growth in participation comes in two ways: (a) by making more individuals and groups eligible to vote through the enactment of new suffrage laws or the enforcement of the old ones; (b) by facilitating participation by those already eligible.

Despite constitutional provision to the contrary, a whole array of formal and informal restrictions on the exercise of suffrage rights by Negroes has developed throughout the Southern states. To penalize these restrictions, it has been recommended that the electoral vote of each state be geared to the actual number of voters instead of basing it upon population. It has been estimated that this would initially cut Southern representation in the House of Representatives by at least 50 per cent. Another line of attack has been the drive to eliminate poll taxes. Thus far the number of poll-tax states has been reduced from eleven to six. Less progress, however, has been made in dealing with discriminatory registration practices.

New laws have been proposed for extending the suffrage to residents of the District of Columbia, to Indian citizens of New Mexico and Arizona, and to eighteen-year-olds (now in effect in Georgia). There have been efforts to relax naturalization laws allowing aliens, regardless of race, color, or national origin, to become citizens and acquire the right to vote. Resident requirements for voting tend automatically to disenfranchise many hundreds of thousands of persons at every election (one extreme estimate puts the figure at 11 million) because of the highly migratory character of the American population. McGovney has suggested that a national standard for the residence requirement be established.[17]

Many persons who are eligible to vote fail to do so because of inconvenience and other difficulties, many of which result from a positive disinterest among certain local groups to facilitate the voting function. Among the recommendations along these lines have been: permanent registration; improved voting hours; more accessible voting places; easier absentee voting, particularly for the increasing numbers of men and women serving in the armed forces; and the use of the short ballot to prevent "voter fatigue."

The participation problem has also been viewed as one in developing incentives for voting. More and better education is a fundamental step in this direction. Broadening the tax base is considered one way to make people aware of their stake in government. Compulsory voting is another device de-

[17] Dudley O. McGovney, "The American Suffrage Medley" (Chicago: University of Chicago Press, 1949), pp. 181–182.

signed to lead *all* the voters to polling booths, thereby compelling a larger number of them to think and choose. Short of compulsory voting, however, perhaps the greatest incentive to voting lies in the character and vigor of the party battle.

Relations among the Three Branches

It is a striking paradox of American life that the provisions of the United States Constitution outlining the tripartite structure of our national government are viewed with awe and reverence by almost everyone except students of government. The result has been a long series of proposals to eliminate the separation between Congress and the executive branch, provide for closer cooperation between them, or modify the legislative veto of the Supreme Court.

Congressional-Executive Merger

The Case against the Constitution. Misconceptions about the British parliamentary system have played a large role in American government and political science. The Founding Fathers thought that the British system at that time was based upon the "separation of powers" described by Montesquieu. They failed to realize that with the development of the Cabinet's power, there had come into being a fusion between executive and legislative agencies.

In 1867 Walter Bagehot weighed the American Constitution and found it wanting. "The English Constitution, in a word, is framed on the principle of choosing a single sovereign authority, and making it good; the American, upon the principle of having many sovereign authorities, and hoping that their multitude may atone for their inferiority." [18]

Woodrow Wilson expressed the same thought in still stronger language:

> The best rulers are always those to whom great power is intrusted in such a manner as to make them feel that they will surely be abundantly honored and recompensed for a just and patriotic use of it, and to make them know that nothing can shield them from full retribution for every abuse of it.
>
> It is, therefore, manifestly a radical defect in our Federal system that it parcels out power and confuses responsibility as it does.[19]

The major case made against the Constitution is that the President and the Congress are independent bodies, with the election and tenure of neither directly dependent upon the will or the action of the other. The result, it is maintained, is to prevent both democracy and effectiveness in the processes of gov-

[18] Walter Bagehot, "The English Constitution," in "World's Classics," No. 330 (New York: Oxford, 1949 ed.), p. 202.

[19] Woodrow Wilson, "Congressional Government" (Boston: Houghton Mifflin, 1925), pp. 284–285.

ernment. Since there is no one central organ of acknowledged leadership, it is impossible to place responsibility for what is or is not done. There is no logical channel through which majority sentiment can be organized. In the absence of majority control, it follows that there is no crystallization of an effective minority to present minority viewpoints and protect minority rights. Congressional activities, therefore, and particularly congressional debates, lack the essential drama to bring them forcibly to public attention and educate the people on political issues. Congress feels compelled to resist attempts at Presidential leadership and to win a place in the sun by public demonstrations of its ability to frustrate or humiliate executive officials.

Moreover, when deadlocks develop at any time other than immediately prior to a Presidential election, there is no method of resolution. With elections occurring at fixed dates rather than at the call of the legislative or executive bodies, it is impossible to take a fundamental legislative issue directly to the people. By the time elections roll around, the issues that have developed since the previous election and the records of men and parties alike tend to be forgotten by everyone except a few powerful pressure groups. Knowing that they need not be prepared at any moment to wage an election campaign and, if successful, assume control of the Government, the political parties have little incentive to concern themselves with basic policy issues. They, therefore, yield command of the legislative battlefield to the pressure groups. Under such conditions, there is no source of control to focus the legislative process on the many matters appropriate to it and to keep it from becoming involved in matters which should be handled rather through administrative or judicial processes. There is no leadership to schedule legislative operations, operate expeditiously, provide for the organization of relevant facts and opinions on proposed measures, or take responsibility for seeing that the laws produced are precisely and intelligibly drafted and consistent with one another.

To a lesser degree, a case has also been made against the separation between the two houses of Congress, between the Supreme Court and the rest of the Federal government, and between the Federal government and the states.

Proposals for British-type Systems. Woodrow Wilson had argued that "Congress must be organized in conformity with what is now the prevailing legislative practice of the world. English precedent and the world's fashion must be followed in the institution of Cabinet government in the United States." [20] The first complete proposal for the reconstruction of the American constitutional system was made by William MacDonald. He wrote:

> If the United States is to have a responsible government, it can only be done by such changes of the constitution as will give to Congress the control of policy. This

[20] Woodrow Wilson, "Committee or Cabinet Government?" *Overland Monthly,* Vol. 3, No. 1, January, 1884, p. 25.

can only be done, in the first place, by creating a ministry or administration—the particular term is not important—which shall represent the majority and which shall give way to another ministry or administration when the majority no longer supports it; and, in the second place, by stripping the President of the control of policy which he now has.[21]

A still more far-reaching reconstruction of the Government has been proposed by Henry Hazlitt. Hazlitt has argued that a popularly elected President would be a potential source of too much power and might impair the leadership of the Cabinet. The President, therefore, would be elected directly by Congress for a term of from five to ten years. The Cabinet would be responsible to the House alone. The Senate would have no direct legislative powers. It would have "the role merely of delaying, revising, forcing the House to reconsider, and telling the people unpalatable or unpopular truths. . . ." [22] There have also been a number of proposals for constitutional structures lying somewhere in between the English system and the American. William Y. Elliott has proposed that the President be given the power to dissolve Congress at least once during every four-year Presidential term. This, he argued, would provide the President with enough power to keep Congress in line and harmonize Executive-congressional operations.[23]

Thomas K. Finletter has made another set of interesting proposals. Using as a starting point Elliott's proposal for giving the President power to dissolve Congress, he argues that there should be no limitation on the number of times that a new election of Congress might be called by the President. He also proposes that in every case the dissolution work both ways, with the President, as well as the members of Congress, being required to face an election. It is also proposed that consultation between the two branches of government be institutionalized by the creation of a joint Executive-legislative Cabinet.[24]

C. Perry Patterson has developed an elaborate plan for placing Executive power in the hands of Congress without any change in the schedule of fixed elections or, for that matter, in the written Constitution itself. He points out that within the framework of the written Constitution there have been many great and revolutionary changes in the actual structure of the Government. The unwritten Constitution now makes the President tantamount to a dictator. New changes in the unwritten Constitution could provide us with responsible government in the hands of Congress. This involves the creation in Congress of "a

[21] William MacDonald, "A New Constitution for a New America" (New York: B. W. Huebsch, 1921), pp. 60*ff*.

[22] Henry Hazlitt, "A New Constitution Now" (New York: McGraw-Hill, 1942), pp. 176–177, 217.

[23] William Y. Elliott, "The Need for Constitutional Reform" (New York: McGraw-Hill, 1935).

[24] Thomas K. Finletter, "Can Representative Government Do the Job?" (New York: Reynal & Hitchcock, 1945).

body of political leaders who will be responsible to the party system and who will initiate legislative policy, and, thereby, serve as a check upon the President by means of the party system in Congress. They cannot be Presidential puppets subject to his dismissal at will. They must be responsible to the Congress through the party organization." This joint committee of both houses of Congress would rule the congressional roost as well as the executive departments. Bicameralism would be reduced to a fiction. The President would become little more than a ceremonial head of state.[25]

The Defects in This Approach. Whether these proposals are desirable or not can be questioned on a number of counts.

First, these proposals are based upon an unrealistic ideal of what government should be like. They are geared to the conception—to use Woodrow Wilson's words—that we should make self-government "a straightforward thing of simple method, single unstinted power, and clear responsibility. . . ." Yet this is a dubious standard for a complex, pluralistic society. One might just as well ask that all future wars be straightforward conflicts, decisively fought upon one front alone.

Second, these proposals are based upon an excessively generous—indeed, romantic—idea of the virtues of the British parliamentary system. The formal structure described by Bagehot and Wilson is delightfully logical. Yet it has not been able to prevent years of instability and confusion during those periods when no one party has been able to obtain a clear majority in the House of Commons. It has not been able to solve the problem of the tremendous gap between Cabinet Ministers, who are supposed to make policy, and the civil-service bureaucracy which has a quasi monopoly of knowledge and thereby often holds the reins of government. In fact, British commentators, similarly dissatisfied with the British system, have also looked admiringly across the seas and proposed measures borrowed from American examples.

Finally, proposals of this type, if adopted, would do little to achieve the objectives sought. If one thinks that they would make elections more meaningful, let him look at city and county governments where there is usually little separation between the legislative and the executive agencies. Nor is there any reason to believe that some form of parliamentary system in the United States could have any significant effect upon party alignments. In fact, James M. Burns maintains—and with considerable validity—that the parliamentary system in America might serve to break down the ties that hold the major parties together and promote the formation of a number of minor parties constantly negotiating alliances with each other for the formation of one Cabinet or the overthrow of another. He describes the power of dissolution, which has customarily been regarded as a method of enforcing the power

[25] C. Perry Patterson, "Presidential Government in the United States" (Chapel Hill, N.C.: University of North Carolina Press, 1947).

of the national government, as "a method applying party discipline, not a cause of that discipline." He also points out that to the extent that centralized government power is found in Britain it is the result not so much of the constitutional system as of the fact that Britain is a more homogeneous country with stronger traditions of class leadership and orientation toward the central government.[26]

Congressional-Executive Collaboration

"The letter of the Constitution wisely declared a separation," wrote Franklin D. Roosevelt in one of his earliest messages to Congress, "but the impulse of common purpose declares a union." [27] The search has led to proposals for various devices and joint organizations that would bring together executive officials and members of Congress, permit consultation and cooperation between the two branches of government, and allow Executive participation from the floor of Congress.

Joint Organizations. The most formidable proposal along these lines, first proposed by Corwin and subsequently advocated by Senator Robert La Follette, Jr., Finletter, and many others, is that the President should "construct his Cabinet from a joint legislative council to be created by the two Houses of Congress and to contain its leading members." [28] Under this proposal the President would become neither a prime minister who is supposed to resign when defeated in Congress nor a figurehead like the king in Great Britain or the president in other countries with parliamentary systems. According to Corwin, arrangements of this type would mean that we would no longer have to depend upon the accidents of crisis or personality to obtain genuine Presidential leadership.

[26] James M. Burns, "Congress on Trial" (New York: Harper, 1949), pp. 144–162. Cf. Ralph M. Goldman, "Party Chairman and Party Faction, 1789–1900" (doctoral dissertation, University of Chicago, 1951), pp. 672–673: "The absence of a meaningful minority leadership in the American system makes all comparison with the parliamentary model of doubtful value in theory or in practice. The privileged status of the Opposition Leader in a parliamentary system is quite as important to that kind of party system as is the Prime Minister. . . . The American system merely has its Residual [National Committee] Chairman. . . ."

To meet this need, Paul T. David has suggested that the defeated Presidential candidate automatically become minority leader, established in Washington with a $50,000 per annum allowance and nonvoting privileges in Congress, until replaced at any time by a minority party national convention or by action of the national committee under rules set out by the national convention. (*Washington Post,* Nov. 24, 1952, p. 8.)

[27] "Public Papers and Addresses of Franklin D. Roosevelt" (New York: Random House, 1938–1950).

[28] Edward S. Corwin, "President, Office and Powers" (New York: New York University Press, 1948), pp. 361–364.

A less pretentious proposal was presented by Leon H. Keyserling in his 1945 prize-winning essay on Post-war Employment Policy. Keyserling suggested the creation of an American Economics Committee composed of three Senators, three Representatives, and three members of the President's Cabinet, together with six representatives of industry, agriculture, and labor, which would "find an American Economic Goal, reflecting America's optimum productive capacity, national income and employment, and correlating these with an 'optimum standard of living within the reach of all American families.' "[29] This proposal was sidetracked by the subsequent framing of the Employment Act of 1946 and by the creation of the President's Council of Economic Advisers, an agency which Keyserling subsequently headed. The drafters of this statute believed that better cooperation could be obtained among the various representatives of the two branches of government if separate planning organizations were established in each and that a joint body could neither provide necessary staff services to the President nor effective economic leadership in Congress.

More specialized proposals have often been made for joint agencies in specific areas. William Y. Elliott has proposed an organization of Cabinet committees which would "bring in responsible leaders of Congress, and, in particular, the chairmen of important committees into the policy-formulating stages on all government policy."[30] These Cabinet committees would cover six crucial areas: national defense and foreign policy, fiscal policy, labor and social welfare, physical resources and development, commercial policy, and government organization.

This approach has been given particular attention by those concerned with foreign policy. Nathaniel Peffer, for example, has proposed the creation of a joint foreign policy council which would include the President, the Secretary of State, the Secretaries in charge of the Armed Forces, the Secretary of the Treasury, and the Chairmen and the two ranking minority members of the foreign affairs committees in the Senate and the House of Representatives.[31]

Rebuttal to Peffer has been provided by Harold Laski.

> Whether its status be that of the convention of the Constitution or of a change made by formal amendment, the subordination of the President implied would make his position intolerable. He could not, in any case, sit in a "cabinet of foreign affairs" where four of his Cabinet officers, all of whom owed their appointments to him, were able to argue against him, to intrigue against him, even to vote against his views; very

[29] L. H. Keyserling, "The American Economic Goal: A Practical Start toward Post-war Full Employment" (mimeographed).

[30] Hearing before the Joint Committee on the Organization of Congress, 79th Cong., 1st Sess., pp. 961–962.

[31] Nathaniel Peffer, "America's Place in the World" (New York: Viking, 1945), p. 216.

early in the evolution of this committee he would clearly require from his Cabinet Members, as a condition of their appointment, that they act solely under his direction.[32]

Yet Laski's skilled polemics should not lead one to think that joint commissions can serve no purpose whatsoever. There are many specific purposes which can be well served by joint bodies representing both branches of government. The Temporary National Economic Committee made economic history in the assembling of important information and in educating people on economic problems. The Hoover Commission on the Organization of the Executive Branch succeeded in paving the way for a number of other reorganization operations that could probably not otherwise have been effectuated. Both these joint bodies, it should be noted, were set up for specific purposes and for limited periods of time.

Consultation and Cooperation. A less formal approach toward the problem of congressional-executive cooperation can be found through the devices of consultation and cooperation. Here one deals with something that is harder to concretize. Consultation and cooperation can be taking place, even though "outsiders" may be complaining that they are not. On many occasions, when observers are taking it for granted that there is consultation and cooperation, there may be a complete vacuum with respect to both.

There are at least four formal methods of promoting consultation and cooperation among the branches of government. One is the formal inclusion of members of Congress in various official bodies or delegations constituted by executive officials. In the field of foreign affairs considerable use has been made of this technique. Another is regular meetings between executive officials and congressional committees. "Excellent relations between the State Department and the foreign affairs committees of both Houses resulted," Kefauver and Levin have observed, "when Secretary of State Cordell Hull took the latter groups into his confidence on the big issues of planning for postwar world organization." [33]

A third method is staff collaboration. "We propose," wrote Kefauver and Levin, "that quarters for liaison staffs for each Federal department and major agency be provided on Capitol Hill." [34]

A fourth method, to use Roland Young's words, is through "having the administrators give Congress more complete and more regular reports on their activities." [35]

[32] Laski, *op. cit.*, p. 524.

[33] Estes Kefauver and Jack Levin, "A Twentieth Century Congress" (New York: Duell, Sloan & Pearce, 1947), pp. 145–149.

[34] *Ibid.*, p. 149.

[35] Roland A. Young, "This Is Congress" (New York: Knopf, 1943), p. 255.

Although all four of the formal methods referred to above have their place in consultative and cooperative relationships among members of Congress and executive officials, there is probably even a much greater role for the use of informal relationships. Genuine consultation is an intimate affair. If it is formalized there is always a danger that it will be postponed until a very late stage in any proceedings and regarded mainly as the perfunctory performance of a ritual. Furthermore, genuine consultation upon major issues is possible only with friends. One can cooperate with opponents but by no means in the same fashion as with one's allies. Informal methods have the advantage of allowing greater selectivity in the making of contacts while more formal methods sometimes bring together people who are animated by little or no common purpose.

Certain prerequisites for successful consultation and cooperation deserve to be mentioned at this point. One of these is time. Many good intentions to consult with members of Congress have been obliterated by an avalanche of hard work and new problems. Another is the ability on the part of an executive official to make up his own mind rather than to be dominated by the last pressure that makes itself felt. It presupposes a capacity to reject advice and at the same time maintain the respect of those whose advice is rejected.

Executive Participation on the Floor of Congress. During the Civil War a Congressman from Ohio proposed the establishment of a system having the heads of executive departments occupy seats on the floor of the House and participate, without voting, in floor activities. This proposal, while never acted upon by either house, has always had a contingent of earnest adherents. It has been hailed by Young, Heller, and Kefauver as one of the best methods of developing constructive relations between the executive and legislative branches. It would, according to them, provide members of Congress with a firsthand opportunity to learn about executive operations. It would prevent department heads from neglecting congressional opinion and require them always to be prepared to defend their operations before Congress.

Laski has argued that the question-period system, while well-suited to a parliamentary form of government, as in England, would "not meet the real problems created by the presidential system." He believed it would give undue prominence and authority to the members of the Cabinet who, in America, are merely the President's appointees and have no recognized status in their own right.[36]

The proponents of this scheme have attempted to counter the objections that have been raised by suggesting the use of various safeguards.[37]

[36] Laski, "The American Presidency" (New York: Harper, 1940), p. 108.

[37] See Robert Heller, "Strengthening the Congress" (Washington, D.C.: National Planning Association, 1945), p. 27. A still more elaborate set of safeguards and conditions is contained in a special memorandum by Herman Finer, entitled "Questions to the Cabinet in the British House of Commons; Their Applicability to the United States Congress," a memorandum

In checking through the dispute on this proposal one cannot help wondering what all the shooting is about. Questions are continuously being submitted to the officials of the executive branch by members of Congress. Many of them are answered in letters that are printed in the *Congressional Record* or in statements that are otherwise made available to the public. A large number of questions are presented to executive officials at committee hearings at which a detailed line of interrogation can be developed, where the opportunities for orderly procedure are much greater than they would be in a larger body and where the spotlight of publicity is probably as strong as it is on comparable debates on the Senate or House floor. In fact, as indicated earlier in the quotation from L. S. Amery, there are many people in England who would like to see a greater use of specialized committees in the British House of Commons in order to enable the members of Parliament to learn more from administrators about what is going on in the various executive departments.

The Supreme Court's Veto

The atmosphere of discussion concerning the relations between Congress and the executive branch is relaxed in contrast to the atmosphere surrounding the recurrent conflicts over the Supreme Court legislative veto. Here the lines are drawn in conflicts over specific and hotly contested cases, and the air is full of vigorous constitutional polemics.

The case for change has invariably been directed against Supreme Court action in overthrowing Federal statutes. There has been little interest in depriving the Court of its power to overthrow state laws. Most critics of the Court would agree with Justice Holmes's observation on this point: "I do not think the United States would come to an end if we lost our power to declare an act of Congress void. I do think the Union would be imperiled if we could not make that declaration as to the laws of the several States." [38]

Nor has there been any demand for alteration in the Court's power to legislate through its interpretation of Federal statutes. The road is always open for changing these interpretations through new legislation. But when a Federal statute is declared unconstitutional, then there is little recourse left to those whom the Court has frustrated. They must either amend the Constitution or else must force the Court to reverse itself, and either of these courses is extremely difficult.

In abstract terms, the case against the Supreme Court's veto—to quote one of the most conservative critics of the Court—is based upon the "danger that the Supreme Court could become a third legislative body more powerful than

submitted on request to the Joint Committee on the Organization of Congress, Joint Committee Print, 79th Cong., 2d Sess., "Suggestions for Strengthening Congress," pp. 49–58.

[38] "Law and the Court," in "Speeches" (Boston: Little, Brown, 1918), p. 102.

Congress and beyond its reach, or beyond the reach of the people." [39] In the more concrete terms used by liberal critics, the case against the Court is based upon the well-documented charge that the majority of the Court has too often served as the protector of propertied interests and as the uncompromising opponent of desirable Federal intervention in the national economy. In the eyes of most observers, however, these charges need to be qualified by the fact that the Court has come to be regarded, to use Charles Beard's phrase, as "the last safeguard for civil liberties." [40]

The gentlest method of dealing with the problem has been to suggest self-restraint on the part of the judges. Justice Marshall himself was the first to make this point: "A just respect for the Legislature requires that the obligation of its laws should not be unnecessarily and wantonly assailed." The traditional method of dealing *roughly* with the Court has been through special efforts to pack it. The size of the Court has been changed by statute seven times. It has been reduced in size twice in order to prevent Presidents from filling vacancies. It has been increased in size five times in order to give Presidents more vacancies to fill. In his famous 1937 attack upon the Court, Franklin D. Roosevelt tried to increase the Court a sixth time but failed. He also failed in the effort to provide for compulsory retirement at the age of seventy though he succeeded in making voluntary retirement more attractive. An effort to pack the Court, no matter what the specific techniques may be and no matter how they may work themselves out in practice, is at least a method of producing self-restraint on the part of the judges. In fact, when allied with organized opposition to given Court decisions, it has probably been the most effective instrument for combating the Supreme Court's legislative veto.

There are two other lines of approach, however, which deserve mention. The first is to amend the Constitution for the purpose of directly affecting the Court's operations. During the 1937 Court fight, Senator O'Mahoney of Wyoming proposed an amendment to provide that the Court could declare a statute unconstitutional only by a vote of at least 6 to 3. Another proposal, offered during the same year, by Senator Wheeler of Montana and Senator Bone of Washington, was to provide that the Court's veto, like a Presidential veto, could be overridden by a two-thirds majority in Congress. Another has been directly to enlarge the scope of the interstate-commerce clause and to limit the scope of the due-process clauses of the Fifth and Fourteenth Amendments. Yet it must be recognized that each of these proposals was a diversionary approach offered for the major purpose of providing a constructive position for those who opposed the Roosevelt program of court reform. Those who proposed amendments of this type in 1937 during the Roosevelt battle subsequently abandoned them.

[39] Hazlitt, *op. cit.*, p. 220.

[40] Charles A. Beard, "The Republic" (New York: Viking, 1943), p. 237.

The second approach is to amend the amending process itself, thereby opening up the way for specific amendments to override specific Court vetoes. Henry Hazlitt has suggested the adoption of the amending process used in Australia. "Amendments to the Constitution of that country may be proposed by a vote of an absolute majority of both the Senate and the House of Representatives. The proposed amendments are then submitted to a direct vote of the people and adopted if they are approved by a majority of the voters in a majority of the States." [41] Other variations have been played upon this theme.

The major case for changing the amending process is that the Constitution is not flexible enough. Yet this argument has weight only if one focuses exclusively upon the written document and the formal process of amendment. In actuality, the Constitution has been undergoing a constant process of change since the time it was written. These changes have been brought about through court decisions, legislation, administrative action, and the development of informal usages and traditions. In fact, some of the most specific of all the Constitution's provisions, such as those dealing with the electoral college, the sending of concurrent resolutions to the President for signature or veto, the size of a quorum, and the recording of Yeas and Nays, have been construed in a manner that constitutes thoroughgoing revision. Formal amendment is merely one—and the least used—of all the methods for revising the Constitution. The availability of many other methods of accomplishing the same objective is a decisive factor in preventing development of any widespread interest or organized effort directed toward easing the amending process.

The Legislative versus the Administrative Process

A final series of general proposals deals with the relationship between administrative and legislative processes. According to many of them, the legislative process would be significantly improved if a better line of demarcation were drawn between the two processes and if the areas of choice permitted to participants and contestants were thereby narrowed. According to others, members of Congress would be able to do a better job with their legislative activities if they approached the administrative process in a different manner.

The Scope of the Administrative Process

Despite a considerable volume of debate as to how much discretion should be allowed within the administrative process, this is not a problem that can be handled by generalizations. This can be demonstrated by an examination of five oft-repeated "principles."

Details through the Administrative Process. The first can be briefly phrased

[41] Hazlitt, *op. cit.*, p. 261.

as follows: "Details should be handled through the administrative process rather than through legislation."

But how to determine what is and is not detail? One man's detail is apt to be another man's burning issue. Decisions on details are sometimes the key to making decisions on "large" policy, without which any purported policy decision might be vague and meaningless. Furthermore, there are many details which can best be handled through the legislative process and which, if not handled thus, will haunt the waking and sleeping days of administrative officials and seriously impair administrative operations.[42]

Broad Policy through the Legislative Process. The second general principle, which is the side of the coin opposite the one discussed above, can be stated in this manner: "The broad general policies of government should be handled through the legislative rather than the administrative process."

This point of view enters in an interesting fashion into the Hayek-Finer controversy over economic planning. Hayek points out that the legislative process can scarcely be used to solve such important economic questions as "how many pigs are to be raised or how many busses are to be run, which coal mines are to operate, or at what prices shoes are to be sold." But if these decisions are handled through the administrative process, he maintains, the result is a breakdown in representative government and a long step forward on the road to serfdom.[43] Government, therefore, should not get involved in such matters, but should confine itself to fixing general rules determining the conditions under which resources are to be used rather than directing their use. Finer, on the other hand, defends large-scale governmental intervention in the economy, but justifies it on the ground that the full framework of economic planning can be constructed through a set of democratically adopted statutes. "The legislature," he writes, "is the heart of the planning process, for it is here that the less authoritative and less definite programs of the parties enter for definition and authorization." [44] Both Hayek and Finer, in effect, advocate "the rule of law," the one regarding it as an alternative to, and the other as the framework of, economic planning.

At times, of course, administrative officials create difficult problems for themselves and the programs they are administering by attempting to handle too many questions themselves instead of channeling them into the legislative process. Two competent observers write:

[42] Charles Hyneman, "Bureaucracy in a Democracy" (New York: Harper, 1950). Chap. 5, "Giving the Bureaucracy Its Job," is one of the few efforts in political-science literature to discuss in broad terms how far legislation should go in prescribing details. The chapter also contains a useful bibliographical note listing various writings that have dealt with some aspects of the problem (pp. 91–93).

[43] Friedrick Hayek, "The Road to Serfdom" (Chicago: University of Chicago Press, 1944), pp. 72–87.

[44] Finer, *op. cit.*, p. 213.

In administrative–legislative relationships the administrator who has a sense of delineation between legislative and administrative functions unerringly feels this sense; and if he respects it, he will be well received. The administrator who lacks faith in democratic methods and hesitates to lay vital issues before the legislative group for final judgment also reveals himself, and he is and should be poorly received.[45]

It is in this sense of delineation rather than any abstract rule that guidance must be found for the participant in the governmental process.

The Administrative Process in Time of Crisis. "In time of crisis and emergency, it is necessary to shift the handling of many problems from the legislative process to the administrative process." This is the third general principle.

There is little doubt that in time of crisis the President and other executive officials must take many drastic steps without waiting for legislative authorizations. Laws that are adopted under such circumstances, moreover, must give executive officials tremendously broad discretion.

This point of view has been presented in persuasive detail by Clinton Rossiter. According to Rossiter, the need for giving executive officials dictatorial powers in time of crisis should be clearly recognized beforehand so that plans can be made to assure its temporary character. He, therefore, suggests eleven criteria to which such dictatorships should be expected to conform in order to be "constitutional." [46]

In time of emergency, the ordinarily perplexing problem of choice between the administrative and the legislative routes multiplies in difficulty. There are matters of both detail as well as general policy that may be handled best through legislation. In the delegation of broad discretion to executive officials, there remains the ever-challenging question as to precisely how much and what powers are to be given to whom. In periods of semiemergency these questions become particularly pressing. In periods of intense crisis, they become critical, the chief problems, in many respects, depending upon the extent to which military authorities should be allowed to declare martial law and upon the extent to which other administrative officials are to be given the authority to restrict the customary civil liberties of individuals—too rigorous curtailment of civil liberties may help the "temporary" dictatorship to remain in power after the end of the crisis which called it into being!

The Administrative Process and Foreign Affairs. "The conduct of foreign affairs is the function of the President and the executive branch."

This fourth principle has often been justified on the legalistic ground that the conduct of foreign relations is an Executive function which has been vested by the Constitution in the President. Yet this is a barren approach to

[45] Jarle Leirfallom and L. J. Metcalf, "Legislation—From an Administrator's Viewpoint," *Public Welfare,* Vol. 6, No. 2, February, 1948.

[46] Clinton Rossiter, "Constitutional Dictatorship" (Princeton, N.J.: Princeton University Press, 1948), pp. 288–314.

the problem. The only monopoly that the President enjoys in the field of foreign relations is a monopoly of "the function of international intercourse." Whether in exercising this monopoly he should serve as the maker of foreign policy or as an instrument of communication is a question that can be resolved only in terms of specific circumstances and specific alignments of power.

The impressive case for administrative as opposed to legislative action in the field of foreign affairs is the frequent need for speed and flexibility. New situations are constantly developing in this field, situations to which policy must be adjusted, without taking time out to initiate legislative action or even in some circumstances to explain the development to many people in the United States. Many of the problems a President faces are of an emergency character, and he can ill afford to cater to minority interests which might attempt to hold up action if he sought decisions through the legislative process.[47]

Furthermore, the President and his representatives need a free hand in negotiations. They are constantly dealing with officials of other nations who can make decisions promptly and they also must be prepared to play a fluid role in the give-and-take process of diplomatic negotiations. This is particularly true about United States participation in the United Nations.

Yet there is also something to be said on the other side. Decisions on foreign policy have a major impact on domestic affairs. It has become increasingly true that the hand that writes our foreign policies rules the country. The excessive use of administrative discretion in this area could thus go a long way toward displacing the legislative process in other areas. It could put the future of the country in the hands of a small group of Government officials whose interests and allegiances are closely tied up with business, military, and diplomatic considerations, and who are often only remotely susceptible to pressure from other equally legitimate interests or to genuine Presidential control.

Safeguards over Administrative Discretion. "More matters can be handled through the administrative process if adequate safeguards are established over the use of administrative discretion."

It is interesting to note that almost all of the safeguards that are proposed in this connection are two-edged swords. They can be put to use not only to facilitate broad administrative discretion but also to prevent it.

Many of these safeguards are of long-standing vintage, having been used for decades and invariably being looked to when new problems of discretion and control are raised. One is the vesting of administrative discretion in multiheaded agencies, presumably responsible to Congress rather than to the Chief Executive. Another is to provide for extensive judicial review of administrative decisions either through the regular courts or special courts established to handle particular programs. Still another is to establish procedures for ad-

[47] This point of view has been fully presented in Thomas A. Bailey, "The Man in the Street" (New York: Macmillan, 1948).

ministrative operations such as requirements for notification in connection with public hearings, consultation with advisory committees, and, in the case of certain agencies, the formal separation between the personnel serving as "prosecutors" and "judges." Each of these approaches has been the focal center for a tremendous amount of debate and discussion concerning Government organization. There is an abundance of learned literature for and against each of these approaches, and a wealth of variations on each.

A more recently proposed "safeguard" is some form of "legislative veto" through the use of concurrent resolutions. Corwin, for example, asks how the line can be drawn between legislative "delegation" and "abdication," and answers his question as follows: "Only, I urge, by rendering the delegated powers recoverable without the consent of the delegate; and for this purpose the concurrent resolution seems to be an available mechanism, and the only one." [48]

It is pertinent to note in passing, however, that reorganization proposals are important weapons in the social struggle. They provide methods for the "outs" to attack the "ins," for the "ins" to consolidate their power, and for almost any type of public or private group to extend or contract governmental operations that they favor or dislike. They provide, above all, a method of pursuing these aims in the name of economy, efficiency, accountability, and other abstract principles that may have little or no connection with the real objectives that are sought.

Congressional Participation in the Administrative Process

In addition to their various activities discussed earlier in this chapter under the heading of "Congressional-Executive Collaboration," and in connection with such quasi-legislative measures as concurrent resolutions, members of the Congress can participate in the administrative process in three ways. They can influence the appointment or removal of executive officials. They can supervise, scrutinize, or investigate the administrative process. They can serve as "errand boys" on behalf of constituents with business before executive officials. Proposals meriting careful attention have been developed in connection with each of these points.

Appointments and Removals. ". . . Congress should restrict senatorial approval of presidential appointments to those officers enumerated in the Constitution. The power to appoint to all positions of a purely administrative character should be lodged in the heads of the respective agencies and the positions should be placed in the competitive classified service." [49]

The effect of proposals of this type unquestionably would be to strengthen the position of the President and other executive officials in both the adminis-

[48] Corwin, *op. cit.*, p. 160.

[49] George Galloway, "Congress at the Crossroads" (New York: Crowell, 1946), p. 237.

trative and legislative processes. It would tend to weaken the capacity of various members of Congress as well as private organizations to use senatorial confirmation as a weapon for opposing executive officials or for undermining party programs.

In so far as removals from executive offices are concerned, the constitutional provisions for impeachment give the members of Congress a weapon which is too burdensome for use. Those who advocate a parliamentary system of government in the United States point out that members of Congress would then have a sharper weapon, at least with respect to the Chief Executive. Others have from time to time suggested that the Constitution be amended in order to make the impeachment process easier. Frequently, lesser executive officials can readily be forced from office by the organized opposition of members of Congress in strategic positions.

During the nineteenth century there were a number of conflicts, particularly during the Presidential term of Andrew Johnson, over the Senate's power to prevent the President from removing an official whose appointment had been subject to Senate confirmation. A Supreme Court decision in 1926 favored the President. "The friction accompanying the controversy over the question," reported Luce, "has naturally led to proposals for amending the Federal Constitution in this particular. Nearly a score of amendments have been introduced, looking to restricting the power of the President." [50] Various statutory restrictions also have been devised with respect to the President's power of removal. The legislative process can be used to install members of regulatory boards and commissions for fixed terms of offices and to fix the grounds upon which they may be removed by the President, conditions which tend to prevent removals except under the most unusual circumstances.[51] A rather unique restriction was written into the Budget and Accounting Act of 1921. Under the provisions of this law, the Comptroller General cannot be removed except by joint resolution.

Preventing the removal of certain executive officials often can be achieved through informal means. Many a bureaucrat maintains his position because of the support of one or more members of Congress who occupy influential positions. Sometimes this support is based upon the backing of private organizations to whom the executive official in question has demonstrated a friendly and cooperative attitude. Many officials in this position enjoy a hidden form of permanent tenure, and any superior officer who tries to unseat them must reckon with a storm of reprisals.

Supervision, Scrutiny, and Investigation. One of the most popular and long-standing theories concerning the relations between the administrative and legislative processes depends upon the proposition that members of Congress,

[50] Robert Luce, "Legislative Problems" (Boston: Houghton Mifflin, 1935), p. 134.
[51] See *Humphrey's Executor v. United States,* 295 U.S. 602 (1935).

preferably through their committees, have an important function to perform in keeping their eye upon administrative operations. Woodrow Wilson maintained that "even more important than legislation is the instruction and guidance in political affairs which the people might receive from a body which kept all national concerns suffused in a broad daylight of discussion." [52] It is useful to analyze these particular activities into three forms or degrees, as follows: supervision, scrutiny, and investigation, each closely related to the others but distinct in certain respects.

"Supervision" connotes a continuing and informed awareness on the part of a congressional committee regarding executive operations in a given administrative area.

> As the powers exercised by the bureaus and commissions are those that have been delegated to them by Congress, Congress should be kept constantly and systematically informed regarding the use to which those powers are being put. If the government agency and the congressional committee could not agree regarding the desirability of a particular regulation or regarding some other policy followed by the agency, then the committee could call the matter to the attention of the whole Congress and offer its recommendations.[53]

"Scrutiny," on the other hand, implies a lesser intensity and continuity of attention to administrative operations. Scrutiny is an exercise of supervisory powers with the flexibility that may be achieved through informal understandings among committee members and executive officials, or, as in the case of the appropriations committees, through "policy guides" which are written into committee reports and which executive officials are expected to follow.

The difficulty which members of Congress may encounter in making a careful distinction between supervision and scrutiny was mirrored in an interesting phrasing problem encountered during the preparation of the Legislative Reorganization Act of 1946. "Without effective legislative oversight of the activities of the vast executive branch," stated the report of the Joint Committee on the Organization of Congress, "the line of democracy wears thin. . . . We feel that this oversight problem can be handled best by directing the regular standing committees of the Senate and House, which have such matters in their jurisdiction, to conduct a continuous review of the agencies administering laws originally reported by the committees." [54] In a subsequent paragraph, "continuous review" was referred to as a "supervisory function."

To get away from the word "supervision," which implied a degree of control not contemplated by all the members of the committee, other words, *e.g.*, surveillance, scrutiny, were used in the section of the Legislative Reor-

[52] Wilson, *op. cit.*, p. 297.

[53] Editorial in *The New York Times,* Jan. 16, 1939.

[54] Report of the Joint Committee on the Organization of Congress, 79th Cong., 2d Sess., Mar. 4, 1946, p. 6.

ganization Act assigning this function to the standing committees (Sec. 136).[55] But the flight from Latin to French and Anglo-Saxon did not resolve the difficulty. The term "surveillance" was challenged on the floor of the Senate by Senator Donnell of Missouri.[56] As a result, the key word in the text was changed from "supervision" to "watchfulness." "Oversight" was left, however (probably by oversight), in the title of the section and stands as a mute reminder of the difficulty faced in making this distinction. This difficulty could probably have been resolved if the word "scrutiny" had been offered as a substitute.

The provisions of the Legislative Reorganization Act with respect to the scrutiny of administrative operations are extensive. The watchfulness mandate was given to every legislative committee and the two appropriations committees. The two Committees on Expenditures in the Executive Departments were given the responsibility of "studying the operation of government activities at all levels with a view to determining its economy and efficiency." Thus provision was made for a six-way scrutiny. To help in discharging this responsibility each committee was authorized to hire a certain number of staff employees. All Senate committees were given the power to subpoena witnesses and documents. Yet this comprehensive approach is still more of a proposal than a fact. "This feature of the Act has met with only partial success to date," George Galloway has observed. "Many standing committees have been too heavily burdened with their legislative duties and limited staffs to keep very close watch upon the executive agencies within their jurisdiction." [57]

The distinction between congressional scrutiny and a congressional investigation is that the former is a more passive process of looking at the facts that are readily available, and the latter involves a more intense digging for facts. If there are many who believe that we need more of the former, there are probably just as many who maintain that we can get along with less of the latter.

Luce has written one of the most vigorous and comprehensive indictments of congressional investigations:

> Prosecution turned into persecution, the ruthless sacrifice of reputation, the vindictive display of prejudice, the mean debasement of partisanship, the advancement of personal fortunes through the use of scurrilous publicity—these are some of the features that make the whole thing a stench in the nostrils of decent men. . . .
>
> The net result of the practice is more harm than good. It interferes sadly with legislative time, especially when overburdened legislators are taken away from legitimate duties for weeks and weeks. . . .

[55] The author of this book feels that he must shoulder part of the blame for the use of the term "surveillance," since it—and, in fact, the entire phrasing of the section—was borrowed from Sec. 2 of the Contract Settlement Act of 1944 which he himself had drafted.

[56] *Congressional Record,* 79th Cong., 1st Sess., p. 6445.

[57] Galloway, "The Operation of the Legislative Reorganization Act of 1946," *American Political Science Review,* Vol. 40, No. 1, March, 1951, pp. 59–60.

It is costly. . . .

It conduces to trial by newspaper. . . .

Worse yet is the effect on the public mind, by encouraging the dangerous belief that all public servants are knaves. . . .

Indeed, what purpose of inquiry is normally legislative unless it involves the making of a law? To that degree and no further can legislative audit, whether by full assembly, or by committee, be justified.[58]

One line of change suggests the delegation of investigations to executive agencies [59] or to special investigating commissions appointed by the Chief Justice of the United States Supreme Court.[60] Another line suggests that there is "greater need for forward-looking inquiries than for backward-looking ones," [61] and Congress should more frequently make "searching investigations into matters of great economic and social significance." [62] Senator Kefauver has expressed the view that the purposes of congressional investigations should be limited. Speaking against the continuation of the Senate Crime Investigating Committee which he had headed, Kefauver stated that "it is not the province of a legislative committee, in my opinion, to pile on cumulative evidence time and time again. I think the byproduct of arousing public opinion is very important, (but) that alone is no justification for having investigations." [63]

The most frequent and most important proposals for reform relate to the adoption through statute, rule, or voluntary acceptance of minimum standards of procedure. In an excellent summation of these proposals, Galloway lists a grand total of 41 possible safeguards. After carefully exploring the question of whether any such safeguards are really needed, he comes to the well-considered conclusion that "a code of fair conduct for all investigating groups might well be adopted by the House and Senate as part of their standing rules. . . . In the Federal Administrative Procedure Act, Congress had provided a code of procedure for administrative agencies. This action should now be matched by the enactment of a code for its own investigators." [64]

"Errand-Boy" Work. If members of Congress spent less time in running errands for their constituents, it is frequently argued, they would have far more time to devote to their legislative duties. One approach to this objective

[58] Luce, *op. cit.*, pp. 446–447.

[59] Nelson M. McGeary "The Developments of Congressional Investigative Power" (New York: Columbia University Press, 1940), pp. 115–160.

[60] Lindsay Rogers, "When Congress Fumbles for Facts," *New York Herald Tribune,* Mar. 29, 30, 31, 1950.

[61] Fritz Morstein Marx, "Congressional Investigations: Significance for the Administrative Process," *University of Chicago Law Review,* Vol. 18, No. 3, Spring, 1951, p. 517.

[62] Heller, *op. cit.*, p. 29.

[63] *Congressional Record* (daily edition), Apr. 24, 1951, p. 4387.

[64] Galloway, "Congressional Investigations: Proposed Reforms," *University of Chicago Law Review,* Vol. 18, No. 3, Spring, 1951, pp. 478–502.

is to provide members with better staff assistance in their personal offices, in the committees to which they belong, and through the Library of Congress.

Another is to provide more information services for constituents. This can be done by channeling requests for information or assistance to congressional committees dealing with the subject matter of any inquiry, to agency liaison offices, or to general information services set up for the use of Congress. Another suggestion is that each state establish special offices in Washington to help represent the interests of private individuals of the state before the various executive agencies.

The American Political Science Association's Committee on Congress has suggested "that Congress might well formulate a Charter of Congressional Freedom from trivial errands. . . ."

> . . . we suggest that the Charter of Congressional Freedom might well prohibit any person from trying to enlist the aid of a legislator in getting a government job below the grade of presidential appointments or in seeking a promotion. . . .
>
> We suggest that Congress forbid its members to intervene in individual cases, contenting themselves with passing the criticism of undue delay on to the appropriate legislative committee.[65]

But before one sets aside the ideas of political scientists as impractical, consider the strange formulation trotted out by a "practical" politician, Representative Robert Ramspeck of Georgia: "I am suggesting that we adopt a constitutional amendment which would prohibit a member of Congress, or Senator, from contacting the executive branch of the Government except in regard to legislation." [66]

If one maintains his hold upon the world of reality, he may well ask himself a number of questions. If the time spent in errand running were cut down, is there any assurance that the vacuum would be filled by attention to legislative duties? In a society which is constantly imposing greater burdens upon the Government, is it reasonable to suppose that the burden on members of Congress can be lightened? Is it not more reasonable to suppose that the burden will constantly grow and that the problem for members of Congress is how to select the matters on which they expend their energies and how to obtain sufficient staff services to help them do a good, instead of a halfway, job? And is errand running something necessarily apart from a member's legislative work? Can it not give him valuable experience on many matters which are dealt with in more general terms in legislative measures? Would he not remain relatively ignorant concerning the practical

[65] Committee on Congress, American Political Science Association, "The Reorganization of Congress" (Washington, D.C.: Public Affairs Press, 1945), pp. 66–67.

[66] Hearings before the Joint Committee on the Organization of Congress, 79th Cong., 1st Sess., p. 296.

problems involved in many legislative proposals if it were not for his work in representing the interests of individual constituents?

A final question is whether or not the errand-boy work of members of Congress may not be of positive value to the administrative process. John Stuart Mill argued that the British Parliament had a major function in serving as "the Nation's Committee of Grievances." [67] In America this function has been well described by Pendleton Herring:

More and more will the Senator, and even more especially the Representative, come to serve as a mediator between his constituency and the operations of government within it. He is in a strategic position to observe how governmental functions actually impinge upon his constituents. He is in a position to advise his constituents how to receive maximum benefits from what the government stands ready to give them and how to make their views felt about desirable fields for governmental action. He is in a position to discover areas where governmental activity should be withdrawn or modified. He is in a position to advise administrative officials how their actions affect the people of his district. Such advice may come as a welcome supplement to the information the administrator receives from his subordinates, from field reports, or from personal inspection, affected as they are by the interests, aspirations, and limitations of the persons making them.[68]

[67] John Stuart Mill, "Considerations on Representative Government" (New York: Macmillan, 1947), p. 172.

[68] Pendleton Herring, "The Politics of Democracy" (New York: Rinehart, 1940), p. 383.

Chapter 8

THE CONTESTANTS AND THEIR POWER

POWER [1] MAY be defined as the ability to influence people through persuasion, compulsion, or—as is usually the case—a combination of the two.

The power displayed by the contestants in the legislative struggle is not easy to measure. The distribution of power is constantly shifting. We have no voltage or kilowatt standards that can readily be applied on a quantitative scale. Also, just as every nation tries to keep its military strength a secret, the wielders of legislative power have erected an elaborate camouflage system. Researchers in social science have barely scratched the surface in penetrating the barriers and in measuring the power of individual groups in specific group conflicts.

Fortunately, a vector analysis of the power exerted by each of the contestants in the legislative process is not essential to the purposes of this book (although a full analysis of power relationships in individual legislative situations would be invaluable). It is enough at this point to indicate the basic factors that serve as the source of any group's power and to show how such power can be multiplied by combining with others. At a later point the effort will be made to show how the power of the various contestants in the legislative process is used to influence the outcome of specific legislative conflicts.

[1] "There is no reasonably adequate study of the nature of social power. The majority of the works on the theme are devoted either to proclaiming the importance of the role of power, like those of Hobbes, Gumplowicz, Ratzenhofer, Steinmetz, Treitschke, and so forth, or to deploring that role, like Bertrand Russell in his *Power*. . . ." Robert MacIver, "The Web of Government" (New York: Macmillan, 1947), p. 458. While MacIver's comment is unquestionably justified, interesting discussions of the nature of social power are to be found in Robert Bierstedt, "An Analysis of Social Power," *American Sociological Review,* Vol. 15, No. 6, December, 1950; Guglielmo Ferrero, "The Principles of Power" (New York: Putnam, 1942); Herman Heller, "Political Power," *Encyclopaedia of the Social Sciences,* Vol. 12 (New York: Macmillan, 1934), pp. 300–305; Benjamin Kidd, "The Science of Power" (New York: Putnam, 1918); Harold Lasswell, "Politics: Who Gets What, When, How" (New York: McGraw-Hill, 1936); and Charles Merriam, "Political Power" (New York: McGraw-Hill, 1934).

THE SOURCES OF POWER

The various factors that are combined to give any group its power can be divided into four closely interrelated categories: (1) wealth, (2) numbers, (3) leadership and organization, and (4) strategic position.[2] Upon examination, each of these turns out to be a vastly complex area in itself.

Wealth

The importance of wealth as a source of power is quite obvious. Over the course of centuries the wealthier groups in any nation have always been among the dominant forces, if not *the* dominant ones. In America the growing concentration of economic power in the hands of a few has consistently, and correctly, been regarded as placing greater political power in the same hands. Throughout the world the case for the nationalization of basic industries has been based mainly upon the desire to wrest political power from the present owners and give it to the state or, in more accurate terms, a competing group.

In fact, there is good reason to believe that the strength of the famous "profit motive" as an important factor in economic behavior derives from the contribution that economic gains can make to the satisfaction of the desire for more power.

> In the age of capitalism, supported by democracy, the rich man is happy whenever his money can give him great influence over his economic inferiors and over public affairs. . . . Biographical studies that speak of the lives of our contemporary plutocrats demonstrate how much of the dynamic force of great industrialists and merchants, directed at reaching the pinnacle of wealth, is basically subordinated to the end of acquiring authority over men and establishing themselves as autocrats of finance.[3]

[2] A somewhat similar breakdown is given in Bierstedt, *op. cit.*: "Power would seem to stem from three sources: (1) numbers of people, (2) social organization, and (3) resources. . . . Given the same social organization and the same resources, the larger number can always control the smaller and secure its compliance. . . . A well-organized and disciplined body of marines or of police can control a much larger number of unorganized majority. . . . Of two groups, however, equal or nearly equal in numbers and comparable in organization, the one with access to the greater resources will have the superior power. . . . Resources may be of many kinds—money, property, prestige, knowledge, competence, deceit, fraud, secrecy and, of course, all of the things usually included under the term 'natural resources.' . . . Power appears only in the combination of all three—numbers, organization, and resources."

One difficulty with this analysis is that the term "resources" is stretched so far that it includes qualities or techniques of leadership that are more logically tied up with social organization rather than with wealth per se. Also, the analysis fails to recognize that a social group can derive power from their occupation of a strategic position.

[3] Robert Michels, "First Lectures in Political Sociology" (Minneapolis, Minn.: University of Minnesota Press, 1949), de Grazia translation, p. 93.

When a given cause of action holds forth the promise of increasing profits but threatens a decrease in power, it is apt to be rejected.

In addition to its direct value as a means of persuasion and compulsion,[4] wealth has the great advantage of providing the wherewithal to obtain other sources of power. To win followers, build an organization, and achieve strategic positions costs money. Generally speaking, the more money available for these purposes, the better the job that can be done. The size of their assets, reserves, and current profits, therefore, is one of the clues to the power of business organizations; the size of their treasuries and dues payments is an indication of the power of labor organizations. Similarly, the size of agency appropriations and the degree of control exercised over agency expenditures are respective guides to the power of executive officials and of members of Congress.

Yet care should be taken not to overemphasize, as most Marxians do, the power potential of wealth.

> The economic strength of any group or class is no longer, as it tended to be under feudal conditions, the measure of its political strength. The relative ease with which powerful economic interests have been defeated in the political arena, the many encroachments of government, by taxation and regulation, on the prerogatives of wealth, the progress of "social legislation" all along the line, and the manner in which various governments, without any proletarian revolution, have taken over such important sectors of capitalistic enterprise as railroads and public utilities, demonstrate the inadequacy of the Marxian thesis to comprehend the complex relationship between economic and political power.[5]

Nor should wealth itself be too glibly equated with economic power, a term which is used to describe power that is to a large degree based upon wealth. The economic power of a nation, a corporation, a union, or a government agency cannot be derived solely from its physical or monetary assets. These are transmuted into power only after being combined with numbers, organization and leadership, and strategic situations.

Numbers

> Rise like Lions after slumber
> In unconquerable number . . .
> Ye are many—they are few.[6]

[4] In the full sense of the term, "wealth" includes not only the more ordinary forms of machinery, goods, and materials but also such "persuasive" forms of property as policemen's blackjacks and atomic bombs. The four factors listed as the sources of power are therefore suitable to the analysis of power not only in situations in which, as with the legislative process, relatively peaceful methods are used but also in conflicts between policemen and racketeers or between nations locked in mortal combat.

[5] MacIver, *op. cit.*, p. 92.

[6] Percy Bysshe Shelley, "The Mask of Anarchy."

With these ringing words, Shelley tried to inspire the workingmen of England to an exercise of their potential power. In fact, this theme has been central to the efforts of every organizer of the underprivileged. There is tremendous strength in the sheer number of followers any group may have.

Even to a small group, numbers are essential. An individual in isolation is weak, and it is only as a number of individuals get together that the possibilities of power emerge. In primitive societies the larger tribes tended to become the more powerful because, given no great disparities in the effectiveness of weapons, a fight can be won by the side with the greatest number of bodies. Even under conditions of modern warfare, "manpower resources" are not to be sneezed at, which is why many militaristic nations have adopted policies to encourage population growth. When disputes are settled by peaceful rather than by violent means, "counting noses" is a widely used technique. It is by a show of numbers in one form or another that elections are won, Supreme Court decisions made, and bills enacted.

Numbers can also provide access to other sources of power. They can provide a source of wealth, if only through dues payments or tithes. They provide the raw materials for organization and leadership. They can lead to a monopoly of certain types of skills or services, thereby putting a group in a highly strategic position.

Organization and Leadership

That the mercantile and manufacturing classes, with all the advantages given them by their wealth, their intelligence, and their habits of co-operation, should have been vanquished by the agricultural masses, may be ascribed partly to the fact that the democratic impulse of the War of Independence was strong among the citizens who had grown to manhood between 1780 and 1800, partly to the tactical errors of the Federalist leaders, but largely also to the skill which Jefferson showed in organizing the hitherto undisciplined battalions of Republican voters. Thus early in American history was the secret revealed, which Europe is only now discovering, that in free countries with an extended suffrage, numbers without organizations are helpless and with it omnipotent.[7]

Only through organization can the full advantage of wealth or numbers be exploited. Indeed, a high degree of organization can often compensate for serious deficiencies in either wealth or numbers. As Ludwig Gumplowicz long ago pointed out:

. . . it is not the size of the social group which determines its power. The lords were always in a minority, and in modern states with millions of inhabitants the power rests with the "upper ten thousand." The intimacy of the union and the resultant organiza-

[7] James Bryce, "The American Commonwealth" (New York: Macmillan, 1907), 3d ed., Vol. II, p. 10.

tion and discipline together with mental superiority complement numerical inferiority giving the minority preponderancy. The minority applies the strategical maxim: march as individuals, strike as one.[8]

In more recent times, the striking power of well-organized minorities has been dramatically demonstrated by the successes of the bolshevist parties in Russia and China. One of the guiding principles of Lenin, Stalin, and Mao Tse-tung has been to draw a sharp line between a mass following, which is to be encouraged, and a revolutionary party, which through tight entrance requirements and successive purges, is to be kept down to a small, compact core of "true believers." [9]

Organization, in turn, is the product of leadership. To some extent, it is the residue left behind by former leaders. Formalized structures, conventionalized procedures, habits of thought—these are the heritage received from leaders of the past. But it is the leaders of the present who must pour new wine into the old bottles, or at least try to prevent the old wine from turning sour.

A powerful organization calls for a variety of leadership skills. Leaders must be perceptive enough to gauge accurately the community of interest upon which people can be brought to act in concert. They must be imaginative enough to create or use the ideals and symbols—the "credenda and miranda" of power, as one writer has put it [10]—that can inspire enthusiasm and loyalty. They must define the objectives of group action, choose the weapons, and develop staff services in the fields of intelligence, planning, and public relations. They must nurture every source of power, extend their group's power through combinations of various sorts, and negotiate the compromises that spell victory or defeat in individual engagements.

Leadership capacity is deeply affected by an organization's general characteristics, including its followers and the problems it faces. It is also the result of such personal qualities as vitality and endurance, decisiveness, persuasiveness, responsibility, and intellectual capacity.[11] Whether an organization can get or maintain leaders with these qualities depends to a large extent on the character of its internal struggle for control. If any one clique goes too far in eliminating rivals and ensconcing itself in control for a long enough period of time, the inevitable result is a hardening of the arteries and a senescence of organizational strength. At the other extreme, if turnover is too rapid, no set of leaders will have sufficient time to become familiar with their tasks and win the confidence of their followers.

[8] Ludwig Gumplowicz, "The Outlines of Sociology" (American Academy of Political and Social Science, 1899, translated by Frederick W. Moore), p. 143.

[9] This useful term is taken from Eric Hoffer, "The True Believer" (New York: Harper, 1951), a profoundly suggestive study of mass movements.

[10] Merriam, *op. cit.*, Chap. 4.

[11] These five leadership qualities are taken from Chester Barnard, "Organization and Management" (Cambridge, Mass.: Harvard University Press, 1948), Chap. 4.

Strategic Positions

At the famous Greek mountain pass of Thermopylae, Leonidas and his band of 300 Spartans held up the advance of the vast Persian army of Xerxes. The entire field of social combat is studded with mountain passes which give organized groups splendid opportunities for both defense and attack. The more complex any situation is, the greater the possibilities of achieving vast power by occupying one or more of these strategic spots or by obtaining access to, and influence over, those who occupy them.

The Government is full of strategic positions. Members of Congress who sit on important committees wield tremendous power within their areas of operation. The same is true for executive officials who have their hands on the controls of a given program and of staff subordinates who have almost monopolistic control of operating facts and procedures. The power of the President's position, of course, comes from the fact that he tends to be the center of the whole works and can play some part—greater or less—in almost any contest. The strategic position of the political parties lies in their virtual monopoly of the machinery of nominations.

Outside Government, the tremendous power of bankers and financiers flows to a large extent from the fact that they are in a position to influence business operations over a tremendous area without incurring a commensurate degree of personal risk. Business managers, unions, farm organizations—each have a strategic position in the process of production and distribution. Business managers have a unique strategic advantage resulting from the community of interest among business managers in general and the managers of newspaper, radio, television, and motion-picture businesses in particular—a community of interest which is nourished by the purchase of advertising space and time and by other financial interrelations. The power of professional organizations, particularly in the legal and medical fields, flows not only from their quasi monopolies of specialized services but also from the access their leaders usually have to influential people outside the professional world.

Strategic positions, however, are only a source of generalized power. The American Medical Association can swing considerable weight to the subject of Government health policies, but its closest friends in Government would not give it much attention on foreign policy. During World War II, when William Green, president of the A.F.L., tried to get Representative Clarence Cannon of Missouri to vote for farm subsidies to bring farm prices down, Mr. Cannon put Mr. Green in his place: "I have always followed Mr. Green on labor bills," he told the press. "But this is not a labor bill. This is a farm bill. On this bill I will follow the farm leaders." [12]

[12] Quoted in an editorial, *New York Herald Tribune,* Nov. 25, 1943.

The Extension of Power through Combinations

The most profound strategic problems in modern warfare, those that are more the province of statesmen than of generals, relate to the forming of combinations. As a basis for initiating World War II, Adolf Hitler developed the Anti-Comintern Axis, a combination composed mainly of Germany, Italy, and Japan. For the purpose of defense and then of counterattack, Roosevelt, Churchill, and Stalin developed a cooperative effort between the United States, England, Russia, and minor allies.

All the contestants in the legislative struggle operate in the same way—the weak in order to build up their power, the strong in order to extend their power and to maintain it. To some extent the formation and dissolution of alliances can be described in the words of James M. Burns: "Like dancers in a vast Virginia reel, groups merge, break off, meet again, veer away to new combinations." [13] To a much greater extent, there is no pattern and less chance in the manner in which partners come together. In agriculture, the cotton, wool, and tobacco interests have traditionally worked together to obtain special legislation. As the lobbyist for the National Wool Growers' Association told a reporter: "It may not be nice to say, but the way you get bills passed is—'you scratch my back and I'll scratch yours.' " [14] The textile manufacturers and the textile unions traditionally cooperate in opposing the reduction of tariffs on textile imports. One of the traditional aims of organized labor has been to form a farmer-labor coalition against business interests. In turn, business interests have aimed—and have often hit the mark—at forming a business-farmer coalition against organized labor.[15] Both groups compete for the

[13] James M. Burns, "Congress on Trial" (New York: Harper, 1949), p. 33.

[14] Tristram Coffin, "No Speech Ever Changed a Vote," *New Republic,* July 14, 1945.

[15] "Nor are all constituents of the farm bloc farmers. There is a powerful voice of business—both big and little. Partly through mutual dislike for organized labor, and partly because of inherent conservatism, the alliance of agriculture and business grows stronger. . . .

The United States Chamber of Commerce, which maintains a temple-like structure across Lafayette Square from the White House, has had an agricultural division for years. . . .

A second point at which industry and the farm bloc converge, though in a minor way, is the National Highway Users Conference, 'a fact-finding, information-giving, and coordinating agency, acting in behalf of the development of highway transportation in the public interest.' . . .

A third item of significance in the effort of industry to hold the moral support of agriculture, sometimes making it a silent partner in farm-bloc proceedings, is the program of the National Industrial Information Committee. Sponsored by the National Association of Manufacturers and composed of the cream of New Deal enemies, the committee functions under the following officers: national chairman, J. Howard Pew, president of the Sun Oil Company; vice-chairman, Ernest T. Weir, Chairman of the Board of National Steel Corporation, and the other vice-chairman, C. M. Chester, chairman of the board of General Foods Corporation." Wesley McCune, "The Farm Bloc" (New York: Doubleday, 1943), pp. 8–10.

support of the veterans, the church, women's organizations, and the other organized groups.

Presidential and executive officials carry this principle even further. The secret of Franklin Roosevelt's power in Congress lay in his ability to bring together behind his proposals Southern Democrats, Northern liberals, the bosses of the big city machines, organized labor, and important blocs of agricultural and business interests. The decline in his power, with respect to practically all domestic measures initiated after his first term in office, stemmed from the formation of a conservative coalition between the Republicans and the Southern Democrats backed by a solid and growing bloc of business and farm interests. Irrespective of political configurations, any President who can get a sufficiently strong coalition of group interest behind a given legislative proposal can succeed in obtaining its passage by Congress. In the same way any department or bureau in the executive branch of the Government which can organize sufficient backing for its own proposals can thumb its nose at the President and more or less have its own way in Congress. This has been demonstrated repeatedly by combinations among the army engineers, the power interests, and certain members of Congress.

The increments of power obtained through combinations, however, are not always "net." The account books will usually show some offsetting factors. At the least, combinations reduce the ease and simplicity with which groups can act and react, extending the area of essential consultation and calculation. They also may require the sacrifice of certain objectives or techniques that might be objectionable to one's allies. It is likely that group power can be extended through combinations only at a discount. While these discounts will vary in size, even when they seem comparatively small, they are an integral part of the power structure of society.

The exchange of legislative support has been persistently held up to scorn as a procedure that threatens the public interest. In its more fleeting forms, it has been branded as "logrolling," a procedure alleged to endanger democratic processes. Yet in any society with more than two groups it is inevitable that every group will try to supplement its inherent sources of power by tapping the power of other groups. In fact, the process of swapping support—with all that it involves in the bringing about of mutual understandings and adjustments and whether it implies a temporary relationship or a long-standing coalition—can be regarded as an essential part of the democratic process.

Logrolling is, however, in fact, the most characteristic legislative process. When one condemns it "in principle," it is only by contrasting it with some assumed pure public spirit which is supposed to guide legislators, or which ought to guide them, and which enables them to pass judgment in Jovian calm on that which is best "for the whole people." Since there is nothing which is best literally for the whole people, group arrays being what they are, the test is useless, even if one could actually find legislative judgments which are not reducible to interest-group activities. And when we have reduced the legislative process to the play of group interests, then logrolling, or give and take, appears as the very nature of the process. It is compromise, not in the abstract moral form, which philosophers can sagely discuss, but in the practical form with which every legislator who gets results through government is acquainted. It is trading. It is the adjustment of interests. . . . There never was a time in the history of the American Congress when legislation was conducted in any other way.[16]

Whether one looks with favor upon any specific combination, whether one regards it as an "unholy alliance" or "a united front in a common cause" depends entirely upon one's own interests and allegiances.

[16] Arthur F. Bentley, "The Process of Government" (Bloomington, Ind.: Principia Press, 1949, reissue), pp. 370–371.

PART II

COMBAT ON THE LEGISLATIVE TERRAIN

Chapter 9

TO HAVE OR NOT TO HAVE A BILL

THE LEGISLATIVE process is only one of the methods through which the contestants in the social struggle pursue their objectives. The concentration of attention on it in this book should not obscure the fact that the most crucial conflicts are often fought on other battlegrounds. In an era of "Big Government," the administrative process has assumed major significance. There are also the processes of judicial action, constitutional amendment, and state and local government. There is the entire field of private action outside the sphere of government. And finally, there are the processes of changing the leadership of government through electoral action or through the most extreme forms of social combat, revolution, and war.

Since the social struggle spills over into all these fields, any attempt to describe the legislative process as though it were the entire universe of struggle, without looking at the manner in which contesting groups weave in and out of the legislative battleground, would give a narrow and distorted picture. "To have or not to have a bill" [1]—that is a question whose pros and cons are repeatedly being weighed by the leaders of private organizations and political parties and by government officials. It is more a question of strategy than of law or of constitutional requirement. It is like the problem of choosing the section of an island on which to establish a beachhead. There are many shores to choose from, each with its peculiar advantages and disadvantages. There is even the possibility of bypassing the island completely. No abstract laws of military science can either guide the generals or provide a basis for an observer to predict exactly how individual generals will behave. Similarly, it would be idle to seek some neat formula by which one could automatically explain decisions on having or not having a bill. In describing how these decisions are made, one must proceed by appraising the alternative choices that lie before legislative strategists and by indicating both the advantages and disadvantages of the legislative terrain.

[1] For purposes of convenience, the word "bill" is used to refer to any type of legislative measure, whether a bill or a resolution. A full distinction between the various types of measures is provided in Chap. 11.

The Area of Choice

There are certain objectives that can be achieved only through the production of Federal statutes and others that can be achieved only through administrative or judicial decisions. There are some things that can be done only by the Federal government, and others only through other organizations. In addition, there is also a broad area of overlapping, an area in which it is entirely possible for contesting groups to embark on two or more courses of action at the same time or else choose between them on the basis of their relative advantages and disadvantages. This area of choice exists because of the flexibility and adaptability of various processes. What rules exist are mostly vague and open to many varieties of interpretation. Contestants with sufficient "know-how" and resourcefulness can often concoct effective devices for their circumvention. Contestants with sufficient power behind them can, in fact, break the rules with impunity. When this is done often enough, the old rules break down and new precedents take their place.

The existence of choice, of course, is a relative matter; it shifts from one situation to another. For many contestants in the social struggle, there is no choice whatsoever; the battleground is picked for them by the action of opponents and competitors. For stronger groups, the area of choice is far broader than for weaker people faced with identical problems; the ability to make choices is itself a good measure of power. For all groups, strong and weak, the availability of alternatives is limited by habit; many of the obstacles to the use of one process as opposed to another flow entirely from an inability to break with customary methods of operation.

The Overlap with the Administrative Process [2]

General Overlapping. The existence of a significant overlap between the legislative process and the administrative process has been touched upon. In the course of the legislative struggle, questions are always arising as to whether or not fundamental policy decisions shall be left to executive officials [3] or shall

[2] For general books which deal with the administrative process and throw some light on the overlap between legislative and administrative processes, see James Hart, "An Introduction to Administrative Law" (New York: Appleton-Century-Crofts, 2d ed., 1950); James M. Landis, "The Administrative Process" (New Haven, Conn.: Yale University Press, 1938); and Herbert A. Simon, Donald W. Smithburg, and Victor A. Thompson, "Public Administration" (New York: Knopf, 1950).

[3] This is often referred to as "the delegation of legislative power," a concept stemming from the old and outworn idea that any uniform rule is "legislative," the administrative role being little more than the clerical application of the rule. It is also associated with the old warning of John Locke that "the legislative cannot transfer the power of making laws to any other hands, for it being but a delegated power from the people, they who have it can-

be by legislative provisions. The geographical distribution of Federal funds can be left entirely up to executive officials, as in the case of the lending operations of the Federal Public Housing Authority, or it can be provided for in accordance with statutory formulas, as in the case of Federal aid to states for the construction of roads and hospitals. The Interstate Commerce Commission may be given broad power to regulate freight rates, while the Agriculture Department may be bound by statutory "parity" formulas in the determination of prices at which farm products are to be supported. Legislation can be used equally either for overthrowing policies and rules established by administrators or for writing them directly into the law. In the course of the administrative process, in turn, many decisions are made which can be legitimately regarded as a substitute for or alternative to legislative action. The appointment of a conservative official to administer a liberal law, or vice versa, can have the same effect as legislative action to amend the law or nullify it. Hence the great importance in the administrative process both of patronage—particularly that form of patronage which stems from an ideological interest in seeing the appointment of people with one's own point of view—and of Senate confirmation of Presidential appointees.[4] Also, congressional investigations and pressure campaigns are habitually used to accomplish through the administrative process what might otherwise be attained through legislation—and used by those who are most intimately connected with the legislative process.

Nevertheless, there are always a large number of cases where the overlapping between the legislative and administrative processes is far from obvious. The relationship between the two has become a subject that is enlivened by endless disputes concerning the alleged propriety of one process being used on matters that are heatedly claimed as the exclusive province of the other. There have been few periods in American history when public life has not been marked by charges from members of Congress that the President or executive officials have exceeded their legitimate powers and have trespassed in the legislative domain. Similarly, there are always continuous laments within the executive branch (though less outspoken, for fear of congressional reprisals) concern-

---

not pass it on to others." "On Civil Government," Book II, Chap. 11. This latter maxim has often been used to support opposition to statutes conferring broad discretion on executive officials. As far back as 1916 the death of this maxim was acknowledged by Elihu Root when he voiced the view that, as a result of the rapid growth of executive agencies, "the old doctrine prohibiting the delegation of legislative power has virtually retired from the field and given up the fight." "Addresses on Citizenship and Government" (Cambridge, Mass.: Harvard University Press, 1916), p. 534. This does not mean, of course, that the doctrine cannot be brought back from the grave as justification for a Supreme Court decision, as in fact happened in the 1935 decision overthrowing the National Industrial Recovery Act.

[4] Senate confirmation is herein regarded as part of the administrative process itself; it would be stretching our words too wide to include in the legislative process the Senate resolutions dealing with Presidential nominations. The type of measures to be regarded as falling within the legislative process is discussed fully in Chap. 11.

ing the usurpation of administrative functions by legislation. To a man from Mars these arguments would sound exceedingly strange, for the charge is always that somebody or some people do not have the power to do what they have already done.[5] These charges of usurpation, however, are usually nothing but a means of arguing or agitating against action which is opposed on substantive grounds. Their effect is to becloud—though actually they document—the fact that the area of overlapping is extremely broad.

Within the entire area of overlapping between the legislative and administrative processes there is an important distinction between essentiality and possibility. The fact that a given objective can be achieved through administrative action and that a new law is not essential does not imply that it is not possible or desirable to achieve the identical objective through legislation. After Pearl Harbor, the Roosevelt Administration could have operated its price-control machinery under the War Powers Act, as was done with the rationing and priorities programs. For reasons of expedience, however, it chose to seek special price-control legislation. In 1943, President Roosevelt set up the Office of War Mobilization by Executive order. A year and a half later a law was enacted changing the name of the agency to the Office of War Mobilization and Reconversion and somewhat broadening its duties, an action that could have been achieved by an Executive order of the President. In the case of the disposition of surplus war property, new legislation was not necessary and the first view of the Roosevelt Administration was that surplus property should be disposed of under existing powers. However, a combination of pressures within Congress forced the Administration to change its mind and the result was the Surplus Property Act of 1944.

To indicate how extensive this area of overlapping really is, let us now look at the area where it is generally assumed that legislative action is indispensable and then at the area that on first thought would appear to be the exclusive province of administrative action. In both cases we will find ample illustrations of the age-old maxim—probably more applicable to the processes of government than to anything else—that there are many ways of skinning a cat.

The "Exclusively Legislative." It is generally regarded as axiomatic that

[5] In ordinary usage, and in the terminology of the previous chapter, the fact that someone has done something is proof that he had the power to do it. But the term "power" is also used in a specialized sense to refer to the rightful use of power. It's as though one said that heavyweight champion Joe Louis does not have power to lick a flyweight pugilist; what would be meant, of course, is that by the rules of the game heavyweights are supposed to fight heavyweights only (at least in the ring). The trouble comes with the presumption that rules can be tight with respect to the subjects with which any given process of government is supposed to deal. In some form or other, all the contestants in the social struggle take part in all the processes of government. The differences among the processes flow more from variations in the role of these various contestants than from any inherent limitations on the scope of the processes or the real powers of any of the contestants.

legislative action is required for the appropriation of funds from the Federal Treasury. Yet the device of setting up a Federal corporation has been developed for the purpose of avoiding, among other things, the annual appropriation process.[6]

While an appropriation may be used to provide the capital stock of a corporation, the initial legislation may also allow the corporation to borrow much larger amounts by selling securities to the Secretary of the Treasury or to private investors; these funds may be used then on a revolving basis. Once legislation of this type has been enacted there may be little or no need for its administrators ever to obtain appropriations; and subsequent requests for legislation may be limited to increases at irregular intervals in the ceilings set upon the borrowing and lending.

It is also regarded as axiomatic that a President cannot make a treaty without Senate ratification (which is a form of legislative action) or declare a war without congressional assent. And in both these cases the axiom corresponds accurately with the formalities of government; the administrative process cannot be used for anything called a treaty or called a declaration of war. But the administrative process can be used to achieve similar or identical ends through other means. The Atlantic Charter, promulgated by President Franklin D. Roosevelt and Prime Minister Winston Churchill, was a dramatic example of purely Executive action. Less dramatic but often fully as important in the arena of international power politics are Executive decisions to recognize this or that government, withdraw this or that ambassador, send a military mission to this country, or direct a Government lending corporation to make a loan to that country. As for military action, a President is Commander in Chief of the armed forces and as such can threaten, or participate in, war by moving military forces into foreign seas or territories. In an age of atomic or bacteriological warfare, moreover, no President would wait for a formal declaration of war before ordering our armed forces to retaliate against an enemy that had struck America. A formal declaration of war can always follow later. In fact,

[6] "The most significant privilege enjoyed by a full-fledged government corporation is its freedom from the customary rules about finance. . . . The government corporation furnishes a method of modifying these principles. A subscription by government to the capital stock of a corporation or an allocation of funds to the corporation removes the money from the Treasury and from annual appropriation control. The funds may be utilized until exhausted whether it takes one year or ten. Earnings of the corporation since they may be corporate funds rather than public revenues, need not be covered into the Treasury but may be retained in the custody of the corporation. They may then be spent at the discretion of the officers of the corporation, though only within the limits of corporate purposes fixed by the charter. If the corporation is engaged in a self-sustaining function, its revenues would enable it to operate on its own resources more or less indefinitely without annual subjection to the presidential and congressional power of the purse." V. O. Key, Jr., "Government Corporations," in Fritz Morstein Marx (ed.), "Elements of Public Administration" (New York: Prentice-Hall, 1946), pp. 244–245.

the exigencies of modern warfare may even make it necessary, in order to avert irreparable losses, for the President to order American forces to strike the first blow.[7]

Is legislation needed to confer on Government agencies new powers or responsibilities not already provided for under the Constitution and existing statutes? History is full of cases in which Executive officials, without waiting for legislative authorization, have taken actions never dreamed of under the Constitution or existing statutes. If the occasion is serious enough and if there are enough supporting interests and groups, Executive officials will often go far into uncharted seas. Was Franklin Roosevelt within his rights when he gave Great Britain 50 overage destroyers in exchange for a ninety-nine year lease of air and naval bases on British islands off the Atlantic Coast? While good lawyers wrote convincing briefs on both sides of the matter, the fact remains that the deed was done. Does the President have power to seize the coal mines or the steel mills when a prolonged strike has threatened to prostrate the economy? If such a strike lasts long enough, any President would take this action even if, like President Truman, he had vigorously opposed legislative action conferring upon him this specific power. In fact, most Presidents in recent decades feel that they are breaking no rules of the game if they take action which is not expressly forbidden by the Constitution or by statute.

This applies even to a relatively unaggressive President like Taft who went beyond specific authorization to bring into the public domain a large tract of land in California in which oil had been discovered. He assuaged his critics and his conscience by subsequently asking Congress for legislation to ratify his action, a procedure that is often used to solidify the administrative actions of Executive officials.

A more aggressive President like the first Roosevelt was less interested in legislative ratification. He wrote:

> I decline to adopt the view that what was imperatively necessary for the Nation could not be done by the President unless he could find some specific authorization to do it. My belief was that it was not only his right but his duty to do anything that the needs of the Nation demanded unless such action was forbidden by the Constitution

[7] In a bitter attack against the foreign policy of Franklin D. Roosevelt, Charles A. Beard complained that "The theory that the President has the power to determine foreign policy, support his policy by arms, and, without appealing to Congress for war authority, strike a designated enemy, has received approval in certain military, naval and civilian circles of the U.S." . . . and that "propaganda in universities, colleges and schools has deeply implanted in the minds of the rising generation the doctrine that the power of the President over international relations is, for all practical purposes, illimitable." Charles A. Beard, "President Roosevelt and the Coming of the War—1941" (New Haven, Conn.: Yale University Press, 1948), pp. 584, 590. Yet what Beard really objected to was the substantive character of the Roosevelt foreign policy. The words he uses are merely another illustration of the good old American habit of seasoning substantive arguments with charges of usurpation.

or by the laws. Under this interpretation of executive power I did and caused to be done many things not previously done by the President and the heads of the Departments. I did not usurp power, but I did greatly broaden the use of executive power. In other words, I acted for the public welfare, I acted for the common well-being of all our people, whenever and in whatever manner was necessary, unless prevented by direct constitutional or legislative prohibition. I did not care a rap for the mere form and show of power; I cared immensely for the use that could be made of the substance.[8]

Furthermore, it should be noted that there are many situations in which administrative action can be used in direct violation of clear-cut legislative or constitutional prescriptions. In fighting the Confederacy, Abraham Lincoln clearly broke the rules of the game when he took money from the Treasury without an appropriation, raised the size of the Army and Navy beyond their statutory limits, and suspended the writ of habeas corpus in various areas.[9] In time of war, martial law can be used to suspend the Bill of Rights itself. The history of Supreme Court decisions on questions of this type shows a strong probability that a majority of the Court will decline to rule against Executive action which seems justified by the situation and which enjoys sufficient support throughout the country.

Finally, administrative action can be used to repeal statutory provisions by the simple method of inaction. As Corwin has pointed out,

any particular statute is but a single strand of a vast fabric of laws demanding enforcement; nor—simply from the nature of the case—can all these be enforced with equal vigor, or with the same vigor at all times. So the President's duty to "take care that the laws be faithfully executed" has come to embrace a broad power of selection among the laws for this purpose; and that this power is today without statable limits the history of the Sherman Act alone is sufficient proof. In a word, the President's very obligation to the law becomes at times an authorization to *dispense with* the law.[10]

[8] Theodore Roosevelt, "Autobiography" (New York: Scribner, 1925), pp. 388–389.

[9] Lincoln justified his action as follows: "My oath to preserve the Constitution imposed on me the duty of preserving by every indispensable means that government, that nation, of which the Constitution was the organic law. Was it possible to lose the nation and yet preserve the Constitution? By general law life and limb must be protected, yet often a limb must be amputated to save a life, but a life is never wisely given to save a limb. I felt that measures, otherwise unconstitutional, might become lawful by becoming indispensable to the preservation of the Constitution through the preservation of the nation. Right or wrong, I assumed this ground and now avow it. I could not feel that, to the best of my ability, I had ever tried to preserve the Constitution, if to save slavery or any minor matter, I should permit the wreck of the government, country, and Constitution altogether." John G. Nicolay and John Hay, "Abraham Lincoln: A History" (New York: Century, 1890), Vol. X, pp. 65–68.

[10] Edward S. Corwin, "The President, Office and Powers" (New York: New York University Press, 1948), p. 149.

This applies to appropriation acts as well as other types of legislation. Although an appropriation is a mandate to spend, Executive officials can refuse to spend. Thus, the military appropriation bill for fiscal year 1950 appropriated funds for a fifty-eight-group Air Force, rather than the forty-eight-group Air Force backed by the Truman Administration. Although he was opposed to this provision, President Truman signed the measure instead of vetoing it. But at the time of signing it, he announced his intention of not spending the extra money. In a statement to the press he said:

> Increasing the structure of the Air Force above that recommended in the 1950 Budget would be inconsistent with a realistic and balanced security program which we can support in peacetime and would interfere with orderly planning for the three services based on a unified strategic concept. I am therefore directing the Secretary of Defense to place in reserve the amounts provided by the Congress in H.R. 4146 for increasing the structure of the Air Force.[11]

The "Exclusively Administrative." At the other extreme, it is commonly supposed that only the administrative process can be used for hiring and firing, dealing with the minutiae of organization and administration, and handling individual cases as opposed to general rules. Yet entirely apart from considerations of desirability, it is blunt fact that the legislative process can be used for each of these purposes. A bill can provide that certain officials meet given statutory requirements. When it is obvious that an incumbent official does not meet these requirements, its passage is equivalent to forcing resignation. By a reduction in the appropriations for a certain division or for a certain type of agency activity, whole groups of employees can be pushed out of government service or, at least, forced to look for other jobs. The only effective limitation on this device, one that can readily be circumvented, is that officials to be fired should not be mentioned by name.[12]

[11] White House press release, Oct. 29, 1949.

[12] In the notorious case of Lovett, Watson, and Dodd, a 1943 appropriation act prohibited all future employment of these three individuals by any agency of Government, except to positions for which they had been confirmed by the Senate. With no dissents, the Court ruled as follows: "Legislative acts, no matter what their form, that apply either to named individuals or to easily ascertainable members of a group in such a way as to inflict punishment on them without a judicial trial are bills of attainder prohibited by the Constitution. . . . When our Constitution and Bill of Rights were written, our ancestors had ample reason to know that legislative trials and punishments were too dangerous to liberty to exist in the nation of free men they envisioned. And so they proscribed bills of attainder. Section 304 is one. Much as we regret to declare that an Act of Congress violates the Constitution, we have no alternative here." (*United States v. Lovett,* 328 U.S. 303.) For a detailed review of this case, see Laurence E. Seibel, "Personal Liberties and the Appropriation Power of Congress," *George Washington Law Review,* Vol. 14, February, 1946, pp. 337–353. Seibel points out that despite judicial decisions, specific individuals could be eliminated from the Government service by a return to the system, used in the first few years

Legislative action can also extend into the minutiae of organization and administration. Appropriations for certain Departments allocate funds so closely to individual bureaus and divisions that the head of the Department has practically no leeway whatsoever to make organizational shifts in his own agency. Many an agency must obtain a special provision of law in order to buy a new car, enlarge its printing budget by $1,000, or subscribe to a few additional technical journals. Legislation for flood control and irrigation projects usually goes still further toward narrowing administrative discretion; individual dams are habitually listed by name together with the sum of money to be spent on each.

Until recently, whenever an army truck collided with Farmer Jones's cow on a country road, the War Department was unable to compensate the farmer for the damages. The poor farmer, if able to survive the deluge of red tape descending from the Adjutant General's office, would very likely call on his Congressman for help. The result would be a private bill for the relief of Farmer Jones. The multiplicity of such private claims, together with similar bills dealing with the grievances of individuals, resulted in the introduction of more than 3,700 private bills during the Seventy-ninth Congress, more than a third of all bills introduced. Almost 900 of these were enacted into law, more than half of all the Federal laws produced during 1945 and 1946. In an effort to relieve the Congress of this burden, the Legislative Reorganization Act of 1946 broadened the discretion of administrative agencies by allowing them to settle private claims up to $1,000. It also extended the jurisdiction of the United States district courts over claims of this nature. Nevertheless, the legislative route is still wide open, and the continued congressional consideration of multitudinous private bills indicates that neither aggrieved individuals nor members of Congress are averse to this overlapping of the legislative and administrative processes.

The Overlap with Other Processes

The area of choice is by no means limited to the overlap between the legislative and administrative processes. The social struggle is punctuated by innumerable instances of groups being faced with a choice of either using the legislative process or going to the courts, trying to obtain a constitutional amendment, seeking action by state or local governments, or carrying on their activities through private and nongovernmental channels.

The Judicial Process. In so far as questions of interpretation are concerned, the position of the judicial process in relation to the legislative process is that

of the Republic, of listing the names of those to be paid under an appropriation, ". . . a forerunner of further repressive legislation in the field of personal liberties."

of the inner circle of two concentric circles. There is nothing that can be done through a judicial decision that could not also be accomplished through legislative action. It could be argued that a judicial decision deals with an individual case rather than a general rule. The answer is that legislation can provide the general rule covering the individual case. A long history of judicial decisions on the Sherman Antitrust Act is one of judicial actions that were equivalent to a detailed series of amendments in the statute itself. The results of any of these decisions could have been attained by prior legislative action. Any of these decisions could have been subsequently reversed by legislative action.

One of the best illustrations of the overlapping between the legislative and judicial processes is to be found in the recent history of railroad legislation. In 1945 the major railroads of the country were attacked by antitrust suits on two major points. The state of Georgia brought an original suit before the Supreme Court charging Northern and Southern railroads with conspiring to maintain a freight-rate system which discriminated against Southern shippers. The Department of Justice launched a similar attack in a Federal district court in Nebraska, charging discrimination against the West. The railroads decided that a passive defense in the courts was not enough; they launched a counteroffensive by backing a bill to exempt the railroads from the antitrust laws and legalize any rate agreements that the railroads may make subject to certain vague controls by the Interstate Commerce Commission. The two efforts proceeded side by side for a number of years. But in June, 1948, the passage of the Bulwinkle bill exempted railroad rate-making practices from the antitrust laws, thus cutting the ground out from under the Supreme Court case. During the early debates on this measure, Senator Alben Barkley, then Senate Majority Leader, bewailed the use of legislation as a means of undercutting the judicial process. He complained:

> The introduction of such bills seems to have become a habit here. I think it is a vicious practice; I think it is a vicious habit; it ought never to have been indulged in. This measure involves the same principle as that involved in the insurance cases. It involves the same sort of situation as existed last week when the Senate passed a bill taking away from the courts its jurisdiction of passing on the tidelands controversies.[13]

A similar, though less lusty, complaint was voiced by President Truman two years later in his veto of the measure.[14] Yet Truman's opposition was not strong enough to stop the congressional supporters of the railroads from overriding his veto. In doing what Truman found "inappropriate" and Barkley, "vicious," they violated none of the rules of the game.

On questions of constitutionality, the relationship of the judicial process to

[13] *Congressional Record,* 79th Cong., 2d Sess., July 27, 1946.

[14] Veto message, June 10, 1948.

the legislative process is one of overlapping rather than concentric circles. The judicial process can be used to annul state and local laws that are beyond the jurisdiction of the national legislative process. The legislative process, on its part, obviously extends far beyond acts of negation and annulment. The area of overlapping—and it is a fairly extensive one—covers all those cases where the Supreme Court can overthrow a Federal law on the ground of unconstitutionality. In such cases, direct legislative repeal is an obvious alternative to judicial action.

Constitutional Amendment. The problem of choice often arises as one of whether a given objective can be achieved through legislation or whether it is first necessary to enlarge the powers of the Federal government through a constitutional amendment.

One of the most historic battles of this type centered around the issue of the income tax. In 1895 legislation was enacted imposing a 2 per cent tax on all incomes over $2,000. A year later a bare majority of five members of the Supreme Court ruled the law unconstitutional. Despite widespread assault, the courts succeeded in blocking off use of the legislative process for two decades until finally, during the Wilson Administration, the Sixteenth Amendment to the Constitution gave Congress and the President specific power to pluck the previously forbidden fruit.

In more recent decades, however, the tendency has been for the Supreme Court majority to sanction the use of the legislative process without prior amendment of the Constitution. An excellent example is found in the history of efforts to have the Federal government prohibit child labor, under the interstate-commerce or the taxing clauses. In 1916 a Supreme Court majority overthrew a Federal anti-child-labor statute on the ground that it exceeded the powers given to the Federal government under the Constitution. As a result, the proponents of this reform embarked on the long and weary path toward having the constitutional amendment approved by two-thirds of the Congress and three-fourths of the state legislatures. Although the first of these objectives was achieved in 1924, it proved impossible to obtain favorable action by enough states. In 1933 the legislative route was again assayed, this time through one of the provisions of the National Industrial Recovery Act. When this Act was itself declared unconstitutional in 1935, it again appeared as though the arduous task of obtaining an amendment to the Constitution must once again be resumed. Yet the opposition within the state legislatures was still strong. In 1937, more than twenty years after the first effort had been blocked, another attempt to use the legislative process was tried. The vehicle was the Fair Labor Standards Act which, in the words of its advocates, consisted of "a floor for wages, a ceiling for hours, and a break for children." In 1941 the Court finally withdrew from the contest by reversing previous rulings and upholding this statute.

Similar decisions in one field after the other have overthrown judicial limitations upon legislative action. In fact, the use of the legislative process coupled with a favorable decision by a Supreme Court majority is not only an alternative to the process of constitutional amendment; for all intents and purposes it constitutes the major way in which we go about amending our Constitution.

State or Local Action. The extent of overlapping between the national legislative process and the processes of state and local governments has been largely determined by the Supreme Court's changing conception of constitutional limitations upon what can be accomplished through Federal action.

There was a time when almost any Federal legislation attempting extensive regulation of industry would be overthrown by a court on the ground that it was an exercise of power reserved to the states and not expressly dedicated to the Federal government. In 1933, for example, the Agricultural Adjustment Act established a system of acreage control as a method of avoiding "overproduction" of farm products and keeping farm prices from falling too low. In 1935, when one Supreme Court decision after another torpedoed New Deal statutes, the Roosevelt Administration tried to protect the Triple A through a set of amendments toning down the original Act. Despite this protective action, a thunderous decision in January, 1936, declared the Act null and void on the ground that the power to regulate agricultural production was a power reserved to the states.[15]

On the heels of the Supreme Court's 1936 decision, President Roosevelt promptly announced his Administration's determination to continue the agricultural adjustment program or "its equivalent." With the cooperation of farm leaders, a new bill was drawn up which regulated acreage control to soil conservation and provided for administration through the states rather than by the Federal government directly. The bill became a law on March 1, less than three months after the Court had ruled that this objective could not be achieved by legislation. This time the acreage-control program weathered all assaults by appeals in the courts. By 1938 the power to regulate agriculture through Federal legislation was so fully accepted by the Court that the Roosevelt Administration was able to obtain a new act superseding the 1936 statute and vastly expanding the Government's activities in the control of agricultural production.

By a long series of decisions in other cases the Court has interpreted almost every form of Federal regulatory action as falling within the province of the constitutional provision authorizing Congress to regulate commerce among the several states. One might go so far as to say that the commerce power has been interpreted so broadly and interstate commerce now affects so many aspects of our economy that it appears very unlikely that future Federal legislation dealing with economic problems will be declared unconstitutional. This

[15] Hoosac Mills decision.

series of decisions has been accompanied by the growing use of Federal grants to state and local governments. By the grant-in-aid device, Federal legislation can provide indirectly for many activities—such as aid to education—in areas where any proposal for direct Federal operations would evoke a storm of organized and unbeatable opposition.

The issue of states' rights versus a powerful Federal government has become, as Wendell Willkie pointed out in 1944, not an issue but a relic.[16] In the same way, the constitutional reference in the Tenth Amendment to powers that are "reserved to the States respectively, or to the people" is hopelessly out of date, for there is no limit on what the Federal government can do through legislation, given sufficient support among private organizations and the members of Congress, executive agencies, and the Supreme Court. The old quip that the British Parliament can do everything but make a woman a man and a man a woman is now almost fully applicable to the national government in the United States.

Private Action. With respect to a large portion of private conflicts, there is little if any recourse to national legislation. This is particularly true of breaches of contract between private parties, where the obvious method of carrying the conflict into public channels is the use of the courts. Yet the more significant any private conflict becomes, the greater are the possibilities that one or another contestant can attempt to gain his objectives through national legislation. In fact, the legislative process is to a large extent a reflection of conflicts between private organizations. The history of labor legislation, for example, is mainly a story of the attempts of both organized labor and employers to attain through the legislative process advantages which they have sought through the nongovernmental processes of collective bargaining. In the same way business and agricultural organizations have not been content to rely upon market competition but have sought legislative action to fortify their position in the business struggle. Thus, the airlines have consistently attempted through legislation to prevent railroads and shipping companies from entering the field of air transportation.

Ballots or Bullets. Both the electoral process and its violent counterpart, revolution, are methods of effectuating changes in the top leadership of government. As such they are not on the same plane of relevance as the legislative process, since they deal with the shift of power from group to group rather than with any group's use of power. Nevertheless, there is a real area of overlapping between these and the legislative process. In the course of the legislative struggle choices are always arising as to whether given ends can be attained through legislation or whether it is not necessary first to effectuate a change in the personnel of government. The extent to which these choices arise and the character of the choice depend not upon any rules or traditions but upon how

[16] Quoted in *The New York Times,* June 12, 1944.

much shift in power and resources is contemplated. Generally speaking, if one aims at a minor shift in power and resources, the legislative process is adequate to the task—although even in such circumstances the defeat or reelection of even one Congressman who is in a strategic position may be helpful. If a greater shift in power and resources is sought, such as legislation which takes long strides toward increasing the power of either organized labor or organized business, legislative action may be impossible until there has been an electoral change in the Presidency or in the composition of Congress. If an extremely radical shift is contemplated, such as the expropriation without compensation of the means of production or the placing of political power in the hands of a fascist dictatorship, then resort to violence would probably be needed as an adjunct of, a preliminary to, or a substitute for, legislative action.

Advantages in the Legislative Process

Among the obvious considerations in the minds of those who ponder whether or not to travel on the legislative highway are the smoothness of the road and the amount of assistance they are likely to obtain along the wayside. When it is believed that a large number of Senators or Representatives will be friendly to a given proposal, there is more reason to seek its embodiment in a bill. Thus, during World War II, business groups that regarded themselves as unduly injured by the "hold-the-line" philosophy of the Office of Price Administration made a habit of floating anti-OPA bills and amendments among their many friends in Congress. When there is slight chance of developing support in Congress, this is reason to drop the idea entirely or use some other avenue. The opponents of early New Deal legislation, for example, made no attempts to seek repeal through legislative action, confining their efforts largely to appeals before the Supreme Court.

Considerations of this type involve an analysis of the disposition of opposing forces and of the best use of one's own available resources. But there are other important considerations that flow more directly from the character of the legislative process itself. To carry the military metaphor one step further, one might say they involve a topographical analysis of the terrain. Apart from the strategic location of friends, enemies, and neutrals, there are unquestioned advantages to be found in the legislative terrain itself. Some of these relate to the mere act of having a bill irrespective of whether the bill ever blossoms into a statute. Some relate to the value of a statute, even under circumstances where the identical objective could be achieved through other processes.

The Importance of a Bill

As a Publicity Device. Introducing a bill in Congress is one of the time-honored methods through which a Senator or Representative can improve his position with constituents and interest groups. In fact, the great majority of bills are not seriously regarded by their congressional sponsors. The process of introducing a bill is easy and painless. It is not even necessary to obtain recognition on the floor. Proposed measures need merely be given to a page boy or carried over to the Bill Clerk in either house. No clearance is needed through any party or congressional machinery. The act of introduction constitutes no commitment as to whether its sponsor will ever lift a finger to advance its progress on the legislative highway. If no action is ever taken on a bill, it is no discredit to the sponsor; most bills die in committee. If there is a chance that it might strike a spark among enough groups to become a going proposition, then there is nothing lost in taking the gamble. The sponsor is in the same position as a millionaire who puts a few dollars on a long shot in a horse race or takes a flier on the stock market. There have even been cases when a member of Congress has introduced a bill for the dual purpose of placing himself in a strategic position to exercise decisive influence to *prevent* its enactment, thereby maintaining the favor of its opponents as well as of its supporters.

One of the reasons why the introduction of a bill can serve as a real favor to an interest group or government agency is its unquestioned value as an educational and propaganda instrument. A bill provides a very concrete symbol to serve as a rallying point for a campaign, whether the purpose be to set up a world government or to increase the pensions of the widows of Spanish-American War veterans. Its official format and trappings give it an important public-relations value. There is nothing like a bill to show that you mean business. It is a good thing around which to organize a campaign, to refer to in a speech, or to mail with a pamphlet. From the viewpoint of those interested in making a living through the conduct of a legislative campaign it is a way of obtaining employment with private organizations, members of Congress, or executive agencies. From the viewpoint of a sponsor, a bill is a good way to supplement a speech and to get a better break in the press or on the radio.

As a Counterweight. A bill is an ideal instrument for warding off charges of negativism and demonstrating that you have a constructive position. It is hard to fight something with nothing. During the Eightieth Congress many of the Senators who were leading the fight against the Taft-Hartley Labor-Management Relations Act introduced an alternative bill of their own. From the political viewpoint, they simply could not afford to be put in a position where it would be charged that they were always against legislation in the labor field and never had any constructive proposals to offer. In the same way, the Senators who led the fight against the Truman Administration's health-insurance legislation could not afford to be in the position of being against the people's health. The logic of the situation called for an alternative measure, and the result was the National Health Bill introduced by Senator Taft and others.[17]

Sometimes following the principle that "you can't fight something with nothing" requires little more than an informal proposal. In January, 1949, for example, Senator Paul Douglas of Illinois was confronted with the problem of what to do about a Veterans Economic Development Corporation Bill which had been referred to a Senate banking and currency subcommittee of which he was chairman. The bill was something of a legislative monstrosity. It proposed to set up a new and heavily financed government corporation which would provide for veterans various services already being made available to broader segments of the population by the Reconstruction Finance Corporation, the Veterans Administration, the Housing and Home Finance Agency, the Departments of Agriculture and Commerce, and many other agencies. The bill was bitterly opposed by all these organizations and by the Bureau of the Budget. Nor did it commend itself to those who were concerned with cutting down special preferential treatment for veterans and developing instead a broad and more balanced array of governmental services. The key proponent of the bill, Colonel Richmond Harris, working in conjunction with the Veterans of Foreign Wars, had brought together a formidable amount of paper support for the measure. Nineteen Senators had been cajoled into serving as sponsors, including the Vice-President-elect, Senator Alben Barkley, and the chairman of the full Banking and Currency Committee, Senator Burnet Maybank of South Carolina. In fact, Senator Maybank had already announced his intention of reporting favorably on the bill to the floor in the near future. Confronted with this situation, Senator Douglas was naturally reluctant to place himself in a position of direct frontal opposition to the measure in the subcommittee. Yet he was equally reluctant to go along on a measure that ran counter to his best judgment and which was so strongly opposed by the executive agencies. The way out of the dilemma was the preparation in draft form of a substitute measure which directed existing governmental agencies to take special precautions against the possibility that the interests of veterans might be neglected in the administration of their programs. To give the bill additional substance, a provision was inserted expanding the lending resources of

[17] "The bill is a political measure only, an assist to Senator Taft's Presidential campaign. It records him as favoring a national health program, which should get him a lot of lay votes, and it assures organized medicine that he wants the program left entirely to its control, which lines up one of the most powerful pressure groups in the United States in his support." Bernard De Voto, "Doctors along the Boardwalk," *Harper's Magazine*, September, 1947, p. 222.

the Reconstruction Finance Corporation. Senator Douglas then sent the draft bill around to various people for comment. This action served to complicate what was previously a straightforward but one-sided issue ("muddied the waters" is the phrase the Veterans of Foreign Wars probably used). As a result of the difficulties involved in reconciling the two drafts, action on the initial proposal was indefinitely postponed.

As an Intellectual Stimulus or Expression. The introduction of a bill is one of the best ways of getting attention in the highly competitive market place of ideas. A bill can serve as an ideal trial balloon for executive officials who are wary of taking a given course of action—particularly if the bill can be planted in Congress in such a manner as to leave the officials who originated the idea free from any responsibility for its preparation. Irrespective of reactions to a bill, the very fact that one or more members of the Congress may introduce it can itself serve to indicate potential support for a given course of action. Furthermore, the availability of the legislative process for the launching of new ideas is one of the factors that helps to protect the Government against hardening of the arteries. In every large governmental organization, there are occasions when people of the highest ability and the greatest creativity find themselves traveling up a dead-end street. Whenever they attempt to get their views before the attention of responsible officials of the highest echelons they find themselves boxed in by intervening superiors who refuse to pass papers along and who issue peremptory instructions on the importance of keeping one's mouth shut. Many a repressed bureaucrat has escaped these restrictions by passing on his ideas in legislative form to a Representative or Senator, either directly or through the intermediary of a private organization. This is all highly irregular, of course, and deserves to be frowned upon by all who believe that the Government should be operated in accordance with organizational blueprints. But in balance it probably adds considerably to the vitality of governmental processes.

Another fundamental advantage of the legislative route is its value in the formulative stages of a program. Since the executive branch of the Government has grown faster than its machinery for the coordinated formulation of executive policies, the only clearinghouse that operates regularly between the multitudinous departments and bureaus is the Legislative Reference Division of the Bureau of the Budget. Under these circumstances sometimes the only possible way to get government agencies working together is by having a draft bill circulated or having a bill introduced unofficially through a friendly Congressman. Agency reactions to it can then be brought together through the Budget Bureau clearance process.

Apart from their need for coordination machinery, many ideas can never be properly crystallized unless they are put into bill form and are thereby subjected to public analysis. The experts who prepare a memo within a government agency can usually coast along on the knowledge that it will be subjected to the criticism of no more than a limited number of officials. When the same men draft a bill, however, they know that their handiwork must be able to withstand the slings and arrows of a far wider circle. They must weigh more precisely the effect of their proposals upon conflicting interests and gauge more accurately the total implications of any course of action that is recommended. This aspect of the legislative process is important irrespective of whether or not the ideas embodied in a bill are finally enacted into law.

In Expediting Executive or Judicial Action. The legislative process can also expedite executive or judicial action. In 1943 Senators Maloney, Taft, and Scrugham introduced a bill aimed at stimulating more attention by the war agencies to questions of civilian supply. During the hearings before the Senate Banking and Currency Committee, testimony brought out many important defects in the operations of the civilian-supply division of the War Production Board. While the chairman of the War Production Board, Donald Nelson, opposed the measure, he took vigorous action independently to achieve the objectives of the bill by strengthening the WPB's civilian-supply division. The bill went through the Senate, but by the time it got to the House it was evident that the case for it had disappeared.

One of the great legislative battles in recent years was centered around President Franklin Roosevelt's highly controversial "court-packing" bill. The purpose of this measure was to change the character of the Supreme Court's decisions by adding more Roosevelt appointees to the bench. Roosevelt lost the legislative battle. But he clearly won the war; for the conflict that developed over the legislation was credited with being instrumental in bringing about the Supreme Court's dramatic reversals in decisions on New Deal legislation.

In Election Campaigns. The use of the legislative process can also be a vital factor in electoral campaigns. Perhaps a classic example is the anti-inflation program which President Truman sent to the Eightieth Congress in November, 1947. Among other proposals of a more or less technical nature, Truman called for the reimposition of price control on a selective basis. There was considerable doubt in the minds of its proponents as to whether or not a price-control act could be administered and enforced—but no doubt whatsoever that enactment of a price-control law by the Eightieth Congress was inconceivable. Nevertheless, by pressing for the inconceivable, the President succeeded in dramatically divesting himself of any responsibility for inflationary price increases, thus putting the Republican leaders of the Eightieth Congress squarely on the spot. By so doing he created an invaluable campaign issue, one that probably meant a large number of additional votes from housewives and low-income families generally. If he had not pressed the legislative fight for price control so vigorously, it is possible that Dewey would have been elected President in November, 1948.[18]

The Importance of a Law

There is something very compelling about a Federal law. It is a document that presumably has the force of the American government behind it. As a pronouncement that has had the approval of a large number of the elected representatives of the American people, it has an aura of prestige and sanctity about it.

To appreciate the attraction exercised by the hope of attaining a law, it is not enough to think of cases where legislation is sought in order to provide an "Open sesame" to the Federal Treasury or a key to a toolbox of Federal powers that would otherwise remain securely locked. Even more revealing are the legislative battles themselves which have centered around objectives that could have been achieved through another route.

As a "Mandate." The struggle over the Employment Act of 1946 was one of the most sharply fought legislative battles during President Truman's first year in the White House. The key provisions of this legislation, in the form first endorsed by the Truman Administration, consisted of a resounding declaration of the Government's responsibility to "assure continuing full employment" and a procedure whereby for the first time the President of the United States would transmit to Congress at the beginning of every regular session a comprehensive economic program. Neither of these provisions necessarily called for legislation. The only objective of the bill that could not have been achieved by Executive action was the provision setting up a Joint Congressional Committee to study the President's economic program, and this could have been accomplished by a simple concurrent resolution of Congress. The opponents of the bill were quick to point this out, contending that the objectives of the provisions could be achieved through Presidential action alone.

Representative Carter Manasco made this the first point in his cross-exam-

18 The fight over price control in the 80th Congress had an interesting epilogue in 1949. Shortly after the Truman election victory, when it became evident that prices were leveling off, Truman was left in the paradoxical position of having campaigned vigorously for something that was no longer a pressing necessity. Nevertheless, if the fight for price control had been suddenly dropped like a hot potato immediately after the election, the President would have opened himself to charges of insincere campaigning. Accordingly, although the case for the reimposition of price control was no longer as valid as when he had first made it, he renewed his request in his messages to Congress in January, 1949. No sooner had he done so than prices began to turn down of their accord and his proposal fell on even more barren ground in the Democratic 81st Congress than it had in the Republican 80th Congress. Yet the introduction of price-control legislation in 1949 had the merit of helping to keep the record straight.

ination of Harold Smith, Director of the Budget, who was the Administration's leadoff witness in the hearings before the House Committee on Expenditures in the Executive Departments.[19] The Budget Director, however, had anticipated this attack in his prepared statement. His line of defense was as follows:

> Some critics say that no law is needed to authorize the President to transmit estimates of the Nation's Budget and recommendations for a coordinated program. They say that the President can transmit and, as a matter of fact, has transmitted estimates of the Nation's Budget and policy recommendations under existing power and authority. It is true that recent Presidential Budget Messages have moved in the direction of the requirements of this bill. This proves, not that the bill is superfluous, but that it is in line with present needs and developments. The appraisals and recommendations required by this bill are of such importance that, in my judgment, they should be transmitted not merely at the discretion of the President, but should become part of his statutory responsibility.

Behind this argument lay a realization that any President, in moving along the lines contemplated by the proposed measure, would much prefer to operate under the provisions of a statute rather than on his own initiative. In the former case he would be merely complying with a procedure agreed to by the Congress. In the latter, he would always run the risk that congressional leaders would attack him for trying to foist upon them some new and foreign kind of economic planning.

The Budget Director's defense, however, was not a complete one. In countering Representative Manasco's question, he confined himself to the procedural aspects of the bill.

A central Administration purpose of the legislation was to obtain specific congressional endorsement of the concept that the Government has a very high degree of responsibility in stabilizing the national economy. It was felt that an endorsement of this type, while having no legal value in the narrow sense, would serve as a psychological springboard from which the Administration could launch many of its individual economic programs dealing with social security, health, resource development, monopoly, taxation, and other economic matters. Conservative groups throughout the country claimed that enactment of the bill with its original strong declaration of policy would lead people to expect too much from the Federal government, and would undermine the foundations of capitalistic free enterprise in America. This point of view made considerable headway in Congress, and by the time the bill became law the declaration of policy was toned down to a carefully qualified statement that aroused very little public expectation of aggressive Government action.

A still more clear-cut example of the value of a legislative mandate was provided in 1944 by the Fulbright and Connally resolutions on foreign policy.

[19] "Full Employment Act of 1945," Hearings before the House Committee on Expenditures in the Executive Departments, 79th Cong., 1st Sess., Sept. 25, 1945.

Both these resolutions consisted of reiterations of policy statements previously made by President Roosevelt and Secretary of State Cordell Hull. Neither added anything to the substance of American foreign policy as proclaimed by the executive heads of the Government. Nor did they have much legal significance. Nevertheless, they proved invaluable in laying the basis for public understanding of the need for international cooperation and for subsequent congressional acceptance of the Administration's work in the formation of the United Nations.

As an Aid in Administration. Richard E. Neustadt, an acute and informed observer, writes:

> Generally speaking, an administrator who wants to undertake a new program gains by prior Congressional sanction quite as much as Congress gains by demonstrating its authority. The more specific the sanction the better. It backs up the administrator. It lightens his load of counter pressures. The fight for Congressional approval enables him to test in advance the forces behind him and in his way. The terms on which approval is obtained give him a blueprint of the alignment of interests with which he will have to deal.[20]

Another example is supplied by James M. Landis:

> Frequently the administration is faced with the need to exercise a power that lies within the limits of its statutory grant; but the subject matter happens to be of such great public concern that it is desirable to have the more direct democratic processes of our government participate in the decision. An illustration from another field may serve to give point to this problem. Under the statutory authority that had already been granted to him, the President had the power to commit the nation to large expenditures in connection with the Florida Ship Canal. The project, however, partly because of the amount of expenditure that it entails and partly because it had for various reasons already become the subject of political debate and conflicting allegiance, differed considerably from the regular public works projects to which the President was authorized to allocate public monies. For these reasons it was an act of political wisdom to put back upon the shoulders of the Congress the basic question as to the desirability of allocating the money necessary for the development of this project.[21]

The lack of a specific legislative mandate can often impair the effectiveness of an executive agency involved in conflicts with other agencies. At an important point in the development of the war production program, for example, the War Production Board officials became convinced that it was necessary to cut back the War Department's plans for building new plants. They pointed out that the Department's construction program would drain needed materials and labor out of current industrial production, and insisted that more emphasis should be placed on better utilization of existing plant facilities. The generals

[20] Richard E. Neustadt, "Presidential Clearance of Legislation" (unpublished doctoral dissertation, Harvard University, June, 1950).

[21] *Op. cit.*, pp. 76–77.

not only protested the WPB's authority to order a curtailment of War Department activity; they made the case that the chairman of the War Production Board received his authority merely on the basis of an Executive order of the President. The War Department, in contrast, received its authority directly from an appropriation act which authorized it to spend money as it saw fit. The importance of this argument cannot be weighed on any legal scales. The fact of the matter is that, to any bureaucrat, statutory authority flowing directly from legislation is regarded far more highly than authority flowing through the intermediate office of the President. This was one of the reasons why legislation was sought, through the War Mobilization and Reconversion Act, to provide a basis for the coordinating functions of the Office of War Mobilization and Reconversion.

As a Basis for Appropriations. A new legislative mandate can always be of value in enhancing the chances of executive agencies in obtaining increased appropriations from Congress. At every session many bills are introduced authorizing or directing this or that agency to undertake activities that it has always been empowered to undertake. To the outside observer these bills seem meaningless. The purpose, however, is usually to mobilize additional support for increased appropriations. The original legislation creating the Bureau of Mines, for example, clearly authorized it to engage in research on all aspects of fuel resources. Yet, during the Eightieth Congress, Interior Department officials arranged to have introduced in Congress a synthetic-liquid-fuels bill providing for up to 30 million dollars to be spent by the Bureau of Mines in experimentation on methods of deriving synthetic liquid fuels from coal and oil shales. With the support of the legislative committees dealing with Interior Department affairs, the bill became law. As a result, the Bureau of Mines was able to obtain Budget Bureau support for a budget request for this purpose and a subsequent appropriation. Without this substantive legislation, which in fact served to restrict the authority of the Bureau of Mines (inasmuch as it set a ceiling on expenditures for synthetic-liquid-fuels research), it is doubtful whether funds for this purpose could have been obtained without a few more years of agitation.

During its brief tenure of existence between 1941 and 1946, the Fair Employment Practices Committee was engaged in a continuous struggle for survival against Southern Democrats who sought to cut off its appropriations. At the outset, funds for the FEPC were obtained from the reserve made available to President Roosevelt for unrestricted wartime expenditures. In 1944, the Southern Democrats wrote into the Independent Offices Appropriations Act a provision forbidding the use of any appropriations whatsoever to pay the expenses of any agency created by Executive order after it had been in existence for a year, unless "the Congress has specifically authorized the expenditure of funds" for this purpose.[22] If the FEPC had received a specific appropriation in the first place, it would have been in a stronger position. Once it was forced to seek its funds through appropriation acts rather than from the President's own funds, it then suffered from the fact that it was an agency operating under an Executive order only, rather than under a statute. Accordingly, a vigorous effort was made to enact legislation giving the FEPC a statutory basis. While this legislation also had the purpose of strengthening its powers and extending its tenure into the postwar period, its most immediate purpose was to help in the struggle for appropriations. All these purposes were frustrated, however, for the bill never became a law, and the agency was terminated by an appropriation provision in 1945 which gave the agency funds for the purposes of liquidation only.

Disadvantages in the Legislative Process

The advantages discussed above are all relative rather than absolute. In any particular situation there are likely to be as many disadvantages in the use of the legislative process as there are advantages, some relating to the hazards of the process itself and some to the futility or disutility of any statute that may eventuate. This necessitates a careful weighing of potential gains and losses rather than automatic decision on a priori grounds.

Here again it is important to point out that appraisals of the legislative terrain cannot be disassociated from judgments made in terms of the disposition of forces. A beachhead which may be beautifully adapted to the landing of large numbers of troops and motorized equipment may also afford an ideal opportunity for opposing forces, if they can reach the vicinity, to crush the attackers.

The Uphill Grind

Delays. The legislative highway is neither short nor easy. Rather it is a long, uphill grind over dangerous terrain with booby traps and pitfalls all along the way. Traffic congestion alone can mean protracted delays. The number of twists and bends in the road is almost endless. At every turn in the road action can be held up by new points of view, new facts, new attacks, new grouping of forces, complex amendments, and alternative proposals. Moreover, the road may be blocked by the opposition of a small minority of Senators and Representatives in strategic positions. Sometimes even a single member can completely stall the progress of a bill either in committee or on the floor. Roland Young has pointed out that this time element is one of the reasons why executive officials often choose the administrative rather than the legislative process.

[22] Public Law 358, June 27, 1944.

Instances continually recur where the position of the President would be bolstered by securing the consent of the Congress to a proposal. This procedure would give Congress a real opportunity to deliberate on and to decide many crucial political problems. And being a political body, Congress should decide these problems. In making decisions, however, the element of time is important, and Congress is not now organized so that it can be relied on to give a quick answer to a problem.[23]

Boomerangs. Another danger is the ever-present possibility that the very act of seeking legislation of one type may stimulate legislative action of the opposite kind. Consider the attitude taken by organized labor toward new labor legislation during the decade between the passage of the Wagner National Labor Relations Act and the Taft-Hartley Labor-Management Relations Act of 1948. It was not long after the passage of the first Act that the leaders of organized labor realized that certain amendments were necessary. Nevertheless, they formed an almost unbroken united front in opposing any and all proposals for an amendment. They steadfastly maintained this position despite a growing outcry on the part of management that organized labor should take a more positive attitude and map out the legislative changes that they would be willing to see made. There is no doubt that this standpat attitude deprived labor leaders of considerable public support that they might have obtained through a more positive and cooperative attitude. They knew, however, that if they should once approve a set of acceptable amendments, the floodgate would be opened and there would be no way to prevent a deluge of destructive amendments. This approach, however unpalatable from the viewpoint of public relations, was clearly grounded on accurate understanding of the legislative facts of life. It yielded concrete results for labor during the legislative work on the 1947 statute, for this stubborn opposition to all legislation unquestionably was an important factor in the Senate's action in toning down considerably the provisions of the bill as it passed the House of Representatives.

One of the most informed observers of the governmental processes finds a disinclination among executive officials to use the legislative process. He writes:

Government agencies hesitate to seek modifications from Congress. They will rather indulge in improvisations and patiently endure the oddest kinds of legal limitation. The reason is obvious. They never know what will emerge from the legislative mill once it begins to turn. Except for the most important questions on which broad public discussion and understanding may be brought to bear, the administrative tendency is to limp along on the existing legal basis, no matter how unsatisfactory it may be. It is regarded as better than to arouse sleeping dogs.[24]

An illustration of the unpredictability of what may emerge from the legislative mill is to be found in the behind-the-scenes maneuvering on the Civilian

[23] Roland A. Young, "This Is Congress" (New York: Knopf, 1946), p. 24.
[24] V. O. Key, Jr., "Legislative Control," in Marx (ed.), *op. cit.*, p. 351.

Supply Bill, referred to earlier in this chapter. The introduction of this measure in the first place was encouraged by various assistants of Donald Nelson who saw in it an opportunity to provide a legislative foundation for the operations of the War Production Board. To their chagrin, however, the congressional sponsors of the measure listened to other advisers and wrote into the bill instead a provision taking the civilian-supply functions away from the War Production Board and setting them up in a new agency. If Donald Nelson's assistants had had any premonition that this might develop, they never would have encouraged the project in the first place and it is probable that the legislation would never have been introduced.

This observation needs supplementation on two scores. Executive disinclination to arouse sleeping dogs can be a means of either frustrating an organized majority of Congress or of preventing an organized minority from dominating a government program. Also, this attitude on the part of executive officials is by no means exclusive to officialdom. It often reflects a strong disinclination on the part of the leaders of some private organizations and of certain members of Congress themselves to use the legislative process.

Another boomerang is the possibility that seeking legislative action may close other routes. In cases where there is a legal doubt concerning the power of the executive branch to achieve a given objective, the act of seeking clear-cut legal authority tends to imply the inadequacy of existing authority. Failure to obtain clarification may be regarded either as conclusive evidence that the doubt should be resolved against the executive branch or that the desired course of action is contrary to the views of the majority of Congress. This danger was undoubtedly one of the factors that led President Franklin Roosevelt to handle on his own the destroyer deal with Great Britain rather than request enabling legislation.

Hollow Victories

A Federal law is after all only a piece of paper with a number, a great many words, and three names signed at the bottom. Whether or not it has any really compelling force behind it depends on the precision with which it is drawn, the will and ability of those who are supposed to administer it, the extent to which the right people know about it, and the amount of organized or potential support it commands. Although many laws are the product of a significant and continuing aggregation of groups and forces, there is, however, as Bentley has pointed out,

> a great deal of "grand-stand-play" law on the federal statute books. . . . There is also much dead-letter law, forgotten by the law officers of the government as well as by the people, which in the terminology of this book is not real law at all, but merely occupies

a favored position, so that with less formality it can again become law if popular initiative or federal attorneys in a representative capacity choose to invoke it.[25]

The day that the Interstate Commerce Act was enacted was an occasion for rejoicing among the farmers and shipping interests, who felt they had won the battle against the malpractices of the railroads. Today the hollowness of this victory is clear. Instead of operating as an agency to control the railroads in the public interest, the Interstate Commerce Commission serves largely as an instrument to protect the railroads. Every time amendments to the interstate commerce legislation have been enacted giving the Commission more regulatory authority, the Commission has exercised its discretion to refrain from using its new powers. Specific instructions which would have resulted in reduction of freight rates or elimination of discriminations have met with interminable delays.[26]

The entire history of antitrust legislation points up the fact that the passage of a statute may produce little more than words on a piece of paper. The original Sherman Antitrust Act stood for years without any real attempt to enforce it. Bentley analyzed the production of this law as follows:

> The enactment of the Sherman law represented a certain stage in a certain group struggle. The presidency stood aligned with the groups which opposed the enactment of such a statute—the fact that a president's signature was appended to the law does not alter this situation. . . . As time went on, the presidency, through certain of the department heads, took gradual steps toward representing the interests in favor of the law. In recent years we have seen the law invoked more vigorously than before, till now we may say in this matter that the presidency is representing the groupings that favor the law much more than those against it. The more or less comes into operation because of the complexity of the agencies united in the presidency.[27]

A more up-to-date appraisal would show that at various times in subsequent years it once again became a meaningless scrap of paper.

In the case of some legislation—and this is true of course of the Sherman Antitrust Act—the responsibility for enforcement does not lie only with executive officials; private parties can also appeal to the courts. But there is a broad realm of statutory law in which judicial action is irrelevant and in which executive officials can completely nullify the enactment. In cases where the effectiveness of the law calls for subsequent appropriations, the refusal of adequate appropriations can carve the innards out of a statute. The Employment Act of 1946 provides another example of the same thing. Its passage was a great victory for all those who believed that the Federal government

[25] Arthur F. Bentley, "The Process of Government" (Bloomington, Ind.: Principia Press, 1949 reissue), p. 353.

[26] On relations between the ICC and the railroads, see Samuel P. Huntington, "Clientalism in Administrative Politics" (unpublished doctoral dissertation, Harvard University, 1951).

[27] Bentley, *op. cit.*, p. 354.

must assume a high degree of responsibility for the stabilization and expansion of the national economy. While the commitment to maintain full employment was weaker than in the original Full Employment Bill, it did represent a long step forward in the enunciation of the Government's economic responsibilities. Yet the bill can well be compared to a check for a large amount signed by a man who has little money in the bank and no intention of making any immediate deposits. Its passage was immediately followed by a series of measures which wrecked the Government's stabilization machinery and precipitated the serious 1946–1948 inflationary boom. Nor did the bill's provisions for congressional machinery meet with any more respect in the initial years than its declaration of policy. The legislation clearly provided that on a given date, shortly after Congress receives the President's Economic Report, the Joint Congressional Committee on the Economic Report should submit to both houses "its findings and recommendations on the major recommendations of the President." Yet when President Truman sent his first Economic Report to Congress, the Joint Committee, all of whose members had voted for the legislation, cavalierly ignored the "mandate of the people." On the appointed day, the Committee brought forth a *pro forma* report that included neither findings nor recommendations but merely pointed out that the President's proposals were of a controversial nature.

Chapter 10

LEGISLATIVE PARENTHOOD

IT IS a few seconds after the noon hour.

The Presiding Officer raps his gavel sharply. The early comers here and there in the chamber lower their eyes, bow their heads, and the Chaplain invokes the blessings of God upon the United States Senate.

The moment the prayer is over there is a confused bustle. A motion is made to approve the Journal for the previous day without reading it. One clerk mumbles an announcement about a conference report that has been disapproved by the House. Another reads the title of a measure that has been received from the President. A half-dozen Senators seek recognition from the Chair.

As these events follow one another in rapid succession, a Senator at one of the desks in the back snaps his fingers. A page boy leaps to his feet and in a second is at the Senator's side. A moment later the boy lays a typewritten document in a tray beside the Bill Clerk, a somber official who sits on the lowest tier of the three-decked rostrum.

The Bill Clerk writes a number on the first page of the manuscript, notes with approval the Senator's suggestion for committee referral, and sets it down in another tray whence, with a dozen or more companions, it will soon be whisked away to the Government Printing Office. A bill has been born!

A similar act of parturition, with only the most minor differences in procedure, takes place each day that the House of Representatives meets. Between the two houses from five to six thousand bills are born every year, or from ten to twelve thousand every session.[1] Any attempt to trace the origins

[1] This estimate is based on the ten-year span from 1937 to 1946. It is surprising to note, however, that during the first ten years of this century, about three times as many bills were introduced during each Congress. In part, the decline in the birth rate is probably due to the increasing ability of the administrative process to achieve objectives that formerly were sought more exclusively through legislation. The decline may also reflect a diminished number of private relief bills. A definitive explanation will not be possible until bills are counted in a manner that identifies both private relief bills and duplicate bills. Some observers have estimated that 40 per cent of all bills introduced represent duplications within and between houses and that, of the 60 per cent remaining, one quarter are private relief bills. See Richard Neustadt, "Presidential Clearance of Legislation" (unpublished doctoral dissertation, Harvard University, June, 1950).

of even one of these bills would involve a tangled network of people, groups, motives, and conflicts. It would mean peering back into the dim past, for "legislation unquestionably generates legislation. Every statute may be said to have a long lineage of statutes behind it." [2]

In general, however, there are typical problems that are encountered in the birth process; problems of legislative parenthood, of drafting original bills, and of preparing amendments. A description of these problems cannot give the same sense of growth and dynamics that can be obtained from a story of one bill's birth, but it can supply a broad view of the birth process itself.

Godparents and Parents

It is a wise child, the saying goes, who knows his own father. In the case of a bill, wisdom is not always enough to identify the real parents. Sometimes nothing short of omniscience will do.

Since the sponsor of any bill has his name publicly inscribed on its first page, it is one of the polite traditions of Capitol Hill to refer to him as its author or drafter, because it is easier to label a bill by the sponsor's name than by using its number or formal title. The press and radio follow this tradition. Yet a bill's sponsor often has taken no hand whatsoever in developing the conception behind it. In most cases he did not draft the specific language. Occasionally, he knows little or nothing about the bill. "In 1890 a bill was passed," wrote an old-time Senator in his autobiography, "which was called the Sherman Act for no other reason that I can think of except that Mr. Sherman had nothing to do with framing it whatever." [3] While the memoir-writing Senator may have been guilty of some exaggeration, there are countless other cases that more readily fit the description.

In analyzing the genesis of a bill, therefore, sponsorship and authorship must be considered separately. Both are essential to the birth of a bill, but just as with a child's father and mother, each has a different function to perform.

The Sponsors

In countries operating under the Cabinet-Parliament system, the administrative arm of the government can introduce legislative proposals by its own action. In England, for example, all major bills are introduced in the House of Commons by members of the Cabinet. In America, however, the separation of agencies precludes formal sponsorship by the Administration. While any-

[2] Woodrow Wilson, "Congressional Government" (Boston: Houghton Mifflin, 1925), p. 297.

[3] George F. Hoar, "Autobiography of Seventy Years" (New York: Scribner, 1903), Vol. II, p. 363.

one from the President to the lowliest lobbyist may prepare a draft for a bill, only a Senator or Representative can introduce it in Congress.

Personal Responsibility of Congressmen. The act of sponsorship carries with it a certain degree of personal responsibility. It is one way of registering a member's point of view—for the benefit of his constituents or a pressure group. It often involves a member of Congress in a host of supplementary activities—answering correspondence on a bill, defending his viewpoint before Congress, and discussing it with proponents and opponents. Sometimes it entails a very high degree of political leadership, a function just as important to the legislative process as the draft of a measure. "If Mr. Sherman had not written a line of the law or contributed a single idea in the course of its enactment, he would be entitled to more credit than any single man in Congress because he alone carried the bill through Congress." [4] In recording the history of the Employment Act of 1946, Stephen Bailey shows that the original measure was prepared for Senator Murray by staff assistants working with executive-agency economists. Yet, fundamentally, Bailey points out, it was Murray's "spark of will which transformed an idea into a specific legislative proposal." [5] The National Labor Relations Act, the Social Security Act, and the United States Housing Act of 1937 are all complicated statutes that were drafted by experts inside and outside the Government. Yet it was Senator Robert F. Wagner of New York who not only introduced the bills which evolved into these statutes but who also became the focal point for the campaign on their behalf. It was Wagner who was always there at the right time to defend each bill in committee, to protect it on the floor, to negotiate with congressional opponents, to handle relationships with the President, to rebut attacks, and to handle (but not necessarily devise) parliamentary maneuvers.

In contrast with his activities on these measures, all of which very properly became known as "Wagner Acts," Senator Wagner's action on behalf of the Urban Redevelopment Bill, introduced during the Seventy-eighth Congress, was limited to the mere act of introduction. On this bill, following the Senator's name, there appeared the words "on request," a device used occasionally to allow a member of Congress to sponsor a bill without necessarily committing himself to its principles. In this particular case the request was made by various real-estate organizations which opposed an extension of public housing but favored the use of public funds for private redevelopment of blighted areas. The limited type of sponsorship was a result of Senator Wagner's obvious interest in assuring real-estate interests that he favored the private redevelopment of blighted areas and at the same time not allowing himself to be regarded as favoring this program as a substitute for public housing. Shortly

[4] W. S. Kerr, "John Sherman" (Boston: French, 1908), p. 206.

[5] Stephen K. Bailey, "Congress Makes a Law" (New York: Columbia University Press, 1949), p. 41.

thereafter, in the Wagner-Ellender-Taft Housing Bill, the Senator joined in sponsoring a measure that combined both approaches.

Sponsorship Power. In the early days of the century, exposés of state legislatures pointed to the introduction of many "strike" bills, bills that could injure a given business enterprise or industry and which were introduced for the purpose of obtaining "protection money." While the strike bill has no direct counterpart in modern legislative practice, nevertheless the principle behind it is not dead. Sponsorship brings with it a certain degree of personal power. The sponsor of a bill is often in the position of exercising a controlling influence over its future. Government officials, members of Congress, and leaders of private organizations will seek him out and ask for amendments. Many will offer various types of inducements to him to seek more rapid action on his bill or to try to hold up action. There are even cases where close observers have been convinced that a member of Congress has introduced a bill for the express purpose of killing it. Although it would be difficult to substantiate a charge of this type in the case of any particular bill, the logic of the situation is clear. No one can be more effective than the sponsor of a bill in counseling against precipitate action or in paving the way toward amendments that would defeat its very purpose—particularly if he should happen to be chairman of the committee to which the bill is referred.

The choice of sponsors, therefore, is one of the primary problems facing anyone who seeks legislative action. An obvious consideration, of course, is whether a member of Congress will regard his sponsorship lightly or whether he will really assume an important degree of leadership.

Choice of Sponsor. A valuable asset in obtaining favorable action on a bill is to have as its sponsor a member—or even better, the chairman—of the committee to which it is referred. The lack of proper committee connections by the sponsors of a bill may mean that it will not even get a hearing. This was the case for many years with the social-security legislation introduced in the Senate by Senators Wagner and Murray, neither of whom were members of the Senate Finance Committee. In the case of the Atomic Energy Act of 1946, for example, Senator Brien McMahon of Connecticut was chairman of the Special Senate Committee on Atomic Energy at the time when he introduced the original bill. This was an invaluable factor in obtaining favorable action by the Congress. In 1937, before the Wagner-Ellenbogen slum clearance and low-rent housing bill could be acted upon in the House, Representative Ellenbogen had to yield the role of House sponsor to Representative Steagall who was chairman of the committee handling it and who demanded the honor of sponsorship as the price of his support.

Party connections are also important. It is usually more effective to get a member of the majority party as the sponsor of a measure. Bills introduced by minority members seldom travel far. In 1944, Senator Maloney, a middle-of-the-road Democrat, succeeded in getting his resolution for a Joint Committee on the Organization of Congress approved by Senator McKellar, head of the Rules Committee subcommittee to which it was referred. Senator La Follette, who became chairman of the committee when Maloney died, would never have succeeded in getting the resolution past McKellar.

In 1947, shortly after the Republicans won a majority in Congress, Representative Hebert of Louisiana, a Democratic member, introduced a bill setting up machinery in the District of Columbia for treating alcoholism as a disease instead of as a crime. The measure attracted national attention as the "Hebert bill." At this point the Republican chairman of the subcommittee handling the subject, Representative Miller of Nebraska, introduced an identical bill. Representative Hebert protested vigorously. "The leadership told me to introduce this bill in my name," retorted Representative Miller at a subcommittee session. "I personally hesitated about doing this but I was told by the leadership to do it. We are the majority party and we are going to be responsible for all good legislation. . . . If it is a good bill we will reintroduce it in our name. We are going to take the cream. You fellows have had your way long enough." [6]

A sponsor's ability as a fighter for his bill or as a symbol evoking certain kinds of group support is also of the greatest importance. Although Senator Wagner was not a member of the Senate Labor Committee, his dogged perseverance and his prestige among organized labor were vital factors in the enactment of the National Labor Relations Act. Although Senator Norris was a member of the minority party after the 1932 election, his deep convictions and understanding regarding TVA legislation were instrumental in its passage in 1933. In 1946, although handicapped by being a member of the minority party and not on the Foreign Relations Committee, Senator Morse led the successful fight for Senate ratification of the World Court Resolution.

Multiple Sponsorship. Although sponsorship by one member is all that is required for introduction, the practice of obtaining multiple sponsorship has developed. In its simplest form this involves cosponsorship by a Senator and Representative in order to obtain a focal point for activity in both houses at the same time. Multiple sponsorship is also used as a method of obtaining the support of key members. Some Senators and Representatives will be interested in working for a measure only if their names are on it. In other cases multiple sponsorship is a valuable symbol of bipartisan support. The sponsorship of the Ball-Burton-Hatch-Hill Resolution by two Republicans and two Democrats symbolized bipartisan support for American participation in an international organization. The sponsorship of the Wagner-Ellender-Taft Housing Bill joined a liberal Northern Democrat, a conservative Southern Democrat, and a conservative Republican, one of the outstanding examples of

[6] Drew Pearson, "Washington Merry-Go-Round," *Washington Post,* Mar. 24, 1947.

sponsorship as a form of legislative strategy. In the case of the Full Employment Bill there was a serious problem in regard to the Senate committee to which the measure would be referred. Had it gone to a committee with an unfriendly chairman, it might have been buried quietly. This contingency was protected against by the fact that among the Senate cosponsors of the measure appeared the chairmen of each of the three committees to which the bill might have been referred. An additional motive was to "take out insurance against competition" on the part of those who were preparing a rival bill. The only committees to which the rival bill could have been referred were the committees of which the three chief sponsors were chairmen.[7]

Occasionally multiple sponsorship is used to build up mass support. In the case of the G.I. Bill of Rights, over 90 members of the Senate were included as its sponsors. In the case of a 1947 housing bill, multiple sponsorship was used to obtain the prior support of the committee to which the measure was referred. Its sponsor stated:

> I call attention to the rather unique fact that this bill is signed and endorsed by every member of the Banking and Currency Committee, of both political parties, which to my mind suggests the scriptural comment, "Behold, how good and how pleasant it is for brethren to dwell together in unity!"[8]

A similar though less successful attempt was made by Representative Patman, the House sponsor of the Full Employment Bill, who built up a bloc of 116 "coauthors and cosponsors."

Multiple sponsorship is frowned upon by many old-timers in Congress who believe in preserving the fiction that the sponsor of a measure is, or should be, its author. Obviously, the extension of multiple sponsorship reduces this tradition to absurdity. Moreover, some members of Congress feel that multiple sponsorship impairs the publicity value for each individual sponsor.

In the House of Representatives, opposition to multiple sponsorship is expressed in the rules themselves, which provide that the name of only one sponsor can be printed on a bill. This provision is consistently evaded, however, by introduction of identical bills by several members. Representative Patman evaded it and at the same time saved on printing costs by making up a list of his 116 "coauthors and cosponsors" and having it printed in the *Congressional Record.*

The Authors

"Who drafted this bill?"

This question is often asked—sometimes as a matter of historical curiosity,

[7] Bailey, *op. cit.*, p. 55.

[8] Senator Charles W. Tobey, *Congressional Record* (daily edition), Nov. 20, 1947, p. 10776.

sometimes as a matter of back-room gossip, more often in order to find a culprit. It is seldom possible to find a factual answer. As Woodrow Wilson said: [legislation] "is an aggregate, not a simple production. It is impossible to tell how many persons, opinions, and influences have entered into its composition." [9]

Complex Backgrounds. The ideas found in most bills have long and complex histories. Their origin is buried in evolving needs and interests, in similar theories evolved by many different people, and in passing through the hands of many "idea brokers" and organizations. Many bills are little more than slightly modified versions of old measures, combinations of old measures, or minute insertions in a long-standing legislative framework.

The process of drafting, moreover, is a continuous one, with amendments and substitutes being offered from all directions at every intersection on the legislative highway. Even at the initial stage, it is usually a conglomerate process with broad participation by many authors. When a private lawyer prepares a bill for a private organization, he usually takes pains to consult widely with various government officials. Many bills are prepared in executive agencies to carry out the views of members of Congress. Preparation of bills in Congress is often merely an assembly job on various parts prepared elsewhere. The bill that became the Contract Settlement Act of 1944, for example, included sections and provisions that were prepared in the War Department, in the Antitrust Division of the Justice Department, in the Bureau of the Budget, by the American Arbitration Association, by the Aeronautical Chamber of Commerce, by a lawyer who represented a major railroad in an important court suit arising out of World War I contracts, and by congressional staff members. Sometimes "congressional preparation" of a bill involves nothing more than a careful checking, somewhere in Congress, of a draft prepared elsewhere.

It is only natural that people associated with one phase of this conglomerate operation very sincerely may regard themselves as the center of the universe and not realize how many other authors are involved. In the development of the Federal Reserve Act, Woodrow Wilson's close adviser, Colonel House, certainly regarded himself as a major force behind the scenes. At least, this was the interpretation of Charles Seymour, editor of Colonel House's intimate papers. Yet to Senator Carter Glass, Colonel House's version of the authorship of the Federal Reserve Act was a scandalous lie. Glass wrote an entire book [10] to set the record straight and to show the real authors of the Act to be Woodrow Wilson, Carter Glass himself, and Glass's staff assistant on the House Banking and Currency Committee, H. Parker Willis.

In writing the history of his activities during the early days of the New

[9] Wilson, *op. cit.*, p. 320.

[10] Carter Glass, "Adventures in Constructive Finance" (Garden City, N.Y.: Doubleday, 1927).

Deal, Raymond Moley tells how the House version of the Securities Act of 1933 was prepared by James M. Landis and Benjamin V. Cohen under the general direction of Felix Frankfurter.[11] A broader view of the authorship of this legislation came some years later from Middleton Beaman, legislative counsel of the House, who testified that he, his assistant, and the members of a House subcommittee under the chairmanship of Representative Rayburn of Texas played an important part in the drafting of the measure.[12]

Stephen Bailey's history of the Employment Act of 1946 is probably the most extensive effort yet made to show how many authors are involved in the process of bill drafting.[13] His account shows that the scores of people in the executive agencies, both houses of Congress, and private organizations were among the authors. Yet even here there are great gaps in the effort to track down the full story of authorship. An interview with Representative Will Whittington of Mississippi indicated that Whittington solicited drafts from the United States Chamber of Commerce, the Committee for Economic Development, and Secretary of the Treasury Fred Vinson. "With the aid of these drafts," Bailey reports, "Whittington pieced together a substitute bill which was finally submitted to the full committee for consideration."[14] But Bailey was still unable to discover the precise origin of the original proposal for a Council of Economic Advisers—whether it came from one of these sources or from Whittington himself.

A complicating factor in any effort to find the author is the fact that many authors, like ghost writers, cover up their tracks. Anyone who advertises his role in preparing a bill for a Senator or Representative runs the risk of undercutting the status and prestige of the member of Congress and of precluding himself from future working relationships with him. A passion for anonymity seems to be as much a qualification for authors of legislative proposals as it is for Presidential assistants. Such a passion often develops in the minds of draftsmen whose yearnings for deference can be assuaged through the vicarious experiences of the sponsors and through the limited personal prestige gained among those who know where the work was really done.

Taboos. Moreover, there are all sorts of taboos concerning the question of who should and who should not draft legislative proposals. Authorship by the Chamber of Commerce or the Congress of Industrial Organizations is often regarded as bordering on the sinful. When it was learned that the Republican National Committee had hired a lawyer to participate in the drafting of the

[11] Raymond Moley, "After Seven Years" (New York: Harper, 1939), pp. 180–181.

[12] Hearings before the Joint Committee on the Organization of Congress, 79th Cong., 1st Sess., p. 422.

[13] An unusual companion piece of this type of political research is Seymour A. Mann, "Congressional Behavior and Labor Policy" (unpublished doctoral dissertation, University of Chicago, 1951), which traces the intricate history of the Taft-Hartley Act.

[14] Bailey, *op. cit.*, p. 166.

Taft-Hartley Act, a hue and cry of protest arose from the opponents of the Act.

Protests of this type are based, of course, not so much upon theoretical principles concerning who should draft a bill but rather upon objections to the substance in a bill and the influence wielded by the drafters. Where there is broad agreement upon the substance of the bill, these taboos tend to be forgotten. The Railway Labor Disputes Act of 1926, for example, originated with a group of railway-management executives and railway labor leaders who formed a drafting committee in 1924 and engaged Donald Richberg to prepare a bill for them. When the bill was introduced in Congress, its origin was not merely admitted; it was stressed. In fact, the argument was made in both houses that it should be approved in the very form in which it was introduced, since railway management and railway labor would feel obliged to abide by it if there were no important changes.

Middleton Beaman once tried to draw a line between who is responsible for the policies in a bill and who writes the words. He also suggested that the important thing is not where a bill has been prepared but whether the legislation, when enacted, expresses accurately the intention of Congress in passing it. "If it meets that test 100 per cent, it makes no difference where it comes from, whether it comes from Heaven, from an executive department, or is written in our office or some other place." [15]

The preparation of a bill is essentially a strategic phase of the legislative struggle nonetheless. It is not merely a method of recording policy or general principles that have been previously formulated. It is part and parcel of the process of policy formulation. It is a job of formulating general principles in a precise form and of making a long series of choices between alternative methods of building upon them. Moreover, bill drafting represents an important act of taking the initiative in formulating issues in a manner most consistent with one's own views and interests. Coming in with the first draft of a bill is like beating the other fellow to the draw. The ability to draft effectively is thus a vital element in the power picture. It has almost as much meaning for the legislative process as nominations have for election campaigns.

All this does not imply that technical advisers on the preparation of bills, such as the lawyers in the Senate and House Office of the Legislative Counsel, are necessarily partisans in the legislative struggle. To a considerable extent they deal only with the surface technicalities of bills prepared by others. Much less often do they do a complete job of bill drafting. But in either case they need be no more partisan than the editorial writer who works for the publisher of two papers in the same town and writes Republican editorials for the morning paper and Democratic editorials for the evening paper. "We have constantly worked, as some of you gentlemen know," Beaman testified, "for both

[15] Hearings before the Joint Committee on the Organization of Congress, 79th Cong., 1st Sess., p. 421.

sides on the same question at the same time, without any suspicion on the part of either that we are betraying their secrets to the other. . . . What we want to do is to express precisely the intent of our client, whether it be a committee or an individual member." [16]

Executive Drafting. The executive official faced with the question of whether or not to submit a bill draft to Congress is often in the position of being "damned if he does and damned if he does not." If he does, he is apt to be charged with attempts to usurp congressional prerogatives and dictate congressional action. "Are you aware also of the extreme unwisdom of irritating Congress," wrote President Theodore Roosevelt to a friend, "by fixing the details of a bill concerning which they are very sensitive instead of laying down a general policy?" [17] On the other hand, if an executive official does not prepare a draft, he is apt to be criticized on the ground that his proposals are too vague and that too great a burden is placed on the meager technical resources of Congress.

It is certainly true that a proposal for legislative action has little meaning unless embodied in a draft of a bill. When President Truman called a special session in November, 1947, to ask for anti-inflation legislation, members of Congress who previously had been in the forefront of protests against executive drafting criticized the Truman Administration for not having submitted draft legislation to Congress. "If the President wants to tell the people that he stands for a certain thing," observed Senator Homer Ferguson of Michigan, "he ought to come out with his proposal. He ought to come to the House and Senate with a message. And he ought to provide a bill if that is exactly what he wants." [18] Representative Joseph Martin of Massachusetts, the Republican Speaker of the House, construed the absence of Administration drafts as evidence that the President really did not want the powers which he had requested.

Generally speaking, there has been an increasing tendency to accept executive initiative in bill drafting. The various departments are regularly expected to prepare specific drafts of legislation affecting their interests.[19] Even in the field of taxation, where congressional prerogatives have long been jealously

[16] *Ibid.*, pp. 414–418.

[17] J. J. Bishop, "Theodore Roosevelt and His Times." Quoted by Wilfred E. Binkley, "President and Congress" (New York: Knopf, 1947), pp. 210–211.

[18] Homer Ferguson, "What Is Your Congress Doing?" *University of Chicago Round Table,* No. 483, 1947, p. 4.

[19] "Most of the bills affecting the Department of Justice, for instance, are prepared in the Department of Justice and are sent up either to the Chairman of the Judiciary Committee or to the Speaker, and then the Chairman of the Committee, or someone on the Committee suggested by him, introduces the bill. That is the usual procedure." Statement by Representative Earl Michener of Michigan. Hearings before the Joint Committee on the Organization of Congress, 79th Cong., 1st Sess., pp. 456–457.

guarded, the legislative committees usually look to executive officials for leadership in the formulation of initial proposals. "This is particularly true," one of America's leading tax experts has pointed out, "when increases in taxes are in prospect." [20]

Most executive proposals are now cleared in advance through the Legislative Reference Division of the Bureau of the Budget, acting as the agent of the President.[21] This procedure aids in the process of executive planning and helps to eliminate or modify jurisdictional conflicts among executive agencies—although many executive officials sidetrack the clearance process by surreptitiously passing draft bills along to friendly members of Congress.[22] In general, however, the procedure has served to enhance the role and power of the Bureau of the Budget. On minor matters the tendency has been for Budget Bureau officials to make the final decision as to whether a bill should be accepted as "in accord with" or as "not inconsistent with" the program of the President, or branded as "not in accord." More important matters come directly to the attention of the President, White House staff, the CEA, and other officials. The Budget Bureau clearance process nevertheless places Bureau personnel in a highly strategic position for influencing the direction of the President's ever-changing legislative program.

It has also become customary for each President to have a key list of "must bills." Many of these measures are drafted in the White House or the Executive Office of the President. To assist in the handling of these measures, specialized personnel has been developed in the White House staff. President Franklin D. Roosevelt established the position of Special Counsel to the President, first filled by Judge Samuel Rosenman, and later by Clark Clifford and Charles Murphy. President Truman expanded this function by employing additional staff members to concentrate upon legislative drafting, review, and clearance.

Presidential participation in drafting, however, does not mean that the President himself transmits the bill to Congress. The Economic Stability Bill of 1949, for example, was drafted by a working group in the Executive Office of the President and then discussed in detail at a series of Cabinet committee meetings. Yet the final draft of the measure was presented to the Congress by the Secretary of Agriculture rather than by the President, thereby relieving the President of responsibility for a multitude of details.

No matter how an executive bill is transmitted to Congress, whether by the President or the head of an agency, whether officially or through the back

[20] Roy Blough, "The Federal Taxing Process" (New York: Prentice-Hall, 1952). See Chap. 5, "The Executive and Tax Legislation," for a detailed review of executive participation in the drafting of revenue measures.

[21] Neustadt, *op. cit.* See in particular Chap. 3, "Current Operating Methods," which includes four remarkably informative case studies.

[22] *Ibid.*, pp. 118–119.

door, it usually commands a certain amount of respect merely on the ground that it has been prepared by an executive agency. This respect is not merely grounded on an appreciation of the familiarity of executive draftsmen with their materials; it also flows from the recognition that an executive draft represents a power potential. It holds a promise of support both by influential executive officials and by the private organizations with which these officials are allied.

Drafting Skills. Far more prevalent than the fiction that sponsorship implies authorship is the notion that any good lawyer can draft a bill. Actually, an excellent lawyer may butcher the draft of a bill. Bill drafting has been one of the neglected phases of law-school training. In fact, the legal profession as a whole has done very little to advance the art of draftsmanship. There are no up-to-date manuals on the legal aspects of the problem, nor has American jurisprudence developed any theoretical handling of legislative drafting that in any way approaches Jeremy Bentham's work in nineteenth-century England.

In any case, bill drafting calls for more talents than can be obtained through abstract legal training, no matter how excellent it may be or become. It calls for an intensive knowledge of administrative regulations, judicial decisions, existing law, and other proposed laws in the field where the work is being done. It requires an understanding of the realities behind the legal forms; above all, it requires an ability to appraise the line-up of interests and the relative strength of conflicting pressures and to assist in the formulation of basically political decisions. It calls for flexibility and dexterity in the use of language, both to convey meaning and, where necessary, to avoid meaning; both to avoid emotional connotations and, where necessary, to arouse emotion. In short, it calls for a wide range of talents and skills in law, administration, economics, politics, and public relations.

Drafting Teams. Since all these qualities are rarely found in one person, the best drafting is done on a teamwork basis. The Bretton Woods Agreement, for example, was drafted by a team composed of Treasury Department lawyers, economic and political advisers of the Treasury and State Departments, and the legislative counsels of the Senate and the House. Occasional checks were made with the three members of Congress who were scheduled to introduce the legislation, Senators Robert F. Wagner of New York and Charles Tobey of New Hampshire, and Representative Jesse Wolcott of Michigan. Under President Truman's Administration the technique of setting up working teams or "task forces" to formulate new bills has been widely used. Sometimes Congress establishes committees of its own for the specific purpose of drafting a bill or of supervising the drafting process. When the movement for reorganization of Congress was getting under way during the last years of World War II, strenuous opposition was expected from many members of Congress, particularly from those who had a strong personal stake in the present committee structure and who might be expected to object to any reshuffling of committees. It was felt that the best way to obtain an effective bill, therefore, was to have one drafted by members of Congress themselves. It was for this purpose that the Joint Committee on the Organization of Congress was established in 1945. Its staff director, George Galloway, went to work in drafting a measure with the assistance of the Office of Legislative Counsel in both the Senate and the House. A year later, this Joint Committee brought forth a bill which, with certain changes, became the Legislative Reorganization Act of 1946.

Timing the Offspring

As in the case of planned parenthood, the choice of time is a vital element in all phases of the legislative struggle. The entire fate of a bill may hinge upon how its supporters or opponents time a campaign on its behalf and their actions with respect to committee handling, floor operations, or Presidential approval or veto. The time question initially arises in connection with the problem of whether or not to use the legislative process. It continues to be a question at every stage of the process. The manner in which it is answered determines the number and the variety of legislative measures and has an obvious bearing upon the type of legislation enacted during any period.

Timing in the Narrow Sense

In the narrow sense, the choice of time involves selecting which part of a Presidential or congressional term would be best for initiating legislative action, and whether or not action should be initiated in one house of Congress before the other.

Between Elections. An ever-present consideration in timing is the problem of the proximity of elections. A Presidential election year is usually regarded as providing an unpropitious occasion for proposing action on measures unpalatable to large groups of voters, such as a widespread increase in taxes. Military leaders had this factor in mind when they persuaded President Truman to send a special message to Congress in 1947 proposing universal military training. They feared that during the election year of 1948 it would be impossible to obtain sufficient congressional support for so stringent a measure. As it turned out, no action was obtained in either year, although Truman added a personal appeal to the Joint Session of March 17, 1948. It was on the same theory that during both 1947 and 1948 no major proposals for the reorganization of the executive branch were made from any source, even though reorganization was ardently advised by many groups. Instead, the Republican leaders and the Truman Administration both supported the resolution which set up the Hoover Commission to study the subject during 1948 and bring in legislative proposals in 1949 after the Presidential election was over.

Another narrow aspect of the timing problem is whether to introduce a bill at the beginning, middle, or end of the two-year period during which a Congress meets. Usually there is a flood of legislative proposals in the early days of the Congress, a flood which tapers off slowly, becomes a steady stream, and then narrows into a trickle toward the end of the two-year period. In most cases, early introduction is the best policy. On certain questions it is imperative. This is particularly true of any measures which are likely to be combated by a filibuster in the Senate or by delaying tactics in the House. At the end of the session, when there are so many competing demands on congressional time, it is much more difficult to deal with dilatory tactics. The early days of a given Congress, when the calendars are relatively free, provide the ideal circumstances under which to handle problems of this type. In the case of amendments to the House rules, these are feasible only on the first day of any Congress when the House adopts the rules to guide it during the following two years.

Finally, there is an end-of-the-season technique for rushing through controversial measures. This was used consistently by the Roosevelt Administration in obtaining extensions of price-control and war-powers legislation. By holding off extensive requests until the last moment, Roosevelt was able to side-step a large amount of debate and obtain many of his objectives at a minimum cost in harmful amendments.

Which House First? One by-product of a bicameral legislature is that it affords a choice among introducing a bill in both houses of Congress at the same time, introducing it first in one house and then in the other, or limiting introduction to one house only. The first of these alternatives is clearly the most advisable in the case of measures that are being pushed forward toward rapid enactment. It also serves the purpose of facilitating a broader campaign than can be carried on when a bill is introduced in one house only. Often the fact that a bill is introduced in one house only is merely indicative that it lacks significant support and is not considered seriously as a legislative vehicle.

On the other hand, there are many instances when the sponsors of legislation have chosen one house as the springboard, postponing until a more favorable time introduction of companion measures in the other house. Sometimes it is felt that the best way for a bill to reach the Senate is in the form of a measure already approved by the House, or vice versa.

The Flow of the Tides

Long-range Cycles. The history of American legislation reveals cyclical trends almost as sharp as the rise and fall in the level of business activity and employment. During the New Freedom era of Woodrow Wilson, reform legislation reached boom levels with the Clayton Act, the Federal Reserve Act, the Federal Trade Commission Act, and the legislation establishing an income-tax system under the Sixteenth Amendment. In the conservative administrations of Harding, Coolidge, and Hoover, legislation of this type sank into a deep slump. With the New Deal of Franklin Roosevelt, it staged a sensational comeback and reached heights never before dreamed of in America. Then, as the New Deal lost its grip and war broke out in Europe, the cycle once more turned downward.

War itself brings on another type of cycle. During the emergency there is a pronounced tendency to look to the President rather than legislation as a source of decision. The aftermath of a war brings a violent shift. The emergency powers of the President are curtailed, and even though the executive officials may be left with a larger residue of power than they ever before enjoyed, there is a renewal of emphasis upon legislative rather than executive solutions to the problems of the day.

Trends of this type have a direct effect on the type of legislation that is introduced. When the outlook for reform legislation seems black, it is natural to postpone its introduction until some more auspicious moment. During periods of prosperity the productivity of ideas for economic reform is low. In depression there is a plethora of proposals for legislative action to benefit disadvantaged groups.

Some legislative measures, of course, have little relation to the economic and political climate. Year in and year out the departments and pressure groups bring in their bills designed to expand a bureau in order to take away certain rights from the Indians and give others back to them; change the status of reserve officers in the Navy; or provide for another attack on hoof-and-mouth disease near the Mexican border. Yet whenever an idea for legislation calls for drastic changes in the *status quo,* there is a natural disposition in favor of waiting until the time is ripe. After the passage of the Employment Act of 1946, many of those groups which had backed the original full-employment proposals felt it was necessary to call for a much higher degree of economic planning. The National Catholic Welfare Conference, for example, issued a circular calling for formation of labor-management councils in each industry as a means of planning a full-production and full-employment program. Other proposals aimed at providing a full-fledged framework of economic planning for America were discussed among labor and left-wing organizations. None of these, however, were embodied in legislative proposals. The feeling seemed to be that the time was not ripe and that until the economic and intellectual atmosphere changed, proposals of this type would evoke more criticism than support. The same delaying attitude was evidenced by business groups whose thinking ran in the direction of reinstituting, as a means toward economic stabilization, the type of controls over production and floors under production that had been experimented with under the NRA.

Catching the Flood Tide. The ability to accurately appraise legislative cycles is of particular importance to a President, whose prestige may suffer from an untimely proposal. The best example of Presidential concern with timing is Franklin Roosevelt's cautious handling of the neutrality versus intervention issue during the years preceding Pearl Harbor. In 1935 Roosevelt signed the neutrality legislation which prevented shipment of munitions to either side in a foreign conflict. Early the next year, however, as civil war broke out in Spain and German troops occupied the Rhineland, it became increasingly apparent that Nazi and Fascist aggression held the seeds of future world conflict. From then on, it is evident that the Roosevelt Administration desired to move away, as fast as possible, from the isolationist stand represented by the Neutrality Act toward a system of collective security. In October, 1937, the President made his famous speech calling upon peace-loving nations to quarantine the aggressors. As described by Roosevelt himself many years later,[23] this speech "was hailed as warmongering; it was even ridiculed as a nervous search 'under the bed' for dangers of war which did not exist." From then on, Roosevelt moved very carefully. Often, in fact, he retreated toward isolationism as though in an effort to catch the tide of public opinion. It was in September, 1939, when Hitler's armies had invaded Poland and there was no doubt that his objective could be achieved, that Roosevelt asked again, this time in clear-cut fashion, for legislation repealing the arms embargo and permitting munitions shipments to countries invaded by the aggressors.

This period of slow searching for the right time stands out in sharp contrast to the situation at the beginning of the Roosevelt Administration in 1933. If ever there was a tide in the affairs of men that, taken in the flood, led on to fortune, this was it. Practically any legislation that Roosevelt might have proposed, short of the socialization of industry, would have been timely. Bill after bill was transmitted from the White House to the congressional leaders and promptly brought back for Presidential signature. Soon, however, the magic "one hundred days" came to an end. The flood tide subsided, and from then on the Administration's proposals had to be paddled strongly against the current.

A similar period came into being on December 7, 1941, when the Japanese bombed Pearl Harbor. The Administration immediately proposed, and Congress approved, legislation giving the President greater war powers than any President had ever before enjoyed in American history. Two years later when Roosevelt proposed compulsory labor service, he was faced with strong opposition in Congress and eventual defeat in the Senate. One may assert from

23 "Public Papers and Addresses of Franklin D. Roosevelt" (New York: Random House), 1939 Vol., p. 28 of Introduction.

the point of view of the necessities of war mobilization that compulsory labor service was not needed that early in the game. From the viewpoint of legislative strategy, however, the discretionary power to clamp on compulsory labor controls whenever necessary might well have been granted if the request had been made before the country had recovered from the initial shock of Pearl Harbor.

The wise legislative strategist recognizes that the legislative tides do not run according to fixed schedule. There are too many fluid factors in the legislative process. Sudden changes in international affairs or in the economic cycle may occur overnight. Pressure groups and politicians often shift positions in an unpredictable fashion. The introduction of a measure itself is a factor which may, under certain circumstances, affect the climate that surrounds it.

Swimming against the Tide. On many occasions the wisest course of action is to swim against the tide. There was certainly no more unfavorable climate for public-power proposals than that existing in the 1920's when Senator George Norris of Nebraska first proposed government utilization of the abandoned Muscle Shoals project in Tennessee. For many years, every effort he made to obtain enactment of his proposals met with defeat. Yet every defeat made him stronger. Finally, in 1933, the combination of widespread unemployment and the Roosevelt Administration tipped the scales in his favor, and legislation was finally enacted setting up the TVA. The same approach was taken by Senator James E. Murray of Montana in 1945 when he introduced his bill to set up the Missouri Valley Authority, a measure which was more of an option on the future than a bid for immediate action. The Murray approach was that the only way to develop a situation in which the enactment of Missouri Valley legislation would be timely was to propose the measure long in advance of its feasibility. The same theory applies even more aptly to the Wagner-Murray-Dingell bill for compulsory health insurance, also first introduced in 1945. Not only was this measure politically inexpedient at the time of proposal; but because of the shortage of hospital facilities and medical personnel it would have been administratively unworkable if enacted. Nevertheless, the bill itself and the campaign on its behalf provided a great stimulus toward the expansion of hospital and other facilities. When the tide of social reform once again starts to rise, the odds should favor early enactment of legislation setting up a more unified development program in the Missouri Valley and some form of government-promoted health insurance.

One great advantage of swimming against the tide is that it provides a long period of maturation and growth. It puts all parties to the legislative struggle on notice. It provides all the contestants with an opportunity to make a careful appraisal of gains and losses and to work out new combinations and coalitions. It gets people accustomed to new ideas and new modes of action, so that when action finally comes, it is more acceptable and more practicable. Chamberlain writes:

> Most of the great mass of regulatory legislation of the past decade, popularly dubbed New Deal legislation, had a well-defined prenatal history extending back several years before it was espoused by the Roosevelt administration. This is true not only of the more conventional fields such as banking, railroads, and taxation, but of the newer areas of social security, holding company regulation, and securities control. Congressional attention to these new fields had not been absent prior to the time the President made his specific recommendations. The normal process has been fairly uniform: an initial reference by one or a few individuals, then a gradually increasing volume of comment accompanied by numerous specific proposals coming from widely divergent sources. In some cases legislation results in a very short time, but more frequently the initial flurries of interest will subside, to be revived from time to time until finally culminating, perhaps with the help of the President, in a law. The long germination period detectable in the genesis of most laws is of the utmost importance: it constitutes one of the most valuable contributions that a legislative body can make.[24]

[24] Lawrence H. Chamberlain, "The President, Congress and Legislation" (New York: Columbia University Press, 1946), pp. 462–463.

Chapter 11

THE ART OF DRAFTING

It is impossible to devise any rigid set of rules to guide the drafting of legislative proposals.[1] Legislative drafting is an art. It cannot be formalized.[2] The authors of a bill are continuously faced with important choices. Each must be decided in the light of the purposes to be achieved and the specific legislative situation.

A bill is not merely a proposal for action; it *is* itself a form of action. It involves the setting of an objective, as the first stage in the push-and-pull process of bargaining. It is a proposal for some change in the distribution of power and wealth. In the determination regarding these types of action lie the major substantive problems faced in the drafting of a bill.

The Substance of a Bill

The Asking Price

When a person thinks of selling a house, three different figures usually come to mind. First, there is the price that he would like to get. Here the sky may be the limit, but let us say he daydreams hopefully about $20,000. Second, there is the price he guesses he may have to settle for in the end—say $15,000. Then there is the asking price. If he asks $20,000 he runs the risk of frighten-

[1] For general material on the preparation of legislation, see Ernst Freund, "Abstract of Statutory Precedent Material Collected and Available for a Manual of Legislative Drafting," Appendix C of "Fiscal Report of the Committee on Legislative Drafting" (*Reports of the American Bar Association,* Vol. 46, 1921); Sir Courtenay Ilbert, "Legislative Methods and Forms" (New York: Oxford, 1901), and by the same author, "The Mechanics of Law Making" (New York: Columbia University Press, 1914); Chester Lloyd Jones, "Statute Law Making" (Boston: Boston Book Co., 1912); Thomas L. Parkinson, "Legislative Drafting" (New York: Academy of Political Science, 1912); and by one of the Parliamentary Counsel to the Treasury, "The Making and Form of Bills," *Parliamentary Affairs,* London, Spring, 1949.

[2] It is possible, however, to list in an orderly form the problems that are met in the drafting process, as is attempted in a general way throughout the rest of this chapter. The most intensive listing of rules that has thus far been made—and it needs revision to extend it and bring it up to date—is found in Freund, *op. cit.*

ing off would-be purchasers. If he asks $15,000 there is little room left for bargaining. The chances are that he will ask for about $17,000 or $18,000.

The framers of a bill face the same problem. In the case of appropriation bills or bills to authorize future appropriations, the considerations are identical. Where bills deal with policies that cannot be measured in quantitative terms, the problem is still very similar. In both cases the primary substantive problem in the initial drafting process is how to strike a mean between what one really wants and what one could ultimately agree to take.

This is not a problem that is easy to approach in a systematic manner. Not many participants in the legislative struggle know what they really want. Those who do have a great strategic advantage. Some merely follow the general principle of wanting as much as they can get—a principle which is so elastic as to have little guiding value. Moreover, wants are highly subjective and difficult to measure; they depend upon a long series of conjectures as to what is desired by group leaders, members, and supporters. Similarly, it is not easy, before the process of legislative tug of war gets under way, to predict what end product may be accepted. Short-run political trends are every bit as baffling as short-run economic trends. He who starts with an unqualified commitment to the battle cry of "unconditional surrender" may end up eager to accept "peace without victory." Furthermore, within limits, the amount you can expect to get often depends upon how much you initially ask for.

Figure Flexibility. The determination of an asking price, therefore, tends to be an arbitrary judgment based upon past relationships and current intuitions. The wisdom in any particular asking price lies less in any inherent value than in one's ability to indicate that it is less than was really desired and at the same time to leave elbowroom for subsequent compromises. The entire process of preparing the Government's appropriation requests fits into this pattern. Since it is usually taken for granted that the Bureau of the Budget makes substantial reductions in agency requests for appropriations, it is easier to justify any agency request that appears in the President's Budget Message. At the same time, the Budget Bureau itself never cuts too far. It leaves room for further cuts to be made in the process of legislative action on appropriation bills.

The preparation of the Marshall Plan by the Truman Administration is another illustration of the pattern. An indication as to the amount of aid desired by the Administration was given in an early trial-balloon speech by a State Department official who suggested the need of 20 billion dollars over a four-year period. At the Paris Conference of European nations, a preliminary report was drafted which indicated the need for closer to 30 billion dollars over the same number of years. Emissaries of the State Department then flew to Paris to advise the Conference that such a preview would scare off members of the Congress. The report was revised to call for 19 billion dollars in American aid. A Citizens' Committee, headed by the Secretary of Commerce, then went to work on the problem of preparing a formal recommendation to the President and to Congress. In their report of November, 1947, it was suggested that the volume of aid be set at between 12 to 17 billion dollars over a four-year period. The practical problem involved in devising this figure was how to allow leeway for bargaining with Congress and at the same time how to avoid the undesirable international complications that might result from too sharp a congressional cut in the Administration's asking price. This problem was solved by planning on very little leeway in the amount to be made available the first year but leaving the door open to congressional limitations on the number of years over which aid will be given.

Ideological Flexibility. The drafting of the Full Employment Bill presents an example in qualitative rather than in quantitative terms. This measure represented a middle ground between what its backers really wanted and what they thought they could get. On the one hand they were interested in the full philosophy represented by Franklin Roosevelt's Economic Bill of Rights, a document that established as a goal not only full employment but also better housing, better education, better health, and other aspects of a constantly rising standard of living. Yet the Full Employment Bill dealt only with the employment goal and scrupulously avoided any suggestion of having the Government assume responsibility for a constantly rising standard of living. It was strictly limited to the purpose of providing employment opportunities for "all Americans willing and able to work." On the other hand, the original bill asked for far more than any of its backers thought could be obtained. Rather than limiting itself to a declaration of the Government's responsibility to promote full employment, it set forth an unqualified responsibility of the Government to "assure" continuing full employment. To have asked for more, in the opinion of the sponsors, would have been to transcend the realm of practical consideration. To have asked for less would have been to draft a bill that would lack the inspirational qualities needed to obtain popular backing.

Evasion or Postponement. One of the fascinating things about the legislative process is the manner in which the problem of the asking price, like many other problems, can be evaded or postponed. The Maternal and Child Health Bill, introduced by Senator Pepper and others in the Seventy-ninth Congress, provided for Federal grants to enable states to give free medical services to all children and to all maternity cases. In essence, it meant that health services for all children and mothers would be provided on the same free basis as public education. Estimates as to how much money would have to be appropriated in order to carry out such a program indicated a figure of close to one billion dollars a year. Sponsors of the measure were thereby faced with a dilemma. On the one hand, the billion-dollar figure was so large that, if presented to a conservative Congress, it would have forestalled consideration of the measure. On the other hand, any figure of less than a billion dollars would have broken down the principle of the bill and would have invited a limitation that would restrict such services only to those who could not pass a means test. This dilemma was avoided by the simple expedient of leaving all figures out of the measure and merely using the language "There are hereby authorized to be appropriated such funds as might be necessary to effectuate the purposes of this Act."

A similar example occurred in the framing of the Sherman Antitrust Act. The aim of the bill was to make unlawful "agreements in restraint of trade." The big problem, however, was how much ground was covered by the term "agreements in restraint of trade." A broad definition would have made the Act more stringent. A narrow definition would have made it relatively unambitious. The dilemma was solved by the simple expedient of not defining the term at all and leaving its interpretation to the courts and to future legislation.[3]

The Distribution of Power and Wealth

Inseparably allied with the problem of how much to ask for are the questions "for whom?" and "from whom?" The greater the number of groups for which one asks benefits, the broader his potential support and the more ambitious his demands may become—although this must be counterbalanced by the fact that the more numerous the portions cut from any piece of pie, the smaller each portion must become. The fewer the groups over which one proposes to establish controls or take resources, the less widespread the resistance will be —although a more aggressive approach may be needed in order to develop enough support to counterbalance the inevitable opposition. In this sense, the handling of "how much?", "for whom?", and "from whom?" is essential not only to the process of preparing a bill but also to the organization of support for it at various stages in the legislative process.[4]

For Whom and from Whom? In the case of the farmer whose cow has been killed by an army truck, the question of "for whom?" is relatively simple. A relief bill asking for damages will provide for a minor transfer of money from the Federal government to a single recipient (although it may be based upon prior understandings concerning a split with the lawyer who handles the bill). On bills of a public character, distribution patterns become much more complex. In the preparation of legislation dealing with Federal aid to education, a major issue has been whether all of the pie goes to public schools or some to

[3] George F. Hoar, "Autobiography of Seventy Years" (New York: Scribner, 1903), Vol. II, p. 364.

[4] This is discussed at greater length in Chaps. 12 and 13.

religious groups. There is also the question of whether aid should be provided for colleges and universities, how it should be distributed geographically, and how much of their own the recipients should be expected to put up. These questions, in turn, open up a multidimensional series of alternatives, each of which favors some groups more than others.

On the other side of the ledger, the Government is continuously faced with the problem of maintaining an inflow of financial resources. It has long been an axiom among those concerned with taxation that the goose will squawk no matter where the feathers are pulled from it. Most private organizations are intensely concerned with having the tax burden shifted as much as possible to others than themselves. In fact, there are few common interests that promote vigorous group activity as much as a common interest in avoiding onerous taxes —particularly on the part of those with substantial resources.[5] Government officials are naturally concerned with distributing the burden in such a way as to confine the squawking to those who are less able to follow squawks with action. A similar problem of "from whom?" is faced in the development of nationwide regulatory measures. The drafters of price-control measures during and immediately after World War II, for example, were faced with the ever-recurring question of what parts of the economy would fall under control and what parts would be exempted.

Governmental Machinery. In the case of most legislative proposals, there are many choices as to which officials are to get more power or funds or, perhaps, be deprived of present power or funds. These choices are no less substantive because they deal with governmental machinery. They are every bit as political as the problems involving the distribution of power and wealth among private organizations. In fact, the decisions on who does what inside the Government are often the answer to the problem of who gets or loses what outside the Government. Hence the tremendous emphasis in legislative struggles upon the details of governmental machinery and the writing of legislative provisions to gear into the existing personnel of Federal agencies rather than in terms of abstract organizational blueprints.[6]

The first problem in deciding "for whom?" within the structure of the Government is: Which Federal officials should get the increased power or funds provided for in a bill? Should they be given directly to the President? If so,

[5] The development of parliamentary institutions in England, for example, was closely associated with the opposition of the country gentry and the burghers to onerous taxes levied by the king. In colonial America, onerous taxes levied by the English led first to the campaign of "No taxation without representation" and then, with other factors, to the Revolutionary War itself. For a full review of this problem in present-day America, see Roy Blough, "The Federal Taxing Process" (New York: Prentice-Hall, 1952), particularly Chap. 2, "Tax Programs and Pressure Groups."

[6] Hence, too, are those public-administration experts who dream of the day when governmental reorganization plans can be divorced from politics doomed to eternal despair.

should he be left free to turn them over to subordinate officials in whatever manner he sees fit? Or should the channel through which the President is to operate be spelled out in the bill? If the power and funds are not to be handed to the President directly, should they be given to the head of an agency that is directly under Presidential control or to a bureau within such an agency? Or should they be given to a so-called "independent board or commission"? Where public works programs are involved, should the projects be built directly by the Federal government? If not, to what extent should funds be channeled to state governments as contrasted with city governments? In either case, how much control should Federal officials be expected to exercise?

And what about relationships with private organizations? An administrative agency can be required or authorized to consult with those who are affected by its activities. More specifically, advisory committees may be established in the bill itself. If so, who are the members to be appointed? Are they to have a semi-independent status of their own, with a chairman of their own choosing? Or are they to operate merely at the beck and call of the administrative agency? Are they to be limited to advisory functions or are they to be given powers and funds of their own?

Then there is the problem of legislative provisions with respect to the courts and the Congress. A bill may subject administrative decisions to a thorough and complete review by the courts. Or it may limit the function of the courts to overthrowing an administrative decision only on the ground that it is "arbitrary and capricious." It may confine judicial review to "questions of law" as distinguished from "questions of fact." [7] Occasionally, judicial machinery may be specially augmented in order to handle the burden of appeals that is anticipated.

A long-standing method of congressional review is the requirement of reports to Congress. Recent legislation has required reports ranging from once a year down to every sixty days. Special reports may be required as an antecedent or a concomitant to a given type of executive action. A special committee can be set up to keep tabs on administrative operations as was provided in the Atomic Energy Act of 1946. Or certain types of executive action may be made susceptible to congressional veto within a given period of time, as was done in the 1945 and 1949 legislation giving the President power to reorganize executive agencies.

Specificity versus Discretion. There is also the vital problem of how much substance should be contained in the bill itself and how much discretion should

[7] The fluidity and usages of these distinctions have been well stated by John Dickinson: "It would seem that when the courts are unwilling to review, they are tempted to explain by the easy device of calling the question one of 'fact,' and when otherwise disposed, they say that it is a question of 'law.'" "Administrative Justice and the Supremacy of Law in the United States" (Cambridge, Mass.: Harvard University Press, 1927), p. 55.

be left to executive officials and the courts. "Modern legislation," it has been said, "should seek to steer a clear course between the Scylla of attempting to anticipate every possible situation and the Charybdis of expressing no policy more definite than some such empty formula as public interest, convenience, or necessity." [8] This ideal is but rarely approximated. When those who support a given bill seriously doubt that the executive officials will do what is desired, the most natural inclination in the world is to spell out the duties of executive officials as fully as possible. This accounts for the extensive use of legislation to deal with the minutiae of organization and administration as already discussed in Chap. 9. At the same time it is particularly difficult to spell out general policies in terms that make them more than an empty formula.

Yet in the process of bill drafting, as in every other phase of the political struggle, all is not always what it seems. Sometimes the most elaborate façade of detail merely hides a tremendous blank-check delegation of power and resources. In the Contract Settlement Act of 1944, paragraph (d) of Sec. 6 listed various costs that would be allowable in the calculation of compensation to war contractors for work done under terminated contracts. It also listed a number of items that "shall not be included as elements of cost." Yet at the end of the section was a provision to the effect that whenever the application of these principles would be impracticable "the contracting agencies may establish alternative methods and standards." In other words, the guides for administrative action with respect to cost items, as with similar standards in many other statutes, had no force whatsoever; they were written into the bill for the sole purpose of supplying window dressing and of giving some members of Congress an illusory feeling of concrete achievement.

Policy Declarations. Declarations of general policy often may seem to be useless ornaments. They are sneered at by many members of Congress who think that all a statute should attempt to do is authorize, direct, or prohibit. Yet increasing weight has been given to policy declarations. Regarding the utility of preambles and textual provisions which describe the necessity for a particular piece of legislation, James M. Landis writes:

> In part this recital takes the place of the old-fashioned preamble, the passing of which many men wise in the law have deplored. Despite the occasional cavalier and cynical treatment of these recitals by the courts, they do help to create the frame of reference within which the administrative is to operate, and to pose the objective that was intended to be reached. It is worth remembering that, at the time of the passage of the Securities Exchange Act of 1934 and the Public Utility Holding Company Act of 1935, representatives of the exchanges and the utilities were considerably disturbed at certain of the recitals. As a result they spent no little effort in an attempt to change some of the language of what professedly is nonoperative phraseology. The years

[8] James Hart, "The Exercise of Rule-making Power," Report of the President's Committee on Administrative Management, p. 316.

have proven that from their standpoint they were right; for both the trend in meaning given the operative provisions of the legislation and the character of subsequent administration was determined, in large measure, by the form and content of the recitals.[9]

The Form of a Bill

What kind of legislative measure should be drafted? How much ground should be covered in one measure? How can it be put together in such a fashion as to stand up under attack? To what extent should deception be used to mislead the opposition? These are the major problems of form that are faced by the sponsors and authors of a bill.

Obviously, they are far from unrelated to the question of the asking price and of the distribution of power and wealth. The two sets of questions must always be considered together, for almost any decision on what may be arbitrarily classified as "substantive" has implications for the form of a measure, and vice versa.

The Type of Measure

The preparation of legislative measures involves choices between various forms of resolutions, between appropriation bills as contrasted with other legislative bills, and between treaties as distinguished from executive agreements. Amendments themselves are also available for use, but there are so many specialized problems involved in amendments that the subject is discussed in a separate section at the end of this chapter.

There are three forms of resolutions: a simple resolution prepared for action in one house of Congress only, a concurrent resolution, and a joint resolution. A Senate or House resolution is the method whereby each house handles its own rules of operating procedures and instructs its committees to engage in studies or investigations. A Senate or House resolution is often used as a method of calling upon the President or an executive agency to submit to either house a report on a given subject. While such a resolution does not have the force of law, it is usually complied with by the President or the appropriate agency. The Federal Trade Commission Act, however, puts the force of law behind a Senate or House resolution directing the Federal Trade Commission to embark upon an investigation.

A concurrent resolution is one that is approved by both houses of Congress but is not sent to the President for signature. It, therefore, does not have the force of law; it merely expresses the intent of the two houses of Congress. In

[9] James M. Landis, "The Administrative Process" (New Haven, Conn.: Yale University Press, 1938), pp. 66–67.

recent years there have been many attempts to use the concurrent resolution as a means of congressional control of the executive branch. In many of the wartime statutes enacted during World War II, Congress was given the authority, through concurrent resolution, to terminate war powers.[10] In the Reorganization Act of 1945 it was provided that a reorganization plan prepared by the President would not go into effect if, within a given number of days, a concurrent resolution of disapproval were passed by both houses of Congress. In the Reorganization Act of 1949 this approach was carried still further by a provision that a Presidential reorganization plan would be ineffective if a simple resolution of disapproval were adopted in either house of Congress.

A joint resolution is, for all intents and purposes, the same as a bill. It is often used in making minor changes in past legislation or in endorsing executive agreements. When so used, it is signed by the President and has the full force of law. It is also used as the vehicle for proposing constitutional amendments, in which case it is not sent to the President for signature or veto.

Theoretically, there is supposed to be a clear distinction between an appropriation bill and all other bills. The former is supposed to be confined to the provision of funds authorized by other legislation. It is not supposed itself to contain new or general "legislation." The rules of each house contain provisions allowing a point of order to be made from the floor against "legislation" in appropriation bills. If the point of order is sustained, the offending item is stricken. Legislative bills, on the other hand, are not supposed to provide funds but merely to authorize subsequent appropriations. Nevertheless, there is a broad borderline area in which either type of measure can be used. If an appropriation act embodies certain prohibitions and limitations on the use of funds, it can be just as effective as substantive legislation. A good example is the appropriation-bill provision enacted during the Eightieth Congress forbidding funds to be used for the employment by the Federal government of members of unions asserting the right to strike. Whether or not this amounted to "legislation" depends entirely upon one's point of view. The advantage of the appropriation-act approach is that an appropriation measure invariably gets passed by Congress in one form or another. Presidential veto is rare. Moreover, the appropriation process is an ideal avenue for those who are afraid of public attention and who want to avoid a full airing of the issues involved. A regular bill, in turn, can be used to direct an agency to use for slightly different purposes money that has already been appropriated. This can have an effect very similar to providing a new appropriation. In the case of government corporations, there is little resort to appropriation bills, and nonappropriation measures are habitually used to make more funds available.

[10] For an interesting historical discussion of the use of concurrent resolutions see Howard White, "Executive Responsibility to Congress via Concurrent Resolutions," *American Political Science Review,* Vol. 36, 1942.

In the field of international relations, there is a clear-cut choice between a treaty and an executive agreement. The former requires a two-thirds majority of the Senate and is not considered in the House.[11] The latter has grown up as a method of attaining an international agreement without having to run the gauntlet of the two-thirds requirement in the Senate. Some executive agreements are handled on the basis of Presidential action only—as was the case with the Atlantic Charter and the Declaration of the United Nations. Others are submitted to both houses of Congress in the form of a bill or joint resolution and require merely a majority vote. Because of the difficulties associated with attaining a two-thirds majority in the Senate, the tendency has been to submit international agreements in the form of executive agreements whenever possible. In fact, the latter vehicle has been used more frequently than the former.

During the course of World War II, for example, one of the major tactics of President Roosevelt and Secretary of State Cordell Hull was to avoid the two-thirds requirement for treaty provisions. Their first step was to initiate a series of purely executive agreements which were not to be submitted to Congress in any form. Members of the Senate Committee on Foreign Relations became alarmed at this prospect and a subcommittee was elected to negotiate with Hull.

> Between them they sought to develop an understanding with the Secretary that would permit the participation of Congress in the negotiation of post-war pacts. In turn, the State Department would receive the authority of the national legislature for negotiating such agreements. The Compromise eventually developed by Senator Green and Assistant Secretary Sayre relied upon the use of the joint resolution. Adoption of a resolution of this character would require only a majority vote in the two houses of Congress. This arrangement would by-pass the minority obstruction in the Senate, while permitting both houses to have a hand in pact-making.[12]

Kenneth Colegrove and others have objected to this use of executive agreements on the ground that it is an evasion of the constitutional limitation of

[11] When the Constitution was written, there was important motivation behind the two-thirds requirement on treaties. New England interests were anxious to protect their fishing rights in the North Atlantic and feared that the majority of the other states might yield these rights in a treaty with England. The representatives of the four Southern states, on the other hand, were interested in navigation on the Mississippi and in the future of New Orleans. This dispute became so heated that consideration was even given to dividing the states into three groups rather than joining them in one union. As part of the over-all settlement of this dispute, the two-thirds provision previously contained in the Articles of Confederation was continued in the Constitution itself.

[12] Kenneth Colegrove, "The American Senate and World Peace" (New York: Vanguard, 1944), p. 94. Other interesting examples are found in the stories of the annexation of Texas and Hawaii, accomplished not by treaty but by congressional joint resolution, as told by Senator George Wharton Pepper. "Family Quarrels: The President, The Senate, The House" (New York: Baker, Voorhis, 1931), pp. 41–42.

treaty making and that no executive agreement can have the sanctity of a treaty. Nevertheless, the availability of the method is hardly a matter of dispute. As Quincy Wright wired to a House committee considering proposals for amending the treaty provisions of the Constitution: "President now has authority, if supported by Congress, to make international agreements on any subject within the delegated powers of Congress." [13]

The Scope

The draftsmen of the bill introduced in 1947 to abolish the Jackson Hole National Monument had no concern with the problem of scope. There was only one monument to be abolished. There were no related subjects which by any stretch of the imagination could have been appropriately dealt with in the same measure. But the draftsmen of the Taft-Hartley Labor-Management Relations Act faced an entirely different situation. They were dealing with an extremely broad and complex field in which there were dozens of points that might properly be dealt with in one bill and dozens of others that might be reserved for separate handling.

Omnibus Measures.[14] The drafters of the Legislation Reorganization Act of 1946 were quick to see the many advantages in an "omnibus bill," a term used to describe a bill composed of many parts, each of which might also stand on its own two feet. The bases for their drafting work were the recommendations contained in a report of the Joint Committee on the Organization of Congress. In all, there were thirty-eight recommendations, divided into eight different categories. There was ample material for from eight to thirty-eight separate bills. The members of the committee decided, however, to have one omnibus measure. The wisdom of this decision was borne out by the results. First of all, the big bill made a big splash. Its very size endowed it with a significance that could never have been achieved by a less ambitious measure. A set of separate measures introduced simultaneously might have had the same initial impact, but public interest would certainly have been weakened and dissipated in the attempt to follow each separate measure on its tedious way through the congressional mill. The omnibus device served, therefore, as a means of both creating and sustaining public interest. It also served to shield and make less objectionable two of the most controversial provisions in the bill—the simplified committee system and the salary raises for members of Congress.[15]

[13] Hearings before subcommittee number 3 of the Committee on the Judiciary, House of Representatives, 78th Cong., 2d Sess., p. 145.

[14] For a full discussion of proposals for omnibus appropriations bills, see Chap. 20.

[15] Another illustration of how controversial provisions can be shielded by less controversial provisions is found in Marriner Eccles' vivid story of the three titles of the Banking Act of 1935, "Beckoning Frontiers" (New York: Knopf, 1951), pp. 196–199.

The omnibus approach also provides the opportunity to execute a hidden ball play. The broader the scope of the measure, the more chance there is of its carrying along to enactment provisions that would otherwise stand no chance of being enacted into law. At the hearings of the Joint Committee on the Organization of Congress, before the drafting of the committee's bill, Professor Fred A. Fairchild of Yale University appeared on behalf of the United States Chamber of Commerce and proposed that a Joint Congressional Budget Committee be established to set annually an over-all ceiling upon appropriations. This recommendation was set forth in the Joint Committee's report and became the basis for a brief and harmless-looking provision in the legislative reorganization bill. It so happened that this provision was drafted in a manner that endowed it with tremendous significance by requiring the President every year to keep expenditures below a ceiling set forth in a concurrent resolution. It would have had the serious effect of depriving the President of any veto power on measures to cut appropriations, thereby strengthening the position of "economy-minded" business interests with active representation in Congress. If this provision had been handled separately, it would have been subjected to careful analysis and would probably have been revised considerably before reaching the Senate floor. Embedded in a broad omnibus measure, however, this provision never received the attention it deserved—either in committee, on the floor, or by the Bureau of the Budget and other executive agencies affected by it. It was not until the bill passed the Senate and reached the desk of the Speaker of the House that the administration had a chance to present its views fully and, at the eleventh hour, have the provision changed.

The combination of separate elements in an omnibus measure also provides the basis for winning the support of diverse interests and pressure groups. In 1933 the National Industrial Recovery Act gave business exemption from the antitrust laws, gave labor the right to organize and bargain collectively, and gave city and state governments the benefits of a large-scale public-works program. The consolidated appeal contained in the measure was one of the major factors in its rapid enactment. A broad bill also provides its backers with a flexibility which is extremely useful in maneuvering. An omnibus bill can contain extra provisions which, like a ship's ballast, can help keep a bill afloat in its long journey through stormy congressional seas. Without resulting in mortal injury to the bill, they can be dropped in a manner that will appease the opposition. In the case of the legislative reorganization bill, for example, the provision calling for a director of congressional personnel was certainly not a fundamental part of the measure but it proved to be useful ballast on the Senate floor when Senator La Follette of Wisconsin agreed to have it deleted at the request of Senator Kenneth McKellar of Tennessee. This flexibility also provides the opportunity to plan the referral of a bill to a friendly committee. If the health-insurance provisions of the Truman Administration's health-insurance bill had been handled separately, the bill would have been referred to the unfriendly Senate Finance Committee. To avoid this, an omnibus measure was prepared which included not only health insurance but also a lengthy title on the public health service. Through this device, it was possible to have the bill referred to the Senate Labor Committee whose chairman was one of the bill's sponsors and who quickly arranged for public hearings.

Narrow Measures. In many situations, a narrowly drafted bill is far more appropriate than an omnibus measure. The bills to exempt railroads, newspapers, and insurance companies from the antitrust laws have all been handled separately. If they had been combined into one measure, the amount of public attention that would have been attracted would have been a great impediment. As it was, the backers of each separate bill made their case for one particular type of exemption. None of them had to assume the onerous burden of defending a measure that would have been attacked as utterly wrecking the American antitrust tradition.

Another consideration is the fact that a number of bills dealing with various phases of the same subject provide an opportunity for a number of Congressmen to serve as the chief sponsors. There is something about being the sponsor of a bill which cannot be gained merely by having the Congressman's name appear on a list with other sponsors. During the Eightieth Congress, private-utility companies gave their strong support to seven different measures, each dealing with various aspects of public-utility regulation and public-power activities.

A narrowly conceived bill can often slip through the crevices of congressional opposition at a time when a broad measure is stalled in its tracks. In 1946 the Case labor-relations bill was vetoed by the President and the veto was upheld in the House of Representatives. The President's veto message, however, did not take issue with the antiracketeering provisions of this omnibus measure. As soon as the veto was upheld, the antiracketeering provisions were handled separately and were quickly enacted into law.

The valley-authority movement has thus far developed on the basis of separate bills. There have been bills to set up a Missouri Valley Authority, to establish a Columbia Valley Authority, and so forth. While Representative John Rankin of Mississippi has introduced an omnibus measure providing for seven TVA's, there has been little support for this approach. It has been felt rather that each river-valley problem should be approached on its own terms, with a special measure aimed at developing the largest possible amount of local support. However, in a period of depression and unemployment, there might develop potential support for drastic action. Under such conditions, the type of bill introduced by Representative Rankin might prove to be the most effective.

Finally, the smaller the scope of a bill, the easier it is to prepare. A narrow bill can be prepared with less drain upon the resources of its backers and with infinitely more speed. Every additional provision means new drafting problems, new pressures to be weighed, and new compromises to be formulated.

Design for Combat

In an item-by-item count, the great bulk of legislative action would seem to consist of purely routine correction and uncontested enactments. Much that goes uncontested in the present would likely have been bones of violent contention in a past day before one or another precedent was established or area of consensus came into being. Other uncontested measures may actually be "out-of-court" settlements, or they may be compromises destined to fail because their sponsors are unwilling to offend powerful groups. If it were possible, however, to separate the relatively few "important" measures from the overwhelming number of "unimportant" ones, it would be found that each of the important bills is a fighting document designed for combat almost as literally and carefully as any tank or artillery piece intended for a battlefield. At the very least, each significant bill is devised to capture a certain amount of attention. At the most, it is aimed at standing up under the shock of attack throughout the legislative, administrative, or judicial processes. From this standpoint, the manner in which a bill is organized and the kind of language that is used are of considerable interest.

Subdivision. The first problem of organization is subdivision. The section is the basic unit of a bill. Each section may be divided into subsections; each subsection into paragraphs; each paragraph into subparagraphs. The various sections can be assembled into titles or even into separately lettered parts of titles. Although there can be no general rule as to where the line can be drawn between any of these segments, experience has proved that a bill's provisions can be understood best if no segments are allowed to become too long and if the various segments are grouped together in a balanced and logical fashion. Draftsmen will often give major emphasis to the strong points in a bill by putting them at the very beginning or by spelling them out with far more language than might otherwise be necessary. More controversial points, on the other hand, can be tucked away at the end in brief and unobtrusive language. Detachability is also a major consideration. "If its several parts are too tightly dovetailed together, if it is so constructed that a modification of one part necessarily involves numerous modifications of other parts, an amendment made in the course of debate may throw it hopelessly out of gear." [16] The careful draftsman, therefore, often erects his structure along the

[16] Ilbert, *op. cit.*, p. 110.

lines of a large, rambling, one-story building rather than of a skyscraper. When this is done, almost any part can be removed without irreparable injury to the other parts. This has the extra advantage of allowing more room for the addition of new provisions. In a particularly complex bill it has also proved helpful to have a subtitle for each section—sometimes even for subsections—and a table of contents listing all the subtitles.

Titles. Increasing use is being made of special sections providing for what is called a "short title." While the regular title which appears before the enacting clause is usually too long for ready reference, the short title provides a convenient label. For example, the regular title of the bill which finally became the Full Employment Act of 1946 was "To establish a national policy and program to assure continuing full employment in a free competitive economy, through the concerted efforts of industry, agriculture, labor, State and local governments, and the Federal Government." Quite a mouthful! But Sec. 1 of this bill ran as follows: "This Act may be cited as the 'Full Employment Act of 1945.'" This short title was invaluable in dramatizing the measure. The charge was often made that the bill was misnamed, since the short title gave the impression that enactment of the legislation would automatically provide full employment. Be that as it may, a more subdued and less challenging title would have served to weaken the chances of obtaining any legislation of this type whatsoever.

Statements of Purpose. Another labeling device is to preface a bill with a preamble or statement of purposes. Such a statement can be invaluable in setting forth the need for a certain type of legislation and the values to be derived from it. It can also serve as a handbook of arguments on behalf of the measure and refutation of the charges made by its opponents. An interesting example is the set of whereases which Senator Vandenberg brought forth as a prelude to the 1947 legislation to aid Greece and Turkey. The major argument against this measure, and against the Truman doctrine on which it was based, was that it side-stepped the United Nations. Senator Vandenberg therefore devised language which indicated why aid to Greece and Turkey was needed and offered a set of six whereases justifying the legislation, the last of which was as follows:

> Whereas the United Nations is not now in a position to furnish to Greece and Turkey the financial and economic assistance which is immediately required; and Whereas the furnishing of such assistance to Greece and Turkey by the United States will contribute to the freedom and independence of all members of the United Nations in conformity with the principles and purposes of the Charter: Now, therefore. . . .

The prefatory language used in this legislation is rather unusual since it appeared before, rather than after, the enactment clause and, technically, was not even a part of the statute itself. It is more customary to use for this purpose the various declarations of policy appearing in early sections of a measure.[17]

Relation to Existing Legislation. With respect to the language of a bill itself, a primary fact to be reckoned with is the prior existence of a tremendous body of related language in statutes, administrative rules and regulations, and judicial decisions. Hence the general character of most bills is commonly "the insertion of a new part in a long-worked machine." [18] A good example is the Interstate Commerce Act which was first passed in 1887 and has since been directly amended by almost fifty separate statutes and indirectly affected by many other acts of Congress. The Act as amended now encompasses about 230 pages. The index to it, including reference to supplementary legislation as prepared by the Interstate Commerce Commission itself, covers more than 150 pages. This labyrinthine body of existing law hangs over the head of anyone who attempts to draft a new measure dealing with the regulation of transportation. It makes it well-nigh impossible to formulate a transportation bill that can be fully comprehensible in its own terms. A similar situation exists with respect to bills dealing with taxes and other long-tilled fields of public policy.

An important decision that must always be faced, therefore, is whether a bill should be drafted in the form of amendments to existing law or as a new measure with or without provisions repealing certain elements in the old law.

> The method of amendment has the advantage of apparent simplicity. It focuses attention upon the proposed change. But it has technical difficulties, other sections of the law may be affected, and later give rise to litigation and judicial interpretation as to implied repeals. A new law offers the advantage of unity of purpose and language, has the difficulty of exaggerating the importance of the change to be made.[19]

The dilemma is often solved by a combination of both approaches.

At times the use of the straight amendment approach is adopted because it has a propagandistic value. An opponent of the Taft-Hartley Act made the following observation:

> It has already been pointed out that key provisions in the act nominally took the form of an "amendment" to the Wagner Act. Why call it an "amendment" when it is a radically different law? The answer is that it was politically wise to do so, because the sponsors knew that large masses of workers would bitterly resent a repeal of the

[17] Statements of this kind may be introduced with such phrases as "It is the policy (or purpose) of the Congress . . . ," ". . . of the Federal Government . . . ," or ". . . of the people of the United States. . . ." At times they are preceded by "findings."

[18] "The Making and Form of Bills," p. 182.

[19] Harvey Walker, "The Legislative Process" (New York: Ronald, 1948), p. 355.

Wagner Act, hence the misleading designation of "amendment" to the Wagner Act, implying that the Wagner Act essentially was retained.[20]

To the extent that amendments are used, another dilemma arises to confront the draftsman. On the one hand, he can merely refer to the previous act, thereby making it almost impossible for anyone to understand the nature of the amendment without looking up the previous act in the statute books. On the other hand, he can reproduce an amended form of the appropriate section of the statute that is being altered. This sometimes has the effect of not indicating in any precise manner the nature of the change. A closely related problem is the extent to which portions of past statutes are to be incorporated by reference without directly repeating the language that is incorporated. This device has the advantage of indicating that what is proposed to be enacted has already received approval in other circumstances. It also serves as a method of accomplishing major objectives in an unobtrusive manner or even in a manner that will prevent many people from finding out what is really being proposed.

Intelligibility. It is sometimes thought that the test of good drafting is whether the product is intelligible to a lay reader. To some extent this is symptomatic of the great illusion that in a democratic society every intelligent citizen should be able to understand every issue of public policy. It may also represent something of a vestigial remnant of Jeremy Bentham's old dream of a comprehensive code that would be "designed for all understandings, and particularly for the less enlightened class." [21]

The germ of truth behind this approach lies in the fact that there is always a certain amount of leeway with respect to using more words or less words, more Anglo-Saxon words or more polysyllabic Latin derivatives, more involved language or more simple language. Some draftsmen still produce unnecessarily torturing language, reminiscent of the "tortuous and ungodly jumble" of the English law in pre-Bentham days. A striking example of this was pointed out by Representative Kitchin back in 1918 when he was defending the legislation that first provided for the Office of the Legislative Counsel in Congress:

> Take the excess- and war-profits-tax title. No tax feature of the bill was at first more complicated and so hard to arrange and simplify. . . . I venture the assertion that not in the knowledge or observation of any gentlemen here was a complicated proposition put into a clearer or more understandable form and terms than are the provisions in the bill relating to this tax. . . . Mr. Beaman put into about five lines

[20] Elias Lieberman, "Unions before the Bar" (New York: Harper, 1950), p. 323.

[21] Jeremy Bentham, "The Theory of Legislation" (New York: Harcourt, Brace, 1931), p. 157.

of this bill what it took a page in the existing excess-profits-tax law, and what it took two or three pages of the English law to state and provide.[22]

Many draftsmen seek, and often attain, the goal of writing legislative provisions so clearly that they cannot be clarified by a paraphrase.

Nevertheless, complex policies cannot be written in a simple fashion. To attempt simplicity in most legislation "is likely to be as profitless as to attempt to turn a Yale lock with a penknife blade." [23] A bill dealing with tax reform, for example, no matter how great an attempt may be made to make the language intelligible, can be understood only by tax experts. The draft which Representative Kitchin found so "understandable" was probably unreadable for, and unread by, most members of Congress. Furthermore, precision itself is a goal which often conflicts with intelligibility. Sometimes the only way to state a thing in clean-cut terms is to use more words, highly technical words, and an intricate exposition of ideas. An effort to achieve a draft that is appealing to the reader may result in creating, beneath the surface appearance of easy intelligibility, one complex ambiguity after another.

Another standard that has sometimes been used to judge the quality of draftsmanship is the ability to write legislative language that leaves no room for interpretation by the courts. One writer on the subject has said:

> It is of prime importance in choosing language for statutes to remember that if the language of the law is clear and plain, courts of justice have no authority, because of evil consequences which would result, to give it a construction different from its natural and obvious meaning. . . . If the bill is exact, it leaves no room for judicial legislation under the guise of an effort to ascertain the legislative intent.[24]

Few bills of any real significance in complex fields of public policy could possibly live up to this standard. Adequate coverage of all conceivable situations is impossible. Although the treatises on the statutory construction of laws provide valuable information on how various judges have construed language in the past, they provide no firm basis whatsoever for predicting how they will do so in the future.

Ultimate precision in the use of language is a sheer impossibility. A word, as Justice Holmes pointed out, "is not a crystal, transparent and unchanged" but "the skin of a living thought and may vary greatly in color and content

[22] *Congressional Record,* 56th Cong., 2d Sess., 1918, pp. 701–702. Mr. Beaman's services had been made available to members of Congress on a demonstration basis by the Legislative Drafting Research Fund of Columbia University. The demonstration proved the utility of having trained draftsmen attached to Congress, and provisions to set up the congressional service with Government funds were written into the Revenue Act of 1918.

[23] "The Making and Form of Bills," p. 182.

[24] Jones, *op. cit.,* p. 110.

according to the circumstances and the time in which it is used." [25] There is a definite limit upon how much of an agreed-upon meaning can be read into the words of any statute. Beyond that limit the field is wide open for creative construction by administrators and judges. In many situations, moreover, the real art of draftsmanship is found not in the ability to state things precisely, for to do so might lose too many votes, but to state things with sufficient generality—or with sufficient ambiguity, if you will—to gain or maintain the necessary support to secure enactment and to provide administrators and judges with the leeway needed to meet new situations.

The Use of Deception

Deliberate intent to deceive is an inescapable element in any conflict. The legislative conflict is no exception to this rule. The bargaining process itself requires a certain amount of deception. Ultimate objectives are concealed. Opponents are prevented from learning the next moves that are to be taken. Sows' ears are talked of as if they were silken purses. It would be miraculous, therefore, if legislative drafting did not on occasion include an important element of deception as to the meaning of a bill's provisions.

The drafting of a bill offers endless opportunities for deception. First, within the framework of a legislative proposal the simplest sentence composed of the simplest words is often far different from what it seems to be. The meaning of most bills can be ascertained only by appraising the interrelationships among a large number of highly complex sentences. A flat prohibition against certain types of activity may be modified by a phrase or proviso in another section or even converted into an open encouragement of the identical activity. Secondly, as indicated earlier, innumerable tricks of concealment are possible in the drafting of provisions amending previous acts or in incorporating parts of them by reference.[26] When provisions of this type are inserted at the end of a long measure or buried within language that attracts attention for unrelated reasons, there are relatively few persons who will take the trouble to find out what they really mean. "You are going to find out that there is more in this bill than may meet the eye," Representative Hartley is quoted as having boasted during a defense of the Taft-Hartley Act.[27]

In addition to the standard tricks of the trade, the substantive ideas in many measures are so complex as to provide endless opportunities for technicians to pull the wool over the eyes of laymen. When such opportunities are fully ex-

[25] *Towne v. Eisner,* 245 U.S. 418 (1917).

[26] Concealment is not something that has recently been invented. It is said that Caligula wrote his laws in very small characters and hung them on high pillars to ensnare his people.

[27] Lieberman, *op. cit.,* p. 315. "This was no idle boast," Lieberman adds, "for the law contains many hidden anti-labor traps calculated to have far-reaching effects on the rights and strength of labor unions in the United States."

ploited, the story of what was done can be unraveled only through an extended explanation.

The United States Housing Act of 1937 provides a first-rate example. When this Act was in the drafting stage, provisions were inserted allowing local housing authorities to obtain loans from the Federal government at an interest rate of 3 per cent and to repay the Government over a period as long as sixty years. In addition, the Government was to give the local housing authority an annual subsidy for the purpose of bringing the rents down to a level that could be afforded by low-income families. Each annual subsidy payment was limited to 3½ per cent of the total cost of any housing project. In order to find out what the net cost would really be to the Government, the average reader of the Act subtracted from the 3½ per cent the Government would pay out the 3 per cent that the Government would get back in the form of an interest payment. This indicated a net loss to the Government of ½ of 1 per cent a year. He then multiplied ½ of 1 per cent by sixty years and came to the conclusion that the Government's net subsidy amounted to 30 per cent of the cost of construction. Since the previous housing program under the Public Works Administration had provided for a capital grant of 40 per cent of the cost of construction, the obvious conclusion was that this new proposal was indeed very moderate.

The bill passed with a substantial majority in both houses. Subsequently, however, many members of Congress, prodded by the real-estate lobby, started to pay a little more attention to the mathematics of this subsidy arrangement. They discovered what would be obvious to a banking expert, the fact that the only way to know the annual charge on repaying a loan is to consult an amortization table. It so happens that any amortization table will show that the annual payment needed to repay a $100 loan over a sixty-year period is $3.50 or 3½ per cent. In other words, the Government's 3½ per cent subsidy to local housing authorities was exactly the amount needed to repay both interest and principle on total cost of any housing project. So far as a local housing authority would be concerned, therefore, the Housing Act of 1937 allowed a 100 per cent subsidy—not 30 per cent—on the cost of the construction. From the viewpoint of government financing, this arrangement seemed better than a lump-sum capital grant, since it spread the 100 per cent subsidy over a period of sixty years, adding only a minor charge to the Federal budget in any single year. From the point of view of low-income families this arrangement was also quite effective. Any smaller subsidy would have meant a rent beyond their means and would have denied access to the housing projects to those who were most in need of decent housing.

If the full implications of this formula had been clear before enactment of the statute, the probability is that the amount of subsidy would have been reduced considerably. On the other hand, the revelation a few years later as to the real meaning of the Act's provisions unquestionably added fuel to the high flames that were lit by the opponents of any type of public housing. In 1939, when President Roosevelt asked for additional funds for the low-rent public-housing program, one speaker after another on the floor of the House denounced the subsidy provisions of the 1937 Act, and the Roosevelt proposal was buried under an overwhelming vote of disapproval.

As this illustration suggests, deception of any kind always runs the risk of leading to serious repercussions. Self-restraint is the safest course in this matter. Jeremy Bentham might well have applied to legislative drafting his comment concerning business practices, "that, if there were no such thing as honesty, it would be a good speculation to invent it, as a means of making one's fortune." [28]

The Arsenal of Amendments

As an observant judge once remarked, "Laws seem to be born full-grown about as often as men are." [29] It is a rare bill that is regarded by anyone, even its proudest authors and staunchest backers, as a finished document to be approved or voted on in the form in which it is introduced. Most bills are regarded by everyone as open to amendment at any time. Occasionally, the amendments are even offered to bills that have no chance of obtaining consideration by a committee. Sometimes the sponsors of a bill will amend their own measure even before it obtains consideration by a committee. If the committee-consideration stage is reached, proposals for amendments fly thick and fast. On the floor, the key maneuvers and the major votes usually relate to amendments rather than to the bill as a whole. The only purpose of a conference committee is to produce amendments that will reconcile the differences between the two houses.

There are many differences between an amendment and a bill. A bill can be vetoed by the President. An amendment cannot be vetoed, since the President has never been given the power, enjoyed by many state governors, to reject a portion of a bill. Amendments, moreover, get less public attention. They usually deal with what seem to be minor details. They are hard for the press or any outside observers to understand. Sometimes they pile up one on top of another in a manner that defies comprehension by anyone except a small handful of members of Congress, experts, and lobbyists.

Amendments for the Offensive

Amendments are peculiarly suited to certain types of offensive fighting. The historic method of opposing a strongly backed measure is to propose crippling

[28] Bentham, *op. cit.*, p. 64.

[29] Judge Dean, *Waters v. Wolf*, 162 Pa. 167.

amendments. This was the strategy used by Senator Henry Cabot Lodge and his small group of irreconcilables in their fight against the League of Nations. Rather than make a frontal attack upon the Versailles Treaty itself, they proposed one reservation after another. They thereby drew public attention away from the major issue, split and confused the Senate supporters of the treaty, and by the time the final vote came, had succeeded in developing a measure that was no longer acceptable to President Wilson.[30] Senator Borah himself took the lead in developing a similar attack some years later against a resolution for American affiliation with the World Court.[31] In this case the Senate accepted the resolution with Borah's reservation, but the League of Nations balked.

More recently, the same strategy was followed in the 1946 struggle on the extension of price-control legislation. The major opponents of price control concentrated their attention upon writing into the extension measure a long series of amendments exempting various commodities and providing for various formulas that would facilitate price increases. The result was what Price Administrator Chester Bowles called a "booby-trap bill."

A striking variant of this approach occurs when members of Congress offer or support amendments which run directly counter to their own views and are intended to make a bill more, rather than less, undesirable. In writing about his experiences in the House of Representatives, former Representative Jerry Voorhis of California tells how this strategy was used by the prolabor group in the House. After the antilabor bloc had succeeded in writing into a pending bill amendments that made it more and more unacceptable to the prolabor group, "the prolabor groups would decide that their best strategy was to 'make the bill as bad as possible so it would be easier to vote against it.' Thus there would be only a handful of the middle group opposing the amendments. And when the final vote came it was almost impossible for a conscientious member to support the bill. . . ."[32]

One of the most effective types of crippling amendments deals strictly with matters of administration and enforcement. When a new function for a Department is proposed, a favorite device is to offer an amendment switching the administration to another agency that is either unfriendly to the program or is incapable of administering it. Another tactic is to provide for such extensive powers of judicial review as to tie up the administrators in unending litigation. Still another is to reduce fines for evasion of any prohibition to an inconsequential sum of money.

30 The essence of this strategy was frankly outlined by Senator Lodge in his "The Senate and the League of Nations" (New York: Scribner, 1925).

31 "Senator Borah had learned a valuable lesson from Lodge," comments Karl Schriftgiesser in "This Was Normalcy" (Boston: Little, Brown, 1948), pp. 232–233.

32 Jerry Voorhis, "Confessions of a Congressman" (Garden City, N.Y.: Doubleday, 1947), p. 98.

During the 1946 and 1947 conflicts on labor legislation, opponents of the Case bill and the Taft-Hartley Act often used the technique of threatening retaliatory amendments. When the Case bill reached the Senate, an amendment was proposed by Senator Byrd requiring unions to give a public accounting of their financial operations. Senator Taylor countered this amendment with a retaliatory proposal that would require members of the Senate to register the amounts and sources of their outside income. While it is difficult to judge whether the Taylor threat was a decisive factor, the Byrd amendment did not succeed. Subsequently, during the drafting of the Taft-Hartley Act, Senator Pepper threatened to propose an amendment increasing regulations upon business for every provision that increased government controls over labor unions. While in this case the threat was never fully carried out, it is conceivable that if an adequate set of retaliatory amendments of this type had been prepared, Senator Pepper might have succeeded in toning down some of the labor controls in the Taft-Hartley Act.

Amendments of this type are often strictly propagandistic in character. One of the earlier advocates of prohibition repeal, for example, habitually made a telling point by repeatedly offering appropriations amendments providing tremendous sums for enforcement of the prohibition laws. During the 1920's, the elder Senator La Follette "showed up the reckless trend of the entire Harding-Coolidge-Hoover era when he sarcastically suggested that all acts of Congress should carry a rider saying that 'this Act shall not apply to any individual or corporation worth $100,000,000 or more.' "[33]

Defensive Amendments

Amendments are also basic to the defense of any proposal. During the Case bill debate, for example, Senator Pepper concentrated his attack upon provisions of an amendment introduced by Senator Byrd to control the operation of union health and welfare funds. Since his attack uncovered many weaknesses in the Byrd proposal, Senator Byrd himself offered numerous modifications upon his own amendment.

The variety of defensive amendments that may be used is well illustrated by the following report on the strategy of a measure's sponsors after it had sustained its first major attack:

> At the conclusion of the hearings on S. 1944 it was obvious to those who had shared in its drafting that some revision would be necessary. Certain amendments were called for because of deficiencies in the bill which had become evident either before or at the hearings. Other amendments seemed desirable because thereby criticism could be met without requiring substantial sacrifices in objectives. Still others,

[33] Schriftgiesser, *op. cit.*, p. 130.

though regretted, seemed inescapable if the opposition to the bill were to be reduced to a point where it could be overcome.[34]

On many occasions the sponsors of a bill will offer strengthening or perfecting amendments before any critic has an opportunity to uncover defects. In this category falls the amendment to the School Lunch Bill of 1946, introduced by Representative Hall, providing that all school lunches subsidized through Federal funds should be handled on a nonprofit basis. Another perfecting amendment introduced from the floor in the case of measures providing for the expenditure of Federal funds is the antidiscrimination amendment frequently recommended by the National Association for the Advancement of Colored People. This amendment usually requires that any services promoted through Federal aid be equally available to Negroes as well as to whites, without prohibiting the use of funds by institutions that segregate Negroes from whites.

Riders

A highly specialized type of amendment, one that has little or nothing to do with the purposes of the bill to which it is offered, is the "rider."

In 1918, when the agriculture appropriation bill was before Congress, the "drys" succeeded in attaching to it an amendment providing for wartime prohibition of intoxicating liquors. In 1925, when a post-office appropriation bill was up for consideration, Senator Walsh of Massachusetts offered an amendment dealing with campaign expenditures, later known as the Corrupt Practices Act. In 1937, Senator Tydings of Maryland attached the Resale Price Maintenance Act to an appropriation bill for the District of Columbia. In each of these cases, the sponsors of the rider succeeded in side-stepping regular committee consideration. Because the riders were attached to appropriation bills on which essential government operations depended, the President had no choice but to approve the legislation.

But appropriation bills are not the only vehicles to which riders may be attached, nor is passage of the rider the only objective. Late in the 1946 session of the Senate, when the Tidelands Oil Bill was being debated, Senator Morse of Oregon offered as an amendment the anti-poll-tax bill that had already been approved by the House. Immediately the Southern Democrats began to filibuster in an effort to prevent a vote on the anti-poll-tax issue. Since the Senate leaders were eager to proceed with their business, and since Morse refused to withdraw his amendment, the effort to obtain action on the Tidelands

[34] David F. Cavers, "The Food, Drug, and Cosmetic Act of 1938: Its Legislative History and Its Substantive Provisions," *Law and Contemporary Problems,* Vol. 6, No. 1, Winter, 1939, p. 10.

Oil Bill was abandoned—which was precisely Morse's objective in the first place. Earlier in the same session a similar ruse was used to defeat a bill raising the minimum-wage level. Senator Russell of Georgia won Senate acceptance of a rider which revised the parity-price formula in a manner wholly unacceptable to the Administration. The amended bill was passed by the Senate. By the time the bill reached the House it became evident that the Senate would accept no bill without the farm-parity amendment and the President would approve no bill that contained it. So the bill was allowed to die.

Any bill which seems destined to achieve final passage tends to attract those who want a "free ride." Samuel Clemens found this out during the course of his labors on behalf of copyright legislation to protect authors against the unauthorized publication of their writings. "See here, Uncle Joe," he complained to Speaker Cannon, "does every fellow who comes here get hitched up to a train he does not want to pull?" [35]

[35] L. White Busbey, "Uncle Joe Cannon" (New York: Holt, 1927), p. 271.

Chapter 12

CAMPAIGN LEADERSHIP AND GROUP SUPPORT

While some of the myths about government are the product of naïveté, others shine with a slick veneer of sophistication. Among the latter is the stereotype picture of myriad lobbyists swarming through the halls of Congress trying to influence legislative decisions. On one side, according to this conception, stand the members of Congress trying to see the issues and make up their minds on competing claims. On the other side are the lobbyists conducting never-ending campaigns for or against this or that bill.

Yet if the total bulk of legislative campaign activities were to be compared to an iceberg, the portion handled solely by professional lobbyists—both those acting on behalf of private organizations and those representing government agencies—would be only a fraction of the segment appearing above the surface of the water. A full-fledged legislative campaign covers not only all phases of the legislative process from drafting to Presidential signature or veto, but also a broad range of variegated activities.

The initiative and the continuing coordination of the activities of a legislative campaign require the most skillful exercise of campaign leadership if they are to be effective. A legislative campaign necessitates the organization of group support. Leadership and its group support will be dealt with in the present chapter. In the chapter that follows it will be seen how leaders and supporters utilize and are affected by the production and dissemination of propaganda and by the development and application of political pressure.

While the lobbyists usually take some part in these aspects of legislative campaigning, the people they speak to and the people they speak for—whether members of Congress, Presidents, executive officials, or leaders of private organizations—are also campaigners. The great difference between the professional lobbyists and the others is that the former include a greater proportion of the foot soldiers and lieutenants and a lesser proportion of the generals.

Campaign Leadership

Of the various sources of power spelled out in Chap. 8 leadership is the active, energizing element. It is leadership which transmits wealth, people, and strategic situations into power, extends such power through organization of support, and puts it to use through the dissemination of propaganda and the application of pressure.

It is pertinent, therefore, to give special attention at this point to the strategy and tactics of leadership and to the organizational foundations of this leadership.

The Strategy and Tactics of Leadership

Strategy can be defined as the development of a basic campaign plan. Tactics can be defined as the application of such a plan at specific points.

Again, this is a distinction which is far from absolute. One man's strategy is another man's tactics. In both strategic and tactical operations, one must calculate alternatives without a precise quantitative measurement of the risks involved and must, in the final analysis, act on hunch.[1] In both, one faces identical problems of defining objectives, developing and executing a combat plan, and negotiating settlements.

Objectives. "First things come first, and I can't alienate certain votes I need for measures that are more important at the moment by pushing any measure that would entail a fight."[2] It was with words such as these that Eleanor Roosevelt's husband customarily countered when she attempted to have him give all-out support to certain types of civil-rights legislation. Presidents, however, are not the only legislative strategists with *must* lists. The major contestants are always in a position where they can win any one objective by concentrating all their resources upon it—but at the expense of sacrificing all other objectives. Every active participant in the legislative struggle must decide what he is going to sacrifice in order to obtain the objectives that count the most. "Pursue one great decisive aim with force and determination," wrote one of the greatest of military strategists, Carl von Clausewitz.[3] Unless this is done, one's resources are bound to be dribbled away in profitless efforts.

It is simpler, of course, if "the great decisive aim" is a clearly-spelled-out, long-range goal. Yet in many situations the "great decisive aim" has to be altered and redefined on the basis of almost continuous improvisation. Objectives are factors that unite or divide one's supporters. In a campaign based upon a loose coalition of sharply divergent groups, any attempt to establish

[1] In "The Theory of Games and Economic Behavior" by John von Newmann and Oskar Morgenstern (Princeton, N.J.: Princeton University Press, 1944), the case is made that in every problem of strategy there can be only a single optimum policy and that it would be irrational to act otherwise. While this theory sounds appealing, the closer one gets to action in given situations, the less applicability it has.

[2] Eleanor Roosevelt, "This I Remember" (New York: Harper, 1949), p. 162.

[3] Carl von Clausewitz, "Principles of War" (Harrisburg, Pa.: Military Service Publishing Co., 1942), p. 19.

fixed and nonflexible objectives would be inconsistent with the maintenance of maximum strength. The broad legislative campaigns of the New Deal and of the Fair Deal both fall into this category.

The scope of any group's objectives, apart from the various priorities that may be applied to them, has a direct bearing upon its decisions to support or oppose candidates for elective (and appointive) posts. Limited-purpose groups often judge members of Congress and executive officials by a single standard, that is, the position taken on one legislative issue. The broader a group's objectives become, the more difficult it is to use a single standard. In the same way a President, whose legislative objectives are invariably multiple despite the changing priorities of the "must list," can never afford to use a single standard. In the distribution of Presidential rewards and punishments he can never forget that even the rebellious Senator who opposes him on most things might be a valuable source of support on a few vital things.

Combat Plans. The development and execution of a combat plan call for attention to special problems associated with given objectives, to strategic positions, to the use of weapons, to intelligence operations, and to bluffing. All these elements are affected by the psychological make-up of leaders. No matter what the objectives may be, sound strategy calls for a full appraisal of strategic positions already occupied or that might be attained in the future. Many opportunities for successful operations can be lost if the possibilities of fully exploiting the former are neglected. Much energy can be wasted in propaganda and pressure that is not carefully directed toward winning support at specific points of influence. Some points of influence—such as committee chairmen, party-policy committees, and the highest officials of executive agencies and private organizations—are obvious. In many other cases—as with individual Congressmen, technical experts, office assistants, and secretaries—their utility is harder to detect or may be nonexistent unless special operations arise into which they may fit.

The use of weapons is also important. There are times when more use of propaganda is needed, others when only direct pressure will suffice. There are some supporting groups that can use only limited forms and media of influence. There are others that, in certain situations, can be called upon to use a variety of weapons. An interesting illustration of skill and restraint in the choice of campaign methods is found in the efforts of the National Association of Real Estate Boards to weaken Senator Taft's support of public-housing legislation. "The quiet and easy way you are handling your political contacts there is quite disturbing to the Senator," wrote a Washington official of the group to the Columbus, Ohio, real-estate board. "The more subtle you can be, the more effective you are. You do not need to exert a public-relations campaign in the press or radio. That helps the Senator. The behind-the-scenes operations with his political cronies are what counts. In my opinion, this is no time for public opinion pressure. It is time for political infighting without fanfare." [4]

Throughout any campaign the strategist-tactician must develop sources of intelligence that keep him minutely informed concerning the lay of the land, the progress of the battle in all theaters of operation, and the plans of his opponents. Only thus can one know *where* to get "fustest" with the "mostest." A good intelligence operation concentrates not so much on learning about public opinion in general but upon the views and intentions of people with power. It is not limited to the analysis of generally available information but penetrates to the innermost recesses of supposedly confidential meetings and conferences.

On the other hand, the strategist-tactician must try to keep opponents from seeing the whole picture. This calls for surprise and diversion. "It is the very essence of politics to set up diversions. . . ." [5] It also calls at times for the deliberate creation of confusion and, more frequently, for deliberate bluffing. Yet if these tactics are to be effective, they cannot be carried too far. As in poker, the opposition must be misled into thinking that most of the time one's moves can be predicted. Moreover, to be safe, one must usually act upon the assumption that in at least some cases one's bluffs will be detected.

As Von Clausewitz has pointed out, the success of any combat plan is greatly affected by the emotional drives of leaders. "A powerful emotion must stimulate the great ability of a military leader, whether it be ambition as in Caesar, hatred of the enemy as in Hannibal, or the pride in a glorious defeat, as in Frederick the Great." Such emotions are needed to maintain "confidence and firmness of convictions" in the face of daily obstacles. They are needed if one is to heed the admonition "Be audacious and cunning in your plans, firm and persevering in their execution." [6] Von Clausewitz might well have added that the more successful leaders know how to arouse and keep aroused similar emotions in their followers.

Settlements. In military combat, physical force always presents the possibility of achieving the desired objective without compromise by destroying the opponent. But none of the weapons found in the arsenal of legislative strategy are based upon physical force. Power, therefore, is less sure, decisions less decisive. No victory is ever total, no defeat unmitigated. As a consequence, the art of compromise is essential in negotiating legislative settlements and in reacting to settlements in the negotiations of which one has not taken a direct part. The skilled leader who wants one loaf of bread will usually ask

[4] "Housing Lobby," Hearings before the Select Committee on Lobbying Activities of the House of Representatives, 81st Cong., 2d Sess., Part 2, p. 885.

[5] E. E. Schattschneider, "Politics, Pressures and the Tariff" (New York: Prentice-Hall, 1935), p. 289.

[6] Von Clausewitz, *op. cit.*, pp. 67, 69.

for two, accept half a loaf rather than nothing at all, and be willing to allow his opponents a few crumbs. Whether a compromise is praised as wise or damned as opportunistic or whether a compromiser is accepted as a realist or accused as a traitor depends upon where the observer stands and how much value he places upon the *quid* and the *quo*. In any case, accusation of betrayal or opportunism are an inevitable part of legislative dynamics.

"I'll never yield on a matter of principle," rings out a familiar battle cry. But principles are usually the first things to be yielded, for the simple reason that they are so rarely a clean-cut expression of fundamental high-priority interests. Because they are sometimes willing to sacrifice principles which are not directly related to basic interests but are rather propagandistic devices for the extension of support, the most effective leaders in the social struggle often appear to be totally unprincipled men. In a world of sharp divisions and dispersed power, they may even have to yield on basic interests. What to yield on and where to stand firm are questions that cannot be intelligently answered until one is able to sense the limits of the obtainable. Franklin Roosevelt was not a lesser man because he made compromises with "Southern Bourbons" and big-city bosses and compacts with Darlan and Stalin but a greater man because he was often able to use such lesser deeds for achieving higher objectives that would otherwise have been unattainable.

Limitations on Strategy and Tactics. Although the above discussion covers all the major factors that enter into the strategic and tactical thinking of more skilled and experienced leaders, it should not be inferred that they enter into all or even most strategic and tactical calculations. Campaign leaders, like everyone else, have their limitations. Some are experts in one type of operation, at a loss in others. Many are eternal amateurs or professional bunglers.

The complexity of American society, moreover, militates against the successful execution of too many pat and well-laid plans. No one individual or group can hold all the strings in one hand all the time. The limits within which legislative campaigns can be effective, no matter how expertly conceived they may be, are defined by the social and economic trends of any period and by the shifting dispersion of power among conflicting groups and interests.

Campaign leaders are often criticized for not having performed the impossible. The facts of life indicate that the most devoted and skillful head can still be broken against a stone wall. Leadership is an essential source of power but not a substitute for power.

In turn, leaders are often praised for strategic wisdom which they do not possess or which may not have been put to any genuine test. The possession and customary exercise of power help in the development of leadership, which in turn can lead to an augmentation of power. The weakest groups participating in the legislative struggle seldom develop the skillfulness and resourcefulness evidenced by the leaders of the large private organizations and government agencies and by the members of Congress who have formidable aggregations of power behind them.

The Organizational Foundations of Leadership

Throughout the entire process of social combat, leadership and organization are closely interrelated. Leaders face the task not only of mobilizing resources but also of dealing with organization itself as a foundation of leadership. High among the problems involved here are those of specialization, of centralization versus decentralization, and of money.

Specialization. The leadership of a legislative campaign involves many kinds of knowledge and activity. It calls for skills in such specialized fields as law, public administration, public relations and publicity, economics, statistics, and governmental procedures. It also calls for the more important abilities to get along with people, influence people, and think in strategic and tactical terms —abilities that have little relation to one's formal training and are often found where one might least expect them to exist.

The full array of needed skills is usually available to large organizations—such as Federal agencies and the national business, farm, and labor organizations—whose purposes extend beyond the legislative process and whose staffs include large numbers of specialized personnel. This is why some of these organizations can conduct the most large-scale and far-flung of legislative campaigns and still show only a small budget allocated directly to legislative work.

Many organizations have separate legislative units. Labor unions and businessmen's associations customarily have "legislative departments" or "legislative representatives." Presidents usually have at least one top assistant specializing in legislative matters, and in recent years the Bureau of the Budget has developed a legislative reference division. Yet specialized units of this type rarely succeed in handling the functions of leadership.[7] Many campaign problems call for the direct attention of the top leadership. Most campaigns require some participation by all branches of an organization. The function of a special legislative unit usually becomes one of advising the top leadership and helping it in the task of mobilizing the rest of the personnel in the organization.

Separate legislative units are sometimes set up outside the formal framework of an organization. In 1939, for example, the American Medical Association collaborated in the creation of the National Physicians Committee, a cam-

[7] For a detailed analysis of the legislative-leadership functions exercised by the Bureau of the Budget and the White House staff, see Richard Neustadt, "Presidential Clearance of Legislation" (unpublished doctoral dissertation, Harvard University, June, 1950).

paign organization whose main objective was to defeat legislative proposals for national health insurance. It would have been beneath the dignity of a professional organization like the A.M.A. to conduct this type of campaign entirely on its own. Subsequently the bulk of the work was turned over to a private publicity firm. In 1946 an opposing organization, the Committee for the Nation's Health, was established to spearhead the campaign on behalf of national health insurance. Previously the campaign work had been handled separately by the congressional sponsors of health-insurance legislation, a few small organizations of doctors who favored this approach to medical service, and the Social Security Board. The Committee for the Nation's Health provided a vehicle for doing a more organized and thorough job than had been done before. Both these organizations had the advantage of being able to concentrate on one single issue in contrast with their affiliated groups, most of which had many irons in the fire. Specialized organizations of this type are of particular value to executive agencies that, for fear of criticism or for lack of funds, prefer to remain behind the scenes rather than conduct active campaigns on their own. For example, during the Eightieth Congress the Committee on the Marshall Plan and the Committee on Peacetime Selective Service played an invaluable role in spearheading the legislative campaign on behalf of the Economic Cooperation Act and the Selective Service Act of 1948.

Specialized campaign organizations can also be hired on a fee basis. Many law firms and public-relations firms provide ready-made organizations for use in legislative campaigns, the former concentrating on bill drafting and the organization of government support, the latter on legislative propaganda and the mobilization of private-group support.

Centralization versus Decentralization. As in any other organizational operation, the leaders of a legislative campaign must always steer a course between one extreme of too little central control and the other of overtight centralization. Some degree of central planning and control is vital. Without it, action taken on one front may totally negate action taken on the other. Without it, objectives cannot be carefully defined, combat skillfully led, or settlements approached in a responsible manner.

Even within organizations that appear to be tightly knit, there is a tendency for those who deal with instruments of power to "go into business for themselves." Unless they can be controlled, they may end up in control. "The Army has lost all control over its chief lobbyist on Capitol Hill, Brig. Gen. Robert Moore," runs a story which illustrates situations that frequently occur. "He has so many friends in Congress that he ignores his bosses in the Pentagon and does as he pleases. When the Army passed over his promotion, Moore's Congressional friends made him a general anyway by writing it into the Appropriation Bill." [8] In many other cases legislative representatives have ig-

[8] Drew Pearson, "Washington Merry-Go-Round," *Washington Post,* Oct. 1, 1951.

nored an organization's views on the vital questions of basic objectives and strategy and have shifted their loyalties to whatever groups seemed to offer the most in personal rewards.

Central control, however, need not be formalized or institutionalized. Informal steering committees and little cabinets will do the job. In fact, they sometimes do the job much more effectively, particularly if formal responsibility is placed publicly on some other group existing on paper only and serving as a "front" to absorb the heat of combat.

The members of a central group are never wise enough to know all the answers or dexterous enough to hold all the strings. In any campaign, large or small, the effort to impose too much direction from a central point merely cuts down the initiative and creative urges of those on the periphery. Von Clausewitz writes:

> The concerted attacks of the divisions and army corps should not be obtained by trying to direct them from a central point. . . . The true method consists in giving each commander of an army corps or division the main direction of his march and in pointing out the enemy as the objective and victory as the goal. . . . We therefore assure the cooperation of all forces by giving each corps a certain amount of independence, by seeing to it that each seeks out the enemy and attacks him with all possible self-sacrifice.[9]

This principle is doubly significant in social combat, where almost every corps whose support is needed has already a certain amount of independence and is bound to assert it, come what will.

Money. While high salaries, sumptuous headquarters, and a large number of employees do not necessarily imply effectiveness, the best campaigns are run by those with enough financial resources to procure the wheels that are needed and keep them greased. A key to the N.A.M.'s effectiveness is the size of its budget. During 1945, according to its financial report for that year, its total income was over $3,600,000. In addition, its members, affiliated bodies, and sympathizers may be regarded as sources of indirect revenue. According to one student of the organization's activities, "the 1936 outdoor advertising campaign for which the Association paid $50,000 would have cost $1,250,000 had not free billboard space been furnished. Similarly, free newspaper space and donated radio time were valued at more than $2,000,000." [10] An accurate estimate of the total financial resources at its command would be impossible to compute. Little help for this is to be obtained from the financial data filed with Congress under the lobby-registration provisions of the Legislative Reorganization Act of 1946. The Act does not provide information on the total budget of pressure groups. It asks only for reports concerning expenditures

[9] Von Clausewitz, *op. cit.*, pp. 25–26.

[10] Alfred S. Cleveland, "NAM: Spokesman for Industry?" *Harvard Business Review,* Vol. 26, No. 3, May, 1948.

for the "principal purpose" of influencing legislation. However broadly or narrowly this may be interpreted (and no accurate definition or standard interpretation has been provided), it can scarcely be construed as covering expenditures for the mobilization of group support and for the more general type of legislative propaganda and pressure activities. In 1949, in a report filed along with a protest against the interpretation that it was required to file at all, the N.A.M. reported legislative expenditures of about $117,000—approximately 1.5 per cent of the organization's total expenditures.[11]

Fund raising is an integral part of any legislative campaign. Pressure groups spend a considerable part of their time in the collection of regular dues and in the solicitation of contributions from members and sympathizers. The most important and most intricate devices for the collection of funds allow for the deduction of contributions from tax payments to the Federal government, thereby providing for an indirect government subsidy. Since contributions to research organizations are tax-exempt, many legislative campaign organizations set up separate affiliates which handle their research functions and can be financed through tax-exempt funds. Others rely on the difficulty of enforcing restrictions on deductions from income taxes [12] and, even though they are on shaky legal ground, succeed in convincing contributors that contributions can be deducted.[13] Business concerns are allowed to deduct any "ordinary and necessary" expenses for doing business. This includes regular dues to pressure-group organizations, as distinguished from special contributions, depending upon the circumstances and the judgment of the Bureau of Internal Revenue and the Board of Tax Appeals. It is also construed to include fees to law firms and public-relations firms, expenditures for institutional advertising, and even for entertainment of government officials.

[11] On Jan. 28, 1948, the N.A.M. brought civil suit against the Attorney General before a special three-judge Federal court in Washington. N.A.M. asked the court to declare sections of the Federal Regulation of Lobbying Act unconstitutional as well as inapplicable to N.A.M. The court declared, on Mar. 17, 1952, that Secs. 303 through 307 of the Act were unconstitutional because (1) the crime established in the Act is not defined with sufficient precision, (2) the Act infringes upon free speech, and (3) the "principal purpose" of a lobby is not sufficiently distinguished from an "incidental purpose." Further congressional action on lobbying will probably await a final ruling by the Supreme Court.

[12] The regulations of the Bureau of Internal Revenue provide that "Sums of money expended for lobbying purposes, the promotion or defeat of legislation, the exploitation of propaganda, including advertising other than trade advertising, and contributions for campaign expenses are not deductible from gross income."

[13] See statement on this contained in a letter from John M. Pratt, Administrator of the National Physicians Committee, to a correspondent who claimed that organization had no right to solicit contributions on the ground that they were deductible from income taxes: "It is generally accepted that 'the proof of the pudding is in the eating.' On this basis, financial contributions to the National Physicians Committee are tax exempt for contributors." "National Health Program," Hearings before the Senate Committee on Education and Labor, 79th Cong., 2d Sess., Apr. 17–24, 1946, p. 884.

The source of funds for legislative campaigns by the executive agencies is the legislation itself. Here the major organizations in the Federal government, particularly the defense establishments, are at a great advantage since their huge budgets allow ample room for the personnel and public-relations expenditures needed in legislative campaigns and include vast amounts of contract expenditures that can be allocated throughout the country in a manner designed to influence individual members of Congress. In 1919 an attempt was made to prohibit legislative campaigns by executive officials. A rider to a deficiency appropriation act provided that

> hereafter no part of the money appropriated by this or any other Act shall, in the absence of express authorization by Congress, be used directly or indirectly to pay for any personal service, advertisement, telegram, telephone, letter, printed or written matter, or other device, intended or designed to influence in any manner a Member of Congress to favor or oppose, by vote or otherwise, any legislation or appropriation by Congress, whether before or after the introduction of any bill or resolution proposing such legislation or appropriation; but this shall not prevent officers and employees of the United States from communicating to Members of Congress on the request of any Member or to Congress, through the proper official channels, requests for legislation or appropriations which they deem necessary for the efficient conduct of public business.[14]

It is not difficult to see why there have been no prosecutions or violations of this legislative restriction. It is relatively easy for an executive official to arrange for requests by friendly members of Congress for the submission of formal recommendations for legislative action. The only effect of this restriction has been to impel executive officials to conduct their legislative campaigns cautiously and at times surreptitiously.

The Organization of Group Support

The very birth of most bills is tied up with group support—in the form either of direct activity to obtain sponsorship or of the sponsors' efforts to estimate potential support. But if they are to make much progress in the legislative process, bills need far stronger backing than is required merely to bring them into being. Just as artillery must be moved into place or an air force readied before an assault upon an enemy stronghold, so group support must be lined up at various points to provide the sources of propaganda and pressure bombardment.

At times, because of a peculiar line-up among contesting forces or because of large previous investments in organizational activities, this support comes more or less automatically. In most cases, however, truly significant support will be forthcoming only if a direct effort is made to develop the most help-

[14] Statutes at Large, Vol. 41, pt. 1, ch. 6, 66th Cong., 1st Sess., 1919.

ful pattern of such support and to cope with a number of difficult problems in organizational relations and management.

Patterns of Support

The initiation of a legislative campaign does not take place in a vacuum. It is merely another incident on the vast battleground of social combat. The initiators operate within an existing alignment of forces. Here stand friends and allies, here a variety of neutrals, here opponents. The obvious steps in developing an effective pattern of support, therefore, are to organize and solidify the support of friends and allies, to win over—or at least prevent opponents from winning—the neutrals, and to split the opposition. Success in these steps, moreover, may transcend the importance of any single bill. The tightening of group lines or a realignment of forces can have profound implications for the outcome of election campaigns, the general course of governmental action, and the direction of economic and cultural change. In fact, a bill or even an entire legislative program is often viewed merely as a means of forging a new coalition to serve in a strategy transcending the legislative process.

Friends and Allies. It might seem that the organization of support among those with interests in common is an easy task. And it is indeed true that unfurling a banner and sounding some clear bugle notes will usually summon a few loyal and eager souls to battle. But to build a solid phalanx around the banner is much harder. Group leaders, particularly the more powerful ones, tend to be busy and overworked. The rank and file tend to be apathetic, even where their most immediate interests are involved.

Considerable effort is needed to build support vertically within a given grouping and keep it at a high level of intensity. Thus a central, and perhaps the crucial, element in the American Medical Association's campaign against national health insurance has been the organization of the medical profession itself in opposition. When the liquor industry is threatened by regulatory legislation, the first step in defense is to line up every company and see that they pass the word down the line to their department heads, factory superintendents, salesmen, suppliers, and customers. When business leaders oppose higher taxes or prolabor legislation, the same pattern is developed on a larger scale. In conducting their campaign against the enactment of the Taft-Hartley Act, and subsequently for its repeal, the national leaders of organized labor spent a large part of their resources whipping up intense resentment against the legislation on the part of local officials, shop stewards, and rank and file members. In developing the campaign for the Brannan Plan, one of the big problems faced by Secretary of Agriculture Charles Brannan was the mustering of support by bureau officials and regional office personnel within the Department of Agriculture itself.

The horizontal organization of support among friendly groups also calls for persistent effort. Common interests must be discovered, nourished, and exploited. Otherwise they cannot lead to common action. One of the chief functions of the "peak" organizations in the business community is to develop unified action among the thousands of separate business groupings. The key to effective campaigning by a labor movement which is organizationally divided is the development of broad support among the rival labor organizations for identical objectives. In the campaign which resulted in the passage of the Employment Act of 1946, "the lining up of a strong phalanx of political forces was considered tc be politically necessary and in truth it is doubtful if S. 380 would ever have passed, even in modified form, without active support of these liberal organizations." [15] The lining-up process was not limited to private organizations. The executive agencies of the Government and both houses of Congress were scoured from top to bottom to discover new sources of strength for the full-employment phalanx. In contrast, the legislative campaign for a Fair Employment Practices Commission has always suffered from an inability to mobilize sufficient support among Negro organizations themselves, the very groups with the largest stake in the fair-employment program.

> Negro organizations, notwithstanding the very considerable contributions of some of the groups discussed, fell short of making a contribution to the movement which was commensurate with their organizational strength and their vital stake in the issue. Rivalry for leadership among Negroes, organizational and ideological struggles, general lack of faith in the National Council for a Permanent FEPC, and distrust of its motives split and debilitated Negro strength. Some small solace can be found in the fact that important Negro groups have rarely been successfully united and activated in political movements requiring extended planning and work. Still FEPC offered a better than average opportunity for united action which was not capitalized upon.[16]

Neutrals. A difficult dilemma is always faced by those who attempt to win friends among groups who would otherwise be neutral. On the one hand, new allies may mean added strength against opponents. On the other hand, the broader one's support becomes, the less one can get depth of agreement and the more one must compromise. The recruitment of support from some one group may create difficult tensions among other supporters and may even alienate them completely. A point usually is reached where additional support is not worth either the additional effort needed or the repercussions that might result. There is, therefore, a principle of marginal utility that cannot be

[15] Stephen K. Bailey, "Congress Makes a Law" (New York: Columbia University Press, 1949), p. 76.

[16] Louis Coleridge Kesselman, "The Social Politics of FEPC" (Chapel Hill, N.C.: University of North Carolina Press, 1948), p. 224.

ignored. The emphasis must be on selectivity and upon a careful weighing of the price to be paid against the benefits that might be received.

There is a tendency among most groups to aim at sources of support that will put them in a "middle-of-the-road" position. This is viewed as a means of distinguishing them from "extremists" on both sides, of putting them in a balance-of-power position, and of facilitating future moves toward developing support on either side. Even those groups that appear to be located at the ultimate extreme have the same interest in balance. The theoreticians of Communist parties, for example, have always inveighed against the twin dangers of "rightist opportunism" and "infantile leftism." This illustrates the barrenness of ranging groups arbitrarily on a one-dimensional line from "right" to "left" —even if, as has been at times suggested, the straight line is transformed into a circle. The infinite variety of in-between positions can be illustrated only by depicting groups as deployed over the length and breadth of a field.

There is a marked tendency toward neutrality and inactivity on the part of groups which are not directly affected by a given issue. Schattschneider has dealt with this tendency by a useful distinction between primary interests and secondary interests. He refers to primary interests as "resolute minorities . . . surrounded by vast marginal aggregates whose impulses to action were almost never able to formulate themselves. The politics of the tariff are apparently predicated on the belief that slumbering and smouldering interests would remain passive while a few men who knew what they wanted acted with decision." [17] The extent to which secondary interests can be activated obviously depends largely upon the ability of primary interests to prod them out of their slumber.

The loose alliances running under the name of national political parties make a special point of staying neutral on the bulk of legislative issues. Their interest in mobilizing a majority vote in national elections makes them wary of taking any position that might antagonize influential groups. The internal logic of a legislative campaign, however, leads the campaigners to an effort to win the support of both parties. Before the 1948 party conventions, for example, the Committee for the Nation's Health set itself the task of committing "both political parties to the insurance principle as the basis of major health legislation." To achieve this objective they saw to it that the case for the health-insurance principle was presented to President Truman and other leaders of the Democratic party, to leading liberals in the Republican party, and to the platform-drafting committees of the Republican and Democratic parties in 1948. While this objective was not attained before the 1948 election, it is interesting to note that the farm organizations, in contrast, succeeded in obtaining almost identical commitments in the platforms of both parties.

[17] Schattschneider, *op. cit.*, p. 122.

Interestingly enough, the effort to build a bipartisan support is not inconsistent with efforts to develop a partisan alignment at the same time. Supporters of the original full-employment bill proclaimed it a nonpartisan measure and bid for, and partially obtained, the support of Republicans. Yet they also attempted to make it a party issue among Democrats, accusing Democratic opponents of disloyalty to the party.

Splitting the Opposition. Divide and conquer is a time-honored maxim of social combat. In its campaign on behalf of the Taft-Hartley Act, business leaders attempted to divide the labor movement's drive against the Act by exempting railway labor organizations from many of its provisions hoping thereby to split off the railway labor unions. The major tactic in the campaign for the Brannan Plan was to divide the American Farm Bureau Federation and the National Grange by winning over and activating a number of favorably disposed state organizations within these two major farm groups. The supporters of the original Full Employment Bill made a special point of trying to split the business opposition to the legislation. "The qualified support of a small number of influential businessmen like Beardsley Ruml and Ralph E. Flanders made it possible for the sponsors of the bill to claim that '. . . small businessmen want full employment. . . . Enlightened big businessmen want full employment.' "[18] No attempt was made to win business support generally. This would have been regarded as a waste of time. In fact, it was felt that a key to splitting the business opposition was to carefully identify that section of business leadership which was the main enemy of the legislation and to concentrate a heavy attack upon them.[19]

The difficulties of splitting a business opposition have been demonstrated on many occasions. Marriner Eccles made the effort in connection with the Banking Act of 1935. "It seemed for a while that a policy of concessions as a price of reducing banker opposition would pay off, but it turned out that the 5-man committee and the conciliatory Executive Council of the ABA were generals without troops. They could not carry the majority of the nation's bankers with them." [20]

A representative of independent oil producers who testified before a congressional committee on the tariff told of the difficulties he found in getting business executives to take an "independent" position:

> I want to say to you that most of the executives of the so-called middle-sized companies and some of the almost major class, even though they are independents, supposed to be independent companies, are afraid to espouse this cause. They are intimidated. They are in favor of a tariff but won't come out in the open. They assured me privately that they are in favor of it but they are afraid of the big boys.

[18] Bailey, *op. cit.*, p. 76.

[19] *Ibid.*, p. 77.

[20] Marriner Eccles, "Beckoning Frontiers" (New York: Knopf, 1951), pp. 201–202.

They cannot go back to New York and borrow the money that they need for developing their properties and carry on their business. At least they think they cannot and are afraid to talk.[21]

Government organization itself provides a splendid opportunity for the divide-and-conquer strategy. Any private organization opposing a legislative proposal originating in an executive agency inevitably tries either to promote interagency or intra-agency squabbles or to create an executive-congressional conflict. The former provides a springboard for bewailing "executive confusion," the latter arousing indignation in Congress toward "executive dictatorship." The ease with which this is so often accomplished arises from the divergent interests underlying governmental activities and is a basic reason why executive officials, even Presidents, often find it impossible to obtain unified agency support for a legislative proposal. The Presidential task of organizing broad interagency support for a legislative program is just as much a three-in-one job of organizing friends, winning over neutrals, and splitting the opposition as any similar task among nongovernmental groups.

The greatest of all opportunities for a divide-and-conquer strategy lies within the political parties. Here one deals with aggregations supported by interests even more divergent than those behind government agencies. Despite abstract talk about the two-party system and the importance of party responsibility, when it comes down to specific issues and campaigns, nobody really wants rigid party lines. A President, for example, who is trying to unify his own party must necessarily try to divide the opposing party. Hence party conflict in the legislative arena becomes a matter of coalition strategy. Both Franklin Roosevelt and Truman suffered from the fact that the opponents to their legislative programs succeeded in maintaining a deep split within the Democratic party ranks. Yet they themselves, while trying to heal this split, were always eagerly looking for sources of support within the Republican party.

Types of Groups. A campaign based upon the support of executive agencies only or that of private organizations only usually cannot go very far. The more effective combinations and coalitions are those bringing together all types of groups—private organizations, political parties or factions, members of Congress, the executive branch, and the judiciary. An interesting example is the National Rivers and Harbors Congress, a private organization which sparkplugs the annual legislative campaign for rivers and harbors appropriations. This organization, according to its own literature, "is the country's oldest and largest water organization and occupies semi-official status by reason of its close liaison with the governmental agencies, legislative and executive, responsible for public works." Its president and most important officials are members of Congress, both Democrats and Republicans, with strategic positions

[21] United States Senate Lobby Investigation Hearings, 71st Cong., 2d Sess., Part 7, p. 3110.

on the legislative committees handling rivers and harbors projects. The closest possible cooperation with officers of the Army Corps of Engineers serves as a means of bringing together representatives of power companies, contractors, coal operators, oil interests, landowners, and railroads. Which of these participants in the rivers and harbors coalition pull the strings and which are the puppets is not only an irreverent question but an irrelevant one. They all pull strings and they all use one another.

Nor can a powerful pattern of support be built if overattention is given only to large and powerful organizations. Small groups of minor importance if operating by themselves can make a major contribution to a legislative campaign. Often they may turn out to be the only ones able to develop a special type of propaganda or to apply pressure on someone in a strategic position. Similarly, individuals who occupy no strategic position in their own right may provide access or entree to individuals and groups of considerable power. Hence, every lobbyist worth his pay attempts to win friends among the lower-level employees, including secretaries and clerks, in private organizations and government agencies.

Organizational Problems

Mixing Ingredients. In making a cake, everything can go wrong if the ingredients are mixed in the wrong order. The same principle applies to the far more difficult task of social engineering involved in organizing mass pressures into a bloc capable of obtaining a given objective on Capitol Hill. On the labor front, for example, it is the practice to seek A.F.L. support before C.I.O. support, for reasons that while the C.I.O. is not so much afraid of the A.F.L. measures, the A.F.L. will shy away from any measures which they regard as sponsored by their energetic rival.[22]

As a corollary to this principle, it sometimes becomes essential to avoid bringing all the supporters of a given legislative objective into close contact with one another. If strange bedfellows become an essential of an effective campaign, an important never-ending problem arises to prevent all the occupants from knowing who else is in the bed. Thus the broad support for the Marshall Plan could hardly have held together if the more radical labor supporters of the proposal had realized how much support it enjoyed on the part of conservative bankers and businessmen. In fact, one of the devices in developing labor support for the Marshall Plan was to build up a bogeyman of conservative opposition.

Limited-purpose Organizations. Every organization has certain primary objectives. If it strays too far afield, there is always a danger it will spread itself

[22] Bailey, *op. cit.*, p. 80.

too thin. The Railway Labor Executives Association, for example, although sympathetic toward the majority of the campaigns waged by organized labor, has an established policy of sticking to its own knitting, campaigning only for those legislative measures that are of the most direct and immediate concern to the railroad workers it represents. It gives sympathy to its labor-union colleagues, but rarely active support.

To win over limited-purpose organizations of this type to a legislative coalition calls not only for high-class salesmanship but also for the shaping of one's legislative objectives to appeal more directly to the organizations whose support is desired. Mutual aims must be hammered out and divergent objectives must be compromised.

Formalization of Support. The formalization of an organization's support also presents a problem. In some cases, the executive board or the legislative representative is given wide discretion with respect to the formation of legislative alliances. In other cases, an organization's support for a legislative campaign can be obtained only through formal action by its convention or by a referendum of its total membership.

Often special subsidiary campaigns are needed to win formal support. In the early stages of the campaign for the Full Employment Bill, for instance, considerable hostility toward the measure was shown by key officials in the C.I.O. national office—despite the bill's closeness to major objectives of organized labor. If the matter had been left in the hands of these hostile officials, C.I.O. support might never have been forthcoming, and the effort to organize liberal support might have ended in frustration. The sponsors of the legislation dealt with this problem by sending the bill with explanatory material to a complete list of individual C.I.O. unions, state-industrial-union councils, and regional directors. The enthusiastic responses to this communication lit a hot fire under the national leaders who slowly and somewhat reluctantly found seats on the band wagon.

Special Machinery. To bring groups together, new machinery is often needed. Where formal support by key groups is impossible or untimely, unofficial support often can be obtained by recruiting group leaders as sponsors or officers of new organizations. Some of these are merely paper organizations which are expected, like Joshua's army before the walls of Jericho, to make enough noise and commotion to convince people that a great army is on the march. Others are designed to organize previously unorganized areas or to tap hitherto unexploited sources of funds. Examples of these are the National Foundation of Home and Property Owners which was established to collaborate in obtaining the legislative objectives of the National Association of Real Estate Boards and the National Association of Home Builders. According to one publicist:

The Foundation is a new catch-all group sired by NAREB to recruit people of its turn of mind who are not in the business of buying and selling real estate. Its membership partly duplicates the rolls of established real estate organizations but the Foundation will admit anybody who holds clear title to a chicken coop or cemetery lot.[23]

Another example is the National Council for Permanent FEPC. This group performed services which no other organization interested in FEPC legislation could possibly handle.[24]

Sometimes special machinery is needed not so much to bring groups together or to organize campaigns as to serve as a clearinghouse for information on the progress of certain measures. The cooperation of church lobbies with other groups, for example, "is facilitated by clearing-house organizations, such as International Legislation Information Service, and Civil Liberties Clearing House." The last-named serves about 75 "non-Communist national organizations interested in the protection and fostering of our civil liberties."[25]

Devices that are particularly appropriate for use by executive agencies are the convening of *ad hoc* conferences and the formation of advisory committees. In May, 1948, with the approval of President Truman, the Federal Security Agency convened a "National Health Assembly" in Washington, D.C. This assembly brought more than 800 representatives of organized groups, including the professional medical organizations, behind every point in the Administration's health program, except national health insurance.

One of the most elaborate advisory committee arrangements, for exclusively legislative purposes, was the one created by the War Department as part of its campaign for peacetime universal military training. Representative Arthur Miller of Nebraska, in a critical speech, has described this effort as follows:

It would seem the military has established a so-called Army Advisory Committee which has for its goal the establishing of these committees in at least 600 representative communities, with an approximate membership of 9,000 civilians. The purpose of these advisory committees, according to a memo signed by Col. James Pierce, issued August 26, 1946, was "preparing a favorable reception for Army policy and discovering the things that hamper Army policy; to advise the Army on all community attitudes which are based on adverse reactions to acts, facts, and policies of the Army; to provide channels for the dissemination of facts and policies of the Army in a manner so that the public will understand and be completely informed."[26]

[23] Alexander L. Crosby, "The Real Estate Lobby," *The American Mercury,* March, 1947, p. 288.

[24] Kesselman, *op. cit.,* pp. 66–67.

[25] Luke Ebersole, "Church Lobbying in the Nation's Capital" (New York: Macmillan, 1951), p. 99.

[26] *Congressional Record,* 80th Cong., 2d Sess., Jan. 19, 1948, p. 319.

Advisory committees have also been used on occasion directly by members of Congress. Thus, advisory committees have been set up by the House Ways and Means Committee on revenue legislation, by the Senate's Finance Committee on social-security legislation, and by the Senate Interstate Commerce Committee on basing-point legislation. In most of these cases the purpose has been dual—to assist in the formulation of a program, and to provide an organizing center for the development of support.

Chapter 13

PROPAGANDA AND PRESSURE

THIS CHAPTER will discuss how the dissemination of propaganda and the application of pressure become tools for the campaign leaders in the achievement of group support and of legislative decisions.

THE DISSEMINATION OF PROPAGANDA

Propaganda acquired its bad reputation in this country during the 1920's when countless writers and scholars exposed the lies which the propaganda machines of both sides disseminated throughout World War I. In addition, "propaganda" is disliked in a democratic society because people feel naïvely that their decisions should be made by themselves and not by someone else. The feeling is naïve because decisions result from past experiences, many of which are usually culturally determined; but it is certainly in keeping with the belief of our society that man, if he only will, can shape his own destiny.[1]

Propaganda is habitually used to refer to *someone else's* efforts to win favorable opinion. One's own efforts are described in terms of "education." Propaganda connotes deception or distortion, as contrasted with "information."

In the sense that propaganda may be defined as an effort to persuade people to favor certain objectives or do certain things, there is no reason why it should necessarily have a derogatory connotation. All the participants in the legislative struggle, from the Catholic church to the Communist party, engage in propagandistic endeavors. Without it they would be at a disadvantage in the organization of group support or the application of pressure. There is effective propaganda and ineffective propaganda. There is honest and deceitful propaganda. There are those who command vast propaganda resources for producing propaganda and those whose output is very meager. Whether specific propaganda activities are judged "good" or "bad" depends on many types of value judgments. The very drafting of legislative measures is part of the propaganda process, although only a small part. The major concern of legislative propagandists is to develop both indirect and direct methods of persua-

[1] Leonard W. Doob, "Public Opinion and Propaganda" (New York: Holt, 1948), p. 242.

sion, to fashion a convincing case, and to disseminate it through the various media of communication.

The Indirect and the Direct

When one thinks of legislative propaganda there inevitably comes to mind such direct operations as the full-page ads, radio orations, and illustrated pamphlets used to defend or attack a pending bill. There are, however, many degrees of direction and indirection in the field of propaganda. Probably the most effective legislative propaganda is the kind which never mentions any specific issue.

> Through the considered use of word-symbols over a couple of generations; through the attention paid by business and big commercial agriculture to rural opinion; through the concerted drive of business organizations to convince the public-at-large that "What is good for business is good for America," the conservative pressures helped to shape the prepossessions which a majority of our national legislators brought with them to the Seventy-ninth Congress. This educational campaign pays enormous dividends.[2]

Goodwill broadcasts by labor, church, and business organizations, "institutional advertising" by large companies,[3] the emphasis upon one or another set of values in schools and churches—all these are of indirect propaganda utility.

Nor is this utility accidental. Bailey refers to the "considered use" of word symbols. Church and school leaders often consciously attempt to influence people's attitudes in certain broad directions. The strategic importance of indirect propaganda can be inferred from the care with which various organizations attempt to commandeer church and school channels. The National Association of Manufacturers, for example, sends to clergymen of all faiths, as well as to seminaries, a regular publication entitled "Understanding." Its subtitle is "A Publication Devoted to Cooperation between Clergymen and Businessmen." It has also organized a nationwide schedule of "Business-Industry-Education days."

> The B-I-E project is based on having one of the familiar "teacher institute" days set by a community's education officials, but instead of attending an "institute" the teachers tour local business companies in groups, see the city's industry at work, hear executives explain company objectives and problems at luncheon, then all dine

[2] Stephen K. Bailey, "Congress Makes a Law" (New York: Columbia University Press, 1949), p. 149.

[3] "Some of the institutional commercials emitted by large manufacturers like the Ford Motor Company are devoted much less to their products than they are to heaping praise upon the over-all wisdom of management, of private ownership, and of our present economic system." Doob, *op. cit.*, p. 477.

together to listen while some of the industrial leaders review the benefits of the American free enterprise system to community and nation.[4]

It is activities of this sort that lay the groundwork for *direct* propaganda on *specific* measures. Indirect propaganda provokes less sales resistance than persuasive efforts of a more specific character. Much direct propaganda, on the other hand, does little more than provide the on-hand supply of ammunition for use by those who already have been made ideologically receptive as a result of many years of influence by indirect propaganda.

Often, the alertness of various powerful groups to the impact of indirect propaganda has led them into forceful action against literature which they regard as potentially dangerous. According to Schriftgiesser, the Pennsylvania Society for the Encouragement of Manufactures and the Mechanic Arts, during the tariff battles of the 1820's, tried to advance the cause of protectionism by "a campaign to remove the textbooks of Adam Smith and J. B. Say, his French disciple, from the schools and colleges, and even hired a German propagandist and economist, one Friedrich List, to write a substitute for these subversive texts."[5] Similar campaigns by business groups have not been unknown in subsequent years—although the object of more recent purge efforts has been literature that departs from the now hallowed concepts of Adam Smith.

In some cases, direct propaganda is almost entirely dispensed with or else directed in a quiet fashion toward only a few carefully selected groups. During the Seventy-ninth Congress the Trademark Act was put through with no public hearings and hardly a word of comment in the press with the exception of certain business and legal publications. General publicity would have militated against it. This method also was used with bills to exempt railroads and newspapers from antitrust laws. By contrast, occasionally a direct propaganda campaign is developed loudly on behalf of one measure to divert attention from simultaneous efforts to slide through a "sleeper" bill. Thus, during the last years of World War II, a vociferous public attack was conducted by business organizations against the existing war-contract-renegotiation legislation. While administration officials and liberal groups ran to the defense of contract renegotiation, the business groups very quietly succeeded in obtaining the enactment of unpropagandized tax legislation that meant far more to them than any possible changes in contract renegotiation.

Building One's Case

Interests. The secret of effective propaganda is the ability to make a case in terms of the interests of those whom one wants to persuade. This means

[4] *N.A.M. News,* Feb. 4, 1950, p. 7.

[5] Karl Schriftgiesser, "The Lobbyists" (Boston: Little, Brown, 1951), p. 7.

sensing what really interests people as contrasted with what someone thinks these "true interests" are or should be. The propagandist who proceeds on the assumption that people can be sold a program that clashes with what they strongly regard as their direct and immediate interest succeeds in little more than deluding himself.

In appealing to the interests of any group, a basic problem is *to demonstrate* that a given legislative proposal will really serve the group's interests. Pure and simple assertion that it will do so will not convince all the people all the time. Many will be bound to assert the contrary. Furthermore, since many legislative proposals are likely to have bad effects as well as good effects, it is necessary to demonstrate that the former are outweighed by the latter. Hence, a full bill of particulars is usually necessary—not because it will be an important or even a major part of a propaganda campaign, but because without it the inevitable criticisms cannot be effectively anticipated and because some people in every group insist upon grubbing into the details. A full bill of particulars usually presents the expected effects of the proposal if it is enacted, discusses alternative approaches, and indicates the precise benefits that might be obtained.

Almost every successful propaganda effort of a major character will contain carefully slanted appeals to a large variety of groups. "Something in it for everyone" is a motto that applies to legislative propaganda as well as to political platforms. At times, of course, separate appeals to divergent interests must be handled separately. Thus, a campaigner for public power may address a business organization one evening on the value of public power to American businessmen and the next evening address a labor or consumer audience on its value as a bulwark against predatory private-business interests.

Similarly, a bill which has been worked out with the bankers and whose original title indicated that its purpose was "to relieve the banks" can be taken by a Franklin D. Roosevelt (as actually happened) and slanted toward a much larger group by calling it a bill to set up a Home Owners' Loan Corporation.

In an era of mass communication, however, it is dangerous to assume that what is said to one group may not be heard by another. Hence, it becomes essential to develop a propaganda approach that has direct appeal to people with divergent interests. Here there is an obvious dilemma: the more one appeals directly to different groups in terms of their immediate interest, the greater is the danger that one's language is meaningless or offensive to some other groups. The favored device for escaping through the horns of this dilemma is to emphasize a broadly desirable objective, such as Recovery or National Security, and de-emphasize the means of attaining the objective. People who will fight to the bitter end among themselves about method can often be united on objectives. Long-range or abstract conceptions, as indicated in subsequent sections of this chapter, can be particularly exciting—so long as they skirt the risk of being so fantastic as to look like "pie in the sky."

The Public Interest. One of the major elements in the art of legislative propaganda is the development and presentation of arguments to the effect that a given point of view will advance "the public interest." Roy Blough, in describing testimony given before congressional committees on tax legislation, observes:

> The purpose of arguments is to persuade the policy-maker that the public interest would be promoted by the adoption of a tax proposal which would financially benefit its advocates. . . . When the witness for a taxpayer interest group appears at hearings before the Congressional Taxing Committee, he does not merely say, and often does not say at all: "Please adopt our proposal because it would benefit us." It is always assumed that each witness thinks he and his group would be benefited by the action he proposes. The argument is usually on a high plane of public welfare. The witness may indeed point out that his industry is subject to an unusual hardship, but even in this case the testimony usually goes beyond the private benefit to consider the public interest. Witnesses do not argue that their proposals would benefit personally the members of the committee, except as these are part of a much larger general group.[6]

Thus, many of the most crucial legislative debates are fought out verbally at the level of conflicting conceptions of the public welfare. If each party to the conflict feels sincerely that his conception of the public interest is sound and that the opposition viewpoint really serves a "narrow interest" or "vested interest," this demonstrates not the accuracy of his observation but rather the intensity with which he adheres to his own conception of the public interest. Mere assertion is never sufficient. A good case on the public-interest aspect of any proposal calls for a full rationale. Blough has made an excellent analysis of the rather limited number of thought patterns that are used in developing rationales on behalf of tax legislation by reducing "public-interest" arguments on taxes to the following 10 propositions: (1) The proposal will increase (decrease) revenue; (2) The proposal will enlarge (diminish) tax fairness; (3) The proposal will promote (destroy) a high and stable level of production and employment; (4) The proposal will encourage (discourage) an important industry or business group; (5) The proposal will repress (promote) socially undesirable consumption; (6) The proposal will improve (make worse) the distribution of wealth and income; (7) The proposal can readily be (cannot be) administered in a complete and uniform manner; (8) The proposal will simplify (complicate) the compliance problems of taxpayers; (9) The proposal will increase (decrease) a "wholesome" tax consciousness; and

[6] Roy Blough, "The Argument Phase of Taxpayer Politics," *University of Chicago Law Review,* Vol. 17, No. 4, Summer, 1950, pp. 605–606.

(10) The proposal will enlarge (contract) the rights and financial independence of the states.[7]

When arguments such as these—which could well be paralleled by similar thought patterns in other fields—are interlarded with copious statistics, quotations from authority, and statements of personal experience, they can be impressive indeed.

Goals, Ideals, Principles. A striking example of long-range goals developed in this context is contained in "The Nation's Health—a Ten-year Program," [8] prepared by the Federal Security Agency's National Health Assembly. This report proposes the following goals:

"1. Twenty years of life added to the average expectancy of individuals at birth

"2. Conquest of certain disastrous epidemics, which have been virtually eliminated as a threat to health in this country

"3. A generation of stronger, better-fed children; and a larger body of knowledge on the child—his physical, mental, and social development—from before birth to the age of six than we have about any other period of human life

"4. A vast storehouse of knowledge about the prevention and treatment of diseases

"5. A sharp reduction in the death tolls from many diseases that were high on the mortality lists of the past"

This is language that everybody can understand. It affects one's life, livelihood, and expectation of survival. It provides a favorable background of ideals within which to propose and debate specific measures to build hospitals, medical centers, train doctors, dentists, and nurses, extend medical research, and provide improved methods of payment for medical care.

In President Truman's Economic Reports to Congress long-range goals of tremendous propaganda value have often been set forth. One of the best illustrations is found in the January, 1950, Report:

Within five years we can achieve an annual output in excess of 300 billion dollars. . . . Expansion to a 300 billion dollar economy within five years would place 30 to 45 billion dollars more per year in the hands of consumers for buying the needs and comforts of life. It would provide opportunity for profitable business investment in plant, equipment, and housing which might run 3 to 6 billion dollars per year above the 1949 level. It would enable farmers to sell about 10 per cent more food for domestic consumption.[9]

Few things move people so deeply as their ideals. Through the ages millions of men and women have died in struggles for ideals—ideals that are often

[7] *Ibid.*, pp. 606–610.

[8] A report to the President by Oscar R. Ewing, Federal Security Administrator (Government Printing Office, September, 1948).

[9] Economic Report to Congress, January, 1950, pp. 6–7.

beyond their understanding and more often unattainable during their lifetime. The greatest of all campaigns are those in which both leaders and followers would sacrifice themselves on behalf of an ideal which they consider greater than themselves. This does not mean that self-interest and ideals are incompatible or contradictory. As Merriam has pointed out, "sacrifice is indeed a form of personal interest"[10] and, at times, those personal interests that are of overwhelming weight are the ones that flow from deep inner frustration, resentment, and hatred.

Nothing attracts people's thinking processes more than a principle. When real-estate propagandists spoke out for the quick removal of rent controls after World War II, they did not say: "Decontrol is needed so that the people I represent can have more money with which to buy more luxuries for themselves and their families and enhance their feelings of prestige and power." They talked rather in terms of abstract principles of housing economics, principles which learned minds labored arduously to devise. A "principle" has a double advantage. On the one hand, it conceals or blurs the direct interests of the propagandists. On the other hand, by stating the case in general terms, it suggests great potentialities of benefit to those on the periphery whose support is being sought. If the general principle advanced under certain conditions should subsequently have implications detrimental to one's own interests, it can then be turned upside down, put on the shelf for use at some later date, or reinterpreted to meet new conditions.

Thus, in the early day of the Republic, business interests propagandized on behalf of a strong central government. But when political conditions changed and when it became evident that a strong central government threatened their interests, they somersaulted completely and became advocates of states' rights. In times of depression, Keynesian economists have developed the principle that public expenditures, particularly for public works, should be varied upward and downward to compensate for the fluctuations in the business cycle.[11] Conservative interests tend to oppose this principle when it means larger expenditures but to leap warmly to its support in times of prosperity when it holds forth the hope of lower expenditures. Liberals tend to desert it when it would lead to a reduction in public spending for social purposes which they value highly.

Symbols. The case for a bill, program, or point of view can be completely lost if presented in terms of a multitude of separate statements. Ideals and principles themselves are sometimes excessively complex. The best way to

[10] Charles Merriam, "Political Power" (New York: McGraw-Hill, 1934), p. 246.

[11] Depending upon their social values, group allegiances, and specialized professional interests, competent and intelligent economists will discuss this principle in many sharply divergent fashions. "Objectively correct" views on public policy aspects of economics, it becomes evident, are a delusion. See this author's review of "The 1950's Come First," *American Political Science Review,* Vol. 45, September, 1951, pp. 867–874.

wrap up many facts and emotions in one package and to make ideals and principles glow with meaning is through the use of symbolism. Contestants in the social struggle have therefore invested heavily in the development of symbols.[12] During the nineteenth century the symbol used most often in attacking someone else's legislative objectives was "unconstitutional." Although still used, this symbol has lost much of its force. Much more effective is the stigma in such terms as "communistic," "socialistic," "red," "radical," "alien," or "un-American."

In buttressing his demands for larger subsidies for silver, one of the Senate leaders of the "Silver Bloc" offered the following alternative to the country: "The Nation must adopt bimetallism or face bolshevism." [13] In attacking the original Full Employment Bill, Merwin K. Hart, president of the National Economic Council, charged that "The real origin of this bill is found in the Constitution of the Union of Soviet Socialist Republics, which states (Art. 118) that its citizens have 'the right to work,' that is, are guaranteed the right to employment and payment for their work in accordance with its quantity and quality." [14] The proponents of the measure, in referring to their opposition, often replied along the following lines: "Those who argue that continuing full employment means regimentation are themselves sowing the seeds of economic and political revolution. No hostile foreign agent could do more to wreck the fabric of our society than to tell our people that unemployment is the price we pay for free enterprise." [15]

Other negative symbols are "political" and "partisan," terms that seem most frequently used by partisan politicians themselves in attacks upon the programs of those with whom they disagree. "Objective," "nonpartisan," and "scientific" are terms used just as frequently—and usually interchangeably—by all sides. These latter symbols appeal deeply to everyone's dream that somewhere in this world of endless struggle and shifting values can be found a firm source of authority. "Impartial experts" are used by all sides in a legislative controversy. One of the best of all propaganda devices is to set up a board composed of "men of unimpeachable integrity and objectivity whose disinterested views will command the respect of everyone." During World

[12] The use of the symbols "civilian control" and "military control" in the conflict over the Atomic Energy Act of 1946, for example, has been carefully analyzed by one of the participants in the struggle. Byron Miller, "A Law Is Passed—The Atomic Energy Act of 1946" *University of Chicago Law Review,* Vol. 15, No. 4, Summer, 1948, pp. 817–819. See also James R. Newman and Byron S. Miller, "The Control of Atomic Energy" (New York: McGraw-Hill, 1948).

[13] Allen Seymour Everest, "Morgenthau, the New Deal and Silver" (New York: King's Crown Press, Columbia University Press, 1950), p. 15.

[14] "Full Employment Act of 1945," Hearings before a subcommittee of the Senate Committee on Banking and Currency, 79th Cong., 1st Sess., p. 890.

[15] "Assuring Full Employment in a Free Competitive Economy," report from the Senate Committee on Banking and Currency, 79th Cong., 1st Sess., S. Rept. 583, p. 22.

War II Bernard Baruch served as a one-man board of this type and the famous Baruch Reports on rubber and postwar adjustment were of inestimable propaganda value to the Roosevelt Administration. In the battle over the Atomic Energy Act of 1946 the atomic scientists were a major factor. "Those Men Who Made the Bomb . . . were awesome creatures indeed to have built the bomb." The fact that few people could understand what they were talking about made them all the more formidable.

When the Council of Economic Advisers was established, its members often reiterated the thesis that they were objective and professional economists.

> There are important values to be derived from having an independent group of economists in a position of high visibility in the government. One result of this position is a dramatic impact on the public, the Congress, and administrators, of the importance of economics as such, and of economic stabilization and growth.[16]

The great bulk of all legislative measures is wrapped up in such symbols as "our democratic institutions," "the American way of life," "national interest," "public interest," "our great traditions," "the ideals for which our fathers died," "national unity," "peace," and "national defense." Some groups concentrate on building up special symbols. The N.A.M. has made extensive use of the phrase, "the American individual-enterprise system," or in abbreviated form, "free enterprise." New Deal propaganda during the period before World War II made similar use of the term "the forgotten man." Later Henry Wallace tried—not too successfully—to develop the symbol of "the common man" and "the century of the common man."

The propagandists are also careful to use symbols of the most timely character. Before Pearl Harbor, Congress was flooded with bills, enactment of which, it was claimed, would build the first line of defense. The first line of defense ranged, it seemed, from recreation and maternity care to the Coast Guard and the FBI. Toward the end of the war, a customary rubric was "postwar planning." When there was wide expectation of serious postwar unemployment, the prevention of unemployment or the provision of full employment was a customary angle. When serious unemployment failed to materialize and instead rising prices became the major domestic problem in the postwar period, almost all economic measures were portrayed as weapons in the fight against inflation.

A bill that itself has recently become law can serve as a symbol to back up future legislation. Thus the major case in selling the British Loan to the American public was that it was needed to make a success of the previously

[16] Roy Blough, "Political and Administrative Requisites for Achieving Economic Stability" (paper presented at American Economic Association, Hotel Commodore, New York City, Dec. 28, 1949).

approved Bretton Woods International Monetary Agreement. In turn, a major part of the case for the Marshall Plan was its value in making the British Loan a success. And part of the case for the Point IV Program of American aid to underdeveloped countries was that it was needed to carry out the objectives of the Marshall Plan.

It is the practice for one group to appropriate the symbols of its opponents. Measures promoted by labor groups and measures calling for greater Federal intervention in the private economy are often described as "promoting free enterprise." Antilabor measures are described as helping to "balance the budget." Huey Long was once quoted as saying, "If fascism ever comes to America, it will come in the name of Democracy." This might well be paraphrased by suggesting that if socialism ever comes to America, it will come in the name of promoting private enterprise. The obvious danger in using the symbols of the opposition, of course, is the possibility that the stolen symbols may sink the stealer.

Some measures, of course, almost defy application of a simple symbol to them. The proposal for a Missouri Valley Authority, for example, has multiple objectives: conservation, irrigation, flood control, power, and navigation. Realizing the difficulty the average person has in grasping so many separate ideas, the propagandists on behalf of this measure have concentrated on trying to sell the administrative concept of a single Federal planning agency located in the Missouri Valley itself. They have attempted to fuse substantive content into this essentially abstract idea, heralding the valley authority as a new form of decentralization that will help democratize American government. Its opponents, in turn, have charged that Federal valley authorities are but another step in the aggrandizement of the Federal bureaucracy and the destruction of local initiative. Both sides put the case in rather abstract terms. More specific symbols were used in the battle over the Taft-Hartley Labor-Management Relations Act of 1948. Organized labor pitched its general propaganda campaign on the theme that it was a "slave-labor bill." In turn, the business organizations behind the Act described it as a measure to combat "labor monopoly."

Defense and Attack. A portion of the time spent in legislative campaign propaganda is always devoted to answering the "unfounded attacks" and "distortions" of opponents. Some campaigners prefer not to answer attacks directly but to do it without making a positive reference to the specific attack. A favorite device is to have the reply emanate from a presumably disinterested source. But just as in warfare, the best method of defense is attack. In the fight for the original Full Employment Bill the offensive was taken at the outset by Senator Murray's testimony before the Senate Banking and Currency Committee linking the opposition to "a small but vocal minority who are against the full employment bill because they are against full employment."[17] This was in sharp contrast to the band-wagon approach, previously taken by most friends of the bill, that "everybody is for full employment." It immediately put the opponents of the bill on the defensive, forced them in self-protection to endorse the objectives of the measure, and gave a psychological advantage to the bill's proponents. In contrast, one of the reasons for the Office of Price Administration's repeated defeats in Congress during World War II was the fact that it spent too much time defending itself. Only sporadically and halfheartedly did it take the offensive and wage a direct case against the opponents of price control.

A difficult decision that faces all legislative propagandists who are campaigning on behalf of a specific measure is whether to present the measure as a basis for discussion or to adopt a more aggressive, change-not-a-line approach. In the early stages of the campaign on its behalf, the original Full Employment Bill was presented as a basis for discussion. "Sound legislation can be developed only by clarifying the differences between conflicting schools of thought," stated Senator James E. Murray.[18] This approach served to develop a friendly attitude on the part of those who liked some things about the bill but objected to others. Seven months later, however, when the bill was brought up in executive sessions of the Senate Banking and Currency Committee, the sponsors produced a revised version and, when the bill was reported from the Committee, the Majority Report argued that "the bill, as reported, adequately meets all valid criticisms . . . no further changes are needed." Referring to proposals for amendments that had been made within the Committee, it stated that "if the bill is not to be converted into a meaningless scrap of paper, it is essential that such amendments be rejected."

Propaganda Media

The great bulk of propaganda relies on use of the printed word. All the tools and tricks known to public-relations experts—from press releases and press conferences to "leg art" and stunts—are used to assault the editors, reporters, and article writers of newspapers and magazines. The National Association of Manufacturers prepares model advertisements for use by local businessmen. These advertisements are described in the *N.A.M. News* of November 1, 1947, as follows: "Your Association has compiled a 'package' of scientifically tested ads with top attention-getting and 'play-back' qualities for use by the regional office staffs in stimulating supplemental advertising in local

[17] "Full Employment Act of 1945," Hearings before a subcommittee of the Senate Committee on Banking and Currency, 79th Cong., 1st Sess., July–September, 1945, p. 16.

[18] "Assuring Full Employment in a Free Competitive Economy," report from the Senate Committee on Banking and Currency, 79th Cong., 1st Sess., S. Rept. 583, p. 2.

media on this key subject of profits." Lesser organizations often arrange to deluge local newspapers with well-prepared "letters to the editor."

Hundreds of labor unions issue papers of their own which keep their members informed on labor's legislative campaigns. The American Legion sends a weekly clip sheet to every community newspaper in the United States and also publishes the *American Legion Monthly* and the *National Legionnaire,* a newspaper which is normally printed every two weeks. Through the provision of a regular weekly news and picture service, it also nourishes about 300 papers that are published by its state, district, county, and post organizations. The N.A.M. does a unique job of preparing specialized periodicals for important groups. In addition to "Understanding," mentioned above, it publishes the following: "Farm and Industry," which "goes primarily to county agricultural agents, to land grant college presidents and deans and to both national and local leaders in the Grange and Farm Bureau"; "Program Notes," which is sent to the program-committee heads of women's clubs as well as to national women leaders; and "Trends," which is circulated "primarily among teachers from the secondary school to the college level." [19]

Frequent use is also made of up-to-the-minute bulletins designed to inform supporting organizations of the latest developments in a legislative campaign and advise them on campaign maneuvers. An interesting example is a mimeographed bulletin entitled "Strategy on Health Legislation" issued by the Committee for the Nation's Health on May 12, 1947. It read in part as follows:

Battle Lines Drawn

With the introduction of the National Health Insurance and Public Health Act, the legislative battle lines for 1947 are visibly drawn.

The issue is between this Bill and the Taft "Health" Bill, which poses as a "substitute" for it—between an adequate, comprehensive health program and a stop-gap measure offered as a sop to divert the demand for a real solution. . . .

The Task This Year

1. Defeat the Taft "Health" Bill. Fight it on the charity issue. Fight it on the administrative issue. Fight it as a sop which doesn't provide nearly enough to accomplish even its own limited purposes.

2. Boost by contrast the health insurance principle by backing the National Health Insurance Bill. Commit both political parties to the insurance principle as the basis for major health legislation.

3. Enact constructive health legislation of a limited nature consistent with our broad national health program.

Many organizations issue legislative pamphlets and leaflets. Under the auspices of the National Physicians Committee, "from 12 to 15 million

[19] *N.A.M. News,* Oct. 4, 1947.

pamphlets were circulated in the attack on the previous Wagner-Murray-Dingell bill, which passed into innocuous desuetude, and many millions of pamphlets are now being circulated through drug stores, supply houses, hospitals, and other medical agencies." [20] Government agencies customarily publish informational brochures making an attractive case for one or another government program. Government documents of this type are usually written in a restrained mood, and their official status gives them a prestige value that cannot be achieved in more out-and-out campaign propaganda.

A favorite device used by both private organizations and government agencies is the reprinting from the *Congressional Record* of speeches by members of Congress. In addition to having an air of authority about it, a reprint from the *Congressional Record* often represents the quickest or cheapest method of printing campaign material. Committee hearings, committee reports, and other congressional documents are also often used. Some of the most valuable propaganda on behalf of national health insurance was contained in a series of committee prints issued during 1946 at the request of Senator James E. Murray in the form of reports to the Senate Committee on Education and Labor. These reports, which were compiled in the Federal Security Agency, included a scholarly memorandum entitled "Need for Medical Care Insurance," questions and answers on the Health Insurance Bill, and the more important statements made for and against the measure.

Occasionally books will be written for the express purpose of serving as legislative campaign propaganda—as with "The American Individual Enterprise System," [21] prepared by the Economic Principles Commission of the National Association of Manufacturers to provide a theoretical justification of the N.A.M.'s general program. A major weapon in the fight for the Taft-Hartley Labor-Management Relations Act was a report entitled "A Labor Policy" prepared by two economists of the Brookings Institution. Documents of this type have a double value. In addition to having the appearance of objectivity (from the viewpoint of the authors, presumably, this is much more than appearance), they provide valuable ammunition for use in other propaganda efforts.

Most of the propaganda carried by radio, television, and moving pictures is of a generalized nature, dealing with broad social values rather than with specific legislative programs. Nevertheless, the broad legislative objectives of business organizations are regularly broadcast by newscasters and commentators. Occasionally a labor organization will sponsor a commentator or even erect a radio station of its own to present its views. Every legislative campaign organization is eager to present its views on the various radio forums and debates and to make other uses of radio time. Government officials make fre-

[20] *Journal of the American Medical Association,* Feb. 3, 1946.

[21] (New York: McGraw-Hill, 1946.)

quent use of the air waves. President Franklin Roosevelt's "fireside chats" were among the most potent propaganda weapons of the "New Deal." Motion-picture propaganda for direct legislative objectives is usually in the form of educational shorts and documentaries.[22] Some of these, such as army shorts on national defense, are customarily played at local movie houses. Most of them, however, are distributed through organizations.

With all the attention that is given to the newer media of mass communication, one should not lose sight of the value of persuasion through personal contact. Other media of propaganda operate more or less in a blunderbuss fashion. Persuasion through personal contact is the only way to deal effectively with specific individuals in strategic positions. There is no other more effective medium of propaganda for use between the leaders of various groups and organizations. Only in this manner, furthermore, is it possible to handle the involved psychological problems resulting from the desire for deference and the fear of being neglected or sidetracked. Nor should it be assumed that in personal contacts major emphasis is necessarily placed upon argumentation and appeals to reason or to emotion. Purely personal interactions, the development of mutual fondness, the discovery of other interests in common—all these can be of inestimable importance. Personal charm itself, in all its innumerable manifestations, is an invaluable influence.

Another of the most effective means of propaganda can be found in "persuasion by participation." Many people never can be won over to the support of a given proposition unless they are consulted at the very outset and asked to play a major role either in formulating the proposition or in criticizing preliminary formulations. This approach is of particular value at the drafting stage. Failure to develop sufficient personal consultation prior to the introduction of a bill can spell serious trouble at later stages. This is borne out by the following commentary on the handling of the Food, Drug and Cosmetic Act of 1938:

> Viewed in retrospect it seems probable that the progress of the legislation would have been facilitated if no attempt had been made to introduce a bill in the special session and, instead, the draft had been made available upon its completion to industrial and consumer groups to obtain their reactions and suggestions. Some of the revisions which were later forced by industry opposition could have been made before the beginning of the regular session in January, 1934. The course followed served to arouse suspicion and hostility which thereafter could never be completely

22 "By and large, film producers in democratic countries have intentionally avoided pictures which can be labelled propagandistic because they have thought of their medium as a vehicle of entertainment. This means, in turn, that the propaganda content of pictures has been mostly unintentional." (Doob, *op. cit.*, p. 504.) Doob means, of course, that the direct propaganda is mostly unintentional. That the indirect-propaganda content of major film productions is intentional is illustrated by the producers' argument that broader distribution of American films abroad will popularize the "American way of life."

allayed. Opposition there inevitably would have been, but it is doubtful that, if the other procedure had been followed, this opposition would have gained the impetus that it did.[23]

A tried-and-tested propaganda device is the convening of special conferences on individual legislative measures. "These conferences," writes Ebersole, "appear to have one or all of three main functions: the political education of constituents and their leaders, furnishing information to public officials, and the organization and promotion of political action." [24] They also serve as a method of getting newspaper attention—particularly when "big-name" speakers can be scheduled to perform.

The Application of Pressure

"Turn on the heat, boys." A President is putting it bluntly to his legislative lieutenants. Or a strategist for a labor union is laying out the next steps toward getting a bill out of committee. Or a Representative, meeting in an anteroom off the House floor with congressional colleagues and representatives of government agencies and private organizations, is appealing for action before the vote is taken on a crucial amendment.

The listeners know the difference between turning on the heat—or pressure—and using the gentler methods of influencing action. The former involves rewards and punishments. It involves the promise or threat that *if* such and such is done, or not done, such and such steps will be taken—or are in process of being taken. The latter relies on the more subtle approach of appealing to interests, ideals, and principles without recourse to rewards and punishments.

In practice, of course, the distinction between the two becomes blurred. Both are used to mobilize group support, and both, in turn, become weapons in the hands of supporters. Both can be used alike for blanket bombardment and for pin-point assaults to influence individuals (although when individuals are propagandized, the usual term is "persuasion"). The two are usually as close as the velvet glove to the iron fist.

Rewards and Punishments

Types. As with propaganda, the pressure that matters most is the indirect variety. In any society, people grow up under a cloud of cultural coercion and restraint. Some things are safe to do or think; others are taboo. By experience

[23] David F. Cavers, "The Food, Drug, and Cosmetic Act of 1938: Its Legislative History and Its Substantive Provisions," *Law and Contemporary Problems*, Vol. 6, No. 1, Winter, 1939, p. 7.

[24] Luke Ebersole, "Church Lobbying in the Nation's Capital" (New York: Macmillan, 1951), p. 100. Ebersole gives a number of interesting examples of conferences and "seminars" conducted by religious organizations. See pp. 100–103.

and example one learns that there is a predictable pattern of rewards and punishments. No matter how much one may rebel this pattern leaves its mark. Many a legislator speaks truly when he claims that he will vote his conscience, come what may, no matter how strong the outcries and threats from his constituents. The thing he may overlook is the fact that the same indirect pressures that molded the consciences of his constituents also molded his own conscience and even helped to put him into office.

Direct pressure does not always appear in the more obvious forms. People want to be liked. They are eager for approval, deference, and prestige. No one, not even the most conspicuously placed of public officials, is so thick-skinned as not to wince under criticism and disapproval. Deference is a potent reward, disapproval a potent punishment.

In its most effective form, direct pressure deals with people's employment. No President or member of Congress can afford to disregard the threats or promises of those who are in a position to affect their continued employment in elective office. Campaign contributions, endorsement and support, and labors to bring out the vote are decisive pressure weapons. Outside the field of elective office, as well, the promise of future employment or the threat of unemployment are also important influences. Business groups are continuously dangling before the noses of government officials the prospect of future employment, a prospect that leads one to avoid stepping on the toes of possible future employers. Patronage also enters the picture. Although it is much less of a weapon than in the days before the growth of the civil-service system, the President and executive officials can often get certain things done by offering or withholding congressional patronage. Private patronage is probably just as widespread. When economic activity declines, the offices of members of Congress become employment centers. Under such circumstances business concerns with direct interest in pending legislation find it to their advantage to find jobs for the constituents of friendly members of Congress.[25]

From a broader viewpoint, the offering of rewards and the threatening of punishments is the very essence of the process of forming a coalition or of making "a deal." Government officials can use their strategic positions to promote or impede public projects for this or that area, contracts for backers and friends, and the favorable handling of cases and claims brought forward by constituents. They can assert their influence at this or that stage in the varying processes of government. Private organizations also have powerful pressure weapons. Businessmen can expand plants or close them down, raise or lower prices, tolerate competition or push competitors to the wall, deal amicably with labor unions or force a strike. Labor organizations can boycott nonunion goods, slow down production, or go out on strike.

[25] The use of "business patronage" in state government is discussed by William V. Shannon in "Massachusetts: Prisoner of the Past," a chapter of Robert S. Allen (ed.), "Our Sovereign State" (New York: Vanguard, 1949), pp. 50–51.

Actions of this type have important implications for the legislative process. In President Wilson's Administration the Adamson Eight-Hour Law was passed under the threat of a general railroad strike. It was also asserted by many that during the period preceding passage of the Taft-Hartley Labor-Management Relations Act certain parties to the controversy precipitated various strikes for the express purpose of assisting the campaign for the law's enactment.

The most extreme pressure, of course, is violence. In other countries legislators have again and again been forced to take their stand under threat of the firing squad or the hangman's noose. In America, happily, such events have not come to pass, although occasional steps in this direction have been made in a number of states. Nevertheless, the implied threat of violence is always in the background. The power of any government rests upon its capacity to suppress revolt and law evasion by direct force. It is also true that the power of many private groups rests in the assumption that if they are pushed too far by national law they may resist by force.

Bribery (see page 38). One of the oldest forms of pressure is direct bribery. In the early days of our Government, votes were bought and sold openly. In his Journal about Senate activities during the First Congress, Senator William Maclay wrote: "In the Senate chamber this morning Butler said he heard a man say he would give Vining one thousand guineas for his vote, but added, 'I question whether he would do so in fact.' So do I, too, for he might get it for a tenth part of the sum." [26] In describing the legislative operations of Alexander Hamilton and his New York banker associates, Maclay commented on the fact that most votes were carried by a majority of only one. The reason for this, Maclay commented wryly, is "the fact that Hamilton and his New York *junto* do business on the principles of economy, and do not put themselves to the expense of hiring more than just the number necessary to carry their point." [27]

Although the incidence of corruption is hard to estimate, observers of the political scene seem agreed that it has declined. The trends have been both from cupidity to probity and from cupidity to timidity. Both givers and receivers have learned to operate more cautiously. In one form or another, bribery still exists—although it would be difficult to uncover many cases that could be sustained before a court of law. "I never have to bribe anybody," a lobbyist has been quoted by a Washington columnist. "It's a bad practice. I just show them how to make a little money. . . ." [28]

[26] "Journal of William Maclay" (New York: Appleton-Century-Crofts, 1890), p. 209.

[27] *Ibid.*, p. 310.

[28] Drew Pearson, "Washington Merry-Go-Round," *Washington Post,* Oct. 24, 1947. For an interesting compilation of cases concerning members of Congress who learned "how to make a little money," see H. H. Wilson, "Congress; Corruption and Compromise" (New York: Rinehart, 1951).

Since most members of Congress maintain some form of business activity in order to pay for homes, offices, and assistance in their constituencies and in Washington, it is relatively easy for business opportunities to be channeled in their direction. It is because there are so many other things that bribes can be called and so many people, including colleagues and relatives, to whom they can be given, that the ominous prohibitions against bribery in the Corrupt Practices Act and the Criminal Code have so little meaning.

Methods. The application of direct pressure is as much an art as the exercise of persuasion. If used too blatantly it may defeat its own purposes. The great bulk of legislative pressures occurs in a hidden or implied form. This is particularly true in the case of campaign support or opposition where, entirely apart from reasons of diplomacy, the issues are so complex that it is dangerous for legislative campaigners to commit themselves too quickly. Moreover, people must be handled with kid gloves. If they are to be pressured into taking a given form of action, they dislike the humiliation involved in being compelled to change positions in public. Rationalizations and face-saving devices are invaluable aids in the application of pressure. The velvet touch of persuasiveness is of the essence.

One of the most effective legislative campaign organizations has stated the case for sweetness and light as follows:

> Never threaten your Congress with loss of your vote. Understandably, such threats only irritate Congressmen, so avoid demands and bullying tactics. Avoid haranguing and the attitude that your belief is incontrovertible.
>
> Yours is a selling job, so apply the same common rules of salesmanship that you use in everyday work. Convince your Congressman you have thought about the issue, and that you are sincere in your position.[29]

An interesting contrast to this approach is provided by the following statement made by William Z. Foster, chairman of the Communist party of the United States, in a speech exhorting the unions to action against pending labor legislation:

> Every union everywhere should adopt resolutions and indignation, union committees should visit Representatives and Senators, mass lobbies should be sent to Washington, protest meetings should be held, citizens' committees should be organized, and if necessary, one-day local protest strikes should be prepared.[30]

Channels for Direct Pressure

Personal Contact. Only an infinitesimal amount of direct pressure takes place in the lobbies off the floor of the Senate and the House of Representatives.

[29] "How to Work with Congress" (Washington, D.C.: The Realtors' Washington Committee of the National Association of Real Estate Boards), p. 8.

[30] *The New York Times*, Jan. 23, 1946.

Discussion in the lobby is necessarily brief, hurried, and conspicuous. Most of the Washington pressure work is done not in the lobbies, but at committee hearings (which will be discussed in detail in Chap. 14) and in government offices. There is hardly a day in the week, particularly while Congress is in session, that hundreds of representatives of private organizations, executive officials, and members of Congress are not using direct pressure, coupled with propaganda, to advance their legislative interests.

According to Senator Harry Cain of Washington,

> . . . there is probably more lobbying going on in nearby country clubs than in the corridors of the Capitol. . . . Here is an intangible manifestation of the political lobby —it is the social lobby—the plethora of elaborate cocktail and dinner parties, sports, junkets and related activities that provide entertainment.[31]

Executive officials in influential positions probably receive as many invitations to social affairs and miscellaneous forms of entertainment as members of Congress. The value of the social lobby lies not so much in the influence of entertainment upon a man's thinking as in the opportunity it provides for obtaining access to someone who is extremely busy during working hours. It is not a "wine, women, and song" kind of influence. It often brings people together for serious consideration of mutual problems. Wesley McCune writes:

> A luncheon club, conducted with informality, may be as productive in lining up support for a unified program as are twice as many hours in congressional office buildings. One such group, called the Farm Hands, meets weekly at the Harrington Hotel to compare notes on the past seven days' grist of announcements and gossip. The forty or more farm representatives, food-trade spokesmen, congressmen, publicity men, journalists, and department officials who keep the club going are one vehicle of the farm bloc. It is they who carry much of the ammunition up front for all-out assaults.[32]

Occasionally personal contact is expanded to group contact in the form of mass lobbying and marches on Washington. During World War II the Consumer Advisory Committee of the Office of Price Administration organized large delegations of housewives to lobby members of Congress on behalf of OPA. In 1945 the C.I.O. brought in large delegations from each of the industrial states to put pressure on their congressional delegation on behalf of a three-point program: expanded unemployment compensation, liberalized minimum-wage provisions, and the Full Employment Bill. Marches on Washington are less frequent. The two great historical marches were those of Coxey's Army at the turn of the century and the famous Bonus March of 1932 on behalf of veterans' legislation. It was a threatened march on Washington which induced President Roosevelt to set up the FEPC by Executive order. Yet

[31] Statement quoted in *Washington Star*, June 9, 1947.

[32] Wesley McCune, "The Farm Bloc" (New York: Doubleday, 1943), pp. 11–12.

when it came to the problem of obtaining congressional action to make the FEPC permanent, the leaders of the Negro organizations decided against another march on Washington for fear that it would serve unduly to antagonize members of Congress.

The People Back Home. Perhaps the most effective channel of personal contact is through "the people back home." One railroad representative has observed:

> All of us have long recognized that the only effective way to influence congressional action is to convince the influential men in each congressional district that the public interest and the interest of the railroads coincide. I have the impression that most of the congressmen, particularly those living in the smaller states and in rural districts, depend for their support upon a comparatively few men in each county in their respective districts. If we could reach the men upon whom a congressman depends for advice and assistance in his political campaign, we could go far toward having the problem solved.[33]

The N.A.M. advises every industrialist and businessman to "map out a sound public-relations program designed especially to keep its Congressman informed of the part industry is playing in the home life of its community." [34] The more successful legislative Representatives stay in the background and concentrate upon developing a general program for contact work with government officials. "I plan the strategy and direct the moves," Purcell Smith, legislative representative of the National Association of Electric Companies, has been quoted as saying, "but it is our company executives who carry the ball." [35] A legislative report of the Citizens' Committee on Displaced Persons, describing direct lobbying in Washington "as an essential but proportionately minor part of the task," advises that "it would be best to concentrate on local instrumentalities. . . ." [36]

Petitions and Memorials. One of the oldest methods of attempting to influence a legislature is the presentation of petitions. In England the legislative process itself was born when the first Parliaments began to petition the king for changes in the law and when, with the reign of Henry IV, individuals and localities began to petition Parliament in turn to petition the king. In America the petition became a major instrument of influence upon the colonial legislatures and "the right to petition the government for a redress of grievances" was written into the Federal Constitution and most of the state constitutions. The use of written petitions, however, has greatly declined. Luce writes:

[33] *United States v. The A.A.R. et al.,* Govt. Brief, Part II, Exhibit G. 207, p. 125. Quoted in John G. Shott, "The Railroad Monopoly" (Washington, D.C.: Public Affairs Institute, 1950), p. 86.

[34] Walter Chamblin, Jr., "Know Your Congressmen" (New York: National Association of Manufacturers, 1944).

[35] Robert S. Allen, "King of the Lobbyists," *New Republic,* Feb. 9, 1948.

[36] Quoted in *Congressional Quarterly Notebook,* Vol. 6, No. 18, May 5, 1948, p. 159.

> Everybody in public life knows perfectly well how easily petition signatures are obtained, how carelessly they are given, how little weight they really deserve. The result is that when they reach an American legislative body, they get scant courtesy. . . . One earnest word spoken to a Representative by a constituent whose judgment inspires confidence is worth a yard of petition signatures.[37]

Another old tradition is the presentation of memorials from state legislatures. In the days when the states loomed much larger on the national scene and when Senators in fact were deemed to be delegates from sovereign state legislatures, the memorial was an important channel of contact. While still used, it also has waned in importance. Robert Luce, who served in the Massachusetts state legislature as well as in Congress, writes:

> Anyone who has served in a State Legislature knows, for example, how scant the attention there given to proposals for memorializing Congress or otherwise affecting Congressional action. These proposals usually prevail with little or no debate. Somehow the legislators feel no responsibility for positions taken in regard to them. Inasmuch as many members of Congress have served in State Legislatures and understand all about this, it is not surprising that the hundred and more memorials sent by the Legislatures to every Congress are ignored. They are that much waste paper.[38]

Letters and Telegrams. But memorials are not the only form of waste paper that descends upon Washington. The waste-paper baskets of members of Congress and executive officials are kept ever full with form letters and form telegrams. Many of these communications are futile because misdirected. Letters from a Negro organization to a Senator from Mississippi can hardly influence the actions of the recipient. Form post cards, canned letters, and telegrams are seldom influential. They tend to call to mind the deluge of fake and inspired telegrams used by utility organizations in the 1934 campaign against the New Deal's holding company bill and exposed by the Senate investigation led by Senator Hugo Black of Alabama. The more seasoned legislative campaigners usually try to follow the advice of former Representative George Outland of California: "One thoughtful letter will outweigh half a dozen which simply say 'vote for this' or 'vote against that.' One spontaneous outburst on your own stationery is worth a hundred mimeographed letters of newspaper clippings in some write-your-Congressman drive." [39] They concentrate on planning for spontaneity. As part of its campaign on behalf of rent control in 1947, the National Association of Consumers evolved a form letter to Senators which told in detail about the writer's personal financial problems and advised its correspondents to make slight alterations of fact and wording.[40]

[37] Robert Luce, "Legislative Principles" (Boston: Houghton Mifflin, 1930), pp. 530–531.

[38] *Ibid.*, p. 483.

[39] "Write to Your Congressman, but Do It Right," *The Reader's Digest*, Vol. 48, June. 1946.

[40] Quoted in *The Wall Street Journal*, June 18, 1947.

In "How to Work with Congress" the National Association of Real Estate Boards, an outspoken opponent of rent control, sent its members these explicit instructions on how to write to members of Congress:

> Whenever possible, make your letters apply to a local situation. Tell specific instances of how legislation affects or would affect your business. Give facts, figures, and sources of information. Avoid confusing Federal with State legislation.
>
> Be brief as possible, but tell your story, simply and naturally. Come directly to the point. Don't bury your requests. Identify, as fully as possible, the legislation about which you're writing. Don't refer merely to the "Jones Bill." Rep. Jones may have introduced several bills, so give the resolution or bill number if possible.
>
> Don't just state that you oppose or favor a certain measure, but also give your reasons for opposing or favoring it. Most Congressmen are more interested in your reasons than in your position.
>
> If you are writing in behalf of an organization, be sure to state your position with the organization, the number of members, and your authority to commit the membership on the issue at hand.[41]

At crucial stages in the legislative struggle, a careful effort is usually made to pick the specific points at which communications can be most useful and to canvass those correspondents who might be most influential. The following letter from a representative of the A.F.L. to labor organizations in California provides a useful illustration:

> Within the next few days a joint conference of the United States Senate and Congress will draft an anti-labor bill, based upon the Taft and Hartley legislation. This bill undoubtedly will be adopted by both Houses. We have every reason to believe President Truman will veto the bill; however, from present indication, the Congress will pass the bill over the President's veto by an overwhelming majority.
>
> In the Senate we are informed that the A.F. of L. needs the support of 7 or more Senators to block the passage of the bill over a veto. Senator KNOWLAND is one of the Senators needed. It is essential that a sufficient number of telegrams, letters and telephone calls be made to Senator KNOWLAND in an attempt to influence him to refuse to override the veto. Thousands of letters from business men are arriving daily, requesting the adoption of this antilabor legislation. However, communications and contacts from members are very light. The united A.F. of L. is, therefore, requesting each union to have each officer, executive board member, and business agent take it upon himself to get 5 persons to wire, write or telephone Senator KNOWLAND within the next week, requesting him to vote against passage over a veto.
>
> In Los Angeles County, A.F. of L. unions have over 5,000 members who are officers in the above capacities. If each of these officers got 5 persons to respond, Senator KNOWLAND will have received word from at least 25,000 citizens. If each officer leaves it to the others, Senator KNOWLAND will receive no correspondence. This is a program that must be carried out. It is a last-ditch attempt to avoid sabotage of the free trade-union movement. Please act immediately.

[41] *Op. cit.*, p. 7.

We will appreciate copies of letters or telegrams sent, or a reply from each officer when he has accomplished the above outlined task.[42]

This letter inadvertently fell into the hands of Senator Knowland himself who inserted it in the *Congressional Record*. In view of the fact that the groups favoring the Taft-Hartley Act undoubtedly used similar methods, it is a credit to Senator Knowland that he merely inserted this letter in the *Congressional Record* without comment rather than using it as a springboard for accusing the A.F.L. of unscrupulous tactics.

Sometimes the sheer bulk of correspondence received on a legislative measure may, if not outweighed by corresponding bulk on the opposite side, have decisive influence. One of the most important issues in the conflict on atomic-energy legislation was military control (as provided for in the May-Johnson bill in the House of Representatives) versus civilian control (as provided for in the McMahon bill in the Senate). A hastily organized group of atomic scientists led a correspondence campaign in protest against the May-Johnson bill.

Professional societies, women's clubs, church federations, labor unions, veterans' groups, and university students adopted resolutions of protest. Letters and telegrams poured into the White House and Congressional offices; the Senate special committee alone received over 75,000 messages, of which the overwhelming majority opposed the provision.

This storm aided the administration, by this time committed to the principle of an exclusively civilian commission, in its effort to keep the May-Johnson bill bottled up in the House. Thus, the issue was brought to a focus in the Senate special committee, where the compromise ultimately incorporated in the act was hammered out.[43]

[42] *Congressional Record,* 80th Cong., 1st Sess., p. 6326.

[43] James R. Newman, "America's Most Radical Law," *Harper's Magazine,* May, 1947.

Chapter 14

THE STRUGGLE FOR COMMITTEE POWER

A LARGE GROUP of people cannot get much work done without some specialization of labor. The 81 members of the First Congress realized this when they met in 1789. After a bill had been considered on the floor, they would usually appoint a special committee to work out the details. Once these committees made their reports, they passed out of existence. At least 350 were born and died during the Third Congress.[1]

As the legislative burden grew heavier and more complex, however, the select-committee system began to bog down. It proved impossible for the Senate and the House themselves to find time to discuss many bills before referring them to a committee. Moreover, select committees proved weak vehicles for the communication of propaganda and pressure between Congress and the executive branch. They lacked the technical proficiency desired by the first Secretary of the Treasury, Alexander Hamilton, in order to establish his control of Congress. They lacked the stability needed by the Jeffersonians to resist Hamilton and later, when Jefferson became President, to carry out their own executive policies.

As a result, more and more use was made of "standing" committees set up to handle all measures in a given field. Less and less effort was made to instruct the committees in advance. By the early 1820's the revolution was complete. Under Henry Clay the standing committees became the automatic recipients of legislative proposals and the focal points of legislative power. By 1885, there had already been ample justification for Woodrow Wilson's pungent

[1] For general material on congressional committees, see Ralph V. Harlow, "The History of Legislative Methods in the Period before 1925" (New Haven, Conn.: Yale University Press, 1917); Lauros G. McConachie, "Congressional Committees" (New York: Crowell, 1898); Ada C. McCown, "The Congressional Conference Committee" (New York: Columbia University Press, 1927); Gilbert Y. Steiner, "The Congressional Conference Committee: 70th to 80th Congresses" (Urbana, Ill.: The University of Illinois Press, 1951). For material on individual congressional committees see Eleanor E. Dennison, "The Senate Foreign Relations Committee" (Stanford, Cal.: Stanford University Press, 1942); and Albert C. F. Westphal, "The House Committee on Foreign Affairs" (New York: Columbia University Press, 1942). For material on committees in state legislatures see C. I. Winslow, "State Legislative Committees" (Baltimore, Md.: Johns Hopkins Press, 1931).

description of the standing committees of Congress as "little legislatures" and of American government as "government by the standing committees of Congress." [2]

Today every bill is automatically consigned to a legislative committee before which it comes, in Lord Bryce's words, "as a shivering ghost stands before Minos in the nether world." [3] The committee members can lock it in "dim dungeons of silence whence it will never return." [4] Or, as is done less frequently, they can arrange for hearings. After hearings, they can let it languish in the files or can report it to the floor. If the latter instance, they can determine the form in which it will be considered by the Senate or House and can exercise great influence on the floor decision. If a bill passes both houses in a form unacceptable to one or the other, its fate is then largely in the hands of a joint conference committee made up of members of the two legislative committees which considered it in the first place.

Hence the real legislative infighting takes place at the committee stage. The legislative contestants are engaged in a ceaseless struggle for positions of committee power. They try to utilize committee hearings as a means of furthering their objectives, to obtain the potent backing of a favorable committee decision, to obtain control of conference committees, and to resist any counter-pressures that operate through the formalized channels of either or both houses.[5]

"Power is nowhere concentrated . . . ," observed Wilson. "It is divided up, as it were, into forty-seven seignories, in each of which a Standing Committee is the court baron and its chairman lord-proprietor." [6]

To understand how power is divided up among committees, it would be futile to map the seignories and list the court barons in any particular year. A few years later both map and list would be out of date. The pattern of committee power is always in flux. The committee system (if something so inchoate can be called a "system") can be understood only by examining the process of struggle and change itself as manifested in the structure and personnel of the committees.

[2] These terms and many others that have become common phrases in American political science come from Woodrow Wilson's "Congressional Government" (Boston: Houghton Mifflin, 1925).

[3] James Bryce, "The American Commonwealth" (New York: Macmillan, 1907), 3d ed., Vol. I, p. 157.

[4] Wilson, *op. cit.*, p. 69.

[5] For an idealistic interpretation differing from the above, see E. Jordan, "Theory of Legislation" (Indianapolis: Progress Publishing Co., 1930), p. 364.

[6] Wilson, *op. cit.*, p. 92.

The Committee Structure

Anyone who has tried to thread his way through the labyrinthine tangle of agencies and bureaus in the executive branch of the Federal government must be prepared to find at least as much complexity, if not more, in the structure of the standing committees of Congress.

Nor is the similarity accidental. The growth of both executive agencies and legislative committees stems from the same factors: the need for specialized organizations to deal with the ever-expanding burdens of the Federal government; the demand for recognition by powerful organizations; and the interest of Congressmen and executive officials in building instruments of personal power or prestige.

The Birth and Death of Committees

It is far easier to create a new legislative committee of Congress than it is to set up a new agency in the executive branch. All that is needed is a simple resolution. The area in which consent must be obtained is therefore far smaller than it would be if a law itself were needed, as is usually the case with executive agencies.[7]

The decision to establish a new standing committee is occasionally worked out ahead of time on the basis of compromise and accommodation between the affected members in either house. These understandings have been eased by the implicit understanding on many occasions that a new committee would not be overactive. Many committees, in fact, have had little function other than to provide additional office space and clerical personnel for the chairman. In 1900 the House Committee on Coast and Insular Survey was set up "for the sole purpose of becoming a burial ground for legislation sponsored by the Navy Department to take over the Coast and Geodetic Survey." This committee "proved an effective defense of the Coast and Geodetic Survey from the inclusion on the part of the Navy Department" without ever making a report.[8]

More often, however, new committees can be born only after a knockdown struggle. In the first decades of congressional history, the creation of new standing committees was slowed down by the opposition of those who pre-

[7] The only legislative committee of Congress established under law is the Joint Committee on Atomic Energy set up under the Atomic Energy Act of 1946. The provisions of the Legislative Reorganization Act of 1946 dealing with the legislative committees of both houses were defined "as an exercise of the rule-making power of the Senate and House of Representatives respectively and as such shall be considered as part of the rules of each House *respectively* or of that House to which they specifically apply." Sec. 101(a).

[8] George H. Haynes, "The Senate of the United States" (Boston: Houghton Mifflin, 1938), Vol. 1, footnote, pp. 281–282.

dicted—and rightfully so—that they would detract from the power of each of the individual members.[9] Once the system of standing committees became firmly established, every proposal for a new one threatened the power and influence of members of one or more existing committees.

The issue of whether or not to establish a new committee is often a struggle over specific legislative policies. Thus, before the Civil War, efforts to set up a Committee on Education and Labor were fought by Southerners, who viewed it as a threat to the slave-labor system in the South. It was impossible to establish this committee until the South had been defeated in the Civil War. Similarly, the abolition of the House Appropriations Committee in 1885 and the creation of eight new committees to take over its functions were the culmination of a decade's conflict over legislative policy on the tariff and internal improvements.

In recent years, the difficulties of establishing new committees have become greater than ever before. During the 1940's only two new legislative committees were created: the House Committee on Un-American Activities and the Joint Committee on Atomic Energy. In both these cases the method used was first to set up a special committee with no standing-committee functions. Once public recognition was won for the work of the special committee, all that remained was the formality of converting the special committees into standing committees.[10]

If the birth rate of standing committees is low, the death rate is still lower.

[9] In 1805, for example, when the House Committee on Rules proposed the creation of a standing committee on public lands, one member who voted against it voiced his fear that a "standing committee, vested with the entire business connected with the public lands, should gain such an ascendancy over the sentiments and decisions of the House, by the confidence reposed in them, as to impair the salutary vigilance with which it became every member to attend to so interesting a subject." *Annals of the Congress of the United States*, 9th Cong., 1st Sess., p. 286.

[10] It is doubtful that these two committees could have been created without resort to special forms of strategy. In January, 1945, when the routine motion of adopting the rules that prevailed during the previous Congress was put before the House, Representative John Rankin of Mississippi, in a surprise maneuver, moved to amend the previous rules by creating a permanent Committee on Un-American Activities. The motion could not be referred to a committee since the House was not yet organized. So it was discussed at once on the floor of the House and was adopted. If Rankin had waited until later and handled his resolution in the ordinary manner, the natural opposition of a number of standing committees with jurisdiction in the same area, combined with that of the liberal members of Congress who objected to the Committee's activities, would probably have resulted in its burial in committee. The Joint Committee on Atomic Energy was established through a relatively minor provision in the broad legislation dealing with atomic energy. If the Senate Special Committee on Atomic Energy had sought instead to create a joint committee by sponsoring a concurrent resolution (and a concurrent resolution is the usual vehicle for setting up a joint committee), the proposal would have run the risk of being killed in the House Military Affairs Committee.

The creation of every new committee necessarily implies the creation of new vested interests in its perpetuation. Many a committee has survived for years and years after all its purposes, save the provision of extra office space and personnel for its chairman, have utterly vanished.

Over the long run, of course, this trend becomes self-defeating. The time always arrives when the number of committees is so great that in the interests of economy and effectiveness, large-scale consolidation becomes imperative. This happened in 1921 when the many individual committees on appropriations and expenditures were merged into two sets of committees on appropriations and expenditures. The most recent amalgamation took place when the Legislative Reorganization Act of 1946 reduced the number of Senate committees from 33 to 15, cut the number of House committees from 48 to 19, and wiped out a large number of special committees that threatened the jurisdiction of standing committees.[11]

In 1946 the obstacles to pruning the luxuriant committee growth were exceedingly great. The strategy for overcoming them lay in the use of an omnibus bill containing many provisions of direct benefit to the members of Congress, such as higher salaries, a retirement program, and more staff assistance. The fact that the amalgamation program as a whole reduced the number of chairmanships then held by the liberal members of Congress probably served as a

[11] The standing legislative committees of Congress, as of January, 1953, were as follows:

Senate:

- Agriculture
- Appropriations
- Armed Services
- Banking and Currency
- District of Columbia
- Finance
- Foreign Relations
- Government Operations
- Interior and Insular Affairs
- Interstate and Foreign Commerce
- Judiciary
- Labor and Public Welfare
- Post Office and Civil Service
- Public Works
- Rules and Administration

House of Representatives:

- Agriculture
- Appropriations
- Armed Services
- Banking and Currency
- District of Columbia
- Education and Labor
- Expenditures in the Executive Departments
- Foreign Affairs
- House Administration
- Interstate and Foreign Commerce
- Judiciary
- Merchant Marine and Fisheries
- Post Office and Civil Service
- Public Lands
- Public Works
- Rules
- Un-American Activities
- Veterans' Affairs
- Ways and Means

Joint Committees:

- Atomic Energy

factor in winning support among the conservative majority in both houses and among the conservative pressure groups that joined in supporting the entire measure.

Only part of the picture is in the full committees. Each full committee has the power to subdivide itself into any number of subcommittees without recourse to permission from the house of which it is a part.[12] This power is customarily exercised by the committee chairman.[13] The tendency, therefore, is for subcommittees to sprout up in great numbers regardless of what is done with the full-committee structure.

Immediately before the Legislative Reorganization Act of 1946 went into effect, there were 140 subcommittees in Congress.[14] A few months after it went into effect, a special count revealed 146 subcommittees, thereby suggesting that the reshuffling had produced a more complex rather than a less complex system.[15] A later count shows that in 1950 there were 131 standing subcommittees: 66 in the Senate and 65 in the House.[16] Unfortunately for the ambitious enumerator, there are no public records that regularly provide a full list of all subcommittees. In fact, some subcommittees have neither name nor formal status and some are set up only as special bodies for the purpose of considering individual bills.

The members of subcommittees enjoy much more power than is generally realized. By refraining from acting on a measure, they can considerably delay action on it, if not kill the measure completely. Many subcommittees, like the 24 subcommittees of the two committees on appropriations, exercise great influence in their own right and are subject to scarcely any review by the full committee of which they are nominally a part.

The Flexibility of Committee Jurisdiction

Since the birth of the standing-committee system, there has never been a period in the history of Congress which has not been enlivened by jurisdictional

[12] A formal resolution on behalf of a subcommittee is needed for the purpose of obtaining additional funds or staff personnel.

[13] This power was challenged in one of the court trials arising from postwar investigation by the National Defense Investigating Committee of the Senate. The appellant claimed that a subcommittee could be established only by formal resolution of the full committee. But the court thought otherwise. ". . . the evidence shows that it is the unvarying practice of the Senate to follow the method of creating and appointing subcommittees which was employed in this instance." *Bennett V. Meyers v. United States,* U.S. Court of Appeals, Decision of Nov. 8, 1948.

[14] Hearings before the Joint Committee on the Organization of Congress, 79th Cong., 1st Sess., 1946, pp. 1040–1043.

[15] *The New York Times,* Apr. 14, 1947.

[16] George B. Galloway, "The Operation of the Legislative Reorganization Act of 1946," *American Political Science Review,* Vol. 45, No. 1, March, 1951, p. 43.

conflicts between rival committees or by the spectacle of individual committees reaching out for more and more territory to control.

In part, this is due to the complexity of the subject matter that comes before Congress. The problems of legislative policy are so interrelated that it would be a sheer impossibility to devise a jurisdictional pattern that eliminated overlapping areas. Even if this miracle could be achieved, new subjects would always arise that were not foreseen in the original pattern.

Jurisdictional conflicts are also due to the efforts of pressure groups and executive agencies to have legislation they want enacted referred to a friendly committee and legislation they oppose referred to a hostile committee. In addition, they arise from the interest of individual members of Congress, particularly committee and subcommittee chairmen, in expanding their personal power and prestige.

The jurisdiction of a committee is determined by two variable factors. The first, and most important, is the subject matter of the bills referred to it. The second is the subject matter on which it chooses to report. As indicated in Chap. 10, careful draftsmanship can often help to steer a bill toward one or another committee. The proper choice of sponsors and a friendly attitude on the part of the Presiding Officer will also contribute. In the Senate, the traditional respect for the prerogatives of the individual Senator has meant that considerable attention is paid to the sponsor's wishes concerning the committee to which his bill should be referred.[17] In the House of Representatives, on the other hand, the wishes of individual sponsors have seldom been an important factor. Discretionary power, except in those cases where the Speaker takes a direct personal interest, has been exercised almost entirely by the House Parliamentarian. In the case of referral to subcommittees, the word of the committee chairman is invariably accepted as final in both houses.

Sometimes an open jurisdictional struggle on the floor of the Senate or House occurs. In 1894, for example, the bill to impose a tax on oleomargarine was referred to the Committee on Ways and Means which had jurisdiction over taxation. This committee, however, was unfriendly to the proposal. The chairman of the Committee on Agriculture, on behalf of his committee, moved that the bill be transferred to his committee. The dairy interests rolled up a majority of 169 to 58 on behalf of the motion.[18] Since then the Committee on Agriculture has always retained jurisdiction over oleomargarine taxation in the House.

There are few restrictions on what a committee chooses to report to the floor. A bill dealing with one subject clearly within a committee's jurisdiction can be

[17] Vice-President Garner was frequently quoted as saying that, so far as he was concerned, he would *always* refer a bill in accordance with the sponsor's wishes. Although the Presiding Officer's discretion was considerably modified by the Legislative Reorganization Act of 1946, this tradition has not been eliminated.

[18] *Congressional Record,* 53d Cong., 2d Sess., Feb. 26, 1894, pp. 2422–2423.

amended in committee to deal with other subjects that would otherwise be under the jurisdiction of other committees. In committee operations possession is often nine points of the law, and possession can often be determined not by what bills are referred to a committee but by the subjects on which a committee may decide to conduct a study or hold a hearing.

The only formal limitations on what a committee may report relate to appropriations. Committees other than the appropriations committees may report bills containing authorizations for subsequent appropriations but are not allowed to report measures which actually appropriate funds. Likewise, the rules forbid appropriations committees from including legislative provisions in their appropriation measures. While the first of these restrictions is always lived up to, the second is habitually violated. In both houses the appropriations committees are prone to include legislative riders in appropriation measures and these violations of the rules are often upheld on the floor.

Often the maneuvering for committee jurisdiction is so intricate that it is extremely hard for any observer to follow the ball, let alone to know who may be calling the signals. The story of jurisdiction over reconversion legislation is an interesting example. The first round in this struggle started during World War II when the referral of a bill to establish an Office of War Mobilization was won by the Military Affairs Committee. Senator Harley Kilgore of West Virginia, a member of this committee, then succeeded in establishing and heading up a War Mobilization subcommittee to which this bill was referred. Somewhat later, Senator James E. Murray succeeded in setting up and becoming chairman of a War Contracts subcommittee, obtaining jurisdiction, at first, over legislation dealing with terminated war contracts and thereby freezing out the Naval Affairs Committee. Then the Murray subcommittee achieved jurisdiction over the disposition of surplus property, an area formerly covered by the Committee on Executive Expenditures. It then took over the field of reconversion legislation and with it the war mobilization legislation formerly considered by the Kilgore committee. "By April, 1944, Murray's War Contracts subcommittee had managed to get control of every important piece of proposed legislation dealing with reconversion and postwar problems." [19]

With the support of both the War Contracts subcommittee and the War Mobilization subcommittee, the full Military Affairs Committee went into the entire subject of unemployment compensation. Encouraged by the representatives of all sections of organized labor, its members had legislation drafted to provide emergency unemployment benefits for the millions of workers and returned veterans who, it was then felt, would be rendered unemployed at the end of the war. The purpose was to bring forth more liberal legislation on this subject than could be expected from the more conservative Finance Committee.

[19] Stephen K. Bailey, "Congress Makes a Law" (New York: Columbia University Press, 1949), p. 33.

The Finance Committee, however, did not sit idly by. In a surprise maneuver it brought an unemployment-compensation bill to the floor of the Senate before the Military Affairs Committee was able to report. The Military Affairs Committee, in turn, promptly reported an omnibus measure dealing not only with unemployment compensation but also very comprehensively with demobilization problems and the establishment of an Office of War Mobilization and Reconversion. When the Finance Committee bill was taken up, the Military Affairs Committee bill was offered as a substitute. The Finance Committee then suddenly broadened its scope far beyond the jurisdiction conferred by the bills that had been referred to it and produced a substitute omnibus measure dealing in a different manner with all the items covered in the Military Affairs Committee bill. This measure was offered as a substitute for the Military Affairs Committee substitute and was adopted by the Senate.

In the House of Representatives the Ways and Means Committee won jurisdiction on the ground that it dealt with social security despite the fact that the bill merely authorized Federal loans to state unemployment compensation systems and did not provide for new taxes. With slight modifications in the Ways and Means Committee and the conference committee, the Finance Committee measure became the War Mobilization and Reconversion Act of 1944.

The cure for jurisdictional tangles has been the goal of many congressional reform movements. One of the recommendations of the Joint Committee on the Organization of Congress was that "the jurisdiction of each reorganized committee be clearly defined so that overlapping and duplication will be eliminated." [20] Accordingly, the Legislative Reorganization Act of 1946 went into great detail in specifying the exact subject matter to be covered by each full legislative committee. This represented a marked change from the past when the jurisdictions of full committees were described in the rules of each house merely by a few general words that never attempted to clarify separate subject-matter areas. The Act also tightened up the Senate rules against the inclusion of legislative provisions in bills reported by the appropriations committees.

Nevertheless, the 1946 legislation did not provide—and could not have provided—a final answer to the jurisdictional problem. This was made clear in the 1947 conflict over proposals to unify the armed services. In the House, this legislation was referred to the Committee on Executive Expenditures which, under the rules, was supposed to handle the entire field of governmental reorganization. In the Senate, a sharp conflict developed between members of the Committee on Executive Expenditures and the Armed Services Committee. The latter claimed jurisdiction on the ground that unification was a problem that dealt exclusively with the armed services. They obtained jurisdiction by winning a majority vote on the floor of the Senate. In 1948, another case oc-

[20] "Organization of the Congress," Report of the Joint Committee on the Organization of Congress, 79th Cong., 2d Sess., S. Rept. 1011, p. 5.

curred when a measure to repeal the tax on oleomargarine was finally forced out of the House Committee on Agriculture by a discharge petition and was adopted by the House. It was then sent to the Senate where traditionally the subject had always been handled by the Finance Committee. Here the butter interests tried a jurisdictional maneuver that had previously been successful in the House. Senator Arthur Vandenberg of Michigan, the President pro tem of the Senate, referred the bill to the hostile Senate Agricultural Committee, but the advocates of repeal challenged his decision and succeeded in reversing him by a 40 to 37 vote on the floor.

The Committee People

We too often tend to think of agencies of government as abstract entities. We too often forget that government "structure" is merely a way of bringing people together to do various things. In the case of congressional committees particularly it should be remembered that committees are people. The struggle for committee power is essentially a struggle to decide who shall be the members of the various committees, who shall be the chairmen, and what kind of staff resources shall be available to whom.

The Members

The assignment of members of Congress to the various legislative committees must be viewed from three vantage points. In strictly formal terms, each house elects members for all its committees.[21] Actually, the formal process of election applies to little more than the assignment of newly elected members to committees and occasionally the transfer of members from one committee to another. By traditional practice, a member who has once served on a committee is regarded as entitled to continue to serve on it so long as he keeps his congressional seat. There is also a tradition that the members with the greatest seniority in either house have a right to any vacancies that develop on the more important committees, such as those dealing with appropriations, taxation, and foreign affairs.

Looked at another way, committee assignments are the responsibility of the major political parties (see pages 87–89). The party with a majority in either house "organizes" the committees in that house. The floor votes by which the members of committees are "elected" usually represent automatic acceptance of lists previously developed by each party. Although the majority party of either house could theoretically exclude the minority party from

[21] Until 1910, the Speaker of the House of Representatives had the power to assign members to House committees. In 1910–1911, however, the famous "revolution" against Speaker "Uncle Joe" Cannon took away the Speaker's power of committee appointments.

membership on legislative committees, it is part of the tradition of Congress that minority members be appointed to every committee.[22] This is usually done in a manner that provides a minority party with committee representation roughly proportionate to its numerical strength in the House as a whole.

Nevertheless, there is room for variation. Thus, in the Eightieth Congress, the Democratic minority received 6 out of 13 committee positions on 11 of the Senate's legislative committees. In three other committees, where majority-party control was regarded more highly, Democrats received only 5 out of 13 posts. On the Appropriations Committee the Democrats received 8 out of 21 positions. The extent of this variation has been limited in recent years by the provisions of the Legislative Reorganization Act which, with only minor exceptions, limits each Senator to membership on two standing committees and each Representative to membership on only one standing committee. When a majority party's margin is not very great, this provision means that the price of a safe majority on some committees is acceptance of a bare majority on other committees.

From a third and more realistic point of view, however, the parties are not actually responsible for committee assignments. Although each party caucus in each house has a Committee on Committees, this group is usually different in membership from the top policy committee of the party in each house. Among the House Democrats, the function of the Committee on Committees has been traditionally performed by the Democratic members of the Ways and Means Committee, a group which, by virtue of the seniority tradition, is to a considerable extent self-perpetuating and which is not directly amenable to control by party leadership or the party caucus. Nor is the national leadership of either party expected to concern itself with the pattern of committee assignment. Even a newly elected President with tremendous popular prestige and with the direct influence that patronage can give him during the first months in office can seldom have more than a very minor effect upon committee assignments. Personal deals and behind-the-scenes horse trading between the party members in each house would probably add up to more than Presidential influence. In the case of the anti-Administration party, the national-party organization outside Congress has no function whatsoever in this field.

This situation creates many favorable opportunities for the use of influence by strong private groups. The farm organizations, for example, have usually succeeded in having the membership of the agriculture committees in both houses limited almost entirely to Senators and Representatives from pre-

[22] Both Thomas Jefferson and Woodrow Wilson objected to representation of minority parties on legislative committees. Jefferson felt that "the child is not to be put to a nurse that care not for it. It is therefore a constant rule that no man is to be employed in any matter who has declared himself against it." (Jefferson's Manual, Sec. 26.) "It is plainly the representation of both parties on the Committees," wrote Wilson, "that makes party responsibility indistinct and organized participation impossible." *Op. cit.*, p. 97.

dominantly agricultural areas. "Until I took my place near the bottom of the committee table," writes former Congressman Jerry Voorhis concerning his assignment to the Agriculture Committee, "I had not realized certain significant facts about the makeup of the committee . . . the committee represented the 'five basic commodities.' The main interests of the overwhelming majority of the committee were—and still are—summed up in 'cotton, tobacco, wheat, corn, and hogs.' "[23]

The interest of the N.A.M. in committee structure is evidenced by its self-satisfied statement on the organization of the House Labor Committee after the Republican victory in the congressional elections of 1946.

> The House Labor Committee completed its organization this week. Its makeup rather well insures the kind of bill the leadership will decide is needed. Not one of the Republicans is regarded as a laborite, and at least half of the ten Democrats are conservatives. Only a little over two years ago, organized labor had such strong representation on the House Labor Committee that any bill which labor favored could be reported favorably—any bill it opposed, bottled up in committee.[24]

Labor, on its part, has long shown the same interest. Speaker "Uncle Joe" Cannon was once accused by Samuel Gompers, head of the A.F.L., of packing House committees with members more friendly to business interests. "Gompers' grievance," commented the Speaker to a newspaperman, "is not that I packed the committees; oh, no; he thinks he was badly treated because I wouldn't pack the committees as he wanted them packed."[25]

The struggle to "pack" or "unpack" a committee is carried on through both parties. The choice of the minority members assigned to a committee can provide the basis for a coalition that can be used effectively to carry a fight against a majority or ultimately to organize a dominant coalition. During the New Deal, conservative Republicans on many committees in combination with conservative Democrats succeeded in overruling many New Deal proposals. In 1947, the liberal Republicans and the liberal Democrats on the Senate Labor and Public Welfare Committee combined to overrule Chairman Taft in the preparation of the Taft-Hartley Act. Although this liberal coalition was subsequently outvoted on the floor, there is little doubt that the final version of the Taft-Hartley Act would have been much more stringent had it not been for the concentrated power of prolabor Senators within the Senate Committee.

In assigning members to major committees, considerable weight is usually given to seniority. Newer members are often assigned posts on the less important committees. The longer a member of Congress serves, the better his chances

[23] Jerry Voorhis, "Confessions of a Congressman" (Garden City, N.Y.: Doubleday, 1947), p. 132.

[24] *N.A.M. News,* Jan. 18, 1947.

[25] *The Boston Globe,* May 2, 1909.

of obtaining the committee assignments he values the most. Since those with the highest seniority cannot be given all the important assignments, choices must be made. These choices are often difficult ones for more than purely personal considerations. An interesting illustration is found in the maneuvers to fill a Republican vacancy on the Senate Foreign Relations Committee at the beginning of the Eighty-second Congress.

Normally the Foreign Relations post would have gone to Senator Morse of Oregon, who had urgently requested representation for the West Coast and had the explicit backing of Senator Vandenberg. But Vandenberg was ill in Michigan, and Taft and Wherry were determined that the liberal and internationalist Morse should not be appointed. Since places on major committees are allotted strictly according to seniority, the conservatives were able to cook Morse's goose by proposing Senator Capehart of Indiana, who outranks Morse. The liberals countered with Senator Aiken of Vermont, who outranks Capehart. The conservatives next advanced Senator Brewster of Maine, who outranks Aiken. The liberals came back with Senator Tobey of New Hampshire, who outranks Brewster. That was when the fun really started.

Tobey already was the ranking Republican on the Banking and Currency Committee and the Interstate and Foreign Commerce Committee. Brewster did not have any top rank on any committee, although he was second to Tobey on Interstate and Foreign Commerce. Delicate negotiations were now begun, with Brewster trying to obtain an assurance from Tobey that if he went to Foreign Relations, he would withdraw from Interstate and Foreign Commerce, leaving Brewster top Republican there. Tobey for his part offered to renounce Foreign Relations if Brewster would do the same, thus clearing the way for Aiken. Brewster and the conservatives did not like this and redoubled the pressure on Tobey to take the Foreign Relations post if he wanted to, but to retire from the Interstate and Foreign Commerce Committee.

Refusing to do any favors for Brewster, Tobey quietly retired from the Banking and Currency Committee, applied for the Foreign Relations post and got it, and held on to his ranking position on Interstate and Foreign Commerce.[26]

The selection of subcommittee members is entirely divorced from the party structure in either house of Congress. Here again, as with the creation of subcommittees and the assignment of bills to subcommittees, the word of the committee chairmen is law. This gives the chairmen considerable discretion in determining whether bills are handled in a friendly or unfriendly fashion. By careful selection, a subcommittee with a conservative majority can be pieced together out of a full committee with a liberal majority. A subcommittee with a liberal majority can be carved out of a bill committee with a conservative majority. In 1945, for example, when the Full Employment Bill was referred to the Senate Committee on Banking and Currency, Senator Robert F. Wagner of New York set up a Full Employment subcommittee to hold hearings on the measure and prepare a report for the full committee. He did this with

[26] Willard Shelton, "Civil War in the G.O.P.," *The Nation,* Jan. 27, 1951, pp. 75–76.

great care, taking pains to see that the conservative members of both parties were represented but at the same time guaranteeing a clear numerical majority that favored the principles of the measure.

The Chairmen

To become chairman of a committee, a Senator or Representative must be assigned to the committee in the first place. If he is reelected enough times, and if he lives long enough, and if his party comes into power, sooner or later he is bound to become a chairman. Once chairman, he is regarded as having the right to continue in his chairmanship so long as he continues to be reelected and continues to live. This is the famous—or rather, infamous—seniority system. Luce comments:

> It is a dangerous system, for sooner or later the man who has started at the tail end of a committee, if reelected enough times, will knock at the door of the chairmanship. He may be unqualified to preside over meetings or at hearings. He may have no capacity for defending committee reports on the floor. He may be a man whose reputation for honor is questioned—there are black sheep in every legislative flock.[27]

The seniority system has often been mistakenly attacked on the ground that it puts too much power in the hands of old men. This argument misses the real implications of the seniority system. Age alone does not cause diminution of mental vigor, alertness, and leadership ability. Nor does it mean that a man becomes more conservative. Some of the outstanding liberals in Congress have been old men who have fought valiantly despite the other handicaps of age. Witness Senator Norris, Senator Wagner, Senator Murray, and Representative Sabath.

The significant effect of the seniority system is that it tends to concentrate political power in the hands of members from "safe and solid" areas of the country, areas where there is very little real competition between the two major parties. This tends to insulate committee chairmanships from the real meanings and mandates of national electoral conflicts. It tends to undermine the ability of party leaders to carry out campaign pledges. Above all, it tends to bring a greater number of conservatives than of liberals into committee chairmanships.

In 1948, President Truman won the Presidential election on the basis of a liberal party platform and a campaign which attacked conservative control of the Eightieth Congress. On the basis of this campaign, the Democratic party won control of both houses of Congress. The liberal and middle-of-the-road Democratic contingent was augmented greatly, outnumbering the hard core

[27] Robert Luce, "Legislative Procedure" (Boston: Houghton Mifflin, 1922), pp. 120–121.

of Southern conservatives. Yet, in the Senate, the seniority tradition gave at least three out of four of the committee chairmanships to the anti-Truman Southerners. The chairmanships of the Senate committees on appropriations, finance, foreign relations, armed services, and the judiciary, for example, were turned over to men who had unquestionably demonstrated their opposition both to the Democratic party platform and to the pledges given to people by the President during the course of his election campaign. In the case of the Senate Banking and Currency Committee, the result of the election was to take the chairmanship away from a liberal Senator, Charles Tobey of New Hampshire, who often favored the President's program, and give it over to a chairman, Senator Burnet Maybank of South Carolina, who had demonstrated opposition toward many fundamental aspects of the President's program.

Immediately after the 1948 election, many people asked the question: "Why don't the Truman Democrats dislodge the anti-Truman Democrats from committee chairmanships?" This is not a question that can be answered easily. There are many factors, including many personal strategies, that are not readily discernible to the outside observer. One of the most important causes of inaction, however, was the blunt fact that the Truman Democrats had a majority only among the Democrats in each house of Congress. They did not enjoy a full majority in either house. The anti-Truman group was in a balance-of-power position and, if aggressive action had been taken against them by the Administration's supporters, they might have joined with their fellow conservatives among the Republican members and put the conservative coalition into formal control of Congress. This ultimate possibility, enhanced by the fact that the rules themselves call for the selection of committee chairmen and committee members by the vote of each house of Congress rather than by party caucuses, was a nightmare that often preyed on the minds of the Truman Democrats.

Seniority rights, however, are not always clear-cut. By one standard they are measured in terms of the length of consecutive service *on a given committee.* By another standard, they are computed in terms of the number of consecutive years served *in the House.* The seniority tradition itself is not sufficiently refined to resolve this ambiguity. An opportunity is thus provided for the various contestants in the legislative struggle to throw their weight in one direction or another. At the beginning of the Eighty-first Congress, Senator James E. Murray of Montana ranked fourteenth among the Senate Democrats. By this standard he was entitled to a chairmanship of one of the 15 standing committees. However, he did not rank first in seniority on any one committee. The weight of the conservative pressures succeeded in denying him a committee chairmanship during the entire Eighty-first Congress.

Another limitation on the seniority principle is the tradition that the member of Congress who successfully proposes the creation of a new committee has a right to the chairmanship. It was on the basis of this tradition that Senator Brien McMahon of Connecticut succeeded in winning the chairmanship of the Senate Special Committee on Atomic Energy. In addition, the Atomic Energy Act of 1946, which provided for a Joint Committee on Atomic Energy, was based upon a measure proposed by Senator McMahon. When the Joint Committee on Atomic Energy was created and the members of the Senate Special Committee were appointed as the Senate representatives of the joint body, Senator McMahon therefore had a double claim to the chairmanship of the new joint committee.

There is far less rigidity in the selection of subcommittee chairmen. Here the decision is entirely in the hands of the full-committee chairmen. In parceling out the more important subcommittee chairmanships, the chairman will usually regard seniority as one factor to be taken into account. But he will also give weight to considerations of policy and personal relationships and feel free to make all sorts of deals. In the Senate where the number of members on each committee is much less than in the House, and where more attention is given to the personal prerogatives of individual members, it is possible for even a newly elected member to win a subcommittee chairmanship.

The Staff

Staff assistance is a vital element in the pattern of committee power. The effectiveness of committee members depends to an important degree on the quality and amount of staff assistance at their command. Likewise, staff aides are often moving forces in their own right. They are delegated important functions with respect to the planning of hearings, the handling of contacts with pressure groups, and the preparation of bills, amendments, and reports. Having direct access to committee members, they are in a strategic position to exercise an influence upon committee decisions.

Only part of the committee-staffing picture can be seen by looking at the official records on congressional employees. Staff assistance for legislative committee work is customarily provided both by executive agencies and private organizations. Organizations conducting legislative campaigns offer this assistance to friendly members of Congress, knowing that it is one of the best ways of advancing their objectives. In many instances, members of Congress request such staff services of them.

In the case of pressure groups, this request is usually made to enable the member to perform more effectively in the interest of the group involved. In the case of the executive agencies, however, the purpose is not necessarily so narrow. Staff assistance from executive agencies is often requested not merely to help serve the ends of interested agencies but also to serve the specific interest of the member or committee making the request. When the same party is in control of the executive branch as in Congress, influential members of Congress, particularly committee chairmen, regard it as a personal prerogative to obtain the assignment of executive personnel from executive agencies to work under their direction. In a limited sense, this is a form of patronage. In a broader sense, there has developed the conception that a committee has a right to assistance from the executive agencies, a right which has in many instances been formalized by statute or congressional resolutions.

In 1921 the Budget and Accounting Act instructed the Comptroller General, at the request of any committee having jurisdiction over revenue, appropriations, or expenditures, to "direct assistants from his office to furnish the committee such aid and information as it may request." (Sec. 312(b).) Similarly, the Atomic Energy Act of 1946 authorized the Joint Committee on Atomic Energy "to utilize the services, information, facilities and personnel of the departments and establishments of the Government." (Sec. 15(c).) Customarily, resolutions providing a special study or investigation either by a legislative committee or a special committee contained language "authorizing" the use of executive services and personnel. The validity of such authorizations, however, is impaired by the fact that a resolution, not having the force of law, cannot authorize executive agencies to use their funds for the purpose of providing services to congressional committees. The Comptroller General has on occasion ruled such use of executive funds illegal and has established certain conditions governing the assignment of executive personnel to congressional committees. Yet these conditions are rarely enforced, for the simple reason that most executive assignments to legislative committees are unofficial.

This entire matter became a subject of contention in the Senate of 1945 when a number of conservative members realized that the full exercise of this right by a number of liberal committee chairmen was a powerful force in the campaign for liberal reconversion legislation. Senator Kenneth Wherry of Nebraska, a staunch Republican conservative, started a campaign to forbid the assignment of executive personnel to Senate committees except on a reimbursable basis. He succeeded in attaining approval of a requirement that the names of all executive personnel assigned to Senate legislative committees be printed monthly in the *Congressional Record*. His efforts also led to a provision in the Legislative Reorganization Act of 1946 forbidding the formal assignment of executive personnel "except with the written permission of the Committee on Rules and Administration of the Senate or the Committee on House Administration of the House of Representatives, as the case may be." (Sec. 202(f).) One effect of Wherry's effort was to weaken the campaign for liberal reconversion legislation. Another was to force executive assignments to congressional committees to be handled in a more subterranean fashion. Still another was to strengthen the case for the employment of professional legislative staffs on the congressional payroll.

For many decades, the theory of congressional staffing seemed to be that each member of Congress was a statesman capable of handling all legislative problems himself. Under this theory any proposal for the formal provision of professional staff services to Congress would be an implied slur upon the capacities of the members themselves. Accordingly, the official staffing of Congress was limited to clerical help in the committees and secretarial help in the offices of the individual members. The only modifications were the creation of the Legislative Counsel's Office to perform technical services on bill drafting and of the Legislative Reference Service in the Library of Congress to perform elementary research services.

The Legislative Reorganization Act of 1946 made a complete break with this tradition. It authorized every standing committee of Congress to hire up to four professional staff members in addition to their clerical staffs. These staff members were to be appointed "by the majority vote of the committee . . . without regard to political affiliations and solely on the basis of fitness to perform the duties of the office." They were to be "assigned to the chairman and ranking minority member of such committee as the committee may deem advisable." In practice, the appointment of professional staff members has been left largely in the hands of committee chairmen and the ranking minority members.

Moreover, two competing patterns have emerged. By one a clear division is made between those staff members assigned to the majority and those assigned to the minority. By the other, staff members are assigned neither to majority nor minority but to the various subjects covered by the committee. "There is no particular reason to assign any of them (staff experts) to the minority or the majority," stated Senator Robert A. Taft during discussion on the floor of the Senate. "They are experts on particular subjects and we have five important subjects within the jurisdiction of the Committee on Labor and Public Welfare, so I think those professional assistants ought to be looked upon as experts performing for the entire committee. . . ."[28] Obviously, this pattern is useful in denying staff services to the ranking minority members or any of the minority members of a committee.

The services provided by the professional staffs of committees cannot be described by any general formula. In some cases staff members make a valiant effort to stand apart from the legislative struggle and provide objective assistance to both sides. When this happens, they pass into the background whenever a really "hot" issue comes up. The genuine staff work, which is necessarily controversial, is thereby left to the staffs of executive agencies and private organizations. In other cases, staff members are required to take sides or do so of their own choosing. When this happens the more imaginative ones are in a better position to mobilize and direct the staff operations of friendly agencies

[28] *Congressional Record,* Jan. 27, 1947, p. 638.

and organizations. The others tend to serve as transmission belts—with some leeway for initiative and judgment—between members of Congress and non-congressional groups.

The Legislative Reorganization Act also expanded the Legislative Counsel offices in both houses. It provided for a well-paid staff of professional experts in the Legislative Reference Service.[29] The Senate version of the Act also would have provided a highly paid administrative assistant to each member of Congress. Members of the House objected to this provision and it was stricken from the final legislation. In a subsequent appropriation act, however, members of the Senate Appropriations Committee picked up this issue and succeeded in inserting a provision which gave each Senator a $10,000-a-year assistant. This assistant was supposed to work on administrative matters, thereby freeing his Senator to devote more time to legislative matters.[30] The net effect, however, has been to provide members of the Senate with more staff assistants in the handling of their committee work.

[29] Under the Act, these experts are to cover the following fields: agriculture; American government and public administration; American public law; conservation; education; engineering and public works; full employment; housing; industrial organization and corporation finance; international affairs; international trade and economic geography; labor; mineral economics; money and banking; price economics; social welfare; taxation and fiscal policy; transportation and communications; and veterans' affairs. (Sec. 203(b)(2).)

[30] This is an amusing survival of the theory that on "legislative" matters a member of Congress needs no assistants.

Chapter 15

THE HEARINGS: STAGING AND PERFORMANCE

"CONGRESS in session," commented Woodrow Wilson, "is Congress on public exhibition, whilst Congress in its committee rooms is Congress at work." [1] This oft-quoted description was written at a time when committee hearings were convened in executive session. Today, with relatively few hearings held behind closed doors, Congress at work on committee hearings is also Congress on public exhibition.

In fact, the committee hearings outrank the floor sessions of Congress—or, for that matter, the policy conference of any other government agency—in the sheer scope and volume of public operations. They provide a means through which members of Congress can educate themselves on the issues involved in a bill. They serve as a clearinghouse for information needed by all the contestants in the legislative process. They provide a springboard for propagandistic and pressure activities. They serve as a testing ground on which preparatory battles can be fought before a measure moves on to a subsequent stage of committee decision. In the case of major legislation it is usually impossible without full and intensive hearings to produce a measure that can stand up on the floor of Congress or prove its value after enactment.

A hearing, like a play, must be staged. The stage managers—that is, the committee and subcommittee chairmen and their staffs—must make a number of important behind-the-scenes decisions, which will be discussed in the following sections. The performance may then proceed.

THE STAGING

Silent Murder or a Hearing

The first decision is whether to have a hearing at all.

Occasionally a committee may act on a bill without having a hearing. This happened in the development of the Legislative Reorganization Act of 1946. Long hearings on the subject were held by the Joint Committee on the Or-

[1] Woodrow Wilson, "Congressional Government" (Boston: Houghton Mifflin, 1925), p. 79.

ganization of Congress. A comprehensive bill was drafted subsequently. But the committee members called no hearings on the bill itself. To have done so would have risked postponement of action until a subsequent session of Congress. Similar maneuvers are used to help prevent the mobilization of effective opposition. In 1948, for example, the House Ways and Means Committee voted suddenly one day to report legislation intended to exclude salesmen and other "independent contractors" from the Social Security Act.

Some decades ago committee action without hearings was the rule.[2] In recent years it has become an exception. The general rule now is that a committee will not report a bill without a hearing and that the denial of a hearing is considered a bill's death sentence.

In American courts a man is presumed innocent until proved guilty. In congressional committees and subcommittees, the ordinary bill is presumed unworthy of attention and automatically sentenced to an ignominious death until enough pressure is brought to give it a hearing. Sometimes the weight of the pressure is against a hearing. For a number of years the coal-mine operators succeeded in preventing hearings in the House of Representatives on legislation for tighter mine-safety regulation.[3] The opposition of committee or subcommittee chairmen is especially potent. Thus, Senator Henry Cabot Lodge, chairman of the Senate Foreign Relations Committee, saw to it that no hearing was ever given to the American-French Treaty which President Wilson forwarded to the Senate in conjunction with the Versailles Treaty.

A strong enough campaign, however, can override a chairman's desire to prevent a hearing. In 1947 the railroad lobby succeeded in having the chairman of the Interstate Commerce Committee in the House order a hearing on legislation which was opposed by the railroad labor unions. But the latter groups then staged a counteroffensive and overrode the chairman.

> When the committee assembled, Congressman "Bob" Crosser, Ohio Democrat, "raised the question of consideration." That means the veteran Cleveland progressive was asking the committee members to vote whether they wished to continue hearings on the bills, or whether they desired to turn to other business. . . . Under parliamentary law, Crosser's "question" was not debatable, so the clerk called the committee roll. Only six members voted to continue the hearing, and twelve against doing so. As a result, the proceedings came to a sudden close.[4]

In the case of a measure that is reasonably sure of being eventually enacted into law in one form or another, all factors usually favor giving a green light to hearings. The advocates and opponents of specific provisions are eager to establish in the hearings a basis for action in subsequent stages in the legisla-

[2] *Ibid.*, p. 83.

[3] For example, see Drew Pearson, "Washington Merry-Go-Round," *Washington Post*, July 6, 1947.

[4] *Labor*, May 24, 1947.

tive process. Members of the committee are anxious to familiarize themselves with the issues involved.

Many groups can get a hearing on almost any measure they want to, particularly if it is referred to a committee on which they have a friend or two in a strategic position. According to McCune, the farm lobbyists were always able to rely on Senator "Cotton Ed" Smith of South Carolina "to convene his committee on Agriculture and Forestry for any purpose—even to hold hearings on bills assigned to other committees. In convening the committee at the drop of a lobbyist's suggestion, Smith is likely to bark to the clerk: 'Call up those butt-heads and tell 'em we're going to have a meeting tomorrow.' "[5]

However, the decision to hold a hearing in no way implies subsequent congressional action. Many hearings merely serve to appease groups that are clamoring for legislative action. A hearing has the virtue of itself giving direct satisfaction of "blowing-off-steam" activity and can often serve as an alternative to subsequent legislative action. Moreover, as indicated below, a hearing can also be staged in such a fashion as to delay or prevent legislative action.

Timing the Show

The most obvious problem of timing is "How soon should hearings be held after the introduction of a measure?" Appropriation-bill hearings usually start in the House of Representatives at the beginning of each session. In fact, the Subcommittee on Independent Appropriations has often started hearings a month before the regular session. On emergency measures, particularly those requested in special Presidential messages, hearings usually are begun quite promptly—sometimes within twenty-four hours.

On the great bulk of measures, however, the chairmen of full committees and subcommittees have a genuine opportunity for the exercise of broad discretion. In the case of the Versailles Treaty Senator Henry Cabot Lodge, chairman of the Senate Foreign Relations Committee, planned a strategic delay before initiating hearings. This was generally interpreted at the time as part of his campaign against the measure. In the case of the Full Employment Bill, Senator Robert F. Wagner, chairman of the Senate Banking and Currency Committee, deliberately postponed hearings for a period of six months after the introduction of the bill. The purpose was to allow time for the organization of group support behind the measure and for the planning of a well-staged set of hearings.

A second problem is "Which committee should begin hearings first?" When two committees in one house are engaged in a jurisdictional struggle, the tendency is for each one to try to beat the other to the draw. The same question also comes up with respect to choosing between House and Senate committees

[5] Wesley McCune, "The Farm Bloc" (New York: Doubleday, 1943), p. 38.

handling identical or similar measures. Each participant in the legislative struggle generally attempts to have hearings started in whichever committee is most favorable to his particular viewpoint. Thus, in the case of the Full Employment Bill, the proponents of the measure succeeded in having hearings begun before the friendly Senate Committee on Banking and Currency. The Senate committee hearings then served as a basis for organizing a stronger presentation and defense of the measure before the hostile House Committee on Expenditures in the Executive Departments.

Coordination with other hearings on related subjects is a rare consideration. Each congressional hearing is run as a separate sideshow only remotely connected with something else members of Congress may be doing. Except for recurrent efforts to keep committee hearings from being held during floor sessions [6] there have been few attempts to develop a general schedule for hearings.

A third problem is "How long should the hearings be?" On minor bills, committee time is of necessity rationed very sparingly. In an atmosphere of dire emergency hearings tend to be brief. The National Industrial Recovery Act, one of the most far-reaching statutes ever to be enacted in American history, was the subject of only three days of public hearings in each house. On major measures, particularly those of a more complex, controversial, or novel character, relatively long hearings are—short of crisis conditions—usually unavoidable. Thirty-one days of hearings were held by the House Committee on Interstate and Foreign Commerce in connection with the Public Utilities Holding Company Act of 1935.

Occasionally long-drawn-out hearings are sought for the express purpose of delaying legislative action. Whenever hearings have been held for proposals on national compulsory health insurance, the American Medical Association and other opponents of this legislation have seen to it that every local medical society in the country demands to be heard. The cumulative effect of long-drawn-out testimony has been to delay the time when proponents of the legislation may move to win affirmative action by the committee. In the House of Representatives where the rules call for a quorum of committee members, dilatory quorum calls may be used for the same purpose. This was done in the case of the Taft-Ellender-Wagner Housing Bill during the Eightieth Congress.

When hearings finally began, the committee set a precedent by scrupulously observing the House rules. Indeed, the rules were so carefully heeded that the commit-

[6] The Legislative Reorganization Act of 1946 provided that "No standing committee of the Senate or the House, except the Committee on Rules of the House, shall sit, without special leave, while the Senate or the House, as the case may be, is in session." (Sec. 134(c).) However, permission to hold committee hearings while the Senate or the House is in session is given rather freely.

tee made no discernible progress whatsoever. Day after day, a conscientious member would point out that a quorum was lacking or that the committee was meeting when the House was in session. . . . Congress adjourned at the end of July and S. 1592 was defunct.[7]

Occasionally an effort is made to hold a "quickie" hearing on a major bill for the purpose of attaining quick congressional action before the opposition has an opportunity to mobilize. Thus a few days after the introduction of the May-Johnson bill on atomic energy, Representative Andrew J. May, chairman of the House Committee on Military Affairs, "opened and closed public hearings on October 9, 1945 and rushed executive committee sessions designed to report the bill out promptly."[8]

This action was only partially successful. Immediately the scientists' organizations, on behalf of civilian rather than military control of atomic energy, demanded more careful consideration of the problem.

> Led by such outstanding men as Drs. Condon, Szilard, and Urey, they descended upon Washington insisting that a single day's hearings limited to favorable witnesses was a shocking abuse of legislative discretion in dealing with such a momentous and largely uncomprehended subject. When their request for further hearing was initially refused, they met informally with a large caucus of congressmen, then used the hearings of a Senate subcommittee considering science legislation as a sounding board for airing the defects of the May-Johnson Bill. Simultaneously, they were calling on prominent private citizens, editors and publishers, on leading figures in the Administration, and on influential senators and representatives. Their efforts so moved Mr. May that he reopened hearings—for a single day.[9]

Open or Closed Doors

As indicated earlier, congressional committees hold a vast number of public hearings on legislative measures at every session of Congress. In fact, the Legislative Reorganization Act of 1946 inserted a provision in the rules requiring committee hearings to be open to the public except "where the committee by majority vote orders an executive session."[10]

A careful peek behind the curtain, however, shows that there are also many closed hearings. In 1947, for example, an able reporter made a tally of his own and concluded that almost half of all committee hearings were secret. "In the first 20 days of March," he wrote, "113 House hearings on the public's

[7] Alexander L. Crosby, "The Real Estate Lobby," *The American Mercury,* March, 1947.

[8] Byron S. Miller, "A Law Is Passed—The Atomic Energy Act of 1946," *University of Chicago Law Review,* Vol. 15, No. 4, Summer, 1948, p. 805.

[9] *Ibid.,* p. 805.

[10] Sec. 133(f). This provision also excepted executive sessions from "marking up bills or for voting." Sessions of this character, however, are entirely different from hearings. They always take place in executive session.

business were held behind closed doors. In the same period 137 hearings were public. A fairly complete list of Senate Committee hearings in the same period showed 47 closed and 56 open." [11] But it is doubtful whether this tally reports the full story. There are many differences of degree between a door that is wide open and a door that is tightly closed. Many hearings that are nominally public are "quickie" operations called on short notice and with no effort to inform all interested parties. Moreover, there are limits on the number of hearings that an overworked press corps can cover. Many public hearings are attended by no one but a handful of witnesses. As far as providing public information goes, they might just as well have been secret in the first place.

Closed hearings are well adapted for favoring "insiders" or weighting the scales against "outsiders." This is probably the reason why the subcommittees of the House Appropriations Committee invariably hold closed hearings on appropriations measures. The reason given is that open hearings would be an invitation to pressure operations by private organizations. It is difficult to conceive, however, how private organizations could be any more interested in Government appropriations than they have always been in the past.

At times, paradoxically enough, the best way to guarantee full news coverage for testimony is to have it presented at a closed hearing. What would be a fairly dull story as it transpired in open hearings can become an exciting piece of headline news if it represents an inside tip on what happened at a hush-hush meeting.

Closed hearings can also be used to prevent unfavorable publicity. Executive officials often ask for the opportunity to testify at executive sessions so that they can deny opponents on the congressional committee the opportunity to use their appearance as an excuse for questioning and speech making that would make the headlines and destroy any useful effect of their own testimony. Secrecy is also a method of sidestepping outside critics. "I can't see that any useful purpose could be served," stated Representative Bertrand Gearhart, in defending closed hearings on the 1948 extension of reciprocal trade agreements, "by listening to spokesmen for a bunch of ladies' sewing societies reading statements on the legislation that have been prepared by the State Department." [12] To those interested in promoting the State Department's program on reciprocal trade, however, the utility of allowing the ladies to make public statements was obvious.

The result of efforts to keep hearings closed sometimes produces a backwater of adverse publicity—particularly when there is a split within the committee itself. When the House Ways and Means Committee decided to close the door on its 1948 hearings on the extension of the Reciprocal Trade Act, ranking minority member Representative Doughton of North Carolina led a public

[11] Charles T. Lucey, *The Washington Daily News,* Mar. 24, 1947.

[12] *The New York Times,* Apr. 30, 1948.

attack on the Republican members,[13] and much of the press echoed his charges that the Republicans were using "star-chamber" methods.

There is no doubt, however, about the utility of closed hearings as a means of promoting a more intimate give-and-take between witnesses and committee members. Many witnesses will speak much more freely at a closed session. Many committee members will behave quite differently when the emphasis is more upon exploring the issues than upon offering opportunities for publicity. Closed hearings are particularly useful in gathering facts for use in the subsequent staging of an open hearing.

But the closing of committee doors offers no real protection against subsequent publicity of confidential information. After a closed hearing on a legislative measure, almost everybody in attendance—committee members, witnesses, and staff aides—is solicited for "leaks" by reporters and representatives of various contestants in the legislative struggle. This is why the executive officials dealing with foreign affairs and the national defense seldom present really confidential information at the many closed meetings in which they participate. The chief benefit for them in closing the doors is that their testimony is thereby surrounded with an aura of high significance.

The Dramatis Personae

"Anytime a bill is presented to the Congress," a small businessman once complained at a Senate hearing, "I can close my eyes and visualize who will appear. They will be about the same people who usually testify for or against a bill. You never have any new blood." [14]

One reason why the same people testify over and over again at one hearing after another is the broad range of interests of those groups that play the largest role in the legislative struggle. During any month, selected at random, the Secretary of Commerce may appear before a dozen committees on a dozen different bills. During the same month, the legislative representative of the National Grange may be just as active. Even where these groups are not themselves anxious to testify, their power and status create a considerable interest on the part of others in finding out what their views may be on pending measures. Another reason is that the job of representing these key groups is largely turned over to a limited number of staff experts or top officers. The former are often the only people in an organization who really have sufficient facts at their finger tips to qualify as informed witnesses. The latter, by virtue of their positions of prominence, provide an essential element of prestige and dignity.

[13] *Congressional Record*, 80th Cong., 2d Sess., pp. 6502–6507.

[14] Testimony of Harry Golden, Hearings before a subcommittee of the Senate Committee on Banking and Currency, 79th Cong., 1st Sess., S. Rept. 380, Aug. 23, 1945, p. 381.

Occasionally a private organization will bring in "grass-root" witnesses. This has the great advantage of adding freshness and variety to a committee hearing. In his vivid book, "Missouri Compromise," which is replete with graphic pictures of committee testimony, Tristram Coffin tells how a welder from Schenectady was brought before a Senate committee to defend price control during the period immediately following World War II.[15] His testimony was brief, human, and moving. "It's a very healthy thing for the Committee to have you here. Nothing is finer than for common people to bring these matters to Congress," remarked one of the Senators. To bring common people before Congress, however, is not easy. It involves transportation and hotel costs. Time must be spent in familiarizing them with the legislative situation and advising them on how to behave before a congressional committee. Hence most grass-root witnesses are brought to Congress by the uncommon people—or, to use more exact language—by organizations representing the more affluent members of the population.

Sometimes, somewhat sparingly, a committee will itself go to the common people. While working on the Agricultural Adjustment Act of 1938, the Senate Agriculture Committee held a series of "gallus" or field hearings throughout the country. Subcommittees of the House Education and Labor Committee did the same in 1949 in developing the case for Federal aid to education in localities affected by wartime activities. These hearings enabled the committee members to meet with lots of "new blood." They also served to stimulate local interest in the measures under consideration.

On important and highly controversial measures a committee may receive many more requests to testify than can possibly be honored. This may simply result from the large variety of interested groups. Or it may be the product of deliberate campaigns to pack or protract the hearing. In either case, the committee members are faced with a problem of rationing the available time. In most instances this responsibility is left in the hands of the committee or subcommittee chairmen. Many of these, in turn, delegate the job to staff assistants.

One way to ration is to set up a schedule that favors friends and supporters. A striking example is found in the health hearings that opened before a Senate subcommittee in May, 1947. "More than nine-tenths of the allotted time," charged Senator James E. Murray, "has been given over to organizations almost all of which represent doctors and hospitals, less than one percent of the people who would be affected by this legislation." This pattern was developed by a staff member who sent out a special news letter to physician and hospital groups in advance of committee plans suggesting that they take steps to request an opportunity to appear. At the same time, the same staff member led the proponents of health insurance up a blind alley by informing them that no schedule for hearings had yet been determined. As a result, the

[15] Tristram Coffin, "Missouri Compromise" (Boston: Little, Brown, 1947), pp. 161–162.

first four weeks of the health hearings were given over to one side and three subsequent days allotted to the other side.[16]

To protect against incidents of this type, special subcommittees are occasionally set up for the sole purpose of serving as a rationing board. In the 1949 hearings on labor relations, the Senate Committee on Labor and Public Welfare decided that the hearing time should be divided equally between the majority and minority members and gave a Democratic Senator (Murray) responsibility for allotting the majority's time and a Republican Senator (Morse) the responsibility of allotting the minority's time.[17]

Where witnesses with a particular point of view are denied an opportunity to testify before one committee, it is sometimes possible to achieve the same objective through another committee. In 1949, for example, the House Judiciary Committee held a brief one-day hearing on the basing-point legislation. Representative Wright Patman of Texas felt that an insufficient opportunity had been granted to the opponents of this measure.

> As chairman of the House Select Committee on Small Business, he undertook himself to hold the hearings on S. 1008 which he said had been denied to him and to small business groups. And for five days, witnesses made appearances before the Small Business Committee or sent statements attacking S. 1008. Professional economists, representatives of small business organizations, wholesale and retail distributors, the National Farmers Union, the American Trucking Association, Inc., and staff of the Federal Trade Commission made a record of protest of 300 pages, the theme of which was that S. 1008 would weaken the anti-trust laws, cancel recent gains in the clarification of the laws, create more confusion and litigation, make it easier for violators to justify infractions, and harder for the Federal Trade Commission to halt such infractions.[18]

Some committees solve the rationing problem merely by trying to divide the time equally between proponents and opponents. Occasionally an ambitious schedule is prepared for the purpose of dividing up the testimony by various aspects of subject matter that may be involved. This was attempted by the House Ways and Means Committee in the hearings that preceded its 1949 recommendations for expanding the social-security system.

Sometimes the amount of time given to any group is not nearly as important as the order of appearance. Many witnesses engage in considerable pulling and hauling for the purpose of being allowed to appear early or late among the list of witnesses. An early appearance allows one to come before a committee while the members are still fresh and untired. It also helps win more prom-

[16] This story is told in a vivid and frankly partisan manner by Nelson Cruikshank in "Playing Politics with Health," *American Federationist,* June, 1947, pp. 24–26.

[17] This arrangement was crystallized and publicized in a resolution in the Daily Digest section of the *Congressional Record,* Feb. 19, 1949.

[18] Earl Latham, "The Group Basis of Politics" (Ithaca, N.Y.: Cornell University Press, 1952), pp. 137–138.

inent attention from the press and radio. A later appearance, on the other hand, often makes it possible to make a careful appraisal of the situation and prepare more definitive answers to questions that may arise.[19]

The juxtaposition of two witnesses whose views are not compatible is a good way to create drama. It also serves to underline conflicts. During the Republican-controlled Eightieth Congress, Republican members of the Banking and Currency Committees in the two houses found that they could undermine the President's proposed anti-inflation program by bringing in one after the other Secretary of the Treasury John Snyder and Marriner S. Eccles of the Federal Reserve Board. It was hoped that the two would take strikingly divergent positions, a hope that partially materialized.

Sometimes the problem is merely one of excluding cranks and crackpots. Announcing hearings on the nomination of Dean Acheson as Secretary of State, for example, the Senate Foreign Relations Committee stated that it would hear all "respectable and creditable" persons. Sometimes unrespectable and discreditable persons who appear on the scene are disposed of by allowing a personal appearance of one or two minutes or by merely inserting their statements in the record of the hearings.

No one has an abstract right to be heard before a congressional committee. Representatives of minor political parties, for example, are often excluded. In denying the American Labor Party an opportunity to testify at the 1947 hearings of the Joint Committee on the Economic Report, the Committee staff director stated that it is often the consensus of committee members "that we ought not to invite as witnesses representatives of any political party, as such. The hearings are set up to deal with the economic question and every effort is being made by the Committee to keep them to a non-partisan basis." [20]

Occasionally all nongovernmental witnesses are ruled as ineligible to appear. This happened at the 1948 hearings of the House Ways and Means Committee. It is only in rare cases, however, that a representative of any substantial organization is ever denied the right to be heard. This is particularly true if the organization has a close friend or two among the committee membership.

It should not be thought, however, that committees are always flooded with requests to testify from people who are interested in a pending measure. Many potential witnesses are reluctant dragons. Sound strategy often calls for withholding testimony entirely or for delaying until the most auspicious moment. In the development of the Clayton Antitrust Act, long hearings were held be-

[19] For an illustration of how delay in appearing can work to a witness's disadvantage see Marriner Eccles, "Beckoning Frontiers" (New York: Knopf, 1951), pp. 205–207. Eccles tells in great detail how Senator Glass, as chairman of the Senate Banking and Currency Committee, delayed for almost a month Eccles' appearance on the Banking Act of 1935 until the views of opposition witnesses "had been firmly fixed in the public mind. . . ."

[20] *The New York Times,* Sept. 15, 1947.

fore the House Judiciary Committee from December, 1913, to April, 1914, but one can leaf through a thousand pages of oral testimony without finding a word from a single government witness. This was probably the result of a wait-and-see attitude on the part of President Wilson. Chamberlain writes:

> It may well be that the decision to keep the Administration position unrecorded during the formative stage was a deliberate one dictated by the strategic needs of the occasion. . . . When it became apparent that the stringency of regulation envisioned in the proposed bill was impossible of realization, Wilson was able to disclaim responsibility for it and demand sweeping changes in the direction of moderation.[21]

Similarly, the United States Chamber of Commerce, although solicited for testimony at the 1945 Senate hearings on the Full Employment Bill, succeeded in dodging all requests and deferring testimony until hearings began in the House.[22]

It follows, therefore, that it is also wise strategy on the part of other contestants in the legislative struggle to try to have reluctant dragons brought into the hearing room. The purpose may be merely to elicit support from timid witnesses who would like to stay on the fence instead of taking a position. Or the purpose may be to bring opponents out in the open rather than allow them to carry on their opposition entirely behind the scenes. It may even be to put opposition witnesses on the spot by having them subjected to antagonistic questioning by committee members. No matter what the purpose, it is only rarely that testimony dodgers are brought before legislative hearings through the use of their committee subpoena powers.[23] In most cases, the method used is to extend a written invitation and use the threat of adverse publicity against a witness who refuses to accept. When subpoenas are used in connection with legislative testimony, it is usually at the instigation of the witness himself. During World War II, for example, many government officials found that by having a committee subpoena them as witnesses they could achieve a dual objective of making their case in public and also of maintaining a record of being opposed to the washing of dirty linen in public.

[21] Lawrence H. Chamberlain, "The President, Congress, and Legislation" (New York: Columbia University Press, 1946), p. 39.

[22] See Stephen K. Bailey, "Congress Makes a Law" (New York: Columbia University Press, 1949), pp. 138–143.

[23] Under the Legislative Reorganization Act of 1946, every standing committee of the Senate was given subpoena power to require the attendance of witnesses and the production of documents. This was part of an effort to merge legislative with investigatory functions and thereby reduce the need for special investigating committees. House committees must obtain this power by special resolution.

The President's Spokesmen

There is one important contestant in the legislative struggle whose name never appears on the list of *dramatis personae*—the President of the United States. It is not merely that Presidential testimony before a congressional committee would be a task too time-consuming for the busiest man in the country; it is also that it would be beneath a President's dignity to subject himself to committee interrogation. Nor has any member of Congress seriously proposed that a President come before his committee as a witness. If there are compelling reasons for a meeting—and there are at times—between a President and a committee, then it is Mahomet who will go to the mountain. In August, 1919, for example, members of the Senate Committee on Foreign Relations wanted more information on the Versailles Treaty proposed by President Wilson. "They therefore instructed me," wrote Senator Lodge, "to ask the President whether he would receive the Committee. He replied in the affirmative, appointed the day and invited the Committee to lunch with him after the conversation had been held." [24]

The question has often arisen, however, as to who should appear before a congressional committee to explain the President's position on specific matters. In a sense, all agency heads are representatives of the President. For this reason increasing efforts have been made during recent years to check agency testimony to see if it conforms with "the President's program." [25] Yet in an equally important sense, every executive agency representative is also on his own, because a President needs to be as free as possible to shift his own position at some subsequent stage of the legislative process.

A more delicate problem arises in connection with the President's closest associates in the White House and the Executive Office. It has generally been the Presidential practice to extend the shield of protection to cover members of the White House staff whether they be shadowy men with a passion for anonymity or more prominent figures, such as the President's Counsel or the Assistant to the President. Officials in various parts of the Executive Office of the President, however, often come before congressional committees to expound the President's program in authoritative terms. This has been done as a matter of course by the Director of the Budget. In the case of the Council of Economic Advisers, there has been some degree of controversy. The first members of the Council of Economic Advisers split publicly on this question. The chair-

[24] Henry Cabot Lodge, "The Senate and the League of Nations" (New York: Scribner, 1925), p. 158.

[25] See Richard E. Neustadt, "Presidential Clearance of Legislation" (unpublished doctoral dissertation, Harvard University, June, 1950) for a realistic appraisal of these efforts during the period from 1921 to 1949. In particular, see section on "Use and Effect of Clearance Phraseology," Chap. 3, pp. 192–196.

man, Edwin G. Nourse, objected to Council appearances before congressional committees on the following grounds:

. . . if the precedent of such appearance is established, the time would come sooner or later when Council members would be asked to testify on matters on which the President has seen fit to take a position definitely contrary to their advice. This would present Council members with the alternative of arguing for the President's position regardless of their own professional convictions, or, on the other hand, of arguing against a policy recommended by the President.

The other two members, Leon H. Keyserling, vice-chairman, and John D. Clark, stated

that both the President and the members of the Joint Committee although occupying "political" office, are strongly predisposed to draw upon objective economic analysis in fulfilling their defined functions under the Employment Act. They feel that, because the Council was established to assist the President in the preparation of his Economic Reports, the intent of the act will best be served if the Council extends cooperative professional assistance to the Joint Committee as, in its turn under the act, it comes to consider the fundamental materials contained in the President's Economic Reports as transmitted to the Congress.[26]

With Nourse's resignation in 1949 this issue was resolved in favor of Council testimony before the Joint Committee on the Economic Report on behalf of the President's general program. There still remained, however, the ever-recurring problem of choosing the specific measures on which the Council members might appropriately appear as the President's representatives.

Executive Reports and Documents

A widespread committee practice is to request written reports on pending bills from executive agencies. This is usually done before a hearing takes place. This practice provides committee members with valuable detailed information. It also helps in the decisions on whether or not to have a hearing and on how a hearing should be planned. In most cases these requests go in a routine fashion to all interested agencies. One variant from the norm is to present detailed questions along with the request for an agency's views. Another is to avoid requesting reports from agencies whose views might be regarded as hostile.

The preparation of agency reports to congressional committees is an important and far-flung operation within the executive branch. Agency officials usually welcome the opportunity to express their views and lay the groundwork for possible testimony in the future. They also recognize that the preparation of these reports is itself a vital part of the policy-formation process.

[26] Edwin G. Nourse and Bertram M. Gross, "The Role of the Council of Economic Advisers," *American Political Science Review,* Vol. 13, No. 2, April, 1948, pp. 290–291.

In fact, it is so vital that the work of the Bureau of the Budget in clearing and coordinating agency reports to congressional committees has become one of the outstanding examples of coordination activities in the executive branch. Agency reports often play a determining role in the legislative struggle. This is particularly true when the reporting process is used as a means of developing a rallying point for agencies, private organizations, and members of Congress.

A perfect illustration of this is found in the history of the school-construction legislation in 1949. Neustadt writes:

> In May of 1949, a letter from the (Budget) Director to the Chairman of Senate Labor Committee set forth the considerations which should govern legislative action in the field of school construction. In so doing he outlined a middle course among the conflicting programs and approaches with which the Committee was confronted. The agencies generally fell in behind the Bureau's line. The rival interest groups joined hands on it. The Senate sponsors of a variety of measures united to support and advance it.
>
> None of this was accidental. The Bureau's letter was the product of three months of appraisal and discussion with the interest groups, the agencies concerned, the White House staff and key members of the Senate. The line which the Bureau took was that worked out informally by a group, composed of a key Senator's secretary, the strategist of a vital interest group and the Presidential assistants most concerned, in addition to its Budget members. The line was mutually satisfactory. It was acceptable to the Budget's technical staff. The agencies could live with it. The risks were removed and the results rendered reasonably certain before the words were spoken.[27]

Occasionally members of a legislative committee are interested in obtaining executive documents that are classified as secret or confidential. In these situations subpoena power may be used. Here again, as with the problem of obtaining witnesses, the great utility of a subpoena is that it provides an excuse for executive officials to make available documents that they want to make available, but with a public display of reluctance. Many officers of government agencies, and of private organizations as well, have collaborated in preparing the details of subpoenas that require them to produce certain very specifically designated documents and letters. When a congressional subpoena meets with strong resistance by agency officials, however, there is no guarantee that it will succeed in producing even a single sheet of paper. The judicial and penal sanctions that ordinarily stand behind a subpoena are simply not applicable to members of a coordinate branch of the Federal government. This was illustrated in March, 1948, when congressional committees attempted to obtain confidential employee loyalty files from a number of government agencies. President Truman immediately directed all executive officials who might receive congressional subpoenas for these files to refer them to the

[27] Neustadt, *op. cit.*, pp. 200–201.

White House.[28] Although it is probable that some of these files were "leaked" to some members of Congress by minor officials, none were obtained through the subpoena technique.

Joint Sessions

The suggestion has often been made that there be more joint hearings between parallel committees of the Senate and the House of Representatives. This suggestion is not the brain child of political scientists alone. It comes from tired and harried legislative representatives who would like to simplify their lives by killing two birds with one stone. It also comes from ambitious folk who would like to stage one big show rather than two small ones.

Joint sessions of this type, however, are extremely rare. The few experiments that have been made merely serve to demonstrate the tendency of Senators to steal the play from Representatives and monopolize the limelight. This tendency is enforced by the fact that the problem of who should be chairman of a joint hearing is usually resolved in favor of a Senator, and the problem of where it will meet is usually resolved in favor of a meeting room in the Senate Office Building or on the Senate side of the Capitol. Senators, therefore, tend to like joint sessions but their inclinations in this direction are usually frustrated by the corresponding disinclination of Representatives.[29]

Within each house somewhat more use is made of joint sessions between committees dealing with related subjects. This practice has been extensively developed to give expression to the community of interests between members of appropriation committees and the members of legislative committees. Designated members of the Armed Services Committees, for example, meet in conjunction with the appropriations subcommittees handling appropriations for the armed services.

Performance at the Hearings

The blustering committee chairman shakes his fist at an intimidated witness. . . . A press agent places a midget on J. P. Morgan's lap. . . . A mysterious "Madam X" tells all. . . .

Incidents like these, confined largely but not exclusively to congressional investigations, have given many people a wrong impression about congressional hearings. It is a rare hearing that is either a sensational spectacle or an outrage upon commonly accepted principles of good taste or fairness. Although

28 President's Directive of Mar. 13, 1948.

29 It is nonetheless true that joint hearings on *ad hoc* basis are easier to arrange than it would be to operate a formal structure of joint legislative committees.

the performance at legislative hearings runs a broad gamut from America at its best to Congress at its worst, the sum total of public hearings held every year is an invaluable part of American political life. To the onlooker, the legislative hearing is "an indispensable key to the puzzles of that vast onward sweep of legislation in the full arena of the House. Here he sees the headsprings of law." [30] To the advocate, it is a crucial point of direct touch with members of Congress.

For the member of Congress, it is one of the principal means of learning the points and bases of conflict. Senator Paul Douglas of Illinois has stated this in language of general applicability.

> If one reviews the Senatorial day, it becomes evident that there is not much chance for a Senator to undertake a profound or cloistered study of a problem. The research personnel in the departments may be of some help to him. His own staff will be of greater help. But in the final analysis, he must learn for himself what is true or false. And he can only find that out in the committee hearings.[31]

Congressional Attendance

Most members of Congress have the feeling that they are always being cut into little pieces by competing demands for their time. This is particularly true of members with important committee assignments, difficult personal projects, or high ambitions. It applies more to Representatives whose constituencies are near Washington than to those whom geography protects from inundations of personal visits. It is more true for Senators than for Representatives. It is more applicable during the hectic closing days of any session.

As a result, it is very unusual to have full committee attendance at public hearings. Advance commitments to attend have little meaning. Until a hearing actually starts, there is no telling who will actually show up. Often a member will rush into a hearing for the sole purpose of making a brief appearance. He will thumb through a witness's prepared statement, ask a question or two, and then, murmuring regrets to the chairman, hastily depart.

Not infrequently one can see more committee staff members at a hearing than members of the committee themselves. Occasionally staff members may in fact run a hearing in the absence of members—although this practice is usually confined to the taking of preliminary evidence in connection with committee investigations. At times a member's staff assistant may attend the hearing on his behalf.

When a person is defending himself in court on charges of perjury before a congressional committee or of failure to comply with a committee subpoena, an obvious point of defense is to attempt to prove that the committee or

[30] Lauros G. McConachie, "Congressional Committees" (New York: Crowell, 1898), p. 63.
[31] *The New York Times Magazine,* Mar. 20, 1949.

subcommittee was acting illegally because of the absence of a quorum.[32] However, most of these questions arise in connection with congressional investigations rather than in hearings on specific legislative proposals. Small committee attendance is only rarely a legal problem. In practical, everyday terms, its effect is to detract from a hearing's significance as a method of getting ideas across to committee members or of obtaining general publicity.

The various contestants in the legislative struggle, therefore, have a direct interest in rounding up committee members, particularly their friends and supporters. This effort is not limited to committee members. Attendance can be augmented by members of Congress who do not themselves belong to a given committee. Most committees, as a matter of courtesy, allow any other member of Congress who so chooses to sit with them at a public hearing.[33] One of the great weaknesses of the Democratic Administration after World War II was the failure to organize the active participation by Administration supporters in Congress in committee hearings on Administration bills. This reflected in part the weaknesses of the private organizations supporting the Democratic Administration. On the other hand, the opponents of the Administration's legislative program were usually extremely active in mobilizing congressional attendance on the part of Republican and conservative Democrats. This, in turn, reflected the energy and resources of the private organizations on their side of the fence.

The Testimony

In advising businessmen how to testify before congressional committees the National Association of Manufacturers once selected as a model the 1939 testimony of petroleum-industry representatives before the Temporary National Economic Committee. The N.A.M. document stated:

[32] This point was raised in the Meyers case, in addition to the question of the subcommittee's legality. The U.S. Court of Appeals agreed with the appellant in part: "On October 6, 1947, however, only two Senators were present at the hearing. Since they were a minority of the subcommittee, they could not legally function except to adjourn. For that reason, the testimony of Lamarre given on that day cannot be considered as perjury nor can appellant be convicted of suborning it." But the court then pointed out the following: "But practically all Lamarre's testimony was given on October 4, when a quorum was present. The proceedings of that day contain the perjurious statements described in all three counts, and his examination on October 6 was largely repetitious." United States Court of Appeals for the District of Columbia Circuit, No. 9797, *Bennett E. Meyers, Appellant, v. United States,* Nov. 8, 1948.

[33] The appropriations committees allow participation by other members of Congress only on the basis of the subcommittee relationships worked out with parallel legislative committees. A few other committees from time to time have also insisted that other members of Congress can take part in their proceedings only as witnesses and not as participants on the committee side of the table.

For weeks the petroleum group studied the TNEC members and watched their conduct of witnesses. When the oil men appeared, they knew the likes and dislikes of each committee member, and they pulled out an organ stop that appealed to everyone on the committee. Even the committee members were high in their praise of what the oil industry had done. And most important of all, it ended the clamor to enact legislation drastically regulating the oil industry.[34]

The oil-industry testimony was based upon more than a mere study of "the likes and dislikes of each committee member." It was the product of a large research organization mobilized in advance under the general direction of the American Petroleum Institute for the specific purpose of developing and documenting the industry's case. It was replete with charts, tables, and statistics, some of which helped to get the industry's points across and some of which gave the industry's presentation that degree of incomprehensibility which is best calculated to impress a not-too-sophisticated listener. Moreover, it is probable that the oil-industry witnesses were not only coached in advance but were also the beneficiaries of dress rehearsals at which their colleagues pretended to be congressional inquisitors.

In these respects the oil-industry testimony was not much different from testimony of any other large and well-financed organization. The appraisal of individual committee members, the use of research techniques, the presentation of elaborate charts and tables, careful advance coaching—these are all elements that go into the preparation of testimony. Although witnesses with meager resources behind them cannot do much along these lines, it is a rare witness indeed who will come before a congressional committee totally unprepared. The organizations that play a serious part in the legislative struggle have learned that a witness who has not organized his case beforehand will, at best, be wasting his time and, at worst, be a lamb led to slaughter.

The Legislative Reorganization Act of 1946 requires witnesses to submit written statements in advance of appearance so that these can be summarized by committee staff members. (Sec. 133(e).) In this way, it was thought, "the tedious oral repetition of oral testimony could be avoided, much valuable time would be saved, and the conduct of committee hearings could be greatly expedited." [35] This requirement, however, is not generally observed. Many witnesses never finish preparing a final draft of their prepared statements until the very last moment. They are not always eager to provide hostile committee members or their staff representatives with an advance inkling of the approach to be taken. When advance statements are submitted, committee staffs often neglect

[34] Walter J. Chamblin, Jr., "Know Your Congressmen" (New York: National Association of Manufacturers, 1944), p. 8.

[35] "Organization of Congress," Report of the Joint Committee on the Organization of Congress, 79th Cong., 2d Sess., S. Rept. 1011, p. 11.

entirely the preparation of digests, or solicit their preparation by the witnesses themselves.

Some witnesses glue their eyes to the text of their prepared statements and deviate not an inch. More expert witnesses, however, ask leave to have their prepared statements inserted in the *Record* and then speak more informally. Some will even plan ahead of time to leave their strongest points out of prepared testimony (particularly if it should be made available to committee members in advance) and save them for more effective use in informal talking.

Informality and spontaneity, of course, are often the product of advance labors. In the preparation of business witnesses against the Full Employment Bill, for example, two research workers prepared mimeographed documents to serve in the preparation of testimony. One of these documents contained a section called "Items for Ridicule." According to Bailey, one of the items suggested several "spontaneous" witticisms.[36]

President Franklin D. Roosevelt, it seems, often lectured his Cabinet members on how to handle themselves before congressional committees. He said:

> We must confine ourselves again to our own business and we must be factual. There has been altogether too much going before committees of Congress and talking about somebody else's work and venturing all kinds of opinion evidence which only is the opinion of the person who happens to give it. . . . In all our testimony before Congress and in all our answers to questions, let us stick to our own last and let us be factual about it. That is one of the most important things that has been said in a long time.[37]

A more extended lecture has been given to businessmen in the "Know Your Congressmen" pamphlet of the National Association of Manufacturers. The five "do's" in the pamphlet are worthy of quotation:

> "1. Before flatly opposing a bill, see if there is not some way of offering a compromise that would be acceptable.
>
> "2. Avoid demagoguery before a committee. It is resented.
>
> "3. The best witness is the man who is doing the job—not somebody to whom he has told the story and who is paid to represent him.
>
> "4. Get directly to the facts. Committees are not much interested in long discussions about the trends of the time.
>
> "5. Get your story told to the committee itself. Any material inserted in the committee record is of little value unless you take the trouble to motivate it yourself."

The four "don'ts" that follow are also of great interest:

> "1. Don't get 'smart.'
>
> An engineer testifying on a bill made a sneering reference to the Antitrust Act.

[36] Bailey, *op. cit.*, p. 138.

[37] Excerpt from Proceedings, Twenty-eighth Meeting, National Emergency Council, Dec. 17, 1935.

He was asked to tell what he knew about the Antitrust Act and was forced into a display of ignorance that destroyed the value of his testimony on the bill.

"2. Don't get off the subject.
A member of a Congressional committee diverted an important business witness into a discussion of the German tariff system, and the witness never got back from Germany.

"3. Don't assume a superior attitude.
It never pays to have a chip on your shoulder. Congressmen are experts at knocking them off.

"4. Don't get pugnacious and stand on your rights.
You haven't any. You only have such privileges as the committee may give you."

Pugnaciousness has its place, however. Sometimes the only effective way of dealing with a domineering interrogator is to hit back instead of merely turning the other cheek. One of the best practitioners of this approach was Harold Ickes who, as Secretary of the Interior, developed a highly effective technique. In 1946, Ickes testified on health insurance on behalf of a private organization with which he associated himself after his departure from the Government. Senator Forrest Donnell of Missouri tried to make the case that Ickes was unqualified to testify because he had not read each section of the bill. Ickes answered with a stinging reply that put Donnell in his place and won for Ickes the support and respect of other committee members. He said:

Well, I was prepared for that question because I understand that is a customary question from the Senator. I have not. I have read a carefully prepared digest of it, and I did not know—I have been appearing before congressional committees for some 13 years—and I did not know that it was a necessary prerequisite to have read carefully a bill, because I have appeared before so many committees the members of which had not read the bill.[38]

In contrast with this display of pugnacity, many witnesses maintain attitudes of deference bordering on the obsequious. When asked stupid questions, they will answer with respect rather than tolerance. When asked difficult or embarrassing questions, they will emphasize their willingness to cooperate and act in conformance with the "doctrine of apparent frankness" (a term coined by a high Government official during World War II to describe his agency's attitude when dealing with congressional committees). When slapped in public, they will turn the other cheek.

Facts are so important that many witnesses will answer factual questions in statistical terms without really being sure of their ground. This is risky business when there is a chance that one's bluff may be called. The risk is minimized, however, by the opportunities that exist for making a revision of the

[38] "National Health Program," Hearings before the Senate Committee on Education and Labor, 79th Cong., 2d Sess., S. Rept. 1606, Part 1, p. 401.

written record before it is printed. To protect themselves on points of fact, many heads of private companies and government agencies will never appear before a congressional committee without being surrounded by a battery of experts who can ply them with notes on questions that arise or who, when asked, can speak directly on a given question.[39] The more experts surrounding a witness, however, the less chance there is of his building up an impression of personal familiarity with his case. Some witnesses, therefore, prefer to take their chances on factual details and appear unattended.

The Interrogation

Seated together in a group facing the witnesses across a committee table, committee members make a most impressive appearance. They enjoy something of the same institutional dignity that surrounds a group of judges in a courtroom. They feel important, too. This can be corroborated by anyone who has sat as a committee member at a public hearing. It is publicly demonstrated by the demeanor of committee interrogators.

And they are important! The behavior of a committee member can make one witness's testimony an outstanding success. He can throw a monkey wrench into the well-laid plans of another witness and convert his presentation into a dismal failure. This was illustrated by the brief hearings on the atomic energy legislation in 1946 by Representative Andrew May of Kentucky when he was still chairman of the House Committee on Military Affairs. "The witnesses favoring civilian control," writes an observant reporter, "were skillfully hushed. Those on the other side were led on with gracious smiles." [40]

Committee interrogation, like cross-examination in a courtroom, is an art in itself. An effective interrogation must be based upon a clear understanding of the objectives to be achieved and a grasp of the basic facts that are involved in the matter at hand.

A friendly interrogation will often start by questions that build up the character and competence of the witness. It will give the witness a chance to make a prepared statement before any questions are asked him. A good example of a rapprochement between the interrogator and the witness is found in the 1948 hearings on basing-point legislation before a subcommittee of the Senate Committee on Interstate and Foreign Commerce.

> Harmony prevailed in the relations between the subcommittee, its chairman, and all other witnesses. With the skill of a conductor on the podium, Capehart led wit-

[39] A witness is customarily allowed to bring advisers with him. The question of whether a witness should be allowed to be accompanied by legal counsel is one that has arisen only in connection with the activities of a few investigating committees.

[40] Coffin, *op. cit.*, p. 233.

ness after witness (once their prepared statements were out of the way) through a series of questions that made it appear that enterprisers were confused by the existing law, that they had no place to go in the government for a definitive answer, and that it was necessary for Congress to come to their rescue and write legislation on the subject. He was his own best witness, and he spoke to the record through many voices.[41]

An unfriendly interrogation is quite different. It may very well start with questions that demonstrate the incompetence or unreliability of the witness. It may then go into the character of the organization which he is representing. In interrogating witnesses who favored national health insurance at a long series of hearings from 1946 to 1949, Senator Forrest Donnell of Missouri habitually asked for facts concerning membership and strength of the organizations represented. He also asked—and in many instances this was extremely damaging—for the facts concerning how and when an organization formally authorized a position in favor of health insurance. This line of interrogation revealed that many witnesses were appearing without the formal support of the organizations in whose name they purported to speak.

Customarily, a witness is allowed to make some sort of preliminary statement before questions are fired at him. This practice gives every witness a distinct initial advantage. Sometimes, however, a hostile committee member will deny a witness this opportunity by initiating a substantive interrogation before he can make a preliminary statement or by breaking in upon the statement without allowing him to finish. If the witness succeeds in making an effective point, the interrogator may then change the subject. In the questioning of an organized-labor spokesman who opposed his position on basing-point legislation, Senator Capehart sidetracked the witness's prepared presentation and "undertook to swoop him off into the imperium of speculation." [42]

A friendly committee member will sometimes give a witness a list of questions in advance. A hostile committee member would never do so. As Senator Fall stated to President Wilson, "If you were on a stand and I were cross-examining you as a witness, I would prefer not to let you see the whole series of questions." [43] As with courtroom examinations, committee interrogators often take great delight in carefully laying a trap for a witness and taking him by surprise.

There is no one source of the questions asked. Many spring extemporaneously from the minds of the committee members. Sometimes these are the most per-

[41] Latham, *op. cit.*, p. 106.

[42] *Ibid.*, p. 117.

[43] From transcript of White House Conference between President Woodrow Wilson and members of the Senate Committee on Foreign Relations, Aug. 19, 1919. Lodge, *op. cit.*, App. 4, p. 346.

tinent of all. Sometimes the committee member "gets tripped up by his improvisations in committee sessions and feels like a fool because of it," [44] or perhaps, while feeling wise, looks idiotic. Some questions are handed to committee members during the course of a hearing by their staff assistants, by reporters or spectators, or even—in a manner that provides an indirect form of cross-examination—by other witnesses. Many witnesses lay the ground for favorable questioning by friendly members by submitting lists of prepared questions in advance. These may even be interlarded in a witness's prepared testimony so that the committee member can interrupt with a helpful question at a desired point. Occasionally, when the subject matter is important enough to warrant it, a witness and a committee member will get together ahead of time to develop a prepared dialogue and may even rehearse it like actors preparing a play.

On matters calling for a high degree of preparation on details, a committee chairman will sometimes allow the interrogation to be handled by members of the committee staff. A staff member who takes on this task, however, always runs the risk of drawing thunder and lightning upon his head if he steals too much of the limelight from committee members or antagonizes any outside groups. Or else he may get in bad with committee members who agree with former Senator James F. Byrnes' dictum that "only members of the committee should be allowed to interrogate witnesses." [45]

The Record

One could compile a good-sized library every year, far more than any one pair of eyes could possibly read, merely by collecting the printed record of congressional hearings. There was a time when the publication of committee hearings was regarded as an infringement of parliamentary procedure. In 1885 Woodrow Wilson observed:

> There is a conclusive objection to the publication of the proceedings of the Committees, which is recognized as of course by all parliamentary lawyers, namely, that those proceedings are of no force till confirmed by the House. . . . It is made a breach of order for any member to allude on the floor of the House to anything that has taken place in committee, "unless by a written report sanctioned by a majority of the Committee." [46]

This procedural objection has long since vanished from the scene. In its place has arisen in the minds of many witnesses and members of Congress an exaggerated regard for the significance of the fine points contained in a pub-

[44] Paul H. Douglas, "Report from a Freshman Senator," *The New York Times Magazine,* Mar. 20, 1949.

[45] James F. Byrnes, "Streamlining Congress," *American Magazine,* February, 1945.

[46] Wilson, *op. cit.,* pp. 83–84.

lished record. This is partly due to the fact that lawyers mistakenly attribute to the written record of a congressional hearing the same legal importance that is more properly ascribed to the record in a courtroom proceeding. They often labor over fine points that are subsequently read and appreciated by no one but themselves.

The real significance of published records of a committee hearing is that they provide a valuable source of information and propaganda. The publication of a statement in a committee report gives it a certain amount of dignity and status. The record is also used as a means of publishing various supplementary memoranda and reports that could not otherwise be readily published or made freely available. Furthermore, committee members can always get a thousand or two thousand copies for free distribution and these can be made available to interested organizations and agencies. At times published hearings on bills or at least some sections of them are so valuable for informational and propaganda purposes that additional copies are ordered from the Government Printing Office for more widespread distribution. The utility of the published hearings generally is diminished by the fact that hearings are seldom organized and edited in a manner that promotes readability. This obstacle, however, is overcome at times by the addition of such editorial aids for the reader as subheads in a text, indices, and so forth.

The published record is not always an accurate reflection of what actually went on at a committee hearing. Both witnesses and committee members are usually given an opportunity to correct their remarks. Theoretically, they are supposed to catch only errors made by the transcribers and improve upon the grammar of an extemporaneous discussion. In practice, this opportunity is habitually used to change the meaning of what was actually said and even to add entirely new material. In addition, the chairman of the committee often makes and allows others to make many off-the-record statements. When this happens, the official reporter rests for a moment. On these occasions some of the juiciest bits of testimony and interrogation are recorded only in the memories of those in the committee room at the time.

Nor is the transcribed record of a committee hearing always published. Economy is the reason that is often given; the publication of hearings costs money. The better reason, however, is a disinclination to tell what has been happening. In 1949, for example, the Senate Committee on Rules and Administration held a "quickie" hearing at which representatives of the Democratic party organizations in the counties immediately adjoining the District of Columbia requested that a pending amendment to the Hatch Act be broadened by the addition of a section that would allow Federal workers in the vicinity of the District of Columbia to take part in local party activities. This proposal was vigorously opposed by other groups in the vicinity of the District of Columbia, particularly in Arlington County. The publication of the printed transcript would have made it easier for the opponents of this proposal to mobilize their forces. Accordingly, the transcripts were never published.

For many years the hearings of the House Committee on Appropriations were never published until after an appropriations bill had come up for consideration on the floor of the House. This had the effect of giving the members of the House Appropriations Committee a monopoly of information. In protest against this practice, the following provision was inserted in the Legislative Reorganization Act of 1946: "No general appropriation bill shall be considered in either House unless, prior to the consideration of such bill, printed committee hearings and reports on such bills have been available for at least three calendar days for the Members of the House in which such bill is to be considered." This requirement has not always been followed by the House Appropriations Committee. Nor is the principle contained in the provision necessarily respected by other committees.

Chapter 16

DECISIONS IN COMMITTEE

"LEGISLATION, as we nowadays conduct it," wrote Woodrow Wilson, "is not conducted in the open. It is not threshed out in open debate upon the floors of our assemblies. It is, on the contrary, framed, digested and concluded in committee rooms." [1]

Although it would be stretching the point to write off floor action as negligible in importance in the legislative process (and in the severity of his attack upon the committee system, Wilson did some stretching), the bulk of congressional decisions on legislative matters is unquestionably framed and digested in committee rooms. The decisions made on the floor of either house by and large represent ratification or modification of committee decisions. Even when floor changes occur, mild or drastic, they are usually the outgrowth of views formulated in committee by a minority group of committee members. The shaping and making of decisions in committee bring our attention to executive sessions of committees, committee reports, and committee voting methods. A very special kind of committee to be examined is the conference committee. Further, there are certain formal devices for bringing influence to bear upon committee choices, and these too shall be noted.

SHAPING DECISIONS IN COMMITTEE

The Executive Sessions

A high navy official was once asked by a Presidential staff member to explain the Navy Department's position on a proposed amendment to an Administration bill dealing with the national defense. "This is no time for us to take a stand," the navy man replied. "We'll develop our position when we go down to the Hill and meet in executive session to help the committee mark up the bill."

This incident illustrates the fact that the executive sessions of congressional committees are centers of vital decision making. Public hearings are merely a

[1] Woodrow Wilson, "The New Freedom" (Garden City, N.Y.: Doubleday, 1913), p. 125.

preliminary. The decisions are made after the hearings are over and the doors are closed. It also points up the fact that the activity in process behind committee doors is often far more significant than that policy-making process behind the closed doors in the executive branch. The nonpublic character of executive sessions promotes the free interplay of ideas among committee members. Compromises and alternatives can be shaped in a fluid environment that could never be approximated at a public meeting.

The executive session also confers a special position of power upon every participant, each one of whom shares the oligopoly of information which is created by the nonpublic character of the meetings. Each participant is in an especially effective position to convey information to outsiders—whether they be the President and other Administration officials, the leaders of private organizations, or other members of Congress—for use in the conduct of their respective campaigns.

These opportunities are seldom allowed to go unnoticed. An "executive session" is far from being a "secret" session. One member may leave the committee room and immediately phone the President or a White House Secretary to ask that the "heat" be put on at a place where it is sorely needed. Another member may move directly from the committee room to a meeting of representatives of government agencies and private organizations called to discuss the next steps in their legislative campaign. Sometimes, through either a legal or an unofficial action, the whole story of conflicts within the committee may be given to the press.

In some instances official statements on the progress of committee decisions are given out at regular intervals. The practice of the House Ways and Means Committee, when working on a major bill, has been described as follows:

> Statements are customarily issued to the press at the end of every session of the Committee by the chairman. Thus, all decisions of the Committee, even of a tentative character, are publicly known almost as soon as they are taken. In one sense, this helps make the decisions final, since there is a certain reluctance to reverse the vote after announcement has been made to the public.[2]

One of the major campaigns in the development of the Atomic Energy Act of 1946 centered around the debate on civilian versus military control which developed at the executive sessions of the Special Senate Committee on Atomic Energy. The disclosure of an amendment presented by Senator Vandenberg "was the signal for a direct offensive by the scientists, the conference of organizations, the emergency committee of prominent individuals, and the many friends of civilian control in the communications fields and elsewhere." [3] Dur-

[2] Roy Blough, "The Federal Taxing Process" (New York: Prentice-Hall, 1952), p. 72.

[3] Byron S. Miller, "A Law Is Passed—The Atomic Energy Act of 1946," *University of Chicago Law Review,* Vol. 15, No. 4, Summer, 1948, p. 811.

ing the same series of executive sessions, committee members "sought advice from leading scientists in close touch with the scientists' organizations and made a determined effort to produce a section which would preserve the maximum secrecy consistent with dissemination of enough data not to hamper research." [4]

When hard and fast lines are drawn among the committee members, it is only natural for opposing groups to meet separately before the committee sessions. On those relatively rare occasions when a decision of this character follows party lines, the Republican and Democratic members may meet separately. Upon conclusion of the public hearings by the Senate Finance Committee on the Tariff Bill of 1929–1930, "the Republican members met as a party group, privately, to rewrite the House bill, and having arrived at a party decision on the bill in secret, went into a regular session of the Finance Committee and by a strictly partisan vote adopted the amendments agreed upon and reported the revised bill favorably to the Senate." [5] The rarity of this method of operation is not only a reflection of the looseness of party operations in Congress but also a contributing factor toward the development of intimate relations between members of opposing parties.

A committee chairman is in a strategic position to influence the operations of an executive session. He can call meetings at a time inconvenient for members whom he would see absent. By delaying the calling of a session, he can provide time for the application of pressure to certain members, or for the preparation of new drafts, or merely for killing time. Unless there is serious objection among his committee colleagues, he can give positions of privilege and potential influence to representatives of government agencies or private organizations by inviting them to the sessions. He can direct the preparation of staff memoranda, drafts, and other documents.

The first problem confronting an executive session is the decision as to what measure will serve as the starting point of discussion. This is not as easy as it might seem. Many bills are skeleton measures introduced to serve as a springboard for hearings, while the period during which the hearings are held is used for the preparation of a more adequate measure. By the time an executive session begins there may be many alternative drafts before the committee. When the Senate Special Committee on Atomic Energy began its 1946 executive sessions, for example, there were three measures before it: a bill introduced by its chairman, Senator Brien McMahon of Connecticut, a bill submitted by Senator Ball of Minnesota, and the May-Johnson bill which was the first measure that had been introduced on the subject and had the support of the

[4] *Ibid.*, p. 812.

[5] E. E. Schattschneider, "Politics, Pressures, and the Tariff" (New York: Prentice-Hall, 1935), p. 35.

War Department. After a preliminary skirmish, Senator McMahon succeeded in having the committee decide to use his bill as a working guide.[6]

"Reading the bill" is a customary procedure in executive sessions. Once various members have had a chance to make general comments on this or that point, the chairman will usually start with the first section and read the measure line by line. When another draft is before a committee, the reading process is sometimes facilitated by a "comparative print." This consists of a large broad-paged booklet in which one column gives the sections of one bill and the other column gives comparable sections of the alternative measure.

The reading of a bill at an executive session is a valuable intellectual discipline. It usually brings the committee members face to face with many points they never before had the time to understand. It brings out hidden meanings that would otherwise lie undiscovered. It is also a grueling operation. The finest points may take up a whole day's discussion. The reading and rereading of a major bill may stretch over many weeks of meetings. The following is a description of this phase of the work of the House Ways and Means Committee:

> If the measure is a major one, the opening session of the Committee is likely to be given over to general remarks by various members of the Committee. The remarks may approach speeches in length and character. . . . After one or more sessions of this preliminary shake-down character, a procedure for discussion and decision is adopted. From then on, the various subjects under consideration are taken up for discussion in a more or less pre-determined order. However, since each subject considered by the Committee is usually related to every other subject, the Committee in its early sessions appears to be moving very slowly towards reaching decisions. This slowness is desirable and is more apparent than real, for after the Committee has thought its way through to an understanding of the problems and a perspective of their inter-relations, discussion moves rapidly toward tentative decisions.[7]

The Committee Reports

The most decisive form of action that a committee can take on a bill is inaction. This negative form of action almost invariably means the death of a measure. Nor is the corpse consigned elsewhere for burial. When committee members kill a bill by inaction, they do not discharge themselves of the measure and report it to the floor. Nor do they even prepare a written report stating why and wherefore.

Occasionally committee members will merely report a measure to the floor with no recommendation for either favorable or adverse action. This is something less than burial but also less than genuine endorsement. Or the mem-

[6] Miller, *op. cit.*

[7] Blough, *op. cit.*, pp. 72–73.

bers of a committee may report a bill to the floor but very specifically reserve the right of committee members to propose amendments when the measure comes up on the floor. This strategy was used by Senator Aldrich in 1907 in connection with the report on the Hepburn Act to strengthen the interstate commerce legislation by the Senate Committee on Interstate Commerce. Its purpose was to deprive the measure of the prestige of the full committee endorsement and to sow the seeds for a floor attack on the bill through amendments capable of mustering widespread support.

An entirely favorable report on the other hand may be nothing but a grandstand play. In 1949 when the House Committee on Interstate and Foreign Commerce reported the O'Hara bill to curb the powers of the Federal Trade Commission, both the proponents and the opponents of the measure agreed that no attempt would be made to call the measure off the calendar and have it taken up for consideration on the floor of the House. The reporting of the bill, therefore, constituted in reality a device for doing nothing.

A committee report almost always invites amendment. These may be of a minor and perfecting nature. They may be "small and immaterial variations intended for the purpose of inducing the House to believe that they had matured the subject well. . . ." [8] They may make major changes or additions. Or else, the committee may, to use the stylized language of a congressional report, "report an amendment in the nature of a substitute."

Once a committee has reported a measure, it need not let go of the subject. Before or during floor consideration, committee members will often come forth with another report offering various proposed changes. Thus, in reporting the Versailles Treaty in September, 1919, the Senate Committee on Foreign Relations proposed four reservations and then reserved "the right to offer other reservations if they shall so determine." Two months later Senator Lodge reported a resolution of ratification and fourteen reservations which included in modified form the four that had been recommended earlier.

When subcommittees report to a full committee, they do so usually in the form of presenting merely the bill itself with any amendments that are being proposed. Sometimes a written report will be prepared but more for the purpose of submitting a proposed draft for the full committee's final report than for the purpose of making a public statement describing the grounds for its action.

The reports of full committees, however, invariably consist not only of the bill and amendments but also of a written report which is given the same calendar number as the reported bill. These committee reports play an important role in the legislative struggle. They serve as campaign documents for use not only in floor debate but in the organization of group support and the development of propaganda. They are useful as a means of exerting pressure

[8] Address by Rep. Hardin, *Annals of the Congress of the United States,* 14th Cong., 1st Sess., Jan. 24, 1816, pp. 747–748.

upon executive officials and of creating a record of "congressional intent" for the purpose of influencing subsequent judicial decisions. The participants in the legislative struggle, therefore, regard the preparation of committee reports as a vital operation. The quality of these reports, no matter what standard may be used in judging them, is a reflection of the ability and resourcefulness of the various contesting groups. The more detailed committee reports are usually prepared by executive officials and representatives of private organizations, with staff members and members of Congress playing a role in the direction of the work. Some of the most vigorous statements on the necessity of congressional independence from the bureaucrats and the pressure groups are to be found in committee reports prepared by executive-agency and pressure-group officials.

One of the recommendations of the Joint Committee on the Organization of Congress was "That a complete and understandable digest of a bill, together with legislative changes made by the bill, written in nontechnical language, accompany the committee report of each bill; and that this digest include a supporting statement of reasons for its passage, of the national interest involved, its cost, and the distribution of any benefits." [9] This recommendation was eliminated from the final version of the Legislative Reorganization Act of 1946. However, the growing tendency has been for reports to contain reasonably full explanations of whatever action is recommended. Experience has proved that information of this type is essential in the prosecution of a legislative campaign and that a committee report is one of the best ways to propagate it. From time to time, however, there will crop up conspicuous examples of a committee report that completely glosses over very important parts of the legislation it is proposing. This usually develops in a situation where there is no dissension within the committee and no clearly organized opposition discernible in the future.

When there is no disagreement among members of the committee, the committee's report will be tagged with neither the term majority nor minority. When there is disagreement, a number of alternative courses are open. With committee members in agreement upon a committee report, one or more members may submit and have printed in document form their "additional or supplemental" views. Or one report may be clearly labeled the majority report and another the minority one. There have even been occasions when the majority group in a committee issued "additional views" to put themselves on record in favor of a principle which they were not altogether willing to embody in a specific legislative proposal.

It is often completely impossible to tell from a committee report exactly what position each member of the committee has taken. A majority report is sometimes printed with only the name of the chairman attached to it. Other

[9] Organization of the Congress, 79th Cong., 2d Sess., S. Rept. 1011, Mar. 4, 1946, p. 8.

members are therefore free to indicate at any future date that they really did not go along with the rest of the committee. Even when there are both majority and minority reports, many members may fail to sign. Moreover, techniques have been developed whereby members can stand clearly on both sides of a given issue. In 1950, for example, the Senate Judiciary Committee reported the Mundt-Ferguson bill outlawing Communist activities by a vote of 12 to 1. Senator Harley Kilgore of West Virginia was one of the 12, but when he was publicly described by a newspaper writer as favoring the measure, he wrote a special letter to the editor of a Washington paper explaining that while he had voted to report the bill out, he was really against it. "As I explained at the time, I voted to report out the bill but reserved the right to oppose it when it was called up for action on the floor of the U.S. Senate. After the legislation was reported out, I wrote to Senator Pat McCarran, Chairman of the Judiciary Committee, and expressed grave doubts about this proposed legislation." [10]

The designation of the committee member who is responsible for preparing a report is handled along hierarchical lines. A committee chairman will often take over the preparation of a report. He may turn it over to the chairman of the subcommittee that handled the legislation in the first instance. Or he may go down the line of seniority and select a ranking member to sponsor the report. One of the most interesting examples of tactical discretion in the selection of the committee member who makes the report occurred in connection with the action of the Senate Committee on Interstate Commerce in 1907 on the Hepburn Act. Skipping over the various Republican Senators who best qualified for the task, Chairman Aldrich moved that the report be made by "Pitchfork" Ben Tillman, who was not only a Democrat but also a bitter personal enemy of President Theodore Roosevelt. Aldrich's motion was welcomed by all the members of the committee who saw in it a hope of splitting the ranks of those who supported the proposed reform.[11]

The Committee Voting

As indicated above, the committee reports do not always give a full record of how committee members have voted on the final product. They are even less informative, however, about the process of voting during strategic points in the committee's work. In some cases, of course, there is very little voting at all. Decisions are made on the basis of nods, assents, mutual understandings, and friendly accommodations among members and their representatives. At other times, a chairman may bypass some of his colleagues and deny them

[10] *The Washington Star,* Apr. 22, 1950.

[11] It so happened that President Roosevelt and Senator Tillman succeeded in overcoming their distaste for each other and cooperated in a successful effort to have the measure enacted.

the opportunity to vote. While the most conspicuous examples of this have occurred in the activities of various investigating committees, the same incidents occur with somewhat less regularity in the operations of legislative committees.

On highly controversial issues, there will often be a long-drawn-out series of votes within the committee. The opposition may start by offering a test amendment at the very outset, the line-up upon which will indicate the relative strength of opposing groups. The voting process is very simple. The chairman will go down the list of committee members, call each member's name, and record the vote beside it. The committee clerk will often keep a whole set of tally sheets and file the tally sheets away when the voting process is completed. It is an unwritten rule that these tally sheets should not be made public. When intracommittee votes are publicized, loud protests may be voiced. During the 1951 debate over the extension of price control, Senator Moody disclosed that during the executive sessions of the Banking and Currency Committee, Senator Capehart had voted for an amendment that would have removed all price and wage controls. "I do not know why the Senator brings up that matter on the floor," protested Senator Capehart, "and whether it is necessary to have persons snooping to see whether a Senator holds up his hand. I wish to say that I do not like such tactics, and I do not think the Senator should make such statements." [12]

A member does not necessarily have to be present to have his vote recorded. Frequent use is made of proxy voting. Much of the strength of committee chairmen in the voting process lies in the fact that they are in an ideal position to obtain proxies from colleagues who are dependent upon them for favors. Some committee chairmen have standing arrangements with other committee members to obtain their proxies in any matters that may come up when they are out of town. Sometimes the voting conflicts within a committee can be handled almost entirely by two members on opposing sides, each one with a pile of proxies in his pocket or on the table in front of him. These proxies may be from people who are out of town, too busy to attend, or sick in bed. It is a well-known fact that for a number of years when Senator Carter Glass of Virginia was too sick to attend any sessions of the Senate or Senate committees, his proxy was invariably handled by Senator Robert F. Wagner of New York. Wagner's opponents invariably charged that Glass's proxy was being cast in favor of proposals that Glass himself would unquestionably have opposed. However, they never succeeded in having a committee vote to overrule this use of Glass's proxy. Nor were they particularly interested in winning this point because from time to time during the same period there were two members on the committee from the Republican side who were also physically indisposed and whose proxies were given to the Republican Senators.

[12] *Congressional Record* (daily edition), June 25, 1951, p. 7205.

People with proxies do not always use them but rather try to accomplish their objectives through persuasion and compromise before they use the blunderbuss weapon of the proxy. The only formal limitation on the use of the proxy is a seldom invoked requirement that no bill shall be reported unless a majority of the committee has actually been present for the vote. Even when there is such a majority present, however, the decisive votes can readily be cast through proxies on behalf of the absent members of the committee. When the quorum requirement is enforced, it serves as an effective device for delaying action. During the long executive sessions of the House Military Affairs Committee on the Atomic Energy Act of 1946,

> the bill encountered such parliamentary obstacles that its chances of stillbirth rose alarmingly. House rules designate a majority of the committee's roster as a quorum and require a quorum for formal action if the point is raised. Several members of the committee were off in Bikini, others were ill or out of town, leaving it within the power of eight or nine members acting in concert to prevent a quorum. The same Republican group then followed the practice of coming to meetings, counting noses, and, if a quorum were present, taking turns leaving the committee room. This process continued for several days despite powerful objections from the public, from the Administration, and from the Speaker of the House.[13]

Although these delaying tactics finally broke down, the use of the quorum calls to prevent votes served as a means of advancing the policies favored by the quorum callers.

Decision Making in the Conference Committee

Every bicameral legislature needs some means whereby its two branches can iron out their inevitable disagreements on policy matters. In the United States this need has been met through the creation of *ad hoc* conference committees selected to deal with individual measures.

Since the members of a conference committee invariably come from the legislative committees which have handled a measure, conference committees must be viewed as an extension of the standing-committee system. They are by-products of the structure of committee power in existence at a given moment. Since conference-committee bills cannot be amended in either house but must be accepted or rejected in toto, the conference committees represent committee power in its most concentrated form. "For practical purposes, in most cases, it is impossible to defeat the legislation proposed by this conference committee. Every experienced legislator knows that it is the hardest thing in the world to defeat a conference report." [14]

[13] Miller, *op. cit.*, p. 814.

[14] George B. Galloway, "Congress at the Crossroads" (New York: Crowell, 1946), p. 99.

To Have or Not to Have a Conference

After losing a point of order against the conference committee report on the Transportation Act of 1940, Senator Bennett Champ Clark of Missouri introduced this resolution in rueful protest against the practice of allowing conference committees to write the basic legislative decisions: "All bills and resolutions shall be read twice and, without debate, referred to conference."

Jesting though he was, his proposal had the virtue of highlighting the tendency to make frequent use of conference committees. The differences between measures approved by each of the two houses are often of crucial importance to individual members of Congress, private organizations, and executive officials. Conference committees become the only practical method of settling these differences. In fact, the realization ahead of time that a conference committee will eventually be set up creates a natural tendency to postpone serious conflict on the floor of each house and pass the buck to the conference committee. When this occurs, almost everything that takes place in committee and on the floor before the appointment of conferees tends to be in the nature of byplay, rehearsal, and preliminary maneuvering.

Often the proponents of an important amendment will refrain from advancing their views on the floor lest a defeat endanger their chance of obtaining the same ends at the conference committee stage. Thus, during Senate consideration of the Displaced Persons Act in 1948, Senator Howard McGrath of Rhode Island indicated that he had an over-all substitute in readiness but that he would not offer it. He was very frank in explaining his reasons for this behavior: "In order not to allow anyone to be able to say that the Senate had already turned down many provisions that are found in the substitute bill, and thereby make it ineligible for consideration in conference, the Senator from New Mexico (Hatch) and myself have reluctantly come to the conclusion not to call up our substitute during the course of this debate." [15]

On the other hand, members of Congress will often accede to amendments that they really oppose on the theory that the place to kill the objectionable proposal is in the conference committee. During the Senate consideration of the Atomic Energy Act, Senator Joseph O'Mahoney of Wyoming offered a floor amendment providing that no one having a part in the development of the bomb project could subsequently benefit by any claim or by location on the public domain deriving from his participation in the project. Senator Milliken of Colorado went along with O'Mahoney's proposal but explained his position as follows: "So, merely to get it out of the way, and although I am in complete disagreement with the theory of the Senator from Wyoming but

[15] *Congressional Record,* 80th Cong., 2d Sess., p. 6900.

not with the ethics involved, I am willing to accept the proviso in the hope that the conference will eliminate the amendment." [16]

The extent to which legislative strategy is based upon the eventual possibility of settling controversies in conference committee, and the immediate character of such a strategy, depend to a large extent upon the distribution of power between and within the two houses. During the Seventieth Congress, for example, the progressive Republicans in the Senate, working in collaboration with many Democrats, produced Senate bills that were much more liberal than the regular Republican organization could tolerate. The formal Republican party position, on the other hand, crystallized in the House. The progressive Republicans usually had less representation in the leadership of Senate committees, and therefore less representation in conference committees. As a result of these circumstances, the conservative Republican viewpoint often came forward in the conference-committee bills, which were then enacted into law. A striking case of this was the Merchant Marine Act of 1931, which contained the very subsidies for private shipping interests that had been opposed at an earlier stage by the progressive Republicans in the Senate.

Similarly, the conference committee can be used to liberalize a measure. During the development of the Public Utility Holding Act of 1935, the Senate passed a bill which contained a strong version of the famous "death-sentence" clause, while the House passed a measure which weakened this provision considerably. Speaker Sam Rayburn refrained from a substantive debate on the issue on the floor of the House. "My position is this," he said. "I should like to see this bill in conference. I have pointed out a great many things in both bills. I think there are frailties in the House measure and also in the Senate measure, but I think we can do a better job in conference than we can here." [17] According to Raymond Moley, who seems to have been close to many of the decisions on legislative strategy adopted during the first term of the Franklin Roosevelt Administration, many legislative campaigns were planned in this manner. In discussing the Securities Act of 1933, Moley says: "This was the first appearance of the strategy that Cohen and Corcoran were to use so often in the years thereafter—ramming a too-severe bill through one House and then using it for trading purposes in the other." [18]

"Blind-fold," writes Luce, "the House puts its interest in the hands of its conferees." [19] Luce's protest is based upon the fact that one house will often ask for a conference without either waiting to see whether the other house will accede to the changes it has made, or, if the changes have been made in the

[16] *Congressional Record,* 79th Cong., 2d Sess., p. 6093.

[17] *Congressional Record,* 74th Cong., 1st Sess., July 2, 1935, p. 10635.

[18] Raymond Moley, "After Seven Years" (New York: Harper, 1939), p. 181, note 12.

[19] Robert Luce, "Legislative Procedure" (Boston: Houghton Mifflin, 1922), p. 404.

other house, without waiting to analyze them carefully and consider the possibility of accepting them.

Yet it is not quite the act of a blind man to do something that has been taken for granted all along. As pointed out above, the intention to have a conference is often accepted by all parties from the very beginning of a legislative campaign, particularly in the case of major measures and measures of an intricate nature. In addition, there are strategic gains in quick action to set up a conference committee. Toward the end of a session, any serious effort to avoid a conference committee through the possibility of accepting a bill as approved by the other house might, under certain circumstances, provoke enough delay to make the enactment of a measure impossible. The members of the house that asks for a conference place themselves in a strategic position also by virtue of the fact that the other house is expected to consider a conference report first. The asking house is thereby put in the position of having the last word.

Situations occasionally arise, however, where even major differences are glossed over in the effort to avoid a conference. Toward the end of a session, initiation of the conference process sometimes threatens sufficient delay as to prevent action. Thus, in the last days of the Seventy-ninth Congress, the Senate yielded completely on House amendments made to the Legislative Reorganization Act of 1946. The House, in turn, yielded to the Senate on legislation to extend social-security benefits for railroad employees.

The conference process may be opposed by those who have reason to believe that disagreement between the two houses would eventuate in a measure going to a conference dominated by members with an objectionable point of view. At the end of the Seventy-ninth Congress, the House yielded to the Senate on the Case bill, which was the precursor of the Taft-Hartley Act. Here the motivation was to avoid a conference committee, the majority of which would have come from two committees dominated by prolabor opponents of the measure. This bill was vetoed by President Truman and the veto was sustained. But if the conference committee had been established, the conferees might have prolonged their deliberations to the point where the veto stage would never have been reached.

The Selection of Conferees

The selection of conferees is even more important than the selection of committee members and committee chairmen, for it is the conferees who often write the final version of a law. In fact, it is because the positions of power established in the standing committees usually carry over into the conference committees that the struggle for power in the legislative committees in each house is often so intense.

Nominally, the conferees from each house are chosen respectively by the presiding officer of the Senate and the Speaker of the House. In actual practice, however, these officials invariably accept the recommendations of the chairmen of the two committees that handled the measure originally.

On the most important measures, a committee chairman will usually head up his list with his own name and that of the ranking minority member. Where a subcommittee has exercised major responsibility, as in the case of appropriation bills, he will often step aside in favor of the subcommittee chairman, who in turn invariably starts off by selecting himself and the ranking minority member of the subcommittee. In the selection of the additional members great weight is given to seniority. On only the rarest occasions will a conferee be appointed who was not a member of the legislative committee that worked on the measure.

In so far as party line-up is concerned, the minority party is always well represented. The ratios usually run 2 to 1, 3 to 2, or 5 to 3. Wherever there is a division along party lines, this practice puts a dissident member of the majority party in a particularly strategic position. By joining with the opposition party, one dissident member can often swing the balance of power.

In so far as size is concerned, committee chairmen have an important degree of latitude. Since the conferees of each house vote as a unit, there is no formal ceiling on the number of conferees that can be chosen from either house. The chairman may select two major-party members and one minority member, or he may set a ratio of 3 to 2, or 5 to 3. This gives him the same leeway in selecting men for or against the viewpoint that he normally exercises in the selection of subcommittees. During the 1948 Senate conflict on the Displaced Persons Act, Senator Wiley of Wisconsin, who was chairman of the Senate Judiciary Committee, selected three Senators as conferees—Revercomb, Ferguson, and Kilgore. This action was taken just as Senator Wiley was departing hastily for his home state. The haste probably explains his failure to realize that Ferguson and Kilgore had both been strong supporters of the more liberal approach with which Wiley himself disagreed and which had already been voted down in the Senate. Upon returning to Washington, therefore, Senator Wiley succeeded in adding to the conferees Senators Donnell and Eastland. These two new conferees, joining with Revercomb, were then able to outvote Ferguson and Kilgore and prevent any liberalization of the measure in the conference committee.

There is no reason to believe that conferees appointed by one house are necessarily interested in defending the bill approved in that house, although this is a general expectation. In fact, if one wanted to stretch the point a little, one might whimsically claim that any similarity between the views of the House or the Senate and those of the conferees representing the House or the Senate is purely coincidental. Many members come to a conference committee eager to defend the views represented in the bill passed by the *other* house or to strike out provisions inserted in their own house. Some are intent upon striking out identical provisions appearing in both bills or upon inserting provisions that appear in neither. Many conference committees include members who voted against the bill in their own house and are equally opposed to the version adopted by the other house and are fully committed to having no legislation whatsoever. During the Senate debate on the Agricultural Adjustment Act of 1938, Senator McNary of Oregon referred to "an unbroken rule of mine that when I oppose a bill I refuse to act as a conferee." [20] McNary's rule has interest because of its rarity. When most members of Congress oppose a bill, they view an opportunity to serve as conferees as a chance to help make the measure less objectionable to themselves or to make it so much more objectionable to others as to enhance the chances of a Presidential veto.

Theoretically, either house may change its conferees if they fail to defend adequately the measure passed by the house or if they prove unable to work out an agreement with the conferees selected in the other house. Actually, this is practically never done. Occasionally, the conferees from one house will, in a situation of deadlock, go back to their house and ask that a new set of conferees be appointed. This invariably leads to the reappointment of the same members, in effect, a device whereby the conferees obtain a vote of confidence which strengthens their position at the bargaining table.

Conference Action

The activities of conference committees are shrouded in secrecy—even more so than the executive sessions of the standing committees in each house of Congress.

Conferees have almost never been known to hold public hearings.[21] Only rarely are the representatives of private organizations allowed to appear at conference-committee sessions. Attendance by representatives of executive agencies is carefully limited. The great bulk of contacts between conferees and outside organizations takes place on a personal basis rather than through the medium of the conference committee itself. Attendance by staff assistants to committee members is usually kept to a minimum. In at least one instance the House members of a conference committee refused to allow their Senate colleagues to continue bringing along an adviser who had been assigned from an

[20] *Congressional Record,* 75th Cong., 3d Sess., Feb. 11, 1938, p. 1818.

[21] One of the few references to formal hearings on the part of conference committees is found in De Alva S. Alexander, "History and Procedure of the House of Representatives" (Boston: Houghton Mifflin, 1916), p. 284. "In one case formal hearings, attended by witnesses and attorneys, aided in eliminating difficulties." But Alexander gives no reference on the case. If a formal record was kept, it was probably never published.

executive agency.[22] There are probably less "leaks" from conference committees than any other brand of secret meeting in the nation's capital. Whatever leaks do take place are usually in the form of information privately piped to colleagues in Congress and supporters in private organizations and executive agencies. Finally, the reports and explanatory statements issued by the conferees rarely give a full and complete explanation of the action taken.

Behind the closed doors of conference committees takes place some of the hardest bargaining and fiercest battling to be found in the entire legislative process. The participants feel that the final language of any law that may be passed is now being written and are eager both to press any minor advantage and to make the final settlements on issues that can no longer be postponed. Their basic weapon is their ability to obtain the support or acquiescence of a majority in their own house. To some extent, the strength of this weapon depends upon the voting line-up on the bill as it originally passed or any instructions that might have been sent along with it. It also depends upon their ability to go back to their house and win consent to a measure that flies in the face of previous floor votes or baldly violates instructions.

Dilatory tactics are another "weapon" in conference-committee battles. Major gains can be won by any group of conferees that is in a position to sit tight and yield little while their opponents are being pressed for speedy action. This is most effective at the end of a session when just a day's delay may mean no opportunity for final action on a conference-committee report. The threat of dilatory tactics on the floor of either house also has implications for a conference committee. This is particularly true of a Senate filibuster. In 1938, Senator Royal Copeland reported to the Senate on how the Senate conferees succeeded in striking from the measure a House amendment which would have labeled whisky "misbranded" if distilled from anything but grain. "I told the House conferees," he said, "that some of the most able filibusterers in the Senate

[22] The adviser in this case was Benjamin Cohen of the famous Corcoran-Cohen team. Cohen had been brought to early conference committee meetings on the Public Utility Holding Act of 1935. The House conferees disliked his effective work on behalf of the Senate version of the "death-sentence clause." They reported to the House "That a conference has been prevented by the unyielding refusal of the managers on the part of the Senate to hold same under conditions consistent with the proper conduct of an executive session and free from the presence and participation of an outsider, who was not an employee of Congress and who is objectionable to the managers on the part of the House." By a vote of 183 to 172 the House backed up its conferees in a demand for Mr. Cohen's exclusion. It is interesting to note that during the debate preceding this vote, one of Mr. Cohen's defenders asserted that "with respect to every one of the supply bills that have been passed after conference for the last twenty years the House conferees have taken with them to the conference any experts they chose, and likewise, the managers on the part of the Senate have had their experts with them in the conference." *Congressional Record,* 74th Cong., 1st Sess., July 29, 1935, p. 12012.

were so opposed to this amendment that we could not accept it, and it was stricken from the bill." [23]

When the conferees emerge from a session on major legislation, they know they have been through a tense experience. Representative Wolcott of Michigan in reporting upon the conference committee that produced the Housing Act of 1937 states:

> When I first came to Congress, I was told that all major legislation was a matter of compromise. I did not know quite what that meant until I took part in some conferences with the Senate on legislation. I did not fully realize what it meant until a conference on this bill, when, after spending eleven and a half hours yesterday giving and taking, adding and subtracting, sparring for advantage back and forth, we finally succeeded in coming to an agreement.[24]

Conferees habitually report back to their respective bodies in tones of despair and fatigue. "It was this bill or nothing," is a refrain echoed again and again in the personal explanations of conferees. In explaining his concurrence to the conference report on the Displaced Persons Act of 1948, Representative Chelf argued that: "we had a gun barrel at our heads . . . it was either this compromise or nothing . . . We did not raise any white flag—had it not been for the time element and immediate adjournment slapping us in the face, I would have hung the jury until Gabriel blew taps on his trumpet. I would never have compromised. I would have demanded the Fellows bill." [25]

One of the best expressions of the weariness usually felt by conferees is made by Representative Carter Manasco when he reported on the Surplus Property Act of 1944: "We thought that the bill as it passed the House was a much better bill than the bill we agreed to, but in 3 weeks' time, when you go up against men who have ideas different from your own, you finally get worn down. I have talked surplus property all day . . . I am tired of it and I want to get rid of it." [26]

The question is often raised as to whether the Senate or the House is stronger in conference committees. Roland Young has answered this question with the assertion that "the Senators are better bargainers than the Representatives in securing both appropriations and legislation." [27] Steiner, in his book on the operations of conference committees, disputes this point of view and after a consideration of 56 pieces of legislation comes to the conclusions that "the influence of the House of Representatives has been found to outweigh that of the Senate to a considerable extent. Thirty-two instances were found wherein House influences dominated the final version of a bill; Senate superiority was

[23] *Congressional Record,* 75th Cong., 3d Sess., June 10, 1938, p. 8738.

[24] *Congressional Record,* 75th Cong., 1st Sess., Aug. 21, 1937, p. 9636.

[25] *Congressional Record,* 80th Cong., 2d Sess., June 18, 1948, p. 8859.

[26] *Congressional Record,* 78th Cong., 2d Sess., Sept. 18, 1944, pp. 7850–7851.

[27] Roland A. Young, "This Is Congress" (New York: Knopf, 1946), p. 233.

found in fifteen cases, while an apparently even break obtained in nine situations."[28] Nevertheless, everything else being equal, the Senators are in a better bargaining position. Of course, everything else is never equal. The major strength of any set of conferees lies in forces beyond themselves and, in fact, outside of either house of Congress. The power line-up in a conference committee can only be appraised in terms of the major social groupings that are actively campaigning on the measure or may be regarded by the conferees as potentially interested in the decisions to be reached. These groups often have more influence on one house than on the other and more on some conferees than on others. Moreover, in the unfolding of any legislative battle, they often change their strategy and objectives as a measure moves from one house to another and then to a conference committee.

New Provisions in Conference Bills

The rules of Congress have almost always contained provisions limiting conferees to the disagreements between the two houses and prohibiting them from bringing in entirely new provisions. These rules have consistently been side-stepped, however, by having one house strike out everything after the enacting clause and offering an amendment in the nature of a substitute. When this happens, everything is technically under disagreement and the conferees are thereby free to start from scratch and write an entirely new measure.

An attempt was made in the Legislative Reorganization Act in 1946 to strengthen the rule by a specific prohibition against the inclusion by conferees in a conference report of "matter not committed to them by either House."[29] However, the same section also provided that the conferees may "include in their report in any such case matter which is a germane modification of subjects in disagreement." This limitation is not much of an obstacle toward the inclusion of new material, for when a subject is in disagreement, almost any change is germane.

In 1938 a Civil Service Retirement Act came from the House with provisions for annuities at the age of sixty, averaging $1,155. The Senate bill provided for annuities averaging $1,090. The conference bill provided for an average annuity of $1,402. In defense of the conference bill, Senator Robert Taft stated:

> It is true that the provision of the conference report results ultimately in a condition somewhat more favorable to the annuitant than resulted from the bill passed either by the House or by the Senate bill, and I think the Senate conferees would have a perfect right to say, "We will take this amendment in some modified form, whether such modified form is more favorable to the employees or less favorable."

[28] Gilbert Y. Steiner, "The Congressional Conference Committee: 70th to 80th Congresses" (Urbana, Ill.: The University of Illinois Press, 1951).

[29] Sec. 135(a).

That does not seem to me to make the report subject to a point of order. One may question the wisdom of the conferees in doing that, but it seems to me there may be circumstances which would lead the Senate to say, "Well, if you are going to change it, we think this is the fair way to change it." So I can see no violation of the La Follette–Monroney Act.[30]

Taft's view was accepted and the bill was approved by voice vote.

When the support for a measure is shaky, however, then it is wise to refrain from introducing new materials. In the development of the Employment Stabilization Act of 1931, the House conferees foresaw that a point of order might be made and sustained against the insertion in the conference bill of a provision for six-year advance planning of public works. Accordingly, the bill was allowed to die in conference. The conference bill was introduced as a new measure. It was then quickly acted upon and passed.

The rules also appear to prohibit conferees from dropping provisions that have previously been agreed upon in both houses. But here again, conferees with adequate support behind them have demonstrated that they have wide latitude whenever the bill adopted by one house is a complete substitute for the one approved in the other house. In the development of the Agricultural Adjustment Act of 1938, Senator McNary and Representative Boileau succeeded in having the Senate and the House respectively adopt an amendment to protect northern dairy-farming interests against the rapid expansion in southern dairy farming. The provision was dropped in the conference committee and a point of order was offered against the conference report on the floor of the Senate. Vice-President Garner ruled against the point of order and explained his action as follows: "It is the reasoning of all the parliamentarians who have ever considered this rule, so far as the Chair can ascertain from all the precedents, that the philosophy should be that where one House passes an entirely new bill as a substitute for the bill of the other House, there is very little limitation placed on the discretion of the conferees, except as to germaneness."[31] He was sustained by a vote of 48 to 31.

Nor do the provisions of the Legislative Reorganization Act of 1946 make any substantial change in this situation. In 1947, when the conference report on the Taft-Hartley Act reached the House, Representative Hoffman of Michigan made a point of order against the section dealing with anti-Communist affidavits. He pointed out that the conference bill had not only inserted new matter but had also eliminated the anti-Communist affidavit as a prerequisite to certification by the National Labor Relations Board for collective-bargaining purposes, a provision that had been previously agreed to in both houses. Overruling the point of order, Speaker Martin explained that "When either branch of Congress strikes out all after the enacting clause of a bill of the other there

[30] *Congressional Record,* 80th Cong., 2d Sess., p. 1740.

[31] *Congressional Record,* 75th Cong., 3d Sess., Feb. 11, 1938, p. 1821.

is unusually wide latitude permitted for the conferees to work on to secure a meeting of the minds between the two bodies." [32]

Formal Influences on Committee Decisions

There is no longer any formal control of committee decisions of the type in existence during the early years of the Republic when committees were set up on the *ad hoc* basis to work out details of measures that had already been agreed upon in general terms on the floor of the House or Senate. Floor control of committee action is now rendered almost impossible by the large and amorphous character of each house as contrasted with the relatively compact character of any committee.

Yet it would be a great error to describe legislative committees of Congress as totally independent, as laws unto themselves. For one thing, members of legislative committees are subjected to a high degree of outside pressure and persuasion from private organizations, executive officials, and other members of Congress. Whether a member of Congress bends like putty under these influences or performs creatively in fashioning an adjustment between competing interests, he operates within an environment that has a marked effect upon his actions. "Independent" is probably the least descriptive adjective that could be used to describe him or his associates.

The formal procedural machinery at times becomes a vehicle for influencing committee decisions. The term "at times" is used advisedly because the formal machinery of the legislative process has no motive power in its own right. It becomes important only when used by forces inside and outside Congress that have their own sources of initiative. The term "influence" is also used advisedly; the word "control" would be an exaggeration. The degree of influence depends upon the amount of power enjoyed by those who use the machinery.

"Instructions" by Resolution

Under the rules of Congress it is perfectly possible for the Senate and the House to pass motions "instructing" legislative committees to do this or that. In actual practice, however, motions to instruct are of only two kinds. The first is a floor motion to recommit a bill to committee with instructions that it bring forth a new bill of a different type. This type of motion is little more than a polite way of applying the kiss of death to a measure on the floor and is discussed in connection with floor operations in Chap. 17. The second is the motion to recommit a bill to conferees with instructions that they bring forth an amended bill. This is the only method of getting a conference bill amended.

[32] *Congressional Record,* 80th Cong., 1st Sess., June 4, 1947, p. 6382.

One of the most effective uses of this latter method occurred in the battle over the Transportation Act of 1940. Representative Harrington had succeeded in having the Committee of the Whole adopt an amendment to the original House bill which would prevent railroad consolidations that might create unemployment among railroad workers. No record vote was attained on this amendment on the floor of the House after the Committee of the Whole had reported. The conferees then dropped this amendment. A motion was then made to recommit the conference bill with instructions that the conferees insist upon the Harrington amendment and two other amendments that had also been made in the Committee of the Whole. This motion was carried by a vote of 209 to 182. Three months later another conference report was brought to the House which included the Harrington amendment but completely eliminated another amendment that had been covered in the motion of instructions. This other amendment had been previously agreed to by both houses in identical form. The second conference report was approved after considerable argumentation in both houses.

Instructions to conferees may also be given before the conference committee starts its work. Such instructions have no binding force, for conferees may violate them without being subjected to a point of order. Moreover, during the course of a conference, the issues may shift in such a way as to render any previous instructions meaningless.

Strenuous objections are usually raised whenever anyone proposes detailed instructions in advance of a conference. When the Senate appointed conferees on the Selective Service Act of 1940, for example, Senator Clark of Missouri moved to instruct the Senate conferees to agree to one House amendment and to refuse to recede at all on one provision of the Senate measure. Senator Burke of Nebraska opposed this motion on the ground that it would not be desirable for the Senate conferees to go to the conference

> bound by any alleged statement made by the chairman of their conferees that they were going to do a certain thing, and with the Senate conferees pledged in advance along a certain line . . . they would meet together with the two bills, the Senate conferees, of course, giving full weight to all the provisions in the Senate bill and the House conferees to their own measure, and then bring back to the respective Houses the best possible bill.[33]

Senator Barkley added that Senate managers "would be woefully handicapped" by instructions that forced them to come back to the Senate and get further instructions before they could negotiate a compromise. The motion to instruct was defeated.

A rather unique form of preconference instructions was developed in the battle over the Transportation Act of 1940. When the House bill came to the

[33] *Congressional Record,* 76th Cong., 3d Sess., p. 11785.

floor of the House, Representative Harrington and his labor supporters suspected that the conferees would drop his amendment for preventing unemployment among railroad workers. Accordingly a petition was circulated reading as follows:

> The undersigned members of the House of Representatives respectfully petition that the Harrington amendment inserted in the Wheeler-Lea Bill, S. 2009, by vote of the House be retained in the conference report. Secondly, we urge and insist in the event you do not retain the Harrington amendment in the conference report that the Harrington amendment be reported in disagreement so that a separate vote on same may be obtained in the House.[34]

The Harrington amendment and other provisions that had been inserted in the Committee of the Whole were dropped in the conference bill. The entire bill was then recommitted with instructions that the deleted provisions be inserted. Three months later a new conference report was brought back which included the Harrington amendment. Thus, the petition device proved a useful one, among other techniques, in developing the campaign on behalf of railroad labor.

"Instructions" by Statute

Perhaps the closest analogy to the ancient system of floor instructions to committees is found in the appropriations process. Appropriations committees are regarded as operating under a framework established by legislation. Their instructions are contained in the statutes authorizing appropriations. These instructions are ironclad when they set a ceiling upon the amount of money that subsequently can be appropriated for a given purpose. The appropriations committees will never report a bill that allocates money in excess of a statutory limit. Ways may be found to achieve the same objective through another method; for example, the appropriation of funds to be channeled to a similar purpose, or the authorizing of a public-debt transaction. But the appropriations committee will never report—and neither house will ever approve—an appropriation measure that directly violates a statutory ceiling.

Attempts have often been made to formulate legislative authorizations that can be regarded as firm commitments to appropriate specified sums of money. But ever since the appropriations function was taken away from the legislative committees and given to the appropriations committees, these attempts have not been successful. Members of appropriations committees have always insisted—and with considerable logic—that, unless there is no real job for the appropriations committees to perform, there is no sense in having separate appropriation bills. And there would be little or no job to perform if measures other than appropriation acts were to contain instructions for specific appropria-

[34] *Congressional Record,* 76th Cong., 3d Sess., p. 5869.

tions as well as ceilings or general authorizations for whatever sums may be subsequently determined necessary and desirable. When one of the appropriations committees brings forth a bill containing a figure lower than the ceiling in the enabling legislation, it usually produces a vehement denunciation of the committee's action as an attempt to "undermine the integrity of legislative committees," [35] or "nullify the action and will of the two Houses and the President." [36]

These arguments are usually countered along the following lines:

> If Congress enacts legislation authorizing an appropriation, is it absolutely binding upon the Appropriations Committees of the two houses and are the Appropriations Committees thereafter foreclosed from looking into the question? . . . I think the time has come when both houses of Congress will have to determine whether or not the Appropriations Committees are merely rubber stamps, or whether they have a duty to look into every appropriation.[37]

The above position has usually emerged victorious. In terms of the actual amounts appropriated, however, the victory of this principle has often been counterbalanced—or one might even say facilitated—by appropriations-committee action to raise the figure in question to the desired level. Whether this is done or not depends upon the amount of power behind the drive for an increased sum, not upon any automatically binding force found in enabling legislation.

On rare occasions a law may contain instructions to specific committees concerning their future legislative activities. When the Revenue Act of 1950 was in its later stages, a sharp controversy arose between those who opposed and those who favored the inclusion of excess-profits-tax provisions. The former fortified their position by promising action on excess profits at a later date and, as a way of making this promise concrete, the following subsection was written into the law:

> The House Committee on Ways and Means and the Senate Committee on Finance are hereby directed to report to the respective Houses of Congress a bill for raising revenue by the levying, collection, and payment of corporate excess profits taxes with retroactive effect to October 1, or July 1, 1950, said bill shall be reported as early as practicable during the Eighty-first Congress after November 15, 1950, if the Congress is in session in 1950 after such date; and if the Congress is not in session after November 15, 1950, said bill shall be reported during the first session of the Eighty-second Congress, and as early as practicable during said session.[38]

[35] Representative Clifford R. Hope of Kansas in debate on agriculture appropriation bill, *Congressional Record,* 80th Cong., 1st Sess., Vol. 93, pp. 5874*ff*.

[36] Senator Carl A. Hatch of New Mexico in debate on Greek-Turkish aid appropriation, *Congressional Record,* 80th Cong., 1st Sess., p. 5482.

[37] Senator Homer Ferguson of Michigan in debate on Greek-Turkish aid appropriation, *Congressional Record,* 80th Cong., 1st Sess., pp. 5482–5483.

[38] Sec. 701(a).

The instructions were complied with faithfully. An excess-profits-tax bill was reported out during December, 1950, and the final legislation was in fact retroactive to July 1, 1950.

Discharge Action

Floor action to "discharge" a bill from a committee that has been refusing to report it out is a blunderbuss weapon through which a majority on the floor of either house can attempt to influence committee decisions. In the Senate any member theoretically can move to discharge a bill from a committee and a majority vote will do the job. Actually, such motions are practically never made. It is always more feasible to seek the same objective through a motion to take a bill out of one committee and refer it to another. In the House it takes a petition signed by a large number of members—currently 218—to bring such a motion up for a vote.[39]

During the twenty-year span from the beginning of the Seventy-first Congress to the end of the Eightieth Congress, 252 discharge petitions were filed in the House but only 29 of these obtained enough signatures to be printed on the calendar. Only 15 bills were discharged from committees.[40] Although most of the bills that were discharged from committees during this period were passed by the House, only one of them, the Wages and Hours Act of 1937, became law—and this was a measure that was discharged from the Rules Committee rather than from a legislative committee.[41] The indirect effect of the discharge operations in the House, however, has probably been greater than this record indicates. The threat of a discharge maneuver has often served to

[39] See Floyd Riddick, "The United States Congress: Organization and Procedure" (Washington, D.C.: National Capitol Publishers, 1949), pp. 241–253, for a detailed historical summary of various changes in the number of names required on the petition. The discharge rule was first adopted in 1910 as part of a coalition attack on the House leadership. The most recent change took place in the 74th Congress when the Democratic leadership succeeded in having the number of names required on a discharge petition raised from 145 to 218.

[40] *Ibid.*, p. 256.

[41] ". . . it seems quite unlikely that any legislation of the type of the wage and hour bill would have been enacted at that session if it had not been for Senator Pepper's victory in the Florida Democratic Primary. The House Labor Committee had already reported out a new bill but it was resting in its usual pigeon-hole in the Rules Committee. Senator Pepper's victory, after a campaign in which the Bill had been an issue, served to open the floodgates, and when the petition to discharge the Rules Committee was opened for signature the required number of names were secured in two hours and 20 minutes. The favorable poll of the Institute of Public Opinion undoubtedly had its effect, also." Louise Stitt, *Law and Contemporary Problems,* "Legislative History of the Fair Labor Standards Act," Vol. 6, No. 3, Summer, 1939, pp. 471–472.

accelerate committee action and even to force committee members to beat a discharge petition to the draw.

There are three disadvantages in the discharge approach. First, a bill that is discharged cannot be perfected through the use of minor amendments and the perfecting process is thrown open on the floor of the house. Second, the members of a committee can beat a discharge petition to the draw by amending the measure in a substantial fashion and then reporting quickly. Third, members of a committee can anticipate this action by reporting a bill out with an unfavorable recommendation and a strong report urging its defeat.

Discharge petitions often serve little purpose other than to allow members of Congress to convince various organizations that they are trying to put up a real fight. For many years in succession discharge petitions have been filed to force out of the House Ways and Means Committee legislation to put into effect the Townsend Plan for old-age pensions. In 1939, this effort forced members of the Ways and Means Committee to counter with an unfavorable report on the Townsend bill. But by 1950 the operation had become a routine affair. An inquiring Washington reporter diagnosed the failure of the discharge petitions as follows:

"As new names go on top of his petition, the old names strangely drop off the bottom. Some party regulars who sign, to add another string to their political bow, are gently 'persuaded to withdraw.' "[42]

In the 1948 struggle over legislation to turn over tideland oils to the states, a dramatic maneuver was attempted by Senator Sheridan Downey of California. The House had already approved a bill to accomplish this objective but the members of the Senate Judiciary Committee were stalling. When the House bill came to the Senate, Downey took advantage of an obscure Senate rule which, on the objection of a single Senator, would keep a House-approved bill on the calendar instead of allowing it to be referred to a committee. The same bill had already been passed by the Senate as well as by the House in the previous year and its enactment was held up only by Presidential veto. Thus, Downey was confident that a majority vote could easily be mustered to support his move. "If the Judiciary Committee does not report the bill in time for the Senate to express its will upon it," explained Downey, "the Senate will then have two methods by which to proceed—either a motion to discharge the committee, or, if this bill is still upon the calendar, a motion to make it the business of the Senate."[43] A few weeks later the Senate Judiciary Committee reported the measure favorably by a close vote of 6 to 5. Because of the imminent end of the session and the certainty of a Presidential veto, the committee bill was allowed to die on the calendar instead of being brought up for a vote.

[42] Robert C. Albright, "Townsend Plan Skeleton Is Rattling," *The Washington Post*, Apr. 2, 1950.

[43] *Congressional Record* (daily edition), May 3, 1948, p. 5297.

This, however, does not minimize the importance of the Downey maneuver as a method of forcing committee action.

Leadership Influence

The distinction should always be kept in mind between the formal *techniques* of influencing committee action and the formal *leadership agencies*—the President, the Speaker of the House, the President of the Senate, the majority and minority leaders, and the majority and minority policy or steering committees—that have prerogatives to influence congressional action.

Motions to instruct or discharge, as formal techniques of directly influencing committees, are usually used by groups other than the leadership agencies. In fact, they often become instruments in the hands of those who seek to weaken, frustrate, or circumvent the formal leadership of Congress. The official leaders of Congress, on the other hand, make only occasional use of these direct techniques. The procedural methods available to them are for the most part of an indirect character. Presidents influence committee action, through the use, or threatened use, of the Presidential veto. This is discussed in detail in Chap 18. The Speaker of the House and the President of the Senate can influence committee action through decisions on the referral of bills as explained in an earlier section of this chapter. The Speaker may also hold up action on a bill that has been passed by the Senate. This was done by Speaker Sam Rayburn in 1946 when he refused to refer the Senate version of the Legislative Reorganization Act to the appropriate committee until agreements had been negotiated to make a number of specific changes in which he was interested. The power of floor recognition is still another technique available to the Speaker for the purpose of influencing committee action.

In so far as party leadership and party-leadership committees are concerned, there are three principal circumstances under which they can affect committee decisions. The first is the selection of committee members and chairmen. When party leadership can determine the personnel of committees, committees become in large part the servants of party leadership. But, as explained in an earlier section of this chapter, the structure of congressional-committee power is usually in the hands of party leadership only in a nominal sense.

The second is control of the floor schedules. To the extent that party leaders can decide which bills may or may not come up for discussion and action on the floor, they can indirectly affect the substantive provisions of committee bills. Favored measures can be given the green light. Unfavored measures can be allowed to die on the calendars. Naturally, the more crowded the calendars are, the more effective this technique becomes. In the House of Representatives the Rules Committee has long enjoyed a high degree of monopoly over this function. In fact, the House Rules Committee has become a leadership institution which often rivals or even outshines and counterbalances the Speaker and the party leaders.[44] An interesting example of how this committee can affect the details of committee action was provided at the end of the Seventy-ninth Congress when the House Ways and Means Committee reported a social-security bill containing equalization provisions to favor areas of the country in greatest financial need. The majority of the House Rules Committee refused to grant this measure a rule unless the equalizations provisions were deleted. The Ways and Means Committee made the amendment and the rule was obtained.

The third is the use of party caucuses to bind all party members to support or oppose a specific action. This device is used infrequently. Because of internal party divisions, caucuses are not held very often and when they are held, it is generally for the purpose of discussing issues rather than reaching a firm party line. Furthermore, the caucus is only rarely used on matters that are directly before a congressional committee. Most caucuses are concerned with measures that have already been processed by committees. Caucus influence, therefore, is necessarily of an indirect character.

An attempt to establish a formal procedure for directly influencing committee action was made in the Employment Act of 1946. Under this legislation, a Joint Committee on the Economic Report would issue reports to "serve as a guide to the several committees of the Congress dealing with legislation" affecting employment, production, and purchasing power. To enhance the prestige and expand the work program of this group, provisions were made for reference to it at the beginning of each year of the President's annual economic program. Although the Committee has issued many reports, there is no evidence to indicate that they have really served "as a guide to the several committees of the Congress." On February 11, 1948, for example, the Joint Committee issued a report recommending allocation powers for the use of grain as part of a program to cope with inflationary trends. In the House of Representatives, the vice-chairman of this Joint Committee, Representative Wolcott of Michigan, was himself the chairman of the committee handling this proposal. However, Wolcott's own committee never even held hearings on the measure and allowed it to die a swift death.

[44] With all the criticism that has been heaped upon the head of the Rules Committee in recent years, it is interesting to note that early in the twentieth century there were those who viewed it as the great solution to the problem of effective leadership in the House. "Here," stated McConachie, "is the new central instrument for equitable and economical distribution of the annual revenue among the great governmental interests. . . . Here is a revival and perpetuation of that unity of lawmaking which characterized those first years when the Committee of the Whole on the State of the Union held the primacy for the formulation of laws. A better century has begun, wherein the American House of Representatives will express more readily and truly the more easily known will of the people." "Congressional Committees" (New York: Crowell, 1898), pp. 206–207.

This listing of the formal techniques available to official leadership agencies should not obscure the fact that these agencies have many informal weapons at their disposal. Essentially, these are the same weapons used by many other participants in the legislative struggle: the organization of group support, the production and dissemination of propaganda, and the development and application of pressure. In fact, the ultimate power of formal leadership agencies to influence committee action depends fundamentally upon the extent to which they become part of a legislative campaign. Official leaders have often been charged with incompetence, deviousness, or downright insincerity for their failure to get committees to do things which, under the existing line-up of social forces, no leaders could ever get them to do. In the same way, various leaders have been branded as "czars" or "dictators" when they have merely served as the instruments for achieving what no one could have prevented.

The power of leadership does not lie in office alone. It lies in the men who are involved and the forces with which they work. At times, the leaders seem to have complete control. Henry Clay, as Speaker of the House, it has been said, "framed his committees so as to force an English war." [45] During the Civil War, Lincoln dominated congressional decisions as had no President before him. During the years immediately after the Civil War, when the frustrated Andrew Johnson took over the Presidency, Thaddeus Stevens, the leader of the Republican radicals, "ruled not only the South but the National Government, through a junto or 'directory,' as Johnson correctly charged. From 1866 to 1868, the year of his death, Stevens, as a sort of prime minister for Congress, virtually ruled in place of the repudiated President, even holding the country's moneybags in his hands." [46]

In the early days of the Republic, according to Harlow, "committees became in a way the specialized agents of the majority, just as they were of the House, and of the executive." [47] According to Harlow, "The real work of legislation was put into shape, not in the legislature, but in secret session of the majority party. In this organization, unknown to the Constitution and beyond the reach of the rules of either chamber, the executive could work with the party following in Congress, and secure the adoption of a pre-arranged program." [48]

And yet one can readily select other periods in history when on a great bulk of legislative measures this picture would be the opposite of the true one. It is unrealistic to talk about the power of leadership in any fixed and static sense. Sometimes it flows through the leaders and sometimes around them. The leaders sometimes seize control and sometimes fail to attain it and sometimes never

[45] Hubert Bruce Fuller, "The Speakers of the House" (Boston: Little, Brown, 1909), p. 273.

[46] Matthew Josephson, "The Politicos" (New York: Harcourt, Brace, 1938), p. 38.

[47] Ralph V. Harlow, "The History of Legislative Methods in the Period Before 1825" (New Haven, Conn.: Yale University Press, 1917), p. 208.

[48] *Ibid.*, p. 145.

try. Moreover, in any given year, the power of leadership over congressional committees shifts from issue to issue. There are all sorts of delicate changes in the structure of power which make it impossible to discuss leadership influence or control in terms of static reference to 1910, to 1946, or to any other specific period, or in terms of Clay, Stevens, or Cannon. The history of leadership influence can be discussed only through full examination of the legislative campaigns as they unfold at specific periods of time, truly a vast and challenging field for historical and political research.

Chapter 17

THE RANGE OF CHOICE ON THE FLOOR

A GOOD WAY *not* to find out what is happening on the floor of either house is to check on the regular order of business.[1] The regular order merely provides a point of departure from which special business is taken up out of order. Few members in either house ever keep track of such recondite information as what the regular order, if followed, would lead to next. To make matters still more like the topsy-turvy world of Alice-in-Wonderland, one of the key devices for departing from the regular order is to recess at the end of the day instead of adjourn. This means that the so-called "legislative day" has not ended. Rather, it keeps on going. Hence when the body meets the next calendar day, there is no need to take up the first items on the regular order of business. It is perfectly proper under the rules for a legislative day to last weeks.

Nor are the rules themselves much of a guide. In both houses they are frequently suspended, evaded, or broken. This is particularly true of the Senate. "Rules are never observed in this body, a President pro tempore of the Senate

[1] Under Rule XXIV of the House, the regular order runs as follows:

First. Prayer by the chaplain.
Second. Reading and approval of the Journal.
Third. Correction of reference of public bills.
Fourth. Disposal of business on the Speaker's table.
Fifth. Unfinished business.
Sixth. The Morning Hour for the consideration of bills called up by committees.
Seventh. Motions to go into Committee of the Whole House on the State of the Union.
Eighth. Order of the day.

While the Senate rules are not so specific, they provide the basis for an order of business somewhat as follows:

First. Morning Hour.
Prayer by the chaplain.
Reading and correction of the journal.
Presiding Officer presents business to the Senate.
Presiding Officer calls for morning business.
Second. Call of the Calendar.
Third. Unfinished business.
Fourth. Motions to proceed to the consideration of executive business.

once observed. "They are only made to be broken. We are a law unto ourselves." [2] In the House, new rules have been written to evade rather than change old rules. A good example is the use of fictions concerning operations on the floor of the House. In order to get around certain requirements on quorums and record votes, the House can meet not only as the House but also in three masquerades—as the Committee of the Whole, the Committee of the Whole House on the State of the Union, and "in House as in the Committee of Whole."

Like the Constitution, the rules of Congress need interpretation. They tend to be what the presiding officers say they are. The source for their rulings are the precedents of the House and Senate,[3] which are comparable to the decisions of the Supreme Court. Moreover, as complex as they are, the rules have not been fashioned to deal with all situations. Traditions and usages, leavened with recurring innovation, fill many a gap.

The first step in understanding floor action is to find out how the participants in the legislative struggle handle rules, precedents, and usages in getting bills to the floor and how, once a bill is on the floor, they choose among the alternative types of decisions available to them.

Getting to the Floor

"The running of trains on a single-track railroad may be likened to the passage of measures through the House," an able observer once wrote in language that is equally applicable to both houses. "The freight gives way to a local passenger train, which sidetracks for an express, which in turn sidetracks for the limited, while all usually keep out of the way of a relief train. Meantime, when a train having the right of way passes, the delayed ones begin to move until again obliged to sidetrack. . . ." [4]

To make the simile still more apt, one should assume that this railroad has no fixed schedule of priorities. One should think of many trains being run by canny engineers who will try to hold back on some occasions and to plow ahead on others. One should then visualize a tremendous number of trains lined up in the railroad yard, with their crews eager to devise means of

[2] J. J. Ingalls, *Congressional Record,* 44th Cong., 2d Sess., Dec. 18, 1876, p. 266.

[3] The House precedents have been compiled by Asher C. Hinds and Rep. Clarence Cannon, respectively, in "House Precedents" and "Cannon's Procedure in the House of Representatives" (U.S. Government Printing Office). The Senate precedents, however, are the private property of the Senate Parliamentarian, who keeps them in a card index. The last available analysis of Senate precedents is Henry H. Gilfrey's, "Precedents, Decisions on Points of Order, with Phraseology, in the United States Senate, 1789–1913," which was published by the Government Printing Office in 1914.

[4] De Alva S. Alexander, "History and Procedure of the House of Representatives" (Boston: Houghton Mifflin, 1916), p. 222.

getting a favorable signal and with gangs of switchmen roaming the yards making efforts to assure that certain trains are permanently sidetracked. Finally, one should realize that every week new trains are lined up in the yards and that every week brings closer the end of the Congress when the yards and tracks are all completely cleared and the entire process of lining-up starts over again.

While the term "legislative graveyard" is probably best suited to describe the standing committees of Congress, where about nine out of ten bills die for lack of committee action, the death rate at the calendar stage is far from negligible. As a result of congestion, accidental collision, or purposeful maneuvering, from one to three out of ten bills reported by committees die silently at the end of every Congress. Even bills that have been passed by one house run the risk of dying on a calendar of the other house. Conference-committee bills, however, are invariably brought up for action.

When to Get There

On some measures there is little problem of deciding upon the best time to obtain floor consideration. "Never" is the best time for a bill one wants to kill. "Any time" is the best for a bill that is in serious danger of dying on the calendar. For measures on which the continuation of vital government activities depends—legislative vetoes that must be approved within a given number of days, crisis bills, or bills that have been reported at the end of a Congress—the best time is "the sooner the better."

With the competition for floor time as keen as it is, however, the best time is often impossible to achieve and the participants in the legislative struggle are faced with the problem of judging between second, third, and fourth choices. On other types of measures the margin of choice is still greater. Between the extremes of "never," "any time," and "the sooner the better" there is a broad area of choice and maneuver.

At what point during a session of a Congress is it most desirable to bring a bill to the floor? Early consideration has distinct advantages. The first weeks of a Congress provide the best occasion to fight off a filibuster. Early consideration allows time to handle sharp attacks and to deal with proposed amendments. Consideration near the end of a session provides an ideal opportunity to kill a measure by insisting on protracted discussion in the Senate even though such discussions are not carried to the extreme of a filibuster. It also provides an opportunity to slip measures through unnoticed. During the last hectic days of a session, when members are tired out and anxious to leave, many a bill can be passed that could never hope to receive favorable consideration during the middle of the session.

Delay toward the end of a session also provides an ideal opportunity for avoiding a conference committee by forcing compliance by the other house. An interesting example of this tactic is the 1947 legislation providing for an elected government in Puerto Rico. In response to the desires of local Republicans in Puerto Rico, Senator Robert Taft was eager to have the legislation include a provision for Presidential appointment of members of the Puerto Rico Supreme Court. This provision was not in the bill which passed the House. It was left out of the bill in the Senate committee because of the danger that it would send the bill to conference and a conference delay would prevent action at the First Session of the Eightieth Congress. Therefore, when the bill came up on the Consent Calendar somewhat earlier in the session, Senator Taft objected to its consideration. At the very last moment of the last day, however, he called it off the calendar himself, moved the amendment, and had the bill passed in the form he wanted it. It was then sent to the House of Representatives which concurred without asking for a conference because there were only a few minutes remaining before the session was to be adjourned.

Delay also proves useful—paradoxically enough—on matters of great urgency. By keeping a bill off the floor for a required length of time, an important measure may be transformed into an urgent one, urgency may be transformed into emergency, and emergency may be made into crisis. Delays of this sort are particularly useful in the case of measures to renew expiring programs. When there is still ample time for action before the expiration date, the opponents of renewal are in a stronger position. On the very eve of an expiration date, however, tables are often completely turned and the proponents are in a dominating position. This has been illustrated again and again in the extension of various control operations such as rent control, export control, and mandatory priorities and allocations initiated during World War II. In these cases the strategy of delay necessarily ties in with the timing of committee action.

Another consideration is timing of floor action in relation to elections and primaries. Congressional elections always take place in November of even-numbered years, usually at the end of the second regular session of every Congress. Primaries are strung out from February to September of the same years. Here again the question of timing relates to the introduction of measures, committee action, and floor action. Floor action is particularly important for members who face difficult primary or election contests. What one says or does on the floor of either house is important news to people back home. It is, therefore, natural for many members to be interested in timing floor consideration in a manner that will be most helpful to themselves. In some cases this involves keeping measures on the calendar until the strategic moment. In others, when the contemplated matter might prove distasteful to constituents, it involves early floor consideration (in the hope that dissatisfied constituents will forget by the time elections roll around) or postponement until after the elections. A typical example of the latter was the Truman Administration's efforts to prevent excess-profits-tax proposals from being considered on the floor of Congress before the 1950 elections. The best way to handle the matter, President Truman was reported as saying at a press conference, would be to wait until after "the election jitters were over."

There is also the problem of relating action in one house to action in the other house. It is sometimes extremely advantageous to call a bill up for consideration first in the house in which it stands a better chance of favorable action. In 1950 President Truman sent to Congress a reorganization plan to curtail the powers of the General Counsel of the National Labor Relations Board. The Administration and organized-labor groups favored this plan and attempted to have a resolution of approval brought up first in the House of Representatives where it had more support, and subsequently in the Senate, where it had less support. The object was to confront the Senate with a House-approved measure. This strategy was frustrated by the insistence of the chairman of the House Appropriations Committee in bringing up an appropriations measure first and by the diligence of the antilabor organizations in speeding up Senate action. The Senate disapproved the plan before the House could get around to acting upon it and since the disapproval of one house is sufficient as a legislative veto, the matter ended there.

Labor groups have often sought House action first for an entirely different reason. In the case of legislation restricting the rights of organized labor, they have usually felt that the liberal forces in the Senate would be in a stronger position if they came into the game later and acted to modify House-enacted provisions. This route was followed again and again in the long series of bills that culminated in the Taft-Hartley Act. The fact that it would tend to give the Senators an upper hand is evidenced by Representative Hartley's frequent but futile insistence that House action should be delayed until after the Senate had passed a bill.

At one point during the history of the struggle over FEPC legislation, factional controversies broke out around the question of "Senate or House first?"

> The National Council (for a Permanent FEPC) felt that success in the House would be comparatively easy to achieve, but that Southern opposition in the Senate was the major stumbling block and unless overcome first, the work on the House of Representatives would go for naught. The left-wingers, conversely, agreed with the American Jewish Congress and several other groups which urged the "House-first" approach. . . . The National Negro Congress asserted in this connection: "It is well known that any bill which has passed one House of Congress has the better chance of passing the other. Hostility in the Senate has been so marked as to make approval of the House almost a necessity before passage by the Senate can be expected." [5]

[5] Louis C. Kesselman, "Social Politics of FEPC" (Chapel Hill, N.C.: University of North Carolina Press, 1948), p. 158.

The above questions are in many ways similar to those faced in the introduction of measures and the scheduling of committee operations. There are others, however, that are more directly geared to the specific terrain of floor consideration. One problem relates to whether one bill should be called up before or after another measure. There are occasions when the best time to consider one subject is in the lull immediately before the consideration of a major measure which will monopolize attention for days or weeks. There are other situations in which the best time to seek action is after a major conflict has been fought and before all the participants can recover from battle fatigue. When two committees have reported rival bills, the advantage often goes to the first brought up for consideration. As in the case of the involved struggle over the War Mobilization and Reconversion Act already referred to, the measure which comes up first is in the favored position. The proponents of the second bill are then put in the position of having to offer primary floor amendments. The supporters of the first measure can then come back with secondary amendments. Since tertiary amendments cannot be offered under the rules, proponents of the secondary amendments are in the position of having the crucial votes taken on their proposals on ground of their own choosing.

Still another problem is providing time for preparation. A bill is sometimes reported from a committee before a formal committee report has been prepared. Still more frequently bills are reported and committee reports submitted before their key supporters have readied their formal talks, prepared formal floor statements, acquainted themselves with the kinds of problems that might arise on the floor, or mapped out their floor strategy. Under these circumstances, a certain amount of delay is essential to adequate presentation.

Another problem relates to floor attendance. One of the most humorous events ever to take place on the floor of the Senate occurred in 1946 when Senator Wayne Morse noticed that, as a result of a protracted harangue by Senator William Langer, all the other members of the Senate except the Presiding Officer, Langer, and himself had left the floor. Taking advantage of this situation, he asked unanimous consent that the anti-poll-tax bill be called off the calendar. "I believe that we are in a position to save the Senate a great deal of time," he quipped, "inasmuch as the Senator and I are about the only members of the Senate now present on the floor." [6] The highly controversial anti-poll-tax bill would then and there have passed the Senate had not some Senate employees who were friendly with the Southern Democrats collared a Democratic Senator and rushed him to the floor to voice a quick objection.

A less playful but somewhat similar maneuver was attempted by Senator McCarran of Nevada in 1949 when he moved to disagree to the House-amended version of the basing-point bill. McCarran had earlier promised the opponents of this legislation, many of whom believed the House version to be more

[6] *Congressional Record,* 79th Cong., 2d Sess., Apr. 18, 1946, p. 3971.

acceptable than any bill that might emerge from a conference committee, that he would inform them before he called the House version up for consideration. On July 26, however, he suddenly called the bill up, moved that it be sent to conference, and secured agreement without objection. "It was my understanding," Senator Long of Louisiana subsequently protested, "that we were to be notified before a motion was made to send that bill to conference. . . . I thought we were to be notified and I was on my way to the Senate chamber at the time the motion was made." [7] McCarran explained his action by pointing out that various opponents of the bill, including Senator Kefauver of Tennessee, were on the floor when the motion was made. Senator Kefauver retorted by charging that McCarran had made his motion in a low tone of voice. "It is true that the junior Senator from Tennessee was on the floor at the time," he added, "but he was talking to the distinguished Presiding Officer at the moment and did not hear the motion. For that matter, several other Senators who are interested in the matter did not hear the motion, either." [8] The issue was then fought out on a motion to reconsider the Senate's action. This was a highly favorable situation for McCarran. Under the Senate rules, a motion to table a motion to reconsider is not debatable, and McCarran thus had the decisive power to shut off debate at any time. If notice had been given in the original motion or if it had been made in a louder voice, the debate would have taken place under circumstances that would have allowed Long, Kefauver, and their colleagues to stall action indefinitely by protracted discussion. The motion to reconsider failed.

A similar tactic was attempted when the conference bill came to the Senate later in the year. Here the effort was made to have the conference bill called up for consideration and acted upon so quickly that its opponents would not realize what had happened. Earl Latham gives this story in detail:

> With the submission of the conference report to the Senate, the opponents of S. 1108 had picked up another ally—time. The Senate was in the last days of the First Session of the Eighty-first Congress, and the Congressmen wanted to expedite their business in order to get home. O'Connor was reported to be confident that he had enough votes to push the bill through. The pressure was so great that the sponsors of the conference report actually managed to slip it through the Senate in a Saturday night session with what Douglas described as "supersonic speed." The action was recalled by the timely attentiveness of Douglas and Long. The Senator from Illinois said that he and Long were standing close to the Chair, but even could not hear the question which was stated, and "we were startled by the almost instantaneous announcement that the report had been agreed to." [9]

[7] *Congressional Record,* 81st Cong., 1st Sess., July 26, 1949, p. 10150.

[8] *Ibid.,* p. 10151.

[9] Earl Latham, "The Group Basis of Politics" (Ithaca, N.Y.: Cornell University Press, 1952), p. 153.

The opponents of the conference bill then succeeded in having its consideration postponed until the beginning of the next year.

How to Get There

How to bell the cat? This is often more difficult than judging the most desirable time to do it.

In the House of Representatives, with its large membership, there has evolved the following exceedingly complex system of rules and usages governing the methods of calling a bill up for consideration: (1) All bills that might be brought before the House are generally classifiable into six types. (2) Some of these bills are highly privileged, others not. (3) Some can be brought up on special days only. (4) Any other bills must be brought up by special orders of the House.

In the smaller-sized Senate, the members work things out with a minimum degree of formality.

Classification of House Bills. All bills that are reported out by committees are divided into (a) public bills dealing with appropriations or revenue, (b) other public bills, and (c) private bills. These three sets of bills are listed in the order in which they are reported. The lists are called, respectively, the "Union Calendar," the "House Calendar," and the "Private Calendar." Any bill on the first or second of these calendars may, if there is no objection, be placed on a fourth list called the "Consent Calendar." A fifth list is the "Discharge Calendar." As explained in Chap. 16, any bill still in committee can be listed on this calendar when a petition with the required number of signatures has been filed with the Clerk of the House. A sixth list is for those bills which come from the President with a veto message, from a conference committee, or, after previous passage, from the other house in amended form. These bills are referred to as "on the Speaker's Table," a calendar by another name.

This process of classification is largely automatic. The only variations for the first three lists are borderline cases. Here the decisions are made by the Clerk of the House. Any member is free to have any bill already on the Union or House Calendars placed on the Consent Calendar. This apparently broad discretion is limited by the fact that subsequently a single objection can prevent it from being taken off the calendar. Controversial bills are thereby excluded and the problem of judgment and choice relates to deciding whether or not to place on the Consent Calendar bills that are slightly controversial. In so far as the Discharge Calendar and the Speaker's Table are concerned, there are no choices and no borderline cases.

Privileged Bills in the House. Special attention is given to revenue-raising bills from the Ways and Means Committee, general appropriation bills from the Appropriations Committee, rivers and harbors bills from the Public Works Committee, and certain bills from the Public Lands and Veterans' Affairs Committees. These committees have the "right to report at any time" on such measures and this right has come to mean consideration at the same time the report is made. This places considerable power over the timing of floor consideration in the hands of the chairman and the dominant group in these four committees. When there are competing claims among these committees, the Speaker uses his power of recognition to favor one or the other. "Any time," however, really means at any time except when business of high precedence is being considered or motions of higher precedence are offered.[10]

Still more highly privileged are measures on the Speaker's Table. Veto messages are promptly presented to the House when received, and action to sustain or override the veto is immediately in order. Consideration can be avoided only by a motion to lay on the table, postpone action, or refer the bill back to a committee. Conference bills can be presented to the House for action at almost any time deemed desirable by the House conference and the party leadership. A request to take up a House bill that has been amended by the Senate is usually coupled with a unanimous consent request to concur or to disagree and ask for a conference. This request must be made by the appropriate committee. If there is objection, the bill can then be called up under a special order from the Rules Committee. Senate-passed bills similar to bills already on the House Calendar can also be called up by the appropriate committee. This means that fast Senate action is one of the best ways to expedite floor consideration in the House.

Special Days in the House. All the bills on the Consent, Private, and Discharge Calendars are specially favored in that specific days of the month are set aside for their consideration. Bills on the Consent Calendar can be taken up on the first and third Mondays of every month, bills on the Private Calendar on the first and third Tuesdays, and bills on the Discharge Calendar on the second and fourth Mondays.

These bills are favored in a limited sense only. When the Consent Calendar

[10] The precedence of business in the House is as follows: "1. Reception of messages. 2. Oath. 3. Quorum. 4. Presentation of conference reports. 5. Adjournment. 6. Entering motion to reconsider. 7. Organization of House. 8. Impeachment. 9. Journal. 10. Election cases. 11. Vetoed bills. 12. Electoral vote. 13. Adjournment or recess of Congress. 14. Privilege. 15. Change of reference to calendars. 16. Calendar Wednesday. 17. Call of Private Calendar. 18. Change of reference to committees. 19. Consideration of conference reports. 20. Reconsideration. 21. Report from Committee on Rules. 22. Special orders. 23. Suspension of rules. 24. Propositions coming over with previous question ordered. 25. Resolutions of enquiry. 26. Amendments in disagreement. 27. Motions to go into Committee of Whole for consideration of revenue and appropriation bills. 28. Bills privileged under right to report at any time. 29. Census. 30. Motions to discharge committees. 31. District Monday. 32. Consent Calendar. 33. Senate bills on Speaker's Table similar to bills on House Calendar. 34. Disposition of Messages." Cannon, *op. cit.*, p. 241.

is ready the Speaker asks: "Is there objection to the present consideration of the bill?" A single objection means that the House moves on to the next bill on the list. Every member thus has a personal veto to use at his discretion.[11] Moreover, the majority and minority leaders customarily assign a few members as "official objectors" to serve as watchdogs and to voice objections, when desirable, on behalf of the party or of absent party members. Accordingly, there is a considerable amount of horse trading and maneuvering surrounding the use of objections. To get a member, for example, to withdraw his objection to bill A, it is sometimes necessary for the sponsor of bill A to withdraw his objection to bill B so that the sponsor of bill B will withdraw his objection to bill C which is close to the heart of the original objector to bill A.

Bills on the Private Calendar are subject to the same procedure. In addition, on the second of the two days per month allotted to this calendar, the Speaker may at his own discretion dispense with this item entirely and recognize members offering motions for other privileged business.

There are two possible obstacles to calling up for consideration a bill that has been listed on the Discharge Calendar. First, under the rules a bill must have been on the Discharge Calendar seven legislative days in order to be called up when Discharge Day rolls around. During this interval the bill can be reported in amended form—and the amendments can make it substantially different—by the committee that had previously failed to act. In this event, the bill would have to be called up from another calendar. A more devious form of circumvention is also possible through the extreme device of recessing the House so that seven legislative days will not be allowed to occur before Discharge Day. This strategy was successfully used in 1934 when the House leadership was eager to stave off action on the Lemke-Frazier farm bill. The Speaker ruled that seven legislative days had not elapsed, even though nine actual days had gone by.[12] His ruling stood unchallenged. By the time of the next Discharge Day, the House had adjourned.

The second obstacle is that the signatures on the petition will not by themselves guarantee consideration of the bill. These signatures must be translated into a majority vote when the actual motion to discharge is made. This calls for a continued campaign. When the motion came up in 1950 to force the discharge of legislation to restore curtailed postal services, Representative Miller of California sounded the call as follows: "I ask the members who have had

[11] It is interesting to speculate on what might happen in the House if some member should someday choose to make frequent use of this veto. Theoretically, he could force less extensive use of the Consent Calendar, or else wrest innumerable concessions from other members on matters in which he was personally interested. Practically, however, every member has such a personal vested interest in having certain measures brought up from the Consent Calendar without objection that he will object to consideration of someone else's bill only when there are clear and present pressures favoring such a step.

[12] *Congressional Record,* 73d Cong., 2d Sess., June 11, 1934, pp. 11063–11065.

the courage to sign this discharge petition to stick with their first and sound decision."[13] The 249 to 81 record vote to take up the bill was testimony to the effectiveness of the postal-clerk campaign that underpinned the gentleman's rallying cry.[14]

There are two other days on which certain bills have a special chance to be considered: District of Columbia Day and Calendar Wednesday. The purpose of the former, which occurs on the second and fourth Mondays of each month, is to provide for the concentrated handling of the many measures rendered necessary by the lack of local self-government in the nation's capital. It is used only when the members of the District of Columbia Committee desire.

The purpose of the latter is to give the various standing committees a chance to call up bills that are not highly privileged in themselves or that have not been given a green light by the Rules Committee.[15] Under it, the committees are called in alphabetical order, and debate on any measure is for all practical purposes limited to one Wednesday. Because of the pressure of urgent business and because of the awkwardness of a procedure under which any given committee may not be called upon for a dozen or more Wednesdays, this procedure is rarely attempted. Moreover, attempts to use it can be frustrated by adjournments and dilatory tactics. A classic example occurred in 1945 when Chairman Mary Norton of the House Labor Committee was trying to obtain consideration of FEPC legislation.

[13] *Congressional Record,* 81st Cong., 2d Sess., Aug. 14, 1950, p. 12449.

[14] An additional obstacle was faced in this case. Since it was the Rules Committee that was being discharged, the result of the above vote was to bring before the House a special order outlining the manner in which the postal-services bill would be considered. This resolution provided that upon the following day Rep. John Walsh of Indiana, the leading proponent of the bill from the Committee on the Post Office and Civil Service (the chairman of the committee had opposed the measure), would be recognized by the Speaker to call up the measure. Rep. Walsh at this moment happened to be on his way to Wisconsin for a radio speech. Without his presence, the rule would be inoperative. This came as a rude shock to Walsh, who had not known that he would have to be on the House floor—and, in fact, the rule was probably designed by Rules Committee members who knew Walsh was away and hoped to catch him off guard. At the last moment, however, Walsh found out what had happened and succeeded in making an airplane connection that brought him back in time to save the day.

[15] The first Calendar Wednesday rule was adopted under Speaker Cannon's guidance in 1909 as a sop to the Republican insurgents. They, in turn, attacked it as inadequate and as threatening to defeat real reform in the rules. "A homeopathic dose of nothingness," George Norris branded it. (*Congressional Record,* 60th Cong., 2d Sess., p. 3150.) Shortly thereafter the Cannon organization itself tried to weaken the Calendar Wednesday rule by bringing up a census bill early on a Wednesday. There ensued a historic debate on whether or not a privileged bill could interfere with Calendar Wednesday. The Republican insurgents and certain Democrats were now in the position of defending the new procedure. It was the overruling of the Speaker's ruling on this matter, by a vote of 163 to 112, that made the first crack in the structure of the Cannon organization and gave Norris the signal for the introduction of his famous resolution to depose Cannon as chairman of the Rules Committee.

On Tuesday, September 25, when the customary request was made for unanimous consent to suspend next day's Calendar Wednesday, she objected. . . . On Wednesday, September 26, however, within fifteen minutes after the session began, William M. Whittington (Dem.-Miss.) moved the adjournment of the House, which was carried by a vote of 74 to 31, thus ending the calendar and legislative day. The friends of FEPC thus learned: Calendar Wednesday could not be utilized unless a firm, stable and continuous majority was at hand to defeat all dilatory motions. . . .[16]

In the Spring of 1946, the effort was repeated. This time the opponents of the FEPC legislation interspersed repeated adjournment motions with dilatory quorum calls that rendered the House almost incapable of legislative action. The FEPC forces finally mustered up a firm majority against adjournment and succeeded in having the call of committees initiated. The Labor Committee, however, was seventeenth on the list and the hope of its ever getting to the top of the list was a vain one. The FEPC strategy was therefore shifted toward getting action through a discharge petition.

At an earlier stage the question of whether to use Calendar Wednesday was a burning issue among the various organizations supporting FEPC legislation. Representative Marcantonio of New York City and others proposed the Calendar Wednesday approach. Rival groups regarded it as a snare and a delusion. For example, the head of one C.I.O. union wired his local unions as follows:

The flimsy charge of Marcantonio that failure to use Calendar Wednesday is solely responsible for inability to get HR 2232 to the floor of the House of Representatives is further evidence of the divisive tactics commonly practiced by those whose endorsement is the kiss of death. The use of Calendar Wednesday was fully explored by proponents of the bill and the consensus was that it would involve more time than the petition method. A bill brought to the floor in this manner must be disposed of in that particular day. Mr. Marcantonio is an expert parliamentarian and was well aware of all these implications.[17]

Special "Rules" in the House. For the first hundred years in the history of the House, any member was theoretically entitled to move that a bill be called off a calendar out of numerical order. Actually, this could not be done unless a member was recognized by the Speaker, who thereby exercised considerable control over the calling up of nonprivileged bills. Gradually, this control came to be exercised through the Rules Committee, which had been chaired by the Speaker since its creation in 1860. By the Fifty-first Congress the Rules Committee was formally given the function of submitting highly privileged resolu-

[16] Will Maslow, "FEPC—A Case History," *University of Chicago Law Review,* Vol. 13, June, 1946, pp. 421–422.

[17] Quoted in Louis C. Kesselman, "The Social Politics of FEPC" (Chapel Hill, N.C.: University of North Carolina Press, 1948), p. 160.

tions—or rules—giving the right of way to any bill of its own choosing. With these rules customarily being adopted, the majority of the Rules Committee had in effect the power to direct an important portion of the legislative traffic in the House.

At times it has seemed as though this power has moved into the hands of the chairman of the Rules Committee. "It makes no difference what a majority of you decide," Rules Committee Chairman Phillip Campbell once told his committee colleagues: "If it meets with my disapproval, it shall not be done; I am the Committee; in me repose absolute obstructive powers."[18] Yet any such obstructive power—and, of course, it could never be absolute—derives from much more than the chairmanship alone. For many years Chairman Adolph Sabath, a New Dealer and Fair Dealer, enjoyed very little power, since the majority of his committee was made up of conservative Southern Democrats and Republicans.

The strategic position given the majority of the Rules Committee has been formally augmented or diminished on many occasions, as changes in the rules have given varying power to the Rules Committee, the Speaker, other party leaders in the House, or the chairmen of the legislative committees. The so-called overthrow of Speaker Cannon in 1910–1911, by diminishing the role of the Speaker, automatically enhanced the position of the Rules Committee and of majority party leaders other than the Speaker. Recurrent fortification of the discharge procedure and Calendar Wednesday strengthened the legislative committees against the Rules Committee and other leaders, although at times they have been used by the party leaders against the Rules Committee.

The last major changes in the rules of the House occurred at the beginning of the Eighty-first and Eighty-second Congresses. In 1949, eager to get action on measures that had loomed large in President Truman's 1948 election campaign, a group of Truman supporters succeeded in having the rules amended to provide a method of obtaining a special rule even when the Rules Committee refused to act. It provided that when the Rules Committee had delayed action for twenty-one days on a reported bill, the chairman of the committee which had reported it, if recognized by the Speaker, could offer a resolution on Discharge Calendar days to call the bill up for consideration. This shifted a portion of the traffic control power from the Rules Committee to the committee chairmen and the Speaker. Since recognition to obtain the floor cannot be automatic, particularly when other members are also striving for recognition, it also put a degree of power back in the hands of the Speaker. During the following months, the anti-Truman Democrats planned a counterattack. In January, 1951, with the support of the great majority of Republicans, they wiped out the two-year-old reform and brought back the previous rule.

If a member of the House (other than a committee chairman operating under

[18] Phillip Campbell, *The Searchlight,* Vol. 6, No. 12, 1922, pp. 5–6.

the twenty-one-day rule adopted in 1949) wants to obtain a special order of the day to call up a bill for consideration, he is not allowed to present a resolution that can be adopted by majority vote. The only courses open are to seek a suspension of the rules, which requires two-thirds approval, or make a unanimous consent request. In either case, previous arrangements usually must be made with the Speaker to win his consent to recognition and the approval of both majority and minority floor leaders must be obtained.

Motions to suspend the rules (which are in order only on the first and third Mondays, the days of the Consent Calendar) are infrequently made, since members who can obtain a two-thirds majority can usually obtain either a special order from the Rules Committee or unanimous consent. Yet the Rules Committee staff will occasionally bring in a special order calling up a bill under suspension of the rules on some day other than the first or third Mondays. The reason for this is that the suspension of the rules procedure can serve as an effective gag rule, since under it debate is strictly limited and no amendments may be offered.

Unanimous consent requests to call up bills are made more frequently. They are used both for the handling of emergency bills and for getting quicker action on minor bills than would be possible by waiting for Consent Calendar day.

The Senate System. The classification of bills is much simpler in the Senate than in the House. As contrasted with the House's five calendars and the Speaker's Table, the Senate has only two calendars. One is the Executive Calendar, on which treaties and nominations are listed; the other is the Calendar of Business, on which are all other bills awaiting Senate action.

As in the House, certain bills are highly privileged. These include vetoed bills, conference bills, Senate bills with House amendments, revenue bills, and appropriation bills (but all appropriation bills, not merely general ones).

Unlike the House, the Senate has no elaborate system of special days. Bills are brought up in two ways, either by taking bills off the Calendar of Business in order or by special action to take up bills out of order. The Calendar of Business may be called at almost any time.[19] Under this procedure—which in some ways is comparable to the House's use of the Consent Calendar and Private Calendar—the Clerk calls off the bills in the order of their appearance on the calendar.

As in the House, official objectors are designated by each party. Objections are usually raised by asking that a bill be passed over—in which case it will come up again at the same place in the calendar. Sometimes an objection will be made merely to delay consideration until a little later the same day. The 1950 legislation to amend the Hatch Act, for example, came up at a time when

[19] Although the call of the calendar is the regular order of business on Mondays at the conclusion of morning business, the calendar also may be called on other days. Usually the party leaders arrange to have it come about twice a month.

Senator Tydings, who wanted to offer an amendment, was not on the floor. "Mr. President, it is my understanding that the Senator from Maryland (Mr. Tydings) intends to offer an amendment to the measure," stated Senator Lucas, the majority leader. "I would respectfully suggest that the bill go to the foot of the calendar until we can confer with the Senator from Maryland." [20] Without objection, the bill went to the foot of the calendar. As a result, the bill came up again in the same afternoon, whereas if it had merely been passed over and left at the same place in the calendar, it might not have come up until the next day the calendar was read.

But an objection does not necessarily prevent consideration. Any member can move to take up the bill. If he wins a majority vote, the measure is then before the Senate despite any objection.[21]

There is nothing in the Senate comparable to the House Rules Committee. The Majority Policy Committee takes the lead in preparing a list of bills to be taken off the calendar. The minority leadership is informally consulted. Special action is then proposed to bring individual bills before the Senate. The most ordinary form of special action is a unanimous-consent agreement. This is required in order to take up a bill during the Morning Hour or while unfinished business is still before the Senate. When not required, it is conducive to cooperative working relations between the party leaders and to the development of an atmosphere in which everyone is expected to perform certain favors for others.

Unanimous consent, of course, is not always feasible. Hence, the rules provide that a motion to call up a bill may be made at almost any time by any Senator. A majority vote is all that is needed under the rules to pass it. The simplicity of the rules on this point, however, is deceptive. A determined minority can stage a filibuster to prevent a vote on such a motion. This happened in the Eightieth Congress during the special session called by President Truman after his nomination at the Democratic National Convention. One of his declared purposes in calling the special session was to obtain passage of the anti-poll-tax bill that had been passed by the House and reported out by the Senate committee. Taking him up on this issue, the acting Republican leader of the Senate, Senator Wherry of Nebraska, moved to call the anti-poll-tax bill off the calendar. A filibuster by Southern Democrats prevented the motion itself from being voted on.

A filibuster on a motion to take up a bill can be prevented by offering the motion during the Morning Hour before 2 P.M. During this period a motion to take up a bill is undebatable. Yet a Morning Hour can take place only at the beginning of a new legislative day. When the Senate takes a recess instead

[20] *Congressional Record,* 81st Cong., 2d Sess., Aug. 9, 1950, p. 12254.

[21] This would not apply, of course, if the calendar is being read under a unanimous consent agreement to take up bills without objection.

of an adjournment at the end of a calendar day, there can be no morning hour on the next day and all motions to take up bills are debatable.

The Questions for Decision

Anyone who has analyzed the voting records of members of Congress knows full well that decision making on the floor of Congress is not simply a matter of accepting or rejecting a bill. The questions that come up for decision may involve complex amendments, rejecting a bill or amendment by indirect means, or the reconsideration of whatever action had been taken earlier. By emphasizing procedural complications, the emergence of clear-cut issues or readily evident indications where each voting member really stands are circumvented.

In the Senate there is more fluidity for this than in the House. On controversial matters it is impossible to predict what types of action may be proposed; almost anything can happen. In the House, floor operations are under tighter control. When a special order is adopted, it often constricts the gamut of action. Motions that are not highly privileged have little chance of being brought before the House. The Speaker will often ask, "For what purpose does the gentleman rise?" If the Speaker does not approve of a motion which the gentleman may want to offer, the gentleman will probably not get the floor. Yet, at times, despite these restrictions on action, the House as well as the Senate finds itself in a situation where a majority of its members and most outside observers have lost track of accumulating amendments and motions and only a handful of members are in a position to unravel the tangled skein of questions before the body.

Amendments

Committee amendments enjoy a privileged status in both houses. Amendments proposed by the majority of a committee are always given central attention on the floor. If a complete substitute is reported—in the form either of an amendment or a new bill—it displaces the original bill as the primary object of discussion. Committee minority amendments are also in a strong position. Both majority and minority amendments are usually buttressed by committee reports and by the full background of hearings, executive sessions, and concentrated campaigning and maneuvering that lie behind the reports.

Amendments offered from the floor by noncommittee members, in contrast, are often attacked on principle. One will find in the *Congressional Record* innumerable instances of members of Congress—usually members of the committee whose bill is up for consideration—strongly asserting that "the place to write a bill is in the committee, not on the floor." [22]

[22] In "Considerations on Representative Government" (New York: Macmillan, 1947 ed.) John Stuart Mill developed in considerable detail the thesis that a representative assembly

The theoretical case against floor amendments can be substantiated in many ways. Although floor amendments may be every bit as important as the bill which is proposed, they are often objected to on the ground that they do not provide enough time or appropriate circumstances for careful study and consideration. Nor should one suppose that just because an amendment is offered from the floor it is necessarily a proposition more "open" in character than if it were presented in committee.

Amendments are supposed to be presented in writing, but there is no requirement that they be printed before they are voted upon. The Senate, however, authorizes members to have amendments printed before they are actually offered so that these advance drafts can be circulated to whomever the individual member wants to keep informed. The House does not allow this practice. In both houses, in fact, many amendments are often discussed and voted upon without much of an opportunity for many members fully to analyze their content or to prevent "hidden ball plays."

At times a committee bill may be snowed under by a large number of unintelligible or even contradictory amendments. Action is sometimes taken to recommit such a bill to the committee in which it originated in the hope that the committee can bring order out of chaos. Or the bill is passed with fervent expressions of hope that the other house or the conference committee will rectify the most obvious errors. On the other hand, there are innumerable advantages in the offering of floor amendments. The most important is that the process of offering amendments from the floor tends to some extent to enlarge the circle of insiders in a larger group. It can bring out facts and issues that might otherwise go unnoticed. The very possibility of having to defend a bill against floor amendments forces committee members to give more thorough consideration to the original provisions of the bill and to prepare more intensive explanations of the reasons for this or that provision. Moreover, the line-up of forces on the floor of the Senate or the House is often much different from the line-up in individual committees. This means that certain groups can have hope of obtaining their ends only on the floor.

A floor amendment provides a member of Congress with a good opportunity to attract attention and build up his record. A member who offers an amendment to an important bill can sometimes move much more into the limelight than by introducing a score of bills that are never acted upon. From the

---

is qualified only to pass or reject a measure, not to alter it. He felt that the work of both original drafting and subsequent amendment could be properly handled by a small expert body. Although British practice has not gone this far, bills brought before the House of Commons by the Cabinet—which is in an important sense the central leadership committee of the House—are not subject to as many floor amendments as are committee bills in the U.S. Congress. In the case of appropriations, no amendments in the House of Commons are allowed to raise the total level of appropriations beyond that recommended in the Cabinet's budget.

strategic viewpoint, moreover, floor amendments provide ideal instruments for consuming time and postponing final decision on a bill. Amendments that succeed in narrowing the support enjoyed by a measure are an ideal way of building up a final coup de grâce. Both sides in a contest find that a vote on even a minor amendment may provide an ideal method of testing the strength of opposing forces and of serving as a guide to subsequent floor strategy.

In the Senate, the amending process is wide open. Rarely is an amendment ever ruled out of order for reason that it is not germane. Even under the tightest unanimous consent agreements, there is usually full opportunity for the presentation of amendments. In the House, the offering of amendments is hardly as open. Amendments to a bill taken off the Consent and Private Calendars or taken up on Calendar Wednesday are never in order. Beyond this fixed limitation, many important legislative struggles center around the procedural issue of whether or not amendments are to be allowed. The Speaker has considerable personal discretion in ruling amendments out of order on the ground that they are not germane.

The Rules Committee also takes action often to directly limit amendments themselves. The Agricultural Adjustment Act of 1933 was considered under a ruling which not only waived all points of order and limited general debate to four hours but also prevented the offering of any amendments whatsoever. Many tax bills are passed under rules that provide that no amendments may be in order "except those offered by direction of the Committee on Ways and Means, and such amendments shall not be subject to amendment." Sometimes all amendments are out of order except certain specified ones. The 1940 act which extended the Sugar Act of 1937 allowed only those amendments "proposing the extension of the provisions of Section 207 of the Sugar Act of 1937." These authorized amendments are usually committee amendments.

Rules of this type are often the subject of bitter controversy. The 1947 debate over the rule dealing with the legislative budget resolution of that year is illustrative. Representative Sabath, ranking minority member of the Rules Committee attacked the rule as "the most drastic gag rule ever submitted to the House since the days of Uncle Joe Cannon's Czaristic control of Congress . . . it deprives you of your rights under the Constitution under the rules of the House."[23] The Republican chairman of the Rules Committee defended this rule by bringing in a full list of similar rules proposed by Democrats during previous years. "I believe the record will disclose," he maintained, "that the Democratic leadership during those many years brought in many closed rules, and the Democratic members, without exception, voted solidly for those closed rules."[24]

[23] *Congressional Record* (daily edition), Feb. 20, 1947, p. 1253.

[24] *Ibid.*, p. 1252.

One of the most illuminating comments on such debates was made by Representative Rankin of Mississippi in connection with a closed rule on a bill to stabilize commodity prices. "The average member of the House," observed Mr. Rankin, "does not want to be gagged on a measure he is against, but he does not mind being gagged on a measure he is for." [25]

In the case of tax bills, "gag rules" are usually an accepted way of doing business in the House of Representatives. Roy Blough summarizes House practices on revenue measures as follows:

> Although revenue measures have priority without a rule, the Ways and Means Committee usually asks the Rules Committee for a "closed" rule which limits debate and forbids amendments to the bill except those sponsored by the Ways and Means Committee. . . .
>
> Restriction of amendment is defended on the ground that amendments made without careful regard to the numerous inter-relations among sections of the Code would result in conflicting provisions and an unworkable law. Moreover, the bill is presumed to represent a balanced program and balance might be seriously affected by amendments. An unemphasized consideration is the fear that superficially attractive but impractical or basically undesirable provisions would be adopted on the floor. . . . Occasionally when sentiment in the House is sharply divided on some issue the rule permits amendment as to that issue alone.[26]

In some respects the offering of an amendment is comparable to the introduction of a bill. Sponsors must be selected, and, at times, cosponsors lined up. A floor amendment may be printed and announced long before the measure at which it is aimed comes up for consideration. In the case of tax measures which are not introduced in original form in the Senate, Senators have often been known to announce and publicly discuss the amendments they plan to propose long before the Senate committee has reported a measure or even before the House has acted. In many other respects there are special tactical problems involved in the offering of amendments on the floor. On certain occasions, a bill is read section by section when the time comes for approval or disapproval. This is done in the case of appropriation bills in both houses. When this is done, an amendment relating to a given section can be offered only at the appropriate time.

There is also the problem of picking the particular stage in the consideration of a measure at which an amendment is to be offered. During the 1921–1922 depression, for example, farm-bloc Senators developed a full strategy for talking on behalf of a farm-relief bill during the hottest days of July. Administration opponents of the bill succeeded in sidetracking them to an im-

[25] *Congressional Record* (daily edition), Dec. 19, 1947, p. 11846.

[26] Roy Blough, "The Federal Taxing Process" (New York: Prentice-Hall, 1952), pp. 76–77.

portant degree by the surprise offer of an Administration substitute. The method by which this substitute was brought before the Senate is related by Karl Schriftgiesser:

> Although Vice-President Calvin Coolidge had quietly encouraged the supporters of the bills to believe that, on the crucial day, he would first recognize one of them, when that day came he slyly evaded his promise by not appearing in the chamber. In his place was Senator Curtis of Kansas, who immediately recognized Senator Kellogg of Minnesota. This clever, tactical manipulation allowed Kellogg to present an administration substitute measure, of which he was the apparent author.[27]

Sometimes the air is so thick with amendments that even the most skilled parliamentarians have difficulty in keeping track of what is happening. An amendment to a pending measure can itself be amended. Although a third-degree amendment is not in order, additional changes can be proposed by offering a substitute for the first amendment. An amendment is then in order to the substitute itself. Four separate proposals for change may thus be in the air at one time.

The order in which these proposals is considered may have a direct bearing on the outcome, since the one which is taken up first may pave the way for other amendments or close the door against them. In both houses, the vote is first taken on an amendment to an amendment. Votes are then taken, respectively, on the amendment to the substitute, on the substitute, and the original amendment itself (although by this time the original amendment may have been significantly changed). In many situations this puts the supporters of the amendment to the amendment in a strategically favorable position, since their proposal must be voted upon first. This is a position which can best be won by the committee majority which had the bill reported to the floor, for all they have to do is wait for an opposition amendment and then regain the initiative by offering a counteramendment.

Sometimes an amendment may be printed and announced but never offered. Or it may be delayed until an occasion arises for proposing its attachment to another measure. Or it may be offered and then, in the light of opposition or because of some informal understanding, may be withdrawn by its sponsors.

Rejection by Indirection

In most cases a bill or an amendment is either passed or defeated. If the former occurs, it can happen in only one way: by actual approval. But in the latter case, members of Congress may avail themselves not only of an outright negative vote but also of five other weapons of rejection. These weapons—recommittal, tabling or postponing, striking out the enacting clause, points of

[27] Karl Schriftgiesser, "This Was Normalcy" (Boston: Little, Brown, 1948), pp. 104–105.

order, and dilatory action—can be used either to force amendments as the price of approval or to defeat a bill or its amendments as conclusively as though it had happened by a direct negative vote.

Recommittal. For the most part, recommittal is merely a delicate way of writing out a death sentence. Lingering doubts may exist as to the future awakening of the corpse but this does not usually detract from the finality of the action.

The recommittal action becomes somewhat puzzling to uninformed observers when the motion to recommit includes certain instructions to the committee. During any typical session motions are offered to recommit one bill for further study, another for a report by a given time,[28] another for the deletion of a specific clause, another for the making of specific amendments. One might get the impression that this is a method of having certain changes made. In the great bulk of the cases, however, the purpose is either to kill the bill or, in the event that not enough votes are available for this purpose, to obtain a record vote on the position presented in the recommittal motion.

This latter alternative is highly popular. It will be noted that a motion to recommit with instructions that certain changes be made provides an ideal method of expressing a negative position on a pending measure. First of all, it is negative in a constructive fashion; it is a way of indicating not blind opposition but opposition *unless* some change is made. At the same time, it expresses more than it is possible to say with an amendment alone, since, in a way, it covers the bill as a whole and the desired amendments. In the House of Representatives, as spelled out more fully in a subsequent section of this chapter, a motion to recommit is often the only way of getting a record vote on amendments.

To a restricted degree, bills may be recommitted at an interim stage before passage. In the case of conference bills, recommittal is a step in the push and pull between the floor majorities of the two houses. In the case of ordinary bills, the purpose may be to have certain changes made in committee that cannot be efficiently handled on the floor, or to arrange for a more relaxed negotiation among competing interests, or to shift the locus of power. It is the last of these that is usually uppermost when a bill is recommitted to another committee than the one from which it was reported. When the Sherman Antitrust Bill was reported from the Senate Finance Committee, those who sought certain amendments adopted the strategy of having it referred to the Senate Judiciary Committee first. They "loaded the bill with a series of humorous amendments, whereupon Senator Sherman who had successfully combatted repeated proposals that the bill be turned over to the Judiciary Committee for revision,

28 In the House, a recommittal motion can call for a report "forthwith," but cannot specify a given date. In the Senate, a report can be requested "forthwith" or at any specific future date.

was no longer able to prevent such reference." [29] The bill was completely rewritten in the Judiciary Committee and was then passed without change by the Senate.

Tabling or Postponing. Theoretically, action to table a question leaves a grain of hope. A question laid on the table may sometimes be taken off the table. Actually, there is little hope of this, because the motion to table is highly privileged and the motion to take off the table is not. A motion to table also has the peculiar virtue of stopping debate, for in both houses the motion is undebatable. This provides a powerful weapon of restriction upon the continuation of debate, but—and this is an all-important qualification—by its very nature, it can be used only by those who are opposed to the pending question. Even in the Senate a filibuster can be stopped by moving to table the measure, although the stopping of debate in this manner would merely represent surrender to the filibuster.

In 1950 Senator Langer of North Dakota expressed his opposition to the pending bill repealing the tax on oleomargarine by offering as amendments the various civil-rights bills dealing with fair employment practices, poll taxes, and lynching. The obvious purpose was to embarrass those supporters of the pending measure who also supported these civil-rights measures. Defenders of the pending bill countered Langer's strategy by moving to table his amendments instead of trying to vote them down directly. This made it easier for the civil-rights supporters to oppose Langer, and subsequently all of his amendments were tabled.

During this same session when a bill to suspend tariff duties on metal scrap was being considered, Senator Wiley offered an amendment curbing Russian fur imports. Senator George succeeded in having it tabled. This killed two birds with one stone. He stopped debate on a rather irrelevant matter and he succeeded in preventing himself and his colleagues from being recorded as directly opposed to an anti-Russian position.

In the House a motion to table is too deadly an instrument to be used very frequently with respect to amendments. Under the House rules a successful motion to table an amendment carries with it to the table all other amendments that are pending and the bill itself. In the Senate a similar rule was in effect many decades ago. Senator Hoar tells in his autobiography how he had changed this so that a successful motion to table an amendment would carry with it only the amendment.[30]

In both houses the motion to table is frequently used with respect to questions other than a bill or an amendment. It is an ideal method, for example,

[29] John D. Clark, "The Federal Trust Policy" (Baltimore, Md.: Johns Hopkins Press, 1931), p. 29.

[30] George F. Hoar, "Autobiography of Seventy Years" (New York: Scribner, 1903), Vol. II, p. 99.

of stopping debate on motions to reconsider and on appeals from decisions of the Chair. In both houses, also, an effect equivalent to tabling can be achieved by postponing a question indefinitely or to a "day certain." But since motions to postpone are debatable and less privileged than motions to table, they are used but infrequently.

Striking Out the Enacting Clause. A somewhat whimsical way of killing a bill is to strike out the "Be it enacted, etc." clause. When such a motion is successful, the effect is just the same as though a vote had been taken to strike out every other word or all the consonants in every word. A typical example occurred during the Eighty-first Congress when Representative Stefan of Nebraska succeeded in having the enacting clause stricken out of a bill which would have authorized the contribution to international relief funds of the money which was earned by conscientious objectors during World War II and was still in the hands of the Government.

The motion to strike out the enacting clause has the minor effect of converting a negative action into a positive motion. As with recommitting and tabling, it puts its supporters in the position of taking the offensive rather than of just voting against something. Of probably much greater importance is the fact that a motion to strike out the enacting clause is in order during the reading of a bill for amendments in the House. In other words, this particular amendment—even though it has the effect of amending a bill out of existence—can come up at a time when amendments only are being considered for action in the House.

Points of Order. When appropriation bills are being considered, a point of order can often be raised against specific provisions of a "legislative" character. In the case of conference bills, points of order may be raised against various provisions on the ground that they contain new material not included in either the House or the Senate version.

If a point of order is sustained by the Chair, the provision against which it was raised is thereby deleted without any direct voting on the floor. However, the decision of the Chair may be appealed and a direct vote can thereby overrule the Chair. In this case the effect is the same as if the point of order had been rejected by the Chair in the first place.

In the House, the Rules Committee often brings out rules to protect bills against points of order that may be raised in an effort to strike out certain provisions of the bill or to defeat certain committee amendments. An interesting rule of this type was brought forth in the case of the Independent Offices Appropriation Bill for Fiscal Year 1948. This rule provided that during the consideration of the measure,

> all points of order against the bill or any provisions contained therein are hereby waived; and it shall also be in order to consider without the intervention of any point of order any amendment to said bill prohibiting the use of the funds appropriated in

such bill or any funds heretofore made available, including contract authorizations, for the purchase of any particular site or for the erection of any particular hospital.[31]

The purpose of this provision was to protect certain budget cuts which had been made in committee through the insertion of legislative provisions and to make it easier for members to propose other cuts from the floor.

Dilatory Action. Dilatory action for the purpose of rejecting a measure is one of the oldest of legislative weapons. It has the double virtue of providing a method for avoiding a clear showdown vote and for eliminating the risks involved in having a measure actually brought up for decision.

In the Senate, dilatory action is easier than in the House. Since dilatory amendments in the Senate are rarely ruled out of order, prolonged senatorial talking, as explained in detail later in this chapter, is extremely hard to stop.

But in both houses the strategists of delay have available many opportunities, particularly if they are well versed in rules and occupy positions of strategic advantage on various legislative and party-leadership committees. They can raise intricate points of order at various points in the course of business. They can appeal the decisions of the Chair and develop full discussions on each appeal. They can use every possible excuse for forcing a roll-call vote, which itself may take fifteen minutes in the Senate and forty-five minutes to an hour in the House. They can slow up the whole process of floor action by forcing recesses or adjournments.

Without a quorum—which, under the Constitution, is a majority of the members—neither house is supposed to be able to transact any business. This requirement is habitually winked at and a considerable amount of business is taken care of in each house without a quorum being present. Nevertheless, any member who can obtain the floor can "suggest the absence of a quorum" and thereby obtain a roll-call vote to determine how many members are really present. The history of the House has been punctuated by many efforts to prevent action by prevention of a quorum. Speaker Clay held that the constitutional provision concerning "a majority of the House" meant one-half of all possible members plus one. By thus pushing to the highest limit the number of members needed for a quorum, it became more feasible for a given number of absentees to prevent a quorum. By the time of Speaker Cannon, however, this limit was reduced by five separate qualifications, each one of which was the result of a bitter parliamentary battle. A quorum now consists of a "majority of those members chosen, sworn and living, whose membership has not been terminated by resignation or by the action of the House."

A still more historic conflict centered around the strategy of refusing to answer a roll call even when present. In many of the legislative battles concerning elections in the South after the Civil War "the Democrats found their most

[31] *Congressional Record,* 80th Cong., 1st Sess., June 17, 1947, p. 7166.

effective weapon in refusing a quorum; in practicing that peculiar art of metaphysics which admits of corporeal presence and parliamentary absence. Even parliamentary law has many fictions; but it seemed a self-contradiction to assert that a member may be present for obstruction and not present for business." [32] In a famous ruling in 1890 Speaker Thomas B. Reed took it upon himself to count those who were present but who had refused to answer when their names were called. Despite violent protests from the Democrats, Reed held firm. Immediately, members tried to rush from the chamber and found to their dismay that Speaker Reed had ordered the doors bolted. On one occasion an irate Southerner kicked open a door in order to escape the count. In the course of a few years, however, even the Democrats accepted the "Reed rules" and the only way to obtain a vanishing quorum was to vanish.

In recent decades a long series of quorum calls has often served to produce protracted delay. The roll will be called; it will be found that less than a majority is present; the names of the absentees will then be called again, while late-comers straggle in; in some cases the sergeant-at-arms will be sent to round up absentees. By the time a full quorum has been reached, many members will have vanished through the doorways and once again the tedious process may be initiated.

One of the major protections against a vanishing quorum in the House is the institution of the Committee of the Whole. By meeting in the guise of "the Committee of the Whole" the House can thereby dodge the constitutional requirement for a quorum. Under the House rules a hundred members—less than half the number required in the House as such—are all that are needed to make up a quorum of the Committee of the Whole.

Reconsideration

The motion to reconsider is one of the few motions known only in American legislative bodies. In most other countries the tradition has always been that a matter should be voted upon only once. This position was shared by Thomas Jefferson who regarded reconsideration as offering an opportunity for a minority to achieve a surprise victory. In one of his letters, Jefferson explained how reconsideration came into being during the Continental Congress. Since the Continental Congress had to serve as the executive body in the direction of the American Revolution, its members renounced the old parliamentary practice of regarding a legislative decision as immutable and adopted the more flexible method of reconsidering their decisions freely.[33] After the adoption of the Constitution, the new Congress maintained the same practice.

[32] Hubert Bruce Fuller, "The Speakers of the House" (Boston: Little, Brown, 1909), p. 219.

[33] Letter to M. deMeusinier, in Thomas Jefferson, "Writings," Ford ed., Vol. IV, p. 149.

A continuing controversy has revolved around the question of who is entitled to move reconsideration. Can it be someone who voted in the minority and wants another chance? Or must it be someone who voted in the majority and has then switched? This question came up in the very first session of the Senate when Senator Maclay of Pennsylvania made a point of order against a motion to reconsider offered by someone who had previously voted in the minority. He was overruled by Vice-President John Adams. Later in the same session, however, Adams reversed himself and ruled on the other side of the issue. After many long controversies Maclay's position is the one which has been generally accepted in both houses.

In actual practice, however, anyone who can get the floor for the purpose can move to reconsider. All that one on the losing side need do is to follow the course of the voting and, when he finds that the vote is definitely against him, switch to the other side. He is then technically on record as having voted with the majority and can move to reconsider.

Another interesting question is how long after the original action is taken can a motion to reconsider be offered. In 1820 when the original Missouri Compromise passed the House, Representative John Randolph moved reconsideration. Speaker Henry Clay ruled the motion out of order "until the ordinary business of the morning, as prescribed by the rules of the House, should be disposed of." Clay then quickly hurried the bill over to the Senate and when Randolph offered the motion again a little later, Clay announced that the bill was no longer before the House and that reconsideration was no longer possible. At present, a motion to reconsider is in order in the House at any time on the same or succeeding day. Two succeeding days of actual session are allowed in the Senate. If the bill has already been forwarded to the other house or to the President, a request may be made for the return of the papers.

A *pro forma* motion to reconsider is usually moved immediately after a measure has been passed. The motion is then habitually voted down or tabled by voice vote. This serves to protect an enacted measure against a sneak surprise attack by its opponents at a later hour or day when its proponents are not on the floor in sufficient numbers. It also has the effect of eliminating any real opportunity for reconsideration.

A genuine motion to reconsider as distinguished from a *pro forma* motion can lead to one of three results. The first is complete failure, as when Senator Kilgore moved to reconsider the Spanish-loan amendment to the Omnibus Appropriation Bill for fiscal year 1951 and saw his motion tabled. The second occurs when the motion to reconsider is carried but when reconsideration itself leads to no change in the original decision. This happened in the case of the same appropriation bill for which Senator Douglas used the reconsideration technique as a means of making a second but futile attack against the funds appropriated for merchant-marine construction. The third possibility is complete victory. When the appropriation bill just mentioned was being considered, the Senate rejected by a division vote an amendment offered by Senator Smith of New Jersey to exempt funds for international-children's-welfare work from a pending 10 per cent across-the-board reduction in the size of the appropriation. Senator Neely of West Virginia offered a motion to reconsider this vote. Senator Wherry of Nebraska moved to table Senator Neely's motion. The tabling motion lost. The motion to reconsider was then passed by 43 to 42. The original amendment of Senator Smith then came before the Senate again and this time was passed by a record vote of 44 to 41.

Chapter 18

ACTION ON THE FLOOR

One of the oldest stories about Congress concerns the little boy who was taken to Washington by his father. For a few days in succession he and his father visited the galleries and saw the chaplain open the sessions with a prayer. After viewing this ceremony a number of days, the boy asked, "Why does the minister come in every day and pray for Congress?" The father replied, "You've got it all wrong, son. The minister comes in every day, looks over Congress, and then prays for the country."

To anyone who views Congress in floor session as Congress at work, a visit to the Senate or House gallery indeed suggests that the country's future is in jeopardy. Floor attendance is usually small. Members will casually stroll in and out. Speakers will use language that sounds formal or stilted. Other members will read newspapers without listening to nearby orators. They will intersperse discussions on one subject with multitudinous irrelevancies. Long periods of time will be filled up by quorum calls and roll calls.

But casual gallery visits provide little basis for finding out what is happening. Floor action is irregular. It fluctuates between deadly dullness and high drama, routine ratification of committee action and momentous decisions. Moreover, it is often of an extremely refined character. Like an East Indian dance, in which the flick of an eyebrow has profound meaning, a harmless-looking minor motion may have tremendous implications. A dreary speech on an irrelevant subject or a bit of frivolous horseplay may provide a smoke screen for behind-the-scenes maneuvering and campaigning. A dramatic clash between opposing members may be nothing but a meaningless performance of stereotyped routines.

The Talking

When King John of England, a few years before the Magna Carta, summoned knights of the shire to the first meeting of "the King's Council in Parliament," the reluctant knights knew full well that what he wanted to do was talk over new taxes before he levied them. The French language was known well enough for all of them to be familiar with the words *parler* and *parlement*. And ever since, talking has been properly regarded as an essential part of the parliamentary process.

It is a customary practice among journalists to lampoon the talking on the floor of Congress as useless babbling. Even among serious students of society there are always some who carry on in the vituperative tradition of Thomas Carlyle, who once referred to the members of the House of Commons as "six hundred talking asses." At the other extreme, the glorification of congressional debate as the ideal method of informing the nation and clarifying issues has been a customary theme among political scientists. Idealists find that congressional debate rarely meets their standards and promptly leap to the conclusion that most of it, therefore, is dross. Neither the skeptic nor the idealist provides a sound approach for realistically describing the talk recorded in the *Congressional Record*. An intimate examination of its purposes and its organization reveals a variety and complexity that can be understood only by using many additional scales of measurement.

Its Purposes [1]

During the early nineteenth-century debates on the Missouri Compromise, a Representative from Buncombe County, North Carolina, was pleading for a chance to talk, despite the fact that other members were impatiently calling for a vote. He explained that he wanted merely to "make a speech for Buncombe." His frank admission of purpose gave American speech two new words: "buncombe" and its shortened form "bunk."

In a very real sense, most floor speeches on pending legislation are buncombe. Their purpose is to build a record for the ultimate consumption of specific audiences whose support or approval is valued. The principle is the same whether a Senator from Nevada is aiming at a news story to enhance his reputation among the folks back home or is seeking the approbation of a

[1] The analysis in this section has much in common with the approach taken on the subject of public debate in Thurman Arnold, "The Folklore of Capitalism" (New York: New York University Press, 1937). The key points in Arnold's analysis are as follows: "Public debate is necessarily only a method of giving unity and morale to organizations. It is ceremonial and designed to create enthusiasm, to increase faith, and quiet doubt. It can have nothing to do with the actual practical analysis of facts. . . . The notion that legislation becomes more expert because of prolonged public discussions of proposed measures is an illusion which follows the notion that public debate is addressed to a thinking man through whose decisions organizations have group free-will. All prolonged public discussions of any measure can do is to reconcile conflicts and get people used to the general idea which the measure represents. . . . Public argument never convinces the other side, any more than in a war the enemy can ever be convinced. Its effectiveness consists in binding together the side on which the arguments are used. . . ." Pp. 379–381.

business leader in Chicago who is a past or potential campaign contributor. It is the same when a member of Congress, either from soaring ambition or a natural interest in personal prestige, plays for a nationwide audience. In no case, however, does the motive of building a personal record necessarily imply either a lack of sincerity on the part of the speaker or an absence of meaningful content in the speech. In fact, the most effective buncombe is both sincere and informative.

Does floor talk play a role in legislative campaigns? Certainly it is not the decisive weapon it seems to those who equate oratorical ability with influence. Speech making alone, no matter how eloquent, cannot by itself organize group support, supplant other forms of propaganda, or apply significant pressure. By the time a bill comes to the floor, the things that Congressmen say generally reflect a well-developed line-up of forces, and the opposing lines are generally drawn tightly enough to resist major changes that may be attempted through speech making alone. One of the ablest orators who ever strode the floor of the Senate was Claude Pepper of Florida. Yet despite his spellbinding, his speeches on behalf of advanced social legislation never brought him into a position of genuine leadership in the Senate. Senator Arthur Vandenberg, however, became an outstanding shaper of foreign policy during the period immediately following World War II. A sterling speaker, his oratory was no whit superior to Pepper's. The difference between the two lay in the relative weakness of the organized forces behind Pepper and the relative strength of those behind Vandenberg.

Nevertheless, it would be a mistake to accept too readily the sweeping oversimplification of Senator Carter Glass: "In the twenty-eight years that I have been a member of one or the other branches of Congress, I have never known a speech to change a vote." [2] There are three distinct purposes (other than that of preventing a vote, a subject discussed separately in the previous chapter) that speech making may serve in a legislative campaign.

The first is to provide a medium of communication between those who are lined up on the same side of a question. The signals passing between leaders and followers are by no means always given behind the scenes. Floor statements are often the quickest and most effective methods of passing the word around among other members of Congress, strengthening the cohesiveness of a group, or fanning the enthusiasm of supporters.

The second purpose is to win additional votes. On most important bills there are usually a number of members who are not able to make up their minds how to vote until the last minute. When the floor amendments raise puzzling new questions and cut members adrift from past commitments, this number may be quite large. Under such circumstances, a well-oriented speech

[2] Quoted in George H. Haynes, "The Senate of the United States" (Boston: Houghton Mifflin, 1938), Vol. I, p. 382.

or series of speeches can often directly influence fence sitters to jump in one direction or another. The most effective speech sets forth an appealing and defensible line of argument, one that can be taken over by a listener and adapted to his own uses. When backed up by a possible exchange of favors among Congressmen and by vigorous campaigning by noncongressional forces, speech making can help in the process of getting members to change their votes, if not their minds also. It can provide both factual guidance and propaganda leadership for other campaigners.

By delaying the final vote, speeches can also provide time for stepping up the tempo of a broad campaign. In early 1945, for example, the Roosevelt Administration succeeded in having the House pass a bill for compulsory control of the civilian labor force. It also succeeded in lining up a majority of votes in the Senate. But before the Senate could vote on the measure, Senators Joseph O'Mahoney and Wayne Morse took the floor of the Senate and launched a vehement and lengthy attack against the measure. During the course of their speech making, labor and business organizations mounted a sharp offensive against the Administration's position. Within a week's time so many Senators had switched into the opposition camp that the Administration leaders dropped the bill like a hot potato rather than risk a resounding public defeat. A similar maneuver was attempted in 1947 when President Truman vetoed the Taft-Hartley Act. Senators Wayne Morse and Glen Taylor staged a delaying action on the motion to override the President's veto. Their motives, they explained, were to give the country a chance to understand and ponder the reasons given by the President in his veto message. While they spoke, leaders of the Administration and of organized labor tried to convince enough Senators either to vote against overriding the veto or else to abstain from voting. This time, when the speaking ended, the campaign failed. Although the speech making was every bit as eloquent as it had been on compulsory-labor service, the power that could be amassed during the speech-making process was not nearly as strong.

The third purpose of speeches in Congress is to help lay the basis for future campaigns. Some of the best floor talks are made by those who are on the losing side and have no immediate hope of winning. Speeches help keep the colors flying. For the winning side, they help in the task of keeping the campaign alive until victory is won in the other house, in the conference committee, or at the stage of Presidential signature. For either side, when a bill is due to become law, they help prepare the ground for carrying on the contest in the administrative and judicial arenas. An innocent-sounding explanation of a section or clause, totally ignored by most members of Congress when first made, may later be used as proof of "congressional intent" and become highly important in administrative or judicial decisions.

However, the contribution of floor speeches to the building of personal records and the conducting of legislative campaigns is not always needed. A strongly entrenched member need not worry much about his record. A steam-roller campaign can gain little from talk on the floor. In fact, too much talking can have the effect of raising troublesome questions and attracting too much attention from latent sources of opposition. Many of the most influential members of Congress are men of few words. This lesson was learned by Speaker Joseph Cannon during his early days in the House. His maiden speech, a long and elaborate defense of a bill to amend the postal code, stirred up the opposition of the older members of the House and of the big-city press. In discussing the speech later he said:

> After that experience, I went back in speechmaking to the method forced upon me when, as a young lawyer traveling a county circuit, I had to prepare my case in the saddle and fight with the catch as catch can plan. I considered the facts I had to deal with and used them if necessary, but did not make speeches to consume time or to cumber the record. More legislation is delayed and embarrassed by too much speaking by the defenders than by the opponents.[3]

Who Talks?

Because of the contribution that floor talking can make to legislative campaigns, the selection of those who speak for a given point of view is seldom left entirely to chance. A routine task of campaign leadership is to line up speakers. This is usually done behind the scenes and well in advance.

Occasionally the solicitation is openly visible on the floor itself. When the United Nations Charter came before the Senate, for example, the isolationist opposition had dwindled to an almost negligible fraction of what it had been many years earlier when participation in the League of Nations was before the Senate. Since little defense for the Charter was needed, few Senators planned to speak on its behalf and there was a genuine danger that an impression of disinterest would be created. As a last-minute measure, the chairman of the Foreign Relations Committee, Senator Connally of Texas, was seen walking around the Senate floor with a pad of paper in one hand and a pencil in the other, buttonholing one Senator after another and beseeching them to speak on behalf of the United Nations.

With many members pressing to be heard, the selection of those who are allowed to talk cannot often be left to chance. The free play of the personal desires of individual members would lead to chaos. Thus, methods have been developed for deciding who can speak and in what order.

In the early Congresses the presiding officers recognized the members who rose first and asked for the floor. With increasing membership and business, it became more and more usual for many members to rise at the same time.

[3] L. White Busbey, "Uncle Joe Cannon" (New York: Holt, 1927), pp. 134–135.

This necessarily concentrated a considerable degree of discretion and control in the hands of the presiding officers. In the House of Representatives, with its larger membership and stricter rules on the length of floor discussion, the power of recognition became—and still is—a powerful political weapon. For decades Speakers of the House have successfully rejected appeals against their refusals to grant recognition.

In both houses the presiding officers habitually keep an informal list of those who are to be recognized. When one member has finished talking, the next speaker will often be selected from the list rather than by the alacrity with which another member jumps to his feet or the shrillness of his shout for attention. "The right of recognition," declared Speaker Randall in 1881, "is just as absolute in the Chair as the judgment of the Supreme Court of the United States is absolute as to the interpretation of the law." [4] Randall's case for absolutism rests only on the ground that the Speakers of the House have succeeded in preventing appeals from their decisions. The decisions themselves are far from being the absolute whims of a czar.

By long-established custom, reinforced by the strategic power of their positions, committee chairmen and ranking minority members have first claims to recognition in both houses. These claims are modified only when other members of the same committee are officially handling a measure. Other committee members and party leaders have similar claims that must be honored by the Speaker and Vice-President. Often, these holders of high priorities themselves present the Presiding Officer with lists of members to be recognized.

To some extent, control of the floor is delegated to individual members other than the Presiding Officer. Under many special orders of the House and unanimous consent agreements of the Senate, a given amount of time is divided equally between the two committee members handling the pro and con of a bill. These members, in turn, subcontract their time by yielding the floor to others for so many minutes at a time. When the leading proponent and the leading opponent are both members of the majority party, problems arise about providing minority members with a chance to speak. Similar problems arise when, instead of two, there are three or more major points of view on a measure. With enough initiative and drive on the part of those who want to speak, these problems are usually resolved without creating much dissatisfaction.

The process of subcontracting extends still further. Under most conditions any individual member may yield to another. "Will the Senator yield?" and "Will the gentleman yield?" are questions heard repeatedly on the floor of the Senate and House. The member who has the floor may yield or not, as he chooses. He may give the petitioner free rein to make a speech of his own or may limit him to the asking of a question. Once a question has been asked,

[4] Asher C. Hinds, "House Precedents," Vol. II (U.S. Government Printing Office), p. 1425.

the talk often flows back and forth between the two members without any repeated requests for yielding. Some of the most skillful and dramatic interchanges of verbal blows take place through this method.

Style and Content

The first thing about talk on the floor that can be observed from the gallery or by reading the record is the stylized form of address.

"Mr. President," a Senator points out, "this bill would undermine all that Americans hold dear."

"Mr. Speaker," a Representative declares, "this amendment is necessary if we are to keep faith with the taxpayer."

Neither of the Presiding Officers may have any interest in what is being said to them. For that matter, they may not even be listening. Yet everything that is said is invariably directed to the man who holds the Chair. Only rarely does a member use such profane language as "you" in referring to a colleague. Rather, it is "the Senior Senator from Ohio" or "the gentleman from Maine." This aversion to personal pronouns even extends at times to the first person. In tones of great dignity members often refer to themselves in "Senator-from" or "gentleman-from" terms.

As a matter of course one member refers to another as "the able" or "the able and distinguished." If perchance he *really* means to convey the meaning customarily attached to these words, he then goes somewhat further—such as, "the able and distinguished gentleman whose learning we all admire and whose sterling capacities for leadership are everywhere appreciated." If he has nothing but contempt and distaste for the member in question, he is apt to go further still and speak as follows: "The gentleman from Virginia has a brilliant mind and a redoubtable command of logic. His well-reasoned arguments are always persuasive, and if not persuasive, at least entertaining, but in this case . . ."

Derogatory language is forbidden by the rules. If a member of the House impugns the motives of another member, his remarks may be expunged from the record. The guilty Senator may be forced to sit down and lose the floor. When passions are boiling in a member's breast, he may attempt an indirect manner of insult. "Mr. President," an excited Senator once asked, although he knew full well what the answer would be, "I wish to know if there is any under the parliamentary rules of the Senate whereby one member may refer to another as a wilful, malicious liar?" After being called out of order, he subsequently restated his views as follows: "The charges made by the Senator from Michigan, I will say, in parliamentary language, are as much without foundation as it is possible for any charges to be." [5]

[5] *Congressional Record,* 69th Cong., Special Sess., Mar. 14, 1925, p. 226. It is interesting

Sometimes an anecdote will be employed as the method of expressing one's sentiments. Senator Connally of Texas, chairman of the Foreign Relations Committee, was on one occasion considerably irritated by a series of questions asked of him by Senator Wherry of Nebraska. He expressed his opinion of Senator Wherry by the following story:

> I feel very much like an old lawyer in my section of the country once did. He had as his legal antagonist a very loud and enthusiastic lawyer, who shouted and foamed at the mouth in addressing the jury, and when it came the turn of the other lawyer to answer him, he stood up and said, "If Your Honor please, Bow- wow- wow- wow."

Whereupon Senator Wherry proceeded to express *his* opinion of Senator Connally by replying: "Bow-wow-wow-wow-wow." [6]

The elaborate formality is pomp; at times, it is also horseplay. But it does have a deeper meaning. The stylized forms of address grew up and have been maintained to serve a purpose: the lubrication of relationships among people who have at one time interests in conflict and interests in common. Flattering words that serve to mask inner animosity between two members make it easier for them to work together on future occasions when they may be on the same side of the fence. They also help avoid the use of direct physical violence between hotly embattled members. Occasionally, it is true, members have assaulted each other with fists, knives, or canes. These are great rarities, however, in contrast to legislative bodies in many other countries where outbreaks of violence are recurrent manifestations of sharp conflicts elsewhere within the body politic.

Another obvious fact about floor talk is its frequent discontinuity. Discussion of a measure to expand the armed forces may be interrupted by a speech on the potato blight in Idaho. While there are rules against irrelevancy, they often lie unenforced, particularly in the Senate. Senators will often wander from one subject to another without any concern for orderly floor discussion. Many members will often talk on the same subject, but at tangents, without directing themselves to the arguments offered by others. This is one of the reasons why the term "debate" is inapplicable to floor talk.

Particularly disconcerting to gallery observers are the frequent quorum calls which completely halt proceedings for ten to fifteen minutes in the Senate or forty-five minutes or more in the House. Supposed to check on the volume of floor attendance or to bring more members to the floor, the motive behind

---

to note that parliamentary language is not required for personal references to individuals who are not members of Congress. In fact, under the constitutional provisions that "for any speech or debate in either House, they shall not be questioned in any other Place," members are secure against any libel suits. This has led to many dramatic instances of vehement personal attacks upon the integrity and loyalty of various individuals. These attacks, however, are usually quite apart from the legitimate legislative operations of Congress.

[6] *Congressional Record* (daily edition), Sept. 7, 1949, p. 12870.

the quorum call is often to end the talking so that various members can huddle together to develop new lines of tactic or strategy.

What one hears from the gallery is not the same as what one may read in the *Congressional Record* the next day. In both houses, members are given the privilege of revising their remarks. Under the rules this is supposed to be limited to the correction of transcription errors and minor grammatical editing. Despite recurrent protests, however, members always succeed in using this privilege as a method of changing the substance of their remarks. In addition, they are given the privilege of turning manuscript copy over to the floor reporters while they are talking and having large portions of their statement, sometimes the entire statement, printed as though they had actually delivered it. This is a convenient way of getting more space in the printed record than one has time to use on the floor itself. It is also a method of making statements that other members might challenge if they heard them on the floor but cannot challenge immediately if inserted in this manner.

Still further removed from public observation is the considerable amount of advance preparation that enters into the preparation of floor statements. When members read from manuscript, as is frequently done, it is obvious that their remarks are not merely spontaneous outpourings. Even when they talk without reference to a manuscript, they may have the guidance of fully prepared notes or of a recent briefing session. Given a set of notes to build upon, some members of Congress can develop splendid orations.

A prodigious amount of ghost writing goes into the preparation of floor statements and speech outlines. This is by no means a reflection upon the personal abilities of members of Congress. It is rather the result of the tremendous complexity of the legislative matters on which members must speak and the necessity for tapping the minds of experts. Many of the most fervent harangues appealing to members to preserve Congress from outside pressure are read verbatim from manuscripts prepared by employees of executive agencies or private organizations. Any self-respecting organization eager to have a member of Congress speak on its behalf must be prepared to provide speech materials. When a member uses such materials, such use makes it his own just as when he introduces a bill drafted by others or signs a letter written by his secretary. The fact that speeches in Congress today are on the whole more informative than they were in the early days of the Republic and that they in fact represent the largest bulk of informative talk done anywhere in the nation flows to a considerable extent from the wide use of specialized writing talent.

The Control of Debate in the House

Talk, once started in a legislative assembly, tends to keep on going. It provides an opportunity for continued self-expression. The longer one member speaks, the greater the chance he will touch on questions which others seek to answer and the more his colleagues may become aware of the impressiveness of a full record as contrasted with a skimpy one. If every member were allowed to speak as long as he chooses, Congress could meet sixteen hours a day every day in the year without keeping up with its business.

The intentional prolongation of talk is a useful weapon of obstruction. It not only can postpone action but under some circumstances can prevent action. Cato and other members of the Roman Senate used this weapon in their struggles against Caesar. It has been used in countless other legislative bodies. Its early use in the United States was so frequent that the colorful word filibuster, which originally referred to a small swift vessel and then to a lawless piratical adventure, was taken over to describe it.

Early in its history, members of the House were faced with the problems of aimless prolongation as well as intentional obstruction. Its membership was considerably larger than that of the Senate. It was the arena for the testing of outstanding political leaders and the resolution of the major political struggles. During the years preceding the War of 1812, for example, New England members who wanted to continue trade relations with England and France and opposed the emerging military conflict used prolonged debate as a major weapon. Their struggle with proponents of the nonintercourse legislation became a battle over whether or not the previous question would be used to conclude debate. In 1812 a filibuster was launched against the declaration of war itself. In order to get the floor and move the previous question, rather novel methods were used. A squad of members suddenly burst into the chamber and ran down the aisles using the spittoons as drums. Completely taken aback, the droning speaker sat down in fright. "A belligerent Democrat snatched the pause to move the 'previous question,' which was seconded, and the declaration of war against Great Britain was thus reached and carried in the House of Representatives of the Congress of the United States in June, 1812." [7]

It became evident over the following decades that the mere use of a motion to end debate—which is what the previous question amounts to—cannot sufficiently control the use of time in so large a body as the House. As a result, an extremely intricate system of additional time controls has been developed. One element in this system is the prohibition of all talk on certain questions. Cannon lists thirty *nondebatable* questions.[8] Included in this list are motions

[7] Henry A. Wise, "Seven Decades of the Union" (Philadelphia: Lippincott, 1872).

[8] Clarence Cannon, "Cannon's Procedure in the House of Representatives," pp. 143–144.

dealing with the previous question itself, adjournment, laying on the table, and certain appeals from the decision of the Chair.

Another is a set of barriers on the length of time that individual members may speak. Under what is called "general debate" a member can speak no more than an hour on any question and another hour on any amendment. The effort is usually made to avoid amendments under general debate and, in fact, general debate itself is forbidden when the House meets "in the House as in the Committee of the Whole."

A special system for amendments is provided in the "five-minute rule." Debate under this rule usually begins once general debate has ended. Any member is allowed to speak for five minutes on an amendment that he himself has offered. Then one opposition statement for five minutes is allowed. This process is frequently prolonged by the use of mock amendments, termed *pro forma* amendments. "Mr. Speaker," a member will state in all seriousness, "I move to strike out the last word." By inviolate custom, the Speaker will then allow him to speak for five minutes. Another member may then rise to say, "I move to strike out the last two words," and so on. Some of the most lively debate in the House occurs under this make-believe procedure.

Finally, various limits are set upon the total time that may be used in debate. On Calendar Wednesday and other special days there are restrictions to prevent debate from spilling over into other days. By unanimous consent, debate may be limited to a given number of hours or days. Special orders proposed by the Rules Committee usually provide a limitation on general debate or even, when the offering of amendments is prevented, upon debate under the five-minute rule as well.

The cumulative effect of all these devices is to give the majority of the House substantial protection against too much talk. The members may not be free to talk indefinitely but at least they are free from indefinitely prolonged discussion. Those who seek to stall action by the House can rarely do so by talking but rather must use other tactics—such as appeals, quorum calls, roll-call votes, amendments, and motions for adjournment or recess—to consume time.

Filibustering in the Senate

When water is dammed up at one spot, it seeks an outlet somewhere else. During the first half of the nineteenth century, at a time before the control of debate in the House had fully matured, filibustering in the Senate was but a mild foretaste of what was to come later. In the latter half of the century, even as floor talk in the House came under more rigid control, in the Senate it became a more frequent and effective legislative weapon. In the eighty-one years from 1865 to 1946, thirty-seven measures, exclusive of appropriation bills, were filibustered to death.[9] Probably four times as many appropriation bills were killed in the same fashion. Countless measures have been defeated, passed, or modified through the mere threat of a filibuster. Many Senators—such as Huey Long and Robert M. La Follette—have made or enhanced their reputations through their filibustering ability.

Who Filibusters? Southern Senators are probably better known than any others for their filibustering activities. The first major filibuster—and one of the most dramatic of all time—took place in 1890 when Southern Senators spoke for 29 days to kill the "Force bill," which would have meant Federal supervision of elections in the South. Southern political leaders have persistently used the filibuster in staving off legislation affecting the status of race relations in the South. Again and again, they have filibustered against antilynching, anti-poll tax, and fair-employment measures. As a result, the ability to talk for long periods has become a positive campaign asset in many areas of the South, and Southern Senators have been known to engage in jealous rivalries over the number of hours they are able to talk without stopping.

Yet the use of the filibuster extends far beyond racial issues and Southern Senators. One of the most notorious of all filibusters was leveled in 1917 against President Wilson's proposal for the arming of merchant ships. Filibustering was unsuccessfully attempted in 1919 against the Versailles Treaty and in 1926 against the World Court Protocol. It has been used in connection with legislation affecting banking, oil, mining, shipping, and power. It has been used by Senators from all sections of the country. It has been supported from time to time by a broad variety of groups who are unable to obtain what they want by a majority vote and feel strongly enough to resort to extreme methods. On this matter, for example, Senator George Norris, one of the greatest of liberal leaders, stood in company with many deep-dyed reactionaries. In his autobiography, Norris expressed his general aversion to filibustering but in frank language justified his leading role in the 1917 filibuster against President Wilson's proposal to arm merchant ships: "I felt the passage of the proposed bill . . . would automatically plunge the United States into the war. . . . Feeling so strongly, I felt the filibuster was justified in spite of my repugnance to the method."[10]

Methods. Talk and discussion are often classified as substitutes for physical force in the settlement of disputes. Filibustering steps over into the borderland between talk and force. In addition to the physical and emotional pain that may be inflicted on listeners, the filibuster itself is an exercise of unabashed

[9] George Galloway, "Limitation of Debate in the United States Senate," Public Affairs Bulletin, No. 64 (Washington, D.C.: Library of Congress, Legislative Reference Service), pp. 20–21.

[10] "Fighting Liberal, the Autobiography of George Norris" (New York: Macmillan, 1946), p. 176.

physical strength. Indispensable to success is the staying power of a Senator's larynx, knees (he can lose the floor if he sits down), and digestive system.

But stamina is not enough. There are many tricks of the trade that the filibuster wielders have developed to make their weapon stronger. The first lies in skillful timing. The most auspicious occasion for a filibuster is when preparations are being made for an early adjournment. Short of this, the best time is when the calendar is crowded with many other bills that are being strongly pressed by groups or agencies that cannot be ignored. A remarkably useful device, if consent is won for its use, is to have material read by the reading clerk. Quorum calls provide excellent rest periods. Appeals and dilatory motions provide useful diversions for talking on other subjects. Probably the most burdensome technique of all is to stick to the subject so that a pretense of meaningful debate may be kept up, public indignation prevented or appeased, and the bare possibility of being ruled out of order for irrelevancy eliminated. When a group of filibusterers are taking turns at speaking, care must be taken to see that the torch of debate is passed on when one member of the group stops. "I warned each member of the filibuster," writes Norris in relating the strategy used in the 1917 fight against the arming of merchant ships, "that he must be ready when the Senator who had the floor surrendered it, and that he must immediately address the presiding officer. If we permitted a moment to elapse, the presiding officer would put the question, and the conference report would be agreed to." [11]

Support from other Senators is also needed. Except for a brief space at the end of a session, a one-man filibuster is impossible. Even then, passive support is usually necessary. The extent of such passive support is usually much wider than is apparent from a mere reading of the *Congressional Record*. The filibustering record of the Senate has demonstrated the great power that can be wielded by a few Senators. Every Senator, therefore, has a potential stake in the preservation of this power. Many Senators who themselves have never filibustered are reluctant to take any steps that could, by way of precedent, interfere with their own use or threatened use of the weapon in the future.

Pressure and propaganda activities by private organizations also have a great bearing on the outcome of a filibuster. This was strikingly illustrated in September, 1950, when the Senate was about to conclude its work before the mid-term elections of that year. A small group of Senators initiated a prolonged series of speeches on behalf of President Truman's veto of an omnibus internal-security bill. One of them, Senator Langer of North Dakota, spoke until he collapsed and had to be carried off the floor on a stretcher. The pressure of business and veterans' organizations and other groups on behalf of the bill was so great that the majority forced continuous sessions of the Senate, wore the speakers down, and overrode the President's veto. In sharp contrast,

[11] *Ibid.*, p. 178.

approval of a conference-committee bill to limit the interstate shipment of slot machines was held up by an eleven-hour-and-ten-minute filibuster by Senator George Malone of Nevada, with only passive encouragement from other Senators. The difference lay in relative weakness of organized group opposition to gambling as contrasted with the strength of group opposition to communism and radicalism.

Restraints. There are a number of Senate rules designed to restrain floor talk. As in the House, many questions are *nondebatable.* These include motions to adjourn, to take a recess, to lay a matter on the table, and nineteen other motions.[12] When the calendar is being called and a bill is allowed to come up for consideration, no Senator may speak more than once or for more than five minutes. On all other bills no Senator is allowed to speak more than once on the same day. Although these restrictions are often suspended or winked at, they help to expedite part of the Senate's business, particularly in routine matters.

Quite frequently the Senate limits itself to a specific number of hours of talking or sets a specific hour at which talk shall cease and a vote be taken. But unlike the House, where this is accomplished by a majority vote on resolutions brought forth from the Rules Committee, the Senate does this by unanimous consent. Debate usually proceeds without limitation for a number of hours before such a step is taken. Meanwhile, the floor leaders canvass the Senators who are most directly concerned with the pending business and try to negotiate a satisfactory arrangement. Once a unanimous-consent agreement to limit debate has been made, it is almost ironclad, for it may later be amended not by a majority vote but only by another unanimous-consent action.

While any Senator's objection can in the first place prevent the limitation of debate through this method, it should also be borne in mind that any Senator who is not on the floor at the time a unanimous-consent agreement is offered may lose not only his right to filibuster but also his right to speak at all. Under Rule 12 of the Senate, a quorum call must be made before the Senate may consider a unanimous-consent request for the taking of a final vote on the passage of a bill or a joint resolution. This does not apply, however, to amendments or to Senate resolutions. Many Senators who have been off the floor for other business and who had been planning to talk on a pending matter have suddenly been surprised by being summoned to the floor to vote without getting any chance to talk.[13]

[12] A full list of the 22 questions that are nondebatable in the Senate may be found in Floyd M. Riddick, "The United States Congress: Organization and Procedure" (Washington, D.C.: National Capitol Publishers, 1949), p. 375.

[13] Sharp protests against the practice of submitting unanimous-consent agreements with prior quorum calls have been made repeatedly by Senator Morse of Oregon. See *Congressional Record,* 80th Cong., 1st Sess., Jan. 22, 1947, pp. 561–562, and May 16, 1947, pp. 5550–5552.

A minor step toward the control of filibustering was taken in the adoption in 1933 of the Twentieth Amendment to the Constitution. Prior to that time, the second session of every Congress, called the "lame-duck session," convened in December after the congressional elections and ended on the fourth day of the following year when the newly-elected President and members of Congress took office. With such a short span of life and such a firm date of adjournment, the closing days of lame-duck sessions offered an ideal filibuster season. The Twentieth Amendment, by providing for two sessions of every Congress beginning in January, removed some of the biennial congestion. As in the case of so many reform actions, however, its effect has proved less than its advocates promised. In addition, the idea of a fixed adjournment date, which provides an auspicious opportunity for filibusterers, was in part brought back by Sec. 132 of the Legislative Reorganization Act of 1946 providing for automatic adjournment, unless direct action is taken for an extension, by the last day in July.

The first frontal attack of consequence came in 1917 when President Wilson made his historic attack on the Senators who were filibustering against his proposal to arm merchant ships:

> The Senate of the United States is the only legislative body in the world which cannot act when its majority is ready for action. A little group of wilful men, representing no opinion but their own, have rendered the great government of the United States helpless and contemptible. . . . The only remedy is that the rules of the Senate shall be so altered that it can act.[14]

Four days later, with only three dissenting votes, the Senate approved the famous "cloture rule." Under this rule, sixteen Senators may present to the Senate a signed petition to close debate. Two calendar days later the Presiding Officer must submit to the Senate the question: "Is it the sense of the Senate that the debate shall be brought to a close?" No debate is allowed on this question. In its original form, cloture would be invoked by a simple two-thirds majority of those present and voting. Once invoked, no Senator could speak more than one hour on anything that might arise concerning the pending measure, including any amendments and motions.[15]

The relative ineffectiveness of the cloture rule is shown by the record of its use during the thirty years from 1917 to 1946. Of nineteen cloture motions presented to the Senate during that period, fifteen failed to get a two-thirds majority. Debate was ordered closed on only four occasions, each of them during the first ten years of its operation.[16] By the end of its first thirty years, the

[14] *The Washington Post,* Mar. 5, 1917.

[15] For other details on the nature of the limitation, see Senate Rule XXII.

[16] Galloway, *op. cit.,* p. 22.

cloture rule broke down almost completely, suffering three devastating blows one after the other. During the 1946 filibuster on fair-employment legislation, the President pro tem of the Senate, Senator McKellar of Tennessee, ruled a cloture petition out of order on the ground that the cloture rule applied only to bills and not to *debate* on amendments to the Journal. In 1948, when the filibuster was in progress against a motion to call up the anti-poll-tax bill, the next President pro tem, Senator Vandenberg of Michigan, held that the cloture rule did not apply to motions to consider a *particular* piece of legislation.

Finally, in 1949, the cloture rule itself was substantially weakened. The Senate Rules Committee reported a resolution to make the existing rule applicable not only to a "pending measure" but also to any "measure, motion, or other matter pending before the Senate, or other unfinished business." In this form, the resolution would have strengthened the cloture rule. But when the motion was made to take up the resolution for consideration, Southern Senators, who regarded it as a prelude to civil-rights legislation, immediately started a filibuster. After long debate a cloture petition was filed to force a vote on the pending motion. An appeal was immediately made. The new Vice-President Alben Barkley reversed his predecessor by dramatically ruling that the cloture rule was applicable to the motion to consider the Rules Committee resolution. But by a narrow vote of 46 to 41, Barkley's ruling was overthrown. A large group of Senators then brought in a substitute for the Rules Committee resolution, one which the Southern Senators agreed to beforehand. Under this substitute, the cloture rule was slightly broadened so that it would cover motions to take up a measure. But a specific exception was made for motions to take up any changes in the rules (including, of course, the cloture rule itself). The voting provision was stiffened by requiring that cloture could be effected only by a vote of at least two-thirds of the Senate membership, irrespective of how many Senators were present and voting. Under this arrangement, with eighty Senators voting—and eighty is a large turnout—one-fifth plus one could prevent debate from being closed.

In a few carefully restricted areas, however, rigid cloture rules have been established. As far back as 1877, the time of the Tilden-Hayes electoral-vote controversy, a law was passed providing that, when an objection is raised to the counting of the electoral votes from any state, no Senator or Representative can speak more than five minutes and no debate can last more than two hours. Without this provision dilatory tactics could be used to prevent the election of President and Vice-President. Under recent executive reorganization acts, Presidential reorganization plans become effective unless disapproved by congressional resolution. To protect against the use of dilatory tactics to prevent congressional disapproval, the Executive Reorganization Act of 1949 provides that, on resolutions disapproving Presidential reorganization plans, debate in either house cannot exceed ten hours and that no motions to amend, recommit, or reconsider shall be in order.

The Voting

After a bill is called up, after the questions for decision are offered, after the talking is over—the time arrives for decision by vote.

If the vote is a roll call, electric bells ring throughout the Senate or House office buildings, and the members come streaming into the chambers from all directions. Roll call or not, the air becomes electric with tension. Even when the outcome is known by everyone, every member knows that what he does will be closely followed by his campaign opponents, his supporters, his rivals, and the many groups that seek his voting allegiance. The bills he introduces, his committee activities, the speeches he makes, the investigations he takes part in, the patronage he obtains, the motions he himself offers—all these have their place. In many cases, they represent a far bigger, though less tangible, impact on government than anything he can achieve by floor votes. But neither separately nor cumulatively can they displace his voting record as the central point of attention on the part of major contestants in the legislative struggle.

Day in and day out, moreover, the problem of how to vote on the floor is always in the back of his mind. His voting decisions comprise the overwhelming majority of all the decisions he must face as a participant in the legislative process. During any given two years his vote may be recorded 200 times and he may participate in an equal number of unrecorded votes. The questions upon which he must express himself cover the broadest conceivable gamut of public-policy issues and extend far beyond his fields of special competence. To a certain extent, the voting process is much the same as in the committees of Congress. Floor voting, however, is more public. It is a more formalized operation. It is subjected to more, and somewhat different, rules of procedure. To understand it, one must give special attention to the number of votes needed on the floor, the methods of recording floor votes and the ways in which floor-voting decisions may be made.

The Number of Votes Needed

In committee sessions, disputed questions are decided by a majority vote. On the floor, the mathematical requirements are more complex. Unanimous consent is required for the approval of bills taken from the Consent and Private Calendars in the House. In both houses, as already indicated, widespread use is also made of unanimous-consent requests to take up bills for consideration and to conduct various activities outside the rules.

Many questions call for a two-thirds vote of approval. A two-thirds vote is needed to override a Presidential veto. It is also needed to approve a resolution proposing a constitutional amendment, to expel a member, or to impeach. In the Senate are found two of the best-known requirements for a two-thirds vote. The first is in connection with treaties. One-third of the Senators voting plus one may reject a treaty, as has been done on several occasions.[17] It is important to note, however, that a treaty can be amended by a simple majority vote and that an executive agreement to accomplish the same objectives can be approved by a majority vote of both houses. The cloture rule is a second occasion calling for a two-thirds vote of the entire Senate. Aside from the provisions for counting a quorum, and for electing the President or Vice-President if a majority in the electoral college is not obtained, this is the only instance in which the full membership of either house of Congress is used as a basis for computing the number of votes.

There are also certain special instances, although less celebrated ones, in which the House of Representatives requires a two-thirds vote. Under the House rules, a two-thirds vote is needed for such action as dispensing with Calendar Wednesday or for the call of the Private Calendar, suspending the rules, or considering a report from the Rules Committee instead of waiting until the following day. In all other cases a simple majority vote is sufficient for approval of a pending question. This, of course, does not mean that a majority of either house—or anything approaching it—is needed. With a bare quorum present and voting, a motion on a bill or an amendment may be carried by one-quarter plus one of the full membership. On unrecorded votes, even a bare quorum is often not present. Moreover, in the Committee of the Whole in the House, where one hundred members constitute a quorum, major amendments can be approved when supported by only 51 votes—less than one-eighth of the total membership in the House.

Critics of the two-thirds needed for Senate approval of treaties are fond of pointing out that under this requirement a treaty may be rejected by a relatively small group of Senators, representing a small minority of the country's population. One might suppose that on questions that can be decided by a majority vote, the winning side has some relationship to a majority of the population. Yet in the Senate, by virtue of the fact that every state has two Senators regardless of population, even a full majority may represent constituencies totaling much less than a majority of the country's population.

In the House, of course, there is a closer relationship between national

[17] As of the close of the 82d Congress, a total of 15 treaties have been rejected in this fashion since the First Congress, as contrasted with 1,128 that have been approved. Another 146 received no final action, have been withdrawn, or remain pending action. See U.S. Department of State, *List of Treaties Submitted to the Senate, 1789–1934* (1935) and the later edition of this listing covering 1934 to 1944.

population and House membership. But this relationship is dissipated by the uneven distribution of those members who actually vote on any given question. Even in the House, the members who line up on the majority side in any individual test of strength may represent a minority of the population, while the minority side may represent a majority of the population.

The Recording of Votes

The question of whether or not a vote is recorded is an extremely important one in the operations of Congress and in the political fortunes of its members. A record vote means a roll call and a roll call consumes a considerable amount of time. A record vote also means that many members must publicly declare themselves on questions concerning which they had hitherto taken an equivocal position or maintained silence. Hence, on the side of avoiding a record vote can be found those concerned with expediting action and those interested in avoiding showdowns. On the side of forcing record votes are those interested in dilatory tactics and those concerned with clarifying the positions of various members.

The overwhelming weight would often be on the side of avoiding record votes if it were not for the constitutional requirement that "the Yeas and Nays of the Members of either House on any question shall, at the desire of one-fifth of those Present, be entered upon the Journal." [18] Under this provision any member may arise and, addressing the Chair, call out, "I demand the 'Yeas' and 'Nays.' "

It is interesting to note that at any typical sessions of Congress there are more roll-call votes in the Senate than in the House. During the Eightieth Congress for example, there were 162 roll-call votes in the House. The records for the Senate for the same period show 248 roll-call votes, more than 50 per cent above the House level. This disparity is largely a reflection of the fact that in the House most of the voting on amendments takes place in the Committee of the Whole and that in the Committee of the Whole the constitutional provision on the Yeas and Nays is evaded.

In both houses, there are two types of nonrecord votes: a voice vote and a division. A voice vote takes place when the Presiding Officer makes a judgment on the basis of the number of members whom he hears calling out "Yea" or "Nay." Many minor and noncontroversial measures are passed by voice vote. This includes a surprising number of conference-committee measures which, before the conference, were the center of major controversies. Under it there are often no objections voiced at all. However, if there is objection and if the vote seems to be close, any member may demand a division. The Chair will then ask those in favor of the pending question to rise and stand until

[18] Art. I, Sec. 5.

counted. The opponents will then be asked to do the same. The Chair will then announce the result of the count but no names will be recorded.

The House has still a third system of providing for a nonrecord vote, namely, the use of tellers. One-fifth of a quorum—44 in the House and 20 in the Committee of the Whole—may demand tellers. Under the teller system, the members leave their seats and gather in the well of the House. Those in favor of the pending question pass in single file up the center aisle and are counted. The opponents then walk down the aisle and are counted. This system has the advantage of providing an accurate vote and at the same time enabling members to have their individual votes go unrecorded. At the same time, it makes it possible for careful observers in the gallery to check off how individual members behave, something that cannot really be done on a voice vote or on a division. Senator Kefauver and Jack Levin tell an interesting story of a "gallery check" that was attempted when the House was voting on the famous "death-sentence" clause in the Public Utilities Holding Company Bill. The House Rules Committee had brought in a special order permitting only a teller vote on this provision. The Scripps-Howard editors, who were supporting the death-sentence clause, felt that a clear record was needed in order to deal with members of the House who, they believed, were dodging the issue.

> On the Scripps-Howard staff at the time was a young reporter with an unusual memory for names and faces. While members, gathering in the well to pass by the tellers, either smiled encouragement or shook their fists at the press gallery, the reporter coolly called off 286 names to four other staffers who recorded the names and passed them to other reporters at telephones. The Scripps-Howard paper was on the streets in 40 minutes with a tally of names that subsequently proved to contain only one error.[19]

Calculations as to how members voted under one form of voting cannot be ascertained when a recount is taken under another form. As visibility regarding a legislator's conduct increases, some votes move from one side to the other or drop out completely.

The Range of Alternatives

In most cases, most members vote a clear "Yea" or "Nay." Yet these are by no means the only alternatives in registering a decision.

Delays and Switches. There are a number of variations in the manner in which a member can cast his vote. The voting process during a roll-call vote takes time. A member can refrain from answering when his name is called, keep a close tally of how the votes are lining up, and can then come in at the very end when the names of those who did not answer at first are being read

[19] Estes Kefauver and Jack Levin, "A Twentieth Century Congress" (New York: Duell, Sloan & Pearce, 1947), p. 63.

again. In this way he can either jump on the band wagon or else vote on the losing side to satisfy one set of interests and prepare himself to tell the interests on the other side that his voting for them would not have helped.

An illustration of this tactic is found in the history of Administration tactics in combating the silver bloc during the early days of the New Deal. Everest records the story as follows:

> Equally effective was the counsel that Administration advisers gave those Senators who sought help in escaping a dilemma. Some of them were not sure bimetallism was sound, but had the "folks back home" to think about, and disliked being recorded in opposition to any inflationary proposal. They were told to absent themselves until the end of the roll call, when they should vote against the bill if there were already thirty votes for free silver, and when they might safely vote for it if there were under thirty votes. Hence the Administration knew that at least ten Senators failed to help the amendment, although they favored inflation of some sort. Since that many additional votes would have secured passage, there was no longer doubt about the inflationary majority in the Senate.[20]

A member can also vote one way when his name is first called and then, after keeping a close tally on the votes and before the outcome is announced, obtain permission to switch to the other side. It was this tactic which succeeded in obtaining a majority vote in the House for the Kerr gas bill in 1950. The first call of the House showed that the bill was about to be defeated by a slim margin.

> However, just before the outcome could be announced, Congressmen from the Southwestern states swarmed into the well of the House, demanding to know how they had been recorded on the roll-call. This was a delaying tactic. . . . Speaker Rayburn, who was presiding, informed Halleck that two more votes were needed if the bill was to be saved from defeat. In other words, it was up to Halleck to produce two switch votes on the Republican side. How well he succeeded may be attested by the fact that not two but three Republicans, who had voted against the Kerr Bill, soon appeared in the House well and informed Rayburn that they would like to change their vote and be recorded for the Bill.[21]

Absence. A member may readily dodge an issue by being absent. Although no statistics on this subject could be compiled, it is obvious to any observer that many members conveniently absent themselves from Washington at the time when difficult questions are up for decision and when it appears safer to take no position at all. Absenteeism may be purposeful even when a member goes to the trouble of stating how he would have voted if present. Through this in-between method of recording one's views a member can express himself

[20] Allan Seymour Everest, "Morgenthau, the New Deal and Silver" (New York: King's Crown Press, Columbia University Press, 1950), pp. 24–25.

[21] Drew Pearson, "Washington Merry-Go-Round," *Washington Post,* Apr. 5, 1950.

for a certain proposition and at the same time go along with those groups who are anxious that he not vote at all rather than that he vote in favor of it.

Many absences, of course, are occasioned by sickness or by important business. On hotly contested measures intense pressure is put on absentees to return. There are many recorded instances of members making dramatic, last-minute airplane flights back to Washington, tottering onto the floor against doctors' orders, or even being brought in a wheel chair or on a stretcher. In 1940, for example, the fate of legislation extending the terms of service for national-guard and reserve officers and Selective-Service trainees hinged on the number of absent Senators who could be brought back to vote. A Senate-approved bill was passed in the House after many changes, by a vote of 203 to 202. It became evident that if the Senate sent the bill to conference, the measure might be killed. The sponsors of the measure then decided to seek Senate acceptance of the House version without alteration.

> . . . This agreed upon, the Senate leaders made sure of an impressive majority, larger than legally necessary, by sending airplanes to bring back as many friendly Senators as possible, and, in the case of several who could not return to Washington, arranging to "pair" them with opposition Senators whose votes would thus be neutralized. On the day of the vote two friendly Senators (Harry S. Truman and Sherman Minton) held the floor and thus deferred the vote until given the assurance that a maximum majority was on hand.[22]

Not Voting. A member may refrain from voting even when present. On this matter one finds a fascinating tangle of conflicting rules and precedents. The rules, for example, indicate that every member must vote unless excused. Attempts during the nineteenth century to compel members to vote proved futile. As early as 1832 John Quincy Adams successfully defied the attempts of other House members to force him to vote. In 1893 when Senator du Bois refused to vote, the Senate, by a large vote, refused to excuse him. The Senator, nevertheless, maintained his silence. In sharp contrast to the written rules in both houses, therefore, there has grown up the unwritten rule of "the right to silence."

Another long-standing parliamentary tradition is that, to use the words of Sec. XVII of Jefferson's Manual, "where the private interests of a member are concerned in a bill or question, he is to withdraw." This principle also is clearly set forth in Rule VIII, Sec. 1, of the House, which provides that every member shall vote on each question put "unless he has a direct personal or pecuniary interest in the event of such question." On rare occasions in both houses members have asked to be excused because of their private financial interests in a pending measure. On equally rare occasions the Speaker of the House has

[22] Mark S. Watson, "Chief of Staff: Prewar Plans and Preparations" (Washington, D.C.: Government Printing Office, 1950), pp. 230–231.

ruled that because of his private interests a member should not be allowed to vote. But with these few exceptions both the ancient principle and the House rule are consistently violated. Members who have the most direct personal or private interests in pending legislation generally have no hesitation in taking part in the voting.

Pairs. A member may enter into a "pair" with another member. The avowed purpose of a pair is to redress the imbalance that is created when one member unavoidably is forced to be absent while a record vote is taken. One member, who would have voted on the other side, presumably enters into a gentleman's agreement with the absentee that neither of them will vote but that the one will be recorded as "paired for" and that the other as "paired against." Some members have "indefinite" or "general" pairs with each other. Under such cases when one party to this two-man agreement is absent, the other is regarded as obliged not to vote unless "released." In other cases, specific pairs are arranged for individual votes or for stated periods of time in both the House and the Senate. Secretaries and clerks are kept busy with the handling of these arrangements.

In actual practice, however, pairs often turn out to be a specialized method of avoiding a vote. "Members pair off, and do as they please," wrote Senator Benton, more than a century ago, ". . . either remain in the city and refuse to attend to any duty, or go off together to neighboring cities; or separate; one staying and one going; and the one that remains sometimes standing up in his place, and telling the Speaker of the House that he had paired off; and so refusing to vote." [23] Benton might have added that the pairing system often becomes a bitter and decisive part of the legislative struggle on the floor of both houses. In preparing for the showdown on any measure where the margin of victory or defeat may be narrow, each side endeavors to convince certain members who are leaning against them that they should "pair against" instead of voting "Nay." On hotly contested party issues, leaders of one party may "declare all pairs off" if they calculate that the other party has a greater number of members who are sick or unavoidably out of town. During the Eightieth Congress's conflict over tax reduction, Senator Lucas of Illinois, who was then minority Whip, charged that the Republican leaders violated "all rules of courtesy and decency" by refusing pairs. When the Democrats were in power, he said, they always arranged for pairs with the Republicans. "If enough Republicans to change the situation were too ill to be present," retorted Republican leader Taft, "we could not get a pair from the Democrats for love or money. They have never given us pairs under those circumstances, and they never will." [24]

[23] Thomas H. Benton, "Thirty Years' View" (New York: Appleton-Century-Crofts, 1856), Vol. II, p. 178.

[24] *The New York Times,* May 27, 1947.

In view of all these variations it is impossible to analyze the recorded votes in the House or in the Senate by merely listing the Yeas and Nays. It is also essential to list announcements by members on how they would have voted if present and to record their pairs. Information on members who neither voted nor paired can be obtained by polling them on how they would have voted if present, as is done regularly by *Congressional Quarterly*. In this manner, *Congressional Quarterly* provides as full an analysis of the voting in Congress as one can get without identifying individual action on voice, division, and teller votes and without going into the motives and pressures that lie behind the members' decisions.

The Pain of Decision

"When the committee hearings and the important books and articles on a proposal are heard; when the mail has been appraised; when the briefs and arguments have been weighed; when the wise men, living and dead, have been consulted, the Senator still faces the task of moving his own lips to say 'Yes' or 'No.' "[25]

The task is often painful. A simple Yes or No, no matter how qualified it may be in explanatory speech making, rarely covers an important issue. There is almost always something to be said on both sides of a question. No one can better appreciate this than a member of Congress subjected to pressure and propaganda from people who are doing the saying on both sides and will probably continue to speak their piece when he next comes up for reelection.

Most members of Congress will probably join with former Representative Voorhis in his rueful comment on the pain of voting: "It would be a great deal easier if only one could answer 'Fifty-five per cent aye,' or 'seventy per cent no,' or 'I vote aye but with the reservation that I do not like Section 3 of the bill,' or 'I vote no, but God have mercy on my soul if I am wrong, as I may very well be.' "[26]

A researcher into the mysteries of congressional voting, after trying to find out how members of the House made up their minds on the 1939 legislation to repeal the embargo provisions of the Neutrality Act, concluded his analysis with the following observation:

> Considering the bewildering complexity of the questions involved, it is with no sense of superiority but profound sympathy and understanding that we close by recording the fact that one member made his decision when a newspaper reporter wrote out a 15-word statement that looked so well in print and offered such a peace-

[25] Paul H. Douglas, "A Senator's Voice: A Searching of the Soul," *The New York Times Magazine,* Apr. 30, 1950.

[26] Jerry Voorhis, "Confessions of a Congressman" (Garden City, N.Y.: Doubleday, 1947), p. 233.

ful refuge from the agonies of indecision that the Congressman adopted and maintained it as his own.[27]

There are few formulas on how to vote that are anything more than witticisms or rough-and-ready guides on unimportant matters. In the first category belongs the overgeneral motto "When in doubt, do right" and the cynical slogan "Vote for every appropriation and against every tax." Of the rough-and-ready type is the formula of voting against a bill when in doubt, presumably on the theory that there is too much legislation anyway. "I have tried to follow a rule," stated Senator Elmer Thomas of Oklahoma during one vote, "that when I do not know a thing about a matter before the Senate, I vote 'Nay.' . . ." [28] On the occasion which prompted this remark the Senator went on to explain that he had just learned more about the subject at hand and that he intended, if a motion to reconsider be offered, to change his vote.

Of somewhat more value as a guide is the action of leaders and blocs with which a member may be associated. On some questions party leadership is important.[29] On others, the example of ranking committee members and individuals whose judgment has been confirmed by experience may be extremely influential. The band-wagon theory also has a role; there is a certain safety in numbers.

On the other hand, these factors tell only part of the story. Leaders who are devoutly followed on some subjects may be respectfully ignored on others. There is also a band-wagon theory in reverse. When there is an overwhelming majority lined up on behalf of a bill, a member may then vote more confidently against it and be able to tell its supporters in all honesty that his negative vote could not have made a particle of difference.

At times it has been suggested that many Congressmen decide how to vote by watching the public-opinion polls. This has been regarded with horror by those who see in the polling operations themselves instruments of irresponsible political power and who believe that members of Congress should guide public opinion rather than follow it. Actually, however, the polls probably play only a very incidental role. This is borne out by the various attempts that have been made to find out from Congressmen themselves exactly what value they place upon public-opinion polls.[30] Public-opinion polls cannot enter very de-

[27] L. E. Gleeck, "96 Congressmen Make Up Their Minds," *Public Opinion Quarterly,* Vol. 4, March, 1940, p. 24.

[28] *Congressional Record,* 73d Cong., 2d Sess., May 22, 1934, p. 9244.

[29] For a detailed study of the role of party policy and other pressures on the roll-call votes of Representatives during four different sessions, see Julius Turner, "Party and Constituency: Pressures on Congress" (Baltimore: Johns Hopkins Press, 1951).

[30] Gleeck, *op. cit.,* pp. 8–9; George F. Lewis, Jr., "Congressmen Look at the Polls," *Public Opinion Quarterly,* Vol. 4, June, 1940, pp. 229–231; J. K. Javits, "How I Used a Poll in

cisively into the thinking of a member of Congress because they do not reflect and appraise the nature and intensities of opinions held by those people in their constituencies whose views, by virtue of the power they represent, count the most.

A member's voting decision is his own reconciliation of all the pressures and propaganda to which he has been subjected. How this reconciliation is made depends upon the legislation situation itself and each member's personal attributes. In situations where the weight of the pressures is all on one side, the decisions naturally tend to move in the same direction. Where members are dealing with more equally balanced conflicts and where their personal advancement depends upon bringing together the support of conflicting groups, the decisions are less predictable. It is on these occasions that a member must truly search his soul. Whether he is an introspective ponderer or whether he relies on a last-minute intuition, it is *his* decision and not that of someone who pulls the strings or gives the signals.

His hour of decision is not seen by the outer world. It can come in the dead of night, in periods of reverie in one's office, after the day's work is done, over the breakfast or dinner table with one's family, or in a taxicab ride to or from the Capitol. It is at these times, I believe, that the final decisions which affect the life of the nation are generally made. The tension of the roll-call merely expresses the decisions which ninety-six widely differing men, with different background, have already made in the quiet of their individual consciences.[31]

Campaigning for Congress," *ibid.*, Vol. 11, Summer, 1947, pp. 222–226. According to Martin Kriesberg, "What Congressmen and Administrators Think of the Polls" (*ibid.*, Vol. 9, Fall, 1945, pp. 333–337), members of Congress place less weight upon public-opinion polls than do administrators. The reason for this may well be that members of Congress are much more interested in the opinions of group leaders in *specific* constituencies, while administrators are more interested in *general* public opinion which might at some time shape itself into forces affecting their agency activities.

[31] Douglas, *op. cit.*

Chapter 19

THE PRESIDENT VOTES: APPROVAL OR VETO

ONCE A BILL has been successfully steered through the tortuous shoals of Congress, it undergoes a rather quick and routinized processing so that a certified product can be presented to the President.[1] It is checked by clerks of the two houses,[2] printed on parchment as an "enrolled bill," and signed by the Speaker of the House and the President of the Senate. A clerk of the house in which it was first passed takes it to the White House where it becomes another piece of paper to burden the most heavily burdened public official in the world.

At previous stages in the legislative history of the measure—from the decision on whether or not to have a bill to the floor action in Congress—the President may have been an active participant or may have had nothing whatsoever to do with it. Now he sits in the center of the picture. If there is no longer any dispute over the measure or if for any combination of reasons his action is a foregone conclusion, there will be little attempt to influence him. If there is still a conflict and any doubt about his decision, the White House now becomes the focal point of the legislative struggle and, for the time being at least, the key concern of other participants in the legislative struggle is the decision making of one man.[3]

[1] For background material on the President's role in the approval and disapproval of legislative measures see Edward S. Corwin, "The President: Office and Powers" (New York: New York University Press, 1948), Chap. 7; Richard E. Neustadt, "Presidential Clearance of Legislation" (unpublished doctoral dissertation, Harvard University, June, 1950); and Norman J. Small, "Some Presidential Interpretations of the Presidency" (Baltimore: Johns Hopkins Press, 1932); Edward C. Mason, "The Veto Power" (Boston: Ginn, 1891); and Charles J. Zinn, "The Veto Power of the President" (Washington, D.C.: Government Printing Office, 1951).

[2] If any errors are found, they may be corrected at this stage by a concurrent resolution. If errors are discovered after a bill has been delivered to the White House, it can be recalled and corrected by concurrent resolution. Once a bill has become law, a joint resolution or another act is required.

[3] There have been many learned debates as to whether the President has any part of the "legislative power." Strict constructionists pointed to the first section of the Constitution: "All legislative powers herein granted shall be vested in a Congress of the United States. . . ." Others have retorted that this section is modified by the provisions of Art. I, Sec. 7, which give the President his veto power. (See Howard L. McBain, "The Living Constitution,"

On questions of how Presidents really function and how pressures operate upon them, there is probably greater public interest and less public knowledge than on any other phase of government. The interest arises from the glamour and high prestige of the Presidency. The lack of public knowledge results in part from the protective shroud of secrecy that necessarily surrounds a President during his period of tenure and from the unfortunate dearth of frank and detailed memoirs by former Presidents or reliable associates. Yet to understand this final stage in the legislative struggle, we must deal as directly as possible with the scope of Presidential choice, the process of Presidential choice, and the decisions themselves.

The Scope of Presidential Choice

The scope of Presidential choice is not unlimited. Constitutional requirements, informal usages, and strategic maneuvering combine to set the limits within which he operates. These limits may be discussed in terms of the measures sent to the White House, the necessity of a President's accepting or rejecting a bill *in toto,* and the time allowed for him to make a decision.

Measures Sent to the White House

When the veto function of the President was being considered in the Constitutional Convention, James Madison observed that "if the negative of the President was confined to *bills,* it would be evaded by acts under the form and name of resolution, votes, etc." [4] Shortly thereafter, Edmund Randolph proposed that the possibility of evasion be dealt with by an additional clause. This resulted in the provision in Article I, Section 7, that "every order, resolution, or vote, to which the concurrence of the Senate and the House of Representatives may be necessary (except on a question of adjournment), shall be presented to the President of the United States" and shall be handled in the same manner as a bill.

The great bulk of measures jointly acted upon by Congress has always been presented to the President. But there are two interesting exceptions to, or rather evasions of, this provision: constitutional amendments and concurrent resolutions.

Exactly two years after Madison, Randolph, and their colleagues had signed the proposed Constitution, the First Congress of the United States presented

(New York: Workers Education Bureau Press, 1927), p. 170. To this writer, at least, such debates about "legislative power" seem to be arid. There is no doubt that the Constitution provides for Presidential participation at many points in the legislative process and not merely at the signature or veto stage.

[4] Arthur Taylor Prescott, "Drafting the Federal Constitution" (Baton Rouge, La.: Louisiana State University Press, 1941), p. 612.

to the state legislatures the first ten amendments which comprised the famous Bill of Rights. These were acted upon by Congress in the form of joint resolutions "to which the concurrence of the Senate and the House of Representatives" was necessary. Yet they were not presented to President Washington. In 1798, almost a decade later, the Eleventh Amendment to the Constitution was ratified by the states after having been handled in the same manner. It was promptly challenged in the Supreme Court on the ground that "the amendment was never submitted to the President for his approbation." One of the arguments used in defense of the procedure that had been used was "that as two-thirds of both Houses are required to originate the proposition, it would be nugatory to return it with the President's negative, to be re-passed by the same number." This argument was countered by the assertion that "the reasons assigned for his disapprobation might be so satisfactory so as to reduce the majority below the Constitutional proportion." It was further stated: "The Concurrence of the President is required in matters of infinitely less importance and whether on subjects of ordinary legislation or of Constitutional amendments, the expression is the same, and equally applies to the act of both Houses of Congress."

On the day after the argument had been made, the judges unanimously threw the case out of Court on the ground that the amendment had been constitutionally adopted. Justice Chase added the following comment: "The negative of the President applies only to the ordinary cases of legislation. He has nothing to do with the proposition, or adoption of amendments to the Constitution." [5]

A more tortured misreading of the clear constitutional provision could scarcely be imagined. And yet if the judges had adhered to the obvious meaning of the Madison-Randolph proviso, they would by that very act of faithfulness to the Constitution have beclouded the validity of the entire Bill of Rights and shaken the foundation of the great compromises which brought the Republic into being. Since then, by the same type of reasoning, *Hollingsworth et al. v. Virginia* has been accepted as constitutional dogma and the whole structure of subsequent formal amendments to the Constitution and of Court decisions concerning these amendments has been based upon the procedural misreading contained in the 1798 decision. Only twice has a President signed a proposed constitutional amendment; Buchanan in 1861, and Lincoln in 1865. The joint resolution signed by Lincoln became the Thirteenth Amendment. It is interesting to note that in this case, after Lincoln notified Congress that he had signed the proposed amendment, the Senate immediately adopted a resolution declaring that Lincoln's signature to the amendment was unnecessary.

Concurrent resolutions represent a more frequent type of evasion of the

[5] *Hollingsworth et al. v. Virginia,* 3 Dall. 378.

requirement for *both* congressional and Presidential participation in lawmaking. During World War II, it was found that congressional opposition to various emergency measures could be circumvented to some degree by providing for the authorization of these measures either by Presidential proclamation or by joint action of the two houses alone through a concurrent resolution. It is deemed highly probable that if it had not been for a provision of this type, the Selective Service Act of 1941 would have been defeated. Similar provisions were also used in the Lend-Lease Act, the First War Powers Act, and the Emergency Price Control Act. In a somewhat different form, provisions have been made for the use of concurrent resolution as a "legislative veto" over action initiated by the President. The outstanding examples are the executive reorganization acts of 1932, 1937, and 1945, under which a reorganization plan promulgated by the President would become effective unless a concurrent resolution disapproving it were enacted within a specified period of time. In 1949 President Truman tried to obtain the same provision in a new Executive Reorganization Act. His intention was frustrated, however, by members of the Senate who were interested in protecting the Army Corps of Engineers and other agencies from being reorganized. They, therefore, succeeded in writing into the 1949 Reorganization Act a provision that a Presidential reorganization plan could be jettisoned by a simple resolution adopted in one house alone.

Questions have been raised as to how the Supreme Court might conceivably rule on provisions of this type. While they certainly seem to violate the prescription of the Constitution, they do so to a lesser degree than already sanctioned in the handling of constitutional amendments. It is easy to develop an impressive theory rationalizing this procedure on the ground that the President is not deprived of the privilege given him by the Constitution just so long as the original act providing for one or another form of legislative veto is handled strictly in accordance with constitutional procedures. Above all, so much legislation and so many decisions affecting the lives of people and agencies have already been handled on this basis that any adverse decision by the Court would be highly improbable.

All or None

Unlike the governors of most states, who have an "item-veto" power,[6] the President cannot approve part of a bill and reject another part. But there are

[6] As of 1947, 38 states provided for an Executive veto of items in appropriations bills. The item veto in the states "has been somewhat less drastically involved than formerly, but it retains a measure of popularity as a 'gun behind the door.'" Frank W. Prescott, "The Executive Veto in American States," *Western Political Quarterly,* Vol. 3, No. 1, March, 1950, p. 112.

three ways in which this procedural fact can be circumvented and in which the President may obtain a wider area of choice.

First, the President may veto an entire bill on the ground that it contains a few items that he disapproves. In the case of appropriation and revenue measures, where delayed action might impede the normal operations of government, such a course is obviously not an easy one. Nevertheless, it has been taken. Both President Hayes and President Wilson have vetoed major appropriation bills because of their objections to particular items. In many instances, the threat of a Presidential veto has served the purpose.

Second, the effect of a selective veto can be obtained by administrative policies. When a rider providing for a loan to Spain was added to the Omnibus Appropriation Act for fiscal year 1951, President Truman disposed of it by simply announcing that he would not proceed with the loan. This type of procedure is regarded as more legitimate on matters of expenditure than in any other fields. In fact, the Federal-budget system makes direct provision for the Presidential impounding of agency funds. The mores of government life, however, are different with respect to regulatory provisions. If President Truman had expressed the same disregard for any provision of the Taft-Hartley Act as he expressed toward the Spanish-loan provision in the 1951 Appropriation Act, the result would have been a public uproar of incalculable proportions. With respect to the labor measure, President Truman solemnly and sincerely assured the country that he would do his best to have every provision fairly administered in accordance with congressional intentions.

Third, a bill passed by Congress could give the President the authority to accept some provisions and disapprove others. This was proposed by President Franklin D. Roosevelt both in 1938 and in 1942. In both instances, however, Congress refused to include the provision of this type. In 1950, President Roosevelt's son, Representative Franklin D. Roosevelt, Jr., of New York, proposed a general budgetary reform measure which would have provided, among other things, a joint rule of Congress to the effect that every appropriation bill must include the specific authorization for the President to disapprove individual items. Under this proposal the President's disapproval could then be overridden by a simple majority vote in Congress, rather than a two-thirds vote. This method, it must be recognized, is more aspiration than possibility, for assent to a procedure of this type would require that powerful groups in Congress voluntarily yield an important part of their power, thereby placing the President in a more strategic position in the legislative struggle.

The Time Allowed

Instead of being given unlimited time in which to make his choice, the President must act in ten days. A number of questions naturally arise as to how the ten days are to be counted. The first is whether or not Sundays are included. This was answered in the Constitution itself, which specifically provided that Sundays are excepted. A second question is, when do the counted days begin. The Constitution gives the President ten days "after it shall have been presented to him." This has been uniformly interpreted as meaning that the first of the ten days is the day after a bill has been presented to the President.

A third question is how much time may elapse between the day that a bill is passed by Congress and the day that it is presented to the President. Here there is no rule, merely a presumption that the officers of Congress should act without undue delay. But since a bill must be printed and then signed by the Speaker of the House and the Presiding Officer of the Senate, a certain amount of delay will take place. This amount can be stretched into a considerable period whenever there is sufficient motive for doing so. When President Wilson went to Europe to negotiate the Versailles Treaty, he reached an agreement with the Speaker of the House and the Vice-President under which they would not sign the bills passed by Congress until he returned to the country, thus permitting him to exercise his power of choice.[7]

A fourth question is whether the President still has ten days if, before the ten days have elapsed, Congress either recesses or adjourns. Some decades ago there were confusion and controversy on this matter. In recent years the Supreme Court has settled this question by ruling that the President may effectively sign a bill at any time within ten calendar days of its presentation to him, whether or not Congress has adjourned or recessed.[8]

A final question is whether an incoming President can handle a bill that had been presented to his predecessor. The Court, viewing the office in terms of the person rather than the institution, has ruled that he cannot.[9]

The Process of Presidential Choice

In a sense, Presidential handling of bills passed by Congress is one of the more institutionalized aspects of the Presidency. "Agency clearance," for example, has become a complicated procedural operation which is winning increasing attention of students of government. Yet it is also as important to understand how Presidential freedom of choice may be measured by previous commitments and how specialized forms of campaigning may be used at this stage by the various participants in the legislative struggle.

[7] *New York Tribune,* Nov. 21, 1918.

[8] *Edwards v. United States,* 286 U.S. 482 (1932).

[9] *Ibid.,* p. 493.

Previous Commitments

In a very major sense, the process of Presidential decision gets under way long before a bill arrives at the White House. The President is committed to specific legislative enactments by the affirmative programs he presents to Congress, by proposals presented by agency officials and congressional leaders, and even by campaign platforms. Affirmative statements of this type provide a series of commitments that serve as a general framework for Presidential decision after a bill has been passed by Congress.

But commitments of this type generally leave ample leeway. A Presidential recommendation for a national-science-research foundation does not commit a President to signing *any* bill that may set up a national-science-research foundation. Thus, a bill dealing with this subject was vetoed during the Eightieth Congress because of administrative arrangements which the President and his advisers on the subject regarded as unsatisfactory. It was not until the following Congress that the bill was passed in satisfactory form.

Even when the President himself may favor or strongly indorse a measure in a very specific form, there is no telling whether or not the bill might be redrafted completely and still meet with his approval. This happened in the case of the Employment Act of 1946: President Truman strongly indorsed the version which was passed by the Senate and criticized the version adopted by the House of Representatives. Yet he willingly signed an entirely different measure which was brought forth by the Conference Committee. In many cases, moreover, legislation moves through Congress without having been initiated by the Administration, and in these cases the proposals of the Administration are no guide for Presidential action.

"Will the President sign this bill or not?" This question is repeatedly asked during the course of the congressional consideration of a measure. It is asked of the President himself, of his closest advisers, of various executive officials, and of members in Congress who presumably are in a position to know. Sometimes the answers are uninformative or misleading. At the end of the Seventy-ninth Congress in 1946 one of the most important measures was the bill to extend price control. Before action on the Conference Committee compromise, reporters at one of his press conferences asked if he would veto the bill. Tris Coffin has recorded his answer: "The President replied primly, 'I never discuss legislation.' "[10] In this particular case Democratic leaders in Congress thought that the President would sign the bill. Yet the President took the position that the bill was unworkable and vetoed it. Coffin has recorded their reaction: "When Kenneth McKellar, the elderly presiding officer of the Senate, heard of the veto he swore a streak of emphatic and colorful profanity. Alben

[10] Tristram Coffin, "Missouri Compromise" (Boston: Little, Brown, 1947), p. 170.

Barkley was stunned. . . . In the House, Representative Spence sat bolt upright, folding and unfolding his fingers. . . ." [11]

In situations like this, it is obvious that if the President does not commit himself ahead of time, both supporters and opponents of a bill may claim that they have been nourished on false hopes or kept in the dark. Nevertheless, Presidents often refuse to predict whether they will sign or veto. "How can I say what I will do about a bill until it comes to my desk and I can see what is really in it?" is the question with which a President often retorts to those who seek a commitment on a pending measure. It is a wise question, for, in many cases, not until the last stage in the congressional phase of the legislative process is completed can anyone know what the words in a bill are really to be; and not for some days later, after careful study by experts, can one find out what these words mean or may be construed to mean.

Presidential action, however, follows no set formula. In some cases the President will state precisely what he will or will not sign. Wilson, for example, was often exceedingly specific, pointing out precisely what provisions must be included in a bill if he were to approve it. Despite his statement that he would never discuss pending legislation, Truman has done likewise. During the Eightieth Congress controversy over tax reduction, he announced that he would veto any bill that would reduce taxes. This immediately met with a blast from Senator Millikin of Colorado, who charged that "It is improper for Mr. Truman to tell Congress in advance what it can or can't do." [12] Millikin later told the Senate that this was the first time in history that a President had vetoed a bill before it had been sent to him.

Rather than make the final commitments in the name of his office ahead of time, the President will often have advance commitments made by members of his staff, heads of agencies, and members of Congress. This has the advantage of providing specific leadership during the course of the congressional process and at the same time of leaving the President free to modify his course, if necessary. A Presidential spokesman can be disowned without the President himself losing face. This was done by President Truman in the case of the basing-point legislation in 1950. Although a high White House official had stated in writing that the bill was in accordance with the President's program, and the Department of Justice had also indicated that it had Administration approval, the President felt that these statements provided no ironclad commitment and he vetoed the bill.

In some cases Administration officials speak for the President without authorization to do so. Members of Congress will do the same. Without authority to commit the President to the acceptance or rejection of a measure, they will

[11] *Ibid.*, p. 172.

[12] *The New York Times*, July 11, 1947.

hint broadly that they know which course the President will follow. There have been cases when both opponents and proponents of a controversial measure have been spreading the word around that the President would act as they wanted him to. When this happens, it is not unusual for the disappointed side to charge that the President has "broken faith."

Agency Clearance

The uninitiated probably think that a President looks at a bill that has been sent to him by Congress and makes up his mind himself after giving the matter whatever amount of thought is necessary. But it is not so simple. From the time of George Washington to the present, Presidents have requested the views of agency heads on whether they should approve or disapprove enrolled bills, particularly in really doubtful cases. It has also been customary for Presidents to ask that agencies recommending a veto submit to him a draft veto message, and that agencies recommending signature submit a draft of any statement that they might feel should be made at the time of signing the measure.

In recent years the task of obtaining agency views on enrolled bills has been handled by the Bureau of the Budget. Without even waiting for an enrolled bill formally to arrive at the White House, the Legislative Reference Division of the Bureau of the Budget obtains printed copies and sends them by special messenger to the various executive agency officials whose views it believes are needed. "In order that your views may be presented with the reports of the Bureau to the President," a typical communication will read, "please send to the Bureau, by messenger, within two working days, in accordance with Budget Circular No. A-9, your comments on this bill."

This enrolled-bill function of the Bureau has been the foundation for its other functions in clearing agency proposals for legislation and reports to Congress. Objections have often been voiced—loudly by some members of Congress, less loudly by some executive officials—to the Budget Bureau's work in policing agency proposals for legislation and agency reports to Congress on pending bills. Its work on enrolled bills, however, has generally escaped such attack; for it is hard to say that the President should not get staff help in discharging his clearly appointed constitutional function with respect to bills that have been passed by Congress.

In the entire process of handling legislation for the President, the Budget Bureau operates under the fiction that its job is merely to ascertain whether or not a bill conforms with the President's program. This fiction suggests that the Bureau is not wandering beyond the realm of budget making, and above all, is not engaged in advising the President on the formation of new policies.

In actual practice, however, the clearance process involves the Bureau of the Budget very heavily in the formation of the President's program—and particularly so at the stage of action upon enrolled bills. The Bureau summarizes the formal recommendations of the other agencies and invariably presents its own recommendations as well. On the great majority of measures this puts the Bureau in a position of tremendous influence. As Neustadt says, "On most of them—particularly the private bills—the Budget file was the 'works.' "[13] On many bills the Budget Bureau file goes right back to the birth of a measure and includes vital documents that were prepared at a time when the proposed measure was first being discussed. On still more measures the file covers the preparation of agency reports to congressional committees. Often it goes back to prior years of congressional handling of similar or identical measures. The information alone in files such as these is a tremendous source of influence.

Many Budget Bureau officials have also developed an uncanny skill to sense what the President wants them to recommend or to rationalize.

> On private bills and similar sorts of issues, one of Bailey's greatest strengths was his ability to anticipate the President's instincts about the equities involved, and provide him with the ammunition to justify them. If, as a matter of budget policy or personal conviction, he could not see his way to recommending what he suspected the President would want, he could and did try to provide a loophole in his own proposals, which the President could use if he so desired. Bailey's record of acceptance for his recommendations was no accident. This was an art, which the Bureau lost somehow in 1948, when its recommendations were reversed on eleven private and five public bills—a low point for the decade. In 1949 the record clearly improved, with the proportion of reversals reduced by half. The artistry has apparently been recovered.[14]

Yet a President cannot always depend entirely upon agency advice or the assistance of the Bureau of the Budget in completely pulling agency views together. Agency recommendations tend to become specialized. Agency officials tend to see the problem in terms of their agency and their personal records rather than from the standpoint of the President. Budget Bureau officials often seem inclined to use technical criteria which are politically unreliable.

The President's problem is an old one. Consider the example of Andrew Jackson and the bill to recharter the Bank of the United States. When the bill was passed by Congress every member of the President's Cabinet, with the exception of the Attorney General, was opposed to Jackson's plan for a strong veto message. Many agency officials suggested an easy veto that would open the door for approval of a modified bill a little later. Sensing the lack of support among the Cabinet, Jackson declined offers of assistance in the preparation of a message and put his "Kitchen Cabinet" to work on a veto message.[15]

[13] Neustadt, *op. cit.*, p. 80.

[14] *Ibid.*, p. 214.

[15] For a useful capsule discussion of this veto message see Marquis James, "The Life of Andrew Jackson" (New York: Merrill, 1938), pp. 600–602.

Most Presidents have solved this problem by entrusting vital clearance matters to their closest associates and personal assistants. This practice has paralleled the growth of the Budget Bureau's clearance function. Franklin Roosevelt and Harry Truman designated specific staff assistants in the White House—although their titles often varied—to maintain general surveillance of the Budget Bureau's clearance work, particularly on the more important enrolled bills. In cases of extraordinary political delicacy a White House aide may take over from the Budget Bureau completely and himself handle the entire job of obtaining agency recommendations, analyzing them, and presenting pertinent views to the President.

Campaigning

One difference between legislative campaigns at earlier stages in the legislative struggle and those after a bill has been sent to the White House is that in the latter instance the campaigning centers more than ever upon the thoughts and actions of one man. At this stage any road that can lead to that one man is usually deemed a worth-while road to travel. Members of Congress and leaders of private organizations will often call upon a President personally or write him beseeching letters in an effort to obtain the decision they prefer. Heavy contributors to the President's election chest may be brought into the picture. In fact, any person who knows a person who knows a person who knows how to get the President's ear fits into this phase of the legislative battle. All the established techniques involved in the organization of group support, the application of pressure, and the dissemination of propaganda may again be called into use.

Behind the formalities of the clearance process, executive-agency officials often enter vigorously into the conflict, if there is one. A Cabinet member who feels strongly about a measure whose future is in doubt will dutifully send his views in writing to the Budget Bureau and, in addition, circumvent the Bureau in an appeal directly to the President. An interesting example is found in the successful efforts of Oscar Chapman, Secretary of the Interior, to have President Truman veto a bill that would have stripped the Federal Power Commission of authority over consumers' gas rates.

Truman had promised Speaker Sam Rayburn to sign the bill, and the promise was still very much in force three days after the measure reached the White House. Then Chapman swung into action. He drafted a lengthy memorandum showing the President in detail that he need not feel bound to his promise to the oil and gas crowd, for they had deceived him in declaring the bill would not raise consumers' gas rates "one red cent." Next, he persuaded Commerce Secretary Charlie Sawyer to write a memorandum counseling a veto because many industries would be adversely affected by an increase in gas rates. Then he collared pussyfooting Mon Wallgren, the odd man on the five-man Power Commission, who had made a hurry-up trip to California in order to escape the backstairs pulling and hauling on the bill. Chapman convinced Wallgren that he should vote for a veto. Wallgren capitulated, and thus the Federal Power Commission went officially on record against the bill by a 3 to 2 count. It was this lightning-fast triple play, with Chapman the man in the middle, that shut out the Kerr Bill.[16]

Budget Bureau officials and members of the White House staff also engage, with the circumspection that their position necessitates, in activities to influence the President's decisions. At times they will go so far as to actively promote agency reports that will embody their own views and thus help to "put the heat on" in support of those views.

The clearance process, of course, is much more than a façade behind which legislative campaigning takes place. It is often a direct vehicle for such campaigning, and, in some instances, the most important one. The essence of a campaign for or against an enrolled bill lies in presenting in specific form both the detailed reasoning behind a desired course of action and an explanation of such a course in terms suitable for public consideration. In many cases the ultimate decision of the President will depend in large part upon whether or not a case has been adequately organized, both in terms of the reasoning that might appeal to the President and in terms of the public position which is most tenable for him to take if he signs or vetoes the measure.

An interesting case of effective campaigning occurred in 1950 when an enrolled bill to amend the Hatch Act reached the White House. The basic provisions of this bill would have allowed the Civil Service Commission to punish violators of the Hatch Act prohibitions against political activities by Federal employees with something less than permanent exclusion from the Federal service. There was little opposition to these provisions. However, the bill contained a provision that had been prepared by old-line Democrats in Virginia for the purpose of helping their state organization to win back control of the governing body in Arlington County, which had been captured by a coalition of liberal Democrats, Republicans, and independent voters who wanted a "new deal." Although the measure had been passed by an overwhelming majority in both houses of Congress, the liberal Democrats in Arlington County led an active campaign for veto. Through many channels they succeeded in conveying the idea to the President that signature of the measure would serve to favor the anti-Truman Democrats in Virginia. At the same time they developed an extremely detailed and effective critique of the measure itself, with particular emphasis upon the points other than the anti-Truman implications of the

[16] Robert S. Allen and William V. Shannon, "The Truman Merry-Go-Round" (New York: Vanguard, 1950), pp. 97–98. Chapman's efforts, it should be noted, did not take place in a vacuum. A group of Senators and Representatives and a number of private organizations played a vital role in the entire campaign.

measure. This point of view was presented to officials in the Department of Justice. As a result, the Justice Department, through the medium of the clearance process, suggested a Presidential veto, preparing as well a draft veto message. The only other point of view urged through the clearance process was that of the Civil Service Commission, which recommended approval of the measure—mainly on the ground that the provisions giving it more discretion for punishing violators of the Hatch Act were sorely needed. The opponents of the bill countered with the argument that the bill as a whole should be vetoed and that immediate steps should be taken to obtain congressional action on the particular provisions so strongly desired by the Civil Service Commission.

If the opponents of the bill had had nothing to rely upon except the conflict between President Truman and the anti-Truman Democrats in Virginia, the bill would probably have been signed. However, the campaign included the following factors: personal appeals to the President, an expertly prepared Justice Department report together with a draft veto message, and a plan for action to obtain through a separate bill the provisions desired by the Civil Service Commission. The sum of these factors succeeded and the bill was vetoed. A few days later a new bill was introduced to handle the provisions desired by the Civil Service Commission, and with strong Administration support it soon became law.

During the course of a campaign for the signature or veto of a measure the President is not necessarily a mere passive recipient of the pressure and propaganda generated by others. The President is invariably fully aware of the swirling conflict around him, knowing that he could not stop or evade it if he wanted to. He will often plunge into the conflict himself. At times his intervention may merely be to encourage one or another group whose potentialities for broader support he wants to put to the test. At other times, he may intervene more directly by laying the basis for the course of action upon which he knows he will embark.

The President's Approval

By the time a bill has surmounted all the obstacles it has faced from the time of introduction to approval by both houses of Congress, the odds are in its favor. In the great majority of cases, the President's decision is to interpose no additional obstacles. The choices that arise at the stage when assent is given are relatively minor, particularly in comparison with the problems involved in disapproval, as outlined in the subsequent section of this chapter. Attention need be paid only to the methods of assent and the use of statements concerning the legislation that has just come into being.

Signing and "Celebrating"

The regular method of assent is very simple. "If he approve," the Constitution provides, "he shall sign it." Most enrolled bills are handled in this manner. But what if he does not approve and yet does not want to disapprove? What if he merely wants to register reluctant acquiescence? It is testimony to the realism of the Founding Fathers that they provided a formula which facilitates the handling of such situations. If the President does not sign an enrolled bill and if at the end of ten days Congress is still in session, "the Same shall be a Law, in like Manner as if he had signed it. . . ."

Over the course of the decades other methods have arisen for registering the degree of Presidential approval or reluctance. One method is to develop the act of signature into a full-fledged ceremony. This can be done only in a limited number of instances, since the ceremonial functions of the President are so extensive entirely apart from the legislative process, and since there are so many bills that he must sign every year. It is usually done when the President wants to attract attention to a legislative victory or when members of Congress, executive officials, or important private organizations can convince him of the desirability of a "victory celebration." On such occasions the President's staff assistants must carefully prepare the list of invited guests, for accidental omissions can seriously wound the feelings of people who regard their own presence as essential. The newspapers will then carry pictures of Very Important People crowding around the President as he signs his name, and the most important of the Very Important People may even carry back with them, for mounting on a wall like a hunting trophy, one of the President's pens.

Statements of Clarification or Qualification

Another method of registering views at the time of signature is the issuance of a public statement. This can be done through the simple medium of a press release whether or not there is an accompanying formal ceremony.

A Presidential statement is an ideal way to underscore the importance of a bill. Sometimes this is needed to provide a bridge between the interest that was aroused during the course of the legislative struggle and the interest that will be needed in the future to support a successful administration of a measure. In the case of the Employment Act of 1946, the President's statement upon signature was designed to deal with those critics in both the "pro" and "anti" camps who had charged that the Act was meaningless because it was so different from the original Full Employment Bill. "In enacting this legislation, the Congress and the President were responding to an overwhelming demand of the people. The legislation gives expression to a deep-seated desire for a conscious and positive attack upon the ever-recurring problems of mass unemployment and ruinous depression." [17] Statements of this type can also serve to orient Administration policy. In the statement referred to above, President Truman described the Employment Act as "a commitment by the Government to the people—a commitment to take any and all of the measures necessary for a healthy economy, one that provides opportunity for those able, willing, and seeking to work." [18] This description of the Employment Act constituted a vigorous interpretation, one based upon a deliberate underplaying of the various limitations contained in the policy section of the Act upon the Government's "commitment to the people."

At times Presidents have used the occasion of signatures to voice much more controversial interpretations. When the Hobbs Anti-Racketeering Act was passed in 1946, President Truman sent a message to Congress which put a special interpretation of his own upon certain ambiguous provisions. Many of the sponsors of the Act had intended it to modify in various respects such labor legislation as the Railway Labor Act, the Norris–La Guardia Act, the Wagner Act, and the Clayton Act. However, the matter was left open for interpretation. The President's message to Congress dealt with this problem as follows:

> The Attorney General advises me that the present Bill does not in any way interfere with the rights of unions in carrying out their legitimate objectives. He bases this conclusion upon the language of the Bill, as a separate measure, and upon the legislative history.
>
> He makes reference, in particular, to Title II of the Bill. That title provides that nothing in the Bill should be construed to repeal, modify, or affect the Railway Labor Act, the Norris–La Guardia Act, the Wagner Act, and specified sections of the Clayton Act, *i.e.,* the great legislative safeguards which the Congress has established for the protection of labor in the exercise of its fundamental rights. The Attorney General also advises that the legislative history shows that the Bill is not intended to deprive labor of any of its recognized rights, including the right to strike and to picket, and to take other legitimate and peaceful concerted action.
>
> On this understanding, I am approving the Bill.[19]

This statement aroused a storm of protest from those who favored a more antilabor interpretation of the measure. A well-known columnist attacked the President's message on the ground that it would now become an essential part of the Legislative Record and enter into judicial consideration of the meaning of the Act.[20] A learned political scientist, however, has maintained that for a court to consider the President's views on matters of this type "would be to

[17] White House press release, Feb. 20, 1946.

[18] *Ibid.*

[19] White House press release, July 3, 1946.

[20] Arthur Krock, *The New York Times,* May 16, 1947.

attribute to the latter (the President) the power to foist upon the houses intentions which they never entertained." [21]

Presidential statements have also been used to voice direct objections to individual provisions, and by so doing help prepare the ground for future legislation that more adequately conforms with the President's standards. In 1910 President Taft signed an important rivers and harbors bill, and, at the same time, submitted to Congress a memorandum in which he pointed out what appeared to him to be some serious defects in the measure. The memorandum concluded with the following statement:

> I do not think, therefore, the defects of the Bill which I have pointed out will justify the postponement of all this important work. But I do think that in preparation of the proposed future yearly bills Congress should adopt the reforms above suggested and that a failure to do so would justify withholding Executive approval, even though a river and harbor bill failed.[22]

One of the most controversial of such statements was presented to Congress in 1947 by President Truman, at the time when he signed a measure to extend the time of rent control. Truman's opposition in Congress had presented him with a difficult dilemma. On the one hand, the bill that was passed by Congress provided for inadequate rent control, and if he had simply accepted it, he might have clearly been held to blame by thousands of tenants when they saw sharp increases in their rent bills. On the other hand, if he vetoed the bill, there was no question but that the result would probably have been no rent control whatsoever. This also would have been a bitter pill for the Truman Administration. The President solved this problem by sending to Congress a message which started as follows:

> I have today signed H.R. 3203, the Housing and Rent Act of 1947, despite the fact that its rent-control provisions are plainly inadequate and its housing provisions actually repeal parts of the Veterans' Emergency Housing Act which have been most helpful in meeting the housing needs of veterans.
>
> Had I withheld my signature, national rent control would die tonight. It is clear that, insofar as the Congress is concerned, it is this bill or no rent control at all. I have chosen the lesser of two evils.

He then proceeded to outline the defects of the bill, called upon governors to help remedy these defects by doing what they could to protect tenants, and proposed a number of other measures to help relieve the housing shortage.

A number of anti-Administration Senators immediately objected. "As I understand the Constitution," said one of them, "the President has no right to file with Congress any memorandum or any document when he signs an act.

[21] Corwin, *op. cit.*, p. 344.

[22] Message to Congress, June 25, 1910.

The only time when the President is permitted to file a memorandum or document is when he returns a bill unsigned, vetoed, and gives his reasons for doing so." [23] A number of Truman supporters in the Senate countered this argument by showing that President Taft had provided a precedent for the Truman message and that the President's constitutional authority to present his recommendations to Congress provided an ample basis for the action President Truman had taken.

Whether or not the President issues a statement upon signing a bill, other participants in the legislative struggle are apt to do so themselves. One group might issue a victory statement, another a blast. One group might use the occasion to point out the things they like and dislike about the measure, while another might call attention to the administrative problems that now must be faced.

The President's Disapproval

From the purely statistical viewpoint, Presidential disapproval of bills that have been approved by Congress is of little consequence. The total number of vetoes from 1789 to 1950 was only 2,002.[24] During the twenty-eight-year period from the beginning of the Sixty-seventh Congress in 1921 to the end of the Eightieth Congress in 1948, the total number of vetoed bills was only about two-tenths of one per cent of all bills enacted into law.

From the broader viewpoint of social combat, however, Presidential disapproval is of major consequence. It provides the most dramatic example of direct conflict between President and Congress. The role of the President in the legislative process cannot possibly be understood without an examination of the role of the Presidential veto, of postveto battles, and of the pocket veto.

The Role of the Veto

The development of the Presidential veto revives a striking example of the sharp contrast that often exists between the intention of the Founding Fathers and the subsequent realities. The men who drafted the Constitution saw in the President's veto power a means of protecting people of property and rank whose interests would presumably be better represented by the Presidency, and against assaults by the masses who might be expected to achieve more effective representation in Congress. With the extension of popular suffrage, however,

[23] Statement by Senator Ferguson of Michigan, *Congressional Record* (daily edition), July 1, 1947, p. 8160.

[24] Secretary of the Senate, "Veto Messages" (Washington, D.C.: Government Printing Office, 1948), p. iv. Daily Digest of *Congressional Record* for data on vetoes during 81st and 82d Cong., 1st Sess.

the "masses" more often than not were given more effective representation through the Presidency than through Congress.

By 1841 a Cabinet officer who served under both Jackson and Van Buren was able to say, with considerable justification, that "the veto power is the people's tribunative prerogative speaking again through their Executive." [25] Seventy or eighty years later there were enough examples of this "tribunative prerogative" to provide a real degree of justification for the following statement by Theodore Roosevelt: "as things now are, the Executive is or ought to be peculiarly representative of the people as a whole. As often as not the action of the Executive offers the only means by which the people can get the legislation they demand and ought to have." [26]

The original intent seems to have been that the President's veto would be used very rarely. Looking backward, our earliest government officials could well recall the attack in the Declaration of Independence against King George's abuse of the veto power: "He has refused his assent to laws most wholesome and necessary for the public good." They regarded the President's veto as something to be used very gingerly—mainly as a shield "against invasion by the legislature: (1) of the right of the Executive, (2) of the judiciary, (3) of the states and the state legislatures." [27] Another justification for the use of the veto was protection of the Constitution itself against legislation which in the President's judgment violated the Constitution. Rarely was the President expected to veto a bill merely because he felt that his judgment was better than that of Congress.

George Washington expressed his views this way: "From motives of respect to the Legislature (and I might add from my interpretation of the Constitution) I give my signature to many bills with which my judgment is at variance." [28] Faithful to this interpretation, Washington vetoed only two bills. In the case of one of these, a major consideration was to demonstrate that the veto power was something that would be used rather than be allowed to die. John Adams vetoed no bills whatsoever. Jefferson vetoed no bills. In fact, Jefferson's opinion was that, "unless the President's mind, on a view with everything which is urged for and against the bill, is tolerably clear that it is unauthorized by the Constitution—if the pro and con hangs so even as to balance his judgment—a just respect for the wisdom of the Legislature would naturally decide the balance in favor of their opinion." [29] With Madison and Monroe, the veto came more into use—with constitutional grounds being

[25] Levy Woodbury, quoted in Henry Jones Ford, "The Rise and Growth of American Politics" (New York: Macmillan, 1898), p. 187.

[26] Theodore Roosevelt, "Autobiography" (New York: Scribner, 1925), p. 282.

[27] Thomas Jefferson, "Writings," Ford ed., Vol. V, p. 289.

[28] Jared Sparks, "Writings of George Washington" (Auburn, N.Y.: Derby and Miller, 1851), Vol. X, p. 371.

[29] Quoted in Mason, *op. cit.*, p. 186.

offered for justification on six out of seven measures vetoed by these two Presidents. John Quincy Adams vetoed nothing.

With Jackson the whole picture underwent a great change. Jackson's twelve vetoes, as one commentator has put it, "descended upon Congress like the blows of an iron flail." [30] From then on the veto was established as a major weapon in the social struggle in America. Although for a little while Presidents continued to garb their judgment in constitutional phrases, it soon became perfectly clear that vetoes were to be based upon the President's judgment of what was right and what was wrong.

This trend was accelerated by the increasing use of the veto after the Civil War as a major protection against private bills which represented personal raids upon the Treasury. Of Grant's 43 vetoes, 29 dealt with private bills. With Cleveland, the proportion rose even higher.

> Cleveland vetoed more bills and resolutions from Congress than all the Presidents together before him. Most of his 250 messages of disapproval concerned private pension bills, which had become almost a racket. The President began reading these acts, sending for the case record, getting the facts and vetoing scores of them; John McBlair had died from epilepsy, not a war wound; Congress should not double Andrew Hill's present pension; another had been lamed as a boy, not in service; here was a man who had never served a day in the Army getting a gratuity . . . and so forth and so on. In June, 1886, he exposed the machinations behind this mass of pension bills giving public money to individuals who had no claim. There had been no real Congressional sanction for these gratuities. In fact, most of these bills had never come before a majority of either House, but passed at nominal sessions held for the express purpose of their consideration, and attended by a small minority of the members. The rebuke had some effect.[31]

A special analysis of Presidential vetoes has shown that since Cleveland's time private bills have remained a major target for Presidential vetoes, and, in fact, represent about 40 per cent of all bills that have been vetoed since 1789.[32]

In the field of public bills two types of measures were long considered safe from possibility of a Presidential veto: appropriation bills and tax bills. In more recent years these taboos have also been broken. Presidents Hayes, Wilson, and Truman have all vetoed appropriation bills. It remained for President Franklin Roosevelt to break the ice on tax measures. In February, 1944, he vetoed the proposed Revenue Act of 1944 on the ground that it would

[30] Ford, *op. cit.*, p. 180.

[31] George Fort Milton, "The Use of Presidential Power" (Boston: Little, Brown, 1944), pp. 157–158.

[32] Clarence A. Berdahl, "The President's Veto of Private Bills," *Political Science Quarterly*, Vol. 52, 1937, p. 508.

provide tax relief "not for the needy, but for the greedy." [33] Following this example, Truman vetoed tax measures on three occasions during the Republican-controlled Eightieth Congress.

Franklin Roosevelt was merely summarizing the practice of a good number of Presidents who preceded him when he told his department heads to review enrolled bills very carefully. He said: "If the decision is close, I want to veto." [34] It had already become clear that a veto can be used as a positive, not merely a negative, weapon in the legislative process. It had also become clear that veto can have a value far beyond its effect upon a particular phase of the legislative struggle. Frequent use of the veto power can place members of Congress on notice that they must reckon with the President. It can build his personal strength with executive officials and private organizations. It can provide a dramatic method for appeals to the country at large, particularly when Presidential action is overridden in Congress. There is little doubt that President Truman's repeated vetoes of major measures during the Republican-controlled Eightieth Congress were a major factor in his successful campaign for election in 1948.[35]

But it must not be thought that the "strength" of a President can be gauged directly by the number of his vetoes. Jefferson, with no vetoes in his record, was one of the strongest of all Presidents. His success in getting Congress to do what he wanted it to do in the first place made veto action unnecessary. In the case of Johnson, who vetoed more bills than any President preceding him, the vetoes were in large part a by-product of Presidential weakness.

Postveto Battles

The term "veto" is misleading. In Latin it means "I forbid." The term is used accurately when applied to the ability of a permanent member of the Security Council of the United Nations, under the United Nations Charter, to prevent many types of action by a single dissenting vote. It is inaccurate when applied to the President's disapproval of a measure, for the simple reason that the President cannot forbid; his disapproval can be overruled by a two-thirds majority in both houses.

[33] White House press release, Feb. 22, 1944. It was on this historic occasion that Senator Barkley dramatically resigned as Majority Leader, only to be reelected unanimously by the Senate Democrats.

[34] Proceedings, Twenty-eighth meeting, National Emergency Council, Dec. 17, 1935, p. 17.

[35] Hindsight, of course, is very helpful in such a judgment. Before the election took place, David Lawrence, an able commentator relying on foresight alone, wrote that "from a Republican point of view, nothing could bring a better break politically than a series of Truman vetoes, for it would furnish the spark for the 1948 campaign which would then be designed to get rid of an obstructionist President." *Washington Star,* Mar. 25, 1947.

Under clear provisions in the Constitution every veto message is supposed to be put to the test. A disapproved bill is to be returned to the house in which it originated, "who shall enter the Objections at large on their Journal, and proceed to reconsider it." This constitutional requirement, conceived at a time when it was thought that veto messages would be few and far between, is followed only when there is a genuine attempt to override the President's veto, rather than as a matter of routine. If no fight is contemplated, the house to which the vetoed bill has been returned simply ignores the constitutional prescription. Rather, the vetoed bill is usually referred to a committee or laid on the table. When one house has overruled the President and sent the vetoed bill to the other house, the second house may likewise avoid reconsideration. In either house, moreover, reconsideration may be delayed for a considerable period of time. It has occasionally happened that a bill has been vetoed by the President at one session of a Congress and reconsidered at the next session of the same Congress.

Some of the most dramatic debates in Congress have taken place upon consideration of a resolution to override the President's veto. Here the conflicting forces reach the last possible stage in the legislative struggle over an individual bill and mobilize their forces of pressure and propaganda to the fullest.

On a postveto bill, voting participation is also unusually high. Under the Constitution the votes must be recorded. The largest of all record votes are usually found on these occasions.

The conflict at this particular point is on an all-or-none basis. Amendments may not be offered. Although a substitute bill may be brought in by a committee, it must be handled as a new bill. And those who attempt to handle it must reckon with the fact that it does not enjoy the same privileged status as a vetoed bill.

Vetoed bills, however, are not customarily passed over the President's disapproval. Of the 1,106 direct vetoes, as distinguished from the 804 pocket vetoes, from the first Administration of George Washington to the end of the Eightieth Congress, only 65 vetoes were overridden—far less than 1 per cent of the total. Even during the Eightieth Congress, when President Truman was opposed by a strongly hostile majority in Congress, only 6 of his 42 vetoes were overridden—or about 14 per cent.[36] It should be kept in mind, however, that a large number of vetoed bills are either private-relief bills or other minor bills on which it is almost impossible to muster a two-thirds vote. On bills of a truly major character, it has been harder for a President to make his veto stick.

Whether a veto is sustained or overridden, however, the legislative struggle usually continues on new measures. When a veto is sustained, the effort is often made to reenact it—sometimes in changed form. During the Eightieth Congress

[36] Secretary of the Senate, "Veto Messages," p. 4.

the Republican leaders who campaigned for tax reduction saw their measures successfully vetoed on two occasions before they were finally able to pass a somewhat liberalized tax-reduction bill over President Truman's third veto. If a veto is overridden, on the other hand, the likelihood is that the effort will once again be made to achieve the objectives sought by the President. After President Truman's unsuccessful veto of the Taft-Hartley Labor-Management Relations Act, for example, both the Truman Administration and organized labor tried repeatedly to effectuate repeal of the Act.

Pocket Veto

There is one form of veto—the pocket veto—in which the President has complete power. Under the Constitution if the President does not sign a bill within ten days, and if the Congress in the meantime adjourns, the bill "shall not be a law." The records of the Secretary of the Senate show that for every three regular vetoes, there have been, on the average, two pocket vetoes.[37]

The end of a session rush, therefore, puts the President in an unusually strong position. Any bill which is sent to the White House during the ten days before adjournment can be prevented from becoming a law by Presidential decision with no possibility of overriding action by Congress. This fact has a direct bearing on the character of legislative campaigning. Because of it, delay in timing strengthens the position of those groups who feel that the President is on their side. Early action puts the President and those allied with him in a somewhat weaker position. At the same time, a postponement of adjournment can be used as a device to prevent the exercise of the President's pocket-veto power. This was one of the major strategies used by President Andrew Johnson's opponents during the embattled reconstruction days.

Until 1934 it was customary for a President to make no public explanations when he used the pocket veto. By virtue of the very circumstances, naturally, no pocket-veto message can be sent to Congress. But in 1934, this tradition was reversed by Franklin D. Roosevelt. In that year he pocket-vetoed 53 bills and gave to the press a full statement of the reasons for not signing each. He explained his course as follows: "The President has desired to take a more affirmative position than this, feeling that in the case of most legislation reasons for definite disapproval should be given." [38] This example was followed studiously by President Truman and will probably be followed by subsequent Presidents.

[37] *Loc. cit.*

[38] *Congressional Record,* 73d Cong., 2d Sess., p. 12456.

Chapter 20

SIGNIFICANT AVENUES OF PROCEDURAL REFORM

THE PREVIOUS prescriptive chapters in Part I dealt with proposals extending considerably beyond the legislative process. This was unavoidable because the activities of private organizations, political parties, and the Federal government cannot be discussed very meaningfully by putting on blinkers and focusing entirely on their direct implications for the legislative process.[1] Similarly, many of the most important proposals for change in the legislative process are those relating to the broader aspects of government and society rather than to the minutiae of legislative operations. In this chapter the perspective is narrowed. Attention is given exclusively to proposals for change in specific legislative activities of members of Congress and executive officials and ideas for the improvement of congressional methods and in certain specialized aspects of lawmaking.

NEW RULES FOR CONGRESSIONAL AND EXECUTIVE CONTESTANTS

Members of Congress

Proposals dealing specifically with members of Congress can be divided into four groups: those dealing with committee activities, with floor action, with staff assistance, and with better methods—particularly television and radio—of obtaining more public attention for legislative activities in Congress.

[1] For background material on proposals relating specifically to the legislative process see: Committee on Congress of The American Political Science Association, "The Reorganization of Congress" (Washington, D.C.: Public Affairs Press, 1945); George Galloway, "Congress at the Crossroads" (New York: Crowell, 1946); "The Operation of the Legislative Reorganization Act of 1946," *American Political Science Review,* Vol. 45, No. 1, March, 1951; Joseph P. Harris, "The Reorganization of Congress," *Public Administration Review,* Vol. 6, Summer, 1946; Joint Committee on the Organization of Congress: Hearings, 79th Cong., 1st Sess., 1945, and Report, 79th Cong., 2d Sess., Mar. 4, 1946; Estes Kefauver and Jack Levin, "A Twentieth Century Congress" (New York: Duell, Sloan & Pearce, 1947); Senate Committee on Expenditures in the Executive Departments, Hearings on Evaluation of Legislative Reorganization Act of 1946, 80th Cong., 2d Sess., 1948; Hearings on Organization and Operation of Congress, 82d Cong., 1st Sess., 1951.

Congressional Committees. STRUCTURE. It is occasionally proposed that steps be taken to go beyond the consolidation of congressional committees which was effected under the Legislative Reorganization Act of 1946. "Sound administration," argue Kefauver and Levin, "requires that the same number of committees exist in both bodies and that they have identical functions. This would facilitate combined hearings and provide for an easy exchange of ideas and information." [2]

While it is doubtful that joint hearings and joint-staff collaboration can be effected through a change in the rules, the most concrete form of joint action is the creation of joint committees. Proposals for joint committees in various fields have abounded and are likely to receive growing support. It is a fairly safe prediction that during future years the same kind of pressures which in the past have resulted in the creation of more committees within each house will express themselves instead through the creation of new joint committees.

A major point of concentration has been to prevent the creation of special committees. The substantive argument against special committees is as follows: "The jurisdiction of the standing committees has been so comprehensively defined in the reformed rules as to govern every conceivable subject of legislation. Thus, to set up a special committee is to trespass upon the assigned jurisdiction of some standing committee." [3] The standing committees have investigatory powers, investigatory staffs, and the power to report legislation developed as a result of their investigations. Special committees, on the other hand, result in the multiplication of committee assignments, duplicating requests for testimony by executive officials, and sporadic, rather than continuous, hearings.

One of the few defenses of special committees as such has been made by Dewey Anderson. He argued that the special-committee approach allows for more flexibility and dynamism. He pointed out that the author of a resolution to set up a special committee usually becomes the chairman of the committee if and when it is established, and that this is an important means of side-stepping the seniority rule. He also argued that special committees "have shown repeatedly that they can command outstanding men for special important tasks. . . . Numerous younger men on the make professionally come to special committees to serve for the relatively brief period of their existence who would be less likely to be attracted by the more routine tasks of a standing committee." [4] It should also be recognized that a special committee is often the only way to give expression to interests and new ideas not sympathetically represented by the leadership of standing committees.

A number of proposals have also been made for dealing with jurisdictional problems. The "grand-reform" approach is to redistribute jurisdiction among

[2] Kefauver and Levin, *op. cit.*, p. 117.

[3] Hearings on Evaluation of Legislative Reorganization Act of 1946, pp. 147–148.

[4] Hearings before the Joint Committee on the Organization of Congress, pp. 626–640.

the various standing committees. It is impossible, however, to devise a classification method that will not yield a considerable amount of overlapping. Once one system of classification is established, new problems will develop or new tactics will be devised which will make it useless. Nor is overlapping, kept within limits, necessarily undesirable. It provides a committee structure more responsive to the needs of a complex society and better protected against the preservation of tight monopolies by individual committees and the groups with which their key members are closely affiliated.

OPERATIONS. "Every committee of Congress could perfectly properly set aside a day in which the individual members of the House or Senate who had filed bills could come before the committee and give their reasons as to why they think their bills should have a hearing, and what witnesses, if any, they know would come before the committee. . . . The committee itself would then vote as to whether a bill should be given a hearing." [5] Occasionally a committee has developed a "docket-day" arrangement of this type. Extension of this practice would unquestionably strengthen the position of bills supported by weaker groups. However, it would not assure action on any given bill, but merely an opportunity for its sponsor to present the case on behalf of action.

Another area of committee operational reform has to do with holding hearings in open session rather than behind closed doors. While closed sessions are certainly appropriate for marking up a bill and voting upon it, some restraints could well be imposed upon the decision of a committee majority to close the doors on other occasions. Safeguards are needed also to help assure compliance with the present requirement for a majority decision. Progress would be made toward both of these objectives by adding a number of conditions to the present authorization for closed hearings when approved by a majority of committee members. One condition would be that the names of those voting for and against closed hearings be recorded and be made publicly available. Another would be that the reasons for closing the hearings be clearly stated and made publicly available.

One of the major problems in connection with congressional hearings is the extent to which an airing is given to various viewpoints. On the one hand, the hearing which develops a clear-cut partisan case is usually the best organized. On the other hand, the hearing which is allegedly an objective and dispassionate dissection of a problem is inevitably colored by the prejudices and predilections of the staff and committee members responsible for the decisions on who testifies and when. Apart from action to prevent unjustified closed hearings, the only formal step that can be taken to deal with this problem is to assure adequate advance notice and opportunity to testify. The growing practice of announcing hearings in advance at the end of the

[5] Testimony of Rep. Herter of Mass., Hearings before the Joint Committee on the Organization of Congress, 79th Cong., 1st Sess., p. 100.

Congressional Record is a long step in this direction. Approved scheduling to prevent conflicts between the hearings and floor operations will make more time available and thus facilitate presentation of views by witnesses. Moreover, committee funds should be allocated more liberally toward the payment of traveling expenses to bring witnesses and committees together. Many representatives of weaker organizations and individuals who have valuable statements to make (including impecunious experts from universities) could well be brought to Washington at committee expense. In some cases, moreover, field hearings by standing committees would go a long way toward providing local organizations and individuals with an opportunity to present their views to congressional committees. If properly planned, they would more than repay the committees for the extra effort expended.

A number of proposals have been made to improve the operations of conference committees. Among the most important is the proposal of the Joint Committee on the Organization of Congress that "Rules governing conferences be clarified and enforced so as to permit consideration only on sections or parts of a bill on which the Houses have, in fact, disagreed and to forbid conferees to change those parts of legislation agreed to by both Houses." [6] The provisions of the Legislative Reorganization Act, however, did not go as far as this recommendation. Particularly, the Act contains no specific prohibition against the deletion of matter agreed to by both houses. One student of congressional conference-committee operations, therefore, has concluded that either the language of the Act should be amended to clarify the situation or the same objective should be obtained through the development of a significant body of precedent under rulings by the Presiding Officer.[7]

Floor Action. CONTROL OF DILATORY ACTION. When one considers the problem of dilatory action other than the filibuster, there are no proposals for changing congressional rules that deal squarely with the issue. True, various minor proposals might slightly circumscribe the use of specific tactics. There would certainly be less use of quorum calls, for example, if it were made more difficult for an individual member to initiate a quorum call, or if the responsibility for counting a quorum were placed in the hands of the Presiding Officer. Similarly, electric voting would reduce the amount of time wasted through either quorum calls or roll calls. Year-long sessions would tend to reduce the number of situations in which, because of the imminence of adjournment, dilatory tactics are particularly effective. Nevertheless, short of a complete concentration of control over floor action in the hands of the Presiding Officer, no changes in rules can strip any group of members of all their opportunities to resort to dilatory tactics through one device or another. Floor

[6] Organization of Congress, 79th Cong., 2d Sess., Rept. 1011, p. 8.

[7] Gilbert Y. Steiner, "The Congressional Conference Committee, 70th to 80th Congresses" (Urbana, Ill.: The University of Illinois Press, 1951), pp. 173–174.

action is so intricate—and necessarily so—that it takes but a moderate degree of ingenuity to develop a new method of delaying action whenever the use of an older method is forestalled. The only effective control of dilatory tactics, therefore, is direct organized opposition by the opposing forces.

In the case of the filibuster, the theoretical possibilities of reform are quite different. It is entirely possible to formulate a set of rules that would allow members of the Senate reasonable opportunities to talk, but at the same time would enable talk to be stopped through a majority vote. One such proposal, for example, would authorize cloture on a two-thirds vote within forty-eight hours after the presentation of the pending question, with cloture by a majority vote possible after fifteen days of debate. Another variation would assign one or two hours of talking time to each individual member of the Senate. It is also easy to draft a rule which is applicable to all pending matters of any type, including resolutions to amend the rules.

In actual practice, however, the problem of filibuster control is one of how to organize an antifilibuster campaign. To an important extent this has always been the case. Under the present cloture rule, which is inapplicable to resolutions to provide for a tighter cloture, it is more so than ever before.

Essentially, the only way to beat the filibuster is to wear down the filibusterers. This can be done only if a majority group is determined to win and is strongly organized. This necessarily involves substantial support from private groups and government agencies. It also calls for skilled leadership. Filibusterers use every parliamentary trick of the trade. A counterfilibuster must proceed on the same basis. An illustration of the many tactics that are available is provided in a memorandum entitled, "How to Beat a Filibuster Without Cloture," which was prepared by Will Maslow of the American Jewish Congress on the basis of his experience with the 1946 filibuster against fair-employment-practices legislation. Because it so fully illustrates the inevitable intricacies of an antifilibuster struggle, it is here reproduced in full:

A resolute majority, determined to uphold democratic rule in the Senate, can beat down a filibuster if enough courage and determination are applied.

1. The bill should be brought to the floor as early in the session as possible, when no vital legislation or appropriation bills are pressing and no end-of-session log jam piles up.

1a. The motion to consider the bill should be made before 2 P.M., when by Senate Rule VIII it is not debatable.

2. At the close of debate on this first day, the Senate should *recess*, not *adjourn*. Thus the legislative day will continue and on the next *calendar* day the Senate will resume its unfinished business where it left off.

3. During the course of the filibuster, the Senate must continue to *recess* from day to day.

4. When the Senate reconvenes after such recess, reading of the Journal is in order and unanimous consent to read it should be denied.

5. If a Senator while speaking uses unparliamentary language or otherwise violates the rules, he should be required to take his seat (Rule XIX).

6. A Senator should not be allowed to yield to another except for a question, and particularly not for a time-consuming quorum call (Huey Long filibuster, June 13, 1935).

7. Permission to yield the floor to transact any business of importance to the filibusterers should be denied.

8. The Senator occupying the floor should not be allowed to make a second quorum call in the absence of intervening business. This prevents dilatory quorum calls.

9. Enforce the rule that a quorum call cannot be made by one Senator while another has the floor.

10. A Senator who makes a quorum call should not himself be allowed to leave the Senate chamber. If he does, the precedent declaring that he loses possession of the floor should be invoked and insisted upon (Huey Long filibuster, May 21, 1935).

11. A Senator should not be allowed to rest on his desk while speaking and the precedent "Keep your feet or take your seat" should be enforced (Reed-Smoot ship purchase filibuster, Jan. 29, 1915).

12. Permission to have the clerk read any material furnished by the filibusterer should be denied.

13. Rule XIV forbidding a Senator to speak more than twice upon any question during the same day (interpreted as *legislative, not calendar* day) should be rigorously enforced. In time therefore the filibusterers will have each spoken twice and thereafter be barred from further debate (O'Daniel OPA filibuster, June 27, 1946).

14. Evening sessions should be held particularly when the Senator holding the floor is unable to make a second quorum call. Such long hours will soon fray the strongest vocal cords.

15. Opponents of the filibuster should not be provoked to reply to the obstructionists, should not seek the floor, and should not interrupt for questions. A filibuster is not a debate; it is an endurance contest. The opposing point of view can be presented at press conferences.

How anyone reacts to antifilibuster efforts is inseparably connected with his general views on party responsibility and with his opinions concerning specific legislative measures. "With the American Executive holding office for a fixed term and never appearing before the legislature to account for his actions," writes Lindsay Rogers, "it is essential that there be some place in the congressional system where the party steam roller will meet an effective barrier. . . . Without the possibility of parliamentary obstruction—that is, filibustering—the party steam roller driven by a President, could move as ruthlessly on the Senate side as it does on the House side of the Capitol." In answer to the argument that a filibuster could hold up essential action in time of national emergency, Rogers suggests that under such circumstances a Presiding Officer could simply ignore the rules and close debate.[8]

[8] Lindsay Rogers, "The Senate and the Filibuster," *Survey,* May, 1949.

On the other side of this issue, the Committee on Political Parties took the position that the present cloture rule represented "a serious obstacle to responsible lawmaking." [9] Others have attacked the filibuster on the ground that it prevents control by any majority whatsoever and places an undue amount of power in the hands of tightly organized minorities. This point of view has been widely publicized by Senator Wayne Morse of Oregon, who has charged that "Under the filibuster, with all its insidious affrontery, the principle of rule by majority is denied the people in the determination of Congressional policy." [10]

Attitudes on this question, of course, are inescapably affected by the character of existing majorities. For example, when Vice-President Dawes launched a vehement but futile attack on filibustering in 1925, the leaders of the American Federation of Labor responded with a rousing attack on Dawes. A statement approved by its national convention in that year branded the Dawes proposal as one that "does not come from the people but emanates from the secret chambers of the predatory interests." The Senate itself was warmly described as "the only forum in the world where cloture does not exist and where members can prevent the passage of reactionary legislation." [11]

In subsequent years the bulk of liberal support was lined up behind measures that were endangered by filibusters and most labor organizations swung into opposition against filibustering. In 1947, when labor and liberal groups were organizing in another futile effort to control filibustering, the National Association of Manufacturers attacked the move as dangerous to the free-enterprise system. "The real reason for the continuous drive to change the rule," the N.A.M. charged, "is to make possible the enactment of socialistic and unsound fiscal legislation." [12]

By 1952 the filibuster question had become a major issue in the internal struggle within the Democratic party. Against the opposition of conservative Democrats, liberal Democrats pressed for a platform pledge to amend the rules. As a result of conciliatory attitudes by certain Southern Democrats, they succeeded in obtaining the following plank: "In order that the will of the American people may be expressed on all legislative proposals, we urge that action be taken at the beginning of the 83rd Congress to improve congressional procedures so that majority rule prevails and decisions can be made after reasonable debate without being blocked by a minority in either House." [12a] See "Additional Comments," pp. 445–446.

CONSTITUTIONAL PROVISIONS ON TREATY RATIFICATION. The proposal to

[9] "Toward a More Responsible Two-party System," *American Political Science Review,* Vol. 44, No. 3, Part II, Supplement, September, 1950, p. 65.

[10] Wayne Morse, "D-Day on Capitol Hill," *Collier's,* June 15, 1946.

[11] American Federation of Labor Information and Publicity Service, Oct. 17, 1925.

[12] *N.A.M. News,* Nov. 1, 1947.

[12a] "The Democratic Platform, 1952" (Washington, D.C.: Democratic National Committee, 1952), p. 43.

amend the constitutional requirement for a two-thirds vote on the ratification of treaties, along with those dealing with the Senate filibuster, the seniority system, and the powers of the House Rules Committee, rounds out the great quadrumvirate of perennial congressional reform measures.

The most eloquent case for amending the treaty provisions of the Constitution has been developed by Kenneth Colegrove, who argues that "the two-thirds rule, permitting the veto of treaties by a minority in the Senate, destroys international cooperation and constitutes a menace to the foreign policy of this country." [13] He recognizes that Executive agreements can achieve the same objectives as treaties and, when followed by legislative resolutions or statutes, have the full effect of law. But he maintains that an Executive agreement lacks the symbolic significance of a treaty and that "an agreement reached between executives, even when supported by joint resolutions of the legislatures, lacks, in the popular mind, that impression of solidarity of mutually accepted obligations, which comes from the solemn covenant negotiated by the Chief Executive and approved by the legislature in the very same form as signed by the minister's plenipotentiary." [14] He, therefore, recommends a constitutional amendment which would make treaty ratification no different from any other majority-vote part of the legislative process. Many Representatives have also emphasized the desirability of including the House of Representatives in the treaty-making process.[15]

Senators have often been hard put to justify their opposition to change in the treaty-ratification provisions of the Constitution. The obvious reason is that, when a treaty is presented to the Senate, the present constitutional provisions for ratification give every Senator at least one thirty-third of a treaty veto and considerably enhance his personal power.

The debate is reduced to relatively inconsequential proportions, however, when one recognizes that through seeking legislative ratification of Executive agreements the President of the United States can achieve Colegrove's objective without a constitutional amendment. Quincy Wright has put the case very bluntly:

> The Senate's tradition and prestige . . . seemed to have obscured from Constitutional jurists the opinion, earlier held, that the treaty process was intended only as an alternative, and that Congress is free to exercise its delegated powers in supporting or authorizing agreements made by the President. The conclusion may be drawn that in the making of international agreements, particularly those concerned with the conclusion of peace and establishment of institutions for perpetuating it, the matter rests in a very real sense in the hands of the President and the people. The

[13] Kenneth Colegrove, "The American Senate and World Peace" (New York: Vanguard, 1944), p. 135.

[14] *Ibid.*, p. 106.

[15] House Judiciary Committee, 78th Cong., 2d Sess., H. Rept. 2061, Dec. 13, 1944, p. 7.

President has ample legal power to negotiate on these subjects, and ample political power if he can command that majority for a peace which the public clearly desires. Difficulties which have in the past been found in the two-thirds vote in the Senate appear to have risen from political timidity and Constitutional misapprehension.[16]

MISCELLANEOUS. Among the most important of the miscellaneous proposals that have been made with respect to floor operations are those dealing with riders, talking opportunities on the floor of the House of Representatives, voting, and the printing of pending bills and amendments.

On a number of these items, Kefauver and Levin have offered or reiterated suggestions. They criticize the practice of the House Rules Committee in bringing forth rules which, by waiving points of order, encourage the insertion of riders in appropriation bills.[17] Yet they suggest no specific prohibition. If it is difficult in many cases to distinguish between a legislative appropriation item and an illegitimate rider to an appropriation bill, it would be still more difficult to make a clear distinction between a germane and a nongermane amendment to an ordinary bill.

Other Kefauver-Levin proposals would allow members of the House more talking time than allowed them under the present one-minute rule or under the usual unanimous-consent arrangement. Electric voting is advocated in order to make more time available. A major obstacle to electric voting is the fact that it would eliminate the roll call as a useful dilatory tactic. Also, under this system members of Congress would have to relinquish their practice of wandering at will while a vote was being taken and would have to appear at their regularly assigned desks in order to insert their voting key into an electric plug.

It has often been suggested that provision should be made for having more record votes on amendments and on the final passage of measures. An electric voting system, of course, would do more than anything else to facilitate record votes. The same objective could be furthered by requiring record votes on certain types of measures or by allowing more record votes in the House of Representatives on bills reported from the Committee of the Whole.

One of the provisions of the Legislative Reorganization Act requires that "no general appropriation bill shall be considered in either house unless, prior to the consideration of such bill, printed committee hearings and reports on such bill have been available for at least 3 calendar days for the members of the house in which such bill is to be considered." (Sec. 139.) This is a procedure which also might well be adapted to all bills, and proposals toward this end have often been advanced by members of Congress who object to voting in the dark. With respect to amendments, it has been proposed that no amendment be

16 "The United States and International Agreements," *American Journal of International Law,* Vol. 38, No. 3, July, 1944.

17 Kefauver and Levin, *op. cit.*, p. 53.

considered unless it is read fully to the House. The difficulty in this approach is that the reading of an amendment by the clerk is scarcely an effective way of acquainting members of Congress with its provisions. In fact, the present practice of reading bills before action is a vestige of an old-fashioned method of telling members what is before the House. It is dispensed with on many occasions and might well be dispensed with completely. To require that amendments be printed, on the other hand, might result in undue delay. This dilemma could probably be escaped through the use of modern duplicating services to make written copies of pending amendments available to all members before a vote is taken.

Staff Assistance.[18] FALLACIES. Before discussing possible improvements, it might be well to touch upon certain fallacies concerning the utility of staff facilities in Congress.

The most shallow fallacy is the assumption that congressional staff facilities could meet the total need that members of Congress have for staff work. Staffs of executive agencies and private organizations have always been used by members of Congress and will always continue to be used. This is not only because the officials of these groups constantly offer staff assistance in order to enhance their own influence. In terms of quantity, members of Congress need far more staff help than could conceivably be placed on congressional pay rolls. In terms of quality, they need the expertise that can be obtained only from people who have been intimately engaged in the operations of executive agencies and private organizations. In many instances skilled congressional staff members are needed primarily to serve as organizers of staff work outside Congress, or as intermediaries through whom staff experts outside Congress can present their work to the members and committees of Congress.

A second fallacy is the idea that larger and more adequate congressional staffs will inevitably provide a counterweight to the influence of executive officials and private organizations. It must be recognized that staff aides often serve as vehicles for the conveyance of outside influences. In fact, it might be said that effective staff work in Congress by employees who are sympathetic with executive officials is essential for good executive-congressional relations. The same might be said for the relationships between any given group in Congress and any given private organizations.

A third fallacy is the thought that the primary need in Congress is for objective staff assistance. In the sense that the word "objective" is taken to mean a quality of mind that induces one to recognize his own biases, this con-

[18] On this increasingly important subject see Lindsay Rogers, "The Staffing of Congress," *Political Science Quarterly,* Vol. 56, March, 1941, pp. 3–20; Gladys M. Kammerer, "The Record of Congress in Committee Staffing," *American Political Science Review,* Vol. 45, December, 1951, pp. 1126–1136; and Kenneth Kofmehl, "Congressional Staffing, with Emphasis on the Professional Staff" (doctoral dissertation in preparation, Columbia University).

tention is undoubtedly valid. But the term is also used to imply that an objective expert is one who does not take sides on issues. In this sense, the need of members of Congress for objective staff assistance is a relatively minor one and can be supplied entirely by the compilations of fact and opinion provided through the Library of Congress. The important need is for qualified staff assistants who take sides on issues and competently assist in the development of legislative positions and legislative campaigning.

A final fallacy is the theory that a more adequate staff will materially lighten the burden of work of the members of Congress. Actually, the provision of staff facilities cannot lighten the burden of work at all. The most it can do is to enable members of Congress to do a better job. But it must be kept in mind that the man who tries to do a better job often turns out to be one who sees that the better job is really a bigger job. Moreover, imaginative staff aides often uncover new problems, new opportunities, and new challenges. They tend to create—or at least attract—heavier burdens.

IMPROVEMENTS. When the exaggerated claims are trimmed down, there still remains an unquestioned need for additional staffing in Congress. First of all, there is a real need for more staff in the offices of most members. Ideally, each member should be authorized to hire a well-paid legislative assistant and a well-paid administrative assistant. With respect to the committees of Congress, the provisions of the Legislative Reorganization Act limiting professional staff to four employees is unduly restrictive. While some committees have not chosen to use this many positions, other committees operate in more than four major areas. Galloway has very pertinently suggested, therefore, "that each standing committee should be authorized to employ at least one staff specialist in each major subject matter within its jurisdiction." [19]

More attention is needed toward providing staff along party lines. "There are situations in the legislative committees of Congress where no specialized staff need be assigned to the minority members of a committee. On the other hand, when the minority members feel that they need staff help under their direction, they should not be dependent upon the good will or charity of the majority members of a committee." [20] The present arrangements providing staff assistance to the majority and minority policy committees in the Senate should be extended to cover the House of Representatives as well.

Many proposals have often been made for some central pool of staff experts available to Congress, but directly controlled neither by individual members nor individual committees. Walter Lippmann's "intelligence bureaus" were designed to achieve this objective. A more recent writer has picked this idea

[19] Hearings on Evaluation of Legislative Reorganization Act of 1946, p. 150.

[20] John Phillips, "The Hadacol of the Budget Makers," *National Tax Journal,* Vol. 4, No. 3, September, 1951, pp. 265–266.

up and has come forth with a proposal for a "National Institute for Policy Analysis," which would "provide Congress with analyses of proposed public policies, examine alternative policies, estimate the probable consequences of each alternative, indicate the degree of consensus or disagreement among qualified experts on the public consequences, and so on." [21] George H. E. Smith has developed the same theme in his proposal for a Congressional Advisory Council on Federal Legislation.[22]

If such proposals are oriented toward providing genuine policy guidance for members and committees of Congress, it is difficult to find much merit in them. If they are aimed at providing members and committees of Congress with analyses of facts and opinions, it should be pointed out that this work is already being done through the admirable facilities of the Library of Congress, and that any improvements in this work could unquestionably be handled best through an expansion or sharpening of the Library's operations.

A number of administrative improvements are needed in order to grease the wheels that result in congressional staffing. A personnel office is needed to serve as an informational clearinghouse between applicants or potential applicants and the members and committees of Congress with positions to fill. Moreover, special attention should be paid to the provision of promotion, salary, vacation, and retirement standards comparable with those enjoyed by personnel in the executive agencies.

Public Attention. "I think the Congress has been badly represented to the people in the public press and the public platform," testified Representative John M. Coffee of Washington. "That is due, in my judgment, to the fact that we do not have a press relations department." [23] What is needed is not a congressional public-relations department, but a number of operations which help make the facts of congressional activity more available to those who are interested in them.

TELEVISION AND RADIO. There is growing interest in proposals to televise and broadcast the proceedings of Congress. Because of its novelty and impact upon both eye and ear, recent telecasting of congressional investigations has had a sensational response from the general public. In radio alone there has been an extensive experience with the broadcasting of legislative proceedings, revealing a rich variety of institutional and technical arrangements developed to overcome difficulties in doing so. The United Nations and the national legislatures of New Zealand and Australia have been on the airways regularly. Saskatchewan Province, New York City, Connecticut, and other states and

[21] Robert A. Dahl, "Congress and Foreign Policy" (New York: Harcourt, Brace, 1950), pp. 159–160.

[22] Hearings on Evaluation of Legislative Reorganization Act of 1946, p. 181.

[23] Hearings before the Joint Committee on the Organization of Congress, p. 320.

localities have put their lawmakers on radio. Nor is broadcasting a novelty for the members of Congress, most of whom have faced the microphone as campaigners, as guest speakers, and in the normal course of their legislative duties.

> A new synthesis of legislative process and mass (communications) media is in the making and seems only to wait upon the appropriate catalyst, for the elements to be combined are many and the inertia to be overcome is great. . . . The American system of radio broadcasting is a complex commercial process, involving relationships among network, regional, and local broadcasters, advertisers, advertising agencies, the Federal Communications Commission, the manufacturers of radio sets, programming organizations, and trade, labor, professional, and audience groups. The United States Congress is an equally complex legislative process, involving relationships among its Members, political parties, pressure groups, constituents, and other branches of the National Government. . . . One thing, however, seems certain. The Congress of the United States should enjoy all the advantages and disadvantages of twentieth-century communications in the same way that the Presidency does. Furthermore, putting Congress on the air would demonstrate for all the world to hear how a democracy is able to create unity out of diversity.[24]

A memorandum, prepared by the New Zealand Legation, concluded that the broadcasting of parliamentary proceedings in New Zealand has assisted in

> . . . maintaining and perhaps improving the conduct of parliamentary proceedings —the listening public having shown themselves to respond very quickly and very critically to conduct which does not conform to accepted ideas of Parliament as a dignified and very serious institution. As a principle it is not now doubted in any quarter that the innovation has created a better informed and more responsible electorate.[25]

There are technical problems, which, in the case of radio, seem easy to master. Electrical recording machines can readily be made available for use at all committee hearings and during all operations on the floors of both houses. In fact, this is the most efficient way of recording testimony or debate for subsequent publication in committee hearings or the *Congressional Record*. It is far more accurate than the use of court reporters or stenotypists; it is less expensive; it is quicker. However, a distinction should be made between recording and actual broadcasting. Radio and television recording can easily be done on a large scale and a nonselected basis. From the materials compiled, selections can be made for use on subsequent radio and television programs. Continuous broadcasting, however, is an entirely different matter. This would

[24] Ralph M. Goldman, "Congress on the Air," Hearings on Organization and Operation of Congress, 82d Cong., 1st Sess., 1952, reprinted from *Public Opinion Quarterly* (Winter, 1950–1951). This article admirably summarizes past experience and continuing obstacles in legislative broadcasting.

[25] Hearings before the Joint Committee on the Organization of Congress, 79th Cong., 1st Sess., p. 944.

require the complete use, during long hours of many days, of time available to two stations, one for the Senate and one for the House. Arrangements of this type would necessarily imply government-owned or government-subsidized facilities.

The big problems, however, are not technical. For one thing, the more extended use of either radio or television makes correction of the record more difficult for members of Congress who are accustomed to revise their remarks before they are printed. A more important result would be tighter control of debate. A Senator may have a right to speak as long as he wants to, but the right to project his voice and image on the air waves as long as he can hold out is something else, something that would unquestionably run into the resistance of colleagues who resented such a monopolization of the channels of personal publicity. Thus, lurking behind any inertia with respect to extending the use of radio and television to the floor of the Senate are the fears of those interested in preserving the filibuster as a major weapon of legislative struggle.

Finally, there is the danger that television of congressional hearings can be "a monster which can destroy innocent individuals, whole corporations, political parties, and entire administrations." Because of this danger, Senator Wiley proposed a study by the Senate Rules Committee to survey the various problems involved in using television, radio, or the motion pictures with respect to the proceedings of Congress and its committees.[26]

CONGRESSIONAL DOCUMENTS. There are a number of methods by which congressional documents can be rendered more useful to those interested in finding out what has taken place during the course of legislative operations.

First of all, much can be done to make printed committee hearings more useful and readable documents. A rare example of good editing is found in the 1945 hearings of the Joint Committee on the Organization of Congress. These hearings contain, in addition to the customary table of contents listing the names of the witnesses, a subject-matter index, a brief summary of each day's hearings, and a critical bibliography prepared by a Library of Congress technician on the entire question of congressional organization. Other hearing volumes have occasionally included subheads in the text to indicate each phase of the testimony or interrogation. Furthermore, it would be extremely helpful if each committee published more extensive reports both weekly and annually, indicating the status of all bills referred to it or reported from it and a summary of all committee reports that have been made, together with an indication of the members whose names are attached to each report. In addition, Kefauver and Levin advocate that "it should be mandatory that committees

26 "Televising of Congress," Hearings on Organization and Operation of Congress, 82d Cong., 1st Sess., 1952, pp. 601–603.

publish all votes on pending legislation and amendments considered, including adverse votes." [27]

A number of proposals have been made concerning improvements in the *Congressional Record*. Kefauver and Levin have suggested that Congress "should dignify it and improve its design and give it a fixed selling price, regardless of size, that would cover manufacturing and distribution costs. It then could be put on sale at news stands all over the country." [28] They also ask that an effort be made to control the insertion of miscellaneous documents and the extension of remarks beyond what was actually said on the floor. Another proposal is for greater control over the corrections that a member is allowed to make in his floor remarks before they are printed in the *Congressional Record*.

It would also be useful to have the Library of Congress prepare a legislative history of every major statute, shortly after it is enacted. No matter how important a piece of legislation may be, the records concerning its development are invariably scattered through scores of separate documents, many of which soon become unobtainable. Within a year or so after the time a proposed bill becomes law, the full story of its legislative development usually is known by only a few persons who were close to the picture. The publication of legislative histories would make this valuable information public property.

The Executive Officials

Proposals concerning the legislative role of executive officials tend to be less abundant than those which relate to members of Congress. The idea that legislation is the job of Congress alone has misled many students of the subject. The more dramatic proposals dealing with the broad problems of congressional-executive relations are discussed in Chap. 6. Here attention will be given to the less sweeping reforms affecting executive proposals for legislation, the President's veto, and executive campaigning.

Executive Proposals for Legislation. Reform recommendations on this aspect of the legislative process are of two types: ideas concerning what the role of executive proposals should be, and ideas concerning the preparation and transmittal to Congress of executive proposals.

THEIR ROLE. There is a widely held conception that the officials of the executive branch—and the President in particular—should occupy a special role in the initiation of legislative proposals. For some, this is the only way to approximate under American conditions the much-admired ideal of Cabinet leadership as exercised under a parliamentary system. For others, it is more the natural consequence of our own political structure. Only the executive officials, it is

[27] Kefauver and Levin, *op. cit.*, p. 140.
[28] *Ibid.*, p. 204.

argued, have the specialized expertise and the familiarity with administrative operations necessary for the preparation of a sound legislative proposal. In these officials alone can one find the aloofness and objectivity needed to protect the public interest against the assaults of private groups. In the President alone can one find a national leader elected by the entire people and responsive to the interests of the entire people.

This point of view is more widely held than the occasions of its formal expressions would indicate. Moreover, when formally expressed, it is usually presented in abstract terms, unaccompanied by specifics.

One of the best expressions of this point of view has been voiced by Luther Gulick in the concluding paragraph of an important journal article:

> In the world into which government is moving, the executive will be called upon to draft the master plan. Deliberative and advisory representative groups will be asked to consider and adopt the broad outline of various parts of this plan. The executive will then be given full power to work out the remainder and the inter-relations of the program and to carry it into effect, not only through the established agencies of government but also through new agencies of a quasi-private character. The legislature of the future will have two primary powers: first, the veto over major policy, and second, the right to audit and investigate. Behind the entire process will be the controlling hand of the mass of citizens in party and pressure groups. These are the bricks and straws from which the new theory of the division of powers must be constructed.[29]

In less general terms, the proposal has often been made that some form of special status be given to Executive-sponsored bills. Galloway, for example, has proposed a semimonopoly for executive officials in the initiation of legislative action.[30] Black has proposed that each house of Congress establish a "Committee on Presidential Bills" to which Presidential recommendations for legislation "could be sent openly and as a matter of usual and formal routine, and not by the devious hands of some unacknowledged agent." When reported, an executive bill would then enjoy a privileged place on the calendar.[31] Others have occasionally proposed a formal method of identifying executive bills, not as a method of bestowing honor, but more in order to place members of Congress on their guard against executive domination of the legislative process.

There is a compelling case, however, against the general approach toward executive leadership, which is exemplified by the Gulick, Galloway, and Black proposals. For one thing, executive officials have no monopoly of expertise and

[29] "Politics, Administration, and the New Deal," *The Annals,* Vol. 169, September, 1933, p. 66. This entire article bears careful reading by those interested in the development of modern thought on American government.

[30] Galloway, *op. cit.,* p. 308.

[31] Henry Campbell Black, "The Relation of the Executive Power to Legislation" (Princeton, N.J.: Princeton University Press, 1919), p. 185.

specialized experience in administrative operations. Many private organizations are far better equipped to initiate legislative action in certain matters than the employees of any government agency. The expertise and experience that exist within the executive branch is often completely disregarded by agency heads and Presidents, or is not made available to them. Various members of Congress often enjoy a better opportunity to harness executive-staff resources. When executive experts engage in informal or "bootleg" work for members of Congress, they are often able to free themselves from the wraps of hierarchical control and perform creative tasks that could never be equaled within the regular procedures of the executive branch.

Furthermore, it is sheer nonsense to regard executive officials, even Presidents, as people who somehow are free of the influence of group pressures and have the interests of the "whole people" at heart. Among many agency heads and their appointees there is as much localism and narrowness of perspective as there is in either house of the Congress. In contrast with a Senator or a Representative, for example, who must deal with many groups with divergent views, the executive official is often responsive only to a limited clientele interested in one objective. In so far as the President is concerned, one finds not freedom from pressures, but a somewhat different orientation toward group interests. A President must necessarily give particularly heavy weight to the interests and views of those who hold the balance of power in pivotal states. This often produces a noticeable leaning toward the views of important mass organizations in urbanized areas rather than the dominant views in Congress, where the formal pattern of representation accentuates the influence of prominent political groups in rural areas. The thought that Congress can develop its own legislative program is even more unrealistic than the idea that it can be developed for them by executive officials only. The point of view here expressed is that it is entirely legitimate for all contestants in the legislative process to have their own sets of legislative proposals, and that there is nothing either inherently desirable or at all practical in the idea that any given set of contestants be given a monopoly of the initiation of legislative proposals.

THEIR PREPARATION AND TRANSMISSION. How can a President best select those legislative proposals which shall be regarded as peculiarly his own, those which other executive officials might be allowed to present as their own, and those which should be killed or revised? Should a President attempt to reconcile all intra-Administration differences before a measure is presented to Congress? "Conflicts and differences between administrative departments concerning proposed legislation, whether on major policies or details," advised the President's Committee on Administrative Management, "should, so far as possible, be adjusted before such bills are presented to the Congress." [32] The

[32] Report of President's Committee on Administrative Management (U.S. Government Printing Office, 1937), p. 20.

merit of this point of view lies in the obvious fact that any President who allows too many policy controversies among his agency heads will seriously weaken his position before Congress and his standing before the country. On the other hand, the settling of all agency disputes before legislation is proposed to Congress seems hardly possible and, in some cases, undesirable. Often the only way to settle an intra-Administration quarrel is for the President to organize enough support in Congress to win over or sidetrack officials who have opposed him within the executive branch. In many cases, also, a constructive compromise can be worked out only after there have been public hearings before congressional committees and a certain amount of congressional debate.

Another aspect of the problem is the location of the legislative clearance function. The President's Committee on Administrative Management recommended a double approach: a legislative counsel on the White House staff to assist the President on major bills, and a legislative clearance function in the Bureau of the Budget to handle the clearance operation on other bills. Both these proposals have been carried out in practice. There is no reason whatsoever to question the utility of a legislative counsel in the White House, but a legitimate question can be raised on whether or not the Bureau of the Budget is the proper location for the remainder of the legislative clearance function.

It would probably be advisable to end the myth that the Budget Bureau's operation on bills is limited to ascertaining whether or not a proposed measure happens to conform to "the President's program." This myth serves to concentrate a considerable amount of policy-making power in the hands of Budget Bureau technicians who may have only limited understanding of the broad problems involved and even less familiarity with legislative and political strategy. Any President would be well advised to insist that Budget Bureau work in this field be openly recognized as dealing directly with the formation of Presidential policy.

Where and how should legislative drafting in the executive branch be done? Many agency officials have made the mistake of regarding legislative drafting as a matter to be handled by lawyers alone. This has often conferred undue policy-initiating power upon lawyers having an inadequate grasp of the total objectives to be sought. It has denied to many agencies the strength which comes from the cross-fertilization of ideas by personnel with varying skills and backgrounds. Moreover, many executive officials are accustomed to handling the drafting process without sufficient consultation with potential supporters in Congress and in private organizations. This attitude stems in part from an unrealistic emphasis upon the theoretical lines which divide the executive branch from Congress, and government from private groups. It is nourished by a psychological frame of mind which places greater value upon the self-expression achieved by writing one's views in a draft bill than upon the actual results to be obtained through the organization of support behind a legislative proposal.

Still another problem is whether executive proposals should be transmitted to Congress seriatim or in some sort of comprehensive listing. Both Woodrow Wilson and Franklin Roosevelt emphasized the former approach. Under Truman, however, much greater emphasis has been given to formal listing. The first major Truman message to Congress, in September, 1945, after the surrender of Japan, listed 21 points for legislative action. The same pattern was followed by Truman in subsequent years in his annual State of the Union Messages and the accompanying Economic Reports and Budget Messages. This approach should be continued. Also, the major executive agencies should follow suit and develop comprehensive legislative programs that can be presented *in toto* to the appropriate committees of Congress at the beginning of each session. This would assist in the elimination of many legislative conflicts among executive agencies and facilitate the planning of an orderly schedule by congressional leaders. Special requests during the course of the year can readily deal with individual matters in greater detail and with unforeseen legislative needs that are always bound to develop.

The President's Veto. The proposals of greatest consequence in this area are those which would in one way or another give the President the power to veto individual items in a measure that has been passed by Congress. In addition, there are a number of other proposals of lesser importance.

THE ITEM VETO. "An important feature of the fiscal procedure in the majority of our states is the authority given to the Executive to withhold approval of individual items in an appropriation bill and, while approving the remainder of the bill, to return such rejected items for the further consideration of the legislature. This grant of power has been considered a consistent corollary of the power of the legislature to withhold approval of items in the Budget of the Executive; and the system meets with general approval in the many states which have adopted it." [33]

In making this proposal, President Franklin Roosevelt echoed the views of Presidents Grant and Arthur and of many students of fiscal affairs. In supporting President Roosevelt's proposal, Senator Arthur Vandenberg of Michigan added an additional argument: "Now that we suddenly confront fabulous appropriation totals . . . it seems more than ever necessary that the Presidential veto should be afforded some degree of that same discretion and selectivity in respect to the component parts of an appropriation bill which the Congress itself enjoys when it formulates and passes these bills." [34] The argument has also been advanced that the Presidential item veto is essential if the President is to trim the pork-barrel appropriations and cope with riders on

[33] Budget Message for Fiscal Year 1939, transmitted to Congress, January, 1938.
[34] *Congressional Record,* 77th Cong., 2d Sess., Mar. 10, 1942, p. 2153.

appropriation bills. This theme is particularly pertinent if and when appropriation measures are merged into an omnibus bill, a position stated by Representative Franklin D. Roosevelt, Jr.[35]

Many arguments have been advanced against the item-veto proposal. Herring comments:

> If the President possessed the selective veto, this would mean an enormous additional increase in his responsibilities. Legislatures would be more prone to give in to the demands of particular interests and include items with the expectation that the President would veto these undesirable elements. Much of the pressure now exerted on Congress would be transferred to the Executive. . . . Congress would become a less responsible body both in its substantive law-making and in the ease with which it could find shelter from political difficulties behind the White House.[36]

In similar terms Young argues that, "It is better for Congress to assume full responsibility for the budget which it passes rather than play hide-and-seek with the President on particular items." [37] Members of Congress have repeatedly attacked the proposal on the ground that it would concentrate too much power in the hands of the President.

The best reasons against the item veto have usually been ignored. First, the President already enjoys the power of curtailing expenditures. To the extent that he exercises it, he is not subject to a congressional resolution overriding his action. Second, once one goes beyond the dropping of individual sums of money in appropriation bills, it is really impossible to contrive an item-veto system which can deal with either legislation in appropriation bills or riders in general. Provisions of this type can be written in such a manner as to make them well-nigh inseparable from the rest of a measure. In part, therefore, the item-veto power is in effect enjoyed by the President and in part it is the kind of power that could not be conferred upon him.

OTHER PROPOSALS. For decades individual members of Congress who have objected to specific Presidential vetoes have proposed that either the President's veto power be abolished or that Congress be given the power to override a Presidential veto by a majority instead of a two-thirds vote. Neither is very practical. A more effective means of undercutting the President's veto power is through the use of concurrent resolutions. The concurrent resolution has the advantage that provisions authorizing its use can be tucked away in a broader measure which has Presidential approval. A concurrent resolution terminating a statute or directing that specific actions be taken need not be transmitted to the White House for the President's approval.

A minor proposal to weaken the President's veto position would eliminate the pocket veto by authorizing a designated representative of either house of

[35] *Congressional Record,* 81st Cong., 2d Sess., Apr. 6, 1950, p. 4928.

[36] Pendleton Herring, "Presidential Leadership" (New York: Rinehart, 1940), pp. 76–77.

[37] Roland A. Young, "This Is Congress" (New York: Knopf, 1946), p. 235.

Congress to receive a vetoed bill during a recess or adjournment.[38] Since there is no limitation upon the number of days in which Congress must act in order to override a Presidential veto, the Clerk of the House or the Secretary of the Senate could then refer the vetoed bill to the House or the Senate for action upon the end of the recess or adjournment. This plan would be still more effective if Congress met in year-round sessions and abandoned the idea of an early adjournment.

A number of minor proposals have been made for strengthening the President's veto. Brogan has argued that a President should be able to combat a measure with which he is in disagreement by going over the heads of Congress and calling for a national referendum.[39] Yet despite the popularity of the referendum in state and local affairs, there has been singularly little interest in this approach toward national affairs. Both the practical problem of handling a referendum on a national scale and the tremendous number of conflicts which might be channelized in this direction if the national referendum were accepted as a method of legislation have tempered the ardor of referendum enthusiasts.[40]

A question that has been long neglected and that deserves more attention concerns the amendment of vetoed measures. It is customary for a President, upon vetoing a bill, to indicate the nature of the changes that would be required to enable him to reverse his position; at times Presidents have offered such amendments in detailed form. Yet under the rules of Congress, a vetoed bill cannot be amended. A new bill embodying the proposals that the President has submitted for a compromise between the President's proposals and the provisions of the vetoed bill must start at the beginning of the legislative process and run the gauntlet of two committees and action on the floor of both houses before it can be sent back to the White House. "The rule is wise," comments Luce, "not only because there must be an end to everything, but also because the work of engrossing ought not to have to be done twice." [41] Yet in effect the rule postpones an end to the consideration of a vetoed matter rather than facilitating a prompt ending; and the clerical work involved in engrossing is too minor a matter to affect the case one way or another. If it were possible for Congress to amend a vetoed bill promptly and then send it back to the White House, it would be possible to save a lot of lost motion and facilitate executive-congressional agreement.

[38] Testimony of Representative Hatton Sumners, Hearings before the Joint Committee on Organization of Congress, 79th Cong., 1st Sess., p. 180.

[39] D. W. Brogan, "Government of the People" (New York: Harper, 1943), p. 382.

[40] For another approach to the use of the referendum, and particularly a national advisory referendum, see Ralph M. Goldman, "The Advisory Referendum in America," *Public Opinion Quarterly,* Summer, 1950.

[41] Robert Luce, "Legislative Problems" (Boston: Houghton Mifflin, 1935), p. 170.

Executive Campaigning. CURTAILMENT. When the Select Committee on Lobbying Activities was set up in the House of Representatives during the Eighty-first Congress, Republican members of the House insisted that the Committee deal not only with lobbying by private groups, but also with "all activities of agencies of the Federal government intended to influence, encourage, promote or retard legislation." [42]

The majority members of the committee developed the point of view that executive officials have the responsibility of "speaking on those issues which transcend group lines or which have no other effective voice," and that executive participation in legislative campaigns is essential to prevent public policy from being "the product of willy-nilly submission to the demands of whatever group has the largest material resources at its disposal." [43] They pointed out that the Constitution gave the President responsibilities for participating in the legislative process, that many executive agencies are required by law to submit legislative proposals to Congress, and that committees and members of Congress continually seek the help of executive officials on legislative matters. At the same time, the majority of the committee stated "that there are limits beyond which executive participation in legislative policy-making may impinge on the authority of Congress and thus endanger our Constitutional system." [44]

When it comes to the question of what might actually be done to curtail executive campaigning the purely abstract or general approach once again breaks down. Unless one would curtail the President's powers under the Constitution, there seems to be no formal procedure for limiting executive influence upon the legislative process.

Should executive lobbyists be required to register under the Regulation of Lobbying Act? Dorothy Detzer thinks so:

> If the LaFollette-Monroney Act were amended to include the government lobbyists, this step, to be sure, would not be an absolute guarantee against misuse of office, any more than the Act now affords complete protection against the nefarious activities of private lobbyists. It would, however, provide an open record, and that record could reveal who lobbied, when, and on what. And with that record, as well as the one now required for private lobbyists, the public would possess a tool with which to secure a new and more effective measure of democratic control.[45]

This proposal was well answered in the testimony of Roger Jones, Director of the Division of Legislative Reference in the Bureau of the Budget, during the hearings of the House Select Committee on Lobbying Activities:

[42] H. Res. 298, 81st Cong., 1st Sess.

[43] Hearings before the Select Committee on Lobbying Activities of the House of Representatives, 81st Cong., 2d Sess., Oct. 20, 1950, General Interim Report, pp. 61–62.

[44] *Ibid.*, p. 62.

[45] *Ibid.*, p. 53.

> In one sense [executive officials] are actually registered. If you will, I think the listing of Executive Branch officials that is contained in the Congressional Directory and in the Official Register of the United States is practically a public notice that anyone there listed may be given a specific job by the proper superior, on up the line to the President of the United States, which could probably be construed as an effort to influence legislation.[46]

Other methods of curtailing executive campaigning are listed in the General Interim Report of the House Select Committee on Lobbying Activities. One method is to use appropriation acts for the purpose of forbidding the expenditure of money for certain public-relations activities. Another is to investigate activities of officials whose actions have been offensive. Still another check is the possibility of having an executive underling fired or voting an administration out of office. Yet all of these techniques, it should be kept in mind, are methods of dealing with specific situations. In effect, they are instruments for countercampaigning rather than for providing a general curtailment in the legislative campaign functions of executive officials.

STRENGTHENING. Quite a number of the proposals already discussed are justified on the ground that they would strengthen the role of the President or other executive officials in the determination of final legislative decisions. Among the most important of these are the proposals for congressional-executive merger and congressional-executive cooperation which were discussed in Chap. 6 and those discussed in this chapter for strengthening the role of executive officials in initiating legislation and extending the President's veto power.

In addition, there are a number of other lines of thought that deserve consideration. The first is the thesis that the greatest potential strength of a President lies in his ability to appeal over the heads of Congress to the American people. In part, it has become a commonplace, when a President's legislative program faces trouble in Congress, for his supporters immediately to suggest that he "go on the air," "get on a train," or otherwise take his case to the people.

This thesis has much to commend it. The White House is an ideal springboard for propaganda activities. Every President is in a peculiarly strategic position to reach vast numbers of people with his message. His message is particularly important when it can appeal to the millions of individuals who are not represented by effective private organizations, but who, through the exigencies of Presidential political campaigns, may become a decisive force at the next Presidential election. In this sense the President's appeals to the people are a method of organizing the unorganized for practical political action.

[46] "The Role of Lobbying in Representative Self-government," Hearings before the Select Committee on Lobbying Activities of the House of Representatives, 81st Cong., 2d Sess., p. 142.

They are also a method of strengthening whatever support he may have among the big-city voters of the pivotal states.

Yet it is also important to recognize a number of major weaknesses in the "Presidential appeal" approach. In the first place, a Presidential appeal to public opinion cannot possibly have the same effect upon electoral behavior in all areas of the country, even if one assumes, for the sake of discussion, a national audience comprising a uniform percentage of the voting population. Furthermore, there is a very real limit—although it can never be precisely measured ahead of time—upon the number and type of legislative issues that the President can take to the public. The President is limited not only by the time available to him, but also by considerations of timing. Long writes:

> When the staff of the Office of War Mobilization and Reconversion advised a hard-pressed agency to go out and get itself some popular support so that the President could afford to support it, their action reflected the realities of power rather than political cynicism . . . the bureaucracy under the American political system has a large share of responsibility before the public promotion of policy. . . .[47]

Further, to emphasize the desirability of propagandizing the public as a means of putting pressure upon Congress may lead to a neglect of the need for directly persuading members of Congress. Many a legislative cause has been weakened in modern-day America because executive officials have used pressure tactics only and disdained to use the more difficult instruments of persuasion. More frequently, many congressional opponents of legislative proposals advocated by executive officials have been goaded into still more bitter opposition by efforts to build fires beneath them without attempting to convince them personally. Although persuasion by itself can scarcely serve as *the* decisive weapon in the legislative struggle, one of the best tests of executive statesmanship is the ability to blend persuasion and pressure in judicious proportions.[48]

Another major approach toward strengthening executive campaigning is found in the thesis that we need more effective political parties. In fact, many of the advocates of stronger parties find that "the best hope for the future of American politics and government lies in a fruitful union between Presi-

[47] Norton Long, "Power and Administration," *Public Administration Review,* Vol. 9, Autumn, 1949, pp. 258–259.

[48] "Fear is in almost all cases a wretched instrument of government, and ought in particular never to be employed against any order of men who have the smallest pretensions to independency. To attempt to terrify them, serves only to irritate their bad humor, and to confirm them in an opposition which more gentle usage perhaps might easily induce them, either to soften, or to lay aside altogether. . . . For though management and persuasion are always the easiest and safest instruments of government, as force and violence are the worst and the most dangerous, yet such, it seems, is the natural insolence of man, that he always disdains to use the good instrument, except when he cannot or dare not use the bad one." Adam Smith, "The Wealth of Nations" (Modern Library edition, New York: Random House, 1937), pp. 750–751.

dential power and party government,"[49] or that the future of the American system lies in "strengthening the only two instruments in our political life, which have an inherent responsibility to the nation as nation: The President and the national political parties."[50] The logic here is that a stronger party organization will not only prevent a President from watching ill-considered legislative ventures, but also provide him with the organized support which is needed to make him a more effective legislative leader.

Anything which is done to strengthen the majority-party organization in Congress and the President's associations with it will obviously strengthen the hand of the President and other executive officials in legislative matters. But nothing effective along these lines can be done unless a combination of private nonparty organizations is brought together to provide the sources of party strength. With any conceivable augmentation in the strength of our national parties, it will still be necessary for both the President and other executive officials to organize support for many legislative measures entirely outside party channels.

Improvements of Congressional Technique in Lawmaking

Finally, attention should be directed to a number of proposals that deal with such legislative methods as the handling of appropriations, the improvement of drafting, the control of congestion, the length of sessions, and codification and revision.

Appropriation Methods

The sheer bulk of appropriation legislation enacted every year and its importance to so many groups and agencies throughout the country have inspired a large number of proposals for changing the manner in which money is appropriated. Among them are the item-veto proposal discussed earlier and the idea that executive proposals for legislative action should be acted upon by Congress through exception or rejection but without an opportunity for amendment.

At this point consideration will be given to the so-called "legislative budget," the omnibus appropriation bill, and a number of minor items.

The Legislative Budget. One of the most ambitious attempts to bring "order" into the handling of appropriation bills in Congress was the ill-fated legislative-budget section (Sec. 138) of the Legislative Reorganization Act of 1946. Under this provision the two committees on appropriations and the two committees on revenue were supposed to meet jointly at the beginning of each regular ses-

[49] James M. Burns, "Congress on Trial" (New York: Harper, 1949), p. 195.

[50] Stephen K. Bailey, "Congress Makes a Law" (New York: Columbia University Press, 1949), p. 239.

sion of the Congress, study the President's budget recommendations, and report to the Congress a concurrent resolution containing "a recommendation for the maximum amount to be appropriated for expenditure in such year, which shall include such an amount to be reserved for deficiencies as may be deemed necessary by such committees." This was supposed to confront Congress with the necessity of discussing and voting upon the total amount of funds to be appropriated for the ensuing fiscal year.

Despite the high hopes held for it, no concurrent budget resolution was adopted in 1947. In 1948, when one was adopted, it was completely disregarded by both houses of Congress as decisions were reached on individual appropriation bills. For a while it seemed to some members of Congress that the concurrent resolution would work out better if the date on which it was supposed to be reported to the two houses of Congress were changed from February 15 to May 1. This change was made in 1949, but from then on no attempt was made to report a concurrent resolution to Congress. The statutory provisions requiring that such a resolution be reported were in effect repealed by congressional inaction.

"The legislative budget went on the rocks," writes Representative John Phillips of California, "for the simple reason that the concurrent resolution setting a maximum amount of appropriations called for a premature commitment by the members of Congress. Moreover, it provided no means of focusing sustained attention upon the relationship between appropriations and revenues." Accordingly, he proposed the complete deletion of the provisions for a concurrent resolution. In its place he would substitute a written report to be presented to Congress every thirty to sixty days and to include "a continuing analysis of such basic information as to the level of the national debt, the conventional deficit or surplus, the cash budget or surplus, and committee and floor actions taken with respect to individual appropriation bills." [51]

Practically every proponent of a revised legislative budget has suggested the formal creation of a joint committee. Many types of joint committees have been proposed. At one extreme, it is suggested that a joint budget committee be given the job of actually preparing the budget; thus, to all intents and purposes, taking over the functions of the Bureau of the Budget.

Hardly less extreme are the proposals that Congress go back to the arrangements existing in the House of Representatives before 1865 and in the Senate before 1867, when both revenue and appropriation bills were handled by the same committees, or to streamline these arrangements by having the entire operation handled by a single joint committee. Roland Young's comment is pertinent:

> There is no need to combine the Revenue and Appropriations Committees, as they were combined before 1865. Congressional practice has become too traditionalized for such change, and there would perhaps be difficulty preserving a committee with

[51] Phillips, *op. cit.*, p. 263.

such great power. Even now, the extensive power of the House Committee on appropriations is occasionally attacked, and one can imagine the reaction of the House if this power were doubled.[52]

Less impractical is the proposal that the two committees on appropriations and the two committees on revenue meet together to frame a general "fiscal policy." The fact remains, however, that the members of these four committees will remain overburdened with the specialized problems of appropriations or of revenue taxation. A strong case can be made that general leadership on fiscal problems can be provided, if at all, by the party-leadership committees in Congress or by the Joint Committee on the Economic Report.

This line of reasoning leads to the conception that any new joint committee in this field should be a joint committee on appropriations which would parallel the Joint Committee on Internal Revenue Taxation. Representative Phillips discusses the jurisdictional relationship between a joint committee of this type and the work of the two committees on expenditures in the executive departments. He suggests that the entire function of checking upon executive expenditures be transferred to the appropriations committees and to his proposed joint committee on appropriations. With this shift in jurisdiction the joint committee could become the recipient of the investigatory reports of the General Accounting Office. This brings his proposal closely in line with previous proposals, such as the one made by Lucius Wilmerding, for the creation of a joint committee on public accounts.[53]

The Omnibus Appropriation Bill. Another major proposal for changing appropriation methods is to consolidate all appropriation bills—with the exception of those deficiency and supplemental bills that cannot be avoided—into one omnibus measure, or "packaged budget." Roland Young believed that the "Budget Bill should be shorn of verbosity and confined to a few hundred, or less, appropriation items . . ." and that it "would contain but a dozen or so pages rather than the several hundred the bills now contained." [54] Both these points of view have been expressed in abstract form by the argument that the consolidated bill would make it easier for Congress to deal with appropriations in an "orderly" fashion.

In 1950, a one-year experiment was attempted.[55] However, it was a short-lived one. In January, 1951, the House Appropriations Committee voted to abandon the omnibus appropriation bill. An analysis of the one-year experiment

[52] Young, *op. cit.*, pp. 262–263.

[53] See Lucius Wilmerding, "The Spending Power" (New Haven, Conn.: Yale University Press, 1943), pp. 253–254, 286–288, 291–292.

[54] Young, *op. cit.*, pp. 260–261.

[55] For divergent congressional résumés of what was accomplished during this experiment, see statements by Representative Clarence Cannon of Missouri, in the *Congressional Record* (daily edition), Jan. 29, 1951, pp. 796–800, and Feb. 27, 1951, pp. 1665–1681. Also see Phillips, "The Hadacol of the Budget Makers."

indicates five interesting conclusions. First, it is difficult to see how the omnibus approach contributed toward the holding down of expenditures. As Representative Phillips has pointed out: "Changing conditions—including the invasion of the Republic of Korea—required the enactment of five deficiency and supplemental bills for fiscal year 1951."[56] Moreover, when the omnibus appropriation bill came before the Senate, the senatorial friends of the Franco regime in Spain succeeded in adding a provision calling for a substantial American loan to the Spanish government. Although President Truman subsequently evaded this requirement, the incident indicated how the omnibus appropriation bill can be a vehicle to which may be attached additional appropriation provisions of all sorts.

Second, the device never succeeded in centralizing additional powers in the hands of the managers of the bill. Although the procedure for the handling of the bill formally called for the creation of an executive committee of ten members in the House Appropriations Committee, the resistance to any "super-duper committee" was so great that the procedure broke down and all questions were referred to the individual subcommittees in the same way as though each portion of the bill were being handled separately. The final bill, of course, was written in the conference committee but the formal selection of nine members of the House Appropriations Committee to serve as House conferees obscured the actual fact that behind this formality each of the individual subcommittees performed the function of conferees with respect to their particular portions of the bill.

Third, the omnibus appropriation bill led to a situation where the President, instead of being weakened by his inability to contemplate the veto of such an important measure, was given an unusually great opportunity to strengthen his political power. Representative Phillips has explained this paradoxical situation as follows:

> The package budget inevitably invites amendments directing the President to cut the total amount by a given sum or percentage. In fact, one of the greatest boasts of the package budget advocates is that the experiment on the fiscal year 1951 bill facilitated the amendment which directed the President to cut down the final total by an amount approximating 550 million dollars. From the viewpoint of high principle, this approach represents an abdication of Congressional responsibility over the power of the purse. From the viewpoint of practical politics, it confers upon the President the power to penalize his political opponents by eliminating expenditures in their home districts. Any President of the United States who wanted to achieve dictatorial control over Congress could hope for little more than the restoration of the package budget and the inevitable move to amend it every year by directing him to make a cut of a given size in any manner he chooses. . . . It is an ironic paradox that members of Congress who shudder at the thought of a constitutional amendment allowing a President to veto individual items in a bill have supported an extra-constitutional

[56] *Ibid.*, pp. 258–259.

device which in effect gives the President the same veto power but allows the Congress no opportunity to over-ride him.[57]

Fourth, the omnibus appropriation bill offered nothing to those who had hoped that it would lead to a reduction in detailed itemization. Rather than being a brief bill of only a dozen or so pages, it ended up as a law of 192 pages. Fifth, rather than contribute to a more "orderly procedure," it assured a more cursory procedure. The measure was so large and so complicated that it defied either careful examination or an approximation to understanding. Less time was spent on each major section in committee; fewer members of Congress had an opportunity to familiarize themselves with the issues in the floor debate. There was less opportunity than usual to obtain a record vote on the floor of the House of Representatives—since under the consolidated-bill procedure only a single motion to recommit was possible.[58]

Despite the countless recommendations relating to the details of the appropriations process, this function will probably continue to be the most complex, cumbersome, and central one confronting Congress. Reviewing a massive budget document within the short time of a few weeks and at the same time equating broad social purposes with dollar units will continue to push legislators from one difficult choice to the next. No number of procedural changes will ever take the place of consensus on broad social purposes as the lubricant of mutual confidence between the askers and the givers of Federal funds. No number of "safeguards" can suffice if demands for "economy" and protestations that "the fat" is out of a budget request evolve into a ritual designed primarily to help avoid the difficult decisions of modern public finance.

The Improvement of Drafting

There are limits on the extent to which either precision or simplicity can be achieved in legislative drafting. Nevertheless, better drafting can help avoid needless conflicts and contribute to understanding of the final product.

First, provisions might well be made for a technical review of every bill that is reported from a congressional committee. In some state legislatures this has been attempted through the use of committees on revision. To saddle members of Congress with a function of this type would hardly be practical. It could be assigned much more satisfactorily to the Office of the Legislative Counsel.

[57] *Ibid.*, p. 261.

[58] For a lucid review of other proposals in this field, see George B. Galloway, "Reform of the Federal Budget," Public Affairs Bulletin, No. 80 (Washington, D.C.: Library of Congress, Legislative Reference Service, April, 1950). These proposals for the most part deal with the President's budget presentation to Congress, the general character of appropriations legislation, the committee and floor procedures in dealing with appropriations bills, and the review or audit of executive expenditures.

Second, steps should be taken toward the preparation of a comprehensive drafting manual. Just as the Government Printing Office issues a manual on the style in which government documents are to be written and printed, the Office of the Legislative Counsel should develop a manual which will deal in comprehensive terms with such matters as the division of a measure into title, parts, sections, and paragraphs, references to existing statutes, abbreviations, amendments, standard clauses and sections, and kindred matters. A manual of this type will promote skillful draftsmanship and make the review process at the committee stage much easier.[59]

Finally, if significant progress is made in the development of a legislative style manual, it might prove desirable to enact a number of style requirements into law. In any such endeavor, however, great care must be taken that requirements of this type not become too complex. The experience of style requirements in state constitutions, as Luce points out, is that in many cases "they have led to a distressing amount of litigation and have brought about the nullification of what might have been useful statutes." [60]

The Control of Congestion

"Congress should jealously guard its time for ample debate and consideration of matters of national and international importance," stated the Joint Committee on the Organization of Congress. "It seems hardly consistent to hear the excuse that Congressional calendars are too crowded to take up and discuss issues of great national interest when so much time is devoted to these minor matters." [61]

Although there is much to commend this logic, it should be pointed out that it also conceals two false assumptions often made regarding the problem of reducing legislative congestion. First, it is often assumed that the time which would be saved by trimming down a portion of the legislative burden would be put to good use. Yet there is little reason for anyone to believe that additional time thus made available would be used in a uniform fashion. Some members of Congress may use it to work on major bills, some to handle their own private affairs, some to give more attention to constituents. Second, it is often forgotten that the volume of legislative business which cannot possibly be reduced is growing so rapidly as to counterbalance any reductions of the legislative burden that could be effected in specific areas. Both American society and American government are becoming increasingly complex. This gives birth to growing pressures for new laws and changes in existing laws. Almost every law which is

[59] An interesting example of a document of this type is "Legislative Procedure in Kansas," published in 1946 by the Bureau of Government Research of the University of Kansas.

[60] Luce, *op. cit.*, p. 558.

[61] Report of the Joint Committee on the Organization of Congress, p. 24.

enacted is a compromise which in turn gives rise to the need for new adjustments and new compromises. Both quantitatively and qualitatively the outlook is clearly one of a major increase in the total legislative burden over the decades that lie ahead.

For those who aim at the elimination of minor bills and the concentration of legislative attention upon major issues only, the easy remedy appears to be a sweeping prohibition against the introduction of broad categories of legislative proposals. "Why not prohibit the introduction of all bills dealing with individual localities?" it is often asked. "Why not confine the introduction of bills to a given number of weeks or months?" Such sweeping proposals are as impractical as the suggestion that legislative initiative be monopolized by executive officials and congressional committees and denied to individual members of Congress. A more discriminating approach is essential.

The Legislative Reorganization Act of 1946 has already banned all bills for the construction of bridges across navigable streams, the correction of military or naval records, the payment of pensions, and tort claims under $1,000. This ban could well be expanded to include tort claims up to $10,000. The adjustment of immigration and deportation cases could be delegated to the Immigration and Naturalization Service and the issuance of land patents to one of the bureaus of the Department of the Interior. The major obstacle to this kind of reform probably lies in the fact that minor bills of this type provide opportunities for members of Congress to perform various favors for constituents and that many members of Congress are probably more interested in continuing to enjoy these opportunities than they are in any program to reduce the legislative burden. It should also be kept in mind that in many cases the prohibition of a certain type of legislation may merely transform a legislative burden into an administrative burden, with the offices of members of Congress being kept busy in arranging negotiations with executive officials to handle the same problems previously dealt with through private legislation.

On the other hand, anything which would take away from the Congress the responsibility of serving as a city council for the nation's capital would make a real contribution toward reducing the number of bills introduced and acted upon at every session. The majority of the proposals that have been presented on this subject aim at the delegation of legislative authority in one method or another to an elected city council. They usually provide that local ordinances enacted by the locally-elected city council will have the force of Federal law unless overthrown by a concurrent resolution of Congress or when ratified by a concurrent resolution of Congress. The most that can be said for proposals of this type is that they represent an important step toward home rule. They would not lift the burden of District legislation from the shoulders of Congress but merely lighten it. Under any arrangements of this type it is inevitable that those who are displeased with actions of the locally-elected council will appeal to members of Congress for the introduction of resolutions or bills which would redress their grievances.

The most direct way to relieve Congress of the burden of legislating for the nation's capital would be to cede the entire District of Columbia—with the possible exception of the Capitol Building, the White House, and the land in between—back to the State of Maryland.[62] Under this plan the city of Washington would govern itself in the same way as the city of Baltimore; and of course, it would no longer be Washington, District of Columbia, but Washington, Maryland. The only legislative matters relating to the District which would come before Congress would be those dealing with the construction or protection of Federal buildings in the city of Washington. The residents of Washington would be able to handle their local affairs for themselves as do the residents of any other city and would be able to have voting representatives in Congress and take part in Presidential elections.

Apart from the problem of the District of Columbia, there is little opportunity for other types of action to reduce the volume of local legislation. Not only are local pressures or local projects extremely strong, but they are in many cases inseparable from national problems. In fact, many of the most important national bills will prove, upon close examination, to be little more than instruments for dealing in some uniform manner with a large number of local projects.

The Length of Sessions

The Legislative Reorganization Act of 1946 provided that Congress should adjourn each year on July 31, unless a decision were made to postpone the date. The major argument offered in defense of early adjournment was that otherwise members would have insufficient time to keep in touch with their constituencies. Under present-day conditions, however, it is becoming increasingly clear that an early adjournment inevitably deprives members of Congress of the time needed to take care of their legislative duties and other congressional burdens. The volume of congressional business is so great that only continuous sessions can provide sufficient time. Year-round sessions would also help eliminate the congestion of bills that usually takes place at the end of the session, reduce the opportunities for success of filibusters, and in most cases do away with pocket vetoes. Nor would they in this day of modern transportation and communication prevent members of Congress from maintaining close contact with their constituents. Year-round sessions could easily be interspersed with a

62 The seed for such a proposal can be found in the writings of Thomas Jefferson, who proposed that the Federal District be limited to a three-mile-square piece of territory rather than the ten-mile square authorized under the Constitution.

number of recesses to provide opportunities for relaxation, mending fences back home, campaigning, and the increasingly popular business of traveling throughout America and the world.

Codification and Revision

There have been many times in the historical development of various countries when the codification and revision of a country's laws have been acts of major political significance. The Corpus Juris Civitis of Justinian, the French *Code Napoléon,* and similar legal compilations have resulted from interest in unifying a nation or an empire, achieving a transition from judge-made law to statutory law, attaining a greater measure of legal stability, or enhancing the prestige of the code's sponsor.[63]

Today, codification and revision are more prosaic enterprises. Codification is of utility to the legislative draftsmen because it brings together past statutes in an orderly arrangement. Revisions serve to eliminate obsolete provisions, simplify language, resolve conflicts, or even fill minor gaps. Both are of use not only in the drafting of new laws, but also in the administrative and judicial processes connected with old laws.

The present United States Code, which consists of 50 titles enacted in 1926, is not an entirely formalized restatement of previous law. It was enacted as "prima-facie evidence" of the law rather than as the law itself, which can be found only in the Statutes at Large.[64]

It is often proposed, therefore, that the United States Code be enacted into positive law, thus making it unnecessary to refer back to individual statutes. However, a formal ratification of the Code would hardly be worth the effort unless a revision were accomplished at the same time. Accordingly the House Judiciary Committee (and its predecessor the House Committee on the Revision of the Laws) has attempted to prepare revisions of individual titles of the United States Code and to have them enacted one by one. As of 1951 eight titles were enacted into law.

The complexity of this has often led to the suggestion that the program be expedited by provision for additional staff facilities. For example, Representative Keogh testified before the Joint Committee on the Organization of Congress in support of a bill which would establish a special office of law-revision counsel in the House of Representatives. As a service to the appropriate

[63] For a trenchant critique of such codes see "The Age of Codification," in William Seagle, "The History of Law" (New York: Tudor, 1946), pp. 277–298.

[64] The United States Code is published by the West Publishing Co. and the Edward B. Thompson Co. and sold commercially. Every year since 1926 an annual cumulative supplement has been prepared which brings each of the volumes up to date. An annotated edition provides references to the relevant judicial decisions on each section.

committees of Congress, the function of the office of the law-revision counsel would be as follows:

> (a) Examine all the public acts of Congress and submit recommendation to such committee for the repeal of obsolete, superfluous, and superseded provision of law contained therein; (b) prepare and submit to such committee a complete compilation, restatement, and revision of the general and permanent laws of the United States, one title at a time, which will conform to the understood policy, intent, and purpose of Congress in the original enactments with such amendments and corrections as will remove ambiguities, contradictions, and other imperfections both of substance and of form with the view of the enactment of each title as positive law. . . .[65]

The Joint Committee, however, felt that this function could be handled by the Office of the Legislative Counsel and recommended additional funds for this office.[66]

Nevertheless, the Office of the Legislative Counsel has been too busy with its regular duties to attempt any sustained work on problems of codification and revision, and it seems obvious that specialized staff resources are needed. Such resources should be provided for on a permanent basis, inasmuch as no revised code can ever be final.

However, staff facilities are not sufficient of themselves. When revisions are made, there is always the possibility that certain changes may be written into the law which unduly strengthen the position of some groups and weaken the position of other groups. It is for this reason that any revisions which attempted to go beyond the technical level and resolve major ambiguities and contradictions would be doomed to failure in advance. The reason that the United States Code of 1926 was not enacted into positive law was that many members of Congress were fearful lest they might find out some years later that unwittingly they had approved of changes which impaired the interests of important groups. This fear could be set to rest by extensive consultation with administrative agencies and private organizations, perhaps through a broadly representative commission for sponsoring revision measures.

Additional Comments

Although the Democrats lost the 1952 election, a number of liberal Democrats—with a bare handful of Republican supporters—decided to pay tribute to their party's pledge by trying to amend the cloture rule at the beginning of the Eighty-third Congress. On January 3, 1953, Senator Anderson of New Mexico submitted a motion "that this body take up for immediate consideration the

[65] Hearings before the Joint Committee on the Organization of Congress, p. 131.
[66] Report of the Joint Committee on the Organization of Congress, p. 12.

adoption of rules for the Senate of the Eighty-third Congress." [67] In defense of this motion Senator Anderson argued that the Senate is not—and should not be —a continuing body and that like the House of Representatives it should adopt new rules every two years. The purpose of the motion was to sweep aside the old rules, particularly the existing cloture rule, so that the Senate could then operate under general parliamentary procedure. It would then be possible to use the previous question (which is decided by majority vote) to curtail debate on the new rules, thus facilitating adoption of a tighter cloture rule.

The supporters of the motion had hoped that a point of order would be raised at once. Vice-President Barkley, who still had about two weeks to remain in office, might then rule the motion in order. The Vice-President, however, was never put to the test. After insisting that the Senate is a continuous body with a continuing set of rules, the new majority leader, Senator Taft, moved to lay Senator Anderson's motion on the table. The motion to table was carried by a resounding vote of 70 to 21.[68]

[67] *Congressional Record,* Jan. 3, 1953, p. 9.

[68] For a detailed presentation of the conflicting viewpoints on this question, see the brief prepared under the auspices of the 1952 Leadership Conference on Civil Rights, *Congressional Record,* Jan. 7, 1953, pp. 182–201, and the brief prepared by the Senate Republican Policy Committee, "Senate Rules and the Senate as a Continuing Body," *Congressional Record,* Jan. 7, 1953, pp. 165–178 (also printed as Sen. Doc. 4, 83d Cong., 1st Sess.).

PART III

CONCLUSION

Chapter 21

THE FUTURE OF THE LEGISLATIVE PROCESS

IN THE concluding chapter of a book dealing with government in America, there are a number of attractive opportunities confronting the author.

On the one hand, he can close with an eloquent peroration which summarizes the proposals for improvement which he himself advocates and in guarded terms suggest that the entire future of American democracy depends upon the fate of these proposals.

On the other hand, in more academic and less personal terms, he can summarize the pros and cons of the most important proposals that have been discussed and assign to the future the challenging task of deciding what shall be done.

But the first of these approaches would be more appropriate to a propaganda document, which this book could scarcely attempt to be. The second would run the risk of becoming pseudoobjective and overstatic.

Both, therefore, will be rejected. Instead, I shall close with a brief attempt to evaluate the dynamics of change in the processes of government, to appraise the special problems involved in campaigns for change in the legislative process, and to discuss the contributions of social scientists to the future of the legislative process.

THE DYNAMICS OF CHANGE

Prediction of the course of future change in the legislative process is necessarily a precarious and pretentious enterprise. However, some basic variables which will probably affect the future of the legislative process can be indicated: the broad sweep of change throughout all of American society, the production of specific proposals for change, and the social power behind such proposals.

The Broad Sweep of Social Change

If the history of the first decades of the twentieth century can be used as a partial guide, a number of probabilities and possibilities can be suggested concerning both short-range swings of the pendulum and underlying long-range trends.

On the international side, we can expect successive periods of international crisis and relapse—with the ever-present possibility of a new World War. On the domestic front, we can expect recurring ups and downs in economic activity—with the possibility that increasing armaments and foreign aid may use so much of our resources as to abolish the specter of large-scale unemployment and intensify the prospect of recurring shortages and inflation. The signs suggest that accelerated advances in technology will make the Industrial Revolution of the nineteenth century look like a mere dash of surf preceding a massive wave. This, in turn, should accelerate the industrialization of the relatively underdeveloped regions, the mechanization of farms, and the urbanization of rural areas.

Another long-range trend holds forth the double promise of new heights in the level of education, with illiteracy abolished, a growing percentage of the population obtaining a college education, and new achievements realized in mass communication through television, radio, motion pictures, the press, and transport.

A number of observations can also be made concerning the major contestants in the legislative struggle. The probability is that private organizations will extend their scope and that increasing power will be concentrated in the hands of dominant groups. For industrial and white-collar labor, this means the further extension of unions. For business and industrial enterprise, it means further growth in mergers, monopolies, monopolistic arrangements, trade associations, and farm associations. There is no reason to assume that any will fail to intensify efforts to use government as an instrument for obtaining their objectives. The extension of industrialization, unionization, and education will also create opportunities for the development of more two-party rivalry in the South and other one-party areas in the United States. Rivalry between business and labor organizations may create situations in which sharper socioeconomic distinctions will be drawn between the coalitions comprising the two major parties.

In government, the long-range outlook seems to favor continued expansion of executive agencies and stronger Federal government as compared with state and local governments on the one hand and the realm of private action on the other. The dominant role in the Federal government's handling of various issues will continue to shift back and forth between executive officials and members of Congress, with the Justices of the Supreme Court, on occasion, adjusting the driver's seat. We can look forward to periods of reform in the social structure and to periods of conservatism.

With the United States playing a larger part in world affairs, an ever-increasing number of issues will arise that can be settled only at the international level. Whether these settlements are made through *ad hoc* diplomatic negotiations, through a loose consultative body like the United Nations, or through a stronger world organization, they will tend to influence the character of policy decisions taken at the national level and to convert national policy making into a subordinate process. Developments of this type will tend to set certain limits within which changes in the processes of government will take place, or, to put it in other terms, they will provide basic materials from which changes in the legislative process will be molded.

The Production of Proposals for Change

There is an important distinction between normative judgments and proposals for change. Every proposal implies a judgment that the *status quo* is not good enough. But every judgment that things might be better does not result in proposals for making them better. In some areas one can find a plentiful supply of suggested remedies, in others a shortage of remedies, and everywhere an abundance of descriptive analyses and of diagnoses.

Negative Approaches. One can be a good music critic without knowing how to write a sonata. In the same way, one can be skilled at describing or finding fault with the legislative process without having either the inclination or the talent to produce proposals for change. In his "Process of Government," for example, Bentley produced an invaluable description of the legislative process. But he limited himself to an explanation and did not attempt a critique. In "Congressional Government," Woodrow Wilson produced a brilliant attack upon congressional operations as he saw them. But, after tilting with the constitutional separation between Congress and the executive branch and pointing out that "the Constitution is not honored by blind worship," he stopped short, barely wetting his toes in the waters of constitutional reconstruction and leaving it for others to jump in to make the proposals for which his own writing prepared a foundation.

Although the negative approach is in part a matter of temperament, the roots of negativism and neutralism go deeper. They are nourished by unsureness. The reflective analyst is often so aware of the difficulties to be surmounted and so doubtful as to the adequacy of what he might propose that he stops short at description and critique. They feed upon cynicism, which itself is often a reflex resulting from an excess of idealism. The idealist, finding out what some aspects of group life can be like, may come to the conclusion that all reform should be left to others who are more innocent about the stubborn realities. He may then confine himself to the task of wielding a scathing analytical scalpel and leaving the body politic exposed to the view of the shocked student and the occasional reader.

Finally, a negative approach may be expected from those whose standards lead them to endorse the *status quo* or accept it without challenge. In times of social quiescence or in times of national emergency when the ordinary pressures of life compel the postponement of thoughts of change, negativism is usually in the ascendancy.

Positive Approaches. Personal temperament is clearly an important factor in the production of proposals for change. For some minds, the development of such proposals offers a fascinating intellectual exercise, like playing chess. It is an exercise that can give one a tremendous sense of power; for, on paper at least, one can build and rebuild the world at pleasure. It can also provide a form of escapism, particularly for those who specialize in the intricacies of institutional gadgetry. It can be a means of talking and acting constructively without direct involvement in conflicts that wound. It is a method of participating in social combat without letting down one's guard. Being for "good government" is as safe as being against sin.

In times of intense national stress, when great shifts of power are imminent or taking place, formal relationships inside and outside government must also be readjusted. Proposals for institutional reform not only provide rational patterns for readjustment but also serve as rallying points around which the major contestants in the social combat can organize their forces. At such times there is always a market for the ideas or services of men and women who can produce the ideas and techniques that meet the needs of particular groups and individual leaders.

The Power behind Specific Proposals

The power of ideas for change in the processes of government should not be minimized. "One person with a belief in a social power is equal to ninety-nine who have only interests," observed John Stuart Mill. "They who can succeed in creating a general persuasion that a certain form of government, or social fact of any kind, deserves to be preferred, have made nearly the most important step which can possibly be taken towards ranging the powers of society on its side." [1]

Many ideas, of course, have no impact at all. The difference between the powerful idea and the weak idea is that the former is one having greater appeal to various interests and is thus more closely bound up with the processes of organizing group support. To enlarge upon Mill's formula, one person with a belief, when supported by ninety-nine with interests to whom this particular belief appeals, can develop social power equal to a thousand separate individuals who have distinct beliefs or interests.

In short, proposals for change in the legislative process are much like

[1] John Stuart Mill, "Considerations on Representative Government" (New York: Macmillan, 1947), p. 117.

legislative bills in that their chances of success depend upon the campaigns waged for and against them. No idea for improvement in the legislative process can have any effect unless it seems attractive enough to have a campaign built around it and unless there are people who develop this campaign.

Sometimes a new twist to an old idea is all that is needed to tap new sources of support and harness new sources of energy behind a campaign effort. Sometimes when new twists or totally new ideas are launched, what is really needed is a new and better approach to sources of support. For instance, efforts to prevent the automatic selection of committee chairmen in accordance with seniority do not need some dramatic new substitute for the seniority principle but rather the organization of sufficient support to force departures of one sort or another from the seniority principle. At some point this necessarily entails a choice between alternative "departures." But an effective choice cannot be made in abstract terms. It must fit into the strategy and tactics of a given campaign.

Campaigns for Change

A variety of motivations is needed for the development of a meaningful campaign for changes in governmental processes. This diversity is usually blended in varying proportions in the minds of campaign leaders. The campaigns themselves follow closely along the lines of any campaign for enactment of a legislative measure. However, such aspects as the choice of objectives, the development of support, and the character of defeats and victories merit special attention.

Objectives

There is hardly a limit to the number of variations and combinations of proposals for change in the legislative process. But there are very substantial limits to the number of objectives behind which any given campaign can be organized. None can cover too much territory. Available resources must be used sparingly, not scattered profusely in the effort to obtain action on a relatively coherent program. A truly comprehensive program can be little more than a stock pile of ideas from which campaign objectives can be drawn from time to time. The more fully and ably developed these ideas are, the more opportunely and successfully can they be selected for use.

As with the drafting of a bill, there is always the problem of how high to set one's sights. To set an objective which requires too great a change from present reality may be to indulge in daydreaming and to mislead supporters into needless activities. On the other hand, too much "realism" can lead to cynicism or smugness. The motto "Make no small plans" often has practical justification.

A high or difficult objective may be useful in evoking support. It may leave more leeway for bargaining and compromise. Moreover, feasibilities cannot be judged in a routine, mechanical manner. A shift in circumstances and the improbable may suddenly be converted into the possible. With the passage of time, the wild-eyed dream may become a highly practical, and indeed moderate, reform.

At times, a paradoxical situation occurs in that, on the one hand, a proposal for change may be impossible to put into effect unless and until there is a marked shift in power between contending forces. On the other hand, if the needed shift in power were to take place, there might no longer be any interest in acting upon the proposed change. This is another way of saying that, when substantive objectives are attained, the support for procedural or organizational reforms that would have contributed to their attainment may no longer be pressed with the same enthusiasm. Yet in some cases the proposed procedural changes will continue to be supported, as a method of consolidating advantages already won.

Another problem is how concretely or specifically an objective should be stated. An abstract principle is hard for many people to understand. A new "gadget," on the other hand, may have great symbolic value. The fact that it is specific may make it easier to understand. If elaborated upon, people may more readily visualize how it will operate. If the details provoke controversy, that also may be an advantage because it brings it to the attention of more people and makes potential supporters out of those critics whose views are accepted. On the other hand, the details of a specific proposal will often be subject to considerable evolution. As a guide to the shifts in detail, therefore, it is always helpful to accompany a specific device with a full statement of the purposes it is supposed to achieve.

Support

The marketing of an idea for changes in governmental processes is fraught with difficulties. Hope for awakening interest in governmental improvement is often pinned on "the responsible, the alert, the active, the informed, and the confident men and women in the street." [2] Yet these citizens often may be puzzled, confused, misinformed, ignorant, disinterested, or groggy from the multiplicity of problems impinging upon them. Or they may be interested in other matters. "Opinion is in most countries too much absorbed with the economic and social aims to which legislation should be directed," wrote Bryce a number of decades ago, "to give due attention to legislative methods." [3]

[2] Barbara Wootton, "Freedom under Planning" (Chapel Hill, N.C.: University of North Carolina Press, 1945), p. 180.

[3] James Bryce, "Modern Democracies" (New York: Macmillan, 1921), Vol. II, p. 356.

Many practical men and women who play leading roles in public affairs are so preoccupied with the specifics of substantive action that discussion of change in governmental processes brings them into a realm where they feel out of place and unprepared to judge. Moreover, a good measure of wariness enters the picture because "No man can be sure that he may not be the victim tomorrow of that by which he may be a gainer today." [4] Nor can he be sure that he may not be the immediate victim of that which has been proposed as causing loss to none.

These difficulties can rarely be overcome without direct, though not necessarily public, appeals to various groups on the hard ground of self-interest. It is for this reason that Burns concludes that if significant congressional reform can ever come "it will doubtless be part of a great popular movement to achieve certain social ends, rather than an isolated effort to improve Congress." [5] This was certainly the case with the 1910 revolt against the powers of the Speaker of the House; the motive power for the anti-Cannon campaign came from the rising forces of social and economic liberalism. Such appeals to various groups can sometimes, particularly with more modest proposals, bring together interests that are usually opposed. When the impact of a proposal is blurred by its very nature or by what is said about it, there is more opportunity to unite divergent groups. Support for the Legislative Reorganization Act of 1946, for example, in addition to being forthcoming from political scientists and publicists interested mainly in abstract principles, was obtained from both conservative and liberal members of Congress, from liberal-reform organizations, and from a number of conservative organizations, the latter particularly appreciative of the economizing potentialities in the legislative budget and favoring a stronger Congress as a means of combating certain liberal tendencies in the executive branch.

Defeats and Victories

As with campaigns on behalf of legislative proposals, efforts to win changes in the legislative process can rarely end in a complete victory. This is inherent in the bargaining nature of the process of change. It also stems from the fact that propaganda to create enthusiastic support invariably gives rise to exaggerated expectations sure to be frustrated if "victory" ever comes.

Moreover, organizational and procedural changes are tools that can be used for a variety of purposes. When they are put to unsuspected uses, those who fought to bring them into existence may conclude that they had created a Frankenstein. Or, such changes, once put into action, may prove to have a blunt cutting edge and to be of little consequence. "It is those who magnify

[4] Federalist Papers.

[5] James M. Burns, "Congress on Trial" (New York: Harper, 1949), p. 140.

gadgets," writes T. V. Smith, "and seek to cure the grudges that attend their malfunctioning who will be disappointed at any and every reorganization of Congress." [6]

The degree to which the outcome of a campaign is regarded as victory or defeat will depend on many factors. One's interest in future combat may lead to exaggeration of the progress already made in order to prevent a sense of defeatism among supporters or to exaggeration of defeats sustained in order to arouse antagonism toward opponents. More broadly, the judgment of defeat or victory will depend upon one's historical perspective and upon the links in the chain of events which one regards as the main objective. Bolles, for example, describes the 1910–1911 curbing of Speaker Cannon's powers as a revolution which freed "the house, the President, the party, and the country from the control of a despot." [7] In reviewing Bolles's book, V. O. Key takes issue with this judgment on the ground that in effect these curbs destroyed an instrument of party leadership.

> Norris and his insurgents could join with the Democrats to deflate the Speaker, but they could not manage the House. Uncle Joe dared the new "majority" to elect a Speaker and to assume responsibility for legislative leadership. They could not do it; and by the "revolution" they destroyed the machinery they might use if and when they became a genuine majority.[8]

But from the perspective of substantive political action, Key's verdict—sound though it may be in the abstract context of governmental forms—seems somewhat narrow. After all, the objectives of the anti-Cannon alliance included, in addition to changes in the House rules, reform of the tariff laws, enactment of a constitutional amendment authorizing income taxes, and other liberal measures. The curbing of Cannonism contributed to the attaining of these objectives and was also a factor in the Democratic march to victory at the polls in 1912 and the oncoming of Wilson's new era. From this viewpoint, it was an operation aimed at removing an obstacle to substantive objectives and was unquestionably a victory.

Sometimes, as a result of untiring efforts, a series of repeated defeats can end in victory. In 1790, for example, a group of Southern Senators started a campaign to require the Senate to open its sessions to the public. The House had set up spectator galleries at its first session in 1789. But the Senate, probably on the ground that its dignity and protection from popular pressure would be enhanced thereby, kept its proceedings secret. Even members of the House were excluded from the Senate's sessions. The Southerners found that in the

[6] T. V. Smith, Review of "Congress at the Crossroads," *Saturday Review of Literature*, Vol. 29, 1946, p. 12.

[7] Blair Bolles, "Tyrant from Illinois: Uncle Joe Cannon's Experiment with Personal Power" (New York: Norton, 1951), p. 224.

[8] *New Republic,* June 4, 1951, p. 18.

secrecy of the Senate, the Federalists would be better able to put across Hamiltonian measures. They believed that with open sessions it would be easier for them to organize a more vigorous opposition to the Federalists. The struggle started in April, 1790, when the two Senators from Virginia moved that the doors of the Senate be opened to the public. When the question was put, only three Senators voted for the resolution. In 1791 the effort was made again, with the leadership this time in the hands of Senator James Monroe of Virginia. Again, the result was failure—but this time nine Senators voted for open sessions, with seventeen supporting secrecy. In 1792 Monroe tried again and failed again, with the opposition at seventeen and the proponents dwindling to eight. By 1793 the issue of open Senate sessions had become still more popular in the South. But increased Southern support led to a decrease in the support that had previously been obtained from Northern Senators. In 1794 another resolution was introduced. In the meantime the Senate agreed to open its doors during the debate on the question of the seating of Albert Gallatin. When the experiment was concluded and it became evident that public sessions were not as fearsome as they had been described by some, the Senate then decided by a vote of 19 to 8 to have public galleries built and to admit spectators at the next session.

The first public sessions were held in 1795. Yet the Senate refused to provide suitable accommodations for reporters. A new struggle ensued and it was not until 1802, twelve years after the original campaign had started, that adequate provision was made for allowing the public to be informed about action on the Senate floor.[9]

In contrast with this memorable example of the fruits of persistence, the passage of time invariably deprives victory of its savor. Any "final" reform is out of the question. John Dewey writes:

> No matter what the present success in straightening out difficulties and harmonizing conflicts, it is certain that problems will recur in the future in a new form or on a different plane. Indeed, every genuine accomplishment, instead of winding up an affair and enclosing it as a jewel in a casket for future contemplation, complicates the practical situation. . . . There is something pitifully juvenile in the idea that "evolution," "progress," means a definite sum of accomplishment which will forever stay done, and which by an exact amount lessens the amount still to be done, disposing once and for all of just so many perplexities and advancing us just so far on our road to a final stable and unperplexed goal. . . .[10]

[9] This account is based on a fascinating article by Elizabeth G. McPherson, "The Southern States and the Reporting of Senate Debates, 1789–1802," *Journal of Southern History,* Vol. 12, No. 2, May, 1946. This action, however, did not apply to executive sessions for the consideration of Presidential nominations. It was not until 1929, after many decades of controversy, that these sessions were also opened to the public.

[10] John Dewey, "Human Nature and Conduct" (New York: Holt, 1944), pp. 284–285.

Social Scientists and Social Change

In previous chapters this writer has tried to deflate pretentious conceptions of the role of social scientists in the process of social change. He has criticized the idea that there can be absolute standards by which governmental forms may be evaluated and has shown that skilled observers may disagree in their judgments of what is good or bad and in their prescriptions for improvement. He has also taken issue with the theory that experts of one variety or another can displace social conflict by some mystic application of science and intelligence, for the resources mobilized behind specific ideas for change depend upon the interests to which these ideas appeal and the amount of support which they are given.

Despite these limitations upon the effectiveness of their work, social scientists should be urged to give more intensive and sustained attention to proposals for change. A review of the proposals discussed in this volume indicates more variety than quality. Many are little more than off-the-cuff suggestions for future thought. Many have never been developed in sufficient detail to be actionable. Few have been carefully analyzed on the basis of a study of the most relevant facts concerning the *status quo* or tested in terms of their probable impact upon the distribution of power. Few efforts have been made to bring separate proposals together into a systematic framework. This is partly the result of a casual, dilettante attitude toward social change and a gnawing cynicism that stifles imagination and undermines sustained creative effort.

Is it an exaggerated conception of the role of social scientists to ask that they give more vigorous and sustained efforts to the production and analyses of proposals for change? The well-adjusted social scientists need not be chagrined at the idea that their conclusions may be something less than apocalyptic revelations, that they cannot themselves bring order out of conflict, and that their power lies in the support they receive. Some can function creatively only when they see themselves at the center of the universe. Perhaps it is better to permit such personalities the luxury of their delusions. It is a simple truism that one man with a mission can contribute more to the march of human thought than a score of cynics who "know" how little a single mind can accomplish and are resolved to prove the accuracy of their knowledge by their collective inertia. That nation which protects and develops its "men with missions," is likely to enjoy the most abundant fruits of human initiative and creativity.

A more wholehearted entry by social scientists into the field of remedial action could have many effects. First, it could serve to enrich the study of "what is." Only when people have reason to believe that their inquiries may serve some purpose can they amass the time and energy needed for intensive descriptive studies. Little stock is to be placed in the notion that facts need or can be gathered in the name of fact gathering alone. Second, it would inevitably lead more and more toward taking sides in the great social issues of the day. This is all to the good. Meaningful research and effective teaching can be handled best by men and women who are in touch with the currents that energize American society. Great theories can be born only from participation in great social developments. To rewrite a phrase of Karl Mannheim, the socially-attached intelligentsia can "play the part of watchmen in what otherwise would be a pitch-black night." [11]

Finally, such participation by social scientists may encourage a move away from overspecialization. No problem in social change is something that can be neatly classified as a problem in political science, jurisprudence, social psychology, public administration, economics, or sociology. These terms refer to specialized tools, many of which are needed to deal effectively with any problem of social change. To argue that any one set of tools may suffice to handle the complexities of social conflict is to prepare the way for stultification.[12] It has become standard practice to seek a bridge for the chasm between overspecialized disciplines by bringing assorted specialists together in joint teaching and research ventures. This has undoubted merit, just as a growth in the tourist trade might contribute to better international understanding. But it is only a fragmentary approach. Joint action by specialists can never be very fruitful without a merger or synthesis of the social-sciences disciplines at the level of general theories of social action. Only through the development of comprehensive and competing theories of social action can all the available tools of analysis, measurement, and judgment be brought to bear upon problems of social change.

This emphasis on theory does not suggest the abandonment of a practical approach. In fact, the more adequate the theory one has, the more satisfactory the analysis of practicalities. The social sciences attain their highest performance at the point where theory and practice merge and realism and idealism can be fused into a meaningful guide to action.

[11] Karl Mannheim, "Ideology and Utopia" (New York: Oxford, 1936), p. 143. Mannheim assigns this part to the socially "unattached." But these are the modern Cassandras; unattached they are also unnoticed. "Guardianship," as stated at the end of Chap. 2, "comes from the affiliations of the guardians—and from the process of social combat itself."

[12] The result of overspecialization may be even worse: "By way of introducing the specialist as a psychological problem, I should like to refer to an accident that occurred several years ago in a system of caves in one of our Southern states. A professional geologist, who had set out to explore the formation of rocks and their enclosures was found dead near the entrance to which he had been unable to make his way back. Traces of his footsteps told of endless, circular, and repetitive wanderings which at many points had come close to the sunlight, never to reach it. The circle this particular specialist described proved fatal to himself, which was strange in view of the fact that he had been a cave explorer for years and was not unfamiliar with the area where death overtook him. He had concentrated on the composition, the texture, and the stratification of rocks as keys to their genesis: he had paid little attention, it appeared, to their topology. . . ." Ulrich Sonneman, "The Specialist as a Psychological Problem," *Social Research*, March, 1951.

INDEX

D

E

F

G

T

U

V

W

Y

Z